PRINCIPLES OF INVENTORY AND MATERIALS MANAGEMENT

Third Edition

PRINCIPLES OF INVENTORY AND MATERIALS MANAGEMENT

Third Edition

Richard J. Tersine
The University of Oklahoma

NORTH-HOLLAND
New York · Amsterdam · London

Elsevier Science Publishing Co., Inc.
52 Vanderbilt Avenue, New York, New York 10017

Sole distributors outside the United States and Canada:
Elsevier Science Publishers B.V.
P.O. Box 211, 1000 AE Amsterdam, The Netherlands

Library of Congress Cataloging-in-Publication Data

Tersine, Richard J.
  Principles of inventory and materials management.

  Bibliography: p.
  Includes index.
  1. Inventory control.   2. Materials management.
I. Title.
TS160.T4 1988   658.7'87   87–13538
ISBN 0–444–01162–5

Current printing (last digit):
10 9 8 7 6 5 4 3 2 1

Manufactured in the United States of America

Contents

Preface   xi
Overview of the Book   xiii

Chapter 1 Introduction   1
Inventory   3
Types of Inventory   4
Organizational Categories and Inventory Problems   4
Functions of Inventory   6
Inventory Problem Classifications   8
Properties of Inventory   11
Inventory Costs   13
Cost Accumulation Profile   15
Conflicting Goals   16
The Inventory Flow Cycle   19
Financial Considerations   20
Business Cycle Influence   25
Just-in-Time   26
Conclusion   27
Questions   28
Cases   29

Chapter 2 Forecasting and Market Analysis   33
The Forecasting Function   37
Time Series Analysis   41
    Forecast Error   43
    Last Period Demand   45
    Arithmetic Average   46
    Moving Average   46
    Regression Analysis   48
    Exponentially Weighted Moving Average (EWMA)   53
    EWMA with Trend Correction   57

EWMA with Seasonal Correction   60
EWMA with Trend and Seasonal Corrections   63
EWMA Overview   65
Box-Jenkins Models   69
Soliciting Opinions   70
Economic Indicators   71
Econometric Models   74
Group Forecasting   75
Conclusion   78
Questions   80
Problems   81
Cases   82
Selected Bibliography   86
Mathematical Abbreviations and Symbols   87
Summary of Formulas   88

Chapter 3 Independent Demand Systems: Deterministic Models

Chapter 3 Independent Demand Systems:
Deterministic Models   89
Fixed Order Size Systems   90
Economic Order Quantity (EOQ)—Single Items   91
Backordering   95
Quantity Discounts   99
Special Sale Prices   106
Known Price Increases   110
EOQ Sensitivity   114
Batch-Type Production Systems   121
Economic Production Quantity (EPQ)—Single Items   121
Make or Buy Decisions   126
Economic Production Quantity (EPQ)—Multiple Items   128
Runout Time (ROT) Method   131
Aggregate Runout Time (AROT) Method   133
Fixed Order Interval Systems   135
Economic Order Interval (EOI)—Single Items   136
Economic Order Interval (EOI)—Multiple Items   139
Conclusion   141
Questions   142
Problems   143
Cases   148
Mathematical Abbreviations and Symbols   152
Summary of Formulas   154
Appendix A. Determination of Single Variable Maximum
    and Minimum Points   156
Appendix B. EOQ Quantity Discount Approximation   156
Appendix C. Derivation of EOQ with Backordering   158

Chapter 4 Discrete Demand Systems: Deterministic Models

Chapter 4 Discrete Demand Systems:
Deterministic Models   160
Lot-for-Lot Ordering   163
Periodic Order Quantity   163
Wagner-Whitin Algorithm   164
Silver-Meal Algorithm   168
Part-Period Algorithm   170
Incremental Part-Period Algorithm   173
Implications for Discrete Lot Sizing   174
Conclusion   176
Questions   177
Problems   178
Cases   180
Mathematical Abbreviations and Symbols   182

Chapter 5 Independent Demand Systems: Probabilistic Models

Chapter 5 Independent Demand Systems:
Probabilistic Models   183
Safety Stock   184
Statistical Considerations   189
    Normal Distribution   192
    Poisson Distribution   193
    Negative Exponential Distribution   193
Known Stockout Costs   193
    Constant Demand and Constant Lead Time   194
    Variable Demand and Constant Lead Time   194
    Constant Demand and Variable Lead Time   206
    Variable Demand and Variable Lead Time   208
Service Levels   211
    Service per Order Cycle   212
    Service per Year   218
    Fraction of Units Demanded   219
    Fraction of Operating Days   222
    Imputed Service Level Stockout Costs   223
Fixed Order Interval Systems   224
Conclusion   226
Questions   228
Problems   229
Cases   233
Mathematical Abbreviations and Symbols   239
Summary of Formulas   240
Appendix A. Probability Distribution Convolutions   241
Appendix B. Normal Distribution   243
Appendix C. Chi-Square Goodness-of-Fit Test   244
Appendix D. Order Quantity and Reorder Point Dependence 248
Appendix E. Joint Probability Distributions   253

Chapter 6 Inventory System Changes and Limitations   261

Inventory System Redesign   263
Releasing Working Capital   266
Inventory System Constraints   266
    Exchange Curves   268
    Working Capital Restrictions   272
    Storage Space Restrictions   274
    Working Capital and Storage Space Restrictions   277
    Overview of Constraints   279
Excess Stock Determination   280
    An Excess Model   282
    Minimum Economic Salvage Value   286
    Lead Time Influence   288
Questions   289
Problems   289
Cases   290
Mathematical Abbreviations and Symbols   295
Summary of Formulas   296
Appendix A. Optimizing Constrained Functions   296

Chapter 7 Single Order Quantities   300

Known Demand, Known Lead Time   302
Known Demand, Variable Lead Time   303
Variable Demand, Known Lead Time   304
    Benefit (Marginal) Analysis   307
    Cost Analysis   310
Variable Demand, Variable Lead Time   314
Conclusion   314
Questions   315
Problems   315
Cases   319
Mathematical Abbreviations and Symbols   324
Summary of Formulas   325

Chapter 8 Dependent Demand Systems:
Material Requirements Planning (MRP)   326

Closed-Loop MRP   328
MRP Inputs   330
MRP Outputs   333
Product Structures   335
    Low Level Coding   338
MRP Computations   338
An EOQ-MRP Comparison   352
MRP Types   364
MRP Overview   365

Capacity Planning and Control   367
Conclusion   373
Questions   374
Problems   375
Cases   379
Appendix A. Bills of Materials (BOM)   385

Chapter 9 Just-in-Time and In-Process Inventory   **395**

In-Process Inventory   396
    Lead Time   398
    Setup Time   400
    Time Cycle Charts   401
    Bottleneck Work Centers   402
    Input/Output Control   403
    Critical Ratio Technique   407
Just-In-Time   409
    Elimination of Waste   410
    Inventory as Waste   411
    Pursuit of Perfection   412
    Repetitive Manufacturing and JIT   415
Conclusion   418
Questions   418
Problems   419
Cases   420

Chapter 10 Distribution Inventory Systems   **425**

Push vs. Pull Distribution Systems   428
Time-Phased Order Point   430
Distribution Requirements Planning   432
Fair Shares Allocations   438
Lot Sizing and Safety Stock   440
Conclusion   441
Questions   442
Problems   442
Cases   444

Chapter 11 Inventory Valuation and Measurement   **446**

Flow of Costs   448
    FIFO   448
    LIFO   451
    Average Cost   453
    Specific Cost   456
Inventory Records   458
    Periodic Count Method   460
    Cycle Count Method   461

Inventory Security   464
Questions   465
Problems   466
Cases   468

Chapter 12 Simulation   **473**
Simulation Categories   475
Monte Carlo Simulation   476
Perpetual Inventory Simulation Problem   479
Periodic Inventory Simulation Problem   484
Simulation of Joint Probability Distributions   486
Length of Simulation Run   489
Conclusion   490
Questions   490
Problems   491
Cases   494
Mathematical Abbreviations and Symbols   499

Chapter 13 Aggregate Inventory Control   **500**
Types of Control Systems   502
    Perpetual Inventory System   504
    Two-Bin Inventory System   505
    Periodic Inventory System   506
    Optional Replenishment Inventory System 508
    Distribution Requirements Planning Inventory System 509
    Single Order Quantity Inventory System 510
    Material Requirements Planning Inventory System 510
    Just-in-Time Inventory System   511
Selective Inventory Control   512
Inventory System Development   516
Inventory System Improvement   519
Aggregate Inventory Measurement   522
Aggregate Inventory Reduction   523
    Raw Materials, Supplies, and Finished Goods 524
    In-Process Inventory   527
Conclusion   528
Questions   530
Cases   531

Bibliography   **537**

Index   **543**

Preface

Management's role in any organization involves the acquisition, disposition, and control of resources that are necessary for the attainment of organizational objectives. These resources (factors of production) typically include labor, capital, equipment, and materials, but the focus of this book is concentrated on materials. Every organization either uses, transforms, distributes, or sells materials of one form or another. As such, they represent a common interest of individual organizations and a significant part of the aggregate national economy.

The management of materials concerns their flow to, within, and from the organization. The efficiency and efficacy of the flow can substantially influence costs and revenue generation and thus hold serious implications for marketing, finance, and production. Materials management seeks a balance between shortages and excesses in an uncertain environment. As it does, marketing is influenced through revenue and customer relations, production through efficiency and cost of operations, and finance through liquidity and operating capital.

In the past, the various materials management activities were performed in a routine manner by clerical personnel. These activities have since evolved into sophisticated functions with a pronounced influence on organizational performance. This increased criticality has buoyed materials management to higher organizational prominence.

This book presents alternative systems for managing materials, more appropriately called inventory. Although inventory refers specifically to material, it can be considered more broadly as any unutilized asset awaiting sale or use. Its control procedures are also applicable to space (seats) on vehicles, water levels in hydroelectric reservoirs, cash in financial management, manpower levels, and general resource allocations. In a general sense, inventory can include any tangible asset such as equipment, machine parts, tools, personnel, vehicles, cash, or support equipment.

The book is designed for students and operating practitioners. At the college level, it can be used in undergraduate and graduate courses in business administration, materials management, operations management, marketing management, industrial engineering, operations research, financial management, and logistics. For organizational practitioners, it will be useful in operations, physical distribution, production control, accounting, purchasing, inventory control, and physical supply. Theory and practice are combined in the book to provide a complete operating philosophy and conceptual foundation.

No attempt is made to develop all the theoretical models found in the literature. Only those models that are adaptable to practical situations are selected. Simple systems are illustrated initially, and more complex models are introduced as the text progresses. Throughout the book, numerous examples of solved problems are included to extend the reader's understanding.

At the end of each chapter there are questions, problems, and short case studies. The questions at the end of chapters provide a review of topics covered. Solving the problems will improve analytical and quantitative skills. The case studies extend the topical coverage into organizational settings. Some chapters have appendixes that provide additional extensions and supporting logic on particular topics.

I wish to acknowledge the colleagues, students, and reviewers who contributed to earlier editions of this text and further to extend my appreciation for the guidance and suggestions donated during its revision. Gratitude is particularly due to Michele Gengler, Rick Toelle, Jack Morris, R. Leon Price, Ianther Calhoun, Melissa Beneway, Mary Jones, Steve Wilson, Paula Reid, and Al Schwarzkopf who offered their professional skills.

Overview of the Book

This book is divided into thirteen chapters. The logic of the text is illustrated in Figure 1. The *Introduction* (Chapter 1) reveals the significance of materials management to modern organizations. It indicates the dimensions of inventory management and its overall importance. *Forecasting and Market Analysis* (Chapter 2) introduces methodologies for forecasting demand levels. *Independent Demand Systems* (Chapters 3 and 5) develop economic lot sizes and reorder points under various types of conditions for independent demand items. *Discrete Demand Systems* (Chapter 4) derives lot sizing techniques for items exhibiting deterministic, time-varying demand. *Dependent Demand Systems* (Chapter 8) formulates scheduling and ordering systems for dependent demand items derived from a master schedule. *Distribution Inventory Systems* (Chapter 10) focuses on time-based material control in a multiechelon distribution network. *Single Order Quantity Systems* (Chapter 7) outlines procedures for nonrepetitive ordering systems. *Inventory System Changes and Limitations* (Chapter 6) considers the problems of changes, constraints, and surpluses on inventory structures. *Just-in-Time and In-Process Inventory* (Chapter 9) investigates the dimensions of the just-in-time philosophy and in-process inventory control. *Inventory Valuation and Measurement* (Chapter 11) studies accounting aspects as well as physical control considerations. *Simulation* (Chapter 12) looks at Monte Carlo simulation as an inventory modeling tool. *Aggregate Inventory Control* (Chapter 13) concludes with a macroview of inventory management.

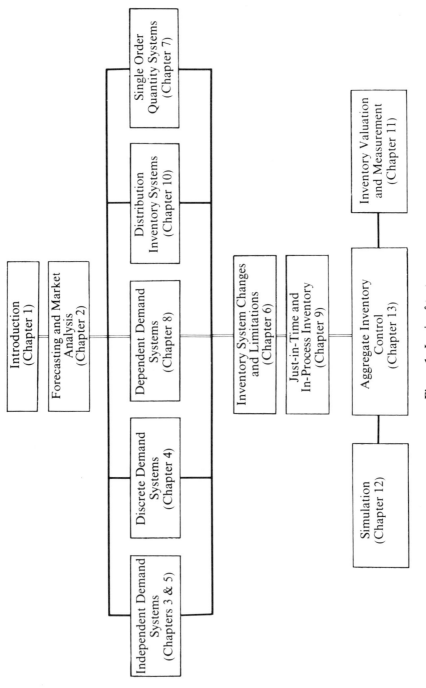

Figure 1. Logic of text.

1 Introduction

INVENTORY

TYPES OF INVENTORY

ORGANIZATIONAL CATEGORIES AND INVENTORY PROBLEMS

FUNCTIONS OF INVENTORY

INVENTORY PROBLEM CLASSIFICATIONS

PROPERTIES OF INVENTORY

INVENTORY COSTS

COST ACCUMULATION PROFILE

CONFLICTING GOALS

THE INVENTORY FLOW CYCLE

FINANCIAL CONSIDERATIONS

BUSINESS CYCLE INFLUENCE

JUST-IN-TIME

CONCLUSION

QUESTIONS

CASES

It is virtually impossible to find an organization that does not either use, transform, distribute, or sell materials of one kind or another, though the uses of materials may vary with the type and scope of operations. The management of materials can have serious implications for the financial, production, and marketing areas of all organizations. Finance is influenced through liquidity and return on investment, production through efficiency and cost of operations, and marketing through revenue generation and customer relations.

Designing, financing, manufacturing, and marketing a product have historically been the major organizational functions. Traditionally management devoted more time to the expenditure of moneys for personnel, plant, and equipment than for materials. Materials were thought of as cheap, readily available, and infinitely plentiful. The realities of the marketplace have changed this myopic view and have added materials management to the list of major organizational functions.

When organizations purchase the same raw materials over and over again, things are simple. Basic raw materials have many uses, and any excesses will eventually be depleted. With increased specialization, organizations tend to make less and buy more of their inputs. Not only does the number of inputs multiply but so does their complexity. Along with basic raw materials, inputs now include complicated components and assemblies. When the quantity and complexity of inputs increase and when any excess inputs might never be needed, difficulties can occur and more materials management skills are required.

With more variegated and specialized inputs, the proportion of expenditures on materials increases. For manufacturing organizations today, materials costs usually are the largest single expenditure. The average manufacturing firm spends over half of its sales revenue on purchased parts, components, raw materials, and services. An even larger portion of the sales dollar of wholesalers, distributors, and retailers is likely to be materials costs. Wholesalers, distributors, and retailers may own little more than inventory, particularly if buildings and facilities are leased. Materials costs range widely, from 15 to 90% of total product cost, but they typically are large enough for serious attention.

Materials management has a tremendous influence on the ultimate cost of a product because it handles the total flow of materials in an organization. The total flow can extend from suppliers to production and subsequently through distribution centers to customers. Encompassed in the management of the material flow is the responsibility for the planning, acquisition, storage, movement, and control of materials and final products. The emphasis is primarily on planning and controlling the flow.

Planning consists of the design of the material flow systems and the policies that govern them. Control consists of the proper execution and maintenance of these systems. Failures in materials management can result from failure in either planning or control. For example, if the material flow system does not function satisfactorily when it performs as designed, that is a planning problem. The wrong system or policies may be its source. However, if the material flow system functions unsatisfactorily when it is not implemented as designed, that is a control problem. Improper execution and maintenance of the system may be its root. Effective materials management systems require both appropriate design and constant surveillance of their operation.

INVENTORY

The control and maintenance of inventory is a problem common to all organizations in any sector of the economy. The problems of inventory do not confine themselves to profit-making institutions but likewise are encountered by social and nonprofit institutions. Inventories are common to farms, manufacturers, wholesalers, retailers, hospitals, churches, prisons, zoos, universities, and national, state, and local governments. Indeed, inventories are also relevant to the family unit in relation to food, clothing, medicines, toiletries, and so forth. On an aggregate national basis, the total investment in inventory represents a sizable portion of the gross national product.

Inventory problems have been experienced by every society, but it was not until the twentieth century that analytical techniques were developed to study them. After World War II a concentrated attack on the risk and uncertainty aspects of inventory was made in the private manufacturing sector. In theory, inventory as an area of organizational operation is now well developed. In practice, it is less advanced. This gap will narrow as educational institutions integrate materials management into their course structures.

The term inventory can be used to mean several different things, such as:

1. stock on hand at a given time (a tangible asset which can be seen, weighed, and counted);
2. itemized list of goods on property;
3. (as a verb:) act of weighing and counting of items on hand;
4. (for financial and accounting records:) value of the stock of goods owned by an organization at a particular time.

In this text, inventory refers to item 1 unless otherwise specified. A more comprehensive definition would refer to inventory as material held in an idle or incomplete state awaiting future sale or use. (In the most general sense, inventory is any idle resource.)

Table 1

Input Source	Inventory Type	Output Destination
Suppliers	Supplies	Administration, maintenance, and production
Suppliers	Raw materials	Production
Production stages	In-process goods (unfinished goods)	Next production stage
Suppliers or production	Finished goods	Storage or customer

TYPES OF INVENTORY

Inventory may consist of supplies, raw materials, in-process goods, and finished goods. *Supplies* are inventory items consumed in the normal functioning of an organization that are not a part of the final product. Typical supplies are pencils, paper, light bulbs, typewriter ribbons, and facility maintenance items. (Factory supplies are called MRO, for maintenance, repair, and operating supplies.) *Raw materials* are items purchased from suppliers to be used as inputs into the production process. They will be modified or transformed into finished goods. Typical raw materials for a furniture manufacturer are lumber, stain, glue, screws, varnish, nails, paint, and so forth. *In-process goods* are partially completed final products that are still in the production process. They represent both the accumulation of partially completed work and the queue of material awaiting further processing. *Finished goods* are the final product, available for sale, distribution, or storage.

The assignment of inventory to any of these categories is dependent on the entity under study. This is because the finished product of one entity may be the raw material of another. For example, a refrigerator manufacturer considers copper tubing as a raw material, but the firm that produces the tubing considers it as a finished good. The customer for finished goods inventory may be the ultimate consumer, a retail organization, a wholesale distributor, or another manufacturer. Table 1 indicates the types of inventory.

ORGANIZATIONAL CATEGORIES AND INVENTORY PROBLEMS

Different types of organizations have different inventory problems. By classifying organizations as retail, wholesale/distribution, and manufacturing/assembly, the extent of inventory problems can be generally delineated. In traversing from retail systems to wholesale/distribution systems to manufacturing/assembly systems, the problems of inventory increase in

Table 2

	Type of Inventory			
Type of Organization	Supplies	Raw Materials	In-Process Goods	Finished Goods
A. Retail systems				
1. Sale of goods	*			*
2. Sale of services	*			
B. Wholesale/distribution systems	*			*
C. Manufacturing/assembly systems				
1. Continuous production system	*	*	*	*
2. Intermittent production system				
a. Open job shop	*	*	*	
b. Closed job shop	*	*	*	
3. Special projects	*	*	*	

magnitude and complexity. Table 2 indicates the organizational category and the types of inventory encountered in each.

Retail systems are organizations that provide the ultimate consumer with goods and services. Inventory is purchased in a salable form and is usable without further processing or conversion. The systems that provide physical products obtain them from wholesalers or directly from factories—for example, stores which sell groceries, clothing, hardware, and varieties of consumer products in departmentalized facilities. They have inventory problems associated with supplies and finished goods. Retail systems that provide services to consumers experience only a supplies inventory problem. Typical organizations in this category are hospitals, financial institutions, universities, and penal institutions.

Wholesale/distribution systems comprise organizations that purchase large quantities of manufactured goods for distribution to retail systems. These organizations do not provide goods to the ultimate consumers but dispense their bulk purchases to retailers in smaller quantities. Therefore, wholesale/distribution systems have inventory problems confined to supplies and finished goods.

Manufacturing/assembly systems comprise organizations that purchase raw materials and change their form to create a well-defined finished good. These systems have the most difficult and complex inventory problems. Manufacturing/assembly systems can be subdivided into continuous production systems, intermittent production systems, and special projects.

Continuous production systems produce a limited number of products in large quantities through fixed routings. Typified by mass production assembly lines, the facility is designed and dedicated exclusively to its products.

Intermittent production systems involve batch production of many different products that must share the capacity of several work centers. They can be subdivided into open job shops and closed job shops. An open job shop will accept orders from any sources that are within its capabilities. A machine shop open to the public is an example. Closed job shops produce goods for only a limited number of customers, in much larger volume than open job shops. These shops may approach the complexity of continuous production systems. Examples are manufacturers that produce items for others under the customer's brand name, such as for Sears (Kenmore).

Special projects are limited-life, one-time events such as the Apollo project, space satellites, and sports stadiums. Special projects usually have explicit statements of the project's goal or numbers of end items. Since only a specified number of end items are produced, no additional finished goods inventory is maintained. From the number of end items the precise requirement for raw materials is obtained, and the production capability is established according to contract specifications. When the specific project is completed, the project organization is either disbanded or assigned to another special project.

FUNCTIONS OF INVENTORY

Inventory exists because supply and demand cannot be perfectly matched. For several reasons, supply and demand frequently differ in the rates at which they respectively provide and require stock. These reasons can best be explained by four functional factors of inventory—time, discontinuity, uncertainty, and economy.

The *time factor* involves the long process of production and distribution required before goods reach the final consumer. Time is required to develop the production schedule, cut raw material requisitions, ship raw materials from suppliers (transit time), inspect raw materials, produce the product, and ship the product to the wholesaler or consumer (transit time). Few consumers would be willing to wait for such an extended period of time on all their purchases. Inventory enables an organization to reduce the lead time in meeting demand. Profitability can be enhanced by a reputation of having products available immediately or within a reasonable time.

The *discontinuity factor* allows the treatment of various dependent operations (retailing, distributing, warehousing, manufacturing, and purchasing) in an independent and economical manner.[1] Inventories make it unnecessary to gear production directly to consumption or to force consumption to adapt to the necessities of production. Inventories free one stage in the supply-production-distribution process from the next, permitting each to

[1] Some authors call the discontinuity factor the decoupling function of inventory.

operate more economically. Raw material inventory isolates the supplier from the user, in-process inventory isolates production departments from each other, and finished goods inventory isolates the customer from the producer. The discontinuity factor permits the firm to schedule many operations at a more desirable performance level than if they were integrated dependently.

The *uncertainty factor* concerns unforseen events that modify the original plans of the organization. It includes errors in demand estimates, variable production yields, equipment breakdowns, strikes, acts of God, shipping delays, and unusual weather conditions. When inventory is available, the organization has some protection from unanticipated or unplanned occurrences.

The *economy factor* permits the organization to take advantage of cost reducing alternatives. It enables an organization to purchase or produce items in economic quantities. Bulk purchases with quantity discounts can reduce cost significantly. Per unit costs can be excessive if items are ordered separately without regard to transportation and lot size economies. Price hedging against impending material cost increases may also favor large quantity purchases. Inventories can be used to smooth production and stabilize manpower levels in undulating and seasonal businesses.

Another way to explain the purposes inventory serves is by introducing functional classifications of inventory. Based on its utility, all inventory can be placed in one of the following broad categories:

1. working stock,
2. safety stock,
3. anticipation stock,
4. pipeline stock,
5. decoupling stock.

Working stock (also known as cycle or lot size stock) is inventory acquired and held in advance of requirements so that ordering can be done on a lot size rather than on an as needed basis. Lot sizing is done in order to minimize ordering and holding costs, achieve quantity discounts, or qualify for favorable freight rates. In general, the average amount of inventory on hand that results from lot sizes constitutes an organization's working stock.

Safety stock (often called buffer or fluctuation stock) is inventory held in reserve to protect against the uncertainties of supply and demand. Safety stock averages out to the amount of stock held during a replenishment cycle as a protection against stockouts.

Anticipation stock (also known as seasonal or stabilization stock) is inventory built up to cope with peak seasonal demand, erratic requirements (strikes or vacation shutdown), or deficiencies in production capacity. It is acquired in advance of requirements to balance production and stabilize the work force level.

Pipeline stock (often referred to as transit stock or work-in-process) is inventory put in transit to allow for the time it takes to receive material at the input end, send material through the production process, and deliver goods at the output end. Externally, pipeline stock is inventory on trucks, ships, and railcars or in a literal pipeline. Internally, it is either being actively processed or moving between work centers.

Decoupling stock is inventory accumulated between dependent activities or stages to reduce the requirement for completely synchronized operations. It isolates one part of the system from the next to allow each to operate more independently. Thus, it acts as a lubrication for the supply-production-distribution system that protects it against excessive friction.

Inventories usually are not held for their own sake but as means to an end. The ends are the objectives established by the organization—its reasons for existence. Clearly there are various types of inventory that are intended to serve a variety of purposes. They cannot be managed in exactly the same way, but must be overseen in keeping with their specific function.

INVENTORY PROBLEM CLASSIFICATIONS

Inventory problems can be classified in many ways. They can be organized according to the repetitiveness of the inventory decision, the source of supply, the knowledge of demand, the knowledge of the lead time, and the type of inventory system. Figure 1 displays the inventory problem classifications with the following subdivisions:

1. Repetitiveness
   a. Single order
   b. Repeat order
2. Supply source
   a. Outside supply
   b. Inside supply
3. Knowledge of demand
   a. (1) Constant demand
      (2) Variable demand
   b. (1) Independent demand
      (2) Dependent demand
4. Knowledge of lead time
   a. Constant lead time
   b. Variable lead time

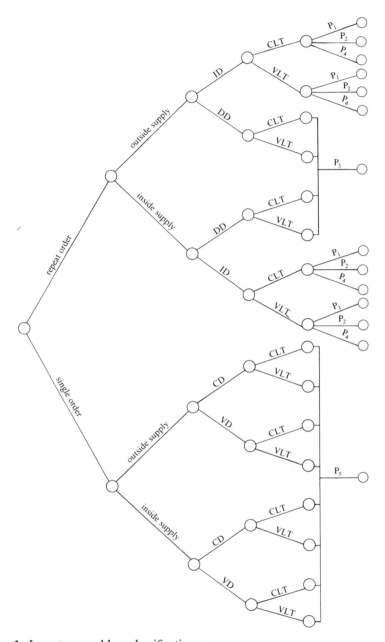

Figure 1. Inventory problem classifications.
KEY: DD = dependent demand, ID = independent demand, CD = constant demand, VD = variable demand, CLT = constant lead time, VLT = variable lead time, P_1 = perpetual inventory system, P_2 = periodic inventory system, P_3 = material requirements planning system, P_4 = distribution requirements planning system, P_5 = single order quantity system.

5. Inventory system
   a. Perpetual
   b. Periodic
   c. Material requirements planning
   d. Distribution requirements planning
   e. Single order quantity

Repetitiveness of the inventory decision refers to the frequency of orders. A single order is placed once and is not repeated, at any rate regularly. Examples of single orders are the acquisitions of materials for the construction of an apartment building, cut trees stocked for the Christmas season, and catered food served at a business or social affair. A repeat order is placed again and again as determined by routine guidelines. Stock or units that are repetitively consumed are replenished or restocked on a recurring basis. Most of the items in supermarkets and department stores are restocked through repeat orders (though high fashion items in a department store frequently are single order items).

The classification by the *supply source* is twofold: outside supply and inside supply. When an item is inside supplied, the company produces the item. In essence one part of the company orders from another part of the company, and work orders are utilized to obtain items in this manner. The issuance of internal work orders compounds the inventory problem with production scheduling problems. When the supply source is outside, items are obtained from approved suppliers. Purchase orders are sent (communicated) to external sources for items manufactured outside the organization.

Another inventory classification pertains to the *knowledge of demand*. The most common assumption about the demand distribution is that the demand is constant over time. The demand can also follow some empirical distribution over time that is not of a standard type, or some specified distribution such as the normal, Poisson, or beta.

An additional subdivision of knowledge of demand includes independent and dependent demand. Independence means no relationship exists between the demand for an item and any other item. In contrast, dependence means the demand for an item is directly related to or the result of demand for a "higher level" item. End items and products are characteristically independent, while raw materials, components, and subassemblies are essentially dependent. Since the demand for dependent items originates elsewhere, it can simply be derived or calculated from the demand for the item of which it becomes a part. Once an organization determines how many independent demand products it will make, it can calculate fairly accurately the number of dependent items it needs (though allowances must usually be made for scrap and other losses). The demand for independent items is less deterministic and generally must be obtained by forecasting.

Inventory problems can also be subdivided according to *knowledge of lead time*. Lead time is usually considered either constant or variable. If the lead time is variable, its distribution may be determined empirically or specified.

Finally, inventory problems can be classified according to the *type of inventory system*. There are many varieties of systems; some of the most common are the perpetual, periodic, material requirements planning, distribution requirements planning, and single order quantity inventory systems. The perpetual inventory system orders stock every time the inventory position reaches a reorder point, so records must be maintained of all inventory transactions. The perpetual updating of the records to reveal inventory status and historical performance is what gives the system its name. The periodic inventory system orders stock on a time cycle. The state of the system is examined only at discrete (periodic) points in time, and decisions on stock replenishment are only made at these intervals. The material requirements planning (MRP) system orders stock only to meet preplanned production requirements. Its mechanisms plan dependent demand requirements for end item production schedules in a time-phased format. The distribution requirements planning (DRP) system orders stock to meet distribution center requirements in multiechelon networks. The single order quantity system orders stock to meet unique or short-lived requirements. All of these systems will be examined in subsequent chapters.

There are other ways of subdividing the inventory problem, but the classifications given above indicate the major dimensions of the problems that can be encountered. To help solve the problems of inventory, it is necessary to build mathematical models which describe the inventory situation. Since it is never possible to represent the real world with total accuracy, approximations and simplifications must be made during the model-building process. These deviations from reality are necessary for the practical reasons that (1) it is impossible to determine what the real world is really like, (2) a very close approximation of reality would be mathematically intractable, and (3) extremely accurate models can be so expensive that their final benefit does not justify their cost. The relevance of a model to a given situation must be based on the reasonableness of its assumptions and limitations. Subsequent chapters will utilize mathematical models for the solution of inventory problems.

PROPERTIES OF INVENTORY

In viewing the properties of inventory systems, several components are universal. Demands, replenishments, constraints, and costs are the most commonly cited. Demands are units taken from inventory; replenishments are units put into inventory; costs are what is sacrificed in keeping or not keeping inventory; and constraints are limitations imposed on demands, replenishments, and costs by management or physical environmental conditions. Demands, replenishments, and constraints are discussed next; costs are described in the following section.

Demands can be categorized according to their size, rate, and pattern. *Demand size* refers to the magnitude of demand and has the dimension of quantity. When the size is the same from period to period, it is constant; otherwise, it is variable. When the demand size is known, the system is referred to as deterministic. When the demand size is not known, it is possible in some cases to ascertain its probability distribution, so that the system is probabilistic. Probability distributions can be discrete or continuous. Discrete distributions can only take on certain values, whereas continuous distributions can take on any value (when purchasing units such as automobiles, it is impossible to obtain fractions of a unit, whereas the purchase of items by volume such as gasoline is not limited to integer values). Standard probability distributions such as the normal, Poisson, and binomial are frequently assumed for demand. The *demand rate* is simply the demand size per unit of time. *Demand patterns* refer to how units are withdrawn from inventory. Units may be withdrawn at the beginning of the period, at the end of the period, uniformly throughout the period, or in some other apparent pattern (e.g., seasonally).

Replenishments can be categorized according to size, pattern, and lead time. *Replenishment size* refers to the quantity or size of the order to be received into inventory. The size may be constant or variable, depending on the type of inventory system. When a replenishment order is received, it usually goes into storage and becomes part of the organization's inventory. It is carried on the balance sheet as an asset until it is sold to a customer or consumed by the organization. The *replenishment pattern* refers to how the units are added to inventory. Replenishment patterns are usually instantaneous, uniform, or batch. Instantaneous receipt indicates that the entire lot is received into stock at the same time. *Replenishment lead time* is the length of time between the decision to replenish an item and its actual addition to stock and can be constant or variable. Probability distributions are used in describing variable lead time, much the same as they are in describing variable demand. The major components of lead time are:

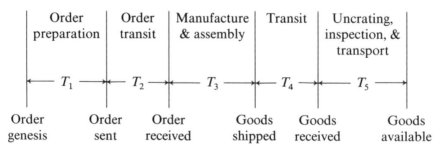

Order preparation	Order transit	Manufacture & assembly	Transit	Uncrating, inspection, & transport
T_1	T_2	T_3	T_4	T_5
Order genesis	Order sent	Order received	Goods shipped	Goods received	Goods available

Mathematically, it can be stated as

$$L = T_1 + T_2 + T_3 + T_4 + T_5 = \text{lead time},$$

where

T_1 = in-house order preparation time,

T_2 = order transmittal time to supplier,

T_3 = manufacture and assembly time,

T_4 = goods transit time from supplier,

T_5 = in-house goods preparation time.

Observe that the variables T_2, T_3, and T_4 are governed by factors outside the ordering organization, rendering them largely uncontrollable. In contrast, the variables T_1 and T_5 correspond to internal activities controllable by the ordering organization. When an organization moves from external to internal manufacturing and assembly of its items, it acquires more control over its replenishment lead time.

Constraints are limitations placed on the inventory system. Space constraints may limit the amount of inventory held; capital constraints the amount of money invested in inventories; and facility, equipment, or personnel constraints the supply capability and operating level of an organization. Management policies (such as never being out of stock on certain items) and administrative decisions (such as reciprocal purchasing agreements) can confine an inventory system in innumerable ways.

INVENTORY COSTS

The objective of inventory management is to have the appropriate amounts of raw materials, supplies, and finished goods in the right place, at the right time, and at low cost. Inventory costs are associated with the operation of an inventory system and result from action or lack of action on the part of management in establishing the system. They are the basic economic parameters to any inventory decision model, and the more relevant ones to most systems are itemized as follows: [2]

1. purchase cost,
2. order/setup cost,
3. holding cost,
4. stockout cost.

Note that for a particular inventory item, only those cost elements that are incremental (out of pocket) are pertinent in the analysis.

The *purchase cost* (P) of an item is the unit purchase price if it is obtained from an external source, or the unit production cost if it is

---

[2] Particularly those related to supplies, raw materials, and finished goods. See R. L. Van DeMark, *Inventory Control Techniques*, Dallas: Van DeMark Inc., 1981, pp. 40–70, for procedures for developing relevant cost parameters.

produced internally. The unit cost should always be taken as the cost of the item as it is placed in inventory. For purchased items, it is the purchase price plus any freight cost. For manufactured items, the unit cost includes direct labor, direct material, and factory overhead. The purchase cost is modified for different quantity levels when a supplier offers quantity discounts.

The *order/setup cost* (*C*) originates from the expense of issuing a purchase order to an outside supplier or from internal production setup costs. This cost is usually assumed to vary directly with the number of orders or setups placed and not at all with the size of the order. The order cost includes such items as making requisitions, analyzing vendors, writing purchase orders, receiving materials, inspecting materials, following up orders, and doing the paperwork necessary to complete the transaction. The setup cost comprises the costs of changing over the production process to produce the ordered item. It usually includes preparing the shop order, scheduling the work, preproduction setup, expediting, and quality acceptance.

The *holding cost* (*H*), synonymous with carrying cost, subsumes the costs associated with investing in inventory and maintaining the physical investment in storage. It incorporates such items as capital costs, taxes, insurance, handling, storage, shrinkage, obsolescence, and deterioration. Capital cost reflects lost earning power or opportunity cost. If the funds were invested elsewhere, a return on the investment would be expected. Capital cost is a charge that accounts for this unreceived return. Many states treat inventories as taxable property; so the more you have, the higher the taxes. Insurance coverage requirements are dependent on the amount to be replaced if property is destroyed. Insurance premiums vary with the size of the inventory investment. Obsolescence is the risk that an item will lose value because of shifts in styles or consumer preference. Shrinkage is the decrease in inventory quantities over time from loss or theft. Deterioration means a change in properties due to age or environmental degradation. Many items are age-controlled and must be sold or used before an expiration date (e.g., food items, photographic materials, and pharmaceuticals). The usual simplifying assumption made in inventory management is that holding costs are proportional to the size of the inventory investment. On an annual basis, they most commonly range from 20 to 40% of the investment. In line with this assumption is the practice of establishing the holding cost of inventory items as a percentage of their dollar value.

The *stockout cost* (depletion cost) is the economic consequence of an external or an internal shortage. An external shortage occurs when a customer's order is not filled; an internal shortage occurs when an order of a group or department within the organization is not filled. External shortages can incur backorder costs, present profit loss (potential sale), and future profit loss (goodwill erosion). Internal shortages can result in lost production (idle men and machines) and a delay in a completion date. The extent of the cost depends on the reaction of the customer to the out-of-stock condition. If demand occurs for an item out of stock, the economic loss depends on whether the shortage is backordered, satisfied by substitution of another item, or canceled. In the one situation, the sale is not lost but only delayed a few days in shipment. Typically a company would expedite an emergency backorder for the item and assume any extra costs charged for the special service (e.g., expediting costs, handling costs, and frequently premium shipping and packaging costs). In another situation, the sale is lost. The actual cost is less identifiable in this case but ranges from the apparent profit loss on the sale to loss of goodwill, which can be hard to specify. It can be seen that the stockout cost can vary considerably from item to item, depending on customer response or internal practice. It can be extremely high if the missing item forces a production line to shut down or causes a customer to go elsewhere in the future. The quantification of these costs has long been a difficult and unsatisfactorily resolved issue.

The central objective of inventory management (though not the sole objective) is usually the minimization of costs. Only those costs which change as the level of inventory changes should be considered in any analysis. For example, amounts expended on heating, lighting, and security services for a warehouse should be disregarded if they do not change as stock levels vary.

COST ACCUMULATION PROFILE

Organizations that manufacture products accumulate costs as manufacturing takes place. Until raw materials are released, no labor or labor-related costs are incurred. But once manufacturing begins, those materials acquire more and more value (cost) as labor and factory overhead are added. Ultimately, completed items reach peak value as they go into finished goods inventory and await shipment to the customer.

Assume an intermittent manufacturing process where material is routed through a series of steps (stages). Value is added at each step, and time is consumed between steps (in queue, transfer, or storage). Assume the product is manufactured in discrete, equal-sized batches. The inventory cost accumulation profile is illustrated in Figure 2. At the beginning of the process, the cost is that of the raw materials; each step (incline) adds additional cost. The horizontal line segments indicate that materials do not change value while in a raw material, storage, or finished goods state. The slope of the line at each step represents the rate at which labor cost is being added. The final vertical rise is the addition of factory overhead to the batch to obtain the total manufacturing cost.

The cost accumulation profile shows the pattern by which costs are incurred (added) for a manufactured product. From an investment point of

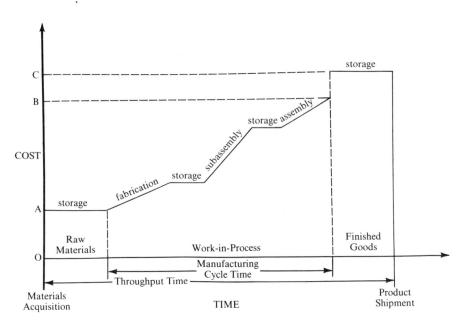

Figure 2. Inventory cost accumulation profile.
$0A$ = material cost, AB = labor cost, BC = factory overhead, $0C$ = total product cost.

view, it is desirable to shorten the throughput time or the total time inventory must spend in an organization from materials acquisition until final product shipment.

CONFLICTING GOALS

The goals associated with materials management are not monolithic or even easily delineated. The major goals of materials management are to minimize inventory investment, maximize customer service, and assure efficient (low cost) plant operation. Some of the common subgoals are low unit cost, high inventory turnover, consistency of quality, favorable supplier relations, and continuity of supply. It is plain to see that these goals can be inconsistent or even in direct conflict.

During a war or a period of extreme scarcity, the simple act of locating sources of supply may become the most important objective. This may also be true if a major supplier is closed because of labor difficulties. With unpredicted upsurges in demand, considerable pressure for supply sources can be experienced.

In a young company that is growing rapidly, cash is perpetually in short supply. Most earnings and borrowings are reinvested in plant and equipment. Since material stocks are essential, there is pressure to keep stock levels low to make cash available for other purposes. To buy in small quantities means passing up quantity discounts. Numerous orders and deliveries are necessary to operate on a "hand-to-mouth" basis. These conditions result in high inventory turnover, which can produce deleterious operational side effects.

Balance is a paramount consideration when goals and objectives are under consideration. Concentration may be on one objective at certain times and on another objective at other times, and tradeoffs must be considered. Concentration on inventory turnover can result in higher unit cost because of smaller, more frequent purchases. Concentration on low unit cost results in large quantity purchases which reduce inventory turnover. A purchasing agent may give undue emphasis to low unit cost while ignoring continuity of supply, quality, and inventory investment. A production manager may overemphasize continuity of supply to the detriment of low unit cost or inventory investment. All too often, the inventory policies in organizations lack perspective—they are aimed at managing the materials, rather than at managing the inventory system as a whole, at a minimum cost.

Inventories are a source of conflict among different managers in an organization. The conflict arises because different managers have different roles to play which involve the use of inventory. Suboptimization is the term used to describe subsystem optimization at the expense of system goals. Suboptimization results from the conflicting roles that managers play.

Start with the production manager. He is faced with the setup costs, scrap, rework, disruptions, and scheduling problems associated with changeovers. To deal with these, he wants to secure long production runs and lead times, ample raw materials inventories, and a large work backlog, and to minimize product variety. The purchasing manager is more interested in volume discounts, price fluctuations, vendor performance, and ordering costs, and consequently he prefers ordering in large quantities at infrequent intervals. Because the warehouse manager ascribes importance to the issues of stockroom and warehouse space, inventory investment, spoilage, turnover, and obsolescence, he would rather adequate stock levels be maintained by frequent orders of small to moderate size. The marketing manager, on the other hand, places value on prompt customer service, maximum product variety, and frequent production runs so the customer can be offered fresh stock and the latest engineering refinements. No stockouts, no production backlogs, minimum lead times, and an ample stock of finished goods are the means to accomplish these ends. Finally, the financial officer is preoccupied with liquidity, cash management, return on investment, minimal stock levels, avoidance of obsolescence, and maximum inventory turnover, and so is inclined to accept a reasonable level of stockouts and only a small investment in inventory.

Table 3. Departmental orientations towards inventory

Functional Area	Functional Responsibility	Inventory Goal	Inventory Inclination
Marketing	Sell the product	Good customer service	High
Production	Make the product	Efficient lot sizes	High
Purchasing	Buy required materials	Low cost per unit	High
Finance	Provide working capital	Efficient use of capital	Low
Engineering	Design the product	Avoiding obsolescence	Low

Tables 3 and 4 depict departmental concerns about inventory.

In reference to supplies and raw materials, it is possible for the financial officer and the purchasing manager to disagree. The purchasing manager usually wishes to purchase items in large quantities so that quantity discounts and transportation economics will result in a low unit cost. The treasurer more likely favors small purchases which would utilize less resources and release funds for other uses.

In reference to in-process goods, it is possible for the production manager and the controller to disagree. The production manager probably desires large inventories which decouple operations and reduce setup costs in high-volume production. The controller is apt to prefer small inventories which decrease storage, handling, transfer, and loss.

In reference to finished goods, the sales manager and the warehouse manager are expected to conflict. The sales manager wants large inventories which can permit quick delivery and increased sales. The warehouse manager likes small inventories which require less space and lower holding costs.

The abovementioned situations can result in conflict or at least differences in opinion and stem from the different roles that managers play. Many promising materials control systems have been wrecked or subverted by interdepartmental rivalries and cross-purposes. The conflicting roles of

Table 4. Conflicting organizational objectives

Area	Typical Response
Marketing/sales	I can't sell from an empty wagon. I can't keep our customers if we continue to stockout and there is not sufficient product variety.
Production	If I can produce larger lot sizes, I can reduce per unit cost and function efficiently.
Purchasing	I can reduce our per unit cost if I buy large quantities in bulk.
Finance	Where am I going to get the funds to pay for the inventory? The levels should be lower.
Warehousing	I am out of space. I can't fit anything else in the building.

managers must not be allowed to impair the organization as a whole. Materials policies must be established that result in the lowest overall costs.

Inventory management is everybody's concern, but it is not uncommon to find everybody's concern nobody's responsibility. Responsibility for inventory is often divided among departments with particular interests. Purchasing may take charge of raw materials and purchased items, while manufacturing looks after in-process goods, and marketing controls finished goods. The allocations of responsibility appear logical, but it is unlikely that the talent and expertise required for proper control are available in all the departments. It is commonly more desirable to put all inventory responsibility in a single location under a materials manager. Departmental conflicts and suboptimization are less likely to occur when inventories are under a materials manager.

Materials management attempts to consolidate activities, improve coordination, and provide a single source of accountability for all material-related activities. It can increase efficiency by providing shorter links between related activities. When these related activities are dispersed throughout an organization, they produce numerous conflicts and spark debilitating power struggles.

The inventory problem cannot be handled in isolation. It is inextricably interwoven with the problems of distribution, warehousing, production, materials handling, purchasing, marketing, and finance. The inventory system is part of a larger operating system and should facilitate the goals of the organization. The management of inventory requires a broad viewpoint and should not be treated as a series of independent decisions on individual items. Inventories are not an island unto themselves but are there to serve the purposes of the organization as outlined in policy statements.

Inventory must be managed, not delegated to clerical routine. To overcome its stormy past, inventory management has been broadened into materials management. Materials management is composed of all material-related functions, such as purchasing, transportation, logistics, production control, inventory, and sometimes even quality. The materials manager is made independent and on the same level as the finance, marketing, and production managers. It is the materials manager's job to strive for organizational goals and not to become the stepchild of any other functional area.

THE INVENTORY FLOW CYCLE

Inventory management involves controlling the rates of flow of material into and out of a system. In reality, it is a scheduling or timing problem. In the initial phase, materials and supplies are procured from suppliers. This reservoir of items forms the first pool of inventory investment that must be managed. The variety and quantity of items purchased should be timed so they will meet the demand for their utilization by the organization. As these items are released to manufacturing, they join another reservoir of inventory called in-process goods. This second reservoir must be managed in relation to the capacity of the facility. As items leave the in-process goods category, they enter another inventory reservoir called finished goods. This third reservoir must be regulated with relation to external demand. The cycle can continue into an additional reservoir if the organization maintains warehouses or distribution centers. A typical manufacturing inventory flow cycle is illustrated in Figure 3. It indicates the areas that regulate the flow into and out of the different inventory categories.

Each of the inventory categories or reservoirs requires a synchronization of the rate of flow into and from it. No particular category can be controlled without respect to the others. When the flow is regulated, an organization can function efficiently. When problems develop in any particular category, it will affect the others and influence organizational effectiveness. It is important that the multistage influence be understood in any inventory flow cycle.

Different organizations may have fewer or more categories to control, but the flow cycle is remarkably similar. For example, retailers and distributors will not have an in-process goods category, since they resell items in the same configuration as they are purchased. However, there are still multistage influences that must be controlled.

The driving force behind the inventory flow cycle is the demand for finished goods. From it, there is a derived demand for all those items that compose it. Whether forecasted or derived from customers' orders, demand starts the particular operational processes necessary to fulfill it. The inventory flow cycle is a vital part of the operational processes that satisfy customer demand.

FINANCIAL CONSIDERATIONS

Organizations are becoming increasingly aware that the overall efficiency and effectiveness of operations are directly related to materials management. The aim of inventory control is to maintain inventories at such a level that the goals and objectives of the organization are achieved. Inventory policies affect cost directly and revenue only indirectly. Inventory does not generate revenue (sales do that), although it makes revenue generation possible.

The relative significance of inventory management to an organization can be gaged by the overall investment in inventory and the magnitude of the material costs for all products. The overall investment in inventory can be ascertained by reviewing the balance sheet of an organization. If the investment in inventory is a large percentage of current assets or total assets, major emphasis should be placed on inventory management. Like-

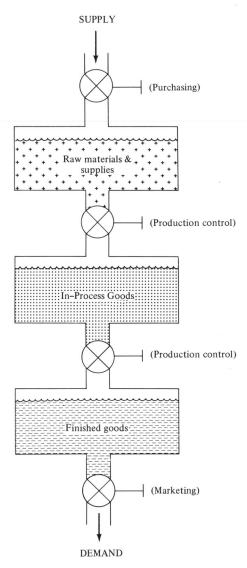

Figure 3. Manufacturing inventory flow cycle.

wise, if material costs are a large percentage of total product costs, inventory management is critical.

Inventories tie up money. For many organizations, the investment in inventories represents a sizable sum. A review of American industry balance sheets reveals that many businesses have 20–40% of their total assets tied up in inventory. Poor control of inventory can create a negative cash flow, tie up large amounts of capital, limit the expansion of an organization through lack of capital, and reduce the return on investment by broadening the investment base. The pressure for capital and the effective utilization of resources has made decision makers more aware of the significance of inventories. Cash invested in inventories could be used somewhere else for profit making, debt servicing, or dividend distribution.

There is an optimum level of investment in any asset, whether it is cash, plant, equipment, or inventory. Having too much can impair income just as much as having too little. With inventories, too much can result in unnecessary holding costs, and too little can result in lost sales or disrupted production. An organization must be careful not to overinvest in inventory that ties up capital and becomes obsolete, yet it must take care not to underestimate needs and run out of materials (thus idling people and equipment) or finished products (thus losing sales and customers).

In regard to inventory as an organizational asset, it should be further understood that inventory is an idle resource and its costs are only justified by the efficiency of operations it makes possible. Therefore, it is to be held only when the other alternatives are either more costly or less profitable.

The scoreboard for profit making organizations is the income statement and the balance sheet. The income statement shows the performance of the organization in profit or loss terms for a given period of time. The balance sheet reveals the general financial condition of an organization at a given point in time. Inventory appears as a current asset on the balance sheet. Its balance sheet entry is usually the accumulated monetary value at cost of all categories of inventory (supplies, raw materials, in-process goods, and finished goods). The importance of inventory for the income statement is that the cost of resources consumed (cost of goods sold) by the organization during a given time period must be allocated before income can be

Table 5. Sample balance sheet

Current Assets			Current Liabilities		
Cash and securities	$	40,000	Accounts payable	$	80,000
Accounts receivable		100,000	Notes payable		20,000
Inventory		300,000	Accrued expenses		10,000
Prepaid expenses		10,000	Current long term debt		50,000
Fixed Assets			Long Term Debt		300,000
Net plant & equipment		550,000			
			Owner's Equity		
			Preferred stock		140,000
			Common stock		300,000
			Retained earnings		100,000
			Total Liabilities		
Total Assets		$1,000,000	& Owners Equity		$1,000,000

Table 6. Sample income statement

Sales		$1,000,000
Direct material	$400,000	
Direct labor	200,000	
Factory overhead	100,000	
Cost of Goods Sold	700,000	− 700,000
Gross Profit		300,000
Selling expenses	50,000	
Administrative expense	100,000	
Total Selling/Administrative Expense	150,000	− 150,000
Operating Income		150,000
Interest Expense		− 50,000
Net Income Before Taxes		$100,000

determined. Abbreviated samples of a balance sheet and income statement are illustrated in Tables 5 and 6.

Liquidity indicates an organization's ability to pay its bills (meet its maturing short-term obligations). Assets are listed in order of decreasing liquidity on the balance sheet. Current assets are expected to be converted into cash within one year, while current liabilities are expected to be paid within one year. Net working capital is defined as current assets minus current liabilities. Liquidity problems are likely if current assets barely cover current liabilities. A current ratio (current assets divided by current liabilities) of 2.0 or greater indicates a healthy working capital, e.g.,

$$\text{current ratio} = \frac{\text{current assets}}{\text{current liabilities}} = \frac{\$450,000}{\$160,000} = 2.81.$$

Another liquidity ratio (from the balance sheet) which excludes inventory is the quick ratio (also called the acid test). It recognizes the importance of the ability to pay current obligations without relying on the sale of inventory:

$$\text{quick ratio} = \frac{\text{current assets} - \text{inventory}}{\text{current liabilities}} = \frac{\$450,000 - \$300,000}{\$160,000} = 0.94.$$

A safe quick ratio is 1.0 or greater.

Inventory is frequently evaluated by *turnover*, a measure of the velocity with which materials move through the organization. Turnover is the ratio of the annual cost of goods sold (from the income statement) to the average or current inventory investment (from the balance sheet). This ratio computes the number of times the inventory has turned over during the year, e.g.,

$$\text{inventory turnover} = \frac{\text{cost of goods sold}}{\text{inventory}} = \frac{\$700,000}{\$300,000} = 2.33.$$

Generally it is assumed that a large inventory turnover is desirable.

A potential distortion problem with this ratio is that the numerator (cost of goods sold) is for an entire year, while the denominator (inventory) is for a point in time. To overcome point distortions, frequently an average of the beginning and ending inventory investments is used. Another potential difficulty with this aggregated ratio is its disregard of the composition of the inventory. This problem can be overcome by having specific turnover ratios for each type of inventory: raw materials, in-process inventory, and finished goods, as well as aggregate inventory. This family of inventory turnover ratios can be very useful for discovering slow-moving items, spotting cost problems, and making comparative analyses between inventory types and between present and past performance.

Inventory turnover also is used to compare an organization's performance with that of other organizations in the same industry. It can be plotted over a number of years and used as a basis for intelligent questioning in identifying or confirming problems. Caution is advised in making comparisons with other organizations, since the turnover performance is a function of many unisolated factors, such as:

1. organizational strategies,
2. degree of vertical integration,
3. nature and type of distribution network,
4. accounting convention (LIFO vs. FIFO),
5. capital intensity (throughput time).

Except for broad comparison purposes, inventory turnover by itself is not an adequate measure of inventory management efficiency or effectiveness. By focusing on the financial aspects of inventory, it neglects important operational features (such as material availability, quantity discounts, and efficient plant operations) and customer service considerations (such as stockouts and customer dissatisfaction). As the turnover is increased, it drives the inventory level down; at some point the reduction of inventory will interfere with operating efficiency and customer service.

An approximation of the throughput time (see Figure 2) for an organization can be obtained by dividing the inventory turnover into the number of operating days in a year. The resulting throughput time is the average amount of time the inventory is in the pipeline, e.g.,

$$\text{throughput time} = \frac{\text{operating days per year}}{\text{inventory turnover}}$$

$$= \frac{360}{2.33} = 154.4 \text{ days.}$$

If the turnover is calculated for each type of inventory, the average cycle times for raw materials, in-process goods, and finished goods can be obtained similarly.

An inventory manager is interested in the economy, efficiency, and effectiveness of the inventory system. Economy refers to the low-cost operation of the inventory system; efficiency refers to how well the inventory system performs in relation to some standard (such as turnover); and effectiveness refers to how well the inventory system serves the goals of the organization. Thus, overall performance might be measured in terms of cost of operation, historical performance standards, and ability to meet customer demands.

BUSINESS CYCLE INFLUENCE

Business cycles are a persistent phenomenon in the national economy. They are recognizable as successive periods of expansion, contraction, recession, and recovery that repeat themselves in the same order, and sometimes over roughly the same time interval, as in the past. While not all industries follow the economy's overall movement, few are immune to its influence. Inventory accumulation and depletion have long been recognized as contributing factors to undulations in the national economy. On an aggregate basis, the flow patterns of inventory contribute to the cyclical behavior of business activity.

Inventory accumulation can accelerate business activities dramatically. When business tapers off, inventories continue to rise for some time and stock levels become excessive. Organizations not only stop buying in excess of demand, but they buy substantially less than current consumption. The underbuying causes production to drop precipitously, which helps to accelerate an economic downturn. Finally, an equilibrium point is reached and recovery commences. The recovery catches organizations unprepared, so sales exceed production and inventory levels drop. When production levels eventually exceed sales and inventories start increasing, the cycle begins all over again. The cycle may involve a time horizon of several years, and it is most relevant to durable goods industries that have long production lead times. Economists refer to the above phenomenon as the accelerator effect.

Organizations that are more "distant from the marketplace" are apt to be more vulnerable to swings in the business cycle. A relatively small change in demand at the consumer level can generate several times the amount of demand change at the producer level in multistage systems. Demand changes at the consumer level get amplified through numerous stages of a logistical network. This amplification occurs because each stage tends to respond to demand fluctuations by modifying its replenishment lot sizes and safety stocks (increased demand results in increased lot sizes and safety stocks, and vice versa). Thus the initial change at the consumer level is greatly multiplied at the highest level in the network (the factory). Of course, time lags in multistage systems further compound the amplification problem.

A long distribution chain or network is likely to set up internal oscillations in demand. A small variation in retail sales can cause giant fluctuations in the stock levels of the manufacturer and disrupt the flow of production. This whipsaw effect creates natural and artificial cyclical processes in inventories and production levels which can combine, cancel, or dampen themselves. Many manufacturers try to obtain information on demand at the retail level, so some guidance in relation to real or artificial undulations is obtained. Ignorance of the consumer's real behavior can result in very erratic demands being made on the manufacturer. The ideal system is one where the manufacturer knows what is actually happening in the marketplace. Management can dampen oscillations by (1) using a forecasting model that disregards short-term demand changes, (2) adopting a single stage (centralized) system so that two or more stages can be under the control of a single group, and (3) instituting direct communication with the ultimate consumer level to obtain real demand data.

The solution is to focus on rates of flow that are based on real demand at the downstream stages of the network where the ultimate consumer resides. If all the stages of the logistical network would produce or order only to real demand at the consumer level, the oscillation problem would largely disappear. The emphasis should be on real demand and not on orders that have passed through several stages of the distribution system.

JUST-IN-TIME

The just-in-time (JIT) concept, developed by the Japanese, challenges the foundations of classical inventory theory in reference to the production of goods. It requires the production of precisely the necessary units in the necessary quantities at the necessary time with the objective of plus or minus zero performance to schedule. This means producing one extra piece is just as bad as being one piece short. Anything over the minimum amount required is viewed as waste, because effort and material expended for something not needed now cannot be utilized now (later requirements are handled later). The JIT concept is counter to American manufacturing philosophy, since good performance has been to meet or exceed the scheduled requirements "just in case" something goes wrong.

Waste, in this view, is anything beyond the absolute minimum resources of material, machines, and manpower required to add value to the product. Value is added only by the actual work performed on a product. Machining, assembling, painting, and packaging add value to a product. Other activities such as moving, storing, counting, sorting, and scheduling add cost to a product but not value. Fork trucks, expediters, and safety stocks add cost but not value. Cost without value is waste. Anything which does not directly add value to the product is waste and should be minimized if not eliminated.

JIT disavows the value of inventory. It is viewed in a negative fashion, not as an asset. It is considered a deterrent to product quality that hides (covers up) problems. Without inventory, problems are exposed, so they can be remedied before they cause trouble. Anything that unnecessarily occupies space consumes a valuable resource. Inventory occupies space. To reduce the resulting waste, it is necessary to plan efficient layouts and material flows.

With JIT, the ideal lot size is *one*. The manufacturing process can be viewed as a network of work centers wherein the perfect arrangement would be to have each worker complete his task on an item and pass it directly to the next worker just as that person is ready for it. The idea is to drive all queues toward zero in order to:

1. minimize inventory investment,
2. shorten production lead times,
3. react faster to demand changes,
4. uncover any quality problems.

Since it is impossible to have all the workers in a network adjacent to one another and it must include outside suppliers, the system must allow for transit time between work centers. However, transfer quantities are kept as small as possible, and lot sizes are a fraction of a day's production. There are no allowances for contingencies. Every item is expected to be correct when received; every machine is expected to be available when needed to produce the item; every delivery commitment is expected to be honored at the precise time it is scheduled. Consequently, there is heavy emphasis on quality, preventive maintenance, and mutual trust between all participants in the manufacturing network.

CONCLUSION

The significance, relevance, and organizational stature of materials management will increase in the future. Numerous forces are dictating changes in this direction. One force is the trend towards increasing the number of highly specialized and complex products. As a result of this development, more organizations in the future will make fewer and buy more of their material requirements. Consequently, materials will represent an increasing percentage of total product costs, and their control will be even more important than it is today. A second major force is the increasing trend toward automation. An uninterrupted flow of materials is required for an automated facility. Failure of supply on a single item can close the facility down. A third major force is the burgeoning cost of materials. An expanding world population with an almost insatiable demand for goods and services is creating shortages in supply which are causing costs to skyrocket. The days of cheap and abundant raw materials appear to be past. These forces and many others indicate that the management of materials is no longer a trivial matter to be delegated to lower managerial levels.

Inventories can be economically puzzling to the casual observer, since they are subject to varied influences. Stock levels may soar if managers expect rising sales or if sales do not measure up to earlier expectations. Inventories may flatten or decline when organizations cannot get all the items they desire, or if decision makers are bearish on future activities. Organizations may hoard inventories when they expect sharply rising prices or materials shortages. In-process inventories can expand rapidly when shortages of key basic materials result in production bottlenecks. It is possible for the same level of inventory to be a blessing and a curse at different points in time. Furthermore, the composition of inventories is frequently just as important as the overall inventory level.

Pressures of the marketplace force organizations into broader product coverage and greater delivery capabilities. As product variety increases, so do the problems of materials management. Greater product variety increases the complexities of forecasting future demand, which escalates the inventory investment needed to maintain customer service levels. Expanded delivery capabilities are established by means of branch warehouses, which also escalate inventory complexity and investment.

All organizations have difficulty managing their inventory. The usual reason is the inability to forecast adequately. When materials are added to inventory, it is in anticipation of demand. If the demand is later than expected or never materializes, the result is excessive stock. If the demand is sooner or stronger than anticipated, the result is inadequate stock. Factors that tend to reduce inventory are better forecasts, improved transportation, improved communications, improved technology, better scheduling, and standardization.

QUESTIONS

1. Why has materials management gained more prominence as a functional area of an organization?

2. What types of inventory and what associated problems are encountered by (i) wholesale/distribution systems, (ii) continuous manufacturing systems?

3. What functions does inventory serve?

4. Based on utility, what are the broad categories of inventory?

5. Define replenishment lead time and specify its major components in their time sequence.

6. What costs are subsumed under the term "holding cost"?

7. What constitutes the purchase (unit production) cost for an internally manufactured item?

8. In what type of situation can a stockout cost be extremely high?

9. Briefly discuss what positions various managers would most likely take in regard to (i) inventory levels, (ii) stockouts.

10. Why is it desirable to shorten the throughput time?

11. In what ways are inventories important for both major types of financial statements (balance sheet and income statement)?

12. What is inventory turnover? State a couple of the potential problems of inventory turnover analysis.

13. What part does inventory play in the traditional business cycle?

14. Give several of the goals of "just-in-time (JIT)."

15. List some examples of materials management problems you personally have experienced.

CASE 1: THREE RING CIRCUS

The general manager was completely frustrated as he walked out of his conference room, where he left a heated argument between some members of his staff—the controller, the marketing manager, and the manufacturing manager. The controller had just presented a financial review of the previous month's performance, and his concluding words were that the inventory was too high and had to be reduced. The marketing manager quickly responded by saying that the finished goods inventory should not be reduced. The customer service performance was bad, and if anything should be changed, it was the finished goods inventory that should be increased. The manufacturing manager turned to the general manager and said, "Don't expect me to reduce the factory inventory if we are to achieve the productivity improvements projected for this year." Then the argument started. When it was evident that no logical conclusion was going to be reached in the present atmosphere, the meeting was adjourned. The general manager went to his office and called the materials manager.

1. Are arguments of this nature inevitable?
2. How should these situations be resolved?
3. Is any party unreasonable or at fault?

CASE 2: ROUGH SEAS

Bay Cove Marine is a distributor that supplies boating paraphernalia to marine companies in the coastal areas of North Carolina and Virginia. Bay Cove distributes several lines of boating equipment plus parts for new and older models of pleasurecraft. The items that Bay Cove distributes to dealers are sold directly to the customer or installed by a service department. The pleasurecraft that the local outlets service include outboards, inboards, outriggers, and small sailing vessels. Bay Cove has always carried complete lines of boating equipment and marine parts. Its excellent reputation has been maintained by a policy of stocking the most complete lines of parts and the widest selection of equipment within the geographical area.

The annual sales profile for Bay Cove has been fairly level over the past two years, with the usual peaks prior to and during vacation periods. The projection for future sales indicates a brief continuation at the present level followed by a gradual and continuing downward trend. Bay Cove has been and expects to be hit doubly hard by major economic problems. The recreational industries are being severely affected by persistent inflation, and the marine industries are having problems related to the high cost of energy.

Bay Cove management recognized the serious position of the industry last year and decided to focus on methods to help them survive the unfortunate economic circumstances. Realizing that the possibility of increasing profits through revenue growth was unlikely, Bay Cove decided to control costs instead. Analysis of the company cost structure revealed that the investment in inventory was the largest percentage of the asset base. Therefore, management concluded that the emphasis in the cost control program should be placed on inventory control.

Knowing that it needs more expertise in inventory management, Bay Cove hired a materials/inventory manager over a year ago. When Mr. Barone was hired, management stipulated that he would be evaluated on his contribution to the company's defined goals. Bay Cove was going to stress all actions that could reduce costs, tie up less capital in inventory, and consequently, improve the return on investment. The terms of Mr. Barone's employment specified that his monetary rewards would be based on the effectiveness of inventory control. His performance would be measured strictly on two criteria, a greater inventory turnover and a greater total asset turnover.

Mr. Barone's first year of employment ended, and the upper level managers were reviewing the past year's performance. The scoresheets were the balance sheet and income statement. The managers calculated the relevant financial ratios and discovered that Mr. Barone's performance had fallen short of the anticipated results. Comparison of the turnover ratios with those of the previous year showed no improvement. Management felt that their analysis had detected some weakness in Barone's ability to control inventory costs. Concentrating solely on the outcome of the turnover analysis, one of the managers, Mr. Rigger, castigated Mr. Barone bitterly. He accused him of employing faulty practices and suggested that he be dismissed.

Mr. Drew, another manager, insisted that Mr. Barone be allowed to explain the statistics. Mr. Barone, quite shocked by the ordeal, babbled a series of expletives and made the following statements in his defense: ratio analysis conducted in an unthinking manner is dangerous; the nature and complexity of Bay Cove's inventory items demand mandatory inventory levels; the company has conflicting and interdependent goals; there is a natural sluggishness associated with optimizing methods; there is a need to consider industry averages; there are inherent fallacies and distortions in turnover ratios.

Mr. Rigger stated that Barone's murmurings were incomprehensible and feeble excuses. He believed that the criteria should stand—nothing short of the discovery of an error in the ratio calculation could be a convincing argument.

1. Does Mr. Rigger have a justifiable cause for Mr. Barone's dismissal?
2. Are Barone's retorts feeble and irrelevant?
3. Are there other reasons Mr. Barone could have cited to strengthen his defense?
4. Did Bay Cove use acceptable performance criteria? What else might have been used to judge Mr. Barone's performance?

CASE 3: A NATURAL

New Commonwealth University is an urban university located in a populous city on the Eastern seaboard. The university has always given attention to the urban community it serves in defining its goals and objectives. NCU is committed to meeting the needs of its students and the regional businesses through teaching, research, and advisory and consulting services.

Key administrative positions in the School of Business have just changed hands. The replacements resulted from a dissatisfaction at the university level with the environment that has developed during the last decade and with the lack of direction toward university goals. The new administration is instituting a program of constructive change in an intense effort to rebuild the School of Business. The administration is determined to strengthen the curriculum for the students and to establish a recognizable resource base for the area.

It is the opinion of the administration and prominent faculty members that the majority of the business faculty have not shown any positive updating of business programs for some time. There has been an obvious lack of advisory and consulting relationships with local clients and an absence of faculty research. In response, all departments are being apprised that they are expected to define a departmental mission and to direct teaching, research, and consulting activities toward the fulfillment of adopted goals.

The Operations Management Department is in the process of revising the curriculum and redirecting its research and consulting projects. Realizing that the faculty has not been active in any area of operations research and has provided only minimal consulting services to this point, its members are attempting to identify an area in which they can fulfill their mission. They know that they cannot achieve proficiency in all areas, so they are trying to focus on a specific portion of their functional area.

Certain criteria become apparent. It is necessary to advise local businesses within the department's chosen area of expertise and to use the results of these advisory projects for publications. They will also have to integrate these faculty efforts with course structures. The courses will have to prepare students for the job market. The department will have to choose an area where the local market will be able to utilize its services. The local market should be large enough to support the program now and in the future.

Niels Holcher, an assistant professor who has just been hired from a large midwestern university, has offered a suggestion. He has told his colleagues that he feels they should emphasize materials management and inventory control in their courses and in their consulting and research efforts. He feels the need exists and is strong enough so that local organizations will request professional assistance. He has stated that while inventory systems are very sophisticated theoretically, there is a great need for practical research and application. In terms of quantity and perplexity of local business problems, it is a natural.

1. Does Niels have a worthwhile suggestion? Will his suggestion satisfy the departmental goals?
2. Should the department specialize in the materials management area? What would the future be in this area and why?
3. Would you have suggested an alternative area? If so, what and why?

2 Forecasting and Market Analysis

THE FORECASTING FUNCTION

TIME SERIES ANALYSIS
  Forecast Error
  Last Period Demand
  Arithmetic Average
  Moving Average
  Regression Analysis
  Exponentially Weighted Moving Average (EWMA)
  EWMA with Trend Correction
  EWMA with Seasonal Correction
  EWMA with Trend and Seasonal Corrections
  EWMA Overview
  Box-Jenkins Models

SOLICITING OPINIONS

ECONOMIC INDICATORS

ECONOMETRIC MODELS

GROUP FORECASTING

CONCLUSION
QUESTIONS
PROBLEMS
CASES
SELECTED BIBLIOGRAPHY
MATHEMATICAL ABBREVIATIONS AND SYMBOLS
SUMMARY OF FORMULAS

Man has always had a fascination with the future. Astrologers, prophets, wizards, and psychics have been foretelling events throughout recorded history. To this day, physical and psychic phenomena not only continue to arouse curiosity but even inspire scientific research into their predictive powers.

In modern organizational settings, looking into the future is done not just for the sake of discovery, to forebode good and evil, or to amuse the curious, but for the purpose of intelligent preparation for what it portends. Corporate planners are interested in the timing, magnitude, and effects of future events that influence their operations. For them, forecasting is the window into the future.

Forecasting is the prediction, projection, or estimation of the occurrences of uncertain future events or levels of activity. Since the future rarely is certain, some system of forecasting, implicit or explicit, is necessary. Forecasting offers an organization some foresight in the premeditation of appropriate courses of action. Its purpose is to make use of the best available present information to guide future activities toward organizational goals. This function is particularly important in the allocation and use of resources.

Absolute accuracy in predicting events and activity levels is unachievable, so there are limits on its potential benefits. Should funds be expended on a venture that is almost always in error? The answer is obviously yes, since the alternative is making decisions in total ignorance. Although forecasts are never perfect, partial knowledge is better than no knowledge. While organizations cannot foresee the future exactly, they desire strong inferences about it when committing large amounts of time and money.

Forecasting is used to predict changeable circumstances so that planning can take place to meet coming conditions. It can be used to predict revenues, costs, profits, prices, rainfall, technological changes, and a host of other variables. In organizational environments, forecasting most often pertains to predicting or estimating future demand. While the focus of this chapter is on demand forecasting, it should be remembered that the same concepts and techniques apply to these other phenomena.

Most organizations are not in a position to wait until orders are received before they begin to plan production facilities and processes, acquire equipment, establish manpower levels, and determine materials requirements. Few consumers would be willing to wait over such a time horizon. Most successful organizations anticipate the future demand for their products and translate this information into factor inputs required to satisfy expected demand. For a business to survive, it must meet its customers' needs at least as quickly as its competitors do. The better management is able to estimate the future, the better it should be able to prepare for it.

Many environmental factors influence the demand for an organization's products and services. It is never possible to identify all of the factors or to

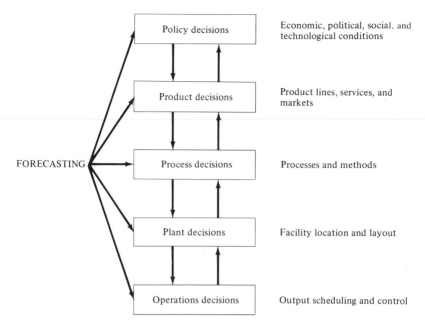

Figure 1. Master forecasting.

measure their probable effects. It is necessary in forecasting to identify the broad, major influences and to attempt to predict their direction. Some major environmental factors are:

1. General business conditions and the state of the economy
2. Competitor actions and reactions
3. Governmental legislative actions
4. Marketplace trends
    a. Product life cycles
    b. Style and fashion
    c. Changing consumer demands
5. Technological innovations

Given the broad spectrum of influences, many types of forecasting are used in organizations. Master forecasting, as illustrated in Figure 1, indicates the major decision categories. While not all organizations have the same forecasting needs, all of them have forecasting requirements. Functional forecasting, as shown in Figure 2, illustrates its influence on each business function. Thus, there are many plans and decisions and many different types of forecasting requirements.

Just as the various plans may require different types of forecasting, they also may require different forecasting bases (units of measure). Revenue,

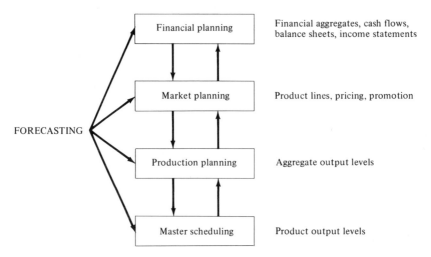

Figure 2. Functional forecasting.

physical units, cost of goods manufactured, direct labor hours, machine hours, weight, volume, and number of customers are common ones. Almost all organizations forecast revenues. Manufacturers typically select additional forecast bases which are more specifically related to their production processes. Among those already mentioned, physical units are commonly used by repetitive manufacturers; cost of goods manufactured, manhours, or machine hours, by intermittent process manufacturers; and weight (pounds, tons, etc.) or volume (liters, gallons, cubic feet, etc.), by continuous process manufacturers. In addition to dollars of revenue, service organizations generally forecast on the basis of the number of customers. The selection of one or more forecasting bases is dependent upon the planning which must take place.

Top-down forecasting and *bottom-up forecasting* are general forecasting patterns used for predicting product demand. Top-down forecasting begins with a forecast of general economic activity (GNP, national income, etc.) for the geopolitical unit where the organization operates. Industry forecasts are developed from the general economic activity forecast. The organization's share-of-the-market forecast is predicted from the industry forecast, and specific product group forecasts are developed from it.

Bottom-up forecasting begins at the product level. Forecasts are made for each product or product groups and are summed to obtain the aggregate organizational forecast. The aggregate forecast can be modified in relation to the general business outlook and the competitive situation. Advertising and promotion may necessitate further forecast revision.

Forecasting, as it is referred to here, is a short-run tool for establishing input-output levels. (By the short run, we mean that products, processes, equipment, tooling, layout, and capacity are essentially fixed.) All statistical forecasting techniques assume to some extent that forces that existed in the past will persist in the future. A forecast is the link between the external, uncontrollable environment and the internal, controllable affairs of an organization. Adequate forecasting procedures can go a long way toward solving many organizational problems.

THE FORECASTING FUNCTION

Forecasting frequently is viewed as a group of procedures for deriving estimates of future activity. From this narrow viewpoint, the line of vision is usually set on the type of forecasting technique to be used. It is more desirable to broaden the view to the forecasting function itself. The forecasting function includes the specific techniques and models, but it also highlights the significance of inputs and outputs (see Figure 3) to the subject of forecasting.

To develop the forecasting function, it is first necessary to determine its outputs. The outputs (and their format) can be specified by a delineation of the intended uses of the forecasts. This chapter already has mentioned numerous uses for forecasts in organizations. When the users obtain the outputs, specific actions will be taken to assure that future demand will be

Figure 3. The forecasting function.
[From Richard J. Tersine and John H. Campbell, *Modern Materials Management*, New York: North Holland, 1977, p. 49.]

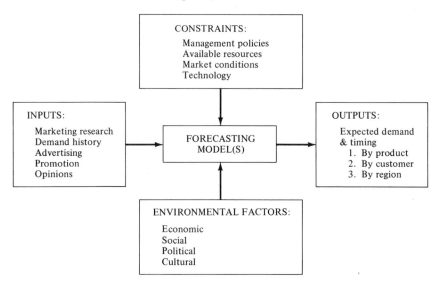

satisfied. Defining the purpose of the forecast helps to set its time horizon, desired accuracy, and units of expression.

The initial specification of outputs can simplify the selection of the forecasting model, but the forecasting function is not complete without the input considerations. No matter how long a system is studied, only a few of its many inputs can be isolated. Fortunately, most systems are relatively insensitive to most of their inputs. Therefore, the size of the problem can be reduced by clearing away the extraneous inputs. Only the significant few need be under close observation for changes in the future.

The data needed to prepare a forecast can be obtained from internal and/or external sources. External sources may provide valuable information on environmental factors such as economic, social, political, and cultural conditions. The selection of forecasting models depends heavily on constraints imposed on the organization by management policies, available resources, market conditions, and technology.

Forecasting is a model-based information system, and there are many models from which to choose. Not only do they differ in techniques but also in effort and cost of implementation. Forecasting models can be classified several ways, such as qualitative or quantitative, formal or informal, intrinsic or extrinsic, statistical or nonstatistical, and descriptive or explanatory. In this chapter the qualitative-quantitative classification is emphasized. Qualitative models rely on opinion, judgment, experience, and expertise; quantitative models rely on the use of historical data or associations among variables to develop forecasts. Some techniques are quite simple, while others are quite complex. Some work better than others, but no single technique works all the time. All forecasts include a degree of inaccuracy, and allowances should be made for it.

By knowing the desired outputs and significant inputs (variables), different forecasting models can be analyzed. Preference for one technique over another depends on several factors such as cost, data availability, staff skills, hardware and software availability, desired accuracy, and time horizon under consideration. Sometimes a specific model will be indicated. If not, several can be tested and the most reliable one adopted.

In general, the forecasting model should be matched to the knowledge and sophistication of the user. Some models require the user to analyze and interpret statistical measures. Managers are reluctant to use results from techniques they do not understand. Fairly crude techniques frequently enjoy widespread popularity because managers are more comfortable using them. Thus, the forecasting approach should fit the organizational environment and the management expertise.

Many models require a substantial amount of historical data. If adequate and relevant historical data do not exist or are prohibitively expensive to accumulate, then many techniques are ruled out. All quantitative forecasting techniques depend upon the existence of adequate and accurate historical data. Elegant forecasting techniques applied to poor data cannot yield good forecasts. The choice of a forecasting technique is often constrained by the available data.

The demand pattern will affect the type of forecasting technique selected. If several components (trend, seasonal, cyclic) are apparent, more advanced techniques are needed. If the demand pattern is unstable over time, a qualitative technique may be needed.

Forecasting usually involves the following considerations:

1. items to be forecasted (products, product groups, assemblies, etc.),
2. top-down or bottom-up forecasting,
3. forecasting techniques (quantitative or qualitative models),
4. units of measure (dollars, pieces, pounds, etc.),
5. time interval (weeks, months, quarters, etc.),
6. forecast horizon (how many time intervals to include),
7. forecasting components (levels, trends, seasonals, cycles, and random variation),
8. forecast accuracy (error measurement),
9. exception reporting and special situations,
10. revision of forecasting model parameters.

In most organizations, a small percentage of the material requirements represents a majority of the investment. These high cost or high usage items should receive the greatest degree of forecasting attention. There are also a great many low cost or low usage items that represent a small percentage of the total investment (although a high percentage of the number of items). Very little effort should be devoted to making forecasts for them. For low cost items, crude forecasts supplemented with large safety stocks are sufficient. Forecasting emphasis should be placed on those items that represent a significant investment.

Fortunately, many items produced by an organization do not need forecasts. Dependent demand items such as components, subassemblies, and services that are part of a finished product can be calculated from the forecasts for the end item. Forecasts should be made only for end items and services that have an uncertain demand.

The presence of randomness precludes a perfect forecast. Forecasts for groups (families) of items tend to be more accurate than forecasts for individual items, because forecasting errors among items in a group tend to cancel. Additionally, error potential increases as the time horizon of a forecast increases. Thus, a short-term forecast is generally more accurate than a long-term forecast.

As shown in Figure 4, there are four basic demand forecasting models—*time series analysis, economic indicators, econometric models*, and *soliciting opinions*. These techniques are short-range forecasting devices, and their value diminishes as the time horizon increases. Many of the techniques

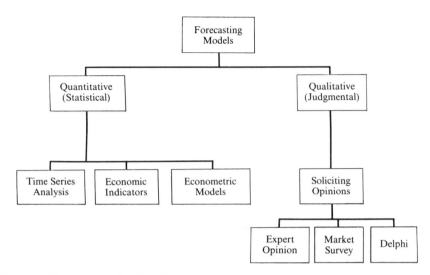

Figure 4. Forecasting classifications.

are based on extrapolation into the future of effects that have existed in the past.

The forecasting approaches to new products and established products are dissimilar. For established products with a demand history, future activity can be based more quantitatively and objectively on past performance. The forecasting techniques of time series analysis, economic indicators, and econometric models can appropriately use conditions which prevailed in the past to approximate the future. New products with little or no history of past demand are unavoidably more interpretative and must rely more heavily on subjective phenomena and solicitation of opinions. The direct survey approach—asking prospective customers of their buying intentions —is frequently used. An indirect survey approach may also be employed: information is obtained from people (salesmen, wholesalers, jobbers) who know how the customers respond. Also, if a comparable or substitute product exists, comparisons with it can be made. Finally, a limited market test of the new product can indicate product acceptability to potential customers.

There is no single forecasting technique that is superior in all cases, and the same organization can use different techniques for different products. It is difficult to ascertain the effect of changes in selling price, product quality, marketing methods, promotion, and economic conditions on forecasts. Regardless of the method adopted, the results provide the decision maker with nothing more than a starting point for making the final forecast. The final forecast usually requires an additional input in the form of judgment, intuition, and experience. Nor should any organization make a forecast and adhere to it blindly without periodic review.

TIME SERIES ANALYSIS

Time series analysis predicts the future from past internal data. A time series is a set of time ordered observations on a variable during successive and equal time periods. By studying how a variable (historical demand) changes over time, a relationship between demand and time can be formulated and used to predict future demand levels. In time series analysis, historical data are analyzed and decomposed to identify the relevant components which influence the variable being forecasted. Time series data may contain up to five interacting components—*levels*, *trends*, *seasonal variations*, *cyclical variations*, and *random variations*. Some or all components may be present. The components (except for the random variations) then are projected forward into the future. If historical components persist into the future, a reliable forecast will be obtained.

The level component is present in all data and represents the central tendency of a time series at any given time. It indicates the scale (magnitude) of a time series. The trend component identifies the rate of growth or decline of a series over time. As illustrated in Figure 5, the trend component indicates the long-term historical pattern between demand and time. It is given by a smooth trend line fitted to the historical data and rarely, if ever, coincides with the precise historical information. Instead, it depicts the general upward or downward movement of demand.

Seasonal variations consist of annually recurring movements above and below the trend line (or level) and are present when demand fluctuates in a repetitive pattern from year to year. The periodicity may be related to weather patterns (nature), tradition, school openings, vacations, taxes, bonuses, model changeovers, or calendar related customs such as holidays. Examples of products with a seasonal pattern are antifreeze, soft drinks, ice cream, toys, snow tires, grass seed, textbooks, air conditioners, and greeting cards.

Before seasonal corrections are included in a forecast model, some conditions should be met. There should be some known reason for the periodic peaks and valleys in the demand pattern, and they should occur at essentially the same time every year. For the seasonal modification to be worth including, it should be of a larger magnitude than the random variations.

Cyclical variations are long term oscillations or swings about a trend line and account for some of the variation between the trend line and raw data points. The cycles may or may not be periodic, but they often are the result of business cycles of expansion and contraction of economic activity over a number of years. The familiar pattern of the business cycle, i.e., prosperity,

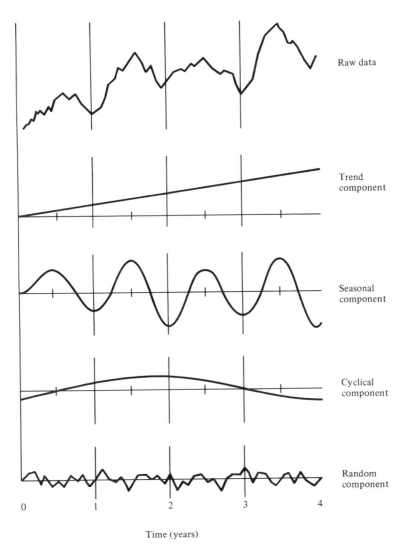

Raw data

Trend
component

Seasonal
component

Cyclical
component

Random
component

0   1   2   3   4

Time (years)

Figure 5. Time series components.

recession, depression, and recovery, may vary as to the time of occurrence, the length of the phases, and the amplitude of the fluctuations. Although the business phases generally trigger some reaction in the plotted variable, the reaction to the cyclical influences within an organization also may be unique and inconsistent. Because the magnitude, timing, and pattern of cyclical movements vary so widely and may be attributed to several causes, there are no generally reliable methods of predicting their repetition. The available methods are beyond the scope of this section.

Random variations have no discernable patterns and often are without specific, assignable causes. They are often referred to as noise, residuals, or irregular variations, and they have such causes as measurement errors, floods, fires, earthquakes, wars, strikes, and other unusual conditions. Random variations represent all the influences not included in trend, seasonal, and cyclical variations. A random component is present in all data series, and its effects are part of the unexplained deviations of the data. An averaging process will help to eliminate its unpredictable influence.

Past trends may be good indicators of the future, but the forecaster should be alert to factors that may cause severe abruption from the past. External factors frequently have a very pronounced effect on the future, and time series analysis tends to neglect them. Time series analysis is somewhat like driving your car down the road with the windshield blacked out, only being able to see through the rear view mirror. You cannot see where you are going, but only where you have been. If something is going to happen in the future which has not happened in the past, there is no way time series analysis can respond to it.

There are many techniques for time series analysis. Some of the most common ones are last period demand, arithmetic average, moving average, regression analysis, and the exponentially weighted moving average. All of the techniques assume some perpetuation of historical forces and that past data are reliable predictions of the future. Inaccuracies result when past conditions change or cease to be operative.

Forecast Error

The decision to adopt a new model or continue with the present one usually rests on some measure of the forecast error. Each technique is tested on the historical data, and the one with the smallest forecast error is selected as the forecast instrument. Several measures of the forecast error are shown in Figure 6.

Forecast errors influence decisions in two different ways. One is in making the choice among various forecasting techniques, and the other is in evaluating the success or failure of a technique in use. Two commonly used measures for summarizing historical errors are the mean absolute deviation (MAD) and the mean squared error (MSE). The MAD is the average absolute error, and the MSE is the average of the squared errors. Neither the MAD nor the MSE considers whether the error is positive or negative (underestimated or overestimated). The difference between the two is that one weights all errors equally, while the other weights errors in proportion to their squared values. The MSE, unlike the MAD, penalizes a forecasting technique more heavily for larger errors than for smaller ones.

The MAD (*mean* is the statistician's term for average; *absolute* means the plus or minus sign is ignored; and *deviation* means the difference between actual demand and the forecast) is obtained by dividing the

1. Mean absolute deviation (*MAD*) — extent:

$$MAD = \frac{\sum\limits_{i=1}^{n} |Y_i - \hat{Y}_i|}{n}$$

2. Mean squared error (*MSE*) — extent:

$$MSE = \frac{\sum\limits_{i=1}^{n} (Y_i - \hat{Y}_i)^2}{n}$$

3. Standard deviation of regression (S_r) — extent:

$$S_r^2 = \frac{\sum\limits_{i=1}^{n} (Y_i - \hat{Y}_i)^2}{n-2}$$

4. Bias — direction:

$$bias = \frac{\sum\limits_{i=1}^{n} (Y_i - \hat{Y}_i)}{n}$$

5. Tracking signal (*TS*) — revision:

$$TS = \frac{\sum\limits_{i=1}^{n} (Y_i - \hat{Y}_i)}{MAD}$$

Figure 6. Forecast error measurement.

number of observations into the sum of absolute deviations.[1] The MAD is calculated from the following formula:

$$MAD = \frac{\sum\limits_{i=1}^{n} |Y_i - \hat{Y}_i|}{n},$$

where

$\hat{Y}_i$ = forecasted demand for period i,

Y_i = actual demand for period i,

n = number of time periods,

$Y_i - \hat{Y}_i$ = algebraic deviation or forecast error,

$|Y_i - \hat{Y}_i|$ = absolute deviation.

Forecasting is probably going to be incorrect, so it is useful to predict the degree of inaccuracy. The MAD can aid in this prediction. It uses past

[1] For a normal distribution, the standard deviation is closely approximated by 1.25 times the MAD. The relationship between the standard deviation and the MAD is important in determining confidence limits for forecasts and in establishing inventory safety stock levels via computer routines.

history as its guide in attempting to estimate forecast error. By comparing the forecasts from different techniques with the actual demands for the same periods, the performance of the techniques can be compared. On the basis of past forecasting abilities, the one considered most desirable has the smallest MAD or the greatest degree of accuracy during the period tested.

While the MAD expresses the extent of the forecast error, it does not indicate the direction. The direction of forecast errors is expressed by the bias, which measures the tendency to consistently overforecast or under-forecast. An ideal forecast technique would have a zero MAD and bias. The bias is calculated from the following formula:

$$\text{bias} = \frac{\sum_{i=1}^{n} (Y_i - \hat{Y}_i)}{n}.$$

A positive bias indicates a tendency to underforecast, while a negative bias indicates a tendency to overforecast. The inaccuracy (error) of a forecast is measured by its MAD and bias.

Statistics of forecast error are needed to (1) judge the suitability and adequacy of a particular forecast model, (2) provide information for adjusting estimates of forecast model parameters, and (3) set service levels on products provided to customers.

Last Period Demand

The last period demand (LPD) technique simply forecasts for the next period the level of demand that occurred in the previous period. No calculations are required, and forecasted values lag behind actual demand by one period. Mathematically,

$$\hat{Y}_t = Y_{t-1},$$

where

$$\hat{Y}_t = \text{forecasted demand for period } t,$$

$$Y_{t-1} = \text{actual demand in the previous period.}$$

The use of the last period demand technique indicates that the immediate future is expected to behave much like the recent past. It works well if there is little variation in actual values from period to period. It responds fairly well to trends; it does not compensate very well for seasonals; and it overreacts to random influences.

Arithmetic Average

The arithmetic average simply takes the average of all past demand in arriving at a forecast. Mathematically,

$$\hat{Y}_t = \frac{\sum\limits_{i=1}^{n} Y_i}{n} = \frac{Y_1 + Y_2 + \cdots + Y_n}{n},$$

where

$\hat{Y}_t$ = forecasted demand for period t,

Y_i = actual demand in period i,

n = number of time periods.

    The arithmetic average technique, unlike the last period demand technique, will smooth out random fluctuations; it will not adequately respond to trends in demand; and it neglects seasonals. Smoothing refers to the dampening or diminishing of random fluctuations and is synonymous with averaging.

    The basic objection to the arithmetic average is that it takes too little account of recent data and is not responsive enough to changes in demand pattern. The arithmetic average works well in a stable situation where the level of demand does not change. It is appropriate for data that are stationary (horizontal) and randomly distributed.

Moving Average

The moving average technique generates the next period's forecast by averaging the actual demand for the last n time periods. The choice of the value of n should be determined by experimentation and often lies within the range of 3 to 8. The objective of the moving average is to include a sufficient number of time periods so random fluctuations are canceled, but few enough periods so irrelevant information from the distant past is discarded. The moving average is computed over time, changing with the addition of new data and the deletion of old data. As data become available for each time period, the latest data are included and the oldest data are excluded from the computation of the mean. Mathematically,

$$\hat{Y}_t = \frac{Y_{t-1} + Y_{t-2} + \cdots + Y_{t-n}}{n} = \frac{\sum\limits_{i=1}^{n} Y_{t-i}}{n},$$

where

$\hat{Y}_t$ = forecasted demand for period t,

Y_{t-i} = actual demand in period $t - i$,

n = number of time periods included in moving average.

This technique gives more weight to the more current time periods. How many periods to use in the average is difficult to say without examining the particular situation. If too few are used, the forecast fluctuates wildly, influenced by random variations in demand. If too many are used, the average is too stable and current trends are not detected. If there is a trend in demand, the moving average will always lag behind it. The lag increases with the number of periods in the average.

The moving average technique is a compromise between the last period demand and the arithmetic average technique with the advantages of both and the disadvantages of neither. If the demand rate is steady, the moving average will respond with fairly constant forecasts, as does the average method. However, when the average demand does change, the moving average forecast, like the last period demand forecast, responds fairly quickly to the change, but without the extreme fluctuations that are characteristic of the last period demand forecast. Increasing the number of periods in the moving average will produce forecasts closer to the arithmetic average forecast. Decreasing the number of periods will produce forecasts closer to last period demand forecast. The moving average dampens random effects, responds to trends with a delay, and does not compensate for seasonals.

EXAMPLE 1

Monthly demand in units for the last two years is listed below. Evaluate the forecasts with the last period demand, arithmetic average, and two-month moving average techniques. Utilizing the mean absolute deviation (MAD) as a criterion, determine the most desirable of the three forecasting techniques. What is the forecast for the twenty-fifth month with each of the three techniques?

Month	Demand	Month	Demand	Month	Demand
1	34	9	38	17	58
2	44	10	44	18	54
3	42	11	36	19	46
4	30	12	46	20	48
5	46	13	42	21	40
6	44	14	30	22	50
7	56	15	52	23	58
8	50	16	48	24	60
				Total	1096

Table 1 compares the three forecasting techniques. The two-month moving average has the smallest mean absolute deviation, 7.27 (160/22); the arithmetic average has a MAD of 7.55 (166/22); and the last period demand has the largest MAD, 8.26 (190/23). The two-month moving average technique is the most

Table 1

Month	Demand	Last Period Demand Forecast Demand	Last Period Demand Absolute Deviation	Arithmetic Average Forecast Demand	Arithmetic Average Absolute Deviation	Two-Month Moving Average Forecast Demand	Two-Month Moving Average Absolute Deviation
1	34	—	—	—	—	—	—
2	44	34	10	—	—	—	—
3	42	44	2	39	3	39	3
4	30	42	12	40	10	43	13
5	46	30	16	38	8	36	10
6	44	46	2	39	5	38	6
7	56	44	12	40	16	45	11
8	50	56	6	42	8	50	0
9	38	50	12	43	5	53	15
10	44	38	6	43	1	44	0
11	36	44	8	43	7	41	5
12	46	36	10	42	4	40	6
13	42	46	4	43	1	41	1
14	30	42	12	42	12	44	14
15	52	30	22	42	10	36	16
16	48	52	4	42	6	41	7
17	58	48	10	43	15	50	8
18	54	58	4	44	10	53	1
19	46	54	8	44	2	56	10
20	48	46	2	44	4	50	2
21	40	48	8	44	4	47	7
22	50	40	10	44	6	44	6
23	58	50	8	44	14	45	13
24	60	58	2	45	15	54	6
25		60		46		59	
	1096		190		166		160

desirable of the three techniques evaluated, and its forecast for the next month is 59 units.

Regression Analysis

Regression analysis establishes a temporal relationship for the forecast variable. The variable to be predicted (demand) is referred to as the dependent variable, while the variable used in predicting (time) is called the independent variable. A cause-effect relationship is often suspected. The simplest type of relationship is a linear association. Regression analysis by the least squares method will fit a straight line to a plot of data. The line fitted by the method will be such that the sum of squares of the deviations about the line is less than that about any other line. The regression line will encompass the trend effect, but not the seasonal effect. The basic equation for a straight line that expresses demand (Y) as a function of time (t) is

$$\hat{Y}_t = \alpha + \beta t,$$

where α is the intersection of the line with the vertical axis when $t = 0$, and β is the slope of the line. The parameters α and β are estimated from the following formulas:

$$\beta = \frac{n \sum_{i=1}^{n} t_i Y_i - \left(\sum_{i=1}^{n} t_i \right) \left(\sum_{i=1}^{n} Y_i \right)}{n \sum_{i=1}^{n} t_i^2 - \left[\sum_{i=1}^{n} t_i \right]^2} = \text{slope,}$$

$$\alpha = \overline{Y} - \beta \overline{t} = \frac{\sum_{i=1}^{n} Y_i - \left[\beta \sum_{i=1}^{n} t_i \right]}{n} = \text{intercept,}$$

where n is the number of periods of demand data included in the calculation.

If the relationship between variables in regression analysis is not perfect, there will be a scatter or variation about the regression line. The greater the scatter about the regression line, the poorer the relationship. A statistic that indicates how well a regression line explains or fits the observed data is the correlation coefficient. The degree of linear association of the forecast variable to the time variable is determined by the correlation coefficient. The correlation coefficient ranges between -1 and $+1$. A high absolute value indicates a high degree of association, while a small absolute value indicates little association between variables. When the coefficient is positive, one variable tends to increase as the other increases. When the coefficient is negative, one variable tends to decrease as the other increases. Figure 7 illustrates typical scatter diagram correlations. The following formula for r^2, the coefficient of determination, is used to compute the correlation coefficient r:

$$r^2 = \frac{\left[n \sum_{i=1}^{n} t_i Y_i - \left(\sum_{i=1}^{n} t_i \right) \left(\sum_{i=1}^{n} Y_i \right) \right]^2}{\left[n \sum_{i=1}^{n} t_i^2 - \left(\sum_{i=1}^{n} t_i \right)^2 \right] \left[n \sum_{i=1}^{n} Y_i^2 - \left(\sum_{i=1}^{n} Y_i \right)^2 \right]}.$$

The simple correlation coefficient measures the strength and direction of the relationship between two variables. The value of r^2 measures the proportion of the total variation of the dependent variable (Y) which is

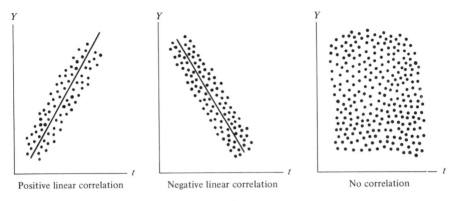

Figure 7. Typical scatter diagram correlations.
[From Richard J. Tersine and John H. Campbell, *Modern Materials Management*, New York: North Holland, 1977, p. 57.]

explained by the independent variable (t). The remainder of the variation $(1 - r^2)$ is due to chance or factors other than the independent variable. It is therefore desirable to have a value of r^2 as close to one as possible.

The following table represents a general rule of thumb for interpretation of the coefficient of correlation.

Absolute Value of Correlation Coefficient	Interpretation
0.90–1.00	Very high correlation
0.70–0.89	High correlation
0.40–0.69	Moderate correlation
0.20–0.39	Low correlation
00.0–0.19	Very low correlation

In linear regression analysis, it is assumed that demand is a normally distributed random variable whose mean is the Y coordinate on the regression line at that point in time. By knowing the standard deviation of the distribution, probability statements can be made about the reliability of the forecasts. It is assumed that the standard deviation S_r can be determined from the following formula:

$$S_r^2 = \frac{\sum_{i=1}^{n} Y_i^2 - \alpha \sum_{i=1}^{n} Y_i - \beta \sum_{i=1}^{n} t_i Y_i}{n - 2}$$

$$= \frac{\sum_{i=1}^{n} \left(Y_i - \hat{Y}_i \right)^2}{n - 2}.$$

Once the linear regression line and the standard deviation have been determined, control limits can be established at one, two, or three standard deviations from the mean. When the actual demand occurs, it can be compared with the control limits to determine if the demand is what could be reasonably expected. If the demand falls outside the control limits, there is reason to wonder if the system has changed. If it has, a new forecasting model should be developed to replace the inadequate model.

Frequently, time series data are autocorrelated or serially correlated. Autocorrelation occurs where one observation tends to be correlated with the next. Autocorrelation violates the conditions required to produce a valid regression estimate. To be valid, each observation on the data in regression analysis should be totally independent of any other observation. Time series data do not usually meet this condition, since most observations in the series can be forecasted by the last observation plus or minus a small change. This is especially true where a strong trend exists. Regression analysis requires that errors about the regression line be small and unrelated to each other and that their expected value be zero.

In some cases a high demand in one period may be an indication of a low demand to follow (the high demand could be due to advance stocking). This condition displays negative autocorrelation. In other cases, a high demand can arise from a cause which will also increase the following period's demand. This condition displays positive autocorrelation.

If autocorrelation exists, regression will underestimate the true variance and result in confidence limits that are too narrow. Autocorrelation may sometimes be corrected for by using first differences. With first differences, the observed datum Y_t is replaced with its first difference $Y_t - Y_{t-1}$. The extent of autocorrelation can be determined by the Durbin-Watson statistic or the von Neumann ratio, an explanation of which can be found in advanced statistics books.

EXAMPLE 2

Annual sales for the last seven years for an organization are given in the following table. Determine (a) the linear least squares regression line; (b) the standard deviation of the regression; (c) the correlation coefficient; (d) the forecasted demand for next year; and (e) the two standard deviation control limits for next year.

Year	Annual Sales
1	$1,760,000
2	2,120,000
3	2,350,000
4	2,800,000
5	3,200,000
6	3,750,000
7	3,800,000

The following table develops the pertinent data:

Year t	Demand Y ($\$10^6$)	tY	t^2	Y^2
1	1.76	1.76	1	3.0976
2	2.12	4.24	4	4.4944
3	2.35	7.05	9	5.5225
4	2.80	11.20	16	7.8400
5	3.20	16.00	25	10.2400
6	3.75	22.50	36	14.0625
7	3.80	26.60	49	14.4400
28	19.78	89.35	140	59.6970

a:

$$\beta = \frac{n\sum_{i=1}^{n} t_i Y_i - \sum_{i=1}^{n} t_i \sum_{i=1}^{n} Y_i}{n\sum_{i=1}^{n} t_i^2 - \left(\sum_{i=1}^{n} t_i\right)^2} = \frac{7(89.35) - (28)(19.78)}{7(140) - 28^2} = 0.3654,$$

$$\alpha = \frac{\sum_{i=1}^{n} Y_i - \beta \sum_{i=1}^{n} t_i}{n} = \frac{19.78 - 0.3654(28)}{7} = 1.3641,$$

$$\hat{Y}_t = \alpha + \beta t = (1.3641 + 0.3654t) \times 10^6 = 1,364,100 + 365,400t.$$

b:

$$S_r^2 = \frac{\sum_{i=1}^{n} Y_i^2 - \alpha \sum_{i=1}^{n} Y_i - \beta \sum_{i=1}^{n} t_i Y_i}{n - 2}$$

$$= \frac{59.6970 - 1.3641(19.78) - 0.3654(89.35)}{5} = 0.01332,$$

$$S_r = 0.1154 \times 10^6 = \$115,400.$$

c:

$$r^2 = \frac{\left[n\sum_{i=1}^{n} t_i Y_i - \left(\sum_{i=1}^{n} t_i\right)\left(\sum_{i=1}^{n} Y_i\right)\right]^2}{\left[n\sum_{i=1}^{n} t_i^2 - \left(\sum_{i=1}^{n} t_i\right)^2\right]\left[n\sum_{i=1}^{n} Y_i^2 - \left(\sum_{i=1}^{n} Y_i\right)^2\right]}$$

$$= \frac{[7(89.35) - 28(19.78)]^2}{[7(140) - 784][7(59.6970) - 391.2484]} = 0.9824,$$

$$r = 0.991.$$

d: $\hat{Y}_8 = 1,364,100 + (365,400)8 = 4,287,300$

e: $\hat{Y}_8 \pm 2S_r = 4,287,300 \pm 2(115,400) = \$4,287,300 \pm 230,800.$

The two standard deviation control limits are $\$4,056,500$ to $\$4,518,100$.

Exponentially Weighted Moving Average (EWMA)

The exponentially weighted moving average, also referred to as exponential smoothing, is a special kind of moving average that does not require the keeping of a long historical record. The moving average technique assumes that data have no value after n periods. Some value (although possibly very little) remains in any datum, and a model that uses all the data with appropriate weightings should be superior to a model that discards data.

Like most forecasting techniques, EWMA uses historical data as its prediction basis. It is a special type of moving average where past data are not given equal weight. The weight given to past data decreases geometrically with increasing age of the data. More recent data are weighted more heavily than less recent ones. The major advantage of the EWMA is that the effect of all previous data is included in the previous forecast figure, so only one number needs to be retained to represent the demand history.

The simplest EWMA model estimates the new average or forecast demand level for the current period from the most recent forecast plus a fraction of the error between the actual demand and the forecasted demand for the most recent period. In other words, a fraction of the difference between the previous period's actual demand (Y_{t-1}) and its forecasted demand ($\hat{X}_{t-1}$) is added to the previous forecast itself to obtain an updated forecast for the current period ($\hat{X}_t$):

current forecast level

$$= (\text{previous forecast}) + a(\text{previous actual} - \text{previous forecast})$$

$$= a(\text{previous actual}) + (1 - a)(\text{previous forecast}),$$

$$\hat{X}_t = \hat{X}_{t-1} + a\left(Y_{t-1} - \hat{X}_{t-1}\right) = aY_{t-1} + (1 - a)\hat{X}_{t-1},$$

where

$$Y_{t-1} - \hat{X}_{t-1} = \text{error in previous forecast},$$

$$a = \text{exponential smoothing constant between 0 and 1}.$$

For example, suppose you are attempting to obtain the forecast level of June sales by the EWMA. The relationships would be as follows:

$$\hat{X}_t = aY_{t-1} + (1 - a)\hat{X}_{t-1},$$

$$\text{June forecast} = a(\text{May actual}) + (1 - a)(\text{May forecast}).$$

The simplest EWMA model assumes only level and random components are in the time series (if only a level were present, the series would be constant or horizontal with time). It attempts to estimate level while filtering out the random component. In this model, the forecast ($\hat{Y}_t$) and the

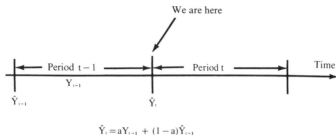

Figure 8. Simple EWMA.

forecast level ($\hat{X}_t$) are equal (when trend or seasonal components are in a time series, the forecast and the forecast level are different). As shown in Figure 8, the forecast ($\hat{Y}_t$) for period t is made at the end of period $t-1$. The origin of time is continuously updated. The time period for the most recent demand observation is always labeled $t-1$, while the upcoming period is always t.

The smoothing constant a lies between zero (no weight to recent actual data) and 1.0 (all weight to recent actual data). Small values of a put greater weight on historical demand conditions and have a greater smoothing effect (maximum stability with minimum responsiveness). Large values of a put greater weight on current demand conditions (maximum responsiveness and minimum stability). Stability is the ability to maintain consistency and not be influenced by random fluctuations, while responsiveness is the ability to adjust quickly to true changes in demand level. The appropriate value of a for a given set of data is determined by trial on a sample of actual past demand (retrospective testing).

Guideline values for a range from 0.01 to 0.30. Larger values of a may be used for short time periods when anticipated changes will occur, such as a recession, an aggressive but temporary promotional campaign, introducing a new product, or discontinuing some products in a line. The value of a should allow the forecast model to track major demand changes while averaging the random fluctuations.

The general formula for the exponentially weighted moving average model is as follows:

$$\hat{X}_t = a\left[Y_{t-1} + Y_{t-2}(1-a) + Y_{t-3}(1-a)^2 + \cdots + Y_{t-k}(1-a)^{t-1}\right]$$
$$+ (1-a)^t \hat{X}_0,$$
$$= a\sum_{k=1}^{t}(1-a)^{k-1}Y_{t-k} + (1-a)^t\hat{X}_0,$$

where

$$\hat{X}_t = \text{forecasted demand level for period } t,$$

$$\hat{X}_0 = \text{forecasted demand level for initial period,}$$

$$Y_{t-1} = \text{actual demand for period } t - 1.$$

The EWMA attributes part of the difference between actual demand and forecasted demand to a real cause and the remainder to chance causes. The EWMA assigns to the demand values of the previous periods weights that decrease in an exponential manner (exponential decay) as the demand data are removed from the present (thus the name exponentially weighted moving average). The weight of past demands decreases exponentially because the fraction $1 - a$ is raised to a power. Notice that all the weights add up to one.

A general formula for expressing the weight of an individual demand value in a future forecast is as follows:

$$\text{weight} = a(1 - a)^{k-1},$$

where k is the number of time periods removed from the current period.

The table below shows the weight that is given to the actual demands of previous periods for a given exponential smoothing constant. When a is low, more weight is given to past data; when it is high, more weight is given to recent data. Note that when a is as low as 0.1, the three most recent periods account for only $0.1 + 0.09 + 0.081 = 0.271$ or 27.1% of the forecast value. However, if a is as high as 0.9, the three most recent periods account for $0.9 + 0.09 + 0.009 = 0.999$ or 99.9% of the forecast. If $a = 1$, the forecast is simply the last period demand.

Exponential Smoothing Constant a	Period Weight				
	$k = 1$ a	$k = 2$ $a(1 - a)$	$k = 3$ $a(1 - a)^2$	$k = 4$ $a(1 - a)^3$	$k = 5$ $a(1 - a)^4$
0	0	0	0	0	0
0.1	0.1	.09	.081	.0729	.06561
0.2	0.2	.16	.128	.1024	.08192
0.3	0.3	.21	.147	.1029	.07203
0.4	0.4	.24	.144	.0864	.05184
0.5	0.5	.25	.125	.0625	.03125
0.6	0.6	.24	.096	.0384	.01536
0.7	0.7	.21	.063	.0189	.00567
0.8	0.8	.16	.032	.0064	.00128
0.9	0.9	.09	.009	.0009	.00009
1.0	1.0	0	0	0	0

Before any simple EWMA model can be tested on historical demand data, it is necessary to estimate its initial forecast value. When sufficient historical data are available, some authors recommend dividing it into two sections—the first to be used to initialize the model, and the second to serve as test data for various values of the smoothing constant. For the initialization step, the average demand in the first portion of the historical data frequently is used as the initial estimate. Other authors suggest that the initial forecast value be set equal to the initial actual (historical) demand, especially when only a few periods of historical data can be obtained. In truth, any reasonable estimate can be used, since the initial forecast value gets discounted strongly after several periods of forecasting. Authoritative analyses of EWMA models conclude that values of the smoothing constant should fall within the range of 0.01 to 0.30. If the simulation on historical data designates a rather large value (over 0.30), use of this EWMA model is inadvisable and a more appropriate forecasting model is indicated.

The basic EWMA model can forecast more than one period into the future, but the more distant estimates are the same as the current estimate. The relationship to forecast n periods into the future when you are at the beginning of period t is thus simply

$$\hat{Y}_{t+n} = \hat{X}_t.$$

The exponential smoothing model reacts slowly to a big change in demand, since the change may be only a random variation. If the change reflects an actual increase or decrease in demand, it will continue in subsequent periods and the exponential smoothing system will track the actual demand and respond to it. The size of the smoothing constant a will determine the sensitivity of the response to changes in demand. Surges in demand can be satisfied by safety stock when a small value of a is used in the forecast system.

There is a direct relationship between the moving average technique and the EWMA without trend or seasonal effects. Just as the sensitivity of a moving average decreases as the number of time periods in the moving average increases, the sensitivity of an EWMA decreases as a decreases. In fact, if n is the number of periods in the moving average, then for the corresponding EWMA we have[2]

$$a = \frac{2}{n + 1}, \quad \text{or} \quad n = \frac{2 - a}{a}.$$

Thus, a moving average model with $n = 7$ is equivalent to an EWMA model with $a = 0.25$ and no trends or seasonal influences.

[2] See Robert G. Brown, *Statistical Forecasting for Inventory Control*, New York: McGraw-Hill, 1959, pp. 58–62.

EXAMPLE 3

From the data below, determine the best forecasting method by using the smallest mean absolute deviation. Evaluate the last period demand, three-month moving average, and EWMA with $a = 0.3$. (Assume the initial LPD and EWMA forecast for month 1 is 185.)

Month	19X0 Demand	19X1 Demand	19X2 Demand
1	180	215	225
2	186	208	225
3	179	195	215
4	170	200	225
5	170	194	210
6	165	185	200
7	155	180	204
8	150	180	195
9	170	181	210
10	192	205	220
11	195	225	240
12	205	235	250

Table 2 compares the three forecasting methods with fractions rounded to whole numbers. The last period demand has the smallest mean absolute deviation, 9.31 (335/36); the EWMA has a MAD of 14.03 (505/36); and the three-month moving average has the largest MAD, 14.24 (470/33).

EWMA with Trend Correction

The simple EWMA model may provide an adequate future forecast if no trend, seasonal, or cyclical effects exist. If a trend is present, the model can be extended to adjust two variables, the average level and the trend. First, the average level for the current period is expanded to include the previous trend:

current forecast level

$$= a(\text{previous actual}) + (1 - a)(\text{previous forecast level} + \text{previous trend}),$$

$$\hat{X}_t = aY_{t-1} + (1 - a)(\hat{X}_{t-1} + T_{t-1}).$$

The current forecast level is then used to update the trend, where the apparent trend for each period is the difference between the consecutive forecast levels ($\hat{X}_t - \hat{X}_{t-1}$). By smoothing the difference with the previous

Table 2

Month	Actual Demand	Last Period Demand		Three-Month Moving Average		EWMA	
		Forecast Demand	Absolute Deviation	Forecast Demand	Absolute Deviation	Forecast Demand	Absolute Deviation
1	180	185	5	—	—	185	5
2	186	180	6	—	—	184	2
3	179	186	7	—	—	184	5
4	170	179	9	182	12	183	13
5	170	170	0	178	8	179	9
6	165	170	5	173	8	176	11
7	155	165	10	168	13	173	18
8	150	155	5	163	13	167	17
9	170	150	20	157	13	162	8
10	192	170	22	158	34	165	27
11	195	192	3	171	24	173	22
12	205	195	10	186	19	179	26
13	215	205	10	197	18	187	28
14	208	215	7	205	3	195	13
15	195	208	13	209	14	199	4
16	200	195	5	206	6	198	2
17	194	200	6	201	7	199	5
18	185	194	9	196	11	197	12
19	180	185	5	193	13	194	14
20	180	180	0	186	6	189	9
21	181	180	1	182	1	187	6
22	205	181	24	180	25	185	20
23	225	205	20	189	36	191	34
24	235	225	10	204	31	201	34
25	225	235	10	222	3	211	14
26	225	225	0	228	3	215	10
27	215	225	10	228	13	218	3
28	225	215	10	222	3	217	8
29	210	225	15	222	12	220	10
30	200	210	10	217	17	217	17
31	204	200	4	212	8	212	8
32	195	204	9	205	10	209	14
33	210	195	15	200	10	205	5
34	220	210	10	203	17	207	13
35	240	220	20	208	32	211	29
36	250	240	10	223	27	219	31
37		250		237		229	
			335		470		505

trend, the trend component for the current period is adjusted as follows:

$$\text{current trend} = b(\text{current level} - \text{previous level})$$
$$+ (1 - b)(\text{previous trend}),$$
$$T_t = b(\hat{X}_t - \hat{X}_{t-1}) + (1 - b)T_{t-1}$$
$$= \text{trend adjustment for period } t,$$

where

$$b = \text{exponential smoothing constant between 0 and 1.}$$

Using the calculations for the current level and the trend adjustment, the forecast for time period t is

$$\hat{Y}_t = \hat{X}_t + T_t.$$

Frequently a forecast of more than one period into the future is desired. Assuming a constant trend for future periods, the forecast for n periods beyond the current period t is determined from the following equation:

$$\hat{Y}_{t+n} = \hat{X}_t + (n + 1)T_t.$$

The EWMA with trend correction assumes level, trend, and random components exist in a time series. It attempts to estimate level and trend while filtering out the random component. The initialization of EWMA with trend must create two starting values, one for both the level and the trend. The initial level can be set equal to the initial actual (historical) demand. The initial trend can be obtained from a linear regression on some portion of the data (perhaps the first five or six periods) by setting it equal to the slope of the regression line. Similarly to the case discussed for the simple EWMA, the available demand history can be divided into two sections. The first section is used to initialize the model, and the second is subsequently administered as test data for various combinations of the smoothing constants.

EXAMPLE 4

From the one-year record of monthly demand in the table below, develop a trend adjusted exponentially weighted forecast with $a = 0.1$, $b = 0.1$, $\hat{X}_1 = 40$, and $T_1 = 0$.

Month	Demand	Month	Demand	Month	Demand
January	47	May	38	September	47
February	42	June	34	October	54
March	16	July	45	November	40
April	47	August	50	December	43

The trend adjusted exponentially weighted forecast is derived in the following table:

Month	Demand Y_t	Level $\hat{X}_t$	Trend T_t	Forecast $\hat{Y}_t$	Deviation $Y_t - \hat{Y}_t$
January	47	40.00	0	40.00	7.00
February	42	40.70	.070	40.77	1.23
March	16	40.89	.082	40.97	− 24.97
April	47	38.47	− .168	38.30	8.70
May	38	39.17	− .081	39.09	− 1.09
June	34	38.98	− .092	38.89	− 4.89
July	45	38.40	− .141	38.26	6.74
August	50	38.93	− .074	38.86	11.14
September	47	39.97	.037	40.01	6.99
October	54	40.71	.107	40.82	13.18
November	40	42.14	.239	42.38	− 2.38
December	43	42.14	.215	42.36	0.64
January		42.42	.221	42.64	

In the above table, the forecast level for February is obtained as follows:

$$\hat{X}_t = aY_{t-1} + (1 - a)(\hat{X}_{t-1} + T_{t-1}) = 0.1(47) + 0.9(40 + 0) = 40.70.$$

The trend adjustment for February is subsequently obtained in the following manner:

$$T_t = b(\hat{X}_t - \hat{X}_{t-1}) + (1 - b)T_{t-1} = 0.1(40.70 - 40) + 0.9(0) = 0.070.$$

Finally, the forecast for February is

$$\hat{Y}_t = \hat{X}_t + T_t = 40.70 + 0.070 = 40.77.$$

All other values in the above table are determined in a similar fashion for the appropriate period. The process is very simple, although manually it is laborious and time consuming.

In analyzing this example, the trend adjustment is much smaller than the error (deviation). In such cases, it is desirable to exclude the trend correction, since it does not have a pronounced effect. The simple EWMA model may be more appropriate for these data.

EWMA with Seasonal Correction

Seasonal demand patterns are characterized by recurring periods of high and low demand. Exponential smoothing models can be modified to take account of seasonal variations. For a seasonal demand pattern, it is necessary to analyze the past equivalent demand periods. Seasonalization can be achieved by a set of seasonal index numbers which represent the expected ratio of demand for individual periods to an average demand.

The following example indicates how indices can be obtained from two years of past monthly data:

| Month | Demand | | | Seasonal Index I_t |
	19X0	19X1	Average	
January	90	110	100	0.962
February	85	95	90	0.865
March	90	100	95	0.913
April	100	120	110	1.058
May	125	141	133	1.279
June	120	130	125	1.202
July	110	120	115	1.106
August	100	120	110	1.058
September	95	105	100	0.962
October	85	95	90	0.865
November	85	95	90	0.865
December	90	90	90	0.865
			$\overline{1248}$	$\overline{12.000}$

$$\text{average monthly demand} = \frac{1248}{12} = 104.$$

The indices in the above table are obtained by dividing the average monthly demand (104) into the respective average for each month. The seasonal index for the month of January is 100/104, or 0.962.

The most common methods of forecasting when there is a seasonal pattern depend on comparing the observed demand with that in a corresponding period in the previous year or with the average of the demand in the corresponding periods in several previous years. The standard for comparison is called a base series, and it has a value for each review period. The commonest base series is the actual demand during the corresponding months last year. If the peak demand shifts back and forth by a month or so from year to year, then the average of the demand in the three months surrounding the corresponding month last year may prove to be a more stable base series.

Exponential smoothing can filter out random effects for both deseasonalized demand and seasonal indices. Actual demand data are deseasonalized by dividing by the index numbers, and the resultant demand (with or without trend effects) is forecasted by a smoothing model. The index numbers also are updated by a smoothing routine:

$$I_{t+m} = \frac{cY_t}{\hat{X}_t} + (1 - c)I_t,$$

where

I_t = seasonal index for the period t,
c = exponential smoothing constant between 0 and 1,
m = number of periods in seasonal pattern ($m = 12$ for monthly data and $m = 4$ for quarterly data with an annual seasonal pattern).

If no trend exists, the forecast level with a seasonal adjustment is as follows:

$$\hat{X}_t = \frac{aY_{t-1}}{I_{t-1}} + (1 - a)\hat{X}_{t-1}.$$

The forecast for period t is the forecast level multiplied by the seasonal index or

$$\hat{Y}_t = \hat{X}_t I_t.$$

Dividing the actual demand by the seasonal index has the effect of deseasonalizing the demand. Multiplying the forecast level by the seasonal index provides the seasonal correction to the forecasted demand.

For forecasting more than one period into the future the forecast is determined as follows:

$$\hat{Y}_{t+n} = \hat{X}_t I_{t+n} \qquad \text{for} \quad n \leq m,$$

where n is the future period beyond the time period t for which a forecast is desired. Forecasts for future periods more distant than m can be made by reusing the appropriate seasonal index.

The EWMA with seasonal correction assumes level, seasonal, and random components are in a time series. It attempts to estimate level and seasonals while filtering out the random component. The season is assumed to be of length m, and the sum of indices over a full season is exactly equal to m. The initialization of EWMA with seasonal corrections must have starting values for the level and each of the seasonal indices. The available demand history can be divided into two sections, the first section being used to initialize the model and the second to test various combinations of the smoothing constants. The initial level can be estimated by averaging actual demand over full seasons. At all times, the sum of indices through an entire season adds to m. Thus, when a specific index is updated, all indices are renormalized to achieve equality to m. If the initial seasonal indices are all close to unity, the seasonal effect is not significant and a seasonal model is inappropriate.

EWMA with Trend and Seasonal Corrections

If both trend and seasonal effects are evident, the EWMA model updates the level, the trend, and the seasonal index each time period. This process is accomplished using the following set of equations:

$$\hat{X}_t = \frac{aY_{t-1}}{I_{t-1}} + (1-a)(\hat{X}_{t-1} + T_{t-1}),$$

$$T_t = b(\hat{X}_t - \hat{X}_{t-1}) + (1-b)T_{t-1},$$

$$I_{t+m} = \frac{cY_t}{\hat{X}_t} + (1-c)I_t.$$

The ratio Y_{t-1}/I_{t-1} is an estimate of deseasonalized actual demand in period $t-1$, while $Y_t/\hat{X}_t$ estimates the seasonal index based on the actual demand observation at the end of period t. The updated results yield a forecast for period t when substituted into the following formula:

$$\hat{Y}_t = (\hat{X}_t + T_t)I_t.$$

For forecasting more than one period into the future the forecast is determined as follows:

$$\hat{Y}_{t+n} = [\hat{X}_t + (n+1)T_t]I_{t+n} \qquad \text{for} \quad n \le m,$$

where n is the future period beyond time period t for which a forecast is desired.

The EWMA with trend and seasonal corrections assumes level, trend, seasonal, and random components are in a time series. It attempts to estimate level, trend, and seasonals while filtering out the random component. The initialization of this model requires the determination of starting values for the level, trend, and seasonal indices. The seasonal indices can be estimated by dividing average demand over a full season (m periods) into the actual demand for each period. If sufficient historical data are available, several full seasons might be averaged to get the initial indices. When a specific index is updated, all indices are renormalized so the sum of indices through an entire season adds to m. The initial level can be estimated by deseasonalizing actual demand for the initial period. The initial trend can be approximated by the slope of annual (full season) data (perhaps by a regression of annual data or of an m period moving average). The full season is used to free the trend of seasonal effects. As touched on in previous sections, the available demand history can be divided into two sections. The first is used to initialize the model, and the second to test various combinations of the three smoothing constants.[3]

---

[3] For recommendations on the range of smoothing constants and other approaches to time series analysis, see E. A. Silver and R. Peterson, *Decision Systems for Inventory Management and Production Planning*, New York: Wiley, 1985.

EXAMPLE 5

From the data given in Example 3 develop an EWMA model with trend and seasonal corrections for 19X2 from the data for 19X0 and 19X1. Assume $a = 0.1$, $b = 0.1$, $c = 0.3$, $\hat{X}_1 = 220$, $\hat{Y}_1 = 220$, and $T_1 = 0$. What is the forecast for March 19X3?

The seasonal indices are developed in the following table:

Month	Demand 19X0	Demand 19X1	Average	Seasonal Index I_t
January	180	215	197.5	1.049
February	186	208	197.0	1.046
March	179	195	187.0	0.993
April	170	200	185.0	0.982
May	170	194	182.0	0.966
June	165	185	175.0	0.930
July	155	180	167.5	0.889
August	150	180	165.0	0.876
September	170	181	175.5	0.932
October	192	205	198.5	1.054
November	195	225	210.0	1.115
December	205	235	220.0	1.168
Total			2260.0	12.000

$$\text{average monthly demand} = \frac{2260}{12} = 188.33.$$

Month t	Demand Y_t	Level $\hat{X}_t$	Trend T_t	Seasonal Index I_t	I_{t+m}	Forecast $\hat{Y}_t$	Deviation $Y_t - \hat{Y}_t$
January	225	220.00	0	1.049	1.041	220.00	5.00
February	225	219.45	−0.055	1.046	1.040	229.49	−4.49
March	215	218.97	−0.097	0.993	0.990	217.34	−2.34
April	225	218.64	−0.120	0.982	0.996	214.59	10.41
May	210	219.58	−0.014	0.966	0.963	212.10	−2.10
June	200	219.35	−0.036	0.930	0.925	203.96	−3.96
July	204	218.89	−0.078	0.889	0.902	194.52	9.48
August	195	219.88	0.029	0.876	0.879	192.64	2.36
September	210	220.18	0.056	0.932	0.939	205.26	4.74
October	220	220.74	0.106	1.054	1.037	232.77	−12.77
November	240	219.63	−0.016	1.115	1.108	244.87	−4.87
December	250	219.18	−0.059	1.168	1.160	255.93	−5.93
January		218.61	−0.110	1.041		227.46	

In the above table, the new seasonal index I_{t+m} for January of the following year is obtained as follows:

$$I_{t+m} = \frac{cY_t}{\hat{X}_t} + (1 - c)I_t = \frac{0.3(225)}{220} + (1 - 0.3)1.049 = 1.041.$$

The forecasted demand level for February is obtained in the following manner:

$$\hat{X}_t = \frac{aY_{t-1}}{I_{t-1}} + (1 - a)(\hat{X}_{t-1} + T_{t-1})$$

$$= \frac{0.1(225)}{1.049} + (1 - 0.1)(220 + 0) = 219.45.$$

The trend for February is obtained as follows:

$$T_t = b(\hat{X}_t - \hat{X}_{t-1}) + (1 - b)T_{t-1}$$

$$= 0.1(219.45 - 220.00) + (1 - 0.1)0$$

$$= -0.055.$$

Thus, the forecast for February is

$$\hat{Y}_t = (\hat{X}_t + T_t)I_t = [219.45 + (-0.055)]1.046 = 229.49.$$

All other values in the above table are determined in a similar fashion for the appropriate period. The advantages of using a computer should be apparent from the tedium of the numerous computations.

The forecast for March 19X3 is

$$\hat{Y}_{t+n} = [\hat{X}_t + (n + 1)T_t]I_{t+n} = \hat{Y}_{t+2} = [218.61 + 3(-0.110)]0.0990$$

$$= 216.09.$$

A summary of the EWMA models outlined in this chapter is contained in Table 3.

EWMA Overview

EWMA facilitates computation and reduces data storage requirements, which are important when many series are being forecasted. Exponential smoothing is computationally simpler and requires much less data retention than other techniques. In numerous instances, the forecast variable is serially correlated.[4] In other words, demand in the present period is closely and naturally related to demand in the previous period. EWMA is an excellent tool for treating serially correlated data, since it gives the heaviest weight to the most recent historical data.

Considerable efforts have been made to obtain the best exponential smoothing constants (a, b, and c). The techniques tend to involve enumerative computer programs that analyze past sales history and determine the best smoothing constants by a trial and error method. For data with no trend or seasonal effects, the only parameter needed is a. Since $1 \geq a \geq 0$, the best parameter value can be approximated by selecting the lowest mean

[4]Autocorrelation analysis, which is beyond the scope of this chapter, will often reveal the existence of trends or seasonality in data.

Table 3. EWMA models.

EWMA Variable	Time Series Components			
	Random	Random + Trend	Random + Seasonal	Random + Trend + Seasonal
Forecast model $\hat{Y}_t$	$\hat{X}_t$	$\hat{X}_t + T_t$	$\hat{X}_t I_t$	$(\hat{X}_t + T_t)I_t$
Forecast level $\hat{X}_t$	$aY_{t-1} + (1-a)\hat{X}_{t-1}$	$aY_{t-1} + (1-a)(\hat{X}_{t-1} + T_{t-1})$	$\dfrac{aY_{t-1}}{I_{t-1}} + (1-a)\hat{X}_{t-1}$	$\dfrac{aY_{t-1}}{I_{t-1}} + (1-a)(\hat{X}_{t-1} + T_{t-1})$
Trend adjustment T_t	0	$b(\hat{X}_t - \hat{X}_{t-1}) + (1-b)T_{t-1}$	0	$b(\hat{X}_t - \hat{X}_{t-1}) + (1-b)T_{t-1}$
Seasonal adjustment I_{t+m}	0	0	$\dfrac{cY_t}{\hat{X}_t} + (1-c)I_t$	$\dfrac{cY_t}{\hat{X}_t} + (1-c)I_t$
Multiperiod forecast $\hat{Y}_{t+n}$	$\hat{X}_t$	$\hat{X}_t + (n+1)T_t$	$\hat{X}_t I_{t+n}$	$[\hat{X}_t + (n+1)T_t]I_{t+n}$

absolute deviation (MAD) from testing a in 0.05 increments. When more than one smoothing factor is required, different possible combinations can be tested to obtain the combination with the least error.

The MAD must be recalculated after each period, and this requires the storage of a long data history. Many analysts recommend a simple exponential smoothing for revision of the MAD:

$$\text{MAD}_t = d\left(Y_t - \hat{Y}_t\right) + (1 - d)\,\text{MAD}_{t-1},$$

where

$$d = \text{exponential smoothing constant between 0 and 1.}$$

The above formulation reduces the data storage requirements and also gives more weight to more recent MAD values. The recommended range of the smoothing constant d is from 0.01 to 0.10.

The forecasting model having the lowest MAD over a period of time is most desirable. Concurrently, the algebraic sum of errors should cancel out (be at the zero level) over a period of time, so no bias remains in the distribution of forecast errors. Forecast errors should fluctuate within reasonable limits around zero. The algebraic sum of errors helps to indicate how well the forecasting system is estimating demand. When the forecast fails to respond to changes in demand, the sum grows larger and larger in a positive or negative direction. Positive errors indicate that demand is rising faster than the forecast, while negative errors indicate a decreasing demand.

After a forecasting model has been selected, it is necessary to monitor its performance. A tracking signal can be used to indicate when the forecasting model should be revised: when a basic change in demand dictates a change in the forecasting model parameters. It is simply a method of evaluating when a forecast exceeds a tolerable error limit. The tracking signal is calculated by the following formula:

$$\text{TS}_t = \frac{\sum_{i=1}^{t}\left(Y_i - \hat{Y}_i\right)}{\text{MAD}_t}.$$

The tracking signal is the ratio of the cumulative forecast error to the corresponding value of the MAD. The resulting tracking signal is compared with predetermined limits, upper and lower. These usually range from ± 3 to ± 8. Errors that fall within limits are judged acceptable, while errors outside limits are a signal that corrective action is needed. If the forecasting model is unbiased, the tracking signal should fluctuate around zero. The tracking signal is reviewed each period and a forecast model revision issued if necessary.

Adaptive control models have been developed to automatically adjust the value of the smoothing constant(s) when the tracking signal exceeds some appropriately chosen bounds (indicating unacceptably large forecast errors). The smoothing constant is increased in order to give more weight to recent data and thereby bring the system more rapidly into line with the changed demand condition. When the out-of-control condition disappears, the smoothing constant is restored to its normal value. Unfortunately, research findings imply that adaptive procedures can create more problems than they solve.

Demand patterns for items are subject to change over a product's life cycle. Such changes dictate revisions of the forecasting model. There are many tests that can indicate the need for a permanent change, but usually a plot of the demand will suffice. Also, there are usually external environmental conditions that cause the demand changes, and managers are well aware of their existence and influence.

Sales promotions as well as other factors influence a forecast to such an extent that predictions based on intuitive judgments and experience may override a statistical extrapolation of past data. Forecasts cannot properly estimate future demand when promotional activities are involved. Special promotions and advertisements may produce an "artificial seasonal" effect. They can also borrow sales from the future and cause cycles. When past data contain unusual promotional effects, it is a good idea to "depromotionalize" the data to a normal level.

When the forecast is for many periods ahead, the EWMA can be a perilous technique. The use of a short term forecasting technique for a long time ahead assumes a stability that may not occur. The longer the projection, the less reliable the forecast becomes.

Time series analysis is best suited to items that have a continuous demand. For items with a discrete or lumpy demand, this mode of forecasting is inadequate. Lumpy demand means that demand is nonuniform or occurs sporadically. It can range from high levels to very low levels or not occur at all during some periods (zero demand). Christmas trees, seasonal agriculture items, high fashion apparel, and repair maintenance items are examples. For such items a probabilistic approach based on expected demand or marginal analysis is appropriate.

In the EWMA only one way of handling trend and seasonality was considered. Trend was considered a linear or additive component, and seasonality was considered a multiplicative or index component. There are situations where trend might be considered as a constant percentage growth component, and seasonality might be applied as an additive component rather than a function of the level itself. There are other extensions that can be included in EWMA. The particular parameters to apply to the forecasting model are a function of demand behavior, and experimentation with the data is necessary before specific models are adopted. Forecasting model selection is a tailoring process.

Box-Jenkins Models

The most sophisticated time series analysis method is that of Box and Jenkins. It is an approach to forecasting and not a specific technique. It is a systematic method that does not assume any specific model, but analyzes historical data in order to determine a suitable model. Their generalized model is called the *autoregressive integrated moving average model* (ARIMA). It consists of several possible separate model combinations. With statistical aids, an analyst rationally eliminates inappropriate model combinations until he is left with an appropriate model. The experience and judgment of the analyst are an important part of the selection process. The ARIMA methodology consists of three steps:

1. identification of a tentative forecast model,
2. estimation of parameters for the identified model,
3. diagnostic checking of the estimated model to determine its appropriateness.

An *autoregressive* model assumes that current data values are dependent on their past values. This means that current performance is a function of past performance. Such a model contains an autoregressive coefficient displaying the portion of the last period's performance affecting or explaining the current period's performance. The autoregressive coefficient is analogous to the slope in traditional regression analysis. A *moving average model* assumes that current data values are dependent on forecast errors of prior periods. The forecast error is the difference between the actual results and the forecasted value. This means that current performance is a function of the difference between the previous period's performance and its forecast. The moving average coefficient represents the proportional effect of deviations from the prior period's forecast on current performance. An *integrated model* is one for which the data have been adjusted for trend and/or seasonality. A given time series may be represented by an autoregressive model, a moving average model, or a mixed autoregressive integrated moving average model. The Box-Jenkins three-step procedure is designed to develop the ARIMA model that best describes the time series to be forecasted.

While the Box-Jenkins procedure can be effective in short-term forecasting, it has not been widely applied to individual item inventory control. The procedure requires large amounts of data for proper use, the tools are difficult to master, and the data must be transformed to achieve stationarity. It is more expensive than exponential smoothing. It is useful where only a few time series need to be forecasted and the extra expense is warranted.

SOLICITING OPINIONS

A subjective approach to forecasting involves the solicitation of opinions concerning future levels of demand from customers, retailers, wholesalers, salesmen, and managers. Through interviews and market research, estimates of future demand can be obtained from customers, wholesalers, and retailers. There are difficulties to this approach, since customers do not always do what they say they will, and it is not uncommon to obtain a broad spectrum of conflicting opinion.

If a sufficient history of past demand is not available, then forecasts must be based on market potential studies, general surveys, and whatever parallel experiences are available. Market research can include personal interviews, telephone surveys, mail questionnaires, consumer panels, and test markets. Internal opinions can be secured from salespersons and managers. Each salesman may be asked to estimate future volume in his territory, and the estimates of all salesmen can be added to obtain a forecast for the entire company. This collective opinion approach is frequently used for new products with no sales history, but it becomes ineffective as the length of the forecast horizon is increased.

This less elaborate and less technical approach makes use of the qualitative knowledge of people in the field and the home office. Forecasts of this type tend to be heavily influenced by immediate events. Also, when an estimate is developed from collective opinion, the final result may be more the opinions of a few influential or persuasive individuals rather than those of the group from which it was drawn.

The Delphi technique is designed to remedy some of the problems which arise in consensus forecasts. It seeks to maximize the advantages of group dynamics while minimizing the problems caused by dominant personalities and silent experts. Without contact with other participants, members of a group of experts submit initial forecasts for a well-defined event and include any supporting arguments and limiting assumptions used to develop the forecast. The individual responses are collected, edited, clarified, and statistically summarized by an analyst who returns the initial results to each expert for a second round of forecasting. Using the edited results, the experts submit their revised forecasts and await further feedback for the next round of forecasting. This iterative procedure continues until consensus is achieved. The Delphi technique commonly is used in forecasting technological events, but it also can be adapted to other forecasting situations.

ECONOMIC INDICATORS

Economic indicators are frequently used to predict future demand. The knowledge of one variable is used to predict the value of another (prediction by association). The decision maker searches for an economic indicator (gross national product, personal income, bank deposits, freight car loadings, etc.) that has a relationship with the forecast variable.[5] A cause-effect relationship is not necessarily implied between the indicator and the forecast variable.

The simplest type of relationship is a linear association. Regression analysis by the least squares method will fit a straight line to a plot of data from two variables. The line fitted by the method of least squares will be such that the sum of squares of the deviations about the line is less than the sum of the squares of the deviations about any other line. A linear function has the form

$$Y = \alpha + \beta X,$$

where

Y = dependent variable (variable to be forecasted),

X = independent variable (economic indicator),

α = intercept,

β = slope.

The parameters α and β are estimated from the following formulas:

$$\alpha = \overline{Y} - \beta \overline{X} = \frac{\Sigma Y - \beta \Sigma X}{n},$$

$$\beta = \frac{n(\Sigma XY) - (\Sigma X)(\Sigma Y)}{n\Sigma X^2 - (\Sigma X)^2}.$$

With the simple regression analysis, the forecaster seeks to discover those variables which have the greatest impact on the forecast variable. What linear regression analysis does is to compute a line which comes closer to connecting the observed points than any other line which could be drawn. It may be used to estimate the relationship between any two or more variables.

A statistic that indicates how well a regression explains or fits the observed data is the correlation coefficient, which ranges between -1 and $+1$. A high absolute value indicates a high degree of association, while a small absolute value indicates little association between variables. When the coefficient is positive, one variable tends to increase as the other increases.

[5] Sources of information on economic indicators include the Federal Reserve Board, Department of Commerce, Department of Labor, trade associations, and university bureaus of business research. Publications such as the *Survey of Current Business*, *Federal Reserve Bulletin*, and *Monthly Labor Review* are typical sources of economic indicators.

When the coefficient is negative, one variable tends to decrease as the other increases. The correlation coefficient is given by

$$r^2 = \frac{(\Sigma xy)^2}{(\Sigma x^2)(\Sigma y^2)} = \frac{\left[n \sum_{i=1}^{n} X_i Y_i - \left(\sum_{i=1}^{n} X_i \right)\left(\sum_{i=1}^{n} Y_i \right) \right]^2}{\left[n \sum_{i=1}^{n} X_i^2 - \left(\sum_{i=1}^{n} X_i \right)^2 \right]\left[n \sum_{i=1}^{n} Y_i^2 - \left(\sum_{i=1}^{n} Y_i \right)^2 \right]},$$

where

$$r = \text{simple correlation coefficient,}$$
$$x = X - \bar{X},$$
$$y = Y - \bar{Y}.$$

The decision maker can verify the statistical significance of any derived simple correlation coefficient by using standard statistical tests found in many texts. A simple t-test can be used to verify if a correlation coefficient differs significantly from zero.

Similarly to time series analysis, the standard deviation of regression S_r is obtained from the following formula:

$$S_r^2 = \frac{\Sigma Y^2 - \alpha \Sigma Y - \beta \Sigma XY}{n - 2} = \frac{\Sigma (Y - \hat{Y})^2}{n - 2}.$$

EXAMPLE 6

Find the least squares regression line and the coefficient of correlation of Y on X from the following data:

Y	68	66	68	65	69	66	68	65	71	67	68	70
X	65	63	67	64	68	62	70	66	68	67	69	71

We have

Y	X	X^2	XY	Y^2
68	65	4225	4420	4624
66	63	3969	4158	4356
68	67	4489	4556	4624
65	64	4096	4160	4225
69	68	4624	4692	4761
66	62	3844	4092	4356
68	70	4900	4760	4624
65	66	4356	4290	4225
71	68	4624	4828	5041
67	67	4489	4489	4489
68	69	4761	4692	4624
70	71	5041	4970	4900
$\Sigma Y = 811$	$\Sigma X = 800$	$\Sigma X^2 = 53,418$	$\Sigma XY = 54,107$	$\Sigma Y^2 = 54,849$

$$\alpha = \frac{\Sigma Y - \beta \Sigma X}{n} = \frac{811 - 0.476(800)}{12} = 35.85,$$

$$\beta = \frac{n(\Sigma XY) - (\Sigma X)(\Sigma Y)}{n\Sigma X^2 - (\Sigma X)^2} = \frac{12(54,107) - (800)(811)}{12(53,418) - (800)^2} = 0.476,$$

$$Y = \alpha + \beta X = 35.85 + 0.476 X,$$

$$r^2 = \frac{\left[n \sum_{i=1}^{n} X_i Y_i - \left(\sum_{i=1}^{n} X_i \right)\left(\sum_{i=1}^{n} Y_i \right) \right]^2}{\left[n \sum_{i=1}^{n} X_i^2 - \left(\sum_{i=1}^{n} X_i \right)^2 \right]\left[n \sum_{i=1}^{n} Y_i^2 - \left(\sum_{i=1}^{n} Y_i \right)^2 \right]}$$

$$= \frac{[12(54,107) - 800(811)]^2}{[12(53,418) - 640,000][12(54,849) - 657,721]} = 0.4937,$$

$$r = 0.702.$$

Many organizations are sensitive to broad economic trends, but finding a particular indicator of how operations will react to economic pressures can be a challenging task. Industrial sales tend to be sensitive to the GNP, but consumer sales are more sensitive to disposable income. There is even a class of products that behave opposite to the general movement of the national economy. The availability and cost of complementary and substitute products can complicate the economic indicator relationship.

An indicator is referred to as leading, coincident, or lagging depending on whether it precedes, parallels, or follows in time the demand it is being used to forecast. It is desirable to use leading indicators, since an economic indicator for a given period will be known only after the period has ended, too late to permit its use to predict sales for that period. If no lag exists, a forecasted value of the economic indicator can be used for prediction.

Multiple linear regression deals with the relationship between the dependent variable (variable to be predicted) and two or more independent variables (variables used to make the prediction). The difference between a simple linear regression and a multiple linear regression is in the number of independent variables used in the analysis. For example, for two independent variables the linear regression equation would be

$$Y = \alpha + \beta_1 X_1 + \beta_2 X_2.$$

In multiple linear regression analysis, more than one independent variable is used to forecast the dependent variable. An F-test is conducted on the multivariate model to determine if the model significantly forecasts the dependent variable.[6] In multiple linear regression analysis, the simple

---

[6] The F-test and t-test determine if the regression coefficients are significant. The F-test determines if $\beta_1 = \beta_2 = \beta_3 = \cdots = \beta_n = 0$, and the t-test determines separately if $\beta_1 = 0$, $\beta_2 = 0$, $\beta_3 = 0, \ldots$, or $\beta_n = 0$.

correlation coefficient is replaced with partial correlation coefficients. Partial correlation coefficients indicate the influence of each individual independent variable on the dependent variable while all other independent variables are held statistically constant. The significance of each independent variable is revealed by a t-test.[6] An insignificant t-test means that an independent variable does not significantly aid in the forecast of the dependent variable. A multiple correlation coefficient is analogous to the single correlation coefficient except it contains the contributions of several independent variables. In determining the multiple correlation coefficient, only those independent variables that have a significant partial correlation coefficient should be included.

With multiple regression analysis, the problem of multicollinearity can arise. Multicollinearity is the situation where there is intercorrelation between independent variables. When two or more of the independent variables are highly correlated, you are in effect using the same variable twice. In this situation, the forecaster simply deletes one of the related variables.

In many cases, the relationship between variables is nonlinear or curvilinear and a more complex type of analysis is required. Straight lines, polynomials, and logarithmic functions are frequently used when trends or growth patterns are present; trigonometric functions (sines and cosines) can be used when cyclic tendencies are present.

It is seldom practical to use economic indicators for item forecasts. They are usually used to forecast product groups or aggregate dollar demand for an organization. Time series analysis is much more practical for item-by-item forecasting.

Economic indicators are *associative*: they depend on the interaction of two or more variables. An important feature of economic indicators (as well as econometric models) is that they can be used to predict turning points in a demand function, based on the changing values of known indicators. In contrast, time series analysis can only predict future demand based on the past demand; it cannot predict upturns and downturns in the demand level.

Simple regression gives equal weight to all historical data, whereas exponential smoothing reduces the weight geometrically with age.

ECONOMETRIC MODELS

An econometric model is usually a set of simultaneous equations that explains the interactions of variables involved in a business situation. The models attempt to show the relationships between relevant variables such as supply, demand, prices, and purchasing power of the consumer. The models can become quite complex, since they analyze the causative forces operating on the variable to be predicted. Usually, they require forecasts of a number of structural variables.

The structural relationships of econometric models can be grouped into four categories—behavioral, technical, institutional, and identities. *Behav-*

ioral relationships include supply curves, demand curves, and other curves that reflect the behavior of particular economic units (consumers, business firms). *Technical* relationships are mainly production functions that show input-output relationships as constrained by technology. *Institutional* relationships are specified by law or regulation and indicate the boundaries of acceptable social behavior (taxes, minimum wages). *Identities* specify balance relationships such as the definition of the gross national product (GNP), which is the sum of personal consumption expenditures, gross private capital formation, government purchases of goods and services, and net foreign trade.

A variant of econometric analysis is input-output forecasting models. These models consider intraperiod as well as interperiod dependences between sectors of the economy. Econometric textbooks treat model development in this area.

In order to capture all the interactions, the econometric model must have many equations. As more equations are added, the model becomes cumbersome in both the initial estimation and the required maintenance. Once a model is developed, its entire structure is known and its assumptions are in full view. Over a period of time, the model can be refined by new research. An econometric model may become very complex, because the phenomenon it is attempting to describe is not simple.

A possible way to estimate future product demand is to determine first the customers, their uses of the product, how much they need for each use, and when they will order the product. A mathematical model can then be built relating all the relevant factors. Because of the number and complexity of factors, a complete model is seldom possible. Approximate models can be built that are worthwhile. A difficulty with this approach is the cost as well as the time consumed in model development.

Econometric modeling usually requires a highly specialized professional staff. Thus it can be very expensive and is usually confined to large organizations or specialized service organizations (Brookings Institution, Chase Econometrics Associates, Data Resources Inc., Wharton Econometric Forecasting Associates, and so forth). While such models are useful in forecasting, their major utilization is in answering "what if" questions. These models allow management to investigate the impact of various changes in the environment on organizational performance.

GROUP FORECASTING

In this chapter several techniques have been outlined for generating individual end item forecasts. These techniques also can be used to forecast the demand for a group or family of items. Organizations that manufacture or sell products usually need item forecasts of expected demand (unless they backlog or backorder products). The generalized choices are to forecast (1) individual end item demand, (2) family item demand, or (3) generic item demand. An end item is a product demanded by a customer. A family or generic item is not a buildable, salable, or identifiable item. It does not physically exist but is a pseudo or artificial parent created to aid in forecasting and planning. In many situations, it is not desirable or economically feasible to independently forecast individual end item demand. By aggregation, family and generic item forecasting can narrow the scope of forecasting. Individual end item forecasts can be dependently derived from family item forecasts. Optional features and major subassemblies can be dependently derived from generic item forecasts. Similarly, the total requirements forecast for a specific end item in many geographic locations can be allocated (disaggregated) to individual locations.

A *family item* is a homogeneous grouping of similar end items (for example, an apparel line of men's shirts consisting of several sizes and colors). A *generic item* is a product which comes with a multitude of options and which can result in a large number of final configurations (for example, a specific model of a car, tractor, or computer). Since multiple option selections interact to create a very large number of unique end items, the individual end items for a generic item are seldom forecasted. The optional features and major subassemblies are dependently derived from the generic item forecast. The individual end items are not assembled until receipt of a specific customer order indicating all of the desired optional features. Thus, the optional features and subassemblies are produced and available, but final assembly does not occur until its configuration is specified by the customer.

In general, an aggregate forecast will be more accurate than individual item forecasts. Unless all items in a group are highly correlated, an aggregate forecast will have reduced variance. The fluctuations in demand for one item tend to offset the demand fluctuations for a related item. When demands for individual end items are very low, end item forecasting is difficult if not impossible. By aggregating into groups, forecasting is facilitated. However, an aggregate forecast must be disaggregated to get the expected demand for individual end items or optional features. This can be accomplished by establishing popularity percentages for each member of the group. The sum of the popularity percentages for each member of a given group is 100%. In this manner, the probability of option selection or of a specific end item within a family is obtained. The forecast for any group member is obtained by multiplying the forecast for the group by its popularity percentage.

Demand lead time is the length of time customers expect or are willing to wait for a product (from the time they place an order for the product until they receive it). Supply lead time is the length of time it takes for a producer (or seller) to make (or order) a product. If the demand lead time is equal to or greater than the supply lead time for a product, no forecast is required, since operations are based on backlogs or backorders of accumulated customer orders. When the demand lead time is less than the supply lead time for a product, some type of forecasting is needed. If there are few end items, forecasts can be developed for each individual end item. When there are many end items, the number of independent forecasts can be reduced if similar end items can be grouped into families and popularity percentages developed for each end item in the family. Similarly, when the large number of end items is the result of highly optioned products, they can be grouped into generics and popularity percentages developed for each optional feature.

The decision process for forecast level selection is outlined in Figure 9.

Figure 9. Forecast level selection.

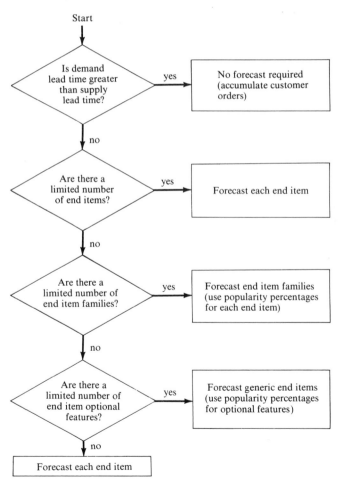

CONCLUSION

Forecasting is predicting, projecting, or estimating some future event or condition which is outside of an organization's control. While forecasting is not planning, it is an indispensable input into planning. Planning sets goals and develops alternative strategies to attain goals. Forecasting deals with the realm of matters outside of management's control. Organizations forecast so they can plan and help shape their future.

A demand forecast is the link between external factors in the organization's environment and its internal structure. The determination of the types of forecasts required and the establishment of procedures governing their generation are fundamental steps in the structure of a well-conceived organization. Forecast techniques depend very much on the number of items being controlled and on the type of operating system. Forecasts need to be made on a routine basis, so the techniques must accommodate the available staff skills as limited by the available computing facilities.

The forecasting of independent demand items is required for supply to be maintained in anticipation of demand. Forecasting is important when an advance commitment (to procure or to manufacture) has to be made. From the forecasts, operational plans are developed. The less flexibility there is in subsequently modifying original plans, the more important the dependability and accuracy of the forecast. There has been a substantial increase in the availability of sophisticated forecasting techniques, but increases in forecasting effectiveness have not been as pronounced. Unfortunately, poor forecasts are often a fact of life. Refinements in forecasting techniques are

Table 4. The realities of forecasts

1. *They are never perfect:*

   Be flexible, not surprised.

2. *They are more accurate for families:*

   Group like items.

3. *They are more accurate for longer time intervals:*

   Use larger time intervals.

4. *They are more accurate for the near term:*

   Keep time horizons short.
   Keep lead times short.

5. *They are necessary for independent demand:*

   Calculate dependent demand.

6. *Recent data are usually more reliable:*

   Focus on current data.

frequently less important than the development of operational flexibility to be able to live with poor forecasts. Several useful generalizations about forecasting are contained in Table 4.

A forecast is only an estimate of expected demand: actual and forecasted demand cannot be expected to agree precisely. Forecasts are only "ballpark" figures that permit the planning function to commence. Frustration should not result from the inability to predict the future precisely. With a properly designed forecasting system, uncertainty is kept to a bearable level.

Forecasters can be somewhat more confident about a range of values than about a single point forecast. A good forecast usually includes not only a single estimate, but an estimate of the magnitude of likely deviations as a guide to its reliability. Deviation is usually expressed by developing the best single estimate (expected value) and then establishing limits above and below that indicate the range of likely variation.

The tracking (forecast errors) of a forecast model is needed to verify the continued integrity of the model. Forecasting models must be revised when they are no longer appropriate. The tracking of a model can provide numerous benefits to management; it can

1. indicate the reliability of the existing model,
2. provide the criterion for forecast model selection,
3. facilitate selection of parameters (months in a moving average, or EWMA smoothing constants),
4. assist in establishing safety stock levels.

Reducing forecast errors requires increasing expenditures on forecasting techniques. Eventually one reaches a point of diminishing returns, and a perfect forecast is in any case an impossibility. Frequently, a much better investment is the development of operational and production flexibility that permits a rapid redeployment of resources in light of market changes.

Forecasting is an ongoing process that requires maintenance, revision, and modifications. The most obvious time to revise a forecast is when it is in error. Some techniques have built-in warning signals that indicate a departure from some predetermined tolerance range. Other techniques require personal surveillance to give the signal. Either way, the existence of the error should be communicated along with an idea of its cause.

It is impossible to design decision rules and forecasting models that will cover every eventuality. The design is primarily concerned with routine, repetitive situations. Unusual situations that cannot be anticipated must result in a managerial override or interrupt. The computer can handle the routine occurrences, and the manager can devote his skill and experience to the nonroutine ones.

The techniques outlined herein are not intended to be exhaustive, but only to summarize prevalent categories. The imagination and ingenuity of a forecaster are vital ingredients in the design of forecasting systems. Although precise mathematical formulas give the impression that forecasting is a science, it still remains an art with a tenuous scientific superstructure.

QUESTIONS

1. Name several common forecasting bases.

2. Discuss how the MAD, the bias, and the MSE are useful in evaluating a forecasting model. Which measure is the best?

3. Describe the areas of application for qualitative, time series, and economic indicator forecasting techniques.

4. Name four components into which time series data usually are decomposed for analysis.

5. Cite some of the advantages and disadvantages of the last period demand, arithmetic average, moving average, and exponentially weighted moving average techniques.

6. Which exhibits a greater degree of linear association, a correlation coefficient of $+1$ or a correlation coefficient of -1?

7. Distinguish the methodology of economic indicator forecasting from time series methodology.

8. How does econometric forecasting differ from regression analysis?

9. Name two difficulties which occur when soliciting opinions for demand forecasting.

10. What independent variables might be used to forecast the following dependent variables: number of applicants to a medical college; annual beer sales for a brewery; demand for residential housing; and demand for farm fertilizer?

11. Distinguish between "fit" and "prediction" when used in a forecasting context.

12. How are the values of the smoothing constant a related to the number of periods in a moving average? How well do low values of a track rapidly changing demand?

13. In what instances would an organization choose to ignore available historical data and use a qualitative forecasting method?

14. Why does the exponentially weighted moving average (EWMA) not require the keeping of a long historical record?

15. What generalized choices for forecasting product demand does a manufacturing organization have?

PROBLEMS

1. From the data below, determine the MAD and bias for the following forecasting techniques: (a) last period demand, (b) arithmetic average, (c) two-month moving average. What is the forecast for period 7 using each technique?

Month	1	2	3	4	5	6
Demand	20	30	40	30	50	58

2. From the data in Problem 1, determine the linear regression equation. Determine the MAD and bias. What is the forecast for period 7?

3. Develop EWMA forecasts from the information in Problem 1 using $a = 0.2$ and assuming the forecasted demand for the first month is the same as the actual demand. From the forecasts, determine the MAD and the bias for the EWMA model. What are the forecasts for periods 7 and 8?

4. Using exponential smoothing and the data in Problem 1, forecast monthly demand if $a = 0.2$ and $b = 0.2$. Assume that the actual demand in the first month is the same as the forecasted demand and that the initial level and the initial trend for month 1 both are 10. From these results, forecast the demand for period 8.

5. From the analysis performed in Problems 1 through 4, which technique is most desirable?

6. If the simple exponential smoothing constant is 0.30, what weight is placed on the current period's demand after an elapse of four additional time periods?

7. Suppose a firm has been using a simple exponential smoothing constant of 0.25. You suspect that the model is overreacting to random fluctuations in demand. Should you try a larger or a smaller smoothing value of a? Why?

8. Suppose your organization has been using a six-month moving average model and has been getting good results. Your boss recently purchased a desktop computer and an EWMA forecasting program. What simple exponential smoothing constant is equivalent to the old moving average model?

9. From the data below, determine the MAD and bias for the following forecasting techniques: (a) last period demand, (b) arithmetic average, and (c) three-month moving average. What is the forecast for period 13?

1.	93	7.	100
2.	105	8.	101
3.	114	9.	81
4.	111	10.	118
5.	106	11.	103
6.	116	12.	114

10. Based on the bias obtained for the techniques in Problem 9, is there a significant trend in the data?

11. From the data in Problem 9, determine the linear regression equation. Does there appear to be a trend? What is the correlation coefficient? What is the standard deviation of regression?

12. From the data in Problem 9, determine the MAD, the bias, and the tracking signal for an EWMA model with $a = 0.2$. Use a forecast for period 1 of 100.

13. From the data in Problem 9, determine the MAD, the bias, and the tracking signal for an EWMA model with $a = 0.1$, $b = 0.2$, an initial forecast of 100, an initial level of 100, and an initial trend of 0. (Assume period 1 as the initial period.) What is the forecast for period 13? Period 15?

14. From the quarterly data below, determine the linear regression equation.

1.	497	7.	821
2.	454	8.	1017
3.	624	9.	709
4.	764	10.	715
5.	631	11.	1794
6.	624	12.	1242

15. Using the data from the first eight quarters in Problem 14, compute the quarterly seasonal indices.

16. Using the data from the last four quarters in Problem 14 and the initial seasonal indices computed in Problem 15, determine the MAD and bias of an EWMA with $a = 0.2$, $b = 0.4$, $c = 0.5$, an initial forecast of 720, an initial trend of 65, and an initial level of 801. What is the forecast for quarter 13? For quarter 15? (Assume period 9 as the initial period.)

CASE 1: PAINT APPLICATION

Peacock Paint Supply is a full-service supplier of a wide range of home repair and construction products to homeowners and commercial contractors. Peacock carries a limited number of name brands and has exclusive privileges to market several brands in its immediate distribution area. The firm prefers to promote high quality merchandise and takes every step to remove itself from direct competition with discount supply houses. Peacock's product lines and personal level of service afford large and small customers a measure of quality unattainable at large discount houses.

The exterior paints Peacock stocks have both market recognition and distinct product advantages. Of its well-known brands, Peacock usually carries the manufacturer's base paint formula in gallon containers and colors it to customer specifications. Although some exterior paint is stocked throughout the year, there always are fluctuations in the demand for the highest quality paints, for two main reasons—first, the overall demand for exterior paint is by nature seasonal (even in Peacock's temperate weather location); and second, the particular brands Peacock carries have application directions which recommend use under specific weather conditions.

For example, Brand X is carried in large quantities during the milder months because of cold weather application problems and the increased demand for paint in general during warm weather periods. The manufacturer of Brand X also produces another exterior paint which has warm weather application problems and is suggested for conditions which run counter to those recommended for Brand X. Several products in Peacock's lines have such complementary demand patterns, but all of these products are considerably more expensive than year-round formulas.

Because of the undulating demand and relative expense of seasonal products, Peacock's manager, Art Plume, realizes that substantial holding cost savings can be gained during low periods of demand if unneeded stock is eliminated. In the case of the exterior paint, he would rather stock only enough paint to meet demand and not have excess paint on hand at the end of its peak season. Art also is aware that forecasting demand for each of the paints is critical to this goal.

The seasonality in demand always has substantially increased the difficulty of making a reliable forecast. Moreover, Art thinks the type of customer is particularly important in the forecasting process. Approximately 60% of paint sales is to local paint contractors, and 40% is to "do it yourself" homeowners. Past demand forecasts for commercial sales have proven to be much more stable than forecasts for homeowners. This contrast is accentuated by the preference of private consumers for prime weather conditions. A late fall or early winter can cause significant fluctuations in the demand.

So far, Art Plume has forecasted demand through experience. The accuracy of the experiential forecasting has been declining, and stocking has become a problem. Art's uneasiness about increased competition and the ever-growing need for efficiency have made him decide to improve upon experience. In addition to his direct observations and general knowledge of Peacock's customers, Art has decided to make specific forecasts. He has categorized past sales by month and customer type. The following table gives the compilation of three years of demand for Brand X:

	Brand X sales[a]					
	Contractors			Homeowners		
	19X3	19X4	19X5	19X3	19X4	19X5
Jan.	10	20	30	10	10	10
Feb.	20	25	30	10	10	16
Mar.	40	50	55	30	45	50
Apr.	55	70	80	75	60	65
May	110	120	140	80	70	80
Jun.	150	160	175	100	95	100
Jul.	170	190	210	100	90	110
Aug.	180	200	210	80	70	70
Sept.	160	170	165	90	100	110
Oct.	50	80	70	70	80	70
Nov.	30	35	60	20	15	20
Dec.	30	50	65	20	30	36

[a] In gallons of base paint.

Art still is flummoxed by the forecasting task. He wonders whether the same technique should be applied separately to each customer category or whether a single forecast should be made by integrating homeowner sales with contractor sales. Besides which forecast method is best in either case, he is concerned with what information other than past data might be useful to the forecasting process.

Use the information given, and:

1. List the points which are important to this forecasting situation in general.
2. Discuss whether Peacock should forecast for product groups or for individual items; whether Peacock should prepare forecasts for separate customer categories.
3. Subjectively analyze which forecasting techniques would perform best for Brand X. Experiment with different forecasting techniques, and check your empirical results against your untested judgments.
4. Discuss other techniques which could be applied if additional information were available. Include the applicability of economic indicators.
5. State what factors may affect and possibly bias forecasting based on historical data or qualitative input. What might be done to compensate for these?

CASE 2: ABBREVIATED DISCS

Hot Records had been a giant in the music industry since the industry's huge growth era of the '60s and '70s and was the undisputed leader in annual record sales in the rock categories. Hot had been the foremost representative for artists introduced in the U.S. on a nationwide scale until the tune changed and the record industry began its four-year decline of 13% of annual sales. The firm, which previously had spent lavishly on high living and frills, incurred serious financial setbacks when the boom went bust.

The music industry suffered for many reasons. A sluggish and inflation-ridden economy, fewer "mega" hits, record counterfeiting, limited radio-station play, high costs of producing and promoting records, poor quality recordings and fierce competition from video games were blamed for driving music sales down. Hot executives believed their particular firm's losses stemmed not only from the causes cited by industry spokespersons but from the large prices charged for long-playing albums, from its inability to sign new artists or get signed artists introduced successfully, and most of all, from home taping. Hot's customers were wary of expensive albums, even those by major artists. The recordings by new artists aroused even more caution. The average customer, young and less able to afford luxuries during economically hard times, preferred to tape recordings and to spend money on video entertainment.

Hot executives now are excited by the apparent end to the downward trend of their maturing industry. While it is too early to label a music recovery a sure thing, a number of trends are running in the industry's favor. The recession is winding down, consumer spending is picking up, and an industry built on hits currently has a few "monster" successes. An important new source of support for records is unexpectedly coming from television. A cable channel which has become a big success is exchanging free air time for videotapes of artists performing their latest songs. The industry also has gone to records which come in more economical sizes and are of higher quality.

To undo the drop in its album sales and ride the crest of the music turnaround, Hot plans to introduce a line of twelve-inch "dance singles" called "shorts" which feature extended versions of hit songs and sell for as little as $3.49. It also plans mini-albums that carry half as many songs as regular albums, sell for $4.49 instead of $6.98, and contain some previously unreleased material. Hot hopes the shorter formats will overcome resistance to purchasing the long-plays. Figuring that these new records will be eye-catching in their reduced size, less expensive, and higher quality (with a cotton substitute for the expensive petroleum additive), Hot believes it has a winner.

The sole purpose of shifting attention to the "shorts" is to increase total sales. The expected increase, due in part to a perceived revival of pop music, is not precisely known. The Hot executives feel they can capture a large part of the album buyer's market and believe the new discs will serve to introduce artists who will later record on the long-plays. Though there is a consensus that the "shorts" are a solution to the sales problem, the management staff would like to know just how successful the undertaking will be. The staff has decided that forecasting should be done prior to the new releases. As to the type of forecasting technique, they are perplexed.

Since this is an entirely new line for Hot, the staff realizes an exact forecast is impossible. They cannot use any of the methods in practice for their established lines, but they wonder if a modification of one might suffice. One executive suggests that multiple linear regression, which is used with the regular album lines, would be suitable. She feels that the independent variables that affect regular discs, such as the general state of the economy, would be equally significant indicators for the new line. However, she welcomes more input from other record executives before she is prepared to declare an end to the sour trend and listen to the sweet music of success.

1. Discuss some difficulties in developing forecasts for new products.
2. Could multiple linear regression be a practical forecasting technique for the new line? For total record sales? What other independent variables could be used in the predictions?
3. What new product features, technological changes, competitive forces, other external decisions or pressures, and industry as well as organizational factors affect the forecast and the selection of a forecasting method?

CASE 3: FROZEN IN TIME

The Grimes Company, a manufacturer of heating, air conditioning, and refrigeration products, has five divisions. One of the divisions is responsible for the manufacturing of truck and trailer refrigeration units. Their units are sold to customers nationwide through a dealer organization consisting of approximately 180 authorized dealers.

The continual use of refrigeration units causes parts to wear rapidly, and their replacement is a frequent occurrence. However, intense usage tends to be seasonal. Grimes finds the demand for refrigeration units to coincide with the demand for replacement parts, and it uses historical data to forecast both requirements. The type and number of replacement parts to order for the upcoming period is obtained by ordering the number of items sold during that period in the previous year.

Grimes receives component parts from various suppliers: for example, clutches from one supplier, engines from another, and compressors from a third. Components must meet Grimes's specifications. It is often impossible to order parts from another supplier in case of an emergency, because an alternative supplier's part usually does not match the specifications.

Dealer orders for parts are filled from stock carried at Grimes. Grimes orders at quarterly intervals from suppliers. It is common for suppliers not to fill orders immediately. When this happens, Grimes often has backorders to fill for the dealers. During the waiting periods, the dealers have been prone to panic. Because of their uneasiness, the dealers have been increasing, even doubling, their orders to Grimes and are consequently carrying more stock.

1. Is Grimes using an effective method for forecasting demand?
2. What problems are occurring at Grimes?
3. What are the possible solutions?

SELECTED BIBLIOGRAPHY

Box, G. E. P. and G. M. Jenkins. *Time Series Analysis: Forecasting and Control*, San Francisco: Holden-Day, 1976.

Brown, R. G. *Smoothing, Forecasting, and Prediction of Discrete Time Series*, New York: Prentice-Hall, 1963.

_____. *Statistical Forecasting for Inventory Control*, New York: McGraw-Hill, 1959.

Chambers, J. C. et al. "How to Choose the Right Forecasting Technique," *Harvard Business Review*, July–August 1971.

Chisholm, R. K. and G. R. Whitaker, Jr. *Forecasting Methods*, Homewood, IL: Irwin, 1971.

Gardner, E. S. "Exponential Smoothing: The State of the Art," *Journal of Forecasting*, Vol. 4, No. 1, 1985, pp. 1–28.

Hax, A. C. and D. Canada. *Production and Inventory Management*, Englewood Cliffs, NJ: Prentice-Hall, 1984.

Landau, E. "On the Non-Statistical Aspects of Statistical Forecasting," *American Production and Inventory Control Society Conference Proceedings*, 1976.

Makridakis, S. and S. Wheelwright. Forecasting Methods and Applications, New York: Wiley/Hamilton, 1978.

McLeavey, D. W. and S. L. Narasimhan. *Production Planning and Inventory Control*, Boston: Allyn and Bacon, 1985.

Montgomery, D. C. and L. A. Johnston. *Forecasting and Time Series Analysis*, New York: McGraw-Hill, 1976.

Silver, E. A. and R. Peterson. *Decision Systems for Inventory Management and Production Planning*, New York: Wiley, 1985.

Tersine, R. J. and W. Riggs. "The Delphi Technique: A Long Range Planning Tool," *Business Horizons*, Vol. 19, No. 2, 1976.

Trigg, D. W. and A. G. Leach. "Exponential Smoothing With an Adaptive Rate," *Operations Research Quarterly*, March 1977.

Wheelwright, S. and S. Makridakis. *Forecasting Methods for Management*, New York: Wiley, 1977.

Whybark, D. C. "A Comparison of Adaptive Forecasting Techniques," *The Logistics and Transportation Review*, Vol. 8, No. 3, 1973.

MATHEMATICAL ABBREVIATIONS AND SYMBOLS USED IN CHAPTER 2

a	Mean exponential smoothing constant between 0 and 1
b	Trend exponential smoothing constant between 0 and 1
c	Seasonal exponential smoothing constant between 0 and 1
d	MAD exponential smoothing constant between 0 and 1
EWMA	Exponentially weighted moving average
I_t	Seasonal index for time period t
MAD	Mean absolute deviation
m	Number of periods in seasonal pattern
n	Number of time periods
r	Simple correlation coefficient
S_r	Standard deviation of the regression line
t	Time period
$\bar{t}$	Mean time period
T_t	Trend adjustment for period t
X	Independent variable (economic indicator)
$\overline{X}$	Mean independent variable
$\hat{X}_t$	Forecasted demand level for period t
Y_t	Actual demand for period t
$\hat{Y}_t$	Forecasted demand for period t
Y	Dependent variable (variable to be forecasted)
α	Intercept
β	Slope

SUMMARY OF FORMULAS IN CHAPTER 2

Model	Formula

Last period demand $\quad \hat{Y}_t = Y_{t-1}$

Arithmetic average $\quad \hat{Y}_t = \dfrac{\displaystyle\sum_{i=1}^{n} Y_i}{n}$

Moving average $\quad \hat{Y}_t = \dfrac{\displaystyle\sum_{i=1}^{n} Y_{t-i}}{n}$

Time series regression $\quad \hat{Y}_t = \alpha + \beta t$

$$\beta = \frac{n \displaystyle\sum_{i=1}^{n} t_i Y_i - \left(\displaystyle\sum_{i=1}^{n} t_i\right)\left(\displaystyle\sum_{i=1}^{n} Y_i\right)}{n \displaystyle\sum_{i=1}^{n} t_i^2 - \left[\displaystyle\sum_{i=1}^{n} t_i\right]^2} = \text{slope}$$

$$\alpha = \bar{Y} - \beta \bar{t} = \frac{\displaystyle\sum_{i=1}^{n} Y_i - \left[\beta \displaystyle\sum_{i=1}^{n} t_i\right]}{n} = \text{intercept}$$

$$r^2 = \frac{\left[n \displaystyle\sum_{i=1}^{n} t_i Y_i - \left(\displaystyle\sum_{i=1}^{n} t_i\right)\left(\displaystyle\sum_{i=1}^{n} Y_i\right)\right]^2}{\left[n \displaystyle\sum_{i=1}^{n} t_i^2 - \left(\displaystyle\sum_{i=1}^{n} t_i\right)^2\right]\left[n \displaystyle\sum_{i=1}^{n} Y_i^2 - \left(\displaystyle\sum_{i=1}^{n} Y_i\right)^2\right]}$$

$$S_r^2 = \frac{\displaystyle\sum_{i=1}^{n} Y_i^2 - \alpha \displaystyle\sum_{i=1}^{n} Y_i - \beta \displaystyle\sum_{i=1}^{n} t_i Y_i}{n-2} = \frac{\displaystyle\sum_{i=1}^{n} (Y_i - \hat{Y}_i)^2}{n-2}$$

EWMA $\qquad\qquad\qquad$ See Table 3.

Economic indicator $\quad Y = \alpha + \beta X$
regression

$$\alpha = \bar{Y} - \beta \bar{X} = \frac{\Sigma Y - \beta \Sigma X}{n}$$

$$\beta = \frac{n(\Sigma XY) - (\Sigma X)(\Sigma Y)}{n\Sigma X^2 - (\Sigma X)^2}$$

$$r^2 = \frac{(\Sigma xy)^2}{(\Sigma x^2)(\Sigma y^2)} = \frac{\left[n \displaystyle\sum_{i=1}^{n} X_i Y_i - \left(\displaystyle\sum_{i=1}^{n} X_i\right)\left(\displaystyle\sum_{i=1}^{n} Y_i\right)\right]^2}{\left[n \displaystyle\sum_{i=1}^{n} X_i^2 - \left(\displaystyle\sum_{i=1}^{n} X_i\right)^2\right]\left[n \displaystyle\sum_{i=1}^{n} Y_i^2 - \left(\displaystyle\sum_{i=1}^{n} Y_i\right)^2\right]}$$

$$S_r^2 = \frac{\Sigma Y^2 - \alpha \Sigma Y - \beta \Sigma XY}{n-2} = \frac{\Sigma(Y - \hat{Y})^2}{n-2}$$

Forecast error
measurement $\qquad\qquad\qquad$ See Figure 6.

3 Independent Demand Systems: Deterministic Models

FIXED ORDER SIZE SYSTEMS
  Economic Order Quantity (EOQ)—Single Items
  Backordering
  Quantity Discounts
    All-Units Quantity Discounts
    Incremental Quantity Discounts
  Special Sale Prices
  Known Price Increases
  EOQ Sensitivity

BATCH-TYPE PRODUCTION SYSTEMS
  Economic Production Quantity (EPQ)—Single Items
    Backordering
  Make or Buy Decisions
  Economic Production Quantity (EPQ)—Multiple Items
  Runout Time (ROT) Method
  Aggregate Runout Time (AROT) Method

FIXED ORDER INTERVAL SYSTEMS
  Economic Order Interval (EOI)—Single Items
  Economic Order Interval (EOI)—Multiple Items

CONCLUSION
QUESTIONS
PROBLEMS
CASES
MATHEMATICAL ABBREVIATIONS AND SYMBOLS
SUMMARY OF FORMULAS
APPENDIX A: DETERMINATION OF SINGLE VARIABLE MAXIMUM AND MINIMUM POINTS
APPENDIX B: EOQ QUANTITY DISCOUNT APPROXIMATION
APPENDIX C: DERIVATION OF EOQ WITH BACKORDERING

One of the major reasons for having inventory is to enable an organization to buy or produce items in economic lot sizes. Organizations which use economic lot sizing often do so when they want to maintain a regular inventory of items which have a fairly uniform, independent demand. This chapter introduces a special collection of deterministic models that apply directly to uniform demand conditions. These models determine the economic lot sizes (optimum inventory policies) for independent demand items, whether they are purchased from a vendor or produced internally.

To determine an optimum inventory policy, information on each of the following parameters is required:

1. demand forecasts,
2. appropriate inventory costs,
3. lead times.

In deterministic models, all of the parameters and variables are known or can be calculated with certainty. The rate of demand for units and the appropriate inventory costs are assumed to be known with assurance. The replenishment lead time also is presumed constant and independent of demand. The real world is seldom as well behaved as described by deterministic models but is more reasonably depicted in probabilistic terms (i.e. in stochastic models, where some or all of the variables are probabilistic). However, deterministic models are frequently excellent approximations, or at least, good starting points for describing inventory phenomena.

It usually is easier to work analytically with inventory models if the variables can be treated as continuous rather than discrete. In cases where inventory demand is sufficiently high, variables can be considered continuous, and it is possible to take derivatives instead of having to work with differences. This collection of models assumes continuous properties and thereby simplifies the task of finding optimizing inventory policies.

FIXED ORDER SIZE SYSTEMS

The two fundamental questions posed to any inventory system are *how many* and *when* to order. The answers depend on the nature of inventory demand and the parameters used to define the system. As previously described, demand in a deterministic fixed order size system is assumed to be known or able to be calculated with certainty and presumed to be continuous. Therefore, the same number of units (how many) always is ordered, and the time between orders (when) is not expected to vary. The stock level is reviewed continuously, and whenever the inventory position reaches a predetermined point, an order for a fixed number of units is placed. Thus, the two defining parameters of the system are the reorder point (B) and the size of the order (Q). The fixed order size system also is

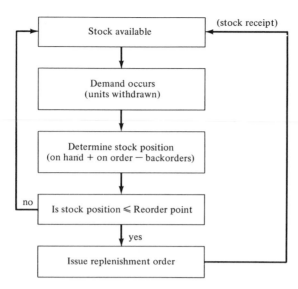

Figure 1. Fixed order size system.

termed a Q-system, since the size of the order (Q) is fixed for each replenishment. A typical example is depicted in Figure 1.

Economic Order Quantity (EOQ)—Single Items

The size of an order that minimizes the total inventory cost is known as the economic order quantity (EOQ). The classical inventory model assumes the idealized situations shown in Figure 2, where Q is the order size.[1] Upon receipt of an order, the inventory level is Q units. Units are withdrawn from inventory at a constant demand rate, which is represented by the negative sloping lines. When the inventory reaches the reorder point B, a new order is placed for Q units. After a fixed time period, the order is received all at once and placed into inventory. The vertical lines indicate the receipt of a lot into inventory. The new lot is received just as the inventory level reaches zero, so the average inventory is $(Q + 0)/2$ or $Q/2$.

If stockouts are not permitted, the total inventory cost per year is graphically depicted by Figure 3 and by the following formula:[2]

total annual cost = (purchase cost) + (order cost) + (holding cost),

$$TC = RP + \frac{RC}{Q} + \frac{QH}{2},$$

---

[1] The classical inventory model is frequently referred to as a sawtooth diagram because of the series of right triangles.

[2] Although we have selected a time period of one year, any time period can be used as long as R and H are on the same time period basis. The model assumes that stockouts will not occur.

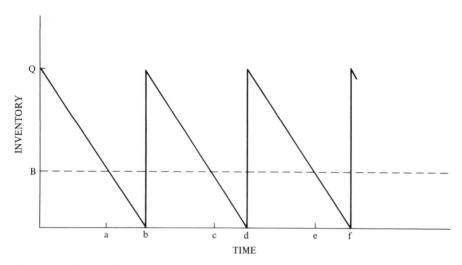

Figure 2. Classical inventory model.
Key: Q = lot size; $Q/2$ = average inventory; B = reorder point; ac = ce = interval between orders; ab = cd = ef = lead time.

Figure 3. Annual inventory costs.

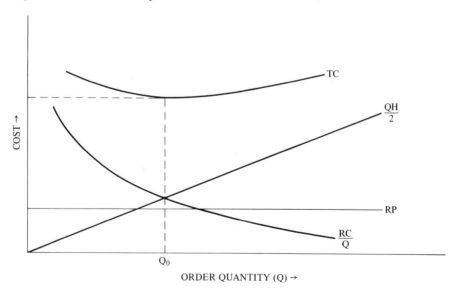

where

R = annual demand in units,
P = purchase cost of an item,
C = ordering cost per order,
$H = PF$ = holding cost per unit per year,
Q = lot size or order quantity in units,
F = annual holding cost as a fraction of unit cost.

In effect, the total annual cost equation determines the annual purchase cost, which is the annual demand times the purchase cost per unit. The annual order cost is obtained as the number of orders per year (R/Q) times the cost to place an order (C). The annual holding cost is the average inventory ($Q/2$) times the annual unit holding cost (H). The sum of the three costs (purchase, order, and holding) is the total inventory cost per year for any given purchased item.

To obtain the minimum cost lot size (EOQ), take the first derivative of total annual cost with respect to the lot size (Q) and set it equal to zero:[3]

$$\frac{d\,TC}{dQ} = \frac{H}{2} - \frac{CR}{Q^2} = 0.$$

Solving the equation for Q, we get the EOQ formula:

$$Q_0 = \sqrt{\frac{2CR}{H}} = \sqrt{\frac{2CR}{PF}} = \text{economic order quantity.}$$

The EOQ results in items with high unit cost being ordered frequently in small quantities (the saving in inventory investment pays for the extra orders); items with low unit cost are ordered in large quantities (the inventory investment is small and the repeated expense of orders can be avoided). If the order cost C is zero, orders are placed to satisfy each demand as it occurs, which results in no holding cost. If the holding cost H is zero, an order (only one) is placed for an amount that will satisfy the lifetime demand for the item.

Once the economic order quantity is known, the expected number of orders placed during the year, m, and the average time between orders, T, can be determined:

$$\text{expected number of orders during year} = m = \frac{R}{Q_0} = \sqrt{\frac{HR}{2C}},$$

$$\text{average order interval} = T = \frac{1}{m} = \frac{Q_0}{R} = \sqrt{\frac{2C}{RH}}.$$

[3] See Appendix A for further clarification of the minimization of a continuous single-variable function.

The reorder point is obtained by determining the demand that will occur during the lead time period. When the stock position [(on hand) + (on order) − (backorders)] reaches the reorder point, an order will be placed for Q_0 units, the economic order quantity. The following formula gives the reorder point when the lead time L is expressed in months:

$$B = \frac{RL}{12} = \text{reorder point in units.}$$

If the lead time L is expressed in weeks, the reorder point is expressed as

$$B = \frac{RL}{52} = \text{reorder point in units.}$$

The goods are assumed to be received when the last item leaves the inventory, and the inventory level is restored to a level equal to the amount ordered. If the lead time is less than the average order interval ($L < T$), there will never be more than a single order outstanding. If the lead time is greater than the average order interval ($L > T$), there will always be at least one order outstanding.

The minimum total cost per year is obtained by substituting Q_0 for Q in the total annual cost equation. A simplified formula for the minimum total cost per year results:

$$TC_0 = RP + HQ_0.$$

The classical EOQ model is based on the following assumptions:

1. The demand rate is known and constant.
2. The lead time is known and constant.
3. The entire lot size is added to inventory at the same time.
4. No stockouts are permitted; since demand and lead time are known, stockouts can be avoided.
5. The cost structure is fixed; order/setup costs are the same regardless of lot size, holding cost is a linear function based on average inventory, and no quantity discounts are given on large purchases.
6. There is sufficient space, capacity, and capital to procure the desired quantity.
7. The item is a single product; it does not interact with any other inventory items (there are no joint orders).

EXAMPLE 1

The Williams Manufacturing Company purchases 8000 units of a product each year at a unit cost of $10.00. The order cost is $30.00 per order, and the holding cost per unit per year is $3.00. What are the economic order quantity, the total annual cost, the number of orders to place in one year, and the reorder point when the lead time is two weeks?

$$Q_0 = \sqrt{\frac{2CR}{H}} = \sqrt{\frac{2(30)8000}{3}} = 400 \text{ units,}$$

$$TC_0 = RP + HQ_0 = 8000(10) + 3(400) = \$81,200,$$

$$m = \frac{R}{Q_0} = \frac{8000}{400} = 20 \text{ orders/year,}$$

$$B = \frac{RL}{52} = \frac{8000(2)}{52} = 307.7 \text{ units.}$$

The economic order quantity minimizes the total cost function under a given set of circumstances. It is based on a given cost structure. It may be more appropriate to find ways to reduce cost parameters, such as the order/setup cost (C). This logic is part of the "just-in-time" philosophy outlined in Chapter 9. A lower order/setup will reduce the EOQ and thus the average inventory.

Backordering

A backorder is an unfilled demand that will be filled, but later than desired. In the backordering situation, a firm does not lose the sale when its inventory is depleted. Instead, the customer waits to have his demand filled when the firm receives its next order. Thus, backordering occurs with loyal, patient, or captive customers.

Backordering may involve expediting (special handling) which is more costly than routine order processing. It may require an alternative external source with a premium price for a shorter lead time, or a more expensive routing as well as overtime for manufactured items. If there were no costs associated with incurring backorders, no inventory would be held. If backorders were very expensive, they would never be incurred. However, there is an intermediate range of backordering costs where it is optimal to incur some backorders towards the end of an inventory cycle.

In this treatment of backordering we assume that all shortages are satisfied from the next shipment. This is referred to as captive demand, as opposed to the situation where unsatisfied demand is totally or partially lost. When the stockout (shortage) cost is finite, an economic advantage may be gained by permitting stockouts to occur. In many cases, the increase in cost due to acceptance of a shortage is more than compensated by the reduction in holding cost.

Figure 4 depicts the backordering inventory model. An order for Q units is placed when the stock on hand reaches the reorder point. The size of the

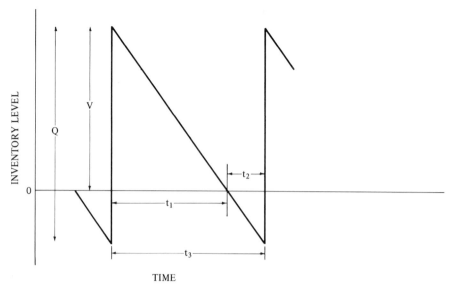

TIME

Figure 4. Backordering inventory model.

stockout is $Q - V$ units, and the maximum inventory level is V units. The backordering cost per unit per year is K, and it is directly proportional to the length of the time delay.

During time period t_3 one order is placed, so the order cost is C. The average holding cost during period t_1 is given as follows:

$$H \frac{V}{2} t_1 = \frac{HV^2}{2R},$$

since

$$\frac{R}{1 \text{ yr}} = \frac{V}{t_1}; \quad \text{then} \quad t_1 = \frac{V}{R}$$

by similar triangles. t_1 is the time period during which there is a positive inventory balance, and t_2 is the stockout time period. The average back-ordering cost during t_2 is as follows:

$$\frac{K(Q - V)t_2}{2} = \frac{K(Q - V)^2}{2R},$$

since

$$\frac{R}{1 \text{ yr}} = \frac{Q - V}{t_2}; \quad \text{then} \quad t_2 = \frac{Q - V}{R}$$

by similar triangles. Therefore, the total cost for one time period of length t_3 is

$$QP + C + \frac{HV^2}{2R} + \frac{K(Q - V)^2}{2R}.$$

There are R/Q order periods of length t_3 in a year, so the total annual cost is obtained by multiplying the above equation by R/Q, which results in

total annual cost = (purchase cost) + (order cost)

+ (holding cost) + (backorder cost),

$$TC = RP + C\frac{R}{Q} + \frac{HV^2}{2Q} + \frac{K(Q - V)^2}{2Q},$$

where

R = annual requirement in units,
P = purchase cost of an item,
C = ordering cost per order,
Q = lot size or order quantity,
H = holding cost per unit per year,
V = maximum inventory level in units,
K = backordering cost per unit per year,
R/Q = number of orders per year.

To obtain optimal values for Q and V, partial derivatives of the total annual cost with respect to Q and V are equated to zero. The following optimum formulas result: [4]

$$Q_0 = \sqrt{\frac{2CR}{H}} \sqrt{\frac{H + K}{K}},$$

$$V_0 = \sqrt{\frac{2CR}{H}} \sqrt{\frac{K}{H + K}}.$$

The inclusion of backordering cost increases the economic order quantity Q_0, but it also results in a smaller average inventory. When the backordering cost (K) is very large, $\sqrt{(H + K)/K}$ approaches one, and the economic order quantity corresponds to the classical case when there is no backorder, or

$$Q_0 = \sqrt{\frac{2CR}{H}},$$

$$Q_0 - V_0 = 0.$$

[4] See Appendix C for derivation of the formulas.

When the backordering cost (K) approaches zero, $\sqrt{K/(H + K)}$ approaches zero, and the maximum inventory level becomes zero. This is the situation where all items are backordered or handled on a special order basis, since V_0 equals zero.

When backorders are permitted to exist, the reorder point calculation is modified (reduced by the size of the backorder). The reorder point is the lead time demand minus the number of units backordered, or

reorder point = (lead time demand) − (backorders),

$$B = \frac{RL}{N} - (Q - V),$$

where

N = number of operating days per year,

L = lead time in days.

Observe that the reorder point could be negative if the lead time demand were less than the size of the backorder. This situation would result in an order not being placed until a certain number of backorders were obtained. Although the reorder point may be positive or negative with backordering, there will always be a period in which there is no stock available. When the backordering cost is finite, the reorder point will always be less than the lead time demand.

With a backordering policy, the longest time a customer will have to wait is a vital piece of information. The longest delay time in years for a backorder is calculated as follows:

$$\text{longest delay time} = \frac{Q_0 - V_0}{R}.$$

If the longest delay time is longer than desired, it can be shortened by increasing K until the longest delay time is acceptable. In effect, K is treated as a management policy variable in arriving at a maximum delay time on backorders.

EXAMPLE 2

From the information given in Example 1, what happens to the economic order quantity if backordering is possible and the stockout cost per unit per year is $1.00?

$$Q_0 = \sqrt{\frac{2CR}{H}} \sqrt{\frac{H + K}{K}} = \sqrt{\frac{2(30)8000}{3}} \sqrt{\frac{3 + 1}{1}} = 800 \text{ units,}$$

$$V_0 = \sqrt{\frac{2CR}{H}} \sqrt{\frac{K}{H + K}} = 200 \text{ units,}$$

$$B = \frac{RL}{52} - (Q - V) = \frac{8000(2)}{52} - 600 = -292 \text{ units,}$$

$$TC = RP + C\frac{R}{Q} + \frac{HV^2}{2Q} + \frac{K(Q - V)^2}{2Q}$$

$$= 8000(10) + \frac{30(8000)}{800} + \frac{3(200)^2}{2(800)} + \frac{1(800 - 200)^2}{2(800)}$$

$$= \$80,600.00,$$

$$\text{longest delay} = \frac{Q_0 - V_0}{R} = \frac{800 - 200}{8000}$$

$$= 0.075 \text{ years} = 3.9 \text{ weeks}$$

When backordering is instituted, the EOQ doubles in size from 400 to 800 units, but the maximum inventory decreases from 400 to 200 units. No order is placed until 292 backorder units are accumulated. The optimum annual cost is reduced by $81,200.00 - $80,600.00 = $600.00 with the backordering policy. However, the longest delay time a customer has to wait increases from zero to 3.9 weeks.

Quantity Discounts

It is a common practice for suppliers to offer lower unit prices on orders for larger quantities as an economic incentive to buyers to purchase in larger lot sizes. The seller benefits from sales of larger quantities by reducing per unit order processing and setup costs and by (at least temporarily) increasing volume. The buyer benefits both by having reduced per unit ordering costs and by paying the lower unit price, but at the cost of having to hold more inventory. The problem faced by the buyer is to identify the lot size that minimizes total costs.

There are two general types of quantity discount schedules offered by suppliers: the *all-units* discount and the *incremental* discount. With the all-units discount, purchasing larger quantities results in a lower unit price for the entire lot. Incremental discounts, however, apply the lower unit price only to units purchased above a specified quantity. Thus, the all-units discount results in the same unit price for every item in a given lot, while the incremental discount can result in multiple unit prices for an item within the same lot. The quantities at which prices change are called price-break quantities for both schedules. Only one schedule usually is applied to a given item, and it may contain one or more price-break quantities.

All-Units Quantity Discounts

The basic economic lot size formula assumes a fixed purchase price per unit. With quantity discounts, the traditional EOQ formulation is not adequate. When quantity discounts are offered, the objective function is still to find the minimum cost point on the total cost curve. However, the total cost curve is not continuous, so the first derivative does not indicate the minimum cost point as readily as it does without discounts. The quantity

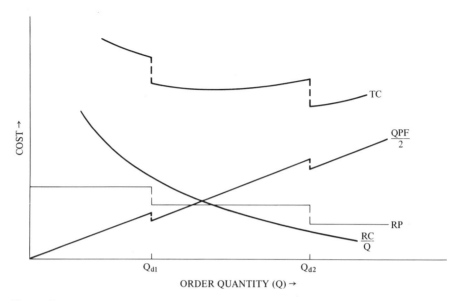

Figure 5. Inventory costs: all-units quantity discounts.

discount creates a discontinuity or disjunction in the total cost curve. Figure 5 shows a hypothetical situation with two price breaks. The minimum cost point will be either at the point of discontinuity or where the derivatives equal zero as determined by the EOQ.

With all-units quantity discounts, the buyer is presented by the supplier with a price schedule consisting of j quantity ranges such that the unit price is equal for all units in an order and decreases with increasing order size. The unit purchase cost is defined as follows:

$$P = \begin{cases} P_0 & \text{for} \quad 1 \le Q < U_1, \\ P_1 & \text{for} \quad U_1 \le Q < U_2, \\ \vdots & \\ P_j & \text{for} \quad U_j \le Q, \end{cases}$$

where $1 < U_1 < U_2 < \cdots < U_j$ is the sequence of integer quantities at which price breaks occur. P_i denotes the unit price applicable to orders whose lot size falls in the interval U_i to U_{i+1} with $P_0 > P_1 > \cdots > P_j$. The last interval $Q \ge U_j$ is unbounded.

Figure 6 shows three possible conditions that might exist with a single price break. Only the solid portion of the total cost curve is relevant; the dashed portion of the curve is not realizable. The solid curve shows the cost function which applies over the entire quantity range. The dashed curve represents extensions of the cost function into nonapplicable regions. The problem is reduced to finding the lowest point on the curve formed by the

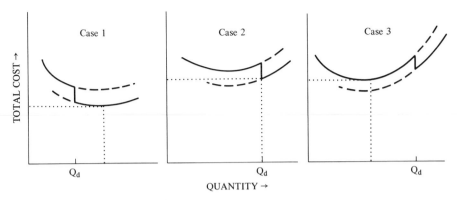

Figure 6. All-units quantity discounts.
Decision rule: Order the quantity with the lowest cost. *Case 1:* order $> Q_d$; *case 2:* order $= Q_d$; *case 3:* order $< Q_d$.

solid portions. Because of the discontinuity of the curve, the least cost quantity cannot always be found by differentiation.

With all-units quantity discounts, there is a separate total cost curve for each unit price. Each curve applies to only a portion of the quantity range where the respective price is valid. The result is a total cost curve with steps (discontinuities) at the price-break quantities. Although the curve for each unit price has a minimum point (EOQ), it is not necessarily valid (feasible). An economic order quantity is valid if it is within the quantity range corresponding to its unit purchase cost. When holding costs are specified as a fraction of unit purchase cost, each curve will have a different EOQ. Lower unit purchase cost results in lower unit holdings costs and larger EOQs. Since each portion of the relevant total cost curve is minimized either at an economic order quantity or at a price-break quantity, the overall optimum lot size can be narrowed to the feasible economic order quantities and the price-break quantities.

The following procedure, as outlined in Figure 7, indicates how to obtain the minimum cost order quantity when one or more all-units quantity discounts are available:[5]

1. Starting with the lowest unit cost, calculate the EOQ at each unit cost until a valid EOQ is obtained.
2. Calculate the total annual cost for the valid EOQ and all price-break quantities larger than the valid EOQ. (A price-break quantity is the lowest quantity for which the price discount is available.)
3. The minimum cost order quantity is the quantity with the lowest total cost in step 2 above.

[5] See Appendix B for an approximation approach to all-units quantity discounts. For a more detailed analysis see R. J. Tersine and R. A. Toelle, "Lot Size Determination with Quantity Discounts," *Production and Inventory Management*, Vol. 26, No. 3, 1985.

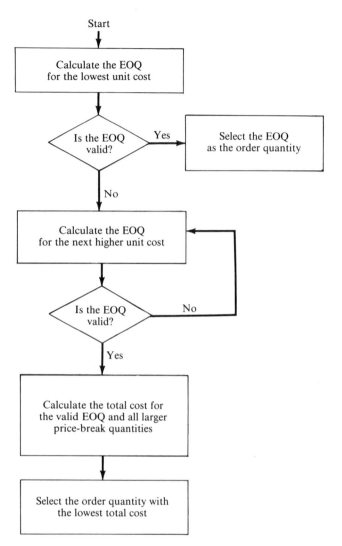

Figure 7. All-units quantity discount logic.

EXAMPLE 3

The Smith Company purchases 8000 units of a product each year. The supplier offers the units for sale at $10.00 per unit for orders up to 500 units and at $9.00 per unit for orders of 500 units or more. What is the economic order quantity if the order cost is $30.00 per order and the holding cost is 30% of per unit cost per year?

The EOQ for each unit price is as follows:

$$Q_{10} = \sqrt{\frac{2CR}{PF}} = \sqrt{\frac{2(30)8000}{10(0.3)}} = 400 \text{ units},$$

$$Q_9 = \sqrt{\frac{2CR}{PF}} = \sqrt{\frac{2(30)8000}{9(0.3)}} = 422 \text{ units.}$$

The EOQ with \$10 is valid. The EOQ with \$9 is invalid, since it is not available for quantities less than 500 units. The total cost of the valid EOQ with \$10 is as follows:

$$TC_{10} = RP + HQ_0 = (8000)10 + 10(0.3)400 = \$81,200.00.$$

The total cost for the single price break quantity of 500 units is as follows:

$$TC_d = RP + \frac{RC}{Q} + \frac{Q(P)F}{2} = 8000(9) + \frac{(8000)30}{500} + \frac{500(9)0.30}{2},$$

$$TC_d = \$72,000 + \$480.00 + \$675.00 = \$73,155.00.$$

Comparing the total costs of the single price-break quantity and the valid EOQ, the minimum cost order quantity is 500 units.

It is possible to obtain the economic order quantity with quantity discounts by graphing total cost versus lot size and selecting the minimum cost point. However, the graphical approach is a tedious and time-consuming process.

Because quantity discounts do not alter demand or lead time, they do not affect reorder point calculations in this situation.

Incremental Quantity Discounts

The only difference in this situation from the previous section is in the type of discount offered. In this situation, the discount applies only to those units purchased in excess of a required price-break quantity. For each order placed, the unit purchase cost is as follows:

$$P = \begin{cases} P_0 & \text{for each of the first } U_1 - 1 \text{ units,} \\ P_1 & \text{for each of the next } U_2 - U_1 \text{ units,} \\ \vdots \\ P_j & \text{for each unit in excess of } U_j - 1, \end{cases}$$

where $P_0 > P_1 > P_2 \cdots > P_j$ and $1 < U_1 < U_2 < \cdots < U_j$ are the price-break quantities. Defining $M(Q)$ as the purchase cost if Q units are ordered, its cost can be calculated *recursively* for any lot size between consecutive price-break quantities $(U_i \le Q < U_{i+1})$ by

$$M(Q) = M(U_i - 1) + P_i[Q - (U_i - 1)]$$
$$= M(U_i - 1) - P_i(U_i - 1) + P_iQ.$$

Thus, the total cost per year can be expressed as

$$\mathrm{TC}_i(Q) = \frac{M(Q)R}{Q} + \frac{RC}{Q} + \frac{FM(Q)}{2} = \frac{[C + M(Q)]R}{Q} + \frac{FM(Q)}{2}$$

$$= \frac{[C + M(U_i - 1) - P_i(U_i - 1)]R}{Q} + P_iR$$

$$+ \frac{F}{2}[M(U_i - 1) - P_i(U_i - 1) + P_iQ].$$

Since the total cost curve for each price is convex, the EOQ for each price level i can be obtained by setting the first derivative of the total cost with respect to Q equal to zero, which results in

$$Q_{0i} = \sqrt{\frac{2R[C + M(U_i - 1) - P_i(U_i - 1)]}{P_iF}}.$$

Since $M(U_i - 1) - P_i(U_i - 1) = \sum_{z=1}^{i}(U_z - 1)(P_{z-1} - P_z)$, Q_{0i} can be expressed as

$$Q_{0i} = \sqrt{\frac{2R\left[C + \sum_{z=1}^{i}(U_z - 1)(P_{z-1} - P_z)\right]}{P_iF}}$$

for $i = 1, 2, \ldots, j$. $M(U_i - 1)$ is the cost of purchasing $U_i - 1$ units under the incremental discount schedule. $P_i(U_i - 1)$ is the discount price multiplied by $U_i - 1$ units; it is what it would cost to buy $U_i - 1$ units if all units could be purchased at the discount price. Since all the units cannot be purchased at the discount price, $M(U_i - 1)$ is greater than $P_i(U_i - 1)$; the difference is the extra purchase cost that results because some units must be purchased at the higher price in order to obtain the discount. This extra purchase cost is, in effect, an additional ordering cost, since it is incurred each time an order is made. Thus, the above formulation is nothing more than a modified EOQ formula with the extra material cost added to the order cost.

The minimum total cost with incremental discounts will never occur at a price-break quantity, but only at a valid EOQ.[6] Even if an EOQ is valid, it is not necessarily optimal, and larger valid EOQs are not necessarily more

---

[6] See G. Hadley and T. M. Whitin, *Analysis of Inventory Systems*, Prentice-Hall, 1963, pp. 62–68 and 323–345, for the proof.

desirable than smaller valid EOQs. In other words, any valid EOQ may be the optimum lot size, and every valid EOQ must be checked. The optimum lot size is determined by calculating the total cost per year for each valid EOQ. An EOQ is valid if $U_i \le Q_{0i} < U_{i+1}$ (the EOQ must fall within the quantity range required for the price break). These observations suggest the following procedure for determining the optimum lot size under an incremental discount schedule:

1. Calculate Q_{0i} for each price level.
2. Determine which Q_{0i} are valid.
3. Calculate the total cost for each valid Q_{0i}.
4. Select the valid Q_{0i} with the lowest total cost.

EXAMPLE 4

The annual demand for an item is 4800 units, the ordering cost is $40 per order, and the annual holding cost fraction is 0.25. What is the optimum lot size if the firm faces the incremental discount schedule below?

Lot Size	Unit Price
< 400	$10.00
400–1199	9.00
1200–4799	8.50
> 4799	8.00

Solution:

i	P_i	U_i	$M(U_i - 1) - P_i(U_i - 1) = \sum_{z=1}^{i} (U_z - 1)(P_{z-1} - P_z)$
0	$10.00	1	0
1	9.00	400	399 ($10.00 - 9.00$) = 399.00
2	8.50	1200	399 + 1199(9.00 - 8.50) = 998.50
3	8.00	4800	998.50 + 4799(8.50 - 8.00) = 3398.00

$$Q_0 = \sqrt{\frac{2CR}{PF}} = \sqrt{\frac{2(40)4800}{10(0.25)}} = 392 \quad \text{(valid)}$$

$$Q_{01} = \sqrt{\frac{2R\left[C + \sum_{z=1}^{i} (U_z - 1)(P_{z-1} - P_z)\right]}{P_i F}} = \sqrt{\frac{2(4800)[40 + 399]}{9(0.25)}}$$

$$Q_{01} = 1369 \quad \text{(not valid)}$$

$$Q_{02} = \sqrt{\frac{2(4800)[40 + 998.5]}{8.50(0.25)}} = 2166 \quad \text{(valid)}$$

$$Q_{03} = \sqrt{\frac{2(4800)[40 + 3398]}{8.00(0.25)}} = 4062 \quad \text{(not valid)}$$

Calculate the total cost for each valid EOQ (Q_{0i}):

$$TC(Q_0) = P_0 R + \frac{RC}{Q_0} + \frac{Q_0 PF}{2} = 10(4800) + \frac{4800(40)}{392} + \frac{392(10)0.25}{2}$$

$$= \$48,979.80$$

$$TC(Q_{02}) = \frac{C + M(U_2 - 1) - P_2(U_2 - 1)}{Q_{02}} R + P_2 R$$

$$+ \frac{F}{2}[M(U_2 - 1) - P_2(U_2 - 1) + P_2 Q_{02}]$$

$$= \frac{(40 + 998.50)4800}{2166} + 8.50(4800) + \frac{0.25[998.50 + (8.50)2166]}{2}$$

$$= \$45,527.57$$

The optimum lot size is the valid EOQ with the least annual cost. The best policy is to order 2166 units at a unit price of \$8.50.

The advantages of quantity discount purchases are lower unit cost, lower ordering cost per year, fewer stockouts, lower shipping costs, and a hedge against price increases. The disadvantages of quantity discount purchases are a larger inventory, increased risk of obsolescence, slower inventory turnover, and an older stock.

Special Sale Prices

A supplier may temporarily discount the unit price of an item during a regular replenishment cycle. Reasons for such a price reduction range from competitive price wars to attempted inventory reduction. The logical reaction to finding an item on sale during a regular replenishment cycle is to order additional units to take advantage of the short-lived price reduction. If a special order is issued, then management must determine the optimum size of the order to place.

Assume that when an order is being placed, it is discovered that the supplier is temporarily reducing the price of the item. The regular price of the item is P, but current purchases can be made at $P - d$, where d is the unit price decrease. Subsequent to the temporary sale, the price of the item will return to P. Order quantities prior to and after the price decrease are

$$Q_0 = \sqrt{\frac{2CR}{PF}} .$$

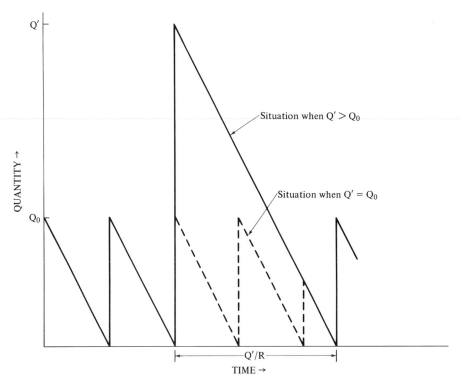

Figure 8. Special sale price.

To obtain the optimal special order size Q', it is necessary to maximize the cost difference during the time period Q'/R with and without the special order. The inventory situation is graphically depicted in Figure 8, where the dashed lines indicate the condition if no special order is placed.

The total cost of the system during the period Q'/R, when a special order $(Q' > Q_0)$ is purchased at the unit price of $P - d$, would be as follows:

$$\text{total cost} = \text{purchase cost} + \text{holding cost} + \text{order cost},$$

$$\text{TC}' = (P - d)Q' + \frac{Q'}{2}(P - d)\frac{FQ'}{R} + C$$

$$= (P - d)Q' + \frac{(P - d)F(Q')^2}{2R} + C.$$

If no special order is placed during the period Q'/R, the total cost of the system when the first order is made at $P - d$ and all subsequent orders are made at P would be as follows:

total cost = purchase cost + holding cost + order cost,

$$TC_1 = (P - d)Q_0 + P(Q' - Q_0) + \frac{Q_0}{2}(P - d)F\frac{Q_0}{R}$$

$$+ \frac{Q_0}{2}PF\frac{(Q' - Q_0)}{R} + \frac{CQ'}{Q_0}$$

$$= PQ' - dQ_0 + \frac{(P - d)FQ_0^2}{2R} + \frac{PFQ_0Q'}{2R} - \frac{PFQ_0^2}{2R} + \frac{CQ'}{Q_0},$$

where

P = unit purchase price before the discount,

d = unit price decrease,

Q' = special order size in units,

C = order cost per order,

F = annual holding cost fraction,

R = annual demand in units,

Q_0 = economic order quantity in units,

$P - d$ = unit purchase price with the discount,

Q'/Q_0 = number of orders during time period Q'/R.

To find the optimal one-time order size Q_0', the difference between TC_1 and TC' must be maximized and the derivative set equal to zero:

$$g = TC_1 - TC' = \text{special order cost saving,}$$

$$g = dQ' - dQ_0 - \frac{dFQ_0^2}{2R} + \frac{2CQ'}{Q_0} - \frac{(P - d)F(Q')^2}{2R} - C,$$

$$\frac{dg}{dQ'} = d + \frac{2C}{Q_0} - \frac{(P - d)FQ'}{R} = 0,$$

$$Q_0' = \frac{dR}{(P - d)F} + \frac{PQ_0}{P - d} = \text{optimum special order size.}$$

Note that then the price discount is zero ($d = 0$), the optimum special order size formula reduces to the EOQ formula ($Q_0' = Q_0$) and the cost saving is zero ($g = 0$). By replacing Q' with Q_0' in the cost saving formula for g, the optimum cost saving is obtained.

$$g_0 = \frac{C(P - d)}{P}\left[\left(\frac{Q_0'}{Q_0} - 1\right)^2\right].$$

EXAMPLE 5

The supplier in Example 1 is offering a special discount and has temporarily reduced his unit price from $10.00 to $9.00. What amount should be purchased to take advantage of the discount?

$$Q_0' = \frac{dR}{(P-d)F} + \frac{PQ_0}{P-d}$$

$$= \frac{1(8000)}{(10-1)(0.3)} + \frac{10(400)}{10-1}$$

$$= 3407 \text{ units.}$$

A special order for 3407 units should be purchased. The amount will last for 0.426 years ($3407/8000 = 0.426$). Thereafter the order quantity should be the EOQ of 400 units. The resultant cost saving would be

$$g_0 = \frac{C(P-d)}{P} \left[\left(\frac{Q_0'}{Q_0} - 1 \right)^2 \right] = \frac{30(10-1)}{10} \left[\left(\frac{3407}{400} - 1 \right)^2 \right]$$

$$= \$1525.85$$

The previous optimizing formulation for special order size Q_0' assumed that the temporary unit price discount was available at the regular time for replenishment (when the stock position reached the reorder point). In some situations, the temporary price discount expires before the regular time for replenishment and management must decide if a special order should be placed on the expiration date. If the special order must be placed before the regular replenishment time and the stock position is q units on the expiration date, the optimizing formulations are:

$$Q_0' = \frac{dR}{(P-d)F} + \frac{PQ_0}{P-d} - q$$

$$g_0 = C \left[\left(\frac{Q_0'}{\sqrt{\frac{P}{P-d}} Q_0} \right)^2 - 1 \right].$$

In this situation, it is not always advantageous to place the special order. The cost savings is only positive when the special order size exceeds $\sqrt{P/(P-d)}$ times the economic order quantity. The decision rule is to place the special order for Q_0' only when $Q_0' > \sqrt{P/(P-d)}\, Q_0$. If $Q_0' \le \sqrt{P/(P-d)}\, Q_0$, ignore the special sale and place the order for Q_0 at the regular replenishment time. Additionally, the above formulation for Q'_0 is derived for a replenishment lead time of zero; if the lead time is not equal to zero, the stock position q at the time the special order is placed must be reduced by the lead time demand (the reorder point).

Known Price Increases

A supplier may announce that a price increase for an item will take place on some future date. As with special sale prices, the logical response is to order additional units to take advantage of the lower (present) price. If a special order is placed before the higher price becomes effective, management's responsibility is to determine the size of the order.

Assume the price of an item will be increased by an amount k as of some date t_1. Unit purchases before t_1 still cost P, but those made after t_1 will cost $P + k$. Thus, purchase quantities prior to the announced price increase

Figure 9. Known price increase.

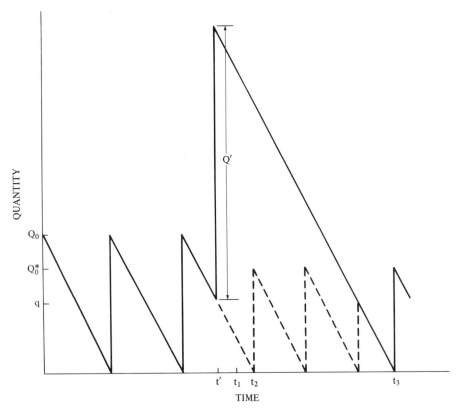

are

$$Q_0 = \sqrt{\frac{2CR}{PF}} = \text{EOQ before price increase.}$$

Since all subsequent purchases will be made at the new price $(P + k)$, the optimal lot size will become

$$Q_0^* = \sqrt{\frac{2CR}{(P + k)F}} = \text{EOQ after price increase.}$$

The known price increase situation is depicted in Figure 9. As shown by the solid lines, a special order of size Q' is purchased at t' $(t' \leq t_1)$, and the stock level at that time is q units. The next purchase will occur at time t_3, after an elapse of $(Q' + q)/R$ units of time (after the special order and stock on hand have been exhausted). If a special order is not placed at t' (as shown by the dashed lines), the next purchase will occur at time t_2, after an elapse of q/R units of time (after the stock on hand has been depleted).

Assuming there is a cost advantage from placing a special order over not placing an order, the objective is to set the size of the order to maximize the cost difference. It is necessary to maximize the difference during the time period $t_3 - t'$; in other words, the special order size should be set so that during $(Q' + q)/R$ units of time the cost difference will be maximized.

The total cost of the system during the period t' to t_3 when a special order Q' is purchased at the unit cost P would be as follows:

total cost = purchase cost + holding cost + order cost,

$$\text{TC}' = PQ' + Q'PF\frac{q}{R} + \frac{Q'}{2}PF\frac{Q'}{R} + \frac{q}{2}PF\frac{q}{R} + C$$

$$= PQ' + \frac{PFqQ'}{R} + \frac{PF(Q')^2}{2R} + \frac{PFq^2}{2R} + C.$$

If no special order were placed prior to t_1, the total cost of the system during the period t' to t_3 when several purchases of Q_0^* are made at the new price $P + k$ would be as follows:

$$\text{TC}_1 = (P + k)Q' + \frac{Q_0^*}{2}(P + k)(F)\frac{Q'}{R} + \frac{q}{2}PF\frac{q}{R} + \frac{CQ'}{Q_0^*}.$$

Substituting the economic order quantity relationship at the higher price into the above equation for Q_0^*, the total cost of the system during the period t' to t_3 if no special order is placed would be as follows:

$$\text{TC}_1 = (P + k)Q' + Q'\sqrt{\frac{2CF(P + k)}{R}} + \frac{PFq^2}{2R},$$

where

k = known price increase in dollars,

P = unit price in dollars before the price increase,

Q' = special order size in units,

C = order cost per order,

F = annual holding cost fraction,

R = annual demand in units,

Q_0 = economic order quantity before price increase,

Q_0^* = economic order quantity after price increase,

q = stock position in units when special order is placed,

t_1 = effective time of price increase,

t' = time when special order is placed,

t_3 = time when special order is depleted,

q/R = amount of time required to deplete stock on hand in years,

Q'/R = amount of time to deplete special order in years,

Q'/Q_0^* = number of orders of size Q_0^* during $t_3 - t_2$.

To find the optimal one-time order size Q_0', the difference between TC_1 and TC' must be maximized and the derivative set equal to zero:

$$g = TC_1 - TC' = \text{special order cost saving}$$

$$= Q'\left[k + \sqrt{\frac{2CF(P + k)}{R}} - \frac{PFq}{R}\right] - \frac{PFQ'^2}{2R} - C,$$

$$\frac{dg}{dQ'} = k + \sqrt{\frac{2CF(P + k)}{R}} - \frac{PFq}{R} - \frac{PFQ'}{R} = 0.$$

The above expression can then be solved for Q' to obtain the optimal special order size:

$$Q_0' = Q_0^* + \frac{k(FQ_0^* + R)}{PF} - q = Q_0\sqrt{\frac{P + k}{P}} + \frac{kR}{PF} - q.$$

By replacing Q' with Q_0' in the cost savings formula for g, the optimum cost savings formula is obtained:

$$g_0 = C\left[\frac{P}{P + k}\left(\frac{Q_0'}{Q_0^*}\right)^2 - 1\right] = C\left[\left(\frac{Q_0'}{Q_0}\right)^2 - 1\right].$$

A special order of Q_0' units results in a cost saving only if $g_0 > 0$, and this occurs only if Q_0'/Q_0 is greater than 1. Thus, a special order should be placed only if the special order size is greater than Q_0 (the economic order quantity at the current price P).

Note that when the optimum cost saving is zero ($g_0 = 0$), the optimum special order size equals the economic order quantity before the price increase ($Q_0' = Q_0$), which can only occur if the price increase is zero ($k = 0$). If the optimum special order size is less than the economic order quantity ($Q_0' < Q_0$), a loss will be incurred by placing the optimum special order. If the optimum special order size is desirable ($Q_0' > Q_0$), it should be placed immediately prior to the price increase. The above formulation is derived for a lead time of zero; if the lead time is not equal to zero, q (the stock position when the special order is placed) must be reduced by the lead time demand (the reorder point). The reorder point is unchanged and will be the same after the price increase as it was before the increase.

EXAMPLE 6

The supplier in Example 1 will increase his unit price from \$10 to \$11 on 1 January. What amount should be purchased and delivered on 31 December before the price increase is effective if the stock position is 346 units? What will be the cost saving of the special purchase?

$$Q_0^* = \sqrt{\frac{2CR}{(P + k)F}} = \sqrt{\frac{2(30)8000}{(10 + 1)0.3}} = 381.4 \text{ units,}$$

$$Q_0' = Q_0^* + \frac{k(FQ_0^* + R)}{PF} - q = 381.4 + \frac{1[(0.3)(381.4) + 8000]}{10(0.3)} - 346$$

$$= 381.4 + 2704.8 - 346$$
$$= 2740 \text{ units,}$$

$$g_0 = C\left[\frac{P}{P + k}\left(\frac{Q_0'}{Q_0^*}\right)^2 - 1\right]$$

$$= 30\left[\frac{10}{10 + 1}\left(\frac{2740}{381}\right)^2 - 1\right] = 30\left[\frac{10}{11}(51.72) - 1.00\right]$$

$$= \$1380.52$$

On 31 December, 2740 units should be purchased. The amount will last for 0.342 years ($2740/8000 = 0.342$). The cost saving of the purchase is \$1380.52. Thereafter, the order quantity should be 381 units at the unit price of \$11.00.

Special sale prices and known price increases may indicate the need to increase the order size substantially. Storage constraints, capital constraints, shelf life, possible engineering changes, and potential changes in demand should be considered when a large increase in order size is contemplated. Some organizations have policies of never exceeding an established time supply for an item (such as never ordering more than a year's supply), to limit holding costs and control excess inventory.

EOQ Sensitivity

Sensitivity analysis determines how the output of a model will be influenced by changes or errors in the input data (parameters). If an input can assume a wide range of values without appreciably affecting the output, the model is insensitive. If a small change in an input can appreciably affect the output, the model is sensitive. The sensitivity of a model will dictate the precision of parameters required for the model. The EOQ model assumes that the annual demand R, holding cost H, and order cost C are deterministic and without variation. Errors by management in determining these parameters will cause variations in output (EOQ and total variable cost). This section will analyze the impact of estimation errors.

In a fixed order size system, the order quantity which minimizes the total variable cost per year dictates the optimum inventory policy.[7] The pertinent mathematical relationships are as follows:

$$Q_0 = \sqrt{\frac{2CR}{H}} = \text{EOQ},$$

$$\text{TVC}_0 = (\text{order cost}) + (\text{holding cost})$$

$$= \frac{RC}{Q_0} + \frac{Q_0 H}{2} = \text{optimum total variable cost per year.}$$

Assume there are errors in the estimation of the parameters R, C, and H by the respective error factors of X_R, X_C, and X_H. The model becomes

$$Q = \sqrt{\frac{2CR}{H} \frac{X_R X_C}{X_H}} = Q_0 \sqrt{\frac{X_R X_C}{X_H}},$$

$$\frac{Q - Q_0}{Q_0} = \sqrt{\frac{X_R X_C}{X_H}} - 1 = \text{order quantity error fraction,}$$

where

Q = order quantity with parameter errors,

Q_0 = economic order quantity,

$X_R = \dfrac{\text{estimated demand}}{\text{actual demand}}$ = demand error factor,

$X_C = \dfrac{\text{estimated order cost}}{\text{actual order cost}}$ = order cost error factor,

$X_H = \dfrac{\text{estimated holding cost}}{\text{actual holding cost}}$ = holding cost error factor.

---

[7]In previous sections, total annual cost has been the measure of effectiveness. The total variable cost per year does not include the purchase cost of the item. It is assumed that no quantity discounts are available and stockouts are not permitted. When quantity discounts are not available, purchase cost ceases to be a relevant incremental cost, and it can be deleted from the formulation.

To examine the effects of errors in estimates of the parameters (R, C, and H), two of the error factors will be set equal to 1 while the third is varied. When all the error factors are equal to 1, the error effect is zero (as you would suspect), and $Q = Q_0$. Thus, with X_C and X_R equal to 1 while X_H is variable, the effect on the EOQ is as follows:

$$\frac{Q - Q_0}{Q_0} = \sqrt{\frac{1}{X_H}} - 1.$$

Similarly, with X_R and X_H equal to 1 while X_C is variable, the effect on the EOQ is as follows:

$$\frac{Q - Q_0}{Q_0} = \sqrt{X_C} - 1.$$

Finally, with X_R varied and X_C and X_H equal to 1, the effect is as follows:

$$\frac{Q - Q_0}{Q_0} = \sqrt{X_R} - 1.$$

Under the single parameter variations just outlined, the effects of errors in estimates of R, C, and H on the sensitivity of the economic order quantity (Q_0) are shown in Table 1. It is readily apparent that errors in parameters are attenuated or dampened when translated into changes in the economic order quantity. For example, if holding costs are in error by a factor of 2, the error in the order quantity is less than 30%. If annual demand (or order cost) is miscalculated by a factor of 2, the error in the order quantity is only 41.4%.

To determine the sensitivity of the total variable cost per year to errors in input parameters, a similar procedure of inserting error factors into the cost formula is used. This model becomes

$$\text{TVC} = \frac{RC}{Q} + \frac{QH}{2}$$

$$= \frac{RC}{\sqrt{(2CR/H)(X_R X_C/X_H)}} + \frac{H\sqrt{(2CR/H)(X_R X_C/X_H)}}{2},$$

which mathematically simplifies to

$$\text{TVC} = \left[\frac{\text{TVC}_0}{2}\right] \frac{X_H + X_R X_C}{\sqrt{X_R X_C X_H}},$$

$$\frac{\text{TVC} - \text{TVC}_0}{\text{TVC}_0} = \frac{X_H + X_R X_C}{2\sqrt{X_R X_C X_H}} - 1 = \text{TVC error fraction.}$$

When all the error factors are equal to 1, the TVC error fraction is zero and $\text{TVC} = \text{TVC}_0$. To examine the influence of errors in parameter esti-

Table 1. Effects of errors in R, C, and H on the EOQ

Error Factor $X_H{}^a$	Effect on $Q_0(\%)^b$	Error Factor X_R or $X_C{}^a$	Effect on $Q_0(\%)^c$
0.1	+216.2	0.1	−68.4
0.2	+123.6	0.2	−55.3
0.3	+82.4	0.3	−45.3
0.4	+58.1	0.4	−36.8
0.5	+41.4	0.5	−29.3
0.6	+28.8	0.6	−22.5
0.7	+19.5	0.7	−16.4
0.8	+11.8	0.8	−10.6
0.9	+5.3	0.9	−5.2
1.0	0.0	1.0	0.0
1.2	−8.8	1.2	+9.5
1.4	−15.5	1.4	+18.3
1.6	−20.9	1.6	+26.4
1.8	−25.5	1.8	+34.2
2.0	−29.3	2.0	+41.4
2.2	−32.5	2.2	+48.3
2.4	−35.5	2.4	+54.9
2.6	−37.9	2.6	+61.2
2.8	−40.3	2.8	+67.3
3.0	−42.3	3.0	+73.2
4.0	−50.5	4.0	+100.0

^{a}Estimated H, R, or C divided by actual value.

^{b}No errors in R and C.

^{c}No errors in C and H (or no errors in R and H).

mates, two of the error factors will be set equal to 1 while the third is varied. Thus, with X_C and X_R set equal to 1 and X_H variable, the effect on TVC_0 is as follows:

$$\frac{\mathrm{TVC} - \mathrm{TVC}_0}{\mathrm{TVC}_0} = \frac{1 + X_H}{2\sqrt{X_H}} - 1.$$

Similarly, with X_R and X_H set equal to 1 and X_C variable, the effect on TVC_0 is as follows:

$$\frac{\mathrm{TVC} - \mathrm{TVC}_0}{\mathrm{TVC}_0} = \frac{1 + X_C}{2\sqrt{X_C}} - 1.$$

Finally, with X_C and X_H set equal to 1 and X_R variable, the effect on TVC_0 is as follows:

$$\frac{\mathrm{TVC} - \mathrm{TVC}_0}{\mathrm{TVC}_0} = \frac{1 + X_R}{2\sqrt{X_R}} - 1.$$

It is obvious from the above formulations that for single parameter variations, the effect on TVC_0 is the same irrespective of the parameter (R,

Table 2. Effects of errors in R, C, and H on TVC_0 [a]

Error Factor X_a^{b}	Increase in TVC_0 (%)
0.1	74.0
0.2	34.2
0.3	18.8
0.4	10.7
0.5	6.1
0.6	3.3
0.7	1.6
0.8	0.6
0.9	0.2
1.0	0.0
1.2	0.4
1.4	1.4
1.6	2.8
1.8	4.4
2.0	6.1
2.2	7.9
2.4	9.7
2.6	11.7
2.8	13.6
3.0	15.4
4.0	25.0

[a] a is any of the three parameters, and there are no errors in the other two. Thus, if a were R, then C and H would have no errors.

[b] (Estimated a)/(actual a).

C, or H). Under the single parameter variations set forth above, the influence of errors in estimates of R, C, and H on the sensitivity of TVC_0 is shown in Table 2 and Figure 10.

It is readily apparent that errors in parameters are attenuated or dampened when translated into their impact on total incremental cost. For example, if holding costs are in error by a factor of 2, the error in TVC_0 is only 6.1%.

To determine the sensitivity of the total variable cost per year to errors in the EOQ, a similar procedure for inserting error factors into the cost formula is used. The model becomes

$$TVC_0 = \frac{RC}{Q_0} + \frac{Q_0 H}{2} = HQ_0,$$

$$TVC = \frac{RC}{X_Q Q_0} + \frac{X_Q Q_0 H}{2},$$

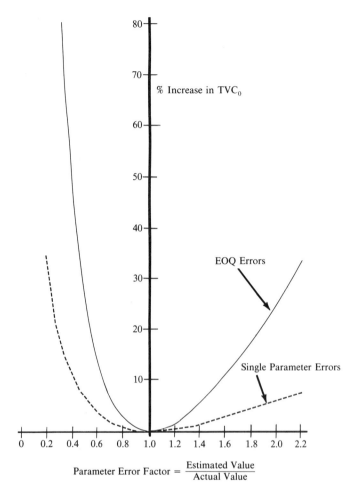

Figure 10. Effect of errors on TVC_0.

where

$$X_Q = \frac{\text{estimated EOQ}}{\text{actual EOQ}} = \text{EOQ error factor.}$$

The error fraction in the total variable cost is as follows:

$$\frac{TVC - TVC_0}{TVC_0} = \frac{\dfrac{RC}{X_Q Q_0} + \dfrac{X_Q Q_0 H}{2} - HQ_0}{HQ_0}$$

$$= \frac{X_Q^2 - 2X_Q + 1}{2X_Q} = \frac{(X_Q - 1)^2}{2X_Q} = \text{TVC error fraction.}$$

Table 3. Effect of errors in Q_0 on TVC_0

EOQ Error Factor X_Q	Increase in TVC_0 (%)
0.1	405.0
0.2	160.0
0.3	81.7
0.4	45.0
0.5	25.0
0.6	13.4
0.7	6.4
0.8	2.5
0.9	.6
1.0	0.0
1.2	1.7
1.4	5.7
1.6	11.3
1.8	17.8
2.0	25.0
2.2	32.8
2.4	40.9
2.6	49.3
2.8	57.9
3.0	66.7
4.0	112.5

When the EOQ error factor is equal to 1, the TVC error fraction is zero and $TVC = TVC_0$. The influence of errors in the EOQ on the sensitivity of TVC_0 is shown in Table 3 and Figure 10. Errors in the order quantity are dampened when translated into their impact on total variable cost. For example, if the economic order quantity is in error by 40% on the high side ($X_Q = 1.40$), it results in only a 5.7% increase over the theoretically possible minimum total variable cost. Errors on the low side are somewhat more costly. An economic order quantity that is in error by 40% on the low side ($X_Q = 0.6$) results in an increase of 13.4% over the theoretically possible minimum total variable cost.

As shown in Figure 10, the cost penalty (increase in TVC_0) is greater for errors of underestimation than for errors of overestimation. This indicates the general desirability for estimates to be on the high side to avoid the larger cost penalty for low estimates.

EXAMPLE 7

In a fixed order size system, the estimated and actual parameter values are given below. What is (a) the individual effect of the holding cost error on TVC_0, (b) the combined effect of the parameter errors on Q_0, and (c) the combined effect of the parameter errors on TVC_0?

Parameter	Estimate	Actual
R	1000 units	2000 units
H	$10	$20
C	$50	$25

Solution:

$$X_R = \frac{\text{estimated demand}}{\text{actual demand}} = \frac{1000}{2000} = 0.50,$$

$$X_H = \frac{\text{estimated holding cost}}{\text{actual holding cost}} = \frac{10}{20} = 0.50,$$

$$X_C = \frac{\text{estimated order cost}}{\text{actual order cost}} = \frac{50}{25} = 2.00.$$

a:

$$\frac{\text{TVC} - \text{TVC}_0}{\text{TVC}_0} = \frac{1 + X_H}{2\sqrt{X_H}} - 1 = \frac{1 + 0.50}{2\sqrt{0.50}} - 1 = 0.0607 = 6.07\%.$$

b:

$$\frac{Q - Q_0}{Q_0} = \sqrt{\frac{X_R X_C}{X_H}} - 1 = \sqrt{\frac{0.50(2.00)}{0.50}} - 1 = 0.4142 = 41.42\%.$$

c:

$$\frac{\text{TVC} - \text{TVC}_0}{\text{TVC}_0} = \frac{X_H + X_R X_C}{2\sqrt{X_R X_C X_H}} - 1 = \frac{0.50 + 0.50(2.00)}{2\sqrt{0.50(2.00)0.50}} - 1 = 0.0607 = 6.07\%.$$

The individual effect of the holding cost error is to increase TVC_0 by 6.07%. The combined error effect of all three parameters is to increase Q_0 by 41.42% and TVC_0 by only 6.07%.

Basic inventory models sometimes are viewed with suspicion because of their restrictive assumptions. A situation can rarely be found where both demand and costs are known precisely and where demand is truly constant. Fortunately, basic inventory models are not very sensitive to errors in the measurement of parameters. Wide variations in demand level and cost parameters do not result in wide variations in model outputs.

Over a considerable range, the total variable cost curve is fairly flat, which indicates that substantial changes in demand, order cost, or holding cost will be attenuated. When EOQs are computed with imprecise estimates, the errors are muted by the presence of the square root function. Therefore, the usefulness of these models is not diluted if exact precision is not available. Within a range of 0.4 to 2.5 times the parameter, the total variable cost changes by less than 11% (see Table 2).

The insensitivity of the basic inventory models to parameter errors is a very advantageous property. Since the total cost is only slightly increased by substantial departures from optimum conditions, the basic models do not require frequent revision (recalculation). Many components of cost parameters are difficult to measure, but the insensitivity renders broad estimates operationally useful. All that is needed is to get into the "right ballpark," and good solutions can be obtained with fairly crude cost data. EOQs can be rounded off without a significant loss in economies. Order sizes can be increased or decreased to the nearest pack or container size; order intervals can be lengthened or shortened to the next convenient time interval.

BATCH-TYPE PRODUCTION SYSTEMS

In batch-type production systems, products are often made to stock in lot sizes (batches). In most cases, multiple products are produced on the same equipment; these products share and even compete for common production capacity as individual items and/or as members of a product family. Planning batch production may involve the determination of the optimum number of units to include in each production run to minimize total annual costs. It also may require coordinating production runs through batch scheduling—that is, determining the order of production and the number of each item to produce before production is changed over to the next product in the sequence. Thus, it may not seek optimum production levels, but allocate production capacity to items in relation to their demands, production rates, and existing inventory levels.

This section describes some of these production planning techniques and their concomitant inventory policies. It introduces the subject of production setups and changeovers. In some batch-type production systems, setups may or may not be required between batches of productions. Where product families are involved, a major setup may be necessary for the family in addition to minor setups for the individual items in the family.

Economic Production Quantity (EPQ)—Single Items

The EOQ formulation assumes that the entire order for an item is received into inventory at a given time. This assumption applies whether the item is purchased externally or produced in-house. If a firm produces a product that has a constant demand and that product is entered into inventory instantaneously, the production order quantity should be determined by the EOQ model. In this case, the order cost will be replaced by a setup cost.[8]

---

[8] The setup cost is essentially the cost of the time required to prepare the equipment or work station to do the job and to dismantle it after the job is finished. Plant output can be substantially affected by the number and length of setups.

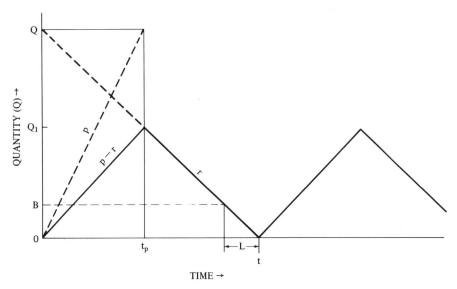

Figure 11. Production order quantity.
Key: p = production rate; r = demand rate $(r < p)$; t_p = production time period; t = time between production runs; $Q_1 = t_p(p - r)$ = maximum inventory; $Q = t_p p$ = production run quantity; $Q_1/2 = [t_p(p - r)]/2 = [Q(p - r)]/2p$ = average inventory; $p - r$ = inventory buildup rate; B = reorder point; L = lead time.

The assumption that the entire order is received into inventory at one time is often not true for in-house production runs. Frequently, replenishment is continuous, and the stock of inventory is being depleted even while the production of an order takes place (finished goods go into inventory gradually). Thus, the EOQ model must be revised to take account of this change in its assumptions. The economic production quantity (EPQ) accommodates this change. Whereas the EOQ assumes discrete instantaneous additions to stock, the EPQ implicitly assumes continuous gradual additions to stock over the production period. Therefore, the EPQ is more suitable to situations where consumption and replenishment simultaneously decrease and increase the stock level.[9]

Units may be taken to the storeroom and added to inventory as they are produced or as they are received from an external source. Whether the item is obtained through purchasing (including intrafirm transfer) or production, the unit cost is usually the most important single cost. If the item is

[9] When the entire purchase or production order quantity is received into inventory at one time, the replenishment rate is called infinite. If the entire order quantity is not received at the same time, the replenishment rate is called finite.

purchased, price determination is usually the responsibility of the purchasing department. If the item is manufactured, the unit production cost will consist of direct labor, direct materials, and factory burden. Direct labor consists of those labor charges conveniently identified with a specified item. Direct material is the cost of the substance from which the item is made. Factory burden includes all manufacturing costs other than direct material and direct labor, such as indirect labor, indirect material, depreciation, taxes, insurance, power, maintenance, supervision, and so forth.

In gradual replenishment situations, the major decision involves the determination of the size of the production run (order). The production run that minimizes the total inventory cost is the economic production quantity (EPQ). Figure 11 depicts a typical cycle for the gradual replenishment of inventory over the time period t_p. Production starts at time zero and ends at time t_p. During the time period from t_p to t, no production occurs and the inventory stock is depleted. At time t, a new production run is started. If there had been no demand during the period zero to t_p, inventories would have risen at a rate p. Hence, $t_p = Q/p$. Since there is a demand at rate r, inventories will increase at a rate $p - r$, where p is greater than r.[10] During the production period, zero to t_p, inventories accumulate at a rate equal to the production rate minus the demand rate, $p - r$. The maximum inventory level is $t_p(p - r)$, or the time of production times the rate of inventory buildup. The average inventory is one-half the maximum inventory, or $t_p[(p - r)/2]$. Since $t_p = Q/p$, the average inventory is given by the following formula:

$$\text{average inventory} = \frac{Q(p - r)}{2p}.$$

The average inventory is not just $Q/2$, but is $Q(p - r)/2p$. The factor r/p represents the fractional amount of the lot size withdrawn from stock during the time the item is being produced. The factor $(p - r)/p$ represents the fractional amount of the lot size remaining in stock at the end of the production period. Since the stock level ranges between a minimum of zero and a maximum of $Q(p - r)/p$, the average inventory is simply one-half of the maximum inventory. If stockouts are not permitted, the total annual inventory cost is as follows:[11]

total annual cost = (production cost) + (setup cost) + (holding cost),

$$TC = RP + \frac{RC}{Q} + \frac{Q(p - r)H}{2p},$$

[10] When $p = r$, the production rate equals the demand rate. In this situation, there are no ordering or holding costs, since production is continuous and perfectly matched with demand.
[11] The model assumes that stockouts will not occur.

where

R = annual demand in units,
P = unit production cost,
Q = size of production run or production order quantity,
p = production rate,
r = demand rate,
C = setup cost per production run,
H = holding cost per unit per year. *carrying cost*

To obtain the minimum cost production order quantity (EPQ), take the first derivative of total annual cost with respect to the production order quantity Q and set it equal to zero:

$$\frac{d\,TC}{dQ} = -\frac{RC}{Q^2} + \frac{(p-r)H}{2p} = 0.$$

Solving the equation for Q, the EPQ formula is obtained:

$$Q_0 = \sqrt{\frac{2CRp}{(H)(p-r)}}$$

= economic production quantity.

Once the economic production quantity is known, the optimum length of the production run can be obtained as well as the production reorder point. If it is assumed that there are N operating days per year, the following relationships apply:

$$\text{optimum length of production run} = \frac{Q_0}{p},$$

$$\text{production reorder point in units} = B$$

$$= \frac{RL}{N} = rL,$$

where L is the scheduling and production setup time in days and r is the daily demand rate. The EPQ is somewhat larger than the ordinary EOQ, because the factor $p/(p-r)$ is greater than one.

Replacing Q in the total annual cost formula by Q_0, the following formula for the minimum total annual cost results:

$$TC_0 = RP + \frac{(p-r)HQ_0}{p}.$$

EXAMPLE 8

The demand for an item is 20,000 units per year, and there are 250 working days per year. The production rate is 100 units per day, and the lead time is 4 days. The unit production cost is $50.00, the holding cost is $10.00 per unit per year, and the setup cost is $20.00 per run. What are the economic production quantity, the number of runs per year, the reorder point, and the minimum total annual cost?

$$r = \frac{R}{N} = \frac{20{,}000}{250} = 80 \text{ units per day,}$$

$$Q_0 = \sqrt{\frac{2CRp}{(H)(p-r)}} = \sqrt{\frac{2(20)(20{,}000)(100)}{(10)(100-80)}} = 632,$$

$$m = \frac{R}{Q_0} = \frac{20{,}000}{632} = 31.6 \text{ runs per year,}$$

$$B = \frac{RL}{N} = \frac{20{,}000(4)}{250} = 320 \text{ units,}$$

$$TC_0 = RP + \frac{(p-r)HQ_0}{p} = (20{,}000)(50) + \frac{(100-80)10(632)}{100},$$

$$TC_0 = \$1{,}001{,}264.$$

Backordering

If stockout costs are finite, the total annual cost must be modified to include their influence. The total annual cost will include the stockout cost as well as the production cost, setup cost, and holding cost. If the stockouts are backordered (no lost demand is encountered), all shortages will be satisfied from the next production run. With infinite stockout costs, shortages were not permitted, and they were not included in the total annual cost model. With finite stockout costs, their inclusion is mandatory.

The economic production quantity with finite backorder cost is obtained from the following formula:[12]

$$Q_0 = \sqrt{\frac{2CRp}{H(p-r)}} \sqrt{\frac{H+K}{K}} = \text{economic production quantity.}$$

The reorder point is obtained from the following formula when the lead time is expressed in days:

$$B = \frac{RL}{N} - \sqrt{\frac{2CR(p-r)}{pK(H+K)}},$$

[12] See W. J. Fabrycky and Jerry Banks, *Procurement and Inventory Systems: Theory and Analysis*, New York: Reinhold Publishing Corp., 1967, pp. 64–68, for the derivation of the formulas.

where

$$K = \text{backordering cost per unit per year,}$$
$$L = \text{lead time in days,}$$
$$B = \text{reorder point in units,}$$
$$N = \text{number of operating days per year.}$$

EXAMPLE 9

If the stockout cost in Example 8 is finite and stockouts are all backordered, what changes occur in the final solution with a backorder cost of $5 per unit per year?

$$Q_0 = \sqrt{\frac{2CRp}{H(p-r)}} \sqrt{\frac{H+K}{K}} = 632\sqrt{\frac{10+5}{5}} = 1095 \text{ units,}$$

$$m = \frac{R}{Q_0} = \frac{20{,}000}{1095} = 18.3 \text{ runs/year,}$$

$$B = \frac{RL}{N} - \sqrt{\frac{2CR(p-r)}{pK(H+K)}} = \frac{20{,}000(4)}{250} - \sqrt{\frac{2(20)(20{,}000)20}{100(5)(10+5)}}$$

$$= 320 - 46 = 274 \text{ units.}$$

Make or Buy Decisions

Make or buy decisions must be made periodically by nearly every manufacturing organization. Normally, the ultimate decision may be assumed to rest upon an analysis of comparative costs. However, there are a number of factors other than product cost that may be of overriding significance. The relevant manufacturing short-term costs are only the incremental (out-of-pocket) costs associated with the make alternative.

Frequently a production or materials manager must make a decision whether to purchase or to manufacture an item. There are numerous factors to consider before a decision can be made, and many of them are difficult to quantify. Some influencing factors might be idle plant capacity, in-house capabilities (personnel, equipment, future capabilities), reliability of supply, reciprocity, employment stabilization, alternative resource uses, and economic advantage. No simple rule can be applied to all cases of make or buy. Each case must be decided on its own merits, and the important issues may vary in different cases or at different times.

If items are purchased externally, the order quantity can be obtained from EOQ analysis. If items are to be produced internally, the order quantity can be obtained from EPQ analysis. A comparison of the make

(EPQ) analysis with the buy (EOQ) analysis can determine the most desirable economic alternatives. From a cost standpoint, inventory analysis can help to solve the make versus buy problem. A simple example will illustrate the method.

EXAMPLE 10

An item may be purchased for $25 per unit or manufactured at a rate of 10,000 units per year for $23. If purchased, the order cost will be $5, compared to a $50 setup cost for manufacture. The annual demand for the item is 2500 units, and the holding cost is 10%. Should the item be purchased externally or produced internally?

1. Purchase:

$$Q_0 = \sqrt{\frac{2CR}{PF}} = \sqrt{\frac{2(5)(2500)}{0.10(25)}} = 100 \text{ units},$$

$$TC_0 = RP + HQ_0 = 2500(25) + 2.50(100) = \$62,750.$$

2. Manufacture:

$$Q_0 = \sqrt{\frac{2CRp}{PF(p - r)}} = \sqrt{\frac{2(2500)50(10,000)}{0.10(23)(10,000 - 2500)}} = 381,$$

$$TC_0 = RP + \frac{(p - r)HQ_0}{p}$$

$$= (2500)23 + \frac{(10,000 - 2500)(2.30)381}{10,000} = \$58,156.$$

The item should be manufactured, since this is the least cost alternative, which results in a saving of $4594 ($62,750 − $58,156) per year.

When searching for potential supply sources, an organization should always consider its own production facilities. The establishment of a new product or a substantial modification of an old product are typical situations requiring make or buy investigations. Make or buy analysis should be an integral part of new product development procedures. If quality, quantity, and service factors are equal, cost considerations are of paramount concern.

In general, a growing new company will tend to buy more items than a mature company. The new organization understandably concentrates its efforts on increasing its output by emphasizing its major product lines. A mature company tends to have facilities, capital, and personnel that can more readily be used for making rather than buying. Thus the growing and mature companies are expanding in a mode most appropriate to their circumstances.

Economic Production Quantity (EPQ)—Multiple Items

Intermittent production processes generally require that a number of products share the same equipment on a rotating basis. Products are often made on a regular cycle in predetermined batches. The overall length of the production cycle is the time to produce one complete sequence of products. The optimum cycle length should be established for the products as a group or family of items rather than for each product independently of the others. The use of single product economic production quantities (EPQs) for each product in the group implies that the equipment will be available when it is needed. Unless the equipment is highly underutilized, there may be scheduling problems and difficulties meeting the requirements of single product EPQs. Therefore, the multiple product scheduling problem should be solved by determining the number of annual cycles (m) that minimizes the total cost of the entire family of items.

Despite its attention to the products as a whole, the methodology for multiple products has some similarity to that for single products. The maximum inventory for a given product is $(p_i - r_i)t_p$, and the average inventory is one-half this amount. It has been established that $Q_i = p_i t_p = R_i/m$ where m is the number of cycles (production runs) per year. Therefore, the average inventory is given by the following formula, where i is a designated product and there are a total of n products:

$$\frac{(p_i - r_i)t_p}{2} = \frac{(p_i - r_i)R_i}{2mp_i} = \text{average inventory.}$$

If stockouts are not permitted, the total annual cost is given by the following formula:

Total cost = (production cost) + (setup cost) + (holding cost),

$$\text{TC} = \sum_{i=1}^{n} R_i P_i + m \sum_{i=1}^{n} C_i + \frac{1}{2m} \sum_{i=1}^{n} \frac{(p_i - r_i)R_i H_i}{p_i}.$$

When $n = 1$, the system reduces to the equation for the single product EPQ with $m = R/Q$. To obtain the minimum cost number of production runs, we take the first derivative of the total annual cost with respect to the number of production runs and set it equal to zero:

$$\frac{d\,\text{TC}}{dm} = \sum_{i=1}^{n} C_i - \frac{1}{2m^2} \sum_{i=1}^{n} \frac{(p_i - r_i)R_i H_i}{p_i} = 0.$$

Solving the equation for m, the optimum number of runs per year is obtained:

$$m_0 = \sqrt{\frac{\displaystyle\sum_{i=1}^{n} \frac{(p_i - r_i) R_i H_i}{p_i}}{2 \displaystyle\sum_{i=1}^{n} C_i}} .$$

The production run size for a given product i is determined by the following formula:

$$Q_i = \frac{R_i}{m_0} .$$

Replacing m in the total annual cost formula by m_0, the following minimum total cost formula is obtained:

$$\text{TC}_0 = \sum_{i=1}^{n} R_i P_i + \frac{1}{m_0} \sum_{i=1}^{n} \left[\frac{(p_i - r_i) R_i H_i}{p_i} \right]$$

$$= \sum_{i=1}^{n} R_i P_i + 2 m_0 \sum_{i=1}^{n} C_i .$$

The optimum number of runs per year (m_0) ignores capacity considerations (it is capacity blind). It assumes there is sufficient capacity available to meet demand. The model is appropriate only if the number of annual operating days equals or exceeds the annual demand time:

$$N \geq \sum_{i=1}^{n} \frac{R_i}{p_i} .$$

When the annual number of days required (demand time) exceeds the annual number of operating days (supply time), production capacity is not sufficient to meet the demand for all products. Therefore, some alternative method for meeting demand must be devised (overtime, expansion, subcontract, etc.).

The multiple items model also assumes setup time is negligible or there is sufficient slack time in each run (cycle) to accommodate it. As shown in Figure 12, the run time for each cycle must equal or exceed the combined run time for each item:

$$\frac{N}{m_0} \geq \sum_{i=1}^{n} \frac{Q_i}{p_i} .$$

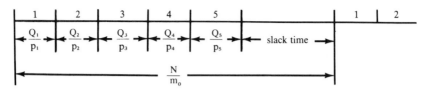

Figure 12. EPQ—multiple items.
$Q_i = R_i/m_0$ = lot size for item i; R_i = annual demand for item i; m_0 = optimum number of runs (cycles) per year; N = operating days per year; n = number of products or items; Q_i/p_i = run time in days per cycle for item i; p_i = production rate for item i in units per day; N/m_0 = run (cycle) time in days; $N/m_0 \geq \sum_{i=1}^{n} Q_i/p_i$; slack time ≥ 0.

EXAMPLE 11

Determine the best production cycle for the group of products in Table 4, assuming 250 working days per year. What is the minimum total annual cost?

The demand per day is obtained by dividing 250 into the annual demand (see Table 5):

$$\sum_{i=1}^{n} \frac{R_i}{p_i} = \frac{5000}{100} + \frac{10000}{400} + \frac{7000}{350} + \frac{15000}{200} + \frac{4000}{100} = 210 \text{ days.}$$

Since the annual operating time $N = 250$ days exceeds the annual demand time of

Table 4

Product	Annual Demand	Unit Production Cost P_i	Daily Production Rate p_i	Annual Holding Cost H_i	Setup Cost per Run, C_i
1	5,000	$6.00	100	$1.60	$40.00
2	10,000	5.00	400	1.40	25.00
3	7,000	3.00	350	.60	30.00
4	15,000	4.00	200	1.15	27.00
5	4,000	6.00	100	1.65	80.00

Table 5

Product	Production Rate p_i	Demand Rate r_i	$\dfrac{(p_i - r_i)R_i}{p_i}$	H_i	(Col. 4) × (Col. 5)	Setup Cost C_i
1	100	20	4,000	$1.60	6,400	$40
2	400	40	9,000	1.40	12,600	25
3	350	28	6,440	.60	3.864	30
4	200	60	10,500	1.15	12,075	27
5	100	16	3,360	1.65	5,544	80
Total					40,483	$202

Table 6

Product	R_i	m_0	Q_i
1	5,000	10	500
2	10,000	10	1000
3	7,000	10	700
4	15,000	10	1500
5	4,000	10	400

210 days, the model is capacity feasible. We have

$$m_0 = \sqrt{\frac{\sum_{i=1}^{5} \frac{(p_i - r_i) R_i H_i}{p_i}}{2 \sum_{i=1}^{5} C_i}} = \sqrt{\frac{40,483}{2(202)}} = 10.0,$$

$m_0 = 10.0$ runs per year.

The production run size for each product is $Q_i = R_i/m_0$, and it is given in Table 6. We have

$$\sum_{i=1}^{n} \frac{Q_i}{P_i} = \frac{500}{100} + \frac{1000}{400} + \frac{700}{350} + \frac{1500}{200} + \frac{400}{100} = 21 \text{ days.}$$

The run time per cycle is $N/m_0 = 250/10 = 25$ days. Since the production time per cycle of 21 days is less than the run time per cycle of 25 days, each cycle has 4 days of slack. Every 25 days would start another cycle. Then

$$TC_0 = \sum_{i=1}^{n} R_i P_i + 2m_0 \sum_{i=1}^{n} C_i$$

$$= (30,000 + 50,000 + 21,000 + 60,000 + 24,000) + 2(10)202$$

$$= \$189,040.$$

This section has described a theoretical way of scheduling production run sizes on one machine or department. Not included in the calculations have been such unknowns as machine breakdowns, operator deficiencies, production of scrap, tooling failures, or quality difficulties. The scheduler must modify any such theoretical model to fit real-world emergencies and contingencies.

Runout Time (ROT) Method

The runout time (ROT) method is a simple heuristic for computing the production sequence for a group (family) of items produced on the same equipment. It schedules the sequence of production lot sizes based on the depletion times and inventory levels of items in the group. At the beginning of a planning period, a runout time (ROT) is calculated for each item as its current inventory position divided by its demand for the period:

$$ROT_i = \frac{\text{current inventory position of item } i}{\text{demand per period for item } i} .$$

The decision rule is to schedule first the item with the lowest ROT and additional items in order of increasing runout times. Hence, the lower the ROT, the more urgent it is to replenish the supply of the item.

EXAMPLE 12

Using the data in Table 7, schedule the production sequence of a family of four items according to the runout time rule. Is there sufficient capacity available if the production capacity for the weekly planning period is 90 hours?

The runout time is calculated in Table 8 with the resulting sequence D, B, A, C. Given the available capacity of ninety hours, the capacity calculations in Table 9 indicate that capacity is inadequate by 20 hours to produce the lot sizes of all items in the family.

Table 7

Item	Standard Hours per Unit	Production Lot Size (units)	Demand Forecast per Period (units/week)	Current Inventory Position (units)	Standard Hours per Lot Size, (Col. 2)(Col. 3)
A	0.10	100	35	100	10
B	0.20	150	50	120	30
C	0.30	100	40	130	30
D	0.20	200	60	100	40
Total					$\overline{110}$

Table 8. Runout determination

Item	Current Inventory Position (units)	Demand per Period (units/week)	ROT weeks, (Col. 2)(Col. 3)	Sequence
A	100	35	2.86	3
B	120	50	2.40	2
C	130	40	3.25	4
D	100	60	1.67	1

Table 9. Capacity requirements

Sequence	ROT (weeks)	Lot Size (units)	Machine Hours per Lot Size	Remaining Capacity (hours)
D	1.67	200	40	50
B	2.40	150	30	20
A	2.86	100	10	10
C	3.25	100	30	−20

Aggregate Runout Time (AROT) Method

The aggregate runout time method schedules the production of items in a family to avoid any shortages of individual items. It adjusts the production lot sizes on the basis of the current inventory levels and allocates capacity to assure capacity feasibility. It schedules just enough production of each item so that the inventory for each item would be depleted at the same time if production were ceased at the end of the period. The runout time for all items in the group (AROT) is calculated as follows:

$$\text{AROT} = \frac{\left(\begin{array}{l}\text{inventory in machine hours}\\ \text{for all items in the family}\end{array}\right) + \left(\begin{array}{l}\text{total machine hours available}\\ \text{during the planning period}\end{array}\right)}{\begin{array}{l}\text{machine hours forecasted per period}\\ \text{for all items in the family}\end{array}}.$$

The AROT method first computes the available and required capacities for the facility for the planning period. Using these values, it calculates the AROT to be used for all items in the family. Gross requirements for each item are obtained by multiplying the AROT by the respective demand forecast per period. By subtracting the current inventory position for each item from its gross requirement, the net requirement or lot size for each item is obtained. The following example will illustrate the procedure.

EXAMPLE 13

How can the stockouts expected from Example 12 be avoided with the aggregate runout time method?

Table 10 develops the data for the AROT calculation. Tables 11 and 12 develop the schedule requirements and capacity requirements. We have

$$\text{AROT} = \frac{93 + 90}{37.5} = 4.88 \text{ weeks.}$$

Table 10. AROT determination

Item	Standard Hours per Unit	Demand Forecast per Period (units/week)	Machine Hours for Demand Forecast, (Col. 2)(Col. 3)	Current Inventory Position (units)	Inventory Machine Hours, (Col. 2)(Col. 5)
A	0.10	35	3.5	100	10.0
B	0.20	50	10.0	120	24.0
C	0.30	40	12.0	130	39.0
D	0.20	60	12.0	100	20.0
Total			37.5		93.0

Table 11. Weekly schedule requirements

Item	Demand Forecast per Period (units/week)	AROT (weeks)	Gross Requirements, (Col. 2)(Col. 3) (units)	Current Inventory Position (units)	Lot Size, (Col. 4) − (Col. 5) (units)
A	35	4.88	171	100	71
B	50	4.88	244	120	124
C	40	4.88	195	130	65
D	60	4.88	293	100	193

Table 12. Capacity requirements

Item	Standard Hours per Unit	Lot Size (units)	Machine Hours Required, (Col. 2)(Col. 3)	Remaining Capacity (hours)
A	0.10	71	7.1	82.9
B	0.20	124	24.8	58.1
C	0.30	65	19.5	38.6
D	0.20	193	38.6	0

Note how the AROT method adjusted the lot sizes so no shortages should occur and the capacity of 90 hours is totally utilized. It did not attempt to establish efficient lot sizes, but allocated the 90 hours so that the following occurs: each item will run out of inventory in exactly 4.88 weeks if production ceases after the current planning period as shown:

item: (current inventory + lot size)/(weekly demand) = runout time

$$A: \quad (100 \quad + \quad 71) \ / \quad 35 \quad = \quad 4.88$$
$$B: \quad (120 \quad + \quad 124) \ / \quad 50 \quad = \quad 4.88$$
$$C: \quad (130 \quad + \quad 65) \ / \quad 40 \quad = \quad 4.88$$
$$D: \quad (100 \quad + \quad 193) \ / \quad 60 \quad = \quad 4.88$$

FIXED ORDER INTERVAL SYSTEMS

The fixed order interval system, also called a periodic inventory system, is based on a periodic rather than a continuous review of the inventory stock position. It is a time based inventory system in which orders are placed at equally spaced, predetermined points in time (when to order). The order quantity (how many to order) is dependent upon the usage (demand) between order review periods.

A maximum inventory level for the item is developed, based on usage during both the lead time and the order interval. After a fixed period of time (T) has passed, the stock position of the item is determined. An order is placed to replenish the stock, and the size of the order is sufficient to bring the present stock level up to the maximum inventory level. Thus, the size of the order is the difference between the maximum inventory level and

Figure 13. Fixed order interval system.

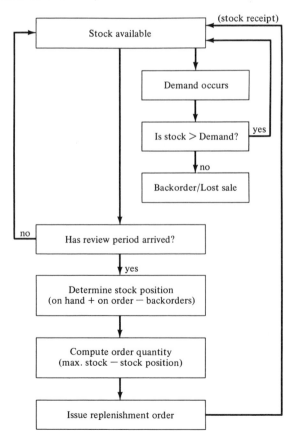

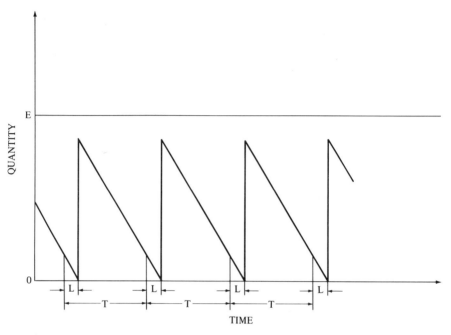

Figure 14. Fixed order interval system.

the inventory position at the time of the review. In deterministic fixed order interval systems, the order size is not expected to vary, because usage (demand) is assumed to be both known with certainty and continuous.

The system, therefore, contains only two parameters to be chosen: the fixed review period T and the maximum inventory level E. From these, all replenishment orders can be found. The fixed order interval system is termed a T-system, since the order interval (when to order) is constant. Occasionally, the order interval is rounded to a weekly, monthly, or some other convenient time basis. A typical fixed order interval system is shown in Figures 13 and 14.

Economic Order Interval (EOI)—Single Items

The basic problem in this system is determining the order interval T and the desired maximum inventory level E. The economic order interval can be obtained by the minimization of the total annual cost. If stockouts are not permitted, the total annual inventory cost is given by Figure 15 and the following formula:

total annual cost = (purchase cost) + (order cost) + (holding cost),

$$\text{TC} = RP + mC + \frac{RFP}{2m} = RP + \frac{C}{T} + \frac{RFPT}{2},$$

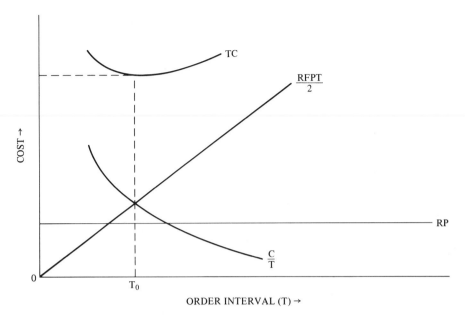

Figure 15. Annual inventory costs.

where

$$m = \frac{1}{T} = \text{number of orders or reviews per year,}$$

$$\frac{R}{2m} = \frac{RT}{2} = \text{average inventory in units,}$$

$$T = \frac{1}{m} = \text{order interval in years.}$$

To obtain the minimum cost order interval, the first derivative of the total annual cost with respect to the order interval T is set equal to zero:

$$\frac{d\,TC}{dT} = \frac{-C}{T^2} + \frac{RFP}{2} = 0.$$

Solving the equation for T, the following formula results:

$$T_0 = \sqrt{\frac{2C}{RFP}} = \text{economic order interval (EOI) in years.}$$

The minimum cost number of reviews per year (m) is simply the reciprocal of T_0, or

$$m_0 = \frac{1}{T_0} = \sqrt{\frac{RFP}{2C}}.$$

In deterministic situations, there is no difference between the fixed order size system and the fixed order interval system. The order quantity for the fixed order interval is simply $Q = RT$, or

$$Q_0 = RT_0 = R\sqrt{\frac{2C}{RFP}} = \sqrt{\frac{2CR}{FP}} = \sqrt{\frac{2CR}{H}}.$$

The maximum inventory level E must be large enough to satisfy demand during the subsequent order interval T and also during the lead time L. The following formula gives the maximum inventory level when the order interval and lead time are expressed in years:

$$E = RT + RL = R(T + L) = Q + B = \text{maximum inventory level.}$$

The following formula gives the maximum inventory level when the order interval and lead time are expressed in days and there are N operating days in the year:

$$E = \frac{RT}{N} + \frac{RL}{N} = \frac{R(T + L)}{N} = Q + B.$$

The minimum total cost per year is obtained by putting T_0 for T in the total annual cost equation. The following formula for the minimum total cost per year results:

$$TC_0 = RP + RHT_0.$$

EXAMPLE 14

The Williams Manufacturing Company purchases 8000 units of a product each year at a unit cost of $10.00. The order cost is $30.00 per order, and the holding cost per unit per year is $3.00. What are the economic order interval, maximum inventory level, and the total annual cost when the lead time is 10 days and there are 250 operating days in the year?

$$T_0 = \sqrt{\frac{2C}{RH}} = \sqrt{\frac{2(30)}{(8000)3}} = 0.05 \text{ years} = 12.5 \text{ days,}$$

$$E = \frac{R(T + L)}{N} = \frac{8000(12.5 + 10)}{250} = 720 \text{ units,}$$

$$TC_0 = RP + RHT_0 = (8000)(10) + 8000(3)0.05 = \$81,200.$$

Every 12.5 days the inventory position would be determined and an order initiated. Note that the optimum total annual cost is exactly the same for the fixed order interval system as for the fixed order size system (see Example 1).

Economic Order Interval (EOI)—Multiple Items

In retailing and wholesaling, a separate order is rarely placed for each item. Frequently, a supplier provides numerous items, and it is more economical to place joint orders. When all items from the same source are ordered jointly, the stock level review for these items can be coordinated and inventory maintenance can be kept to a minimum. Furthermore, the monitoring of stock levels often is less frequent and can be scheduled to fit comfortably with other organizational activities. Logistics and transportation cost savings also may be possible because of smaller materials handling costs and weight breaks in the transportation rate structure.

In preparing joint orders, the quantity of each item to order depends on the time interval between orders for the entire group. The basic problem in this situation is the determination of the time interval T which will minimize inventory costs for the group as a whole. Once the optimum time (order) interval is established, the desired maximum inventory level E_i for each item can be set in relation to it. From there, the individual order quantities can be calculated as the difference between each item's maximum inventory level and its stock position at the time of the order review.

The economic order interval can be obtained by minimizing the total annual cost. Neglecting stockout cost, the formulation is

total annual cost = (purchase cost) + (order cost) + (holding cost),

$$TC = \sum_{i=1}^{n} R_i P_i + \frac{(C + nc)}{T} + \tfrac{1}{2} TF \sum_{i=1}^{n} R_i P_i,$$

where

R_i = annual requirement for item i,

P_i = purchase cost of item i,

n = total number of joint order items,

C = order cost for the joint order,

c = order cost associated with each individual item,

T = order interval in years,

F = annual holding cost as a fraction of purchase cost.

The minimum cost order interval is obtained by taking the first derivative of the total annual cost with respect to the order interval (T) and setting it equal to zero:

$$\frac{d\,TC}{dT} = \frac{-(C + nc)}{T^2} + \tfrac{1}{2} F \sum_{i=1}^{n} R_i P_i = 0.$$

Solving the equation for T, the EOI formula results:

$$T_0 = \sqrt{\frac{2(C + nc)}{F\sum_{i=1}^{n}R_i P_i}} = \text{economic order interval in years.}$$

The maximum inventory for each item must be large enough to satisfy demand during the subsequent order interval and also during the lead time L. The amount to order of each individual item is simply the maximum inventory level (E_i) minus the inventory position. The maximum inventory is determined as follows when the order interval and lead time are expressed in days, and there are N operating days in the year:

$$E_i = \frac{R_i T}{N} + \frac{R_i L}{N} = \frac{R_i(T + L)}{N}$$

$$= \text{maximum inventory for item } i.$$

EXAMPLE 15

A firm orders seven items from the same vendor. The order costs are \$1.50 per purchase order and \$.50 per item. If carrying costs are 20% per year, what is the minimum cost order interval? If lead time is 1 month, what is the maximum inventory level for each item?

See Table 13. We have

$$T_0 = \sqrt{\frac{2(C + nc)}{F\sum_{i=1}^{n}R_i P_i}} = \sqrt{\frac{2(1.50 + 3.50)}{0.20(2000)}} = 0.158 \text{ years.}$$

Table 13

Item	Annual Demand	Unit Cost	Purchase Cost
A	150	$1.00	$150
B	400	.50	200
C	125	2.00	250
D	100	3.00	300
E	800	.50	400
F	70	5.00	350
G	175	2.00	350
			$2000

Table 14

Item (i)	Maximum Inventory (E_i)
A	37.5 or 38
B	100
C	31.25 or 31
D	25
E	200
F	17.5 or 18
G	43.75 or 44

The minimum cost order interval is 0.158 years, or 1.9 months. Every 2 months you would enter a new order for the seven items. The maximum inventory level (Table 14) is obtained as follows:

$$E_i = \frac{R_i(T + L)}{12} = \frac{3R_i}{12} = \frac{R_i}{4}.$$

The formulas developed for the fixed order interval system assume that the demand rate, lead time, price per unit, ordering cost per order, and holding cost per unit are constant; that no stockouts are permitted; and that the complete order quantity is received at one time. In actual situations, many of these assumptions are violated. The important consideration is how useful the decision model becomes when there are assumption variances. If assumption violations are not critical, the model can be an excellent surrogate for reality.

CONCLUSION

An important result of deterministic inventory analysis is the realization that economic order quantities do not vary directly with demand but as the square root of demand. This nonlinear relationship could explain why many organizations experience inventory problems. Intuitive inventory policies are undermined by difficult-to-grasp nonlinearities.

Although the models developed in this chapter are evidently applicable to many situations, they are fraught with many limiting assumptions. The reasonableness of model assumptions and their sensitivity to actual conditions determines the utility of any particular model. For example, all of the models assume that the demand for an item is known with certainty. There are few items that enjoy such a preordained future. Stockouts (shortages) either are not permitted to exist or are backordered and satisfied when replenishments are received.

It is further assumed that the holding cost per unit per year is known. Typically, it is not known and it is subjected to gross estimation. In addition, the order cost is treated as a fixed dollar amount per order placed.

Actual situations are not usually so simple. Lead times are assumed to be constant (another less than accurate characterization).

These limitations and shortcomings are not highlighted as an attempt to discourage the use of basic models. Quite the contrary, a better understanding of relevant matters can increase the use of models within their range of applicability. Fortunately, sizable deviations of parameter values produce rather small cost penalties. The robustness of the EOQ, EPQ, and EOI helps justify their widespread use. When deterministic models are insensitive to parameter changes, they provide an excellent approximation to real-world phenomena.

QUESTIONS

1. List several of the assumptions leading to the classical economic order quantity (EOQ).

2. When is the practice of backordering economically feasible?

3. When would negative reorder points occur in a backordering situation?

4. What distinguishes the *all-units* from the *incremental* quantity discounts schedule?

5. Over what period of time are the cost differences between placing and not placing a special order compared in a known price increase situation?

6. Are EOQ inventory models justifiably suspect because of their restrictive assumptions? Explain.

7. Does the effect of errors on the minimum total variable cost (TVC_0) tend to be greater when the EOQ has been overestimated or underestimated?

8. Why is the EOQ model frequently unsatisfactory in determining production order quantities?

9. What is the maximum inventory level that is reached when the organization receives lot (batch) sizes on a gradual basis?

10. What models would be used when an organization must decide whether to receive inventory from a supplier on an instantaneous or a gradual basis?

11. How can capacity and scheduling problems be foreseen in a multiple item EPQ approach?

12. What is the methodology behind using the runout time (ROT) method of production planning?

13. How does the aggregate runout time (AROT) method correct some of the problems associated with the basic ROT method?

14. If a high-technology manufacturer believed that possible advances in the state of the art precluded the holding of large inventories, how could it incorporate this belief into its inventory models?

15. How are the EOQ and the economic order interval (EOI) similar?

16. How are the order sizes established for individual items within the multiple item EOI approach?

PROBLEMS

1. The Star Equipment Company purchases 54,000 bearing assemblies each year at a unit cost of $40. The holding cost is $9 per unit per year, and the order cost is $20. (a) What is the economic order quantity? (b) How many orders will be placed in one year? (c) If the lead time is 1 month, what is the reorder point for the assemblies? (d) If the lead time is reduced to 2 weeks, what will be the reorder point?

2. The Hercules Machine Company purchases 38,000 units of a component each year at a price of $4.00 per unit. The ordering cost is $9.00 per order, and the annual holding cost is estimated at 25% of the unit value. (a) What is the economic order quantity for the component? (b) What is the total annual inventory cost for the component if it is ordered in economic quantities? (c) What is the maximum number of components in inventory? (d) What is the approximate order interval in weeks if the most economic ordering policy is followed and the firm operates 52 weeks each year?

3. The Never-Die Hospital purchases gauze in lots of 1500 boxes, which is a 6-month supply. The cost per box is $10; the ordering cost is $25 per order; the annual holding cost is estimated at 25% of unit value. (a) What is the total annual cost of the existing inventory policy? (b) How much money could be saved if the economic order quantity were applied to the purchase of the gauze? (c) What should be the reorder point if the lead time is 2 weeks?

4. Assume that the following data pertain to an inventory item: annual demand = 6000 units; unit purchase price = $15; ordering cost per order = $25; annual holding cost per unit = $3; lead time = 3 weeks (when the firm operates 50 weeks/year). If the firm's customers do not object to backordering and each unit backordered costs $2 per year, then: (a) What is the size of the economic order quantity? (b) What is the maximum inventory level? (c) What

is the reorder point? (d) When the reorder point is reached, how many more units will be demanded before the next order arrives? (e) How many units will be backordered during each order cycle?

5. Assume that the same information given in Problem 1 applies except that backordering is a possibility. If backordering is acceptable, the shortage cost per unit per year will be $3. (a) What will happen to the original economic order quantity if backordering is instituted? (b) If each unit requires two square feet of space, how much space will be needed if backordering is used? if backordering is not allowed? (c) Could the company save any in total annual costs if it could use backordering?

6. A mobile home fabricator has an annual demand of 10,000 units for a small refrigerator. The supplier sells the units for $100 in order quantities below 125 and for $95 in order quantities above 124 units. The order cost is $5, and the annual holding cost is 10% of unit value. (a) In what quantities should the item be purchased with an all-units quantity discount? (b) What will be the maximum inventory level?

7. If an incremental quantity discounts schedule is in effect, what is the optimum lot size for the refrigerator described in Problem 6?

8. The supplier to the Hercules Machine Company is offering a special discount and temporarily reducing the unit price of the component described in Problem 2 by $.20. What lot size should Hercules order to take advantage of the discount?

9. The supplier mentioned in Problem 2 has decided to increase the unit price of its component from $4.00 to $4.20 tomorrow. If the reorder point is 1500 units and the current stock position is 2200 units, (a) what lot size should Hercules order today? (b) what cost savings will be sacrificed if no special order is placed prior to the price increase?

10. An electronics company uses 20,000 particle beams each year. The supplier of the beams offers them at the following prices:

Quantity Ordered	Unit Price
1–799	$11.00
800–1199	10.00
1200–1599	9.00
≥ 1600	8.00

The cost of an order is $50, and the holding cost is 20% of the unit value per year. (a) What size order should be placed to minimize costs with an all-units quantity discount? (b) How long will each order last?

11. A firm has an annual demand for a component of 3000 units. A fixed cost of $250 is incurred each time an order is placed, and holding costs are computed

at 25% of unit value per year. Source A will sell the component for $10 regardless of the order size. Source B will only accept orders of at least 600 units at a unit price of $9.50. Source C will charge $9.00 per item but requires a minimum order of 800 units. (a) What quantity should be purchased and from which source? (b) What are the cost savings in comparison with the other two sources?

12. If incremental quantity discounts are offered to the electronics company mentioned in Problem 10, what would be the optimum lot size under these conditions?

13. Volatile Industries originally estimated its annual demand for item XYZ as 800 units per year and its holding cost for this item as $1 per year. Volatile has discovered at the end of the year that annual demand is only 600 units and holding costs per unit per year are closer to $2. The only good news is that Volatile figured orders cost them $25 to place when they really cost just $20 each. Volatile now wants to know the significance of these mistakes on last year's decisions. (a) What was the combined effect of these errors on the economic order quantity for item XYZ? (b) What was the individual effect of each error on item XYZ's economic order quantity? (c) What was the combined effect of the errors on the minimum total variable cost of item XYZ for the year? (d) What was the individual effect of the error in demand on the minimum total variable cost for last year?

14. If a company overestimates its annual demand for an item by 50% and underestimates its ordering cost by 20%, by what percentage (of the economic order quantity) will the order quantity be too large?

15. A tire manufacturer plans to produce 40,000 units of a particular type of tire next year. The production rate is 200 tires per day, and there are 250 working days available. The setup cost is $200 per run, and the unit production cost is $15. If holding costs are $11.50 per unit per year, (a) what is the economic production quantity? (b) how many production runs should be made each year? (c) If the production lead time is 5 days, what is the reorder point?

16. Rick wants to determine the optimum amount of money to withdraw from an automatic teller machine (ATM) per transaction. The bank charges $.30 per ATM withdrawal transaction and a flat service charge of $5.00 per month. Rick spends an average of $10.00 per day. He figures there is a 10% chance that he will lose his wallet or be robbed in any given year. The bank pays 6% per year on checking account balances. (a) What is the optimal withdrawal amount per transaction? (b) How might the amount of Rick's withdrawals be altered if he moved to a high crime area?

17. A firm produces five products in a work center. The available information is shown in the table. If there are 250 working days available, (a) what is the best

production cycle? (b) what is the optimum production run size for each product? (c) what is the annual demand time?

Item	Annual Demand	Unit Production Cost P_i	Daily Production Rate p_i	Annual Holding Cost H_i	Setup Cost C_i
1	6,000	$6.00	300	$2.10	$ 80
2	20,000	4.00	500	1.40	40
3	8,000	6.00	160	1.80	100
4	8,000	2.00	200	.50	50
5	15,000	4.00	200	1.50	50

18. A company produces six products on a single machine. The information available on the products is shown in the table.

Item	Annual Demand	Unit Production Cost P_i	Daily Production Rate p_i	Annual Holding Cost H_i	Setup Cost C_i
1	3,000	$8.00	100	$2.00	$ 70
2	8,000	8.00	200	1.80	100
3	5,000	4.00	100	1.20	120
4	5,000	2.00	250	.60	80
5	12,000	5.00	600	1.50	250
6	6,000	2.00	100	.50	160

(a) What is the optimum production cycle if there are 250 working days available? (b) What are the product production run sizes? (c) What is the length of a complete production cycle in days? (d) What is the slack time per run?

19. Suppose the setup costs in Problem 18 were actually overestimated by 20%. (a) How much difference would the error make in the production run sizes for each product? (b) What difference would the error make in the length of a complete production cycle?

20. The demand for an item is 9 units per period. The holding cost is $.10 per unit per period. The demand can be met by either purchasing or manufacturing, as described by the following data:

	Purchase	Manufacture
Item cost	$ 8.00	$ 7.50
Order/setup cost	$20.00	$200.00
Replenishment rate	∞	18 units/period

What are the minimum cost source and order quantity?

21. A chemical processor uses 500 gallons/day of a solvent. The holding cost is $.002 per gallon per day. The processor is thinking about synthesizing the solvent in house. Relevant data are as follows:

	Purchase	Manufacture
Item cost	$14.00	$ 13.90
Order/setup cost	$ 8.00	$100.00
Replenishment rate	∞	2100 gallons/day

What are the minimum cost source and order quantity for the solvent?

22. Kaiser Karts fabricates four different components on the same piece of equipment. Kaiser is planning its production schedule for next week. The expected demands and inventories on hand, fabrication hours required per part, and standard lot sizes are shown in the table:

Part	Standard Hours per Part	Lot Size	Demand	Inventory on Hand
A	0.02	400	300	300
B	0.04	300	250	400
C	0.04	400	350	500
D	0.05	300	350	600

The fabrication process operates 40 hours per week. (a) Use the runout time method to develop a fabrication schedule for the four parts. (b) Does there appear to be a capacity problem?

23. Using the information given in Problem 22, develop a 40-hour fabrication schedule which is capacity feasible. (Hint: Try the aggregate runout time method.)

24. Given an annual demand of 8000 units and an economic order quantity of 600 units: (a) What is the economic order interval for the item in weeks? (b) What maximum inventory level should be established if the lead time is one week and there are 52 operating weeks per year in an economic order interval system?

25. A firm orders eight items from the same vendor, as shown in the table. The ordering costs are $10 per purchase order and $.25 per item. Carrying costs are 15% per year. (a) What is the economic order interval? (b) If the lead time is 1 month, what is the maximum inventory level for each item?

Item	Annual Demand	Unit Cost	Purchase Cost
A	175	$1.00	$175.00
B	425	.60	255.00
C	115	2.10	241.50
D	90	3.00	270.00
E	810	.75	607.50
F	70	4.00	280.00
G	190	5.00	950.00
H	210	2.00	420.00
			$3,199.00

26. The demand forecast for a product during the next year is given in the table below. The lead time for the product is 3 days, and the demand rate is uniform during any one month. The order cost is $30 per order, and the annual holding cost is 30% of the unit cost. The purchase cost is $5.00 per unit for lot sizes less than 500, and $4.90 for lot sizes over 500 units. The organization has a policy of ordering units in lot sizes of 1-month, 2-month, or 3-month supply. What is the lowest cost policy from the three alternatives?

Month	Demand (Units)	Month	Demand (Units)
1	180	7	130
2	220	8	360
3	190	9	110
4	140	10	280
5	270	11	250
6	210	12	160

CASE 1: A LITTLE KNOWLEDGE

A welding distributor has been buying its office supplies from the same supplier for some time. George Ouch, the salesman for the office supply company, has been calling on Hot Tips Incorporated for over three years. Much to George's dismay, it has always been the practice of Hot Tips to buy the smallest lot size available of a particular four-part preprinted billing form at a cost of $611 for 10,000 forms. The rationale for this particular buying policy was to expend the least amount of money possible (at any one time) on office supplies, for reasons of liquidity.

Tom Erudite, in an effort to enhance his position with the company, has been attending evening classes. Recently, he took a course which dealt with inventory systems and materials management. Tom was anxious to save the company money (and also look good himself) by applying the techniques he learned in class to his job.

When George contacted Tom he was amazed to discover that he wished to purchase the largest lot size available of the four-part billing form. It was 30,000 forms at $1700. George could not believe the sudden change in policy. Upon questioning Tom, he found that he used something called an EOQ model. Tom explained that by analyzing all the relevant costs, he could save $80 annually by purchasing the larger quantity of billing forms.

1. What is your opinion of this sudden change in inventory policy?
2. Should office supplies always be purchased in the largest quantity available? Why?
3. Explain the annual cost saving of the larger order.

CASE 2: MAKE OR BUY

The Alphabet Valve Company is a small plumbing supply firm which produces several small items for a local market. The firm manufactures some of its subassemblies and relies on contractors for others. Final assembly operations take place on the premises of Alphabet. One of the products, a common exterior water valve, is presently under study by the company officials.

The company has an agreement with one of its contractors to produce the handles for the valve under consideration. The handle is milled from stainless steel to the company's specifications and shipped to a supply point at Alphabet. The handle is attached to the valve body. The entire assembly is then given a coat of corrosion-resistant paint and packaged for shipment. The other major components of the valve are made in Alphabet's plant (presently operating at 80% of capacity).

The reason the valve has come under study is a price increase announced by the handle company. The contractor has a new price of $2.25 per handle. Alphabet's president does not believe that the market will support a price increase for the valve and he wishes to evaluate alternative sources.

The purchasing agent has researched the problem and has located a used milling machine (price $7000; life 5 years, no salvage value). He estimates that the machine will cost $1000 per year to operate and that they can produce the valve handle for $1.50 (variable cost per unit) with a volume of 4000 valves per year. The purchasing agent has placed the problem before the other officers of the firm and is soliciting their recommendations.

1. What recommendation would you make to the president?
2. If the handle is manufactured in house, should it be the same handle as was purchased?

CASE 3: MR. OLDER VERSUS MR. YOUNGER

Mr. Thomas, president of Thomas Manufacturing Company, and Mr. McDonnell, vice president, were discussing how future economic conditions would affect their product, which is vacuum cleaners. They were particularly concerned about inflation, which was causing their costs to increase at an alarming rate. They had increased the prices of their products last year, and felt another price increase would have an adverse affect on sales. They wondered if there was some way to reduce costs in order to maintain the existing price structure.

Mr. McDonnell had attended a meeting the previous night and heard a presentation by the president of a hand tool company on how they were solving the inflation problem. Apparently, they had just hired a purchasing agent with a business degree who was reducing costs by 15%. Mr. McDonnell thought some new ideas might be applicable to Thomas Manufacturing. The present purchasing agent, Mr. Older, had been with the company for 25 years and they had no complaints. Production never was stopped for lack of material. Yet a 15% cost reduction, in the present economy, was a possibility which could not be ignored. Mr. Thomas suggested that Mr. McDonnell look into this area and come up with a recommendation in 3 weeks.

Mr. McDonnell contacted several business schools in the area. He said he would be interested in hiring a new graduate, majoring in purchasing. One of the requirements of the applicants was a paper on how they felt they could improve the company's purchasing function. Several applicants visited the plant and analyzed the purchasing department before they wrote their papers. The most dynamic paper was submitted by Tim Younger. He recommended:

1. Lower the stock reorder levels from 60 to 45 days for many items, thus reducing inventory.

2. Analyze the product specifications on many parts of the vacuum cleaners with an idea toward using plastics instead of metals.
3. Standardize many of the parts on the vacuum cleaners to reduce the number of items kept in stock.
4. Analyze items to see if more products can be purchased by blanket purchase orders with the ultimate goal of reducing the purchasing staff.
5. Look for new and lower cost sources of supply.
6. Increase the number of requests for bids, in order to get still lower prices.
7. Be more aggressive in negotiations. Make fewer concessions.
8. Make sure all trade, quantity, and cash discounts are taken.
9. Buy from the lowest price source, disregarding local public relations.
10. Stop showing favoritism to customers who also buy from the company. Reciprocity comes second to price.
11. Purchase as current requirements demand, instead of according to market conditions. Too much money is tied up in inventory.

After reading all the papers Mr. McDonnell was debating with himself what he should recommend to Mr. Thomas. Just last week at the department meeting Mr. Older was recommending many of the opposite actions. In particular he recommended an increase in inventory levels, anticipating rising prices. Mr. Older also stressed the good relations the company had with all its suppliers and how they can be relied upon for good service and possible extension of credit if the situation warrants it. Most of their suppliers bought their vacuum cleaners from Thomas Manufacturing. Yet, Mr. Younger said this practice was wrong and should be eliminated. Mr. McDonnell was hesitant as to what action he should recommend. He had only one day to make his decision.

1. What recommendation would you make if you were Mr. McDonnell? Why?
2. Analyze Mr. Younger's recommendations. Do you agree or disagree with them?

CASE 4: HEALTHY INDIGESTION

Nutrition Specialists, Inc. is a chain store operation in the retail health food business. NSI operates a number of small retail health food stores which are located within mall complexes throughout a southern metropolitan area. The outlets are generally small in size but offer a full line of health food items. The broad assortment of items is presently being purchased for the chain. The items are delivered to a central warehouse and then distributed to the outlets almost on an as-needed basis.

Over the past few years the NSI managers, Joe and Mike Minardo, have gained an awareness of the competitive nature of their business and the need for efficient operating practices. They have discovered that they are in a much better position than the smaller independent retail health food stores, due to their significant purchasing power and computerized inventory system. NSI has actively engaged in price competition and placed major emphasis on cost control. Thus far, its strategies have proven correct. The company has been expanding and recently has opened two new outlets.

From its inception NSI has adhered to the policy of dealing primarily with one supplier in order to achieve sales volume discounts. The major supplier furnishes the company with most of their staple health food items, such as vitamin pills, packaged teas and herbs, health food literature, beauty products, grains, fruit juices, and dairy items. This supplier, like others in the industry, hesitates to extend credit because of the nature of the industry. NSI has been one of the few that are able to overcome this reluctance.

Presently, NSI is encountering two pressing problems. Stockouts within the individual outlets occur frequently. When this happens store managers send customers elsewhere, and institute a special order for the item from the central warehouse. Because of space constraints in the warehouse, NSI is considering a possible expansion, or alternatively, purchase of a second facility.

Joe Minardo, the younger of the two managing brothers, feels measures should be taken to prevent shortages and to increase the internal efficiency of the firm. His position comes as a reaction to an announced price increase from the major supplier. Due to inflationary pressures on his costs, the supplier announced an across-the-board increase of 10% on all items to become effective in four weeks. Joe, therefore, feels that the company should stock up on all items before the increase comes into effect. He wants to increase all order quantities beyond normal lot sizes and to initiate special orders for items that would not typically be ordered before the price increase. Joe maintains that this action would delay purchase of the items at higher prices and thereby provide a substantial cost saving to the company. He also asserts that the additional stock would be a temporary solution to stockout problems and would postpone a facility decision if the larger orders could be expedited to the outlets.

Mike opposes Joe's assertions vehemently, on the basis that Joe would be taking a risky step during times when forecasts for the industry as well as the economy are grim. Mike refuses to authorize orders for larger lot sizes or place orders ahead of schedule. He insists that the gains that Joe is promising are questionable and an unworkable solution to their problems. Mike thinks Joe has finally gone too far with his cost cutting schemes.

1. What purchasing and inventory factors should be considered in order to resolve the conflict?
2. What types of risks are involved in Mike's position?
3. Does Joe have a valid argument? Mike?
4. What recommendations would you make to the brothers?

CASE 5: INGENIOUS CONTRIVANCES

I & C, Inc. produces a myriad of stainless steel and aluminum kitchen utensils as well as several patterns of stainless steel flatware. Its product lines are in continuous flux, because the company is constantly adding new kitchen gadgets to its already overwhelming number of contrivances. I & C takes great pride in its ability to create an item suitable for every conceivable kitchen need. There is heavy emphasis on product innovation and market leadership. The firm has been quite successful at entering the kitchen convenience market with a "never heard of before" but "can't live without" device.

Currently, I & C is undergoing new product development for an aluminum vegetable steamer and is in the process of formulating production decisions for the device. The steamer can be inserted in different size cooking pots, enabling the user to steam various quantities of food with the same implement. It consists of eight pieces of aluminum mesh that can expand to the size of the cooking appliance and collapse for storage.

Since I & C has a wide array of products, it is imperative that the items be produced on a regular cycle. The company stresses the need for full utilization of its equipment. Given the short product life of many items, as well as small yearly sales of others, I & C avoids purchasing equipment that would be dedicated to a specific product. Fortunately, the engineering and production managers have determined that the steamer is producible on existing equipment, since it is simply a modification of a straining utensil that has been in production for several years.

The critical decision now is the scheduling of production for the steamer. A determination must be made for the size and the frequency of the production run. Various members of the management team have been consulted. Marketing is excited about the prospects for the steamer, due to the popularity of steamed vegetables. They expect sales during the first year to be 50,000 units. The production manager has issued the following estimates: $200 setup cost, $5 per unit production cost, and 300 units per day production capability for the 250 day working year. The firm's inventory analyst estimates an annual holding cost of $.80 per unit. Applying the concept of scheduling production in economic quantities to initial figures, the analyst stipulates a production run of 8660 units approximately 5.8 times a year. He feels that this size and frequency of runs meet the forecasted demand most efficiently.

Mr. Kaiser, the general manager, has reservations. He has just finished reviewing a product proposal for an item that would compete for machining time with the steamer and the strainer. He also is having difficulty ascertaining his actual production capability and questions the validity of the capacity figures he has been receiving. He is beginning to wonder if basic operating principles are being overlooked.

1. Should I & C adopt the initial figures as its production plan?
2. Has any necessary information been overlooked? Should the theoretical model be modified?
3. What production, operating, and marketing factors could alter or influence this type of decision?

MATHEMATICAL ABBREVIATIONS AND SYMBOLS USED IN CHAPTER 3

AROT	Aggregate runout time
b	Price reduction fraction
B	Reorder point in units
C	Ordering cost or setup cost

d	Unit price discount in dollars
E	Maximum inventory level in units
EOI	Economic order interval
EOQ	Economic order quantity
EPQ	Economic production quantity
F	Annual holding cost fraction
g	Cost saving of special order
H	Holding cost per unit per year
K	Backordering cost per unit per year
k	Unit price increase in dollars
L	Lead time
m	Number of annual orders or production runs
m_0	Optimum number of annual orders or production runs
n	Number of products
N	Number of annual operating days
p	Daily production rate
P	Unit purchase or production cost
P_d	Unit purchase cost with discount
q	Stock level in units at a given time
Q	Order quantity in units
Q'	Special-order quantity in units
Q_d	Quantity discount break quantity
Q_0	Economic order quantity in units
Q_{0i}	EOQ for price level i
Q_0^*	EOQ after price increase
r	Daily demand rate
R	Annual demand in units
ROT	Runout time
T	Order interval in years
T_0	Economic order interval in years
TC	Total annual inventory cost
TC_0	Optimum total annual cost
TVC	Total variable cost per year
TVC_0	Optimum total variable cost per year
U	Price-break quantity in units
V	Maximum inventory level in units
V_0	Optimum maximum inventory level in units

X_C Order cost error factor
X_H Holding cost error factor
X_R Annual demand error factor
X_Q EOQ error factor

SUMMARY OF FORMULAS IN CHAPTER 3

Model	Formula

Basic EOQ

$$Q_0 = \sqrt{\frac{2CR}{H}}$$

$$B = RL/N$$

$$TC = RP + \frac{RC}{Q} + \frac{QH}{2}$$

$$TC_0 \doteq RP + HQ_0$$

EOQ with backordering

$$Q_0 = \sqrt{\frac{2CR}{H}} \sqrt{\frac{H+K}{K}}$$

$$V_0 = \sqrt{\frac{2CR}{H}} \sqrt{\frac{K}{H+K}}$$

$$B = \frac{RL}{N} - (Q - V)$$

$$TC = RP + \frac{CR}{Q} + \frac{HV^2}{2Q} + \frac{K(Q-V)^2}{2Q}$$

EOQ with special sales price (regular replenishment)

$$Q_0' = \frac{dR}{(P-d)F} + \frac{PQ_0}{P-d}$$

$$g_0 = \frac{C(P-d)}{P} \left[\left(\frac{Q_0'}{Q_0} - 1 \right)^2 \right]$$

EOQ with special sales price (before regular replenishment)

$$Q_0' = \frac{dR}{(P-d)F} + \frac{PQ_0}{P-d} - q$$

$$g_0 = C \left[\left(\frac{Q_0'}{\sqrt{\frac{P}{P-d}} Q_0} \right)^2 - 1 \right]$$

EOQ with known price increase

$$Q_0' = Q_0 \sqrt{\frac{P+k}{k}} + \frac{kR}{PF} - q$$

$$g_0 = C[(Q_0'/Q_0)^2 - 1]$$

Model	Formula
EOQ sensitivity	$$\frac{Q - Q_0}{Q_0} = \sqrt{\frac{X_R X_C}{X_H}} - 1$$ $$\frac{\text{TVC} - \text{TVC}_0}{\text{TVC}_0} = \frac{X_H + X_R X_C}{2\sqrt{X_R X_C X_H}} - 1 = \frac{(X_Q - 1)^2}{2 X_Q}$$
EPQ	$$Q_0 = \sqrt{\frac{2CR(p)}{H(p - r)}}$$ $$TC_0 = RP + \frac{(p - r) H Q_0 \cdot}{p}$$ $$B = RL/N$$
EPQ with backordering	$$Q_0 = \sqrt{\frac{2CRp}{H(p - r)}} \sqrt{\frac{H + K}{K}}$$ $$B = \frac{RL}{N} - \sqrt{\frac{2CR(p - r)}{pK(H + K)}}$$
EPQ—multiple items	$$m_0 = \sqrt{\frac{\sum_{i=1}^{n} \frac{(p_i - r_i) R_i H_i}{p_i}}{2 \sum_{i=1}^{n} C_i}}$$ $$Q_i = \frac{R_i}{m_0}$$ $$TC_0 = \sum_{i=1}^{n} R_i P_i + 2 m_0 \sum_{i=1}^{n} C_i$$
EOI	$$T_0 = \sqrt{\frac{2C}{RFP}} = \frac{Q_0}{R}$$ $$TC = RP + \frac{C}{T} + \frac{RFPT}{2}$$ $$E = \frac{R(T + L)}{N} = Q + B$$ $$TC_0 = RP + RHT_0$$
EOI—multiple items	$$T_0 = \sqrt{\frac{2(C + nc)}{F \sum_{i=1}^{n} R_i P_i}}$$ $$E_i = \frac{R_i(T + L)}{N}$$

APPENDIX A. DETERMINATION OF SINGLE VARIABLE MAXIMUM AND MINIMUM POINTS

The determination of a maximum or minimum value for a continuous differentiable function of one variable is easily handled by differential calculus. The slope of a curve at a point is simply the derivative at that point. At a maximum or minimum point on a curve, the slope is zero. Therefore, the maximum or minimum point can be determined by setting the first derivative of the function equal to zero. If a function is defined by

$$y = f(x),$$

the maximum or minimum point is where

$$\frac{dy}{dx} = 0.$$

To determine if the point is a maximum or a minimum, it is necessary to take the second derivative. After the second derivative is taken, the value of x obtained from the first derivative is substituted into the equation for the second derivative, and the sign indicates if the point is a maximum or a minimum. The point is a maximum if the second derivative is negative; it is a minimum if the second derivative is positive.

Whenever

$$\frac{dy}{dx} = 0,$$

y has a maximum value if

$$\frac{d^2y}{dx^2} < 0;$$

y has a minimum value if

$$\frac{d^2y}{dx^2} > 0.$$

APPENDIX B. EOQ QUANTITY DISCOUNT APPROXIMATION

The basic decision with quantity discounts is whether a larger quantity should be ordered to take advantage of a unit-price reduction.

When the order cost (C) is very small compared to the purchase cost (PQ) of an order, an approximation formula can be used to decide on the discount. The formula will determine the maximum quantity that economically could be purchased with the discount. If the quantity necessary to qualify for the discount is larger, do not take the discount; if smaller, order the optimum quantity or just enough to qualify for the discount. The maximum quantity that can economically be ordered to qualify for a quantity discount is as follows:[13]

$$Q_m = \frac{2bR}{F} + (1 - b)Q_0 = \text{maximum discount order quantity},$$

where

R = annual demand in units,

F = annual holding cost fraction,

Q_0 = economic order quantity without the quantity discount,

$b = (P - P_d)/P$ = price reduction fraction,

P = unit price without quantity discount,

P_d = unit price with quantity discount.

Note that when there is no discount ($b = 0$), the maximum quantity is equal to the EOQ ($Q_m = Q_0$). The above formula applies when the order cost is very small compared to the total invoice cost ($C \ll P_d Q$). An example can illustrate the use of the discount procedure.

EXAMPLE B-1

A supplier sells copper elbows to a refrigerator manufacturer. The list price is $.80 per unit, with a discount price of $.76 per unit in lots of 2000 or more. The annual demand is for 10,000 elbows, and the order cost is $10 per order. If the holding cost fraction is 25%, should the discount be taken? What should be the order quantity?

$$Q_0 = \sqrt{\frac{2CR}{PF}} = \sqrt{\frac{2(10)10,000}{0.80(0.25)}} = 1000 \text{ units},$$

$$b = \frac{P - P_d}{P} = \frac{0.80 - 0.76}{0.80} = 0.05,$$

$$Q_m = \frac{2bR}{F} + (1 - b)Q_0 = \frac{2(0.05)10,000}{0.25} + (0.95)1000 = 4000 + 950,$$

$$Q_m = 4950 \text{ units}.$$

The discount should be taken, and the order quantity should be 2000 units. Note that the order cost is much less than the purchase cost of an order.

---

[13] See Robert G. Brown, *Decision Rules for Inventory Management*, Holt, Rinehart and Winston, 1967, pp. 199–200 for the mechanics of the derivation.

APPENDIX C. DERIVATION OF EOQ WITH BACKORDERING

The total annual inventory cost is as follows:

$$TC = RP + \frac{CR}{Q} + \frac{HV^2}{2Q} + \frac{K(Q-V)^2}{2Q},$$

$$TC = RP + \frac{CR}{Q} + \frac{HV^2}{2Q} + \frac{KQ}{2} - KV + \frac{KV^2}{2Q},$$

where

$R =$ annual requirement in units,

$P =$ purchase cost of an item,

$C =$ ordering cost per order,

$Q =$ lot size or order quantity in units,

$H =$ holding cost per unit per year,

$V =$ maximum inventory level in units,

$K =$ stockout cost per unit per year.

To obtain optimal values for Q and V, the partial derivatives of the total annual cost with respect to Q and V are equated to zero. The two resulting equations are solved simultaneously to obtain the optimal values for Q and V. The partial derivative of total annual cost with respect to Q is as follows:

$$\frac{\partial TC}{\partial Q} = -\frac{CR}{Q^2} - \frac{HV^2}{2Q^2} + \frac{K}{2} - \frac{KV^2}{2Q^2} = 0,$$

$$\frac{1}{Q^2}\left(-CR - \frac{HV^2}{2} - \frac{KV^2}{2}\right) + \frac{K}{2} = 0,$$

$$Q^2 = \frac{2CR}{K} + \frac{HV^2}{K} + V^2.$$

The partial derivative of total annual cost with respect to V is as follows:

$$\frac{\partial TC}{\partial V} = \frac{HV}{Q} - K + \frac{KV}{Q} = 0,$$

$$\frac{1}{Q}[HV + KV] - K = 0, \qquad \frac{V(H+K)}{Q} = K,$$

$$Q = \frac{HV}{K} + V, \qquad V = \frac{KQ}{H+K}.$$

The optimal value for V is obtained by substituting the above value of Q into the previously derived relationship:

$$Q^2 = \frac{2CR}{K} + \frac{HV^2}{K} + V^2 = \left[\frac{HV}{K} + V\right]^2,$$

$$\frac{2CR}{K} + \frac{HV^2}{K} + V^2 = \frac{H^2V^2}{K^2} + \frac{2HV^2}{K} + V^2,$$

$$\frac{2CR}{K} = \frac{H^2V^2}{K^2} + \frac{HV^2}{K},$$

$$\frac{2CR}{K} = \frac{V^2H}{K}\left[\frac{H}{K} + 1\right] = \frac{V^2H}{K}\left[\frac{H+K}{K}\right],$$

$$V^2 = \frac{2CR}{H}\left[\frac{K}{H+K}\right],$$

$$V_0 = \sqrt{\frac{2CR}{H}}\sqrt{\frac{K}{H+K}}$$

$$= \text{optimum maximum inventory level.}$$

By substituting the optimal value of V into the previously developed relationship for V, we can obtain the optimal value of Q:

$$V = \frac{KQ}{H+K} = \sqrt{\frac{2CR}{H}}\sqrt{\frac{K}{H+K}},$$

$$Q = \left[\frac{H+K}{K}\right]\sqrt{\frac{2CR}{H}}\sqrt{\frac{K}{H+K}} = \sqrt{\frac{2CR}{H}}\sqrt{\frac{(H+K)^2K}{K^2(H+K)}},$$

$$Q_0 = \sqrt{\frac{2CR}{H}}\sqrt{\frac{H+K}{K}} = \text{optimum order quantity.}$$

4

Discrete Demand Systems: Deterministic Models

LOT-FOR-LOT ORDERING

PERIODIC ORDER QUANTITY

WAGNER-WHITIN ALGORITHM

SILVER-MEAL ALGORITHM

PART-PERIOD ALGORITHM

INCREMENTAL PART-PERIOD ALGORITHM

IMPLICATIONS FOR DISCRETE LOT SIZING

CONCLUSION

QUESTIONS

PROBLEMS

CASES

MATHEMATICAL ABBREVIATIONS AND SYMBOLS

The lot sizing techniques developed for continuous and independent demand items (EOQ, EPQ, and EOI) assume that demand occurs with certainty at a constant rate. Although the static EOQs, EPQs, and EOIs are insensitive (robust) to variations from their underlying assumptions (including demand variations), there are situations where time variations in demand are so pronounced that the constant demand rate assumption is seriously violated. Even though demand may be deterministic or known with certainty, its pattern may vary so drastically over time that it cannot appropriately be addressed by techniques that approximate average inventory by a repeating sawtooth pattern.

Demand which exhibits time varying patterns is characterized as discrete. Discrete demand patterns can occur in either independent or dependent demand items, and hence represent another departure from the applications associated with the lot sizing techniques suitable to continuous, independent demand situations. The emphasis in this chapter is on lot sizing models for items exhibiting deterministic, time varying demand, whether that demand is independent or dependent. Such is the case for components with lumpiness of demand in an MRP system, as well as for end items with a pronounced trend and/or seasonal effect.

When the demand rate varies with time, an exact analysis is more burdensome than the fixed order sizes used with continuous demand items. It is necessary to analyze demand over a finite period from the present to a specified planning horizon where the length of the planning horizon can have a substantial effect on the lot size decisions. Furthermore, a dynamic rather than a static lot sizing policy must be put into effect, and it is often necessary to adopt a rolling schedule. Replenishment quantities are computed over the entire planning horizon, but only the imminent (immediate) decision is implemented. As the schedule rolls forward in time, new demand information is appended so that the constant length of the planning horizon is maintained.

Various approaches have been devised to handle varying demand rates. A simplistic approach is to ignore the variation and apply the EOQ formulation with an average demand rate. In lot-for-lot ordering, the order for each period is the exact quantity in that period. Wagner and Whitin developed a dynamic programming procedure to determine the optimum varying order size.[1] Silver and Meal developed a heuristic algorithm for order size determination.[2] Groff as well as Kicks and Donaldson developed a mar-

---

[1] H. M. Wagner and T. W. Whitin, "Dynamic Version of the Economic Lot Size Model," *Management Science*, Vol. 5, October 1958, pp. 89–96.

[2] E. A. Silver, and H. C. Meal, "A Simple Modification of the EOQ for the Case of Varying Demand Rate," *Production and Inventory Management*, Vol. 10, No. 4, 4th Qtr., 1969, pp. 52–65; E. A. Silver and H. C. Meal, "A Heuristic for Selecting Lot Size Quantities for the Case of a Deterministic Time-Varying Demand Rate and Discrete Opportunities for Replenishment," *Production and Inventory Management*, Vol. 14, No. 2, 2nd Qtr., 1973, pp. 64–74.

ginal cost algorithm for lot sizing.[3] The part-period algorithm also derives varying order sizes for varying demand patterns.[4] Several of these approaches will be discussed in subsequent sections herein.

There are a number of assumptions made regarding lot sizing decisions in this chapter. They include the following:

1. The demand is known and occurs at the beginning of each period, but changes from one period to another.
2. The planning horizon is finite and composed of several time periods of equal length.
3. Lot sizes must include one or more integer time periods of demand taken in the same sequence as the chronology of the planning horizon.
4. The entire requirements for each period must be available at the beginning of that period. All replenishments are constrained to arrive at the beginning of periods (no replenishments arrive part way through a period).
5. There are no quantity discounts, so the unit cost of an item is without variation.
6. All items are treated independently of other items, with no benefits from joint review or replenishment.
7. The entire order quantity is delivered at the same time, and no shortages or stockouts are allowed.
8. Items required in a period are withdrawn from inventory at the beginning of the period. Thus, the holding cost is applied to the end-of-period inventory and is only applied to inventory held from one period to the next. Items consumed during a period incur no holding cost.
9. The inventory costs (ordering and holding) and lead times are known with certainty and are time invariant.
10. Orders placed at the beginning of a period are assumed to be available in time to meet the requirements of that period (zero lead time). This assumption is not a serious limitation, because the lot sizes for a nonzero lead time can be offset (set back) by the lead time.
11. No provisions are made for holding inventory beyond the last period in the planning horizon (assume demand beyond the planning horizon is zero).
12. The initial inventory level is zero. If the initial inventory is not zero, it must be subtracted from the demand requirements in the first

---

[3] G. K. Groff, "A Lot Sizing Rule for Time-Phased Component Demand," *Production and Inventory Management*, Vol. 20, No. 1, 1st Qtr., 1979, pp. 47–53; P. Kicks and W. A. Donaldson, "Irregular Demand: Assessing a Rough and Ready Lot Size Formula," *Journal of the Operational Research Society*, Vol. 31, No. 8, 1980, pp. 725–732.

[4] J. J. DeMatteis, and A. G. Mendoza, "An Economic Lot Sizing Technique," *IBM Systems Journal*, Vol. 7, 1968, pp. 30–46.

period to obtain an adjusted requirement for that period. If the initial inventory exceeds the first-period demand, the adjustment process is continued until all the inventory is consumed.

LOT-FOR-LOT ORDERING

Lot-for-lot (LFL) ordering is the simplest approach of all. Items are purchased in the exact quantities required for each period. There is no forward buying beyond the immediate period. This approach minimizes the inventory holding cost, since no items are ever held over from period to period. However, it ignores the costs of placing an order. It is suitable for very expensive items or items with a highly discontinuous demand where excellent inventory control must be maintained. It is also well suited to high-volume, continuous production (assembly lines).

PERIODIC ORDER QUANTITY

A periodic order quantity (POQ) approach to discrete demand results in varying lot sizes which each encompass the demand for a fixed period of time. The fixed time period is given as an economic order interval (EOI) or economic order quantity (EOQ) expressed as a time supply. The EOI is calculated using an average demand rate, instead of a constant demand rate per period as with continuous models. The calculated economic order interval is rounded to the nearest integer greater than zero, so the lot sizes obtained from its use will cover exactly the requirements for an integer number of periods. The EOI is found as follows:

$$\text{EOI} = \frac{\text{EOQ}}{\overline{R}} = \sqrt{\frac{2C}{\overline{R}Ph}} \, ,$$

where

EOI = economic order interval in periods,

C = ordering cost per order,

h = holding cost fraction per period,

P = unit purchase cost,

$\overline{R}$ = average demand rate per period.

The lot sizes are simply the accumulated demand for the rounded EOI time supply. Order receipts are only planned for periods with a positive demand. If zero demand exists for an order receipt period, the order receipt is moved forward to the first subsequent period with a positive demand.

EXAMPLE 1

An item has a unit purchase cost of $50, an ordering cost per order of $100, and a holding cost fraction per period of 0.02. Determine the lot sizes by the period order quantity from the data below.

Period	Requirements (units)
1	10
2	3
3	30
4	100
5	7
6	15
7	80
8	50
9	15
10	0
	310

Solution:

$$\text{EOI} = \sqrt{\frac{2C}{RPh}} = \sqrt{\frac{2(100)}{31(50)0.02}} = 2.54.$$

Rounding to the nearest integer, a 3-period supply would result in the following lot sizes:

Period	1	2	3	4	5	6	7	8	9	10
Lot Size	43	0	0	122	0	0	145	0	0	0

WAGNER-WHITIN ALGORITHM

An algorithm is a procedure which will lead to a solution of a given problem by a repetitive process. An algorithm is more complex than substituting into an equation, and it requires considerably more computation. The Wagner-Whitin algorithm obtains an optimum solution to the deterministic dynamic order size problem over a finite horizon with the requirement that all period demands must be satisfied. The time periods in the planning horizon must be of a fixed determinate length, and orders are placed to assure the arrival of the goods at the beginning of a time period.

The Wagner-Whitin algorithm is a dynamic programming approach which uses several theorems to simplify the computations. The algorithm proceeds to determine the minimum controllable cost policy. It involves the following three-step procedure:

1. Calculate the total variable cost matrix for all possible ordering alternatives for a time horizon consisting of N periods. The total variable cost includes ordering and holding costs. Define Z_{ce} to be the total variable cost in periods c through e of placing an order in period c which satisfies requirements in periods c through e.

$$Z_{ce} = C + hP \sum_{i=c}^{e} (Q_{ce} - Q_{ci}) \qquad \text{for} \quad 1 \le c \le e \le N,$$

where:

$$C = \text{ordering cost per order,}$$
$$h = \text{holding cost fraction per period,}$$
$$P = \text{unit purchase cost,}$$
$$Q_{ce} = \sum_{k=c}^{e} R_k,$$
$$R_k = \text{demand rate in period } k.$$

2. Define f_e to be the minimum possible cost in periods 1 through e, given that the inventory level at the end of period e is zero. The algorithm starts with $f_0 = 0$ and calculates $f_1, f_2, \ldots, f_N$ in that order. The f_e is calculated in ascending order using the formula:

$$f_e = \text{Min}(Z_{ce} + f_{c-1}) \qquad \text{for} \quad c = 1, 2, \ldots, e.$$

In other words, for each period all combinations of ordering alternatives and supplementary f_e strategies are compared. The best (lowest cost) combination is recorded as the f_e strategy to satisfy requirements for periods 1 through e. The value of f_N is the cost of the optimal order schedule.

3. To translate the optimum solution (f_N) obtained by the algorithm to order quantities, apply the following:

$f_N = Z_{wN} + f_{w-1}$ The final order occurs at period w and is sufficient to satisfy demand in periods w through N.

$f_{w-1} = Z_{vw-1} + f_{v-1}$ The order prior to the final order occurs in period v and is sufficient to satisfy demand in periods v through $w - 1$.

.
.
.

$f_{u-1} = Z_{1u-1} + f_0$ The first order occurs in period 1 and is sufficient to satisfy demand in periods 1 through $u - 1$.

EXAMPLE 2

An item has a unit purchase cost of $50, an ordering cost per order of $100, and a holding cost fraction per period of 0.02. Determine the order quantities by the Wagner-Whitin algorithm from the demand given below. Assume the initial inventory is zero at the beginning of period 1.

Period	1	2	3	4	5	6
Demand	75	0	33	28	0	10

The total variable cost matrix shown in Table 1 is calculated as follows:

$$Z_{ce} = C + hP \sum_{i=c}^{e} (Q_{ce} - Q_{ci}),$$

$Z_{11} = 100 + 1(75 - 75) = 100,$

$Z_{12} = 100 + 1[(75 - 75) + (75 - 75)] = 100,$

$Z_{13} = 100 + 1[(108 - 75) + (108 - 75) + (108 - 108)] = 166,$

$Z_{14} = 100 + 1[(136 - 75) + (136 - 75)$

$$+ (136 - 108) + (136 - 136)] = 250,$$

$Z_{15} = 100 + 1[(136 - 75) + (136 - 75)$

$$+ (136 - 108) + (136 - 136) + (136 - 136)] = 250,$$

$Z_{16} = 100 + 1[(146 - 75) + (146 - 75) + (146 - 108)$

$$+ (146 - 136) + (146 - 136) + (146 - 146)] = 300,$$

$Z_{22} = 100 + 1[(0 - 0)] = 100,$

$Z_{23} = 100 + 1[(33 - 0) + (33 - 33)] = 133,$

Table 1. Total variable cost matrix Z_{ce}

			Z_{ce}			
c	$e = 1$	2	3	4	5	6
1	100	100	166	250	250	300
2		100	133	189	189	229
3			100	128	128	158
4				100	100	120
5					100	110
6						100

$$Z_{24} = 100 + 1[(61 - 0) + (61 - 33) + (61 - 61)] = 189,$$

$$Z_{25} = 100 + 1[(61 - 0) + (61 - 33)$$
$$+ (61 - 61) + (61 - 61)] = 189,$$

$$Z_{26} = 100 + 1[(71 - 0) + (71 - 33) + (71 - 61)$$
$$+ (71 - 61) + (71 - 71)] = 229,$$

$$Z_{33} = 100 + 1[(33 - 33)] = 100,$$

$$Z_{34} = 100 + 1[(61 - 33) + (61 - 61)] = 128,$$

$$Z_{35} = 100 + 1[(61 - 33) + (61 - 61) + (61 - 61)] = 128,$$

$$Z_{36} = 100 + 1[(71 - 33) + (71 - 61) + (71 - 61) + (71 - 71)] = 158,$$

$$Z_{44} = 100 + 1[(28 - 28)] = 100,$$

$$Z_{45} = 100 + 1[(28 - 28) + (28 - 28)] = 100,$$

$$Z_{46} = 100 + 1[(38 - 28) + (38 - 28) + (38 - 38)] = 120,$$

$$Z_{55} = 100 + 1[(0 - 0)] = 100,$$

$$Z_{56} = 100 + 1[(10 - 0) + (10 - 10)] = 110,$$

$$Z_{66} = 100 + 1[(10 - 10)] = 100.$$

The minimum possible cost in periods 1 through e (f_e), shown in Table 2, is determined as follows:

$$f_e = \text{Min}(Z_{ce} + f_{c-1}),$$

$$f_0 = 0,$$

$$f_1 = \text{Min}(Z_{11} + f_0) = (100 + 0)$$
$$= 100 \quad \text{for} \quad Z_{11} + f_0,$$

$$f_2 = \text{Min}(Z_{12} + f_0, Z_{22} + f_1) = \text{Min}(100 + 0, 100 + 100)$$
$$= 100 \quad \text{for} \quad Z_{12} + f_0,$$

Table 2. Total variable cost alternatives and f_e

c	$e = 1$	2	3	4	5	6
1	100	100	166	250	250	300
2		200	233	289	289	329
3			200	228	228	258 ←
4				266	266	286
5					328	338
6						328
f_e	100	100	166	228	228	258

$$f_3 = \text{Min}(Z_{13} + f_0, Z_{23} + f_1, Z_{33} + f_2) = (166 + 0, 133 + 100, 100 + 100)$$
$$= 166 \quad \text{for} \quad Z_{13} + f_0,$$
$$f_4 = \text{Min}(Z_{14} + f_0, Z_{24} + f_1, Z_{34} + f_2, Z_{44} + f_3)$$
$$= (250 + 0, 189 + 100, 128 + 100, 100 + 166)$$
$$= 228 \quad \text{for} \quad Z_{34} + f_2,$$
$$f_5 = \text{Min}(Z_{15} + f_0, Z_{25} + f_1, Z_{35} + f_2, Z_{45} + f_3, Z_{55} + f_4)$$
$$= (250 + 0, 189 + 100, 128 + 100, 100 + 166, 100 + 228)$$
$$= 228 \quad \text{for} \quad Z_{25} + f_1,$$
$$f_6 = \text{Min}(Z_{16} + f_0, Z_{26} + f_1, Z_{36} + f_2, Z_{46} + f_3, Z_{56} + f_4, Z_{66} + f_5)$$
$$= (300 + 0, 229 + 100, 158 + 100, 120 + 166, 110 + 228, 100 + 228)$$
$$= 258 \quad \text{for} \quad Z_{36} + f_2.$$

In the example $f_6 = f_N$ is the combination of Z_{36} and f_2, so the last order will be placed in period 3 and will satisfy the requirements from periods 3 through 6, or $33 + 28 + 0 + 10 = 71$ units; f_2 is the combination of Z_{12} and f_0, so the order will be placed in period 1 and will satisfy requirements from periods 1 through 2, or $75 + 0 = 75$ units. The optimal order schedule and cumulative variable costs are as follows:

Period	1	2	3	4	5	6
Demand	75	0	33	28	0	10
Order Quantity	75	0	71	0	0	0
Cumulative Var. Cost	100	100	238	248	258	258

SILVER-MEAL ALGORITHM

Edward Silver and Harlan Meal developed a variation of the basic EOQ that approaches the optimality of the Wagner-Whitin algorithm for a given time horizon. This heuristic selects a lot size that includes an integer number of period requirements such that the total relevant costs (TRC) per time period for the duration of the lot size are minimized. The total relevant costs are the ordering and the holding costs. If an order arrives at the beginning of the first period and it covers requirements through the end of the Tth period, the criterion function can be expressed as

$$\frac{\text{TRC}(T)}{T} = \frac{C + \text{total holding costs to the end of period } T}{T}$$

$$= \frac{C + Ph \sum_{k=1}^{T} (k-1) R_k}{T},$$

where

$$C = \text{ordering cost per order,}$$
$$h = \text{holding cost fraction per period,}$$
$$P = \text{unit purchase cost,}$$
$$Ph = \text{holding cost per period,}$$
$$\text{TRC}(T) = \text{total relevant cost over } T \text{ periods}$$
$$T = \text{time supply of the replenishment in periods,}$$
$$R_k = \text{demand rate in period } k,$$
$$\text{TRC}(T)/T = \text{total relevant cost per period based on } T \text{ periods.}$$

The objective is to select T to minimize the total relevant costs per unit time. The heuristic evaluates increasing values of T until[5]

$$\frac{\text{TRC}(T+1)}{T+1} > \frac{\text{TRC}(T)}{T}.$$

When the total relevant cost per unit time starts increasing at $T + 1$, the associated T is selected as the number of periods' supply for the replenishment order. The replenishment quantity Q associated with a particular value of T is

$$Q = \sum_{k=1}^{T} R_k.$$

The Silver-Meal (SM) heuristic guarantees only a local minimum for the current replenishment. It is possible that larger values of T could yield even lower costs per unit time, but the likelihood of improvement in most real cases is small.

The justification for using a less than optimal heuristic is a combination of simplicity and reasonable cost performance. In most cases the average cost penalty is less than 1% from the "optimal" Wagner-Whitin algorithm, and often there is no cost penalty. When the heuristic is tested in a rolling-horizon environment, it may outperform the dynamic programming algorithm. Two situations where the heuristic does not perform well are:

1. when the demand rate decreased rapidly with time over several periods,
2. when there are a large number of periods with zero demand.

EXAMPLE 3

From the data given in Example 2, determine the order quantities by the Silver-Meal heuristic.

[5] The actual Silver-Meal algorithm modifies the expression to $T^2 R_{T+1} > C/Ph + \sum_{k=1}^{T}(k-1)R_k$ and selects the value of T that first satisfies the inequality.

Table 3

Period	T	Demand R_T	Incremental Holding Cost $Ph(T-1)R_T$	Cumulative Holding Cost $Ph\sum_{k=1}^{T}(k-1)R_k$	TRC(T) (C + col. 5)	TRC(T)/T (col. 6/T)
1	1	75	50(0.02)(0)75 = 0.00	$0.00	$100.00	$100.00 ←
2	2	0	50(0.02) (1)0 = 0.00	0.00	100.00	50.00
3	3	33	50(0.02)(2)33 = 66.00	66.00	166.00	55.33 ←
3	1	33	50(0.02)(0)33 = 0.00	0.00	100.00	100.00
4	2	28	50(0.02)(1)28 = 28.00	28.00	128.00	64.00
5	3	0	50(0.02) (2)0 = 0.00	28.00	128.00	42.67
6	4	10	50(0.02)(3)10 = 30.00	58.00	158.00	39.50

Table 3 indicates the computations required to determine the replenishment quantities. The total relevant cost per period decreases from period 1 until it increases in period 3. The initial replenishment in period 1 would be enough units to last through period 2 or 75 + 0 = 75 units. The next replenishment in period 3 would be enough units to last through period 6 or 33 + 28 + 0 + 10 = 71 units. Note that in this situation the Silver-Meal heuristic arrived at the same replenishment decisions as the optimizing Wagner-Whitin algorithm with much less computation. The Silver-Meal heuristic ordering schedule and cumulative variable costs are as follows:

Period	1	2	3	4	5	6
Demand	75	0	33	28	0	10
Order Quantity	75	0	71	0	0	0
Cumulative Variable Cost	100	100	238	248	258	258

PART-PERIOD ALGORITHM

This algorithm selects a number of periods to be covered by the replenishment such that accumulated holdings costs equal the ordering cost. Exact equality is usually not possible because of the discrete nature of requirements, so an order size is increased as long as the accumulated holding costs are less than or equal to the ordering cost. The objective is to determine the lot sizes that include an integer number of period requirements so that

$$Ph\sum_{k=1}^{T}(k-1)R_k = C,$$

$$\sum_{k=1}^{T}(k-1)R_k = \frac{C}{Ph},$$

where

$$C = \text{ordering cost per order,}$$
$$h = \text{holding cost fraction per part-period,}$$
$$Ph = \text{holding cost per part-period,}$$
$$C/Ph = \text{EPP} = \text{economic part-periods,}$$
$$\sum_{k=1}^{T} (k-1) R_k = \text{APP} = \text{accumulated part-periods.}$$

The economic part-periods (EPP) represent a breakeven point that converts ordering cost and holding costs to a part-period measure. The part-period is the period demand times the number of periods inventory will be held beyond the order period. The lot size is sequentially increased by the requirements of successive periods until the APP exceeds the EPP. The initial order is placed in period 1. The next replenishment order is planned for the first period when the APP value exceeds the EPP value. The magnitude of subsequent orders is obtained in a similar manner to the initial order. The replenishment quantity associated with a particular value of T is

$$Q = \sum_{k=1}^{T} R_k.$$

EXAMPLE 4

From the data given in Example 2, determine the order quantities by the part-period algorithm.

Solution:

$$\text{EPP} = \frac{C}{Ph} = \frac{100}{50(0.02)} = 100.$$

Table 4 indicates the computations required to determine the replenishment quantities. In period 4, the APP of 150 exceeds the EPP of 100, so the initial replenishment

Table 4

Period	T	R_T	$(T-1)R_T$	$\text{APP} = \sum_{k=1}^{T}(k-1)R_k$
1	1	75	$0(75) = 0$	$0 < 100 \leftarrow$
2	2	0	$1(0) = 0$	$0 < 100$
3	3	33	$2(33) = 66$	$66 < 100$
4	4	28	$3(28) = 84$	$150 > 100 \leftarrow$
4	1	28	$0(28) = 0$	$0 < 100$
5	2	0	$1(0) = 0$	$0 < 100$
6	3	10	$2(10) = 20$	$20 < 100$

in period 1 would be enough units to last through period 3, or $75 + 0 + 33 = 108$ units. The next replenishment in period 4 would be enough to last through period 6, or $28 + 0 + 10 = 38$ units. The part-period replenishment schedule and cumulative variable costs are as follows:

Period	1	2	3	4	5	6
Demand	75	0	33	28	0	10
Order Quantity	108	0	0	38	0	0
Cumulative Var. Cost	138	166	166	276	286	286

Refinements to the part-period algorithm (PPA) have been developed to improve its performance. These refinements, called *look-ahead* and *look-backward*, can improve performance when there are large requirement variations surrounding the replenishment order periods. However, they require additional computations and do not necessarily result in optimality.[6]

The look-ahead and look-backward features are intended to prevent stock covering peak demands from being carried for extended periods of time, and to avoid orders being keyed to periods with low demands. The adjustments are made only when they improve conditions. The look-ahead test is made first. If it fails, the look-backward test is made. If both tests fail, no additional action is taken and the orders from the part-period algorithm are implemented.

The look-ahead test looks at the periods beyond the tentative order period to see if there are any unusual demands coming. The first order takes place in period 1 and is for T periods of supply. The next order is to be placed in period $T + 1$. If it is moved forward, it will be placed in period $T + 2$ and the initial order will be revised to cover $T + 1$ periods of supply. The steps are as follows:

1. Determine the tentative order period by the part-period algorithm.
2. Look ahead at the demand in the next period:
   a. If the demand in the next period $T + 2$ equals or exceeds the part-period value in the tentative order period $T + 1$, the order period is moved ahead to the next period. Otherwise the tentative order period is accepted. To move the order period ahead, the following condition is necessary:

$$R_{T+2} \geq TR_{T+1}.$$

   b. The look-ahead test is repeated in successive periods until it fails.

The look-backward test is not invoked if the look-ahead test moves the order to a future period. If the look-ahead test does not move the order

---

[6] The part-period algorithm without the look-ahead and look-backward refinements is also termed the least total cost (LTC) approach by some authors.

ahead, the look-backward test is applied as follows:

> Multiply the demand in the tentative order period $T + 1$ by 2. If the demand in period T is larger, the order is moved back one period. Otherwise, the tentative order period is accepted. To move the order period backward, the following condition is necessary:

$$R_T > 2R_{T+1}.$$

Although the look-ahead and look-backward tests are not infallible, they add precision when demand is fluctuating violently.

INCREMENTAL PART-PERIOD ALGORITHM

The part-period algorithm introduced in the previous section increased an order as long as the *accumulated* holding cost was less than or equal to the fixed ordering cost. The incremental part-period (IPP) algorithm increases an order as long as the *incremental* holding cost is less than or equal to the fixed ordering cost. Part-periods are not accumulated, but are stated on an incremental basis. The objective is to determine the lot sizes that include an integer number of period requirements so that

$$Ph(T - 1)R_T = C,$$

$$(T - 1)R_T = \frac{C}{Ph},$$

where

C = ordering cost per order,

h = holding cost fraction per period (part-period),

P = unit purchase cost,

T = number of periods of demand included in a replenishment,

R_T = demand rate in Tth future period,

C/Ph = EPP = economic part-periods,

$(T - 1)R_T$ = IPP = incremental part-periods.

The lot size is sequentially increased by the requirements of successive periods until the IPP exceeds the EPP. The initial order is placed in period 1. The next replenishment order is planned for the first period when the IPP value exceeds the EPP. The magnitudes of subsequent orders are obtained in a similar manner to the initial order.

EXAMPLE 5

From the data given in Example 2, determine the order quantities by the incremental part-period algorithm.

Table 5

Period	T	R_T	IPP $= (T - 1)R_T$
1	1	75	$0(75) = 0 < 100 \leftarrow$
2	2	0	$1(0) = 0 < 100$
3	3	33	$2(33) = 66 < 100$
4	4	28	$3(28) = 84 < 100$
5	5	0	$4(0) = 0 < 100$
6	6	10	$5(10) = 50 < 100$

Solution:

$$\text{EPP} = \frac{C}{Ph} = \frac{100}{50(0.02)} = 100.$$

Table 5 indicates the computations required to determine the replenishment quantities. Since the IPP through six periods never exceeds the EPP of 100, the initial order in period 1 would be enough units to last through period 6, namely, $75 + 0 + 33 + 28 + 0 + 10 = 146$ units. The incremental part-period replenishment schedule and cumulative variable costs are as follows:

Period	1	2	3	4	5	6
Demand	75	0	33	28	0	10
Order Quantity	146	0	0	0	0	0
Cumulative Var. Costs	171	242	280	290	300	300

The virtues of the incremental part-period algorithm are that it is easy to understand and requires fewer calculations than other heuristics such as the Silver-Meal and the part-period algorithms.

EXAMPLE 6

Compare the performance of the discrete lot sizing approaches on the data given in Example 2.

See Table 6 for a comparison of the results from the solutions in Example 2, Example 3, Example 4, and Example 5.

IMPLICATIONS FOR DISCRETE LOT SIZING

All of the approaches in this chapter identify the order receipt points and lot sizes across the planning horizon for a single item. None of the approaches considers the consequences of lot sizing within a multi-item or multilevel planning structure; to be specific, none examines the impact of

Table 6

Period	Demand	Lot Size			
		Wagner-Whitin	Silver-Meal	Part-Period	Incremental Part-Period
1	75	75	75	108	146
2	0	0	0	0	0
3	33	71	71	0	0
4	28	0	0	38	0
5	0	0	0	0	0
6	10	0	0	0	0
Variable cost:		$258	$258	$286	$300

lot sizing at a higher level in a product structure upon lower level items. Although lot sizing generally is considered effective at the end product level and less effective at lower levels, its use at higher levels can have far-reaching effects. For a product with many levels, differing and fluctuating lot sizes at upper levels in the product structure can create difficulties in lot sizing at lower levels. Changes in top levels are transmitted down through the lower ones, producing system nervousness (exaggerated responses at component levels to small changes at parent levels).

In multistage systems (systems where parts and components are dependent upon subassembly and assembly policies and where subassemblies and assemblies are dependent upon end item schedules), the effect of lot sizing policies on the system as a whole should be considered. It is important to determine how different policies perform within the system, based on the costs which result from their use. As discussed here, all of the approaches are myopic in this sense. They consider only one item at a time and ignore any costs associated with dependent (related) items.

Another important consideration in the use of lot sizing techniques is their suitability to dynamic environments. In practice, lot sizing policies are usually made sequentially on a rolling horizon basis. After the end of one period, the demand schedule is updated by deleting the consumed (first) period, adding a new period to the end, and adjusting the schedule to reflect the demands from the period following the deleted period through the appended period. In this manner, the number of time periods in the planning horizon is maintained (fixed) each time the schedule is rolled forward to adjust for the period that has just elapsed. Although lot sizes may be computed over the entire planning horizon, only the most imminent decision is usually implemented. Those decisions appearing later in the schedule remain in the planning phase.

These updates can present a problem. Research indicates that results obtained from static conditions are likely to be spurious in a rolling schedule environment. This is especially true for lot sizing algorithms that are horizon sensitive (those in which a change in the number of periods or the addition of new demand requirements will alter some, if not all, of the ordering decisions). New requirements at the end of the horizon may cause earlier decisions to be revised and new orders added.

The Wagner-Whitin algorithm spans the entire time horizon to determine current planned orders and is sensitive to changes in more distant future periods in the planning horizon. All of the less-than-optimal approaches (except the periodic order quantity, which is insensitive because of the square root function) plan orders considering only the requirements of the immediate future periods (less than the complete planning horizon). Thus they are less sensitive to demand changes in more distant future periods. This myopia is advantageous in reducing instability and is attractive in a rolling schedule environment, where the Wagner-Whitin algorithm ceases to be optimal and other simpler heuristics may outperform it.

The rolling schedule environment is frequently used in MRP systems. The demand (requirements) schedule for an item is the time-phased net requirement. The replenishment schedule derived from the selected lot sizing procedure becomes the planned order receipt schedule for an item. Planned order receipts become planned order releases through offsetting for lead time. As periods are deleted (consumed), the current planned order releases change into scheduled receipts in the periods in which they were shown as planned order receipts. As the schedule is rolled forward, another demand (time-phased net requirement) is appended to the terminal period.

CONCLUSION

Some of the assumptions made in regard to classical inventory models (EOQ, EPQ, and EOI) are inappropriate for demand which varies from period to period. Since demand does not always occur at a constant rate, but can follow a discrete pattern, the indiscriminate use of fixed order sizes can result in larger than necessary inventory costs for these situations. Therefore, several alternative, optimum-seeking approaches for determining lot sizes when the demand rate is not constant have been outlined.

These lot sizing approaches focus on controlling the costs of holding inventory and processing orders. None of the approaches, with the exception of the Wagner-Whitin algorithm, assures an optimal or minimum cost solution for time-varying demand patterns. The more complicated Wagner-Whitin dynamic programming algorithm can minimize cost for a deterministic, fixed horizon demand series. For this reason, it often serves as a benchmark against which to measure the performance of non-optimal but less complex lot sizing approaches. Because the Wagner-Whitin commonly is criticized as being difficult to explain and compute, the various heuristic procedures have been developed and tested against it.

The heuristic approaches are similar in the way they arrive at lot sizing decisions. Each starts with the present period (period 1) and scans each successive period until a stopping criterion is met. Then an order is placed to satisfy requirements up to or through the stopping period. The procedure is then repeated for periods beyond the stopping period. Orders for subsequent periods are planned by reapplying the logic. The ordering cost is charged each time an order is placed, and a holding cost usually is charged for each unit carried forward from the previous period. Costs are controlled within the established criteria, but they are not necessarily minimized.

Lot-for-lot ordering seeks to minimize holding costs by never batching any orders. Orders are simply placed for the exact requirements in each period. The periodic order quantity determines a time period (interval) in which holding costs and ordering costs presumably are minimized. The stopping criterion is based on an integer number of periods, and lot sizes cover the demand which occurs within the time interval. The Silver-Meal heuristic algorithm selects a lot size that includes an integer number of period requirements such that the total relevant costs per time period for the duration of the lot size are minimized. The stopping criterion is based on an increase in the total relevant cost per unit of time. Both the part-period and the incremental part-period method calculate an economic part-periods value that converts ordering and holding costs to a part-period measure. The part-period algorithm bases its stopping criterion on the relationship between accumulated part-periods and the economic part-periods, whereas the incremental part-period algorithm uses the relationship between incremental part-periods and the economic part-periods as its criterion.

All of the lot sizing approaches seek to minimize costs for a single item and do not consider items as part of a multistage inventory system. They do not address the cost consequences of lot sizing for the system as a whole, nor do they consider any workload balances in a multistage system. When other factors are given consideration, some lot sizing policies have more advantages than others. Even though the Wagner-Whitin algorithm can assure optimality in some circumstances, it may not perform as well as simpler techniques in a rolling schedule environment.

QUESTIONS

1. What inventory cost is minimized by lot-for-lot (LFL) ordering?

2. What assumption is made regarding the withdrawal of inventories in the lot sizing techniques described in this chapter?

3. Describe what happens if the demand is zero for an order receipt period when the periodic order quantity model is in effect.

4. State the first step involved in the three-step procedure of the Wagner-Whitin algorithm.

5. In what situations does the Silver-Meal algorithm not perform well?

6. What do the economic part-periods (EPP) represent in the part-period algorithm?

7. When do the look-ahead and look-backward refinements usually improve the simple part-period algorithm?

8. Distinguish between the part-period and the incremental part-period algorithms.

9. When are orders placed in the incremental part-period model?

10. Where is lot sizing thought to be effective in MRP systems?

11. What impact does a nonzero lead time have on the algorithms outlined in this chapter?

12. What does a rolling planning horizon do to the optimality of the Wagner-Whitin algorithm?

13. Are the heuristic algorithms in this chapter desirable in single level or multi-level inventory systems? Why?

PROBLEMS

1. An item has a unit purchase cost of $50, an ordering cost per order of $100, and a holding cost fraction per period of 0.02. Determine the order sizes by the Silver-Meal algorithm using the data below:

Period	1	2	3	4	5	6	7	8	9	10
Demand (units)	10	3	30	100	7	15	80	50	15	0

2. From the information given in Problem 1, determine the order sizes by the part-period algorithm.

3. From the information given in Problem 1, determine the order sizes by the incremental part-period algorithm.

4. From the information given in Problem 1, determine the optimum order sizes by the Wagner-Whitin algorithm.

5. An item has a unit purchase cost of $100, an ordering cost per order of $200, and a holding cost fraction per period of 0.02. Determine the lot sizes by the

periodic order quantity from the data below:

Period	Requirements (units)	Period	Requirements (units)
1	10	7	250
2	10	8	270
3	15	9	230
4	20	10	40
5	70	11	0
6	180	12	10

6. From the information given in Problem 5, determine the lot sizes by the Silver-Meal algorithm.

7. From the information given in Problem 5, determine the lot sizes by the part-period algorithm.

8. From the information given in Problem 5, determine the lot sizes by the incremental part-period algorithm.

9. From the information given in Problem 5, determine the optimum lot sizes by the Wagner-Whitin algorithm.

10. A component has a unit production cost of $200, an ordering cost per order of $300, and a holding cost fraction per period of 0.01. Determine the size of the replenishments by the periodic order quantity from the data below:

Period	Net Requirements (units)	Period	Net Requirements (units)
1	120	7	0
2	50	8	85
3	0	9	205
4	360	10	0
5	70	11	70
6	0	12	145

11. From the information given in Problem 10, calculate the size of the replenishments by the Silver-Meal algorithm.

12. From the information given in Problem 10, calculate the size of the replenishments by the part-period algorithm.

13. From the information given in Problem 10, calculate the size of the replenishments by the incremental part-period algorithm.

14. From the information given in Problem 10, calculate the size of the optimum replenishments by the Wagner-Whitin algorithm.

CASE 1: CASTING A LOT

Mohawk Industries builds transmissions for a large automobile manufacturer. One of its transmission assemblies requires part#HD234, purchased from a supplier within the same industrial park. Because of the close proximity of its supplier, the lead time for part #HD234 is negligible.

The demand for part #HD234 varies according to the orders received from the automobile manufacturer. The requirements schedule for the next ten periods is shown below:

Period	1	2	3	4	5	6	7	8	9	10
Demand	15	35	50	40	150	225	175	70	20	0

This requirements schedule is considered fairly average. Furthermore, the cost of placing an order with the nearby supplier is $100.00, and the inventory holding cost per unit per period is $.50.

Mohawk is in the process of assessing different lot sizing policies. It is interested in several that have been suggested. Before it can decide among them, Mohawk wishes to test each on part #HD234. Those which will be tested include:

  a. lot-for-lot (LFL) ordering,
  b. the periodic order quantity (POQ),
  c. the part-period algorithm (PPA) with and without the look-ahead and look-back (PPA/LALB) refinements,
  d. the incremental part-period algorithm (IPPA).

To assist Mohawk in its examination of the policies, address the following:

  1. Compare the ordering policies and total costs of each by subjecting the requirements schedule given for part #HD234 to each model.
  2. Explain the cost components for each rule. Account for any differences in the costs calculated for the various lot sizing rules.
  3. If any rule performed poorly, explain why.

CASE 2: ROLLING ON

Baby Boomers, Inc. emerged in the early eighties as a successful, rapid-growth enterprise which was then able to capitalize on the innovative ideas of its youthful founders. It now finds itself in a position where its once revolutionary products are part of the status quo and its once burgeoning operations are stunted. In short, Baby Boomers has reached the end of an era and is passing into a more mature phase of its existence.

Revolution having given way to stability, Baby Boomers is preparing itself to age gracefully. One area where impulse and individual discretion are conceding to more established practices is in the inventory control division. Having been rather loosely managed by BB's liberal arts major, the division is in dire need of stricter, more conservative policies. Some of the policies in question are the tenuously set fixed order sizes for items known to follow time-varying demand patterns. Now more sensitized to standard operating practices, the inventory manager is interested in lot sizing algorithms for these items.

Her interest has led her to the belief that lot sizing policies should be appropriately set by intermediate-range planning. She would like to use an 8-period (week) planning horizon to test the performance of three different lot sizing techniques under the same conditions. She intends to simulate three weeks of planning (three separate order schedules) for each technique using the demand data for one particular item. This is to be accomplished by rolling an initial 8-period schedule forward twice (simulating an initial schedule prepared in one week, a second schedule prepared the following week, and a third schedule prepared the third week). The demand data she has available at the start of this project are as follows:

Week	11	12	13	14	15	16	17	18	19	20
Demand	60	40	30	70	50	0	80	70	40	100

She plans to establish an initial schedule for weeks 11–18. This schedule will be rolled forward and augmented with the 40-unit demand in week 19. The augmented schedule will be rolled forward to prepare the third schedule and itself augmented with the 100-unit demand in week 20. In addition to rolling the schedules forward and appending the appropriate data, she wishes to revise the two rolled schedules further to reflect more real-life (changing) conditions. The proposed changes to the rolled schedules are:

1. In the first rolled 8-period schedule (weeks 12–19), the previous demand of 80 units in week 17 will be moved ahead to week 16, leaving the demand in week 17 at zero units.
2. In the second rolled 8-period schedule (weeks 13–20), the zero demand in week 17 will be increased to 60 units because of an additional requirement. Furthermore, the previous demand in week 14 of 70 units will be increased to 100 units.

Whenever the schedule is rolled forward (to enact the passing of one planning period), it is assumed that any order scheduled for the period dropped from the schedule (the first period) is placed. The units included in this order in excess of the demand in the dropped period will be used to reduce the demands in the beginning period(s) of the rolled schedule. In other words, the demand requirements for the first period of the rolled schedule will be adjusted for the available inventory. If the available inventory exceeds the first-period demand, the adjustment process will continue until all the available inventory is consumed.

The three lot sizing techniques to be used in the study are the periodic order quantity (POQ), the incremental part-period algorithm (IPPA), and the Silver-Meal heuristic algorithm. The algorithms will be used to devise the rolling schedules, and the cost of each schedule will be examined. The item used in the analysis has a holding cost fraction per period of 0.03 and a per unit purchase cost of $100.00. Each time BB places an order for the item, a $200.00 cost is assessed. (Assume the lead time on all orders is zero.)

Conduct the study for the inventory manager by completing the following:

1. An initial 8-period schedule (weeks 11–18), a first revision (weeks 12–19) and a second revision for the POQ, the IPPA, and the Silver-Meal heuristic algorithm.
2. Cumulative costs for all of the order schedules.
3. A brief comparative analysis of the results.

MATHEMATICAL ABBREVIATIONS AND SYMBOLS USED IN CHAPTER 4

APP	accumulated part-periods
C	ordering cost per order
EOI	economic order interval in periods
EPP	economic part-periods
f_e	minimum possible cost in periods 1 through e with zero inventory at the end of e
h	holding cost fraction per period (or part-period)
IPP	incremental part-periods
LFL	lot-for-lot
N	number of periods in the time horizon
P	unit purchase cost
POQ	periodic order quantity
Q	lot size in units
Q_{ce}	lot size in units to meet requirements from period c through e
$\overline{R}$	average demand rate per period
R_k	demand rate in period k
T	time supply of the replenishment in number of periods
TRC(T)	total relevant cost over T periods
Z_{ce}	total variable cost of an order received in period c to satisfy requirements through period e

5 Independent Demand Systems: Probabilistic Models

SAFETY STOCK

STATISTICAL CONSIDERATIONS

  Normal Distribution

  Poisson Distribution

  Negative Exponential Distribution

KNOWN STOCKOUT COSTS

  Constant Demand and Constant Lead Time

  Variable Demand and Constant Lead Time

    Backorder Case: Stockout Cost per Unit
    Backorder Case: Stockout Cost per Outage
    Lost Sales Case: Stockout Cost per Unit
    Lost Sales Case: Stockout Cost per Outage

  Constant Demand and Variable Lead Time

  Variable Demand and Variable Lead Time

SERVICE LEVELS

  Service per Order Cycle

  Service per Year

  Fraction of Units Demanded

  Fraction of Operating Days

  Imputed Service Level Stockout Costs

FIXED ORDER INTERVAL SYSTEMS

CONCLUSION

QUESTIONS

PROBLEMS

CASES

MATHEMATICAL ABBREVIATIONS AND SYMBOLS

SUMMARY OF FORMULAS

APPENDIX A: PROBABILITY DISTRIBUTION
  CONVOLUTIONS

APPENDIX B: NORMAL DISTRIBUTION

APPENDIX C: CHI-SQUARE GOODNESS-OF-FIT TEST

APPENDIX D: ORDER QUANTITY AND REORDER
  POINT DEPENDENCE

APPENDIX E: JOINT PROBABILITY DISTRIBUTIONS

In Chapter 4 deterministic models for independent demand systems were introduced. This chapter will deal with the same type of inventory models except that they will be described in probabilistic terms. If demand and lead time are treated as *constants*, they are called deterministic; if they are treated as *random variables*, they are called probabilistic or stochastic. The models in this chapter assume that the average demand remains approximately constant with time and that it is possible to state the probability distribution of the demand. In particular, since the lead time is the usual period of concern, attention is focused on the distribution of demand during the lead time. Lead time demand is a random variable if at least one of its primary components (demand and/or lead time) is a random variable.

Traditional inventory models (economic order quantity and economic production quantity) take no account of risk and uncertainty in their formulation. Some of their common assumptions (limitations) are as follows:

1. The demand is known, uniform, and continuous.
2. The production rate is known, uniform, and continuous.
3. The lead time is known and constant.
4. The order/setup cost is known and constant.
5. The holding cost is known, constant, and linear.
6. There are no resource limitations (dollar limits or space limits).
7. Stockouts are usually not permitted (infinite stockout cost).
8. The cost of the inventory analysis is negligible.

Inventory of independent demand items can be divided into working stock and safety stock. Working stock is what is expected to be used during a given time period. The average working stock is one-half the order quantity (lot size), which may be determined by the EOQ formula or some variant of it. The working stock varies with the square root of annual usage. Safety stock, unlike working stock, does not usually depend on lot sizes. It is not held because an organization expects to use it, but because it might. It is held because an organization believes in the long run it is more efficient (it will generate more revenue or reduce costs). Safety stock is determined *directly* from a forecast. Since forecasts are seldom exact, the safety stock protects against higher than expected demand levels.

SAFETY STOCK

Risk and uncertainty enter the inventory analysis through many variables, but the most prevalent are variations in demand and lead time. Such variations are absorbed by provision for safety stocks, also referred to as buffer stocks or fluctuation stocks. Safety stocks are extra inventory kept on hand as a cushion against stockouts due to random perturbations of nature

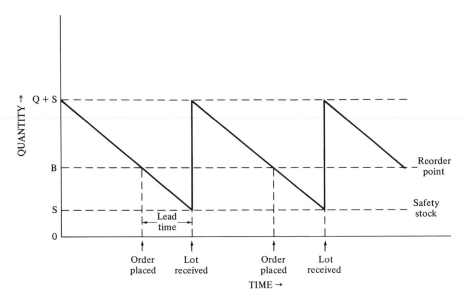

Figure 1. Ideal inventory model.

or the environment. They are needed to cover the demand during the replenishment lead time in case actual demand exceeds expected demand, or the lead time exceeds the expected lead time. Safety stock has two effects on a firm's cost: it decreases the cost of stockouts, but it increases holding costs.

Under the fixed order size system (Q-system), there is a fixed order quantity that is ordered every time the reorder point is reached. Safety stock is needed to protect against a stockout after the reorder point is reached and prior to receipt of an order. This time period during which a stockout could occur is known as the lead time. The fixed order quantity Q and the reorder point B completely define the fixed order size system. Safety stock is an important constituent of the reorder point. In fixed order size systems, the reorder point B is composed of the mean lead time demand $\overline{M}$ plus the safety stock S.

In an ideal inventory system, as shown in Figure 1, the average demand pattern always prevails with no variance. In actual inventory systems, as shown in Figure 2, the pattern of demand over time will be discrete and irregular. Figure 2 shows three cycles of an inventory system. In the first cycle, the demand during the lead time is so great that it results in a stockout. In the second cycle, the demand during the lead time is less than expected, and the replenishment is received before the safety stock is reached. In the third cycle, the demand during the lead time is greater than expected, but the safety stock is sufficient to absorb the demand.

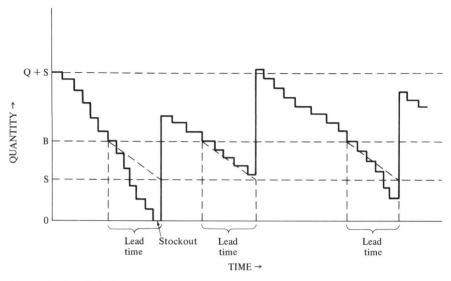

Figure 2. Realistic inventory model.

Safety stocks are needed because forecasts or estimations are less than perfect and suppliers sometimes fail to deliver goods on time. There should be some protection against these two unfavorable contingencies:

1. a higher rate of use than was forecasted,
2. a late delivery of goods.

Either or both of these situations can lead to a stockout in the absence of safety stock. Each additional increase in safety stock provides diminishing (decreasing) benefit. The first unit of stock in excess of expected demand provides the largest increment of protection against stockout; the second unit provides less protection than the first unit, and so on. As the size of the safety stock is increased, the probability of a stockout decreases. At some safety stock level, the cost of holding additional units plus the expected stockout cost is at a minimum. This level is the optimum level, and a net loss results from moving in either direction.

Warehouses and retail outlets maintain safety stocks to be able to supply customers when their rate of demand is irregular or unpredictable. Factories maintain safety stocks to be able to replenish retail and field warehouse stocks when their demand is above average. Extra stock in a semifinished form is carried to normalize production among manufacturing departments when work loads are unbalanced. These additional stocks are often part of a business philosophy of serving customer and internal needs without delay in order to assure the long-run effectiveness of the organization.

It would be fallacious to believe that additional stock is maintained for altruistic purposes. Stockouts result in external and internal shortages. External shortages can result in backorder costs, present profit loss (loss of sales), and future profit loss (goodwill erosion). Internal shortages can result in lost production (idle men and machines) and a delay in a completion date (cost penalty).

The customer's reaction to a stockout (shortage) condition can result in a backorder or a lost sale. With a backorder, the sale is not lost, but only delayed in shipment. Typically, a company will institute an emergency expediting order to get the item, or the customer will be served from the next order of items to arrive. The backorder results in expediting costs, handling costs, and frequently extra shipping and packaging costs. With a lost sale, the customer's demand for the item is lost and presumably filled by a competitor. The stockout cost for a lost sale ranges between the lost profit on the sale to some unspecified loss of goodwill. A goodwill loss can result in a customer not returning to the outlet to purchase other items in the future. A stockout can result in an extremely high cost if it is in a raw material for a production line that must then be shut down. Often, the cost of a stockout for a manufacturing company is so great that none can be tolerated. It can be seen that the stockout cost (whether due to a backorder or to a lost sale) can vary considerably for different items, depending on customer or internal usage.

In many cases, organizations can use countermeasures to prevent, avoid, or mitigate stockouts. Typical countermeasures are expediting, emergency shipping, special handling, rescheduling, overtime, and substitution. The countermeasures have a prevention cost that can be considered a stockout cost (even though the stockout does not occur).

When referring to stockout cost it is necessary to be explicit to avoid confusion. A stockout can result in a backorder or a lost sale. In the backorder case, the customer has his demand satisfied upon initial receipt of an order (e.g., a captive market, as in a factory). In the lost sale case, the demand is not satisfied and it is lost forever. At the retail level, a stockout of an item usually results in a lost sale, since the customer will go elsewhere to make the purchase. At the manufacturing level, a supply bin stockout of an item usually results in a backorder. In the backorder case, the customers are patient; in the lost sales case, the customers are impatient and purchase from other sources.

Just after a shipment (order quantity) is received, the inventory level is high. Just before the next shipment is received, the inventory level is low. The average inventory level on hand just before the receipt of a replenishment order is the safety stock (over many cycles, the inventory level will sometimes be more than the safety stock and sometimes less, but it will average to the safety stock). There is no problem in giving good service just after a shipment arrives, for stocks are high and demand can be filled

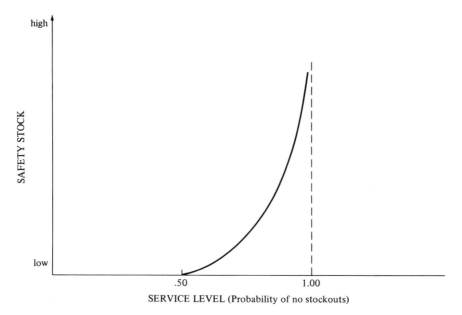

Figure 3. Safety stock vs. service level.

promptly. The only time there is danger of not meeting demand is just before the next shipment is received (during the lead time). Of course, the larger the order quantity, the fewer the annual orders, which means the fewer the opportunities (lead times) for stockouts to occur.

Safety stock can be considered a fairly permanent investment in inventory. On an average, safety stock is always on hand—similar to a fixed asset. In deterministic fixed order size models, the average inventory is approximated as $Q/2$. When safety stock is held, the approximate average inventory becomes $S + Q/2$, where S is the safety stock quantity and Q is the order quantity.

Safety stocks (and thus the reorder point) will be larger for

1. higher stockout costs or service levels,
2. lower holding costs,
3. larger variations in demand,
4. larger variations in lead time.

The relationship between safety stock and service level is shown in Figure 3. It shows safety stock or investment along the vertical axis and service level along the horizontal axis. For a single item, the relationship is straightforward: the curve slopes upward throughout, indicating that additional safety stock (investment) will always increase the level of customer service. The curve gives no indication of what the level of service or investment should be. Management must decide if the additional expenditure is justified in a particular case. As the customer service level is raised by larger safety stock, the investment increases. Thus, the customer service level directly affects safety stock but does not affect working stock. Usually the investment in working stock is determined before considering safety stock.

There is no fixed formula or rigid procedure to follow in determining the safety stock. The calculations of different methods available are based on demand, lead time, and stockout costs. The information known about these variables determines the complexity of the calculations. The safety stock is simply the difference between the stock available for the replenishment period (reorder point) and the average demand during the replenishment period. The reorder point is defined as the stock position at which an order is triggered. In the formulations to be developed in this chapter, it will be assumed that the order quantity can be determined by an economic balance of the relevant inventory costs, but it will be assumed independent of the reorder point.[1]

There are two schools of thought on how to establish safety stocks (and reorder points) for a fixed order size system. The first approach deals with known stockout costs: explicit costs can be allocated to shortages. The second approach deals with unknown stockout costs: management specifies a service level based on some probability distribution of demand during the lead time. Both of these approaches will be outlined and investigated. The remainder of the chapter will emphasize safety stock and reorder point determination. The demand and lead time will be assumed independent and distributed in future time periods with time invariant parameters.

STATISTICAL CONSIDERATIONS

When the demand is probabilistic (not deterministic), rather than minimize cost, it is necessary to minimize the expected cost. If the demand distribution is discrete, the expected cost is obtained by summing the different costs for each strategy weighted (multiplied) by their respective probabilities and then selecting the strategy (demand level) with the lowest expected cost. If the demand distribution is continuous, the minimum expected cost expression is obtained by taking the derivative of expected cost with respect to the variable and then setting it equal to zero.

Two of the best-known and most widely used statistics for describing distributions are the arithmetic mean and the standard deviation. The arithmetic mean is a measure of central tendency, while the standard

[1] See Appendix D for the procedures for obtaining optimality when the order quantity and reorder point are dependent. With dependence, the expressions are cumbersome and iterative. Fortunately, the exact minimum cost solution based on dependence is closely approximated by the simpler solution methods based on independence of the order quantity and reorder point.

deviation is a measure of dispersion of a distribution. The arithmetic mean $\overline{M}$ for a continuous distribution is

$$\overline{M} = \int_0^\infty Mf(M)\, dM = \text{mean lead time demand,}$$

and the standard deviation σ is the square root of the variance,

$$\sigma^2 = \int_0^\infty (M - \overline{M})^2 f(M)\, dM = \text{variance of lead time demand.}$$

For discrete data, the following formulas apply:[2]

$$\overline{M} = \sum_{M=0}^{M_{\max}} MP(M) = \text{mean lead time demand,}$$

$$\sigma^2 = \sum_{M=0}^{M_{\max}} (M - \overline{M})^2 P(M) = \text{variance of lead time demand,}$$

where

$$M = \text{lead time demand in units (a random variable),}$$

$$f(M) = \text{probability density function of lead time demand,}$$

$$\sigma = \text{standard deviation of lead time demand,}$$

$$P(M) = \text{probability of a lead time demand of } M \text{ units,}$$

$$M_{\max} = \text{maximum lead time demand in units.}$$

The probability of a stockout for a given item is simply the probability that the demand during the lead time will exceed the reorder point. When continuous distributions are employed, the stockout probability is the first definite integral of the probability density function of demand during the lead time from the reorder point to infinity, or

$$P(M > B) = \int_B^\infty f(M)\, dM.$$

The expected stockout quantity during the lead time is the second definite integral of the probability density function of demand during the lead time from the reorder point to infinity, or

$$E(M > B) = \int_B^\infty \left[\int_M^\infty f(M)\, dM \right] dM = \int_B^\infty (M - B)f(M)\, dM.$$

[2] For discrete distributions, replace integrals with summations and density functions $f(M)$ with probabilities $P(M)$.

Table 1. Statistical considerations

Variable	Continuous Distributions	Discrete Distributions
Mean lead time demand, $\overline{M}$	$\int_0^\infty Mf(M)\,dM$	$\sum_{M=0}^{M_{max}} MP(M)$
Lead time demand variance, σ^2	$\int_0^\infty (M - \overline{M})^2 f(M)\,dM$	$\sum_{M=0}^{M_{max}} (M - \overline{M})^2 P(M)$
Probability of a stockout, $P(M > B)$	$\int_B^\infty f(M)\,dM$	$\sum_{M=B+1}^{M_{max}} P(M)$
Expected stockout quantity, $E(M > B)$	$\int_B^\infty (M - B)f(M)\,dM$	$\sum_{M=B+1}^{M_{max}} (M - B)P(M)$

For discrete data, the following formulas apply:

$$P(M > B) = \sum_{M=B+1}^{M_{max}} P(M),$$

$$E(M > B) = \sum_{M=B+1}^{M_{max}} (M - B)P(M),$$

where

$P(M > B)$ = probability of a stockout,

B = reorder point in units,

$f(M)$ = probability density function of demand during the lead time,

$E(M > B)$ = expected stockout in units during lead time.

A summary of the relevant statistical measures outlined in this section is contained in Table 1 for both continuous and discrete distributions.

The normal, Poisson, and negative exponential distributions have been found to be of considerable value in describing demand functions. The normal distribution has been found to describe many demand functions at the factory level; the Poisson, at the retail level; and the negative exponential, at the wholesale and retail levels. Of course, these distributions should not be automatically applied to any demand situation. Statistical tests should establish the basis for any standard distribution assumption concerning a demand function.

Standard distributions should not be employed in inventory analysis merely for their computational efficiency. Before any standard distribution is employed, it should be verified by a goodness-of-fit test that the distribution is a reasonable representation for the demand or lead time. One such test is the chi-square test of fit. Appendix C at the end of this chapter outlines the chi-square goodness-of-fit test.

Normal Distribution

When demand is treated as continuous, the most frequently used distribution is the normal (also called the Gaussian) distribution. The normal distribution is easy to work with, and it is well tabulated. More importantly, the normal distribution tends to reasonably approximate phenomena encountered in practice. It has two defining parameters, the mean and standard deviation.

The normal distribution is a symmetrical bell-shaped curve with the three measures of central tendency (mean, median, and mode) equal. To the extent that these three measures of central tendency are the same or nearly identical, a frequency distribution can be approximated as normal. A basis for prediction with a normal distribution is the standard deviation of observations about the measures of central tendency. For a normal distribution 68.27% of all events occur within ± 1 standard deviation, 95.45% occur within ± 2 standard deviations, and 99.73% occur within ± 3 standard deviations of the mean. In inventory analysis, the standard deviation provides a means of estimating the safety stock required to provide a specific degree of protection above the average demand.

The normal distribution can take on an infinite number of symmetrical shapes about its mean, but in all of them demands are equally likely to be above or below the mean. The shape in any individual case is dictated by the standard deviation. For low levels of average demand, the normal distribution is inadequate, since its symmetrical nature would dictate the possibility of negative demand. Since negative demand is impossible, other distributions such as the Poisson are used for low levels of demand.

The general formula for the normal distribution is cumbersome and difficult to use. Fortunately, standardized normal distribution tables have been developed which simplify use. When demand is normally distributed, the reorder point can be obtained from the following formula:

$$B = \overline{M} + S = \overline{M} + Z\sigma = \text{reorder point in units,}$$

where

$\overline{M}$ = average lead time demand in units,

S = safety stock in units,

Z = standard normal deviate,

σ = standard deviation of lead time demand.

The standard deviation is frequently cumbersome to calculate; it is adequately estimated as 1.25 times the mean absolute deviation (MAD) of forecast errors. Further elaboration on the normal distribution can be found at the end of this chapter in Appendix B.

Poisson Distribution

The normal distribution is restrictive because of its symmetrical form. A further disadvantage is that the range of the distribution includes negative values. For items of low demand, the discrete Poisson distribution is a very likely candidate for the demand distribution. The Poisson distribution is defined by a single parameter, the mean. The mean rate of demand can be determined by dividing the total number of units demanded over the relevant historical period by the length of the time interval. The standard deviation of the Poisson distribution is simply the square root of the mean ($\sigma = \sqrt{\overline{M}}$).

The Poisson distribution is not symmetrical with respect to the mean; there are more values to the right of (greater than) the mean than to the left. For this reason, the Poisson distribution is said to be skewed to the right. If average demand is large, the Poisson distribution is indistinguishable from the normal distribution. As a rule of thumb, the normal approximation to the Poisson is usually adequate when the mean is 12 or greater.

The Poisson distribution is not commonly applicable to distributions with mean values above 20. Only slow-moving retail items are commonly described by this distribution. As a general rule, the smaller the mean, the greater the degree of skewness in the distribution. There are instances where demand is sporadic, discontinuous, and not particularly symmetrical. The Poisson distribution can be very helpful when these conditions occur. It is a good fit for small, infrequent demand where the demand rate is fairly constant.

Negative Exponential Distribution

The negative exponential distribution has been found to describe demand for some retail and wholesale situations. This continuous distribution is a single-parameter distribution, being completely defined by its mean. The standard deviation of the negative exponential distribution is the same as its mean ($\sigma = \overline{M}$).

The normal, Poisson, and negative exponential distributions have been reduced to tables, which simplify the solution to inventory problems. Statistical tables will be introduced later in the chapter.

KNOWN STOCKOUT COSTS

Stockout cost is usually the most difficult inventory cost to ascertain. Stockout cost may be due to backorders or lost sales, and it may be expressed on a per unit basis, a per outage basis, or some other basis. The diversity of ways of stating stockout cost adds to the difficulty, which is compounded by uncertainty about the effect of dissatisfied customers' actions on future demand. This section will develop solution techniques for establishing the reorder point and safety stock when stockout costs are known (stockout costs will include backorder cost per unit, backorder cost per outage, lost sales cost per unit, and lost sales cost per outage) and the demand and lead time may be constant or variable.

When demand and lead time are variable, it is necessary to describe the relevant variation in some numerical fashion such as a frequency distribution. Unless dynamic factors are known to exist (trends, seasonals, and cyclics), the variation is assumed static and due to random or chance causes. When a distribution is used to describe demand, it is assumed that trends, seasonals, or cyclic effects are not present or they have been removed by standard statistical techniques. The distribution should contain only random variations. Dynamic variations which are due to nonrandom causes can be treated by adaptive forecasting techniques.

Constant Demand and Constant Lead Time

If demand and lead time are constant, there will be no safety stock, since inventory decisions are made under certainty. Since there is perfect knowledge of demand and lead time, a manager simply plans the inventory level to match demand. Under these conditions, the inventory will be at the zero level when the replenishment order is received. This assumption of perfect knowledge is usually unrealistic. But in certain cases, some products may exhibit a high degree of regularity which permits the deterministic treatment as outlined in Chapter 3. Traditional inventory models frequently assume constant demand and lead time.

Variable Demand and Constant Lead Time

The assumption of constant lead time is frequently realistic for many items. When the variation in lead time is small in relation to the average lead time, probabilistic lead times can be closely approximated by a constant lead time. Also, contractual stipulations can render the lead time nearly certain. When the supply is from an internal source (one department or division supplying items for another department or division of the same organization), the lead time is controllable. Figure 4 exemplifies the variable demand, constant lead time situation.

If an historical distribution of demand is available, the safety stock can be determined by selecting a safety stock level that results in the lowest expected cost. It is easy to determine the safety stock using this method. The objective is to minimize the sum of the cost of holding the safety stock and the cost of the stockouts. As the size of the safety stock increases, the holding costs increase but the stockout costs decrease. As the safety stock decreases, the stockout costs increase but the holding costs decrease.

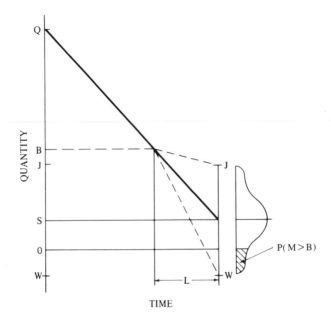

Figure 4. Variable demand and constant lead time.
Key: B = reorder point; Q = order quantity; L = constant lead time; S = safety stock; $B - S$ = expected lead time demand; $B - J$ = minimum lead time demand; $B - W$ = maximum lead time demand; $P(M > B)$ = probability of a stockout.

The danger of a stockout occurs only during the lead time. There are R/Q lead times per year.

Frequently, the demand distribution is expressed on a time basis that is different from the lead time. Under these conditions, it is necessary to modify the demand distribution so it specifies the demand during the lead time. The technique of modifying the demand to allow for varying-length time periods is termed convolution. Probability distribution convolutions are described at the end of this chapter in Appendix A.

Backorder Case: Stockout Cost per Unit

With backorders, there is no loss of sales, since the customer awaits the arrival of the order if stock is not available. The expected safety stock is defined as

$$S = \int_0^\infty (B - M) f(M)\, dM$$

$$= B \int_0^\infty f(M)\, dM - \int_0^\infty M f(M)\, dM = B - \overline{M},$$

where $\overline{M}$ is the expected lead time demand, and the number of backorders per lead time is zero if $M - B \leq 0$ and $M - B$ if $M - B > 0$. The expected number of backorders per lead time is

$$E(M > B) = \int_B^\infty (M - B)f(M)\, dM.$$

The appropriate mathematical notation is as follows for a continuous distribution when the stockout cost is on a per unit basis:

Annual safety stock cost = (holding cost) + (stockout cost),

$$TC_s = SH + \frac{AR}{Q} \int_B^\infty (M - B)f(M)\, dM$$

$$= H(B - \overline{M}) + \frac{AR}{Q} \int_B^\infty (M - B)f(M)\, dM$$

$$= H(B - \overline{M}) + \frac{ARE(M > B)}{Q},$$

where

TC_s = expected annual cost of safety stock,

$B = \overline{M} + S$ = reorder point in units,

S = safety stock in units,

H = holding cost per unit of inventory per year,

A = backordering cost per unit,

R = average annual demand in units,

Q = lot size or order quantity in units,

M = lead time demand in units (a random variable),

$\overline{M}$ = average lead time demand in units,

$f(M)$ = probability density function of lead time demand,

$M - B$ = size of stockout in units.

By taking the derivative of the expected annual cost of safety stock with respect to the reorder point and setting it equal to zero, the following optimizing relationship results:[3]

$$P(M > B) = P(s) = \frac{HQ}{AR} = \text{optimum probability of a stockout.}$$

The above formula can be applied to both discrete and continuous probability distributions of lead time demand. Knowing the probability

---

[3] See L. A. Johnson and D. C. Montgomery, *Operations Research in Production Planning, Scheduling, and Inventory Control*, Wiley, 1974, pp. 59–62, for the mechanics of the derivation. If $HQ/AR > 1$, it indicates the cost of a stockout is so small that it is always desirable to incur backorders.

distribution permits the determination of the value of B which has the minimum expected annual cost. When discrete distributions are employed, the exact optimum stockout probability is frequently unattainable because of the discrete nature of the data. When the optimum stockout probability cannot be attained, the next lower attainable stockout probability is selected. A simple example will illustrate the procedure.

EXAMPLE 1

What is the optimal reorder point for the inventory problem specified below and in Table 2?

$$R = 1800 \text{ units/year,}$$
$$C = \$30.00 \text{ per order,}$$
$$F = 15\%,$$
$$P = \$2.00/\text{unit,}$$
$$A = \$1.00 \text{ per unit backordered.}$$

To solve the above problem, it is necessary to determine the economic order quantity and then the optimum probability of a stockout:

$$Q_0 = \sqrt{\frac{2CR}{PF}} = \sqrt{\frac{2(30)1800}{2(0.15)}} = 600 \text{ units,}$$

$$P(s) = \frac{HQ}{AR} = \frac{0.30(600)}{1(1800)} = 0.10.$$

By consulting the last column in Table 2 for $P(s) = 0.10$, we see the computed

Table 2

Lead Time Demand M	Probability $P(M)$	Probability of Stockout $P(M > B)$
48	0.02	0.98
49	0.03	0.95
50	0.06	0.89
51	0.07	0.82
52	0.20	0.62
53	0.24	0.38
54	0.20	0.18
55	0.07	0.11
56	0.06	0.05 ←
57	0.03	0.02
58	0.02	0.00
	1.00	

value is between 0.05 and 0.11. Selecting the smaller value (0.05), the reorder point is 56 units. The fixed order size system would function with $Q = 600$ units and $B = 56$ units.

Backorder Case: Stockout Cost per Outage

The formulations previously developed for the backorder case have been for determining the safety stock when the stockout cost is on a per unit basis. The stockout cost may also be on an outage basis. A stockout cost per outage is a fixed amount and can occur at most once during a replenishment cycle. Since a stockout occasion can occur only once per lead time period, the stockout cost is independent of the magnitude or duration of the stockout. One possible interpretation would be the cost of the countervailing action necessary to avert the impending shortage. The number of times the organization is exposed to a stockout of an item is equal to the number of times an order is placed. In an annual period there are R/Q opportunities for a stockout. When the stockout cost is a constant amount for each outage without reference to the number of units out of stock, the following formula applies for a continuous distribution:

$$\text{annual cost of safety stock} = (\text{holding cost}) + (\text{stockout cost}),$$

$$TC_s = SH + G\frac{R}{Q}\int_B^\infty f(M)\, dM$$

$$= H(B - \overline{M}) + \frac{GRP(M > B)}{Q},$$

where

$\quad TC_s$ = expected annual cost of safety stock,

$\quad B = M + \overline{S}$ = reorder point in units,

$\quad S$ = safety stock in units,

$\quad H$ = holding or carrying cost per unit per year,

$\quad G$ = backordering cost per outage,

$\quad R$ = average annual demand in units,

$\quad Q$ = lot size or order quantity in units,

$\quad f(M)$ = probability density function of lead time demand,

$\quad \overline{M}$ = average lead time demand in units.

If the derivative of the expected annual cost of safety stock with respect to the reorder point is taken and set equal to zero, the following relationship is obtained:[4]

$$f(B) = \frac{HQ}{GR}.$$

The above optimum relationship was developed for a continuous distribution, but frequently only integer values of inventory are possible. When the optimum reorder point lies between two integer values, select the integer with the larger $f(B)$.

For the standard normal distribution the optimum reorder point is *not* obtained from the above formula, since the ordinate $f(B)$ undergoes a change of scale when it is transformed to the standard normal distribution. Thus, if we are to find where $f(B) = 0.05$, we must find where the standard normal distribution has an ordinate of 0.05σ. The standard normal deviate Z for the optimum stockout probability can be obtained directly from the standard normal table if $\sigma f(B)$ is known (see Table 3).

If the demand follows a normal distribution, the optimizing safety stock can be determined from Table 3 and the following formulas:

$$Z = \frac{B - \overline{M}}{\sigma} = \frac{B - \overline{DL}}{\sigma_D \sqrt{L}} = \frac{S}{\sigma_D \sqrt{L}},$$

$$S = Z\sigma = Z\sigma_D \sqrt{L},$$

where

Z = standard normal deviate,

$B = \overline{DL} + S$ = reorder point in units,

$\overline{M} = \overline{DL}$ = average lead time demand,

σ = standard deviation of lead time demand,

L = lead time,

S = safety stock in units,

σ_D = standard deviation of demand.

EXAMPLE 2

Weekly demand is normally distributed with a mean of 20 units and a standard deviation of 4. What is the optimum reorder point if holding costs are $5.00 per year, the backorder cost is $10.00 per outage, the order quantity is 26 units, and the lead time is 1 week?

$$\sigma f(B) = \frac{\sigma HQ}{GR} = \frac{4(5)26}{10(52)20} = 0.05.$$

[4] See Martin K. Starr and David W. Miller, *Inventory Control: Theory and Practice*, Englewood Cliffs, NJ: Prentice-Hall, 1962, p. 63 for the mechanics of the derivation.

Table 3. Standard normal distribution

Standard Normal Deviate Z	Probability of a Stockout $1 - F(Z)$	Ordinate $f(Z)$	Partial Expectation $E(Z)$
− 4.00	.9999	.0001	
.00	.5000	.3989	.3989
.05	.4801	.3984	.3744
.10	.4602	.3969	.3509
.15	.4404	.3945	.3284
.20	.4207	.3910	.3069
.25	.4013	.3867	.2863
.30	.3821	.3814	.2668
.35	.3632	.3752	.2481
.40	.3446	.3683	.2304
.45	.3264	.3605	.2137
.50	.3086	.3521	.1978
.55	.2912	.3429	.1828
.60	.2743	.3332	.1687
.65	.2579	.3229	.1554
.70	.2420	.3123	.1429
.75	.2267	.3011	.1312
.80	.2119	.2897	.1202
.85	.1977	.2780	.1100
.90	.1841	.2661	.1004
.95	.1711	.2541	.0916
1.00	.1587	.2420	.0833
1.05	.1469	.2300	.0757
1.10	.1357	.2179	.0686
1.15	.1251	.2059	.0621
1.20	.1151	.1942	.0561
1.25	.1057	.1826	.0506
1.30	.0968	.1714	.0455
1.35	.0886	.1604	.0409
1.40	.0808	.1497	.0367
1.45	.0736	.1394	.0328
1.50	.0669	.1295	.0293
1.55	.0606	.1200	.0261
1.60	.0548	.1109	.0232
1.65	.0495	.1023	.0206

(continued)

Table 3 *(continued)*

Standard Normal Deviate Z	Probability of a Stockout $1 - F(Z)$	Ordinate $f(Z)$	Partial Expectation $E(Z)$
1.70	.0446	.0940	.0183
1.75	.0401	.0863	.0162
1.80	.0360	.0790	.0143
1.85	.0322	.0721	.0126
1.90	.0288	.0656	.0111
1.95	.0256	.0596	.0097
2.00	.0228	.0540	.0085
2.05	.0202	.0488	.0074
2.10	.0179	.0440	.0065
2.15	.0158	.0396	.0056
2.20	.0140	.0355	.0049
2.25	.0122	.0317	.0042
2.30	.0107	.0283	.0037
2.35	.0094	.0252	.0032
2.40	.0082	.0224	.0027
2.45	.0071	.0198	.0023
2.50	.0062	.0175	.0020
2.55	.0054	.0154	.0017
2.60	.0047	.0136	.0015
2.65	.0040	.0119	.0012
2.70	.0035	.0104	.0011
2.75	.0030	.0091	.0009
2.80	.0026	.0079	.0008
2.85	.0022	.0069	.0006
2.90	.0019	.0059	.0005
2.95	.0016	.0051	.00045
3.00	.0015	.0044	.00038
3.10	.0010	.0033	.00027
3.20	.0007	.0024	.00018
3.30	.0005	.0017	.00013
3.40	.0004	.0012	.00009
3.50	.0003	.0009	.00006
3.60	.0002	.0006	.00004
3.80	.0001	.0003	.00002
4.00	.00003	.0001	.00001

$$Z = \frac{B - \overline{M}}{\sigma}, \qquad t = \frac{M - \overline{M}}{\sigma},$$

$$f(Z) = \frac{e^{-Z^2/2}}{\sqrt{2\pi}} = \sigma f(B), \qquad F(Z) = \int_{-\infty}^{Z} f(t)\, dt = 1 - P(M > B),$$

$$E(Z) = \int_{Z}^{\infty} (t - Z) f(t)\, dt = \frac{E(M > B)}{\sigma}.$$

From Table 3 an ordinate of 0.05 gives a Z of 2.03. Thus

$$S = Z\sigma = 2.03(4) = 8.12, \text{ or } 8 \text{ units,}$$

$$B = \overline{M} + S = 20 + 8 = 28 \text{ units.}$$

The optimum safety stock is 8 units, with a reorder point of 28 units.

If demand follows a Poisson distribution, the optimizing inventory policy can be obtained from Poisson tables such as Table 4. A simple example can best illustrate the use of the Poisson table.

Table 4. Poisson distribution

Reorder Point B^b	$\overline{M}^c =$ 2	3	4	5	6	7	8	9	10	11	12
2	.271										
3	.180	.224									
4	.090	.168	.195								
5	.036	.101	.156	.176							
6	.012	.050	.104	.146	.161						
7	.003	.022	.059	.104	.138	.149					
8	.001	.008	.029	.065	.103	.130	.139				
9		.003	.013	.036	.069	.101	.124	.131			
10		.001	.005	.018	.041	.071	.099	.119	.125		
11			.002	.008	.023	.045	.072	.097	.114	.119	
12			.001	.003	.011	.026	.048	.073	.095	.109	.114
13				.001	.005	.014	.029	.050	.073	.093	.106
14					.002	.007	.017	.032	.052	.073	.091
15					.001	.003	.009	.019	.035	.053	.072
16						.001	.005	.011	.022	.037	.054
17							.002	.006	.013	.024	.038
18							.001	.003	.007	.015	.026
19								.001	.004	.008	.016
20									.002	.005	.010
21									.001	.002	.006
22										.001	.003
23											.002
24											.001

[a] The fractions in the table are the probabilities associated with exactly B demands during a lead time with an average demand of $\overline{M}$ units.

[b] B = reorder point = $\overline{D}L + S = M_a$.

[c] $\overline{M}$ = average lead time demand = $\overline{D}L$.

EXAMPLE 3

The weekly demand for an item is Poisson distributed with a mean of 5 units. What is the optimum reorder point level if holding costs are $5.00 per unit per year, the backorder cost is $5.00 per outage, the lead time is 1 week, and the order quantity is 13 units?

$$R = \bar{x} + z(s)$$

$$f(B) = \frac{HQ}{GR} = \frac{5(13)}{5(52)5} = .05.$$

In the Poisson table for a lead time demand of 5 units, .05 is found between .036 and .065. Selecting the larger $f(B)$, the optimal reorder point is 8 units and the safety stock is 3 units.

Lost Sales Case: Stockout Cost per Unit

The treatment of lost sales does not differ substantially from that of the backorder case. With lost sales, all stockouts (shortages) are lost and not recovered. The average number of annual cycles is no longer R/Q, but is $R/[Q + E(M > B)]$, where $E(M > B)$ is the expected stockout quantity per cycle. Usually $E(M > B)$ is a small fraction of the quantity, so it will be assumed that the average number of annual cycles is still R/Q.

The only difference between the lost sales case and the backorder case is in the safety stock expression. The expected amount of safety stock on hand when a new order arrives has previously been established as

$$S = \int_0^\infty (B - M)f(M)\, dM = B - \overline{M};$$

however, since all stockouts are lost, the safety stock is zero whenever $M \geq B$, and the expression can be rewritten as

$$
\begin{aligned}
S &= \int_0^B (B - M)f(M)\, dM \\
&= \int_0^\infty (B - M)f(M)\, dM - \int_B^\infty (B - M)f(M)\, dM \\
&= B\int_0^\infty f(M)\, dM - \int_0^\infty Mf(M)\, dM - \int_B^\infty (B - M)f(M)\, dM \\
&= B - \overline{M} + \int_B^\infty (M - B)f(M)\, dM.
\end{aligned}
$$

Note that in the backordering case (no lost sales), the safety stock was simply $B - \overline{M}$, or the reorder point minus the average lead time demand. In the lost sales case, the safety stock is greater than $B - \overline{M}$ by the expected number of lost sales for each cycle. The expected number of lost sales per cycle is precisely the same as the expected number of backorders per cycle in the previous analysis. The expected number of lost sales per lead time is

$$E(M > B) = \int_B^\infty (M - B)f(M)\, dM.$$

The appropriate mathematical notation is as follows for a continuous distribution with stockout cost on a per unit basis:

Annual cost of safety stock = (holding cost) + (stockout cost),

$$TC_s = SH + \frac{AR}{Q} \int_B^\infty (M - B)f(M)\, dM$$

$$= H(B - \overline{M}) + \left(\frac{AR}{Q} + H\right)\int_B^\infty (M - B)f(M)\, dM,$$

$$TC_s = H(B - \overline{M}) + \left(\frac{AR}{Q} + H\right)E(M > B),$$

where

TC_s = expected annual cost of safety stock,

S = safety stock in units,

B = reorder point in units,

H = holding cost per unit of inventory per year,

A = lost sales cost per unit,

R = average annual demand in units,

Q = order quantity in units,

M = lead time demand in units (a random variable),

$\overline{M}$ = average lead time demand in units,

$f(M)$ = probability density function of lead time demand,

$M - B$ = size of stockout in units.

By taking the derivative of the expected annual safety stock cost with respect to the reorder point and setting it equal to zero, the following relationship results:[5]

$$P(M > B) = P(s) = \frac{HQ}{AR + HQ}.$$

The above formula gives the optimum probability of a stockout. It can be applied to both discrete and continuous probability distributions of lead

---

[5] See Lynwood A. Johnson and Douglas C. Montgomery, *Operations Research in Production Planning, Scheduling and Inventory Control*, New York: John Wiley and Sons, 1974, pp. 64–65, for the mechanics of the derivation.

time demand. Knowing the probability distribution permits the determination of the value of B which has the minimum expected cost.

EXAMPLE 4

An organization orders an item in lots of 1000 units for which it has a 5000 unit yearly demand. The holding cost per unit per year is $10, and the lost sales cost per unit is $50. Determine the minimum cost reorder point from the demand history in Table 5 during a constant lead time period.

$$P(s) = \frac{HQ}{AR + HQ} = \frac{10(1000)}{50(5000) + 10(1000)} = 0.038.$$

The optimum probability of a stockout is 0.038, which is between the probabilities of 0.10 and 0.03 associated with 350 and 400 units. The reorder point should be set at 400 units.

Table 5

Demand M	Demand Probability $P(M)$	Probability of Stockout $P(M > B)$
150	.01	.99
200	.04	.95
250	.21	.74
300	.55	.19
350	.09	.10
400	.07	.03 ←
450	.03	.00

Lost Sales Case: Stockout Cost per Outage

The appropriate mathematical notation for a continuous distribution with stockout cost on an outage basis is

$$TC_s = SH + \frac{GR}{Q} \int_B^\infty f(M)\, dM,$$

$$TC_s = H(B - \overline{M}) + H \int_B^\infty (M - B) f(M)\, dM + \frac{GR}{Q} \int_B^\infty f(M)\, dM,$$

$$TC_s = H(B - \overline{M}) + HE(M > B) + \frac{GRP(M > B)}{Q},$$

where G is the lost sales cost per outage. To minimize the above expression, the derivative of the expected annual safety stock cost with respect to B is set equal to zero:

$$\frac{d\,\mathrm{TC}_s}{dB} = 0 = H - HP(M > B) - \frac{GR}{Q}f(B),$$

$$\frac{f(B)}{1 - P(M > B)} = \frac{HQ}{GR}.$$

The above relationship is cumbersome to use except for tabulated distributions such as the normal and Poisson, where the ordinate $f(B)$ is divided by the cumulative distribution function $F(B) = 1 - P(M > B)$. Because of the infrequent application of the lost sales case with stockout cost per outage, no further elaboration is provided.

Constant Demand and Variable Lead Time

When the lead time is variable, it is possible to establish the reorder point in terms of the minimum lead time, average lead time, or maximum lead time. With respect to the minimum or maximum limits, the reorder points would be substantially different. A reorder point based on the minimum

Figure 5. Constant demand and variable lead time.
Key: Q = order quantity; B = reorder point; S = safety stock; L_m = maximum lead time; $\overline{L}$ = expected lead time; $P(M > B)$ = probability of a stockout; $B - S$ = expected lead time demand.

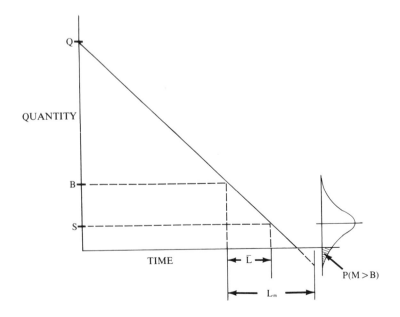

lead time would tend to provide inadequate protection, and one based on the maximum lead time would result in excessive stock levels. If the impact of a variable lead time is not evaluated statistically, the most common practice is to base the reorder point on the average lead time. If substantial variation in lead time is experienced, a more formal statistical analysis is warranted.

When the demand is constant and the lead time is variable, the solution techniques are similar to the variable demand, constant lead time case. The basic difference is that the demand during the lead time is obtained by multiplying the constant demand by the frequency distribution for the lead time. The mathematical formulations and computations are similar. Figure 5 exemplifies the constant demand, variable lead time situation.

EXAMPLE 5

An organization has a yearly demand of 260 units for a product purchased in lots of 25 units. The weekly demand is constant at 5 units. The holding cost per year is $10, and the backorder cost per unit is $10. What is the optimum reorder point if the weekly lead time is defined by the distribution shown in Table 6?

Table 6

Lead Time L	Probability $P(L)$
3	0.25
4	0.35
5	0.25
6	0.10
7	0.05
	1.00

Table 7

Lead Time Demand M	Probability $P(M)$	$MP(M)$	Probability of Stockout $P(M > B)$
15	0.25	3.75	0.75
20	0.35	7.00	0.40
25	0.25	6.25	0.15
30	0.10	3.00	0.05 ←
35	0.05	1.75	0.00
	1.00	$\overline{M} = 21.75$	

The optimum stockout probability for backordering with stockout cost on a per unit basis is obtained as follows (see Table 7):

$$P(s) = \frac{HQ}{AR} = \frac{10(25)}{10(260)} = 0.096.$$

The optimum reorder point is associated with a stockout probability of 0.096, which is between the probabilities 0.15 and 0.05 associated with demand levels of 25 and 30. The optimum reorder point is 30 units, which results in a safety stock of 8 units.

If the lead time follows a normal distribution, the optimizing reorder point can be determined from Table 3 and the following formulation:

$$B = \overline{M} + Z\sigma$$
$$= D\overline{L} + ZD\sigma_L,$$

where

D = constant demand rate per day,

σ = standard deviation of demand during lead time,

σ_L = standard deviation of lead time,

$\overline{L}$ = average lead time in days.

It is desirable for an organization to have short average lead times and consistent lead times. Both conditions permit safety stock levels to be at a minimum.

Variable Demand and Variable Lead Time

When both demand and lead time are variable, there is an increase in problem complexity. As in the previous sections, however, the objective is to set the reorder point at its lowest expected cost.

It is in fact rare to find a situation in practice where the lead time is known exactly. The factors that make up the lead time are subject to random variation, so that lead time is better described by a probability distribution than by a point estimate. In the case where both demand and lead time uncertainties are accounted for simultaneously, a joint probability distribution can be created that gives the probabilities for various combinations of demand level and lead time length. The range of the joint probability distribution is from the level indicated by the product of the smallest demand and the shortest lead time to the level indicated by the product of the largest demand and the largest lead time. The joint probability distribution is then used with the formulas developed in the previous

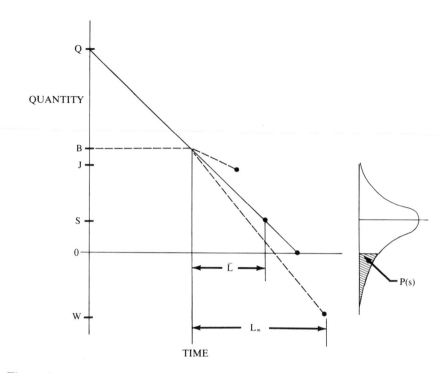

Figure 6. Variable demand and variable lead time.
Key: Q = order quantity; B = reorder point; S = safety stock; L_m = maximum lead time; $\overline{L}$ = expected lead time; $P(s)$ = probability of a stockout; $B - S$ = expected lead time demand; $B - W$ = maximum lead time demand; $B - J$ = minimum lead time demand.

section for the lead time demand. To deal with the joint probability approach in a rigorous mathematical manner is extremely difficult, and consequently, only models of limited applicability have been developed. See Appendix E at the end of this chapter for further elaboration on the analytical joint probability approach. Figure 6 exemplifies the variable demand, variable lead time situation.

Where the demand and lead time distributions are independent, the mean and variance of the demand during the lead time are given by[6]

$$\overline{M} = \overline{D}\overline{L},$$

$$\sigma^2 = \overline{L}\sigma_D^2 + \overline{D}^2\sigma_L^2,$$

[6]See Robert G. Brown, *Smoothing, Forecasting, and Prediction of Discrete Time Series*, Prentice-Hall, 1963, pp. 366–367.

Table 8. Fixed order size system formulas (deterministic case)

	Stockout Cost per Unit	
Stockout Case[a]	Economic Order Quantity Q_0	Reorder Point B
No stockouts permitted[b]	$\sqrt{\dfrac{2CR}{H}}$	RL
Backordering	$\sqrt{\dfrac{2CR}{H}}\sqrt{\dfrac{H+K}{K}}$	$RL - (Q - V)$
Lost sales	$-^c$	$-^c$

[a] Symbols: H = holding cost per unit per year; R = average annual demand in units; C = order cost per order; K = backorder cost per unit per year; L = lead time in years; V = maximum inventory level in units; $Q - V$ = number of backordered units.

[b] When no stockouts are permitted, the stockout cost is infinite; when stockouts are permitted, the stockout cost is finite.

[c] With a deterministic fixed order size system, no lost sales will occur, since the demand is known and can be satisfied.

where

$$\overline{L} = \text{average lead time length in days,}$$

$$\overline{D} = \text{average demand per day,}$$

$$\sigma_D = \text{standard deviation of demand distribution,}$$

$$\sigma_L = \text{standard deviation of lead time distribution,}$$

$$\sigma = \text{standard deviation of demand during lead time,}$$

$$\overline{DL} = \text{average demand during lead time.}$$

If the demand and lead time distributions are not independent, the mean and variance of the demand during the lead time are given by

$$\overline{M} = \overline{DL},$$
$$\sigma^2 = \overline{L}^2\sigma_D^2 + \overline{D}^2\sigma_L^2 + \sigma_D\sigma_L.$$

If it is not desirable to use the analytical joint probability approach, an equally appropriate approach is Monte Carlo simulation.[7] The Monte Carlo method approximates the solution to the problem by sampling from a random process. Monte Carlo simulation will be outlined in a subsequent chapter.

In summary, for fixed order size systems with known stockout costs, a comparison can be made between deterministic and probabilistic formulas.

---

[7] See Claude McMillan and Richard F. Gonzales, *Systems Analysis: A Computer Approach to Decision Models*, Homewood, IL: Richard D. Irwin, 1968, Chapter 7, for the analytical and Monte Carlo simulation approaches to establishing joint distributions.

Table 9. Fixed order size system formulas (probabilistic case)

Stockout Case	Economic Order Quantity $Q_0{}^a$		Reorder Point B^b	
			Known Stockout Cost	
	Stockout Cost per Unit	Stockout Cost per Outage	Stockout Cost per Unit	Stockout Cost per Outage^c
Backordering	$\sqrt{\dfrac{2CR}{H}}$	$\sqrt{\dfrac{2CR}{H}}$	$P(M > B) = \dfrac{HQ}{AR}$	$f(B) = \dfrac{HQ}{GR}$
Lost sales	$\sqrt{\dfrac{2CR}{H}}$	$\sqrt{\dfrac{2CR}{H}}$	$P(M > B) = \dfrac{HQ}{AR + HQ}$	$\dfrac{f(B)}{1 - P(M > B)} = \dfrac{HQ}{GR}$

^{a}It is assumed that the deterministic EOQ is an adequate approximation because of its insensitivity. See Appendix D for more exact mathematical relationships without the deterministic assumption.

^{b}The formulas in the table give the optimum reorder point for the appropriate lead time demand distribution.

^{c}For the standard normal distribution, the ordinate of the distribution is $\sigma f(B)$.

For deterministic systems, the demand and lead time are constant. The order quantity and reorder point formulas for deterministic systems are contained in Table 8. For probabilistic systems demand and lead time can either or both be variable. The order quantity and reorder point formulas for probabilistic systems are contained in Table 9.

SERVICE LEVELS

Perhaps the most common situation is when an organization does not know its stockout costs or feels very uneasy about estimating them. Under these conditions, it is common for management to set service levels from which reorder points can be ascertained. A service level indicates the ability to meet customer demands from stock.

There are several ways to measure a service level. It can be computed on units, dollars, transactions, or orders. It is frequently defined for some specified time period when orders are normally filled from stock. It may be specified in general as the percentage of demand filled "on time," that is, within a specified time period after receipt of the customer's order. No one service level measure will be appropriate for all the items in inventory. Different levels of control may be desirable for different classes of inventory items.

The establishment of service levels is a subjective management judgment that is based on convenience rather than scientific justification. The choice by management of a service level implies a cost attributed intuitively or indirectly to service failure.

If a customer always receives his order when demanded, the service level is 100%. Anything less than 100% means some disservice or stockout. The service level and the stockout level sum to 100%. Not only is it extremely difficult to guarantee that demand will always be satisfied, but also it is likely that such a guarantee will be far too costly. A policy of never having a stockout is generally not economic. The principle of diminishing returns applies. As the service level approaches 100%, the investment in safety stock often increases drastically. It may not cost much to increase from 85 to 90%, but going to 99% may be prohibitively expensive. Thus, most organizations consider a "reasonable" number of stockouts acceptable because of the high cost of trying to eliminate them altogether.

There are environments where service levels at or near 100% are necessary. In manufacturing organizations failure to provide a needed part can bring a production line to a halt. Inventory in this environment is better suited to an MRP system than to a fixed order size system.

The service level takes on different meanings depending upon how it is stated as a decision criterion. Four commonly used service levels are:

1. frequency of service per order cycle,
2. frequency of service per year,
3. fraction of units demanded,
4. fraction of operating days.

The reorder points or safety stocks developed under the different service concepts will be different. The selection of the type and level of service is a management policy decision.

Service per Order Cycle

A service level based on frequency of service per order cycle will indicate the probability of not running out of stock during the replenishment (lead time) period. This approach does not concern itself with how large the shortage is, but with how often it can occur during the lead time (order cycle). It is defined as the fraction of replenishment cycles without depletion of stock:

service level fraction per cycle

$$= 1 - \frac{\text{number of order periods with a stockout}}{\text{total number of order periods}}$$

$$= 1 - P(M > B),$$

$$P(M > B) = 1 - (\text{service level fraction per cycle})$$

$$= \frac{\text{number of order periods with a stockout}}{\text{total number of order periods}}.$$

The $P(M > B)$ is the stockout level fraction per order cycle, or the probability of at least one stockout while awaiting a supplier's delivery. It is also a measure of the fraction of lead time periods during which the demand will exceed the reorder point. The magnitude of the stockout is ignored with this approach.

The safety stock is determined as follows when a service per order cycle is adopted:

$$\text{safety stock} = S = M_a - \overline{M} = M_a - \overline{D}L,$$

where

$M_a = B = $ lead time demand at acceptable service level in units,

$\overline{M} = $ average lead time demand in units,

$L = $ constant lead time in days,

$\overline{D} = $ average daily demand in units.

EXAMPLE 6

What should be the order quantity and reorder point for the inventory problem specified below and in Table 10? What is the expected stockout quantity per cycle?

$$\text{Stockout level fraction per order cycle} = 0.125,$$
$$R = 18{,}000 \text{ units/year,}$$
$$C = \$200 \text{ per order,}$$
$$H = \$5 \text{ per unit per year,}$$
$$L = 1 \text{ day.}$$

Solution:

$$Q_0 = \sqrt{\frac{2CR}{H}} = \sqrt{\frac{2(200)18{,}000}{5}} = 1200 \text{ units,}$$

$$\text{average demand} = \overline{M} = \sum MP(M) = 60 \text{ units.}$$

Table 10

Lead Time Demand in Units, M	Probability $P(M)$	$MP(M)$	Probability of Stockout $P(M > B)$
30	0.025	0.75	0.975
40	0.100	4.00	0.875
50	0.200	10.00	0.675
60	0.350	21.00	0.325
70	0.200	14.00	0.125 ←
80	0.100	8.00	0.025
90	0.025	2.25	0
	1.000	60.00	

Consulting Table 10 for $P(M > B) = 0.125$, we obtain

$$M_a = B = 70 \text{ units},$$

$$\text{safety stock} = S = M_a - \overline{M} = 70 - 60 = 10 \text{ units}.$$

The order quantity would be 1200 units and the reorder point 70 units. Then

$$
\begin{aligned}
E(M > B) &= \sum_{70}^{90} (M - B) P(M) \\
&= (70 - 70)(0.20) + (80 - 70)(0.10) + (90 - 70)(0.025) \\
&= 1.50 \text{ units}.
\end{aligned}
$$

The expected stockout quantity per cycle is 1.50 units. The expected stockout quantity per year is $E(M > B) R/Q = 1.50\,(18{,}000/1200) = 22.50$ units.

EXAMPLE 7

From the information given in Example 6, what would be the reorder point under the conservative method (100% service level)?

$$S = M_{max} - \overline{M} = 90 - 60 = 30 \text{ units},$$

$$B = M_{max} = 90.$$

Reorder point determination can be simplified considerably if the demand follows some known distribution such as the normal, Poisson, or negative exponential. Since these distributions have no upper bound, the 100% service level or conservative method cannot be used with them. The stockout service level can be readily used with a standard distribution.

The normal distribution is completely defined by its mean $\overline{D}$ and standard deviation σ_D. A service level of 95% indicates that you will be out of stock 5% of the cycles. Table 11 indicates how the demand at an acceptable service level is obtained when the normal distribution applies.

Table 11. Standard normal distribution

Reorder Point $M_a = B$	Probability of Stockout, $P(M > B)$
$\overline{D}L + 3.09\sigma_D\sqrt{L}$	.001
$\overline{D}L + 2.58\sigma_D\sqrt{L}$	.005
$\overline{D}L + 2.33\sigma_D\sqrt{L}$	.010
$\overline{D}L + 1.96\sigma_D\sqrt{L}$	.025
$\overline{D}L + 1.64\sigma_D\sqrt{L}$	.050
$\overline{D}L + 1.28\sigma_D\sqrt{L}$	.100
$\overline{D}L + 1.04\sigma_D\sqrt{L}$	.150
$\overline{D}L + 0.85\sigma_D\sqrt{L}$	.200
$\overline{D}L + 0.67\sigma_D\sqrt{L}$	.250

EXAMPLE 8

If the distribution given in Example 6 is assumed normal with a standard deviation of 20 units, what will be the safety stock if a 95% service level per order cycle is desired?

$$M_a = B = \overline{D}L + 1.64\sigma_D\sqrt{L} = 60(1) + 1.64(20)\sqrt{1} = 92.8,$$

$$\text{safety stock} = S = M_a - \overline{D}L = 92.8 - 60 = 32.8 \approx 33 \text{ units.}$$

EXAMPLE 9

If the annual demand for an item is a normally distributed random variable with a mean of 8000 units and a standard deviation of 1000 units, what should be the safety stock and reorder point be if the lead time is $\frac{1}{2}$ month? (Assume management has decided it is willing to be out of stock in 5% of the order cycles.)

Since the mean and standard deviation are expressed on an annual basis and the lead time is on a $\frac{1}{2}$ month basis, they must be convoluted to the lead time period:

$$\overline{M} = \overline{D}L = \frac{R}{2(12)} = 333,$$

$$\sigma = \sigma_D\sqrt{L} = 1000\sqrt{1/[2(12)]} = 204.12,$$

$$M_a = \overline{D}L + Z\sigma = 333 + 1.64(204.12) = 668,$$

$$S = M_a - \overline{D}L = 668 - 333 = 335 \text{ units.}$$

The safety stock is 335 units, and the reorder point is 668 units.

The Poisson distribution is completely defined by its mean $\overline{D}$. The standard deviation of the Poisson distribution is the square root of its mean $(\sigma_D = \sqrt{\overline{D}})$, so knowledge of the average demand is sufficient to describe the distribution. To use an order cycle service level with the Poisson distribution assumption requires the use of a statistical table of the summed Poisson distribution. Table 12 is an abbreviated summed Poisson table. To use the summed Poisson table, locate the average demand column and descend on it until you obtain the stockout probability. The desired inventory level M_a is then read from the corresponding value in the first column.

EXAMPLE 10

The average daily demand for an item is 2 units, and the lead time demand is Poisson distributed. What should be the reorder point if a 96.6% service level per order cycle is desired? (Assume a lead time of 4 days.)

Table 12. Cumulative Poisson distribution

Reorder Point B[b]	$\overline{M}^c =$	2	3	4	5	6	7	8	9	10	12
2		.323									
3		.143	.353								
4		.053	.185	.371							
5		.017	.084	.215	.384						
6		.004	.033	.111	.238	.394					
7		.001	.012	.051	.133	.256	.401				
8			.004	.021	.068	.153	.271	.407			
9			.001	.008	.032	.084	.169	.283	.413		
10				.003	.014	.043	.098	.184	.294	.417	
11				.001	.005	.020	.053	.112	.197	.303	
12					.002	.009	.027	.064	.124	.208	.424
13					.001	.004	.013	.034	.074	.135	.319
14						.001	.006	.018	.041	.083	.228
15							.002	.008	.022	.049	.156
16							.001	.004	.011	.027	.101
17								.002	.005	.014	.063
18								.001	.002	.007	.037
19									.001	.003	.021
20										.002	.012
21										.001	.006
22											.003
23											.002
24											.001

[a] The fractions are the stockout probabilities associated with a given reorder point and an average lead time demand.

[b] Reorder point $B = \overline{D}L + S = M_a$.

[c] Average lead time demand $\overline{M} = \overline{D}L$.

From the summed Poisson table for an average lead time demand of 8 units, we find that B is 13 units for a stockout level of 0.034:

$$\text{safety stock} = S = B - \overline{D}L = 13 - (2)4 = 5 \text{ units.}$$

The negative exponential distribution is also defined by its mean $\overline{D}$. The standard deviation of the distribution is equal to its mean ($\sigma_D = \overline{D}$). To use a service level policy with the negative exponential distribution requires the use of a statistical table. Table 13 is useful in determining the reorder point when the demand follows a negative exponential distribution.

Table 13. Negative exponential distribution

$\frac{B}{\overline{DL}}$	$\frac{M_a}{\overline{M}}$	$\frac{\overline{DL}+S}{\overline{DL}}$	Stockout Probability $P(M>B)$	$\frac{B}{\overline{DL}}$	$\frac{M_a}{\overline{M}}$	$\frac{\overline{DL}+S}{\overline{DL}}$	Stockout Probability $P(M>B)$
	0		1.000		2.80		0.061
	0.10		0.905		2.90		0.055
	0.20		0.819		3.00		0.050
	0.50		0.607		3.10		0.045
	0.75		0.472		3.20		0.041
	1.00		0.368		3.30		0.037
	1.10		0.333		3.40		0.033
	1.20		0.301		3.50		0.030
	1.30		0.273		3.60		0.027
	1.40		0.247		3.70		0.025
	1.50		0.223		3.80		0.022
	1.60		0.202		4.00		0.018
	1.70		0.183		4.20		0.015
	1.80		0.165		4.40		0.012
	1.90		0.149		4.60		0.010
	2.00		0.135		4.80		0.008
	2.10		0.122		5.00		0.007
	2.20		0.111		5.20		0.006
	2.30		0.100		5.40		0.005
	2.40		0.091		5.60		0.004
	2.50		0.082		5.80		0.003
	2.60		0.074		6.00		0.002
	2.70		0.067				

EXAMPLE 11

If the average daily demand for an item is 2 units and the lead time demand is negative exponentially distributed, what should be the reorder point if a 95% service level per order cycle is desired? Assume a lead time of 4 days.

A stockout level of 0.05 gives $M_a/\overline{M}$ = 3.00, from Table 13; thus

$$\text{reorder point} = M_a = 3\overline{M} = 3\overline{DL} = 3(2)4 = 24 \text{ units,}$$

$$\text{safety stock} = S = M_a - \overline{M} = 24 - 4(2) = 16 \text{ units.}$$

A service level based on the frequency of service per order cycle does not indicate how frequently stockouts will occur over a given time period for all products. This unfortunate situation exists because the order cycle will vary from product to product. If an organization replenishes stock monthly with a 90% service level, there will be 1.2 (12 × 0.1) stockouts in a year, whereas if a firm replenishes stock weekly with a 90% service level, there will be 5.2 (52×0.1) stockouts per year. The more frequently stock is replenished in a given time period, the larger the number of expected stockouts.

Service per Year

A service level based on frequency of service per year allows for uniform treatment of different products. When the service level is based on the order cycle (as in the previous section), the stockout frequencies of different products are not comparable, since each product may have a different lead time. Fortunately, it is easy to convert from service per order cycle to service per year. The service level fraction per year is obtained by raising the service level fraction per order cycle to the power of the number of annual order cycles (R/Q):

$$\text{service level fraction per year} = (\text{service level fraction per cycle})^{R/Q}.$$

The stockout level fraction per order cycle is obtained as follows from the stockout level fraction per year:

$$P(M > B) = 1 - (\text{service level fraction per year})^{Q/R}.$$

EXAMPLE 12

From the information given in Example 6, what should be the reorder point if the 0.125 stockout level fraction per order cycle is changed to a 15% stockout level fraction per year?

$$P(M > B) = 1 - (\text{service level fraction per year})^{Q/R}$$

$$= 1 - (0.85)^{0.067} = 0.01.$$

Consulting the $P(M > B)$ column in Table 10, 0.01 is between 0.025 and 0.000, so the smaller is chosen, which gives

$$B = M_a = 90 \text{ units.}$$

The order quantity would be 1200 units and the reorder point 90 units.

EXAMPLE 13

From the information given in Example 9, what will be the service level fraction per year if there are four order cycles per year?

$$\text{Service level fraction per year} = (\text{service level fraction per cycle})^{R/Q}$$

$$= (0.95)^4 = 0.81.$$

Fraction of Units Demanded

Often the fraction of units demanded (or dollars demanded) and instantaneously filled from stock is a meaningful service index. The service level fraction for units demanded can be defined as

service level fraction for units demanded

$$= \frac{\text{number of units supplied}}{\text{total number of units demanded}},$$

stockout level fraction for units demanded

$$= \frac{\text{number of units short}}{\text{total number of units demanded}}.$$

The above relationships must be measured over some time period, which may be a week, a month, a year, or the duration of the lead time.

The expected number of stockouts during an order cycle has already been developed earlier in the chapter as

$$E(M > B) = \int_{B}^{\infty} (M - B) f(M) \, dM.$$

To obtain the stockout level fraction for units demanded during the order cycle, it is necessary to divide by the quantity demanded (Q) during the order cycle:

$$\text{stockout level fraction for units demanded} = \frac{E(M > B)}{Q}.$$

For a normal distribution, the expected number of stockouts during an order cycle is the partial expectation $E(Z)$ times the standard deviation, or

$$E(M > B) = \sigma E(Z),$$

which results in

$$\text{stockout level fraction for units demanded} = \frac{\sigma E(Z)}{Q}$$

for a normal distribution. $E(Z)$ is the partial expectation or standardized stockout quantity for a standard normal distribution. By knowing the stockout level fraction, the standard deviation of the lead time demand, and the order quantity, the partial expectation $E(Z)$ can be determined. By consulting a standard normal table (see Table 3), the standard normal deviate Z can be obtained for the derived partial expectation, and the reorder point obtained from the following formula:

$$B = \overline{M} + Z\sigma.$$

The formulations developed in this section apply to the case of complete backordering. For complete lost sales, the units demanded during the order cycle are $Q + E(M > B)$, which results in

$$\text{stockout level fraction for units demanded} = \frac{E(M > B)}{Q + E(M > B)}.$$

Since the lot size Q is usually much larger than the expected number of stockouts during the order cycle, $E(M > B)$, the complete backordering formulation can usually be applied to the lost sales case without any significant difference. The service level fraction for units demanded is insensitive to backorders or lost sales and gives essentially similar results in either case or any mix of these two extremes.

EXAMPLE 14

What is the order quantity and reorder point for the following problem (see Table 14):

$$\text{stockout level fraction for units demanded} = 0.01,$$
$$R = 1800 \text{ units/year},$$
$$C = \$3.00 \text{ per order},$$
$$H = \$3.00 \text{ per unit per year?}$$

Solution:

$$Q_0 = \sqrt{\frac{2CR}{H}} = \sqrt{\frac{2(3)1800}{3}} = 60 \text{ units},$$

$$E(M > B) = Q \text{ (stockout level fraction for units demanded)}$$
$$= 60(0.01) = 0.60 \text{ units.}$$

Table 14

Lead Time Demand M	Probability $P(M)$	$P(M > B)$
48	.02	.98
49	.03	.95
50	.06	.89
51	.07	.82
52	.20	.62
53	.24	.38
54	.20	.18
55	.07	.11
56	.06	.05
57	.03	.02
58	.02	.00
	$\overline{1.00}$	

Table 15

Reorder Point B	Probability $P(B)$	$\sum\limits_{M=B+1}^{M_{max}} (M-B)P(M) = E(M>B)$
58	.02	0
57	.03	$1(0.02) = 0.02$
56	.06	$1(0.03) = 0.03$ $2(0.02) = \underline{0.04}$ $\overline{0.07}$
55	.07	$1(0.06) = 0.06$ $2(0.03) = 0.06$ $3(0.02) = \underline{0.06}$ $\overline{0.18}$
54	.20	$1(0.07) = 0.07$ $2(0.06) = 0.12$ $3(0.03) = 0.09$ $4(0.02) = \underline{0.08}$ $\overline{0.36} \leftarrow$
53	.24	$1(0.20) = 0.20$ $2(0.07) = 0.14$ $3(0.06) = 0.18$ $4(0.03) = 0.12$ $5(0.02) = \underline{0.10}$ $\overline{0.74}$
52	.20	$1(0.24) = 0.24$ $2(0.20) = 0.40$ $3(0.07) = 0.21$ $4(0.06) = 0.24$ $5(0.03) = 0.15$ $6(0.02) = \underline{0.12}$ $\overline{1.36}$

The expected lead time stockout is 0.60 units, which in Table 15 is between 0.36 and 0.74 units. Selecting the smaller value, the reorder point is 54 units. The order quantity is 60 units, and the reorder point is 54 units.

EXAMPLE 15

If the distribution given in Example 14 is assumed normally distributed with a mean of 53 and a standard deviation of 2 units, what should be the reorder point?

$$E(Z) = \frac{Q}{\sigma}(\text{stockout level fraction for units demanded}) = \frac{60(0.01)}{2} = 0.30.$$

Consulting the normal table for the partial expectation $E(Z) = 0.30$, a standard normal deviate Z of 0.22 is obtained. The reorder point can be obtained as follows:

$$B = \overline{M} + Z\sigma = 53 + 0.22(2) = 53.4 \text{ units.}$$

Fraction of Operating Days

Another measure of stockout or shortage is the length of time an out-of-stock situation exists. Stockouts may be defined as the fraction of days out of stock. This results in a service level policy based on the time out of stock, and it can be written as

service level fraction for operating days

$$= \frac{\text{number of operating days without stockout}}{\text{total number of operating days}}$$

$$= 1 - \frac{\text{number of operating days with stockout}}{\text{total number of operating days}},$$

stockout level fraction for operating days

$$= \frac{\text{number of operating days with stockout}}{\text{total number of operating days}}.$$

If an item is out of stock 10% of the time, it is reasonable to assume that 10% of the time demand is unsatisfied. Thus the service level based on the fraction of operating days is very similar to the service level based on the fraction of units demanded. For practical purposes, the two approaches can be considered equivalent.

Before we leave the topic of service levels, a word of caution is in order. Some organizations set safety stock levels at some average time supply for each item. That is, they use a specified number of days or weeks of supply as the criterion for determining the amount of safety stock. This is a poor practice that should be avoided. The fallacy in using a fixed time supply is that safety stock is set as a function of the level of demand, whereas it should be set as a function of the variability of demand. A fixed time supply gives too much protection to high volume items with relatively predictable demands and not enough protection to low volume items with more variable demands. In actual practice, high volume items tend to exhibit less relative variability of demand.

Table 16. Imputed stockout costs

Stockout Level (1 − Service Level)	Stockout Cost[a]	
	Backorder Cost/Unit	Lost Sales Cost/Unit
Stockout level per order cycle, $P(s)$	$\dfrac{HQ}{AR}$	$\dfrac{HQ}{AR + HQ}$
Stockout level per year, $1 - [1 - P(s)]^{R/Q}$	$1 - \left[1 - \dfrac{HQ}{AR}\right]^{R/Q}$	$1 - \left[1 - \dfrac{HQ}{AR + HQ}\right]^{R/Q}$
Stockout fraction of units demanded,[b] $E(M > B)/Q$	$\dfrac{HQ}{AR}$	$\dfrac{HQ}{AR + HQ}$

[a] The formulas in the table give the optimum probability of a stockout. To obtain the appropriate stockout cost, solve the formula for A.

[b] For the stockout fraction of units demanded, it is necessary to solve for $E(M > B)$ and find the associated $P(s)$ before the appropriate formula can be solved for the stockout cost.

Imputed Service Level Stockout Costs

Whenever an organization uses a service level to establish a reorder point because of an inability to determine stockout cost, it really does establish a stockout cost. Associated with a given service level is an imputed or implicit stockout cost. It is a simple matter to determine the imputed stockout cost for a given service level from previously developed optimum formulations for the probability of a stockout. Table 16 outlines the formulations for determining the imputed stockout costs from the various service level concepts. A few examples can best illustrate the procedure.

EXAMPLE 16

From the information given in Example 6, what is the imputed backorder cost per unit?

$$P(s) = \frac{HQ}{AR} = 0.125 = \frac{5(1200)}{A(18,000)},$$

$$A = \frac{5(1200)}{0.125(18,000)} = \$2.67 \text{ per unit backordered.}$$

EXAMPLE 17

If the stockout level fraction per order cycle of 0.125 in Example 6 were changed to a stockout level fraction per year, what would be the imputed backorder cost per unit? What would be the imputed lost sales cost per unit?

$$\text{Stockout level per year} = 1 - \left[1 - \frac{HQ}{AR}\right]^{R/Q}$$

$$0.125 = 1 - \left[1 - \frac{5(1200)}{A(18,000)}\right]^{15},$$

$$A = \$37.04 \text{ per unit backordered};$$

$$0.125 = 1 - \left[1 - \frac{HQ}{AR + HQ}\right]^{R/Q}$$

$$= 1 - \left[1 - \frac{5(1200)}{A(18,000) + 5(1200)}\right]^{15},$$

$$A = \$36.70 \text{ per unit lost.}$$

EXAMPLE 18

From the information given in Example 14, what is the imputed backorder cost per unit? What is the imputed lost sales cost per unit?

$$0.01 = \frac{E(M > B)}{Q}, \qquad E(M > B) = 0.01(Q) = 0.01(60) = 0.6.$$

From the information in Example 14, the reorder point associated with 0.6 is 54 units, which has a stockout probability of 0.18. Thus

$$P(s) = \frac{HQ}{AR} = 0.18 = \frac{3(60)}{A(1800)},$$

$$A = \frac{3(60)}{0.18(1800)} = \$.56 \text{ per unit backordered};$$

$$P(s) = \frac{HQ}{AR + HQ} = 0.18 = \frac{3(60)}{A(1800) + 3(60)},$$

$$A = \frac{3(60) - 0.18(3)60}{0.18(1800)} = \$.46 \text{ per unit lost.}$$

FIXED ORDER INTERVAL SYSTEMS

All of the models developed in this chapter have focused on fixed order size systems with an emphasis on the reorder point and the demand distribution during the lead time period. With minor modifications the models also can be applied to fixed order interval systems.

In the fixed order interval system (T-system), there are a fixed order period and a varying order size. At predetermined intervals, the inventory is reviewed and an order is placed. The size of the order is determined by subtracting the amount on hand from a predetermined total (when the fixed order period is shorter than the lead time period, the stock on hand must include units on order but not yet received). The order interval T and the predetermined total E completely define the fixed order interval system. The operating doctrine under this system is sometimes called the "order up to E" doctrine.

In the fixed order size system (Q-system), safety stock is needed only for the lead time period. In the fixed order interval system, safety stock is needed for the lead time and the order interval. Once an order is placed at time t, another order cannot be placed until $t + T$, and the second order will not be filled until the lead time period has elapsed, at time $t + T + L$. Thus, safety stock protection is needed for the lead time L plus the order interval T.

The order interval and maximum inventory level formulas for probabilistic conditions are contained in Table 17. The service levels are similar, with the reorder point (B) replaced by the maximum inventory level (E), the service per order cycle replaced by service per order interval, and the lead time demand distribution replaced by the lead time plus order interval demand distribution. The revised service levels are as follows, with M equal to the demand during the lead time and the order interval (a random

Table 17. Fixed order interval system (probabilistic case)

| | | Known Stockout Cost[a] | |
| | | Maximum Inventory Level E[b] | |
Stockout Case	Economic Order Interval $T_0 = Q_0/R$	Stockout Cost per Unit	Stockout Cost per Outage[c]
Backordering	$\sqrt{\dfrac{2C}{RH}}$	$P(M > E) = \dfrac{HT}{A}$	$f(E) = \dfrac{HT}{G}$
Lost sales	$\sqrt{\dfrac{2C}{RH}}$	$P(M > E) = \dfrac{HT}{A + HT}$	$\dfrac{f(E)}{1 - P(M > E)} = \dfrac{HT}{G}$

[a] It is assumed that the deterministic EOI is an adequate approximation because of its insensitivity.

[b] The formulas give the optimum maximum inventory level for the appropriate demand distribution during the lead time plus the order interval. Symbols: H = holding cost per year; R = average annual demand in units; C = ordering cost per order; T = order interval in years; A = stockout cost per unit; G = stockout cost per outage; $P(M > E)$ = probability of a stockout during the order interval; $f(E)$ = ordinate; σ = standard deviation of demand for lead time and order interval.

[c] For the standard normal distribution, the ordinate of the distribution is $\sigma f(E)$.

variable):

service level fraction per order interval

$$= 1 - \frac{\text{number of order intervals without a stockout}}{\text{total number of order intervals}}$$

$$= 1 - P(M > E),$$

service level fraction per year

$$= (\text{service level fraction per order interval})^{1/T}$$

$$= [1 - P(M > E)]^{1/T},$$

service level fraction for units demanded

$$= \frac{\text{number of units supplied}}{\text{total number of units demanded}}$$

$$= 1 - \frac{E(M > E)}{TR}.$$

Imputed stockout costs can be derived from the fixed order interval service levels just as they were for the fixed order size service levels in Table 16.

CONCLUSION

The fixed order size system is completely defined by the order quantity Q and the reorder point B. The risk of stockout occurs after the reorder point is reached and before the next incoming order is received. Although the risk of stockout is dependent on both the order quantity and reorder point (with large order quantities, there is less exposure over a time horizon to potential stockouts), near-optimum results can usually be obtained by treating the order quantity and reorder point as independent. In this manner, risk is only considered in establishing the reorder point. The order quantity does not enter into the risk adjustment, and it is set by deterministic procedures (EOQ and EPQ) outlined in previous chapters. The safety stock is the risk adjustment to the reorder point to protect against stockouts. The reorder point consists of the mean lead time demand plus the safety stock. Safety stock levels can be obtained by the minimization of the expected cost of safety stock (holding and stockout costs) or by the creation of service levels. The fixed order size system under risk is schematically represented in Figure 7.

There are two approaches to establishing risk adjusted reorder points, depending on whether stockout costs are known or unknown. If stockout costs are known or can be ascertained, optimizing formulas can be derived depending on the stockout case (backorder or lost sale) and on the cost

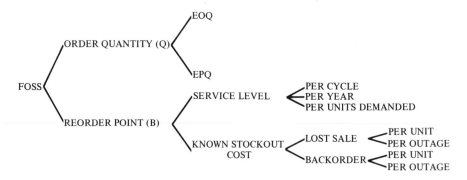

Figure 7. Risk: fixed order size systems.
Key: FOSS = fixed order size systems; EOQ = economic order quantity; EPQ = economic production quantity.

category (stockout cost per unit or per outage), as outlined in Table 9. If stockout costs are unknown, management can set service levels indicating the ability to meet customer demands from stock. The more typical kinds of service levels are service per order cycle, service per year, fraction of units demanded, and fraction of operating days. Since stockout costs are difficult to determine, service levels are more commonly used. The type of service level adopted depends on the industry, organizational peculiarities, ease of application, and type of products involved.

Demand when an item is out-of-stock can be either backordered or lost; in fact, a combination of the two is likely. From a mathematical standpoint the case of complete backordering is usually easiest to model. Because of the relatively low frequency of stockout occasions under any reasonable policy, the use of the simpler "complete backorders" model usually leads to a policy that produces a negligible cost increase over the more exact lost sales model, even when all demands in an out-of-stock situation are lost.

The treatment of risk in fixed order size systems involves the analysis of the demand distribution (continuous or discrete) over the relevant lead time. Empirically derived distributions or standard distributions (normal, Poisson, negative exponential, etc.) can be employed to describe the demand pattern. Standard distributions that are well tabulated provide the benefit of easy calculation and development. Of course, standard distributions should not be employed unless they adequately describe the demand phenomenon.

In establishing optimal solutions, numerous assumptions were made which rendered the models mere approximations to the optimal solution. While these approximations cast some doubt on the models, they should not limit their use. Within the range of parameter estimates required to utilize any inventory model, the assumptions establish an excellent first approximation. In many cases, because of the insensitivity of total inventory cost to changes in parameters and variables, the approximations are near optimal.

QUESTIONS

1. For what period of time are safety stocks necessary in a fixed order size system? Are they carried only during this period of time?

2. Why is the most conservative approach to establishing reorder points not ordinarily the optimum approach? In what situation would the most conservative approach be desirable?

3. What effect would ordering in larger quantities have on stockouts?

4. What conditions generally call for larger safety stocks?

5. What three statistical distributions were used to describe demand? In what demand situations would they most likely be used, and would any of them be inadequate in certain situations?

6. What level of safety stock should be maintained when both demand and lead time are constant?

7. When stockout costs are unknown, how are reorder points established?

8. Why and when is the convolution of a demand distribution required in probabilistic systems?

9. Why is the next lower attainable stockout probability selected when the optimum stockout probability cannot be attained in a discrete distribution?

10. Why does the expected annual cost of safety stock include holding costs on the expected stockout quantity for a lost sales case but not for a backordering case?

11. How is the constant demand and variable lead time solution technique similar to the variable demand and constant lead time solution technique?

12. What methods can be used to determine the lead time demand when both demand and lead time vary?

13. What is the limitation of a service level based on the frequency of service per order cycle?

14. Does an organization really establish a stockout cost when it uses a service level approach?

15. How does the service level approach for fixed order interval systems differ from the approach for fixed order size systems?

PROBLEMS

1. An industrial distributor sells water pumps and other related supplies. A particular water pump is purchased for $60 from the manufacturer. The average sales per day are 5 units, and the annual holding cost is 25% of unit cost. The annual demand for the pump is 1500 units, and the order quantity is 300 units. The backorder cost per unit is $50, and the lead time is 20 days. The demand during lead time is given in the table below:

Demand	Number of Occurrences
70	3
80	3
90	4
100	80
110	6
120	4
	100

(a) What is the reorder point? (b) How much safety stock should be carried? (c) What is the expected annual cost of the safety stock?

2. An automotive parts dealer sells 1200 carburetors a year. Each carburetor costs $25, and the average demand is 4 units/day. The order quantity is 120 units, and the lead time is 25 days. The backorder cost per unit is $20, and annual holding cost is 20% of unit cost. The lead time demand is given in the table below. Determine the safety stock level and the reorder point.

Demand	Number of Occurrences
90	25
95	25
100	5
105	20
110	15
115	10
	100

3. Assume that the information given for the water pumps in Problem 1 is still true except that lead time demand follows a normal distribution with a mean of 100 units and a standard deviation of 5 units. (a) What should be the reorder point? (b) What is the safety stock? (c) What is the expected stockout quantity per order cycle?

4. What should be the safety stock in Problem 2 if the lost sales cost per unit is $20?

5. A pet shop's monthly demand for Angora cats is normally distributed with a mean of 20 and a standard deviation of 4. Holding costs are $50 per cat per

year, the backorder cost per outage is $60, the order quantity is 25, and the lead time is 1 month. Determine the reorder point for Angora cats.

6. A pet shop's monthly demand for black snakes is Poisson distributed with a mean of 2 snakes. The order quantity is 6 snakes, holding costs are $5.00 per snake per year, the backorder cost per outage is $12.00, and the lead time is 2 months. At what level should the snakes be reordered?

7. A gasoline service station's daily demand for regular gasoline is normally distributed with a mean of 1200 gallons and a standard deviation of 400 gallons. If the lead time is 4 days, what reorder point should be set so as to be out of regular gasoline during only 1% of the order cycles?

8. A discount store's daily demand for its basic electronic calculator is Poisson distributed with a mean of 3 units. The reorder time period is 4 days. (a) What should be the reorder point if the desired stockout probability per order cycle is 0.10? (b) What is the expected stockout quantity per order cycle when the desired stockout probability per order cycle is 0.10?

9. The city of Connubial's demand for marriage licenses is negative exponentially distributed with a mean of 5 per day. The printer's lead time is 5 days. What should be the reorder point on marriage licenses if a service level per order cycle of 99% is desired?

10. A pizza-parlor owner is concerned about maintaining an optimum stock of pie crust, since a stockout would mean a loss of customers. He has consulted a local business student, who has sampled the pizza demand over a period of weeks and found that it was normally distributed with a mean of 106 per week and a standard deviation of 23. The owner informed the student that the lost sales cost would be $20 per unit, and the cost of maintaining a supply of pie crusts is $10 per crust per year (crusts are ordered in quantities of 100 with a lead time of 3 weeks). (a) What is the optimum reorder point for pizza crust? (b) What is the expected stockout quantity for pizza crust each order cycle?

11. A commercial crabber who fishes 350 pots per day orders bait in quantities of 50 crates per order. Because of weather conditions, he is unable to fish his pots with any regularity, so his weekly demand for bait is normally distributed with a mean of 25 crates and a standard deviation of 5. Since the bait must be refrigerated, the annual holding costs are $10 per crate, with backorder costs of $15 per outage. If it takes him a week to have bait ordered and delivered, what should be his reorder point?

12. Smith Concrete has an average monthly demand for 1000 bags of cement. Replenishment orders of 2000 bags require a lead time of 1 week. Holding costs are $5.00 per bag per year, and lost sales costs are $10 per bag. If the

weekly demand for concrete is as given in the table below, what should be the reorder point?

Demand M	Demand Probability $P(M)$	Probability of Demand > M
100	.01	.99
125	.04	.95
150	.11	.84
175	.14	.70
200	.40	.30
225	.12	.18
250	.10	.08
275	.06	.02
300	.02	.00

13. A plant that produces executive office chairs has a yearly demand of 5200 with a constant weekly demand of 100. The managers have experienced some inventory difficulties with the leather covering, which must be ordered from an outside supplier. Because of a manufacturing irregularity with the supplier, its delivery time has been variable over the past year. Leather is ordered in precut strips of 500, with annual holding costs of $20 per strip. The plant wants to ensure a suitable inventory on hand, since the backorder cost per strip is $15. What is the optimum reorder point if the weekly lead time is defined by the following distribution?

Lead Time (weeks)	Frequency f
1	10
2	20
3	35
4	26
5	9
	$\overline{100}$

14. The daily demand for an item is represented by the empirical distribution given below. What safety stock should the plant maintain to ensure that stockouts will not be incurred in more than 5.5% of the order cycles if the lead time is 1 day? What would be the safety stock under the conservative method?

Daily Demand D (units)	Frequency f
5	10
10	35
15	65
20	32
25	8
	$\overline{150}$

15. A grocer stocks several different brands of cereal. Because of the large number of boxes on hand, storage both on the display shelf and in the stockroom has become a problem. He has begun to analyze the demand for each brand, and he is willing to run short of a particular brand in 10% of the order cycles. He has found that the annual demand for a certain brand is a normally distributed random variable with a mean of 1000 boxes and a standard deviation of 150 boxes. What should his safety stock and reorder point be if it takes him $\frac{3}{4}$ month to get a new delivery?

16. A large business machine wholesaling company was experiencing a variation in both the demand for typewriters and the lead time in ordering them. In order to establish an efficient inventory level, an analysis of the demand and lead times was conducted, yielding a weekly demand that was normally distributed with a mean of 50 typewriters and a standard deviation of 10. The lead time was also normally distributed, with a mean of 16 days and a standard deviation of 5 days. If weekly demand and lead time are independent, what reorder point should be established to provide a 97.5% service level per order cycle?

17. The demand for an item averages 100 units per month. Actual demand data for the last 10 months are given in the table below (no seasonal, trend, or cyclical effects are in the data). The lead time is 2 months to replenish the inventory. What reorder point will ensure a service level per order cycle of 94%?

Month	1	2	3	4	5	6	7	8	9	10
Demand	100	90	80	110	90	120	130	70	100	100
Error	0	−10	−20	10	−10	20	30	−30	0	0

18. The weekly demand for a product is given in the table below. The lead time is 2 weeks. What is the probability distribution for the lead time demand?

Demand	Probability
0	.05
1	.40
2	.30
3	.25

19. An item has the following characteristics:

$$P = \$13.00/\text{unit}, \qquad F = 20\%,$$
$$R = 130 \text{ units/year}, \qquad L = 3 \text{ weeks},$$
$$C = \$9.00/\text{order}, \qquad \sigma_R = 26 \text{ units}.$$

The annual demand is normally distributed. If the manager will tolerate only one backordering outage per year, compute the economic order quantity and reorder point for the item.

20. Daily demand for hamburger buns at a fast food outlet is as follows:

Daily Demand	Midpoint	Probability
350–449	400	.20
450–549	500	.50
550–649	600	.30

(a) What should be the reorder point with a lead time of one day and a service level per order cycle of 85%? (b) What should be the reorder point with a lead time of three days and a service level of 90%?

21. Assume the following data pertain to a single inventory item: average annual demand = 500 units; holding cost per unit per year = $50.00; ordering cost per order = $5.00; lead time = 1 day; operating days per year = 250; demand follows a Poisson distribution; desired service level fraction (per order cycle or per order interval) = 97%. (a) If the item were controlled by a Q-system, what should be the reorder point? (b) If the item were controlled by a T-system, what should be the maximum inventory level? (c) What is the difference in units between the safety stocks required under the two systems?

22. Assume that all the data given in Problem 21 still pertain. (a) What is the imputed stockout cost per unit if backordering is allowed? (b) Using the imputed stockout cost from part (a), what is the expected annual cost of safety stock if a Q-system is used to control the item?

23. Inventory item KG34 has the following information in its inventory record: an economic order quantity of 300 units; an average weekly demand of 50 units; a standard deviation of weekly demand equal to 20 units; an annual holding cost of $13.00 per unit; a stockout cost per unit of $8.00; a lead time of 2 days. The firm which has these data on file operates 50 weeks (5 days/week) each year. (a) If the stockout cost is on a backordering basis, what is the reorder point for item KG34? (b) If the stockout cost is on a lost sales basis, what is the reorder point? (c) How do the safety stock requirements under the two stockout cases differ?

CASE 1: HIGHER SERVICE LEVELS

Hopson Steel is a distributor of steel and metal products. It has sales territories in twelve states which are served from six warehouses. Each warehouse is autonomous and carries enough inventory to cover sales in two states.

Profits and sales at Hopson Steel have not changed appreciably over the last five years. To the dismay of the major stockholders, the profits of competitors have increased. In an effort to institute change, Mr. Benton, the President, has replaced the company's general manager with Mr. Arnold Cohen. With considerable effort and a substantial salary offer, Mr. Cohen was persuaded to leave his position with a sporting goods firm.

Upon arrival at the firm, Mr. Cohen examined sales records and market forecasts for the steel industry. He predicted a substantial increase in demand for several products. After commenting several times that increased sales were the salvation for Hopson Steel, he issued the following directives to each of his six material managers.

1. Purchase and stock at each warehouse *all* items listed in the general supply catalogue.
2. Purchase large quantities of products for inventory so quantity discounts can be utilized.
3. If economically possible, purchase economic order quantities (EOQs).
4. Inventory levels will rise, but the larger holding cost will be offset by increased sales (the higher service level will increase sales).
5. All managers who exceed last year's performance will receive bonuses.

Within a few months, sales increases were reported along with predictions of even greater increases by year end. The warehouses reported the largest stock of steel products in the company's history. Labor negotiations between the steel industry and labor unions were at an impasse and it appeared that a strike was imminent. Fearing that a strike would deplete inventory levels when sales were increasing, Mr. Cohen urged the procurement of even larger quantities of steel products from any source available.

Although a strike did occur, it lasted for only a week. At the end of the year, Mr. Benton reported a sales increase for the company but a loss on operations. He attributed the poor performance to high inventory levels and other unexpected costs. With some reservation, Mr. Benton predicted a brighter year ahead with increased sales and a return to profitability. He professed continued trust in Mr. Cohen's ability.

1. Discuss the merits of each of Mr. Cohen's directives to his material managers. Do you agree with them?
2. Do you share Mr. Benton's trust in Mr. Cohen?
3. As a stockholder, what are your opinions about the president's comments on the future of the company? Do you foresee any major problems?

CASE 2: KNOT HOLES

Woodcraft, Inc. produces sundry items that are made primarily from wood and wood by-products. Their line of products includes baker's racks, wine racks, paper towel holders, chopping blocks, bread boxes and canister sets, and other wooden storage items. Although the basic material for all the products is wood, each item is made from a certain grain and grade, and the raw materials are not considered interchangeable. Woodcraft purchases most of its materials from a North Carolina supplier who ships them to the Maryland plant in numerous precut sizes.

Mr. Ash, the production manager, has the responsibility of purchasing and controlling the raw materials inventory. This has proved to be a tedious task. The supplier is unable to promise delivery dates and has been unreliable in his estimates of delivery schedules. The lead times of certain grains and grades run the gamut from speedy deliveries to seemingly endless delays. The volatility of lead times is due to the infrequency of lumber cuttings and the difficulties of cutting, preparing, and shipping the wood.

Mr. Ash, however, feels that he has finally developed an infallible system for dealing with lead time fluctuations. By "infallible" he means successful in avoiding production stoppages because of materials outages. Mr. Ash orders the lumber in economic order quantities. He has set the reorder points at arbitrarily high levels, resulting in the establishment of large safety stocks. He boasts that inventory levels may be high, but his production schedule always runs smoothly.

Mr. Teak is a subordinate in Mr. Ash's department. He agrees that Woodcraft needs to ensure adequate inventory levels, but he challenges Mr. Ash's wasteful methods. Mr. Teak cites the astronomical inventory carrying costs as testimony to poor inventory practices. More obvious evidence of exceedingly high stock levels is the stacks of rotten lumber stored in the lot adjacent to the manufacturing facility.

Mr. Teak told his superior that he is appalled at the gross mismanagement of material resources. As a starting place, he has decided to establish more efficient inventory policies for the company's most popular product, a 12″ × 16″ counter-top cutting board. The board has a very stable demand and is produced evenly throughout the year. It is made from a medium grade of oak that arrives from the supplier in uniformly cut sizes.

Because the oak has been consistently difficult to obtain, the supplier has suggested an alternative type of material. The alternative wood is of lesser quality and is slightly more porous. However, the supplier has been able to ship it to a custom counter-top maker in Baltimore from 3 to 7 weeks after order receipt.

The choice between the two materials is clear-cut to Mr. Ash. He is eager to start purchasing the new precut material but is uncertain about the application of the EOQ formulation. He knows that to minimize his total costs he should order in 150 unit lot sizes, but he is uncertain as to when to initiate his orders. Because there would still be variability in the lead time, he has decided to set the reorder point by a trial and error method. He will reduce the reorder point from the previously high level set by Mr. Ash and decrease it incrementally until it is in an acceptable range. This method, he hopes, will reduce the safety stock level and still allow for manufacturing regularity.

1. Is Mr. Teak's solution logical? Is it an oversimplification of the problem?
2. Is Mr. Ash's method in error? Should the order quantity and reorder point be established independently?
3. Describe the inventory situation for the cutting board, and recommend a method for establishing appropriate inventory policies.

CASE 3: MANAGING MOLLUSKS

Tando's Restaurant of Virginia Beach offers one of the most varied and unusual menus in the resort city. The restaurant has acquired a fine reputation for exquisite and unique dishes. They are best known for three entrees that are ethnic adaptations of sea scallops. Due to the unusual preparation of the scallop dishes, this seafood has become the largest selling menu item.

The scallops are not purchased locally, but are shipped from a purveyor who serves a sister operation, Tando's of Branford, Connecticut. For quality and price reasons, the scallops are not bought from local dealers. The owners find that transportation charges are minimal compared to the value derived from the other factors. The New England purveyor has an established route to other local operations, and he has been able to fill orders within three days.

Daniel Speas, one of the proprietors, was an operations management major and has always tried to utilize the inventory management tools he learned as an M.B.A. student. Dan had been ordering the scallops by intuition until he could become familiar with the beach trade. He has been dissatisfied with the results. Tando's has experienced spoilage and shortages too frequently. Dan is certain that now is the time to test theoretical inventory methods.

Dan has spent the greater part of a week determining the cost data for the scallops and has itemized his results as follows:

$$R = 2500 \text{ doz./yr}, \qquad P = \$7/\text{doz.},$$
$$C = \$25 \text{ per order}, \qquad A = \$3.50/\text{doz.},$$
$$F = 0.50.$$

Knowing that customers are unpredictable, Dan cringes at estimating daily demand. Even though scallops are a perennial favorite, the demand is erratic. Based on scanty documentation, Dan has constructed a table of the daily demand distribution for the mollusk:

Demand (doz./day)	Frequency
6	35
7	35
8	15
9	10
10	5

Dan assumes this distribution does not differ significantly from the Poisson distribution. Assured that the theoretical distribution is an adequate surrogate for his distribution, Dan's computations are simplified. His calculations yield a reorder point of 16 dozen units with an apparent safety stock of 3 dozen scallops.

1. Has Dan done a thorough and precise job?
2. How should inventory policies for sea scallops be established? What permutations could alter or destroy the formulations?
3. What type of inventory problems may be unique to restauranteurs? What types of analysis should be recommended to them?
4. Briefly describe selection of demand distributions for this menu item.

CASE 4: FLORIDA FLORA IN GEORGIA

Ashley Wynne operates a greenhouse, The Southern Nursery, in Augusta, Georgia. The name is a misnomer, because the company does not grow any of its plants from seedlings nor propagate any new plants. All of the plants are shipped from Florida and are cared for in Southern's greenhouses until sold. The only part of the operation that resembles a nursey is the greenhouse that is designated for unhealthy or diseased plants.

The lush ferns that Ashley buys in Florida are his prime product. Ashley had a 1600 unit demand for the ferns last year. The demand is increasing, because the area is becoming a tourist attraction. Many are taken home as examples of Georgian greenery. The ferns arrive in baskets suitable for hanging and are sold individually or in bulk purchases to commercial customers. At times, Ashley has also sold his baskets to other nurseries, depending on his supply and the success of price negotiations with the nurserymen. Because of the diversity of his clientele, Ashley's prices vary widely.

Ashley intends to continue his practice of serving many markets; he enjoys the bartering process. However, his pricing policy, or lack of one, complicates the establishment of stockout costs. Ashley assumes he can use $3.00 per unit, but feels very uncertain that it is a valid stockout cost for ferns. He finds estimating the holding cost less complex. He has assigned a $2.00 holding cost per plant.

The time between order initiation and delivery is uncertain. The Florida supplier usually delivers the order within 5 days, and the ordering cost is $15.00. Ashley sold his ferns during the past year according to the following lead time distribution:

Lead Time Demand	Probability
21	.03
22	.04
23	.07
24	.12
25	.09
26	.20
27	.22
28	.13
29	.06
30	.04

Ashley has raised the possibility that his reordering policies and practices need revision. He figured his operation is currently servicing only about 85% of his demand. He would like to be able to satisfy approximately 95% of customer demand for ferns.

To achieve a higher service level Ashley is contemplating becoming his own supplier. He is examining the steps necessary to cultivate the luxuriant ferns himself. Expansion seems to be the key to approaching a 95% service level or better; Ashley is intrigued with the idea of vertical integration.

1. Discuss Ashley's plans.
2. Can Ashley revise his reordering policies and accomplish his goal without vertically integrating?
3. How can Ashley compute stockout costs?
4. Discuss inventory problems that are probably occurring at The Southern Nursery.

CASE 5: INHARMONIOUS ACCORD

Radio Hut sells a large variety of products, from small transistor radios to very expensive and sophisticated component stereo systems. It is apparent that Radio Hut has been making mistakes in the determination of safety stock levels for small tape recorders. The demand for the recorders is erratic and difficult to predict; it peaks during the Christmas season. Even though the suppliers are reliable, the lead time is quite long; so the risk of stockouts is high, and outages frequently occur. Radio Hut's policy is to satisfy the customers to avoid losing them to competitors. These conditions force Radio Hut to maintain a high safety stock. However, the space available for storage is not large enough to satisfy actual demand. Faced with these problems, Radio Hut's manager, Fidel High, appointed two assistant managers to establish the correct level of safety stock necessary to meet actual demand.

Manager One decided that the best way to determine the safety stock was to determine the stockout cost. He assumed that at the retail level a stockout would result in a lost sale, because customers choose to purchase from a competitor rather than wait. He calculated the sum of losses of present sales and losses of future sales to obtain a stockout cost per unit of $7.00. The annual demand is approximately 1200 units; the ordering cost is $30.00; the holding cost just increased from 20% to 25% of the purchase price of $65; and the lead time demand is distributed according to the following table:

Lead Time Demand	Probability
20	.08
25	.16
30	.24
35	.22
40	.19
45	.07
50	.04

After conducting computations, he came up with a safety stock of 15 units.

Manager Two thought that determining a stockout cost was much too uncertain and involved too many variables. He based his study on the service level per order cycle. He estimated a service level of 95% would be adequate and found a safety stock of 20 units would be appropriate at this level.

Now Radio Hut faces several problems:

1. Which safety stock level would be best?
2. Should an average be taken?
3. Why are there discrepancies between the two estimates?
4. How can Radio Hut prepare for the peak demand at Christmas?

Solutions to these questions are still in the initial phases, yet Mr. High has decided to throw more suggestions at the two assistants. He wants them to investigate the probability of reducing stockouts by shortening lead time or by increasing lot sizes, the possibility of informing suppliers of Radio Hut's expected annual demand so that they could manage to deliver the tape recorders in the quantity needed at the moment required, and the chance of using local or multiple suppliers as a partial solution.

Given the information and the additional suggestions:

1. What should Radio Hut do?
2. Are Mr. High's suggestions likely to solve the inventory problem? If so, then how?
3. Discuss the effects of stiff competition and seasonality on the establishment of safety stock levels.

MATHEMATICAL ABBREVIATIONS AND SYMBOLS USED IN CHAPTER 5

A	Stockout cost per unit
B	Reorder point in units
C	Ordering cost per order
D	Daily demand in units (a random variable)
$\overline{D}$	Average daily demand in units
D_a	Daily demand at acceptable service level in units
$D_{\max}$	Maximum daily demand in units
E	Maximum inventory level in units
$E(M > E)$	Expected order interval stockout quantity in units
$E(M > B)$	Expected lead time stockout in units
EOI	Economic order interval
EOQ	Economic order quantity
f	Frequency of occurrence
$f(M)$	Probability density function of lead time demand
G	Stockout cost per outage
H	Holding cost per unit per year
L	Lead time in days
$\overline{L}$	Average lead time in days
L_a	Lead time at acceptable service level in days
$L_{\max}$	Maximum lead time in days
M	Lead time demand in units (a random variable)
$\overline{M}$	Average lead time demand in units
M_a	Lead time demand at acceptable service level in units
$M_{\max}$	Maximum lead time demand in units
MAD	Mean absolute deviation
P	Unit purchase cost
$P(D)$	Probability of a daily demand of D units
$P(L)$	Probability of a lead time of L days
$P(M)$	Probability of a lead time demand of M units
$P(s)$	Optimum probability of a stockout
$P(M > B)$	Probability of a stockout during lead time
$P(M > E)$	Probability of a stockout during order interval
Q	Order quantity in units
Q_0	Economic order quantity in units
R	Average annual demand in units
S	Safety stock in units
T	Order interval in years

T_0 Economic order interval in years
TC   Expected annual cost of inventory
TC_s Expected annual cost of safety stock
Z Standard normal deviate
σ Standard deviation of lead time demand in units
σ_D Standard deviation of daily demand in units
σ_L Standard deviation of lead time in days

SUMMARY OF FORMULAS IN CHAPTER 5

Model	Formula

Basic EOQ

$$Q_0 = \sqrt{\frac{2CR}{H}}$$

Reorder point with
  known stockout costs:

Backorder case

$$P(M > B) = \frac{HQ}{AR}$$

$$f(B) = \frac{HQ}{GR}$$

$$B = \overline{M} + S = \overline{M} + Z\sigma$$

Lost sales case

$$P(M > B) = \frac{HQ}{AR + HQ}$$

$$B = \overline{M} + S = \overline{M} + Z\sigma$$

Reorder point with
  service levels:

Service level per
  order cycle

$$SL_C = 1 - P(M > B)$$

Service level per year

$$SL_Y = (SL_C)^{R/Q} = [1 - P(M > B)]^{R/Q}$$

Fraction of units
  demanded

$$SL_U = 1 - \frac{E(M > B)}{Q} = 1 - \frac{\sigma E(Z)}{Q}$$

Basic EOI

$$T_0 = \sqrt{\frac{2C}{RH}} = Q_0/R$$

SUMMARY OF FORMULAS IN CHAPTER 5 (*continued*)

Model	Formula
Maximum inventory level with known stockout cost: [a]	

Backorder case
$$P(M > E) = \frac{HT}{A}$$

$$f(E) = \frac{HT}{G}$$

$$E = \overline{M} + S = \overline{M} + Z\sigma$$

Lost sales case
$$P(M > E) = \frac{HT}{A + HT}$$

$$E = \overline{M} + S = \overline{M} + Z\sigma$$

Maximum inventory level with service levels [a]

Service level per order interval
$$SL_T = 1 - P(M > E)$$

Service level per year
$$SL_Y = (SL_T)^{1/T} = [1 - P(M > E)]^{1/T}$$

Fraction of units demanded
$$SL_U = 1 - \frac{E(M > E)}{TR} = 1 - \frac{\sigma E(Z)}{TR}$$

[a] For the reorder point model, M and σ apply to the demand during the lead time period; for the maximum inventory level model, M and σ apply to demand during the lead time period and the order interval.

APPENDIX A. PROBABILITY DISTRIBUTION CONVOLUTIONS

Frequently, it is necessary to know the probability distribution of the demand for varing-length time periods. If the demand is stationary with no integral time series modifications and if the demand in subsequent periods is independent of the demand level in previous periods, then the probability distribution of the demand for varying-length time periods can be easily obtained. The revised probability distribution of the demand is derived by convolutions of the original probability distribution with itself.[8] The convolution process permits the extension of a probability distribution of demand for a given fixed time period to the demand distribution for any integral multiple of that time period.

For a discrete distribution, the binomial expansion can be utilized to obtain the desired convolution. For example, suppose the demand distribution shown in Table A-1 applies to an item for a weekly period. What would be the demand distribution for a 2-week period? The 1-week demand

[8] For a more complete discussion of convolutions see G. Hadley and T. M. Whitin, *Analysis of Inventory Systems*, Englewood Cliffs, NJ: Prentice-Hall, 1963.

Table A-1

Demand	Probability
0	.10
1	.40
2	.30
3	.20

can be written in binomial expansion terms as follows:

$$.1 + .4X + .3X^2 + .2X^3,$$

where the exponent of X equals the demand ($X^0 = 1$), and the coefficient of X is the probability of the respective demand level. To obtain the probability distribution of demand for n weeks, the expression is raised to the nth power and the results are read using the same convention. Thus, the demand distribution for two weeks is obtained as follows:

$$(.1 + .4X + .3X^2 + .2X^3)^2 = .01 + .08X + .22X^2 + .28X^3$$
$$+ .25X^4 + .12X^5 + .04X^6,$$

which results in the two-week demand distribution shown in Table A-2. The use of the binomial expansion in developing convolutions, while correct, can become mathematically tedious. For this reason it is desirable to use standard distributions (normal, binomial, and Poisson) which are well behaved in relation to convolutions. When normal, binomial, or Poisson distributions are convoluted, the same respective distribution results, regardless of the number of convolutions.

For a stationary distribution with mean $\overline{X}$ and standard deviation σ, n convolutions will result in a mean of $n\overline{X}$ and a standard deviation of $\sigma\sqrt{n}$. Thus, we can easily determine the demand for any integral multiple of a time period if the demand distribution is normally distributed in the time period.

Table A-2

Demand	Probability
0	.01
1	.08
2	.22
3	.28
4	.25
5	.12
6	.04

APPENDIX B. NORMAL DISTRIBUTION

The normal distribution is described in general terms earlier in the chapter. There are three functions related to the normal distribution that are used to derive decision rules in inventory management. They are the probability density function (pdf), the cumulative distribution function (cdf), and the partial expectation. The ordinate (height) of the probability density function is $f(M)$ at any point M. The cumulative distribution function $F(M)$ is the area under the pdf to the left of any point M. The probability of a stockout (probability that demand during the lead time exceeds the reorder point) is one minus the cdf: $P(M > B) = 1 - F(B)$. The partial expectation function $E(M > B)$ is the expected stockout quantity during a given period. It is the area under the cdf to the right of any point B. These relationships are illustrated in Figure B-1.

Figure B-1. Normal distribution.

$$f(M) = e^{-(M-\bar{M})^2/2\sigma^2}/\sigma\sqrt{2\pi} \text{ for } -\infty < M < \infty;$$
$$f(B) = e^{-(B-\bar{M})^2/2\sigma^2}/\sigma\sqrt{2\pi};$$
$$F(B) = \int_{-\infty}^{B} f(M)\, dM = P(M \le B) = 1 - P(M > B);$$
$$E(M > B) = \int_{B}^{\infty} (M - B)f(M)\, dM.$$

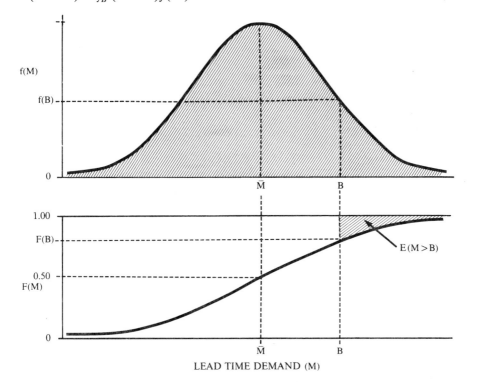

LEAD TIME DEMAND (M)

The standard normal distribution, also called the unit normal distribution, is a special case of the normal distribution where the mean value is 0 and the standard deviation is 1. For the standard normal distribution, the pdf is $f(t)$, the cdf is $F(t)$, and the partial expectation is $E(Z)$. These relationships are shown in Figure B-2. Any normal distribution with a mean $\overline{M}$ and a standard deviation σ can be transformed to a standard normal distribution by the relationship $t = (M - \overline{M})/\sigma$. Appropriate statistical information concerning any point B of a normal distribution can be obtained by transforming it to $Z = (B - \overline{M})/\sigma$ and consulting a standard normal distribution table such as Table 3. A summary of properties of the normal distribution is contained in Table B-1.

APPENDIX C. CHI-SQUARE GOODNESS-OF-FIT TEST

When the standard statistical distributions can be used in inventory analysis, they can simplify the analysis and reduce the computational effort.

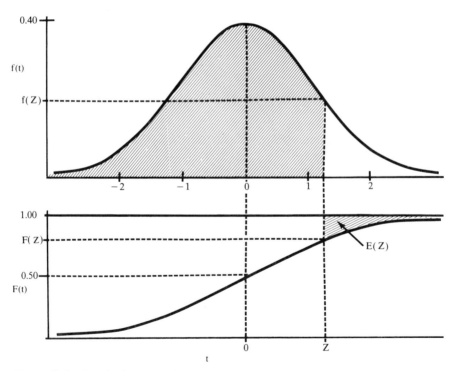

Figure B-2. Standard normal distribution.
$t = (M - \overline{M})/\sigma$; $Z = (B - \overline{M})/\sigma$; $f(Z) = e^{-Z^2/2}/\sqrt{2\pi}$; $f(t) = e^{-t^2/2}/\sqrt{2\pi}$; $F(Z) = \int_{-\infty}^{Z} f(t)\, dt = 1 - P(M > B)$; $E(Z) = \int_{Z}^{\infty}(t - Z)f(t)\, dt = E(M > B)/\sigma$.

Table B-1. Properties of the normal distribution[a]

Variable	Normal Distribution (in M)	Standard Normal Distribution (in t)
Probability density function (ordinate)	$f(M) = \dfrac{e^{-(M-\overline{M})^2/2\sigma^2}}{\sigma\sqrt{2\pi}}$	$f(t) = \dfrac{e^{-t^2/2}}{\sqrt{2\pi}}$
Mean	$\overline{M} = \displaystyle\int_{-\infty}^{\infty} Mf(M)\,dM$	$\bar{t} = \displaystyle\int_{-\infty}^{\infty} tf(t)\,dt = 0$
Variance	$\sigma^2 = \displaystyle\int_{-\infty}^{\infty} (M - \overline{M})^2 f(M)\,dM$	$\sigma_t^2 = \displaystyle\int_{-\infty}^{\infty} (t - \bar{t})^2 f(t)\,dt = 1$
Probability of a stockout	$1 - F(B) = 1 - \displaystyle\int_{B}^{\infty} f(M)\,dM$	$1 - F(Z) = 1 - \displaystyle\int_{-\infty}^{Z} f(t)\,dt$
Expected stockout quantity	$E(M > B) = \displaystyle\int_{B}^{\infty} (M - B)f(M)\,dM$	$E(Z) = \displaystyle\int_{Z}^{\infty} (t - Z)f(t)\,dt$

[a] $t = (M - \overline{M})/\sigma$; $Z = (B - \overline{M})/\sigma$; $P(M > B) = 1 - F(B) = 1 - F(Z)$; $E(M > B) = \sigma E(Z)$.

Before standard distributions such as the normal, Poisson, and negative exponential are employed, it is necessary to establish the goodness of fit of the distribution. A test based on the chi-square distribution can determine if any real difference exists between an empirical (actual) distribution and the standard distribution it is assumed to represent. The chi-square goodness-of-fit test will indicate if the difference between two distributions (empirical and theoretical) is statistically significant.

To measure the compatibility of actual (observed) and theoretical (expected) frequencies, it is necessary to calculate the chi-square statistic. The calculated chi-square statistic is compared with a value obtained from a chi-square table for a given level of significance and number of degrees of freedom. If the calculated chi-square statistic is less than the value obtained from the statistical table, the theoretical distribution is accepted as an adequate surrogate for the actual distribution. A chi-square statistic of zero represents a perfect fit; the larger the chi-square statistic, the poorer the fit. Chi-square tables can be found in any statistics book.

The chi-square statistic is obtained from the following formula:

$$\chi^2 = \sum \frac{(f_0 - f_e)^2}{f_e} = \text{chi-square},$$

where

$$f_0 = \text{observed frequencies},$$
$$f_e = \text{expected frequencies}.$$

The most frequently used levels of significance are 0.05 and 0.10. The degrees of freedom are $k - 3$ for the normal distribution and $k - 2$ for the Poisson distribution (k is the number of frequency classes). A few simple examples can illustrate the test.

Table C-1

Demand per Day D	Observed Frequency
0	40
1	30
2	20
3	10
	$\overline{100}$

Poisson Distribution Example

The demand per day for an item is given in Table C-1. Determine whether the daily demand can be considered Poisson distributed at the 0.10 level of significance.

We have

$$\overline{D} = \frac{\Sigma fD}{\Sigma f} = \frac{100}{100} = 1.$$

The arithmetic mean $\overline{D}$ of the above distribution is 1 unit. By consulting a Poisson distribution table for a mean of 1 unit, the probabilities of each expected demand level are obtained and transformed to the expected frequencies in Table C-2.

Consulting a chi-square table for level of significance 0.10 and 2 degrees of freedom ($k - 2 = 4 - 2$), we find $\chi^2 = 4.605$. Since the computed value (2.17) is less than the table value, the Poisson distribution can be used to describe daily demand.

Table C-2

Demand per Day, D	Frequency of Demand		$f_0 - f_e$	$(f_0 - f_e)^2$	$\dfrac{(f_0 - f_e)^2}{f_e}$
	$f_0{}^a$	$f_e{}^b$			
0	40	36.8	3.2	10.24	0.28
1	30	36.8	−6.8	46.24	1.25
2	20	18.4	1.6	2.56	0.14
3	10	6.1 ⎫	2.0	4.00	0.50
4	0	1.5 ⎬ 8.0			
5	0	0.3			
6	0	0.1 ⎭			
					$\overline{2.17}$

[a] For 100 days.
[b] $f_e = 100P(D)$.

Table C-3

Lead Time Demand, M	Frequency f
≤ 39	12
40–44	26
45–49	80
50–54	130
55–59	104
60–64	42
≥ 65	6
	$\overline{400}$

Normal Distribution Example

The lead time demand for an item is shown in Table C-3. Before the data were grouped, the mean and standard deviation were calculated to be 52.5 and 6.6 units respectively. Determine if the lead time demand can be approximated by a normal distribution at the 0.05 level of confidence.

The expected frequencies are obtained in the following manner:

1. $Z = \dfrac{M - \overline{M}}{\sigma} = \dfrac{39.5 - 52.5}{6.6} = -1.97.$

From the normal table a Z of 1.97 gives 0.47558.

$$f_e = (0.5000 - 0.47558)400 = 9.768.$$

2. $Z = \dfrac{M - \overline{M}}{\sigma} = \dfrac{44.5 - 52.5}{6.6} = -1.21.$

From the normal table a Z of 1.21 gives 0.38686.

$$f_e = (0.47558 - 0.38686)400 = 35.488.$$

3. $Z = \dfrac{M - \overline{M}}{\sigma} = \dfrac{49.5 - 52.5}{6.6} = -0.45.$

From the normal table a Z of 0.45 gives 0.17364.

$$f_e = (0.38686 - 0.17364)400 = 85.288.$$

4. $Z = \dfrac{M - \overline{M}}{\sigma} = \dfrac{54.5 - 52.5}{6.6} = 0.30.$

From the normal table a Z of 0.30 gives 0.11791.

$$f_e = (0.17364 - 0.11791)400 = 116.62.$$

Table C-4

Lead Time Demand M	Frequency of Demand		$(f_0 - f_e)$	$(f_0 - f_e)^2$	$\dfrac{(f_0 - f_e)^2}{f_e}$
	f_0	f_e			
≤ 39	12	9.8	3.2	10.24	1.045
40–44	26	35.5	−9.5	90.25	2.542
45–49	80	85.3	−5.3	28.09	0.329
50–54	130	116.6	13.4	179.56	1.539
55–59	104	95.0	9.0	81.00	0.853
60–64	42	44.1	−2.1	4.41	0.100
≥ 65	6	13.8	−7.8	60.84	4.409
	$\overline{400}$				$\overline{10.817}$

5. $Z = \dfrac{M - \overline{M}}{\sigma} = \dfrac{59.5 - 52.5}{6.6} = 1.06.$

From the normal table a Z of 1.06 gives 0.35543.

$$f_e = (0.35543 - 0.11791)400 = 95.008.$$

6. $Z = \dfrac{M - \overline{M}}{\sigma} = \dfrac{64.5 - 52.5}{6.6} = 1.82.$

From the normal table a Z of 1.82 gives 0.46562.

$$f_e = (0.46562 - 0.35543)400 = 44.08.$$

7. $Z = \dfrac{M - \overline{M}}{\sigma} = \dfrac{64.5 - 52.5}{6.6} = 1.82.$

From the normal table a Z of 1.82 gives 0.46562.

$$f_e = (0.50000 - 0.46562)400 = 13.752.$$

Hence we have Table C-4.

Consulting a chi-square table for level of significance 0.05 and 4 degrees of freedom ($K - 3 = 7 - 3$), we find $\chi^2 = 9.488$. Since the computed value (10.817) is greater than the table value, the normal distribution does not adequately describe the actual distribution.

APPENDIX D. ORDER QUANTITY AND REORDER POINT DEPENDENCE

In fixed order size inventory models involving uncertainty, it becomes apparent that the order quantity and reorder point are interdependent. The interaction is frequently and justifiably ignored to simplify inventory control. Analysis is needed, however, to check this assumption. The risk of stockout occurs only after the reorder point is reached. The size of the order quantity will determine how frequently the reorder point is reached. The larger the order quantity, the less frequent the exposure to stockouts (the risk of depletion varies inversely with the size of the order quantity).

Backorder Case: Stockout Cost per Unit

The possibility of a stockout only occurs during the lead time (after the reorder point is reached).[9] In an annual period, if there is no more than one order outstanding at any given time, the number of time periods during which a stockout could occur is R/Q, or the annual demand divided by the order quantity. To account for the dependence between order quantity and reorder point, the expected annual cost formula for a continuous distribution with backordering can be written as

expected annual cost = (purchase cost) + (order cost)
$$+ \text{(holding cost)} + \text{(stockout cost)},$$

$$\text{TC} = RP + \frac{RC}{Q} + H\left[\frac{Q}{2} + \int_0^\infty (B - M)f(M)\, dM\right]$$
$$+ \frac{AR}{Q}\int_B^\infty (M - B)f(M)\, dM,$$

where

R = average annual demand in units,
P = purchase cost per unit,
C = ordering cost per order,
Q = order quantity in units,
H = holding cost per unit per year,
B = reorder point in units,
M = lead time demand in units (a random variable),
A = stockout cost per unit,
$f(M)$ = probability density function of lead time demand,
$$S = B - \overline{M}$$
$$= \int_0^\infty (B - M)f(M)\, dM = \text{expected safety stock in units,}$$
$$E(M > B) = \int_B^\infty (M - B)f(M)\, dM$$
$$= \text{expected lead time stockout in units,}$$
$$AE(M > B) = \text{expected lead time stockout cost.}$$

[9] The lead time demand is the total demand that occurs during the lead time. For deterministic models, it is simply the product of the demand rate and the lead time. When demand and lead time are independent random variables, the lead time demand is a random variable.

The expected annual cost formula can be simplified to the following:[10]

$$TC = RP + \frac{R}{Q}[C + AE(M > B)] + H\left[\frac{Q}{2} + B - \overline{M}\right].$$

The first term gives the annual purchase cost of the item. The second term gives the fixed cost per order cycle (order cost plus stockout cost) times the number of annual cycles (R/Q). The final term is the holding cost, which amounts to half the order quantity plus the safety stock ($B - \overline{M}$).

By taking partial derivatives of the expected annual cost with respect to Q and B and setting them equal to zero, optimum expressions for Q and B can be obtained:[11]

$$\frac{\partial TC}{\partial Q} = \frac{-R}{Q^2}[C + AE(M > B)] + \frac{H}{2} = 0,$$

$$Q_0 = \sqrt{\frac{2R[C + AE(M > B)]}{H}}$$

$$= \text{economic order quantity in units,}$$

$$\frac{\partial TC}{\partial B} = -\frac{RAP(M > B)}{Q} + H = 0,$$

$$P(M > B) = P(s) = \frac{HQ}{AR} = \text{optimum probability of a stockout.}$$

Lost Sales Case: Stockout Cost per Unit

When stockouts result in lost sales, the expected annual cost formula is modified as follows:

$$TC = RP + \frac{R}{Q}[C + AE(M > B)] + H\left[\frac{Q}{2} + (B - \overline{M}) + E(M > B)\right].$$

The first term gives the purchase cost of an item times the units demanded. The second term gives the fixed cost per order cycle (order cost plus stockout cost) times the number of annual order cycles (the number of order cycles is slightly less than R/Q because of lost sales, but that effect is

---

[10] The formula developed assumes that sales are delayed (not lost) in a backorder situation. In most situations the differences between results obtained from backorders and from lost sales are slight.

[11] For derivations of optimal expressions, see Harold Bierman, Charles Bonini, and Warren H. Hausman, *Quantitative Analysis for Business Decisions*, Homewood, IL: Irwin, 1969, pp. 169–177; Martin K. Starr and David W. Miller, *Inventory Control: Theory and Practice*, Englewood Cliffs, NJ: Prentice-Hall, 1962, pp. 120–124; and Lynwood A. Johnson and Douglas C. Montgomery, *Operations Research in Production Planning, Scheduling, and Inventory Control*, New York: Wiley, 1974, pp. 59–66.

assumed negligible). The third and final term is the holding cost, which includes one-half the order quantity plus safety stock. The stock remaining when Q arrives is expected to be $B - \overline{M}$; however, if shortages occur, the expected depletion will be less than $\overline{M}$ by the expected number of units short, $E(M > B)$. Thus, the average inventory will be larger by the shortage quantity.

By taking partial derivatives of the expected annual cost with respect to Q and B and setting them equal to zero, optimum expressions for Q and B can be obtained:

$$\frac{\partial TC}{\partial Q} = -\frac{R}{Q^2}[C + AE(M > B)] + \frac{H}{2} = 0,$$

$$Q_0 = \sqrt{\frac{2R[C + AE(M > B)]}{H}}$$

$$= \text{economic order quantity in units,}$$

$$\frac{\partial TC}{\partial B} = -\frac{RAP(M > B)}{Q} + H - HP(M > B) = 0,$$

$$P(M > B) = P(s)$$

$$= \frac{HQ}{AR + HQ}$$

$$= \text{optimum probability of a stockout.}$$

Summary

For the backordering case, the optimum formulas for the fixed order size system with dependence have been derived and are as follows:

$$Q_0 = \sqrt{\frac{2R[C + AE(M > B)]}{H}} = \text{EOQ,}$$

$$P(M > B) = P(s)$$

$$= \frac{HQ}{AR}$$

$$= \text{probability of a stockout.}$$

For the lost sales case, the optimum formulas for the fixed order size system with dependence have been derived and are as follows:

$$Q_0 = \sqrt{\frac{2R[C + AE(M > B)]}{H}} = \text{EOQ,}$$

$$P(M > B) = P(s) = \frac{HQ}{AR + HQ} = \text{probability of a stockout.}$$

To obtain the optimum values when order quantity and reorder point are dependent, an iterative procedure can be used which converges to the optimum solution. The procedure, which uses the formulas developed, is as follows:

1. Select appropriate case (backorder or lost sales formulas).
2. Compute Q with $E(M > B) = 0$.
3. Use computed Q to obtain $P(M > B)$ and B.
4. Use computed B to obtain a value for $E(M > B)$.
5. Recompute Q with $E(M > B)$.
6. Repeat steps 3, 4, and 5 until convergence occurs.

The above procedure is a cumbersome but simple task, and usually not more than one iteration is required to obtain convergence. Because of insensitivity, the independence assumption usually provides an excellent approximation to optimality. A simple example can best illustrate the technique.

EXAMPLE D-1

Determine the parameters for a fixed order size system from the data given below and in Table D-1:

$$R = 1800 \text{ units/year},$$
$$C = \$30/\text{order},$$
$$F = 15\%,$$
$$P = \$200/\text{unit},$$
$$A = \$8.00 \text{ per unit backordered}.$$

Table D-1

Lead Time Demand M	Probability $P(M)$	Probability of Stockout $P(M > B)$
48	.02	.98
49	.03	.95
50	.06	.89
51	.07	.82
52	.20	.62
53	.24	.38
54	.20	.18
55	.07	.11
56	.06	.05
57	.03	.02
58	.02	.00
	1.00	

To solve the above problem, we use the procedure outlined in the previous section and find the deterministic economic order quantity:

$$Q_0 = \sqrt{\frac{2CR}{PF}} = \sqrt{\frac{2(30)1800}{200(0.15)}} = 60 \text{ units,}$$

$$P(M > B) = P(s) = \frac{HQ}{AR} = \frac{30(60)}{8(1800)} = 0.125.$$

By consulting Table D-1 for $P(s) = 0.125$, we see that the computed value is between 0.11 and 0.18. Selecting the smaller value, we obtain a reorder point of 55 units. The next step is to compute $E(M > B)$, the expected lead time stockout in units:

$$E(M > B) = \sum_{M=B+1}^{M_{max}} (M - B)P(M)$$

$$= (56 - 55)0.06 + (57 - 55)0.03 + (58 - 55)0.02 = 0.18.$$

It is now necessary to recompute the order quantity using $E(M > B)$ as follows:

$$Q_0 = \sqrt{\frac{2R[C + AE(M > B)]}{PF}} = \sqrt{\frac{2(1800)[30 + 8(0.18)]}{200(0.15)}}$$

$$= 61.4, \text{ or } 61 \text{ units,}$$

$$P(M > B) = \frac{HQ}{AR} = \frac{30(61)}{8(1800)} = 0.127.$$

Consulting Table D-1 for $P(s) = 0.127$, we obtain the reorder point of 55 again. The problem is solved. Since the reorder point has not changed, it will result in the same economic order quantity, 61 units. Convergence has been obtained. The optimum inventory policy for the fixed order size system is $Q_0 = 61$ and $B = 55$ units.

Although convergence will not always be as easy as in the above example, the independent treatment is frequently an excellent approximation to the optimum solution. In the above example, the independent solution was $Q_0 = 60$ and $B = 55$, while the optimum dependent solution was $Q_0 = 61$ and $B = 55$. If the stockout cost per order cycle, $AE(M > B)$, approaches or exceeds the order cost per cycle, C, then the assumption of independence between the order quantity Q and the reorder point B weakens. In that case the order quantity and reorder point should be determined jointly.

APPENDIX E. JOINT PROBABILITY DISTRIBUTIONS

When demand and lead time are two independent distributions, they can be combined to form a single distribution of the demand during the lead time. Unless a computer is used, the forming of joint probability distributions is

Table E-1

Daily Demand D (Units)	Probability $P(D)$	Lead Time L (Days)	Probability $P(L)$
0	.40	1	.25
1	.30	2	.50
2	.20	3	.25
3	.10		1.00
	1.00		

an arduous task even for the simplest of discrete distributions. This section will illustrate the statistical technique for developing a joint probability distribution.

We develop a joint probability distribution of demand during lead time for the independent distributions shown in Table E-1.

From the two distributions it is apparent that the demand during the lead time could be as low as 0 and as high as 9 (a demand of 3 units on each of 3 lead time days). The joint probability distribution will range from 0 to 9 units. To determine the probability of each given lead time demand, it is necessary to sum the various probabilities of ways a specific lead time demand could occur.

Lead time demand = 0:

1. first day	0 demand	0.40(0.25)		= 0.1000
2. first day	0 demand	0.40(0.40)0.50		= 0.0800
second day	0 demand			
3. first day	0 demand	0.40(0.40)0.40(0.25)		= 0.0160
second day	0 demand			
third day	0 demand			
Total				= 0.1960

Lead time demand = 1:

1. first day	1 demand	0.30(0.25)		= 0.0750
2. first day	1 demand	0.30(0.40)0.50		= 0.0600
second day	0 demand			
3. first day	1 demand	0.30(0.40)(0.40)0.25		= 0.0120
second day	0 demand			
third day	0 demand			
4. first day	0 demand	0.40(0.30)0.50		= 0.0600
second day	1 demand			
5. first day	0 demand	0.40(0.30)(0.40)0.25		= 0.0120
second day	1 demand			
third day	0 demand			

6. first day	0 demand	0.40(0.40)(0.30)0.25	= 0.0120
second day	0 demand		
third day	1 demand		
Total			= $\overline{0.2310}$

Lead time demand = 2:

1. first day	2 demand	0.20(0.25)	= 0.0500
2. first day	0 demand	0.40(0.20)(0.50)	= 0.0400
second day	2 demand		
3. first day	2 demand	0.20(0.40)0.50	= 0.0400
second day	0 demand		
4. first day	0 demand	0.40(0.40)(0.20)0.25	= 0.0080
second day	0 demand		
third day	2 demand		
5. first day	0 demand	0.40(0.20)(0.40)0.25	= 0.0080
second day	2 demand		
third day	0 demand		
6. first day	2 demand	0.20(0.40)(0.40)0.25	= 0.0080
second day	0 demand		
third day	0 demand		
7. first day	1 demand	0.30(0.30)(0.50)	= 0.0450
second day	1 demand		
8. first day	1 demand	0.30(0.30)(0.40)0.25	= 0.0090
second day	1 demand		
third day	0 demand		
9. first day	1 demand	0.30(0.40)(0.30)0.25	= 0.0090
second day	0 demand		
third day	1 demand		
10. first day	0 demand	0.40(0.30)(0.30)0.25	= 0.0090
second day	1 demand		
third day	1 demand		
Total			= $\overline{0.2260}$

Lead time demand = 3:

1. first day	3 demand	0.10(0.25)	= 0.0250
2. first day	3 demand	0.10(0.40)0.50	= 0.0200
second day	0 demand		
3. first day	0 demand	0.40(0.10)0.50	= 0.0200
second day	3 demand		
4. first day	3 demand	0.10(0.40)(0.40)0.25	= 0.0040
second day	0 demand		
third day	0 demand		
5. first day	0 demand	0.40(0.10)(0.40)0.25	= 0.0040
second day	3 demand		
third day	0 demand		

6.	first day	0 demand	0.40(0.40)(0.10)0.25	= 0.0040
	second day	0 demand		
	third day	3 demand		
7.	first day	2 demand	0.20(0.30)0.50	= 0.0300
	second day	1 demand		
8.	first day	1 demand	0.30(0.20)(0.50)	= 0.0300
	second day	2 demand		
9.	first day	2 demand	0.20(0.30)(0.40)0.25	= 0.0060
	second day	1 demand		
	third day	0 demand		
10.	first day	2 demand	0.20(0.40)(0.30)0.25	= 0.0060
	second day	0 demand		
	third day	1 demand		
11.	first day	1 demand	0.30(0.20)(0.40)0.25	= 0.0060
	second day	2 demand		
	third day	0 demand		
12.	first day	1 demand	0.30(0.40)(0.20)0.25	= 0.0060
	second day	0 demand		
	third day	2 demand		
13.	first day	0 demand	0.40(0.20)(0.30)0.25	= 0.0060
	second day	2 demand		
	third day	1 demand		
14.	first day	0 demand	0.40(0.30)(0.20)0.25	= 0.0060
	second day	1 demand		
	third day	2 demand		
15.	first day	1 demand	0.30(0.30)(0.30)0.25	= 0.0067
	second day	1 demand		
	third day	1 demand		
Total				= $\overline{0.1797}$

Lead time demand = 4:

1.	first day	3 demand	0.10(0.30)0.50	= 0.0150
	second day	1 demand		
2.	first day	1 demand	0.30(0.10)0.50	= 0.0150
	second day	3 demand		
3.	first day	3 demand	0.10(0.40)(0.30)0.25	= 0.0030
	second day	0 demand		
	third day	1 demand		
4.	first day	3 demand	0.10(0.30)(0.40)0.25	= 0.0030
	second day	1 demand		
	third day	0 demand		
5.	first day	2 demand	0.20(0.20)0.50	= 0.0200
	second day	2 demand		

6. first day	2 demand	0.20(0.20)(0.40)0.25	= 0.0040
second day	2 demand		
third day	0 demand		
7. first day	2 demand	0.20(0.40)(0.20)0.25	= 0.0040
second day	0 demand		
third day	2 demand		
8. first day	2 demand	0.20(0.30)(0.30)(0.25)	= 0.0045
second day	1 demand		
third day	1 demand		
9. first day	1 demand	0.30(0.10)(0.40)0.25	= 0.0030
second day	3 demand		
third day	0 demand		
10. first day	1 demand	0.30(0.40)(0.10)0.25	= 0.0030
second day	0 demand		
third day	3 demand		
11. first day	1 demand	0.30(0.20)(0.30)0.25	= 0.0045
second day	2 demand		
third day	1 demand		
12. first day	1 demand	0.30(0.30)(0.20)0.25	= 0.0045
second day	1 demand		
third day	2 demand		
13. first day	0 demand	0.40(0.10)(0.30)0.25	= 0.0030
second day	3 demand		
third day	1 demand		
14. first day	0 demand	0.40(0.30)(0.10)0.25	= 0.0030
second day	1 demand		
third day	3 demand		
15. first day	0 demand	0.40(0.20)(0.20)0.25	= 0.0040
second day	2 demand		
third day	2 demand		
Total			= $\overline{0.0935}$

Lead time demand = 5:

1. first day	3 demand	0.10(0.20)0.50	= 0.0100
second day	2 demand		
2. first day	3 demand	0.10(0.20)(0.40)0.25	= 0.0020
second day	2 demand		
third day	0 demand		
3. first day	3 demand	0.10(0.40)(0.20)0.25	= 0.0020
second day	0 demand		
third day	2 demand		
4. first day	3 demand	0.10(0.30)(0.30)0.25	= 0.00225
second day	1 demand		
third day	1 demand		

5. first day	2 demand	0.20(0.10)0.50	= 0.0100
second day	3 demand		
6. first day	2 demand	0.20(0.10)(0.40)0.25	= 0.0020
second day	3 demand		
third day	0 demand		
7. first day	2 demand	0.20(0.20)(0.30)0.25	= 0.0030
second day	2 demand		
third day	1 demand		
8. first day	2 demand	0.20(0.30)(0.20)0.25	= 0.0030
second day	1 demand		
third day	2 demand		
9. first day	2 demand	0.20(0.40)(0.10)0.25	= 0.0020
second day	0 demand		
third day	3 demand		
10. first day	1 demand	0.30(0.10)(0.30)0.25	= 0.00225
second day	3 demand		
third day	1 demand		
11. first day	1 demand	0.30(0.20)(0.20)0.25	= 0.0030
second day	2 demand		
third day	2 demand		
12. first day	1 demand	0.30(0.30)(0.10)0.25	= 0.00225
second day	1 demand		
third day	3 demand		
13. first day	0 demand	0.40(0.10)(0.20)0.25	= 0.0020
second day	3 demand		
third day	2 demand		
14. first day	0 demand	0.40(0.20)(0.10)0.25	= 0.0020
second day	2 demand		
third day	3 demand		
Total			$= \overline{0.0478}$

Lead time demand = 6:

1. first day	3 demand	0.10(0.10)0.50	= 0.0050
second day	3 demand		
2. first day	3 demand	0.10(0.20)(0.30)0.25	= 0.0015
second day	2 demand		
third day	1 demand		
3. first day	3 demand	0.10(0.30)(0.20)0.25	= 0.0015
second day	1 demand		
third day	2 demand		
4. first day	3 demand	0.10(0.10)(0.40)0.25	= 0.0010
second day	3 demand		
third day	0 demand		

5. first day	3 demand	0.10(0.40)(0.10)0.25	= 0.0010
second day	0 demand		
third day	3 demand		
6. first day	2 demand	0.20(0.10)(0.30)0.25	= 0.0015
second day	3 demand		
third day	1 demand		
7. first day	2 demand	0.20(0.20)(0.20)0.25	= 0.0020
second day	2 demand		
third day	2 demand		
8. first day	2 demand	0.20(0.30)(0.10)0.25	= 0.0015
second day	1 demand		
third day	3 demand		
9. first day	1 demand	0.30(0.10)(0.20)0.25	= 0.0015
second day	3 demand		
third day	2 demand		
10. first day	1 demand	0.30(0.20)(0.10)0.25	= 0.0015
second day	2 demand		
third day	3 demand		
11. first day	0 demand	0.40(0.10)(0.10)0.25	= 0.0010
second day	3 demand		
third day	3 demand		
Total			= $\overline{0.0190}$

Lead time demand = 7:

1. first day	3 demand	0.10(0.10)(0.30)0.25	= 0.00075
second day	3 demand		
third day	1 demand		
2. first day	3 demand	0.10(0.20)(0.20)0.25	= 0.0010
second day	2 demand		
third day	2 demand		
3. first day	3 demand	0.10(0.30)(0.10)0.25	= 0.00075
second day	1 demand		
third day	3 demand		
4. first day	2 demand	0.20(0.10)(0.20)0.25	= 0.0010
second day	3 demand		
third day	2 demand		
5. first day	2 demand	0.20(0.20)(0.10)0.25	= 0.0010
second day	2 demand		
third day	3 demand		
6. first day	1 demand	0.30(0.10)(0.10)0.25	= 0.00075
second day	3 demand		
third day	3 demand		
Total			= $\overline{0.0053}$

Lead time demand = 8:

1. first day	3 demand	0.10(0.10)(0.20)0.25	= 0.0005	
second day	3 demand			
third day	2 demand			
2. first day	3 demand	0.10(0.20)(0.10)0.25	= 0.0005	
second day	2 demand			
third day	3 demand			
3. first day	2 demand	0.20(0.10)(0.10)0.25	= 0.0005	
second day	3 demand			
third day	3 demand			
Total			= 0.0015	

Lead time demand = 9:

1. first day	3 demand	0.10(0.10)(0.10)0.25	= 0.00025	
second day	3 demand			
third day	3 demand			
Total			= 0.0003	

At this point the reader should be convinced of the laboriousness of the enumeration approach to developing joint probability distributions for even the simplest discrete distributions. Table E-2 contains the joint probability distribution for the lead time demand for the simple example.

To avoid much of the tedium of developing joint probability distributions, Monte Carlo simulation can be directly incorporated in determining inventory management policy. The calculation of joint probability distributions of lead time demand by Monte Carlo simulation requires several hundred replications to assure a reliable estimate. Monte Carlo simulation will be discussed and outlined in Chapter 12.

Table E-2

Lead Time Demand M (units)	Probability $P(M)$	Probability of Stockout $P(M > B)$
0	.1960	.8040
1	.2310	.5730
2	.2260	.3470
3	.1797	.1673
4	.0935	.0738
5	.0477	.0261
6	.0190	.0071
7	.0053	.0018
8	.0015	.0003
9	.0003	.0000
	1.0000	

6

Inventory System
Changes and Limitations

INVENTORY SYSTEM REDESIGN

RELEASING WORKING CAPITAL

INVENTORY SYSTEM CONSTRAINTS
 Exchange Curves
 Working Capital Restrictions
 Storage Space Restrictions
 Working Capital and Storage Space Restrictions
 Overview of Constraints

EXCESS STOCK DETERMINATION
 An Excess Model
 Minimum Economic Salvage Value
 Lead Time Influence
QUESTIONS
PROBLEMS
CASES
MATHEMATICAL ABBREVIATIONS AND SYMBOLS
SUMMARY OF FORMULAS
APPENDIX A: OPTIMIZING CONSTRAINED FUNCTIONS

Inventory systems develop as the inventory control needs of an organization evolve. When an organization is small or in its infancy, inventories are generally small. Elaborate systems of inventory control are unnecessary, so fairly unsophisticated methods of control are implemented. As an organization develops new products or pursues other forms of diversification, the problem of control increases. Coping with growing needs all too often results in the mere expansion of the existing, unsophisticated inventory system. Eventually, the expanded system becomes overloaded and extremely inefficient. At this point, it is necessary to redesign the inventory system in its entirety in light of current and future needs.

The signal for greater inventory control and system redesign can come from many sources. If the system loses orders, does not adequately indicate inventory status, causes too many stockouts, accumulates excessive and surplus inventory, does not serve the purposes of its users, or simply fails when measured for performance, it is time to consider system redesign. Overlooking any of these signals can be harmful. For instance, management may believe the system is adequate if items are always available when requested and no stockouts occur. An inadequate inventory system to some can appear efficient through an overinvestment in inventory. This can occur because top management is more alerted to stockouts than to overstocks. An overstock is indicated by a large investment in inventory and a low stock turnover ratio. If stockouts never occur, it is likely that the inventory investment is too high, and the current inventory system may need some degree of revision.

On the other hand, it must be recognized that an inadequate or outdated system design is only one source of control problems. Poor results can emanate from inappropriate operating procedures, the system not operating as designed, personnel shortcomings, external and economic factors, etc. Before a system is redesigned or even changed, the alteration must be weighed carefully. Systems which must be revised for small changes in operating conditions are of limited value. It is also untenable to require a mathematical genius for routine decisions. The relative value of alternative inventory systems should be measured by the capital investment and by the customer service and operating cost advantages of one over another.

Frequently inventory systems and levels are reevaluated under duress, in an economic downturn or recession. Organizations experiencing liquidity or cash problems usually limit their investment in inventory. Inventory systems should be evaluated periodically (perhaps yearly) as to their effectiveness in attaining organizational goals. Although inventory inefficiencies are highlighted during periods of economic stress, larger efficiencies and savings also are available during periods of economic growth.

INVENTORY SYSTEM REDESIGN

Before any changes are considered, the various objectives of the inventory system should be delineated. It is essential to define what objectives are to be sought and their relative importance. The relative importance of various objectives may change over time or as dictated by economic conditions. It is practically impossible to design an effective system without a thorough understanding of the purposes it will serve.

When considering a change in an inventory system, a good starting point is to review the existing system, so as to determine whether or not to change it, in what way it should be changed, and to what extent. In this respect, the decision to change an inventory system can be treated like any other capital investment analysis.

The redesign of an inventory system should be based on the resultant system's benefit to the organization. The benefit can be expressed in incremental cost savings and/or improved customer service. Since a revised system affects manpower levels, paperwork, information flow, and accounting functions as well as inventory levels, it is difficult to establish a precise point estimate of total cost savings. It is easier to determine the cost savings that result from changes in the level of average inventory. Before any revised inventory system is implemented, an incremental cost analysis should be conducted to indicate the potential benefits of redesign. The final decision should not be based solely on a cost analysis, since other intangible or unquantifiable factors also must be considered. The interested parties and personnel who use or work in the existing inventory system should be part of the redesign study.

It is generally too costly and time-consuming to analyze every item. Conclusions can be drawn from a sample of items, preferably a random sample. When relevant information is scarce or when the inventory involves thousands of items, data collection can involve all the high dollar usage items and only a sample of the remaining items.

When feasible, simulation is an excellent analysis tool for determining the impact of different system designs without actually implementing them. The principle involved in any simulation is to design a model in mathematical or symbolic terms which behaves in the same manner as the real system. Different systems with various features can be tested via simulation models, and the best system selected. Simulation will be treated more thoroughly in Chapter 12.

Frequently, a pilot study of the inventory system can reveal the potential benefits of redesign. It can be conducted in the following manner:

1. A representative sample of inventory items is selected and analyzed.
2. Using the appropriate inventory models, theoretical and actual performance are compared.

3. The potential cost savings and resultant benefits are determined.
4. A decision is made to continue the study, stop the study, revise the inventory system, or make no changes in the inventory system.

Another approach, which provides maximum security, is to run the new and old systems in parallel. This costly approach provides the greatest amount of comparative information. The new plan should be adopted with a schedule that contains milestones indicating continuation or termination. Finally the umbilical cord of the old system must be severed and the new system must stand alone.

It is sometimes advisable to install a new computerized system with a small range of items and gradually expand it to other items or locations. The gradual implementation provides time to correct errors and miscalculations. Rapid installation based on a "sink or swim" philosophy can be devastating for systems with major flaws or weaknesses that are not apparent until after installation. A stepwise installation provides time for unanticipated adjustments and modifications.

Special caution should be exercised in reviewing a new inventory system for several periods after its implementation. Stock levels and service levels are likely to be higher than planned for some time. The replenishment of understocked items will usually be more rapid than the depletion of overstocked items. The net result will be a temporary increase in stock. Months or even years may be required to realize the full benefits of a control system.

A new system will not be perfect, and it will not produce optimum results. The important thing is that any new system be an improvement over present methods. It should produce schedules and plans that are reasonably good. It is unrealistic to rely on everything going right. There must be reserve built into any system in the form of contingencies to cope with emergencies or unusual events. A fallback capability or a failure mode is necessary.

EXAMPLE 1

An organization with an inventory of five items is considering a change from a periodic to a perpetual inventory system. Currently, each item is ordered at the end of the month. The ordering cost per item is $10 per order, and the holding cost is 20% per year. Relevant item data are listed in Table 1. Should the organization adopt a perpetual inventory system?

The cost of the periodic inventory system is as follows:

$$\text{periodic annual cost} = (\text{order cost}) + (\text{holding cost})$$
$$= 10(60) + 0.2(4200) = \$1440.$$

Table 1

Item	Annual Demand R_i	Unit Cost P_i	Orders per Year	Average Inventory $P_i R_i/24$
1	600	$ 3.00	12	$ 75.00
2	900	10.00	12	375.00
3	2400	5.00	12	500.00
4	12000	5.00	12	2500.00
5	18000	1.00	12	750.00
			60	$4200.00

Table 2

Item	Optimal Dollar Order Size $P_i Q_i$	Orders per Year $P_i R_i/P_i Q_i$	Order Size Q_i
1	$ 424.26	4.24	141
2	948.68	9.49	95
3	1095.44	10.95	219
4	2449.49	24.49	490
5	1341.54	13.42	1342
	$6259.51	62.59	

To determine the cost of the perpetual inventory system, it is necessary to calculate the EOQ in dollars for each item. The optimal dollar order size for each item is obtained by multiplying the optimal order size by the unit cost, or

$$\text{EOQ in dollars} = P_i Q_i = P_i \sqrt{\frac{2R_i C}{FP_i}} = \sqrt{\frac{2P_i R_i C}{F}} .$$

Using the above expression, the optimal order size in dollars can be calculated (see Table 2). The cost of the perpetual inventory system is as follows:

$$\text{perpetual annual cost} = (\text{order cost}) + (\text{holding cost})$$

$$= 10(62.59) + \frac{0.20(6259.51)}{2}$$

$$= 10(62.59) + 0.20(3130)$$

$$= \$1252.$$

The adoption of the perpetual system will result in annual savings of $1440 − $1252 = $188. The perpetual system will reduce costs by 13% from the existing periodic system.

A comparison of a perpetual and an MRP inventory system for an item with dependent demand is illustrated in Chapter 8.

RELEASING WORKING CAPITAL

If money is tight, an organization can release working capital by decreasing its investment in inventory. This can be done by reducing lot sizes below current quantities and placing orders more frequently. The net effect of placing smaller orders is to raise the holding cost fraction in order to lower the average inventory investment. While ordering in smaller quantities may appear uneconomical by previous standards, liquidity pressures can bear upon holding costs and effectively alter the wisdom of carrying larger quantities. The limitation of the inventory investment for working capital reasons is illustrated in the next section.

Organizations should be careful in arbitrarily reducing lot sizes for liquidity purposes. The smaller lot sizes will increase the exposure to stockouts for independent demand items and thus lower the service level. Additionally, quantity discounts may be lost. All the ramifications for operational performance should be considered before implementing such a policy. For example, if service levels are to be maintained while lot sizes are reduced, it will be necessary to increase safety stocks. All the facets of inventory management should be kept in view when attempting to change systems.

INVENTORY SYSTEM CONSTRAINTS

In determining the optimal inventory system, it has been assumed that no limitations are placed upon it. Frequently, management will impose physical and economic limitations that render the optimal system unacceptable. Since the inventory system is only a single subsystem in an organization, management may be required to suboptimize the inventory system for the overall good of the organization. Stringent budget requirements can sometimes necessitate that inventory levels be less than optimal. This is not uncommon when the liquidity preference increases. In essence, the liquidity condition necessitates an increase in the holding cost fraction and negates the previously determined optimal order quantities. The determination of the increased holding cost fraction is a relatively simple matter.

Suppose first that an organization with a perpetual inventory system and an average inventory investment of $3130 (Example 1) must reduce its average inventory investment to $2000 because of liquidity necessities. If the existing holding cost fraction is 0.20, what will be the new, higher holding cost fraction? The ratio of the old average inventory investment to the new is as follows:

$$\frac{\left(\sum_{i=1}^{n} \frac{P_i Q_i}{2}\right)_1}{\left(\sum_{i=1}^{n} \frac{P_i Q_i}{2}\right)_2} = \frac{3130}{2000} = \frac{\sum_{i=1}^{n} \sqrt{\frac{P_i R_i C}{2F_1}}}{\sum_{i=1}^{n} \sqrt{\frac{P_i R_i C}{2F_2}}} = \sqrt{\frac{F_2}{F_1}},$$

$$\frac{3130}{2000} = \sqrt{\frac{F_2}{0.20}},$$

$$F_2 = 0.489.$$

Thus, the holding cost fraction increases from 0.20 to 0.489. The economic order quantity for each inventory item would be recalculated with the holding cost fraction of 0.489, which would ensure that the total average inventory investment would be $2000.00. In a subsequent section, the same type of problem will be solved with the more versatile mathematical technique of Lagrange multipliers.[1]

Now suppose an organization with a periodic inventory system and an average inventory investment of $4200 (see Example 1) must reduce its average inventory investment to $3150 for liquidity reasons. If the existing economic order interval is 1 month and the holding cost fraction is 0.20, what will be the new economic order interval and the new holding cost fraction? The ratio of the old inventory investment to the new is as follows:

$$\frac{\sum_{i=1}^{n} \frac{R_i P_i T_1}{2}}{\sum_{i=1}^{n} \frac{R_i P_i T_2}{2}} = \frac{T_1}{T_2} = \frac{4200}{3150},$$

$$\frac{1}{T_2} = \frac{4200}{3150},$$

$$T_2 = 0.75.$$

Thus, the review period decreases from 1 month to 0.75 months. The maximum inventory level will have to be recalculated for each item, using the shorter review period. The increased holding cost fraction is determined

---

[1] For a further elaboration of Lagrange multipliers, see Appendix A at the end of this chapter.

as follows:

$$\frac{T_1}{T_2} = \frac{\sqrt{\dfrac{2C}{F_1 \sum_{i=1}^{n} P_i R_i}}}{\sqrt{\dfrac{2C}{F_2 \sum_{i=1}^{n} P_i R_i}}} = \sqrt{\frac{F_2}{F_1}},$$

$$\frac{1}{0.75} = \frac{F_2}{0.2},$$

$$F_2 = 0.27.$$

The holding cost fraction increases from 0.20 to 0.27.

Exchange Curves

At times it is difficult to obtain explicit values for the fixed cost per order (C) and the annual holding cost fraction (F) to be used as inputs to an EOQ. Not only is it troublesome to designate their values, but it may even be undesirable to use explicit values to minimize costs on an individual basis. Under some circumstances, it is more appropriate to permit management to control aggregate inventory levels without being burdened with individual item decisions. Management may more fittingly deal with the design of the total inventory system and impose broad limitations on the amount of inventory held in general. With this approach, the aggregate inventory investment and the total number of replenishments per year become management policy variables. They can be set at levels acceptable to management under particular operating and financial conditions and allowed to change as conditions warrant.

If management attempts to use the total average inventory investment and the total number of annual replenishments as decision variables, it will find that at a prescribed value for one variable there will be a tradeoff (or exchange) for the other. Specifically, if management plans to decrease the total average investment in inventory, it concomitantly increases the total number of annual replenishments. This tradeoff between management policies can be shown by a method called *exchange curves*. An exchange curve shows the optimal tradeoffs that can be achieved between two or more aggregate measures of performance. Management may select an acceptable operating point on an aggregate exchange curve of total average inventory investment versus total number of annual replenishments. At the selected point, values for C and F will be implied, and order quantities for individual items will be based on the ratio C/F. These quantities will lie within the chosen limitations and conform to aggregate policies.

The construction of the exchange curve is based on the assumption that the fixed cost per order (C) is the same for all inventory items under consideration and will be determined implicitly. If an EOQ is used for each item in the (deterministic) system, the total average inventory investment (for a group of n items) is

$$U = \sum_{i=1}^{n} \frac{P_i Q_i}{2} = \sum_{i=1}^{n} \sqrt{\frac{CP_i R_i}{2F}} = \sqrt{\frac{C}{F}} \sum_{i=1}^{n} \sqrt{\frac{P_i R_i}{2}},$$

and the total number of annual replenishments is

$$V = \sum_{i=1}^{n} \frac{R_i}{Q_i} = \sum_{i=1}^{n} \sqrt{\frac{P_i R_i F}{2C}} = \sqrt{\frac{F}{C}} \sum_{i=1}^{n} \sqrt{\frac{P_i R_i}{2}}.$$

Both of the policy variables (U and V) are shown to be dependent on the value of the ratio C/F. The multiplication of the above formulas for U and V results in the following hyperbolic expression:

$$UV = \left(\sum_{i=1}^{n} \sqrt{\frac{P_i R_i}{2}} \right)^2.$$

Division of the formula for U by the formula for V gives

$$\frac{U}{V} = \frac{C}{F},$$

so that any point on the hyperbolic curve implies a value of C/F. In cases where either C or F is known explicitly, the value of the other parameter is implied from the implicit value of C/F.

The general effects of the ratio C/F apply to all items considered in the analysis. As C/F increases, each order quantity increases, which in turn increases the total average inventory investment and decreases the total number of annual replenishments. By varying C/F, the aggregate exchange curve can be traced. By selecting a desirable operating point on the curve, a value for C/F is implied. Using the C/F value in the EOQ formula for each individual item gives the desired operating characteristics for the entire system.

EXAMPLE 2

From the subsequent data (from Example 1) for a perpetual inventory system, derive the following: (a) the hyperbolic exchange curve for total average inventory investment and the total number of annual replenishments, (b) the optimal total number of annual replenishments for a total average inventory investment of $3130.00, (c) the parameter C/F for a total average inventory investment of $3130.00, (d) the optimal total number of annual replenishments for a total average inventory investment of $2000.00, (e) the parameter C/F for a total average inventory investment of $2000.00, (f) the optimal total average inventory investment for 100 total annual inventory replenishments, (g) the annual holding cost fraction for parts c and e above if the order cost is $10.00 per order, and (h) the optimal individual order sizes for a total average inventory investment of $3130.00.

Item	Demand R_i	Unit Cost P_i	Annual Investment $P_i R_i/2$	$\sqrt{\text{Col. 4}}$
1	600	$ 3.00	$ 900.00	30.00
2	900	10.00	4,500.00	67.08
3	2,400	5.00	6,000.00	77.46
4	12,000	5.00	30,000.00	173.21
5	18,000	1.00	9,000.00	94.87
			$50,400.00	442.62

Figure 1. An exchange curve ($UV = 195,912$).

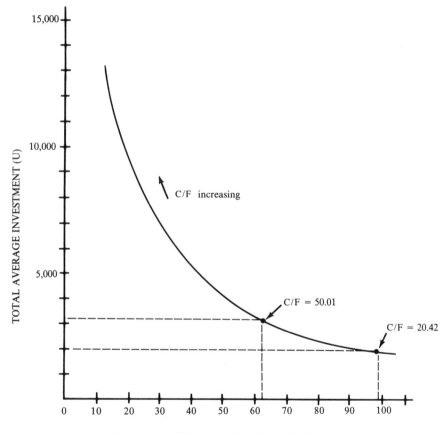

TOTAL NUMBER OF ANNUAL REPLENISHMENTS (V)

a:

$$UV = \left(\sum_{i=1}^{n} \sqrt{\frac{P_i R_i}{2}} \right)^2 = (442.62)^2 = 195{,}912.$$

The exchange curve is illustrated in Figure 1.

b:

$$V = \frac{195{,}912}{U} = \frac{195{,}912}{3130} = 62.59 \text{ annual replenishments.}$$

c:

$$\frac{C}{F} = \frac{U}{V} = \frac{3130}{62.59} = 50.01.$$

d:

$$V = \frac{195{,}912}{2000} = 97.96 \text{ annual replenishments.}$$

e:

$$\frac{C}{F} = \frac{U}{V} = \frac{2000}{97.96} = 20.42.$$

f:

$$U = \frac{195{,}912}{V} = \frac{195{,}912}{100} = \$1959.12.$$

g:

$$\frac{C}{F} = 50.01;$$

$$F = \frac{C}{50.01} = \frac{10}{50.01} = 0.20 \text{ for part c,}$$

$$F = \frac{C}{20.42} = \frac{10}{20.42} = 0.498 \text{ for part e.}$$

Note that the holding cost fractions are the same as those used in the previous section on inventory system constraints.

h: From part c above for $U = 3130$, the C/F value is 50.01. Then

$$Q_{0i} = \sqrt{\frac{2CR_i}{P_i F}} = \sqrt{\left(\frac{C}{F}\right)\left(\frac{2R_i}{P_i}\right)}.$$

The optimal individual order sizes (Q_{0i}) are tabulated in the last column of the table below:

Item	C/F	$2R_i/P_i$	$Q_{0i} = \sqrt{(\text{col. 2})(\text{col. 3})}$
1	50.01	400.00	141
2	50.01	180.00	95
3	50.01	960.00	219
4	50.01	4,800.00	490
5	50.01	36,000.00	1342

The optimal individual order sizes are the same as those listed in Table 2 for Example 1.

Working Capital Restrictions

If working capital restrictions limit the size of the average inventory investment to J dollars, the determination of the best inventory levels can be determined by the Lagrange-multiplier method. Appendix A at the end of this chapter outlines the procedures for optimizing constrained functions by this method. The problem can be stated as:

$$\text{Minimize} \quad G = (\text{order cost}) + (\text{holding cost})$$

$$= \sum_{i=1}^{n} \left[\frac{R_i C}{Q_i} + \frac{Q_i P_i F}{2} \right]$$

$$\text{subject to} \quad g = \sum_{i=1}^{n} \frac{P_i Q_i}{2} = J.$$

From the above minimization problem subject to a single constraint, the following Lagrangian expression can be developed:

$$h = C \sum_{i=1}^{n} \frac{R_i}{Q_i} + F \sum_{i=1}^{n} \frac{P_i Q_i}{2} + \lambda \left[\sum_{i=1}^{n} \frac{P_i Q_i}{2} - J \right].$$

To minimize the original objective function G subject to the restriction requires the minimization of h with respect to Q_i and λ. This is accomplished by taking the partial derivatives and setting them equal to zero:

$$\frac{\partial h}{\partial Q_i} = -\frac{C R_i}{Q_i^2} + \frac{F P_i}{2} + \frac{\lambda P_i}{2} = 0,$$

$$\frac{\partial h}{\partial \lambda} = \sum_{i=1}^{n} \frac{P_i Q_i}{2} - J = 0.$$

The simultaneous equations above can be solved for Q_i and λ:

$$Q_i = \sqrt{\frac{2 C R_i}{(F + \lambda) P_i}},$$

$$\lambda = \frac{C \left(\sum_{i=1}^{n} \sqrt{P_i R_i} \right)^2}{2 J^2} - F.$$

An example can best illustrate the technique.

EXAMPLE 3

The optimal average inventory investment in Example 1 is $3130. Suppose the organization has a shortage of working capital and can only afford an average inventory investment of $2000. Given the information in Example 1 and the $2000 restriction on the average investment, what is the best perpetual inventory policy?

The problem can be stated as the minimization of the cost

$$G = (\text{order cost}) + (\text{holding cost})$$

$$= 10 \sum_{i=1}^{n} \frac{R_i}{Q_i} + 0.20 \sum_{i=1}^{n} \frac{P_i Q_i}{2}$$

subject to the restriction that

$$g = \sum_{i=1}^{n} \frac{P_i Q_i}{2} = 2000.$$

To solve the problem, the Lagrange-multiplier technique must be applied. Its application results in the following optimum expressions:

$$\lambda = \frac{C \left(\sum_{i=1}^{n} \sqrt{P_i R_i} \right)^2}{2J^2} - F = \frac{10(625.95)^2}{2(2000)^2} - 0.20 = 0.289,$$

$$Q_i = \sqrt{\frac{2CR_i}{(F + \lambda) P_i}} = \sqrt{\frac{20 R_i}{0.489 P_i}}.$$

Table 3 develops the order size for each item.
For item 1, the order size is determined in the following manner:

$$Q_i = \sqrt{\frac{20(600)}{0.489(3.00)}} = 90 \text{ units.}$$

Table 3

Item	$P_i R_i$	$\sqrt{P_i R_i}$	Order Size Q_i	Orders per Year R_i/Q_i	Dollar Order Size $P_i Q_i$
1	$ 1,800	42.43	90	6.66	$ 270.00
2	9,000	94.87	61	14.75	610.00
3	12,000	109.54	140	17.14	700.00
4	60,000	244.95	313	38.33	1565.00
5	18,000	134.16	858	20.98	858.00
		625.95		97.86	$4003.00

For all other items in the table, the values are obtained in a similar fashion. The cost of the constrained inventory policy is

$$G = (\text{order cost}) + (\text{holding cost})$$

$$= 10(97.86) + \frac{0.20(4003)}{2} = \$1379.$$

It can be seen that the annual cost increases from \$1252 for the optimal policy to \$1379 for the constrained policy. An increase in the annual cost of \$127 (\$1379 − \$1252) allows the organization to cut the average inventory level by \$1130 (\$3130 − \$2000). The value of λ (0.289) is of interesting economic significance. It represents the increment added to the annual holding cost fraction when the inventory restriction is placed on the average investment. Had the holding cost fraction in the original problem been 0.489 (0.20 + 0.289) instead of 0.20, the optimal inventory policy would have indicated a total average inventory investment of \$2000.00.

The procedure outlined in this section puts a limitation on the average inventory investment. Sometimes the limitation will be on the total investment in inventory at any given time. The only difference in the procedure is a change in the constraint to the following:

$$\sum_{i=1}^{n} P_i Q_i = \sum_{i=1}^{n} P_i R_i T = J.$$

The previous example illustrates the impact of a liquidity restriction on inventory. The Lagrange-multiplier method exhibits the optimum redesign of the inventory system to accommodate the capital constraint. This calculus-based method can be extended beyond the single constraint of the previous example to multiple constraints as well as other types of restrictions.

Storage Space Restrictions

If storage space restrictions limit the maximum inventory size to W cubic feet, the determination of the best inventory levels can be obtained by using Lagrange multipliers. The problem can be stated as:

$$\text{minimize} \quad G = (\text{order cost}) + (\text{holding cost})$$

$$= \sum_{i=1}^{n} \left[\frac{R_i C}{Q_i} + \frac{Q_i P_i F}{2} \right]$$

$$\text{subject to} \quad g = \sum_{i=1}^{n} w_i Q_i \leq W,$$

where

$$W = \text{total storage volume for all inventory items,}$$

$$w_i = \text{storage requirement for each unit of item } i.$$

The constraint makes sure that even if all items reach their maximum inventory positions simultaneously, the storage space will still be able to contain them all.

From the previous minimization problem subject to a single constraint, the following Lagrangian expression can be developed:

$$h = C \sum_{i=1}^{n} \frac{R_i}{Q_i} + F \sum_{i=1}^{n} \frac{P_i Q_i}{2} + \lambda \left[\sum_{i=1}^{n} w_i Q_i - W \right].$$

To minimize the original objective function G subject to the inequality restriction requires the simultaneous solution of the following equations:

$$\frac{\partial h}{\partial Q_i} = -\frac{CR_i}{Q_i^2} + \frac{FP_i}{2} + \lambda w_i = 0,$$

$$\lambda(g - W) = \lambda \left[\sum_{i=1}^{n} w_i Q_i - W \right] = 0,$$

where

$$\lambda = 0 \quad \text{if} \quad g - W < 0,$$

$$\lambda > 0 \quad \text{if} \quad g - W = 0.$$

When $\lambda = 0$, the storage capacity limitation is not binding and the optimal solution is to use the independently determined economic lot sizes for each item.

From the simultaneous equations above, the following expression for Q_i can be obtained:

$$Q_i = \sqrt{\frac{2CR_i}{FP_i + 2\lambda w_i}}.$$

By testing different values of λ, it is possible to determine the optimum order quantities Q_i that meet the requirements of the constraining condition g. Manually, the enumerative process is laborious, but it is easily handled with the aid of a computer. The iterative process requires that λ be set equal to zero and small increments be added to it until the problem conditions are met. An example can best illustrate the technique.

EXAMPLE 4

If the maximum storage space available in Example 1 is 2000 cubic feet, what is the optimal perpetual inventory system? Assume the unit volume requirement in Table 4.

The problem can be stated as the minimization of the following cost equation:

$$G = (\text{order cost}) + (\text{holding cost})$$

$$= 10 \sum_{i=1}^{n} \frac{R_i}{Q_i} + 0.20 \sum_{i=1}^{n} \frac{P_i Q_i}{2}$$

subject to the restriction that

$$g = \sum_{i=1}^{n} w_i Q_i \le 2000.$$

By trial and error or an enumerative computer program, the optimum value of λ is found to be 0.14. Table 5 develops the relevant order quantities for each item. For item 1, the order quantity in Table 5 is obtained in the following manner:

$$Q_i = \sqrt{\frac{2CR_i}{FP_i + 2\lambda w_i}} = \sqrt{\frac{2(10)600}{0.2(3) + 2(0.14)1}} = 117 \text{ units.}$$

The other order quantities are found in a similar manner. The storage space constraint results in smaller order quantities than in the unconstrained solution in Example 1. The reduction in order sizes ensures that the maximum storage space

Table 4

Item i	w_i (ft^3)
1	1.0
2	1.5
3	0.5
4	2.0
5	1.0

Table 5

Item	R_i	P_i	w_i	Q_i	$w_i Q_i$ (ft^3)
1	600	$ 3.00	1.0	117	117.0
2	900	10.00	1.5	86	129.0
3	2,400	5.00	0.5	205	102.5
4	12,000	5.00	2.0	392	784.0
5	18,000	1.00	1.0	866	866.0
					1,998.5

requirement of 2000 cubic feet is not violated. The value of λ has a useful economic interpretation: it is the marginal value of warehouse space and means that the cost saving per year from one more available cubic foot is $.14.

Working Capital and Storage Space Restrictions

Working capital and storage space considerations may both constrain the operation of an inventory system. If the average inventory investment is limited to J dollars and maximum inventory storage space to W cubic feet, the best inventory level can be obtained by using Lagrange multipliers with the Kuhn-Tucker conditions. The problem can be stated as:

$$\text{minimize} \quad G = (\text{order cost}) + (\text{holding cost})$$

$$= \sum_{i=1}^{n} \left[\frac{R_i C}{Q_i} + \frac{Q_i P_i F}{2} \right]$$

$$\text{subject to} \quad g_1 = \sum_{i=1}^{n} \frac{P_i Q_i}{2} \leq J,$$

$$g_2 = \sum_{i=1}^{n} w_i Q_i \leq W.$$

From the above minimization problem, subject to two constraints, the following Lagrangian expression can be developed:

$$h = C \sum_{i=1}^{n} \frac{R_i}{Q_i} + F \sum_{i=1}^{n} \frac{P_i Q_i}{2} + \lambda_1 \left[\sum_{i=1}^{n} \frac{P_i Q_i}{2} - J \right] + \lambda_2 \left[\sum_{i=1}^{n} w_i Q_i - W \right].$$

To minimize the original objective function G subject to the two inequality restrictions requires the simultaneous solution of the following equations:

$$\frac{\partial h}{\partial Q_i} = -\frac{CR_i}{Q_i^2} + \frac{FP_i}{2} + \frac{\lambda_1 P_i}{2} + \lambda_2 w_i = 0,$$

$$\lambda_1 (g_1 - J) = \lambda_1 \left[\sum_{i=1}^{n} \frac{P_i Q_i}{2} - J \right] = 0,$$

$$\lambda_2 (g_2 - W) = \lambda_2 \left[\sum_{i=1}^{n} w_i Q_i - W \right] = 0,$$

where

$$\lambda_1 = 0 \quad \text{if } g_1 - J < 0, \qquad \lambda_2 = 0 \quad \text{if } g_2 - W < 0,$$
$$\lambda_1 > 0 \quad \text{if } g_1 - J = 0, \qquad \lambda_2 > 0 \quad \text{if } g_2 - W = 0.$$

From the first equation, the following expression for Q_i can be obtained:

$$Q_i = \sqrt{\frac{2CR_i}{FP_i + \lambda_1 P_i + 2\lambda_2 w_i}}.$$

Substituting the Q_i expression into the two remaining simultaneous equations, the following expressions are obtained:

$$\frac{\lambda_1}{2}\left[\sum_{i=1}^{n}\sqrt{\frac{2CR_i P_i^2}{FP_i + \lambda_1 P_i + 2\lambda_2 w_i}} - J\right] = 0,$$

$$\lambda_2\left[\sum_{i=1}^{n}\sqrt{\frac{2CR_i w_i^2}{FP_i + \lambda_1 P_i + 2\lambda_2 w_i}} - W\right] = 0.$$

By testing different combinations of values of λ_1 and λ_2, it is possible to determine the optimum order quantities Q_i that meet the requirements of the constraining conditions g_1 and g_2. The enumerative process requires a computer. The process begins with λ_1 and λ_2 set equal to zero, and then one is held constant while the other is increased in increments, and vice versa. An example will illustrate the procedure.

EXAMPLE 5

Assume the maximum storage space available in Example 1 is 1500 cubic feet, and the unit space requirements in Table 6 apply to each item. If working capital is restricted so that the average inventory investment must not exceed $2000, what is the best inventory system?

The problem can be stated as the minimization of the following cost equation:

$$G = (\text{order cost}) + (\text{holding cost})$$

$$= 10\sum_{i=1}^{n}\frac{R_i}{Q_i} + 0.20\sum_{i=1}^{n}\frac{P_i Q_i}{2}$$

Table 6

Item	Volume w_i (ft^3)
1	1.0
2	1.5
3	0.5
4	2.0
5	1.0

Table 7

Item	R_i	P_i	w_i	Q_i	$w_i Q_i$	$P_i Q_i/2$
1	600	$ 3.00	1.0	92	92.0	$ 138.0
2	900	10.00	1.5	73	109.5	365.0
3	2,400	5.00	0.5	178	89.0	445.0
4	12,000	5.00	2.0	302	604.0	755.0
5	18,000	1.00	1.0	609	609.0	304.5
					1503.5	$2007.5

subject to

$$g_1 = \sum_{i=1}^{n} w_i Q_i \leq 1500,$$

$$g_2 = \sum_{i=1}^{n} \frac{P_i Q_i}{2} \leq 2000.$$

With an enumerative computer program, the values of $\lambda_1 = 0.03$ and $\lambda_2 = 0.37$ are obtained. Table 7 establishes the optimal order quantities for each item. For item 1, the order quantity is obtained as follows:

$$Q_1 = \sqrt{\frac{2CR_1}{FP_1 + \lambda_1 P_1 + 2\lambda_1 w_1}} = \sqrt{\frac{2(10)600}{0.2(3) + 0.03(3) + 2(0.37)(1)}} = 92.$$

The other order quantities are obtained in a similar manner. Because of the inability to stock fractional units, the goal of $2000 and 1500 cubic feet cannot be precisely attained. However, the solution comes very close. All of the respective order quantities are less than those in the unconstrained solution obtained in Example 1. The multiplier values ($\lambda_1 = 0.03$ and $\lambda_2 = 0.37$) indicate the marginal benefits from relaxing the constraints. The overall impact of capital and space limitations is to increase the holding cost of an item.

Overview of Constraints

What may seem like optimum policies for individual items (evaluated in isolation) may be less than optimal when the overall aggregate inventory condition is considered. There are many types of constraints that can be put upon inventory systems.[2] The Lagrange-multiplier method can be utilized to obtain optimum solutions for single, and frequently double, constraining conditions.

[2] R. J. Tersine et al., "Varying Lost Sizes as an Alternative to Undertime and Layoffs in Aggregate Scheduling," *International Journal of Production Research*, Vol. 24, No. 1, 1986.

An American Production and Inventory Control Society (APICS) special report developed another technique for optimizing order quantities under a number of orders (setups) limitation.[3] The technique is called the "lot-size inventory management interpolation technique," or LIMIT. The LIMIT technique calculates the optimum lot sizes when the EOQ lot sizes are infeasible. It revises all lot sizes by the same proportion to bring them within the limit. When capital or storage space is insufficient, the lot sizes are reduced; when capacity is insufficient, the lot sizes are increased. The LIMIT technique produces the same results as Lagrange multipliers for systems faced with only one constraint.

When constraints exist, the optimum solution techniques increase in complexity. Fortunately, constraints are frequently inactive. An inactive constraint does not modify the optimum solution by its existence. In other words, it can be ignored when solving the problem. Active constraints are those that modify the optimum solution by their existence, and they must be included in obtaining the solution to the problem.

It is a simple matter to determine if constraints are active or inactive. First, determine the order quantities by ignoring the constraints (assume all constraints are inactive). If the order quantities satisfy the constraints, the solution is optimal. If the unconstrained order quantities do not satisfy the constraints, determine the optimal solution for one constraint at a time (assume only one constraint is active) and establish its suitability. If the singly constrained order quantities satisfy all constraints, the solution is optimal. If none of the singly constrained order quantities satisfy all the constraints (more than one constraint is active), solve the problem treating multiple constraints as active, as in Example 5.

The effort required to solve a problem increases rapidly with the number of constraints.

EXCESS STOCK DETERMINATION

Many organizations find themselves in a situation where inventory levels are excessive. The impact of excessive inventory on the fiscal health of an organization makes it imperative that reductions be made. Often this condition results in a mandate to materials managers to achieve a lower level by a given point in time. Reasonable or not, material managers must respond with their best effort to achieve the goal without serious disruptions in operations.

Reduction of inventory can be accomplished in three ways: (1) increase the outflow (demand) of items, (2) limit the inflow (supply) of items, and (3)

[3] James H. Greene (Ed.), *Production and Inventory Control Handbook*, New York: McGraw-Hill, 1970, pp. 16–17 to 16–22.

reduce the level of surplus items. The outflow can be increased by aggressive marketing efforts such as market penetration, advertising, and special sales promotions. The inflow can be limited in several ways. Safety stock levels can be reduced by decreasing service levels, maintaining production schedules, improving the quality of inflows, and shortening lead times. Lot size levels can be lowered by increasing the holding cost fraction and reducing setup (ordering) costs. In-process inventory levels can be lowered by reducing lead times, improving efficiency, emphasizing and controlling quality, and improving input-output control (scheduling). Before any of the above considerations are implemented, there should be an overall review of inventory policy variables to determine their impact on operating procedures.

The third major way to reduce inventory concerns surplus items. These usually include obsolete and slow-moving items. However, it is also possible to have excessive levels of fast-moving items. Obsolete items for which there are no known future requirements should be sold or salvaged. For other items it is necessary to determine if excessive levels exist.

Excess inventory is a negative asset that is dead weight. It uses valuable storage space, depletes working capital, eliminates other opportunities, inflates assets, and reduces return on investment. Excess and obsolete items should be subjected to disposal. Periodic review can identify items that need not be carried in stock or items whose quantity should be reduced.

The reasons for surplus and obsolete items are varied. They may result from:

1. a redesign of a product;
2. a change in methods of production;
3. a reduction in demand for a product;
4. new technological innovations;
5. forecast errors;
6. overzealous purchasing practices;
7. record keeping errors; or
8. the introduction of new products.

Even when there is a future demand for an item, its stock level may exceed what should be available. The accrued holding costs for these excessive quantities for extended periods of time can be a financial burden to an organization. It may be economically advantageous to sell or salvage a fraction of such stock levels. The benefits from such a transaction are the revenue generated from the salvage sale plus the savings in holding costs.[4]

The starting point for inventory reduction is analysis of the current composition of the inventory. A report showing the quantities of inventory

[4]R. J. Tersine and R. A. Toelle, "Optimum Stock Levels for Excess Inventory Items," *Journal of Operations Management*, Vol. 4, No. 3, 1984, pp. 245–258.

available for each item should be prepared. The quantities should be expressed in units and dollars. If the data are not available from records or if the records are unreliable, a physical inventory is necessary. Once inventory levels are ascertained, it is necessary to compare them with current and future requirements. Items with significant variances from requirements should be highlighted. A master list of all potential excess items should be developed.

There are only two alternatives for an organization with excess inventory. It can attempt to sell the stock or hold onto the stock until it is demanded. A price reduction is usually necessary to sell the excess, and it can range from a modest discount to a writeoff at some minimal salvage value (perhaps zero). With stock retention, the more the excess, the longer it will be until it is depleted. Some stock levels may exceed any foreseeable demand.

The perpetual inventory system is frequently used for independent demand items. This system is defined by an economic order quantity (EOQ) and a reorder point. When the stock position reaches a reorder point quantity, an order for a fixed lot size (Q) is placed. The maximum inventory for an item is the lot size plus the safety stock. Any quantity above the maximum should be considered as excess and reduced through attrition or considered for disposal.

In the next section, an excess inventory model will be developed for a deterministic perpetual inventory system. The excess model is predicated on the following assumptions:

1. There is an ongoing demand for the item. If any portion of the available stock is salvaged, it must be repurchased at a future date to satisfy an ongoing demand.
2. The annual demand rate (R) is known and constant.
3. The current unit cost (P) is known, and no quantity discounts are relevant.
4. The ordering cost per order (C) and the annual holding cost fraction (F) are known and constant during the relevant time period.
5. Stockouts are not permitted.
6. There are no constraints on space or capital.
7. The item is not perishable, and it does not deteriorate as a function of time.

An Excess Model

To establish if there is excess of an item, it is necessary to determine the economic time supply for the item. Any stock above the economic time supply should be sold. This situation is illustrated in Figure 2, where there

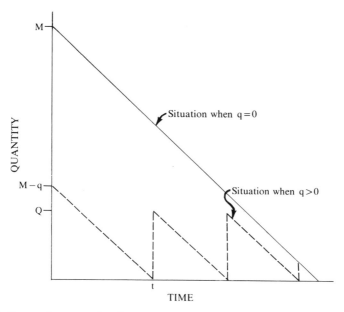

Figure 2. Excess inventory levels.

are M units of stock available, of which q units are excess. It is assumed that there is an ongoing demand for the item and that any units sold as excess will be repurchased at a later date. The net benefit (cost savings) resulting from the sale of excess is as follows:

$$\text{net benefit} = \text{salvage revenue} + \text{holding cost savings}$$

$$- \text{repurchase costs} - \text{reorder costs},$$

$$\text{salvage revenue} = qP_s = P_s(M - tR) = P_sM - P_sRt,$$

$$\text{holding cost savings} = \frac{M^2PF}{2R} - \frac{(M-q)^2PF}{2R} - \frac{QqPF}{2R}$$

$$= \frac{M^2PF}{2R} - \frac{RPFt^2}{2} - \frac{MQPF}{2R} + \frac{QPFt}{2},$$

$$\text{repurchase costs} = Pq = PM - PRt,$$

$$\text{reorder costs} = \frac{Cq}{Q} = \frac{CM}{Q} - \frac{CRt}{Q},$$

where

$$q = M - tR = \text{excess inventory in units,}$$
$$t = \text{time supply in years,}$$
$$t_0 = \text{economic time supply in years,}$$
$$C = \text{ordering cost per order,}$$
$$F = \text{annual holding cost fraction,}$$
$$M = \text{available stock in units,}$$
$$P = \text{unit cost or market value of the item,}$$
$$P_s = \text{unit resale or salvage value of the item,}$$
$$Q = \text{lot size in units,}$$
$$R = \text{annual demand in units.}$$

Figure 3. Net benefit curve.

$$t_0 = \frac{P - P_s + C/Q}{PF} + \frac{Q}{2R} = \frac{t_1 + t_2}{2}, \qquad t_2 = \frac{M}{R},$$

$$t_1 = \frac{2(P - P_s + C/Q)}{PF} - \frac{M - Q}{R}.$$

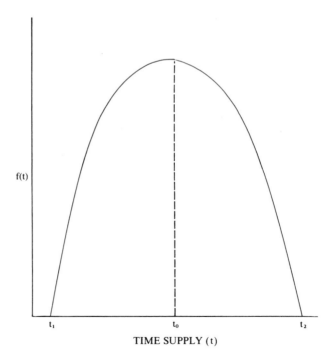

TIME SUPPLY (t)

The resultant net benefit formulation is as follows:

$$f(t) = -\frac{RPFt^2}{2} + \left(PR - P_sR + \frac{QPF}{2} + \frac{CR}{Q} \right)t$$

$$+ \frac{M^2PF}{2R} - \frac{MQPF}{2R} + P_sM - PM - \frac{CM}{Q}.$$

The above formulation is a parabola, as shown in Figure 3. By taking the first derivative of the net benefit with respect to t and setting it equal to zero, the economic time supply t_0 is obtained:

$$f'(t) = -RPFt + \left(PR - P_sR + \frac{QPF}{2} + \frac{CR}{Q} \right) = 0,$$

$$t_0 = \frac{P - P_s + C/Q}{PF} + \frac{Q}{2R}.$$

Since the second derivative of $f(t)$ is negative, it is known that the above relationship gives the maximum point. A simple example will illustrate the use of this relationship.

EXAMPLE 6

An item with 200 units in inventory and a unit cost of $20 has an annual demand of 100 units. The lot size is 20 units, the order cost is $10 per order, and the annual holding cost fraction is 0.25. If the salvage value is $15 per unit, should any of the items be sold as excess?

The available stock represents a 2 year supply ($200/100 = 2$). The economic time supply is as follows:

$$t_0 = \frac{P - P_s + C/Q}{PF} + \frac{Q}{2R} = \frac{20 - 15 + 0.5}{5} + \frac{20}{200} = 1.2 \text{ years.}$$

Since 1.2 years' supply is optimal and there is a 2-year supply available, 0.8 years of supply, or 80 units (0.8×100), are excess. The 80 units should be sold at $15, with a resultant inventory level of 120 units. The net benefit of the disposal is obtained by solving for $f(t)$ with $t = 1.2$; the resultant cost saving obtained is $160.00 as shown in Table 8.

Table 8

Time Supply Retained, t (years)	Net Benefit $f(t)$
.00	$ − 200.00
.25	− 65.63
.50	37.50
.55	54.38
.60	70.00
.65	84.38
.70	97.50
.75	109.38
.80	120.00
.85	129.38
.90	137.50
.91	138.97
.92	140.40
.93	141.77
.95	144.38
1.00	150.00
1.05	154.38
1.10	157.50
1.15	159.38
1.19	159.97
1.20	160.00 ←
1.21	159.98
1.25	159.38
1.30	157.50
1.35	154.38
1.40	150.00
1.45	144.38
1.50	137.50
1.75	84.38
2.00	0.00

Minimum Economic Salvage Value

The minimum economic salvage value indicates the unit salvage value P_s for which the net benefit $f(t)$ is zero. There is a net benefit to be derived if an item can be salvaged above this value. If the item cannot be salvaged above this value, there is no benefit to be obtained and all units should be retained. Thus, the minimum economic salvage value indicates the lowest unit price for which an item should be offered for salvage sale.

When the economic time supply t_0 equals the actual time supply M/R, the net benefit is zero. Thus,

$$t_0 = \frac{M}{R} = \frac{P - P_s + C/Q}{PF} + \frac{Q}{2R}.$$

Solving for P_s, the minimum economic salvage value (P_s^*) is obtained:

$$P_s^* = P + \frac{C}{Q} - \frac{PF(M - Q/2)}{R}.$$

All values of P_s greater than P_s^* result in a net benefit, while all smaller values result in a net loss.

EXAMPLE 7

From the information given in Example 6, what is the minimum economic salvage value?

$$P_s^* = P + \frac{C}{Q} - \frac{PF(M - Q/2)}{R}$$

$$= 20 + \frac{10}{20} - \frac{20(0.25)(200 - 10)}{100},$$

$$P_s^* = \$11 \text{ per unit.}$$

Table 9. Minimum economic salvage value

Unit Salvage Value P_s	Economic Time Supply t_0 (years)	Net Benefit $f(t_0)$
$ 0	4.2	
1.00	4.0	
2.00	3.8	
3.00	3.6	
4.00	3.4	
5.00	3.2	Infeasible
6.00	3.0	
7.00	2.8	
8.00	2.6	
9.00	2.4	
9.24	2.3	
10.00	2.2	
11.00	2.0	$ 0.00 ←
12.00	1.8	10.00
13.00	1.6	40.00
14.00	1.4	90.00
15.00	1.2	160.00
16.00	1.0	250.00
17.00	0.8	360.00
18.00	0.6	490.00
19.00	0.4	640.00
20.00	0.2	810.00

The item should not be sold as excess if the salvage price per unit is less than or equal to $11.00. The net benefit for a range of salvage values is shown in Table 9.

Lead Time Influence

The lead time L for an item influences the magnitude of the excess stock determination by putting a lower limit on the economic time supply t_0. If stockouts are to be avoided, the retained inventory should not be less than the lead time demand LR. Thus, with lead time greater than the economic time supply $(L > t_0)$, the retained inventory should be the lead time

Figure 4. Excess stock determination.

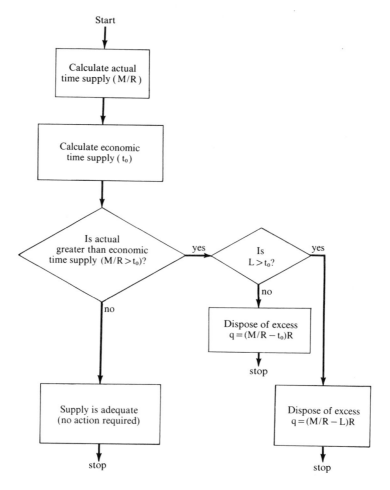

demand; with lead time less than or equal to the economic time supply, the retained inventory should be economic time supply. The logic for the excess stock determination is contained in Figure 4.

QUESTIONS

1. What are some of the signs of an overloaded or inefficient inventory system?

2. Name three limitations which may render the optimal inventory system unacceptable?

3. What are active and inactive constraints? How do they enter into the problem of finding the optimal solution if three constraints exist, one of which is active?

4. What is the net effect of reducing lot sizes due to working capital restrictions?

5. How are individual lot sizes determined when exchange curves are in use for aggregate inventory planning?

6. How are optimal solutions determined for constrained inventory systems?

7. In inventory problems, what units are assigned to the Lagrange multiplier? What do they represent?

8. How are problems involving inequality constraints solved?

9. Once a constrained solution is found, how is its optimality verified?

10. What inflows and outflows are taken into account when determining the net benefit (cost saving) resulting from the sale of excess inventory?

11. Define the minimum economic salvage value.

12. How does the lead time for an item influence the magnitude of its excess stock?

13. Define a convex function for both one- and two-variable functions.

PROBLEMS

1. A firm with an inventory of five different items is considering a change from a periodic to a perpetual inventory system. Each item is currently ordered quarterly, with an order cost of $25. The holding cost per year is 30% of unit

cost. Relevant data are listed below:

Item	Annual Demand R_i	Unit Cost P_i	Orders per Year	Average Inventory $P_i R_i/8$
A	300	$ 8.00	4	$ 300
B	800	10.50	4	1050
C	1500	4.00	4	750
D	2150	4.00	4	1075
E	2600	2.60	4	845
			20	$4020

Should the organization adopt a perpetual inventory system?

2. In Problem 1, should the organization adopt a perpetual inventory system if the holding cost per year is 10% per unit?

3. The optimal average inventory investment in Problem 1 is $2537. Suppose the firm has a shortage of working capital and can only afford an average inventory investment of $1500. What is the best perpetual inventory policy, given the information in Problem 1 with the above restriction imposed?

4. A perpetual inventory system item with 400 units in stock and a unit cost of $10.00 has an annual demand of 150 units. The ordering cost is $25.00 per order, and the annual holding cost fraction is 0.30. If the salvage value is $5.00 per unit, should any of the units be sold as excess?

5. From the information given in Problem 4, what is the minimum economic salvage value for the item?

6. Suppose $R = 5000$, $C = 150.00, $P = 15.00, and five setups are required in a year. What is the implied annual holding cost fraction for an item in a perpetual inventory system?

CASE 1: RUNNING ON THE INSIDE TRACK

Buz Hodges, the junior sales representative for Jocko Wholesale Sporting Goods, recently flew from his home base in Houston to the Dallas–Fort Worth area. As luck would have it, he was seated next to the assistant coach of Texas Technical Institute's highly successful football team. The young coach's father, by coincidence, is the Chairman of the Board of Hercules Sports Shops, an affiliate of Texas Conglomerates. Conglomerates owns the top-ranked professional football team, a chain of indoor tennis clubs, and the fastest growing franchise of roller rinks. The huge enterprise is also the prestigious sponsor of the nationally organized Middle League of Amateur Baseball.

Realizing his good fortune, the junior salesman swiftly displayed his marketing "gimmickry." Due to his occupational glibness, wit, and charm, he was able to commission a deal to supply uniforms to Coach Schumacher's summer football camp. Even more impressive was his attainment of commercial leads. Not only was he able to talk with the coach's father during his Dallas visit, but he obtained "inside tracks" that could result in acquisition of some of the industry's most sought-after accounts.

Upon his return to Houston, he spoke to the marketing vice president about his phenomenal success. He had negotiated a deal with one of the Conglomerate executives to supply 1500 units of merchandise to a central warehouse every week for the next two months. He is in the process of working out the details of supplying Fleet Feet, a subsidiary of Conglomerates, with a complete line of jogging shoes for the more than 30 stores. In addition, he has several large orders pending approval of other purchasing departments.

This recent wave of good fortune is not unique. Since his arrival at Jocko, the young sales wonder has bestowed unbelievable windfalls on the firm. However, the unprecedented sales have come unexpectedly and are causing planning difficulties for the other functional areas.

Surprisingly, the difficulties associated with the discontinuous sales seem to have trickled to his own department. During his sales report Buz is able to glean that the marketing vice president is less than exuberant about his news. This negative reaction to his accomplishments stirs the enthusiastic Hodges. Comprehending that his firm commitments, let alone his projected sales, may not be met, Buz voices the following refusal to retrench:

> If the company is unable to meet my quotas, then a company expansion plan is the only alternative. If the company wants aggressive sales, then they should prepare for them.
>
> Support for my new style of sales must come from an adequate inventory. These manufacturers should be called at once, and the shipments should be expedited. Let's get the goods here and "blast" our infernal interval ordering periods. Lead times and other delay excuses used by our manufacturers are hypocritical—I'm doing them a favor as well.
>
> Limitation of my sales is asinine—the only logical solution for these pending orders is instantaneous receipt of goods and prior stocking of merchandise. If the company wants to do this systematically, then we need to design a system that can do it.

The marketing vice president admits that the present system cannot support a highly aggressive marketing program. The system is simply overloaded. The company receives orders from manufacturers in economic intervals, but the present interval system is clearly inadequate. However, an abrupt change would not be well received. Some improvement over the old system might be a more realistic goal.

1. What is the relationship between the company's goals and its inventory system? What would appear to be reasonable goals for Jocko?
2. How can it handle the influx of orders? What should its policy be toward Texas Conglomerates?
3. What may be the limitations of the systems? Would limitation of sales be a possibility in the short or long run?

4. Can great variations in demand affect the selection and operation of the inventory system?

CASE 2: RESTRICTED CAPITAL FLOW

David Friedman & Sons sell air conditioning and heating units in the Oklahoma City metropolitan area. Numerous members of the Oklahoma City Homebuilders Association do business with Friedman & Sons, and the most reputable builders are regular clients of the firm. The majority of its air conditioning unit sales are to residential builders, but there are some sales of special size units to commercial contractors as well as single unit sales to private homeowners.

Friedman carries 15 different models of air conditioning units in stock. The four manufacturers of the models are implementing technological changes in order to satisfy the demand for more efficient units. The rapidity of the technological changes is forcing Friedman to reevaluate its present stocking policies. The firm wants to include the updated models in its inventory ordering system and yet be flexible enough to include even more efficient models as they are developed.

The company has usually held a small inventory; keeping the inventory investment at a minimum has been an important company policy. Friedman forecasts sales on a quarterly basis. The forecast is derived by accumulating the actual orders and adjusting them with an additional amount for uncommitted, but projected, sales. These figures are kept at a conservative level so that, when translated into an inventory investment, the amount stays within a low range.

Friedman's purchases are based on a reorder point and economic order quantity. The firm uses a manual inventory system. Each model is inventoried on a file card with pertinent information on the model, such as price, reorder point, EOQ, and lead time. Sam Levinson calculates the EOQ periodically; he tries to keep the EOQ as accurate as possible in view of fluctuating demand. So far, the executives believe that the EOQ system is functioning fairly well.

One problem that the firm is encountering with the present system is control of the physical inventory. There are some problems in keeping track of unit serial numbers with the manual system. There are physical problems in locating and updating the status of individual units. Some of the problem is attributed to general accounting inaccuracies. The control problem often is not discovered until a unit is allotted for sale. It is not uncommon to find the unit is defective or has been dismantled so that some of the parts could be used on other units or sold as spare parts. The physical stock and the condition of the stock seldom are accounted for correctly on the file card.

An even more pressing problem is a general economic one. Management is forecasting a critically slow period for the homebuilding industry with residual effects on their own sales. New housing starts are decreasing. Actual orders for air conditioning units have dropped appreciably, and the forecast is extremely bleak. Business is so bad that the firm has received the fewest firm orders in five years, and the accounts receivable are aging. The builders are operating on credit, because they are holding sizable inventory investments of their own.

It is becoming very difficult to forecast sales in the present economic situation. The forecasting problem is compounded by a change in the builders' ordering habits. The builders are giving less advance notification on much smaller orders. These changes on the demand side, coupled with the builders' needs to seek credit on their orders, are hastening Friedman's inventory dilemma and working capital shortages.

Sam Levinson's inclination is to change the depth of the in-stock line. He contends that the firm should reduce the number of models in all of the manufacturers' lines carried by Friedman. For instance, one of the more popular lines should include only the most frequently purchased models and a slightly larger number of each. Sam prepared a table illustrating the models in this line he would select to carry, with his estimate of each model's annual sales under present conditions:

Model	Price	Yearly Sales
Z 210	$650	170
Z 310	690	240
Z 410	740	220
X 520	750	260
X 530	780	180

David Friedman agrees that this is a good initial cutback, but would like to see a more quantitative analysis showing the plan's desirability. A further improvement would be simply to apply a working capital restriction to the investment in inventory. David feels that the limit on this particular line should approximate $30,000. He is anxious to develop a system that will cut back on inventory and enhance the liquidity of the firm.

1. Given $F = 0.25$ and $C = 30, construct an inventory policy for the firm's most popular line.
2. What other inventory changes should be incorporated?
3. What further economic changes would affect the development of the inventory system? Will the new system correct the other inventory problems?
4. Is Levinson's reduction plan the sole solution, and should it be extended to the other lines?

CASE 3: MRP OR BUST

Rollo Fishbein, President of Alpha Electronics, has recently become a member of APICS, an organization for production and inventory control professionals. Through APICS, Rollo has gained considerable knowledge about modern production and inventory control systems. He has become particularly interested in material requirements planning (MRP) systems as solutions to many present day inventory problems—the types of problems which exist at Alpha.

Alpha Electronics is a small but rapidly growing manufacturer of electrical meters and test equipment such as voltmeters, potentiometers, ohmmeters, and galvanometers. All of the end products are high quality, expensive items sold primarily to industrial firms or to educational institutions. Alpha purchases over

1000 parts and manufactures approximately 1500 parts and assemblies of its own. Some of the parts are used on more than one instrument, and a few simpler parts are used on at least 40% of the finished items. Production lots are mostly small, as usual for precision instruments. Alpha is using a fixed order size system to control inventories of both parts and end items. EOQs and reorder points are calculated for all items.

Because of the rapid expansion of the firm, there is a recurrent cash crunch. In order to improve the liquidity position, Rollo would like to see inventories minimized. He has become enthusiastic about MRPs capability of substantially reducing production costs and inventory investments. His convictions about the advantages of MRP systems are so strong that he has declared that Alpha will implement an MRP system immediately with a target completion date of less than one year.

Judging from what he has heard and read, Rollo has determined that Alpha meets all the product requirements for successful implementation of an MRP system. The other requirements of the organization dictate computerized data processing methods, and the functional requirements of the production and inventory departments require a sophisticated MRP system. Rollo has deemed further investigation of alternative systems unnecessary and has chosen to bypass some of the system design phases. For instance, he has overridden the material manager's request for detailed systems design proposals from competing firms; Rollo has requested a design for an entirely new system and requisitioned information pertaining only to conversion to an MRP system. His short-cut procedure stipulates that the only detailed design is to be the selection of an MRP package. Rollo is so confident of his decision and so eager to begin the process that he has already contacted a software consultant to come in and tailor an existing MRP package to Alpha's needs.

The selection of the software consultant has anticipated the selection process for computer hardware. Rollo is circumventing the tedious process of choosing hardware and is ready to match the computer configuration to his stated system requirements and MRP software needs. Rollo has decided that the power and capabilities of the computer configuration should exceed the present system requirements by a wide margin. Thus, he is prepared to purchase more computing power for the firm and will simply select a system that is compatible with the MRP system undergoing development. Rollo is pleased that his software consultant is affiliated with a company well known for general purpose equipment. Not only is the computer company respected for its highly versatile equipment, but Rollo's APICS associates have informed him that this company could best meet his selection criteria—low cost and familiarity with the software.

As a further step toward a speedy implementation Rollo is proposing a direct conversion. This "cold turkey" approach is based on two important considerations. First, there should be an abrupt discontinuation of the old system, as it is obsolete and so drastically different from the new system that nothing could be gained from its continuation. Second, the conversion should be made quickly and inexpensively.

Rollo has assured his personnel that there will be an educational program, but it will have to come subsequent to the developmental phase. All system operators will receive on-the-job training, and all management and staff personnel will attend a session designed to explain the system outputs. In addition, management and staff will be required to attend an acceptance meeting near project completion and a follow-up meeting at project termination. Rollo has also promised that he will allocate funds for new positions; people with computer backgrounds and experience will be hired to execute a smoother transition and to ensure optimum operating efficiency.

1. Is the proposed system a good way of handling the firm's expansion problem? Realizing that perfect results are unlikely, have the potential benefits of the redesign been exaggerated?
2. What are the behavioral implications of this system conversion? Has Rollo Fishbein initiated the change in a manner that will lessen resistance?
3. What implementation approach would you suggest?
4. Is it essential that Alpha undergo a system redesign? If so, what needs to be redesigned?

MATHEMATICAL ABBREVIATIONS AND SYMBOLS USED IN CHAPTER 6

C	Order cost per order
EOQ	Economic order quantity
$f(t)$	Net benefit from salvage of an excess item
F	Annual inventory holding cost fraction
G	Total annual incremental cost = (order cost) + (holding cost)
J	Maximum size of average inventory in dollars
L	Lead time in years
M	Available stock in units
n	Number of inventory items
P_i	Unit purchase cost of item i
P_s	Unit salvage value for an item
P_s^*	Minimum economic salvage value for an item
q	Excess inventory in units
Q_i	Order quantity for item i in units
R_i	Annual demand for item i in units
t	Time supply of inventory of an item in years
t_0	Economic time supply in years
T_i	Order interval for item i
U	Total average inventory investment
V	Total number of annual replenishments
w_i	Storage volume requirement for each unit of item i
W	Maximum total storage volume for all items
Y	Maximum number of annual orders
λ	Lagrange multiplier

SUMMARY OF FORMULAS IN CHAPTER 6

Model	Formula
EOQ exchange curves	$U = \sum_{i=1}^{n} \dfrac{P_i Q_i}{2}$
	$V = \sum_{i=1}^{n} \dfrac{R_i}{Q_i}$
	$UV = \left(\sum_{i=1}^{n} \sqrt{\dfrac{P_i R_i}{2}} \right)^2$
Working capital restrictions	$Q_i = \sqrt{\dfrac{2CR_i}{(F + \lambda) P_i}}$
	$\lambda = \dfrac{C \left(\sum_{i=1}^{n} \sqrt{P_i R_i} \right)^2}{2 J^2} - F$
Storage space restrictions	$Q_i = \sqrt{\dfrac{2CR_i}{FP_i + 2\lambda w_i}}$
Excess stock: Economic time supply	$t_0 = \dfrac{P - P_s + C/Q}{PF} + \dfrac{Q}{2R}$
Minimum economic salvage value	$P_s^* = P + \dfrac{C}{Q} - \dfrac{PF(M - Q/2)}{R}$

APPENDIX A. OPTIMIZING CONSTRAINED FUNCTIONS

In many models developed in this text, a general cost function has been minimized. Generally, the only constraints on the solution were boundary conditions, such as that the order quantity must be nonnegative. However, it is common to find certain restrictions on controllable variables. Frequently, physical resources, such as capital and floor space, put limitations on the optimum solution. The method of Lagrange multipliers can be used to find a minimum value of a function subject to constraints.

The Lagrange method specifically applies to equality constraints. When the Lagrangian method is combined with the Kuhn-Tucker conditions, problems involving inequality constraints can be solved. However, the solutions obtained with the equality constraints and inequality constraints are only optimal if the functions meet the test of convexity for minimization problems.[5] Tests for convexity are outlined in a later section.

[5] For solution techniques for optimizing constrained functions when the convexity requirement does not hold, see G. Hadley and T. M. Whitin, *Analysis of Inventory Systems*, Englewood Cliffs, NJ: Prentice-Hall, 1963, pp. 433–437.

In inventory problems, the function f usually represents the expected annual cost, and the constraints g_i are usually capital or floor space. The Lagrange multiplier is the value or cost per unit of resource; it represents the amount by which the minimum cost can be reduced by adding one additional unit of the limiting resource. The Lagrange multipliers can be considered imputed values or shadow prices of the resources.

One Equality Constraint

To minimize a function $f(X_1, \ldots, X_n)$, subject to an equality constraint $g(X_1, \ldots, X_n) = a$, where both functions are continuous and differentiable, simply minimize the unconstrained function

$$h(X_1, \ldots, X_n, \lambda) = f(X_1, \ldots, X_n) + \lambda[g(X_1, \ldots, X_n) - a],$$

where λ is a Lagrange multiplier unrestricted in sign.

To minimize the unconstrained function $h = f + \lambda(g - a)$, the partial derivatives of h with respect to X_j and λ are set equal to zero:

$$\frac{\partial h}{\partial X_j} = \frac{\partial f}{\partial X_j} + \lambda \frac{\partial g}{\partial X_j} = 0, \qquad j = 1, \ldots, n,$$

$$\frac{\partial h}{\partial \lambda} = g - a = 0.$$

By simultaneously solving the above equations for X_j and λ, the minimum point $f(X_1, \ldots, X_n)$ is obtained. If the multiplier is positive, it indicates the rate at which f will decrease per unit increase in the parameter a.

More Than One Equality Constraint

The method for one equality constraint can be extended to more than one. To minimize a function $f(X_1, \ldots, X_n)$, subject to two equality constraints $g_1(X_1, \ldots, X_n) = a_1$ and $g_2(X_1, \ldots, X_n) = a_2$, where all the functions are continuous and differentiable, simply minimize the unrestrained function

$$h(X_1, \ldots, X_n, \lambda_1, \lambda_2) = f(X_1, \ldots, X_n) + \lambda_1[g_1(X_1, \ldots, X_n) - a_1]$$

$$+ \lambda_2[g_2(X_1, \ldots, X_n) - a_2],$$

where λ_1 and λ_2 are Lagrange multipliers unrestricted in sign.

To minimize the unconstrained function $h = f + \lambda_1(g_1 - a_1) + \lambda_2(g_2 - a_2)$, the partial derivatives of h with respect to X_j, λ_1, and λ_2 are set equal to zero:

$$\frac{\partial h}{\partial X_j} = \frac{\partial f}{\partial X_j} + \lambda_1 \frac{\partial g_1}{\partial X_j} + \lambda_2 \frac{\partial g_2}{\partial X_j} = 0,$$

$$\frac{\partial h}{\partial \lambda_1} = g_1 - a_1 = 0,$$

$$\frac{\partial h}{\partial \lambda_2} = g_2 - a_2 = 0,$$

where $j = 1, \ldots, n$. By simultaneously solving the above equations for X_j, λ_1, and λ_2, the minimum point $f(X_1, \ldots, X_n)$ is obtained.

One Inequality Constraint

The Lagrangian method can be supplemented with the Kuhn-Tucker conditions to solve the minimization problem subject to a single inequality. To minimize a function $f(X_1, \ldots, X_n)$ subject to an inequality constraint $g(X_1, \ldots, X_n) \leq a$, where both functions are continuous and differentiable, simply minimize the unconstrained function

$$h(X_1, \ldots, X_n, \lambda) = f(X_1, \ldots, X_n) + \lambda[g(X_1, \ldots, X_n) - a],$$

where λ is a nonnegative Lagrange multiplier.

To minimize the unconstrained function $h = f + \lambda(g - a)$, the Kuhn-Tucker conditions for the minimization of a function subject to an inequality constraint are invoked as follows:

$$\frac{\partial h}{\partial X_j} = \frac{\partial f}{\partial X_j} + \lambda \frac{\partial g}{\partial X_j} = 0, \qquad \lambda(g - a) = 0,$$

where $j = 1, \ldots, n$. By simultaneously solving the above equations for X_j and λ, the minimum point $f(X_1, \ldots, X_n)$ is obtained.

More Than One Inequality Constraint

The method for one inequality constraint can be extended to more than one. To minimize a function $f(X_1, \ldots, X_n)$ subject to two inequality constraints $g_1(X_1, \ldots, X_n) \leq a_1$ and $g_2(X_1, \ldots, X_n) \leq a_2$, where all the functions are continuous and differentiable, simply minimize the unconstrained function

$$h(X_1, \ldots, X_n, \lambda_1, \lambda_2) = f(X_1, \ldots, X_n) + \lambda_1[g_1(X_1, \ldots, X_n) - a_1]$$
$$+ \lambda_2[g_2(X_1, \ldots, X_n) - a_2],$$

where λ_1 and λ_2 are nonnegative Lagrange multipliers.

To minimize the unconstrained function $h = f + \lambda_1(g_1 - a_1) + \lambda_2(g_2 - a_2)$, the Kuhn-Tucker conditions for the minimization of a function subject to two inequality constraints are invoked as follows:

$$\frac{\partial h}{\partial X_j} = \frac{\partial f}{\partial X_j} + \lambda_1 \frac{\partial g_1}{\partial X_j} + \lambda_2 \frac{\partial g_2}{\partial X_j} = 0,$$

$$\lambda_1(g_1 - a_1) = 0,$$

$$\lambda_2(g_2 - a_2) = 0,$$

where $j = 1, \ldots, n$. By simultaneously solving the above equations for X_j, λ_1, and λ_2, the minimum point $f(X_1, \ldots, X_n)$ is obtained.

Tests for Convexity

The procedures outlined herein for obtaining the optimum solution to a minimization problem only give candidates for the optimum solution. To ensure that a solution is optimum, both the objective function f and constraints g_i must be convex. A convex function always bends upward. A straight line (linear) function is both convex and concave.

A function $F(X)$ with one variable that is continuous and possesses a second derivative is convex if its second derivative is greater than or equal to zero:

$$\frac{d^2F(X)}{dX^2} \geq 0.$$

A function $F(X_1, X_2)$ with two variables that is continuous and possesses second derivatives is convex if

$$\left(\frac{\partial^2 F}{\partial X_1^2}\right)\left(\frac{\partial^2 F}{\partial X_2^2}\right) - \left(\frac{\partial^2 F}{\partial X_1 \partial X_2}\right)^2 > 0, \qquad \frac{\partial^2 F}{\partial X_1^2} > 0, \qquad \frac{\partial^2 F}{\partial X_2^2} > 0.$$

For the determination of the convexity of functions with more than two variables, see McMillan.[6]

[6] Claude McMillan, Jr., *Mathematical Programming*, New York: John Wiley and Sons, 1970, pp. 419–424.

7 Single Order Quantities

KNOWN DEMAND, KNOWN LEAD TIME

KNOWN DEMAND, VARIABLE LEAD TIME

VARIABLE DEMAND, KNOWN LEAD TIME
   Benefit (Marginal) Analysis
   Cost Analysis

VARIABLE DEMAND, VARIABLE LEAD TIME

CONCLUSION
QUESTIONS
PROBLEMS
CASES
MATHEMATICAL ABBREVIATIONS AND SYMBOLS
SUMMARY OF FORMULAS

The single order quantity model is concerned with the planning and control of inventory items that are purchased only once during a time period, or for which only one production run may be initiated. The familiar inventory models (EOQ, EOI, and EPQ) do not readily apply to the single order situation because (1) the demand is not continuous, (2) the demand level may change drastically from time period to time period, and/or (3) the product's market life may be very short due to obsolescence or perishability.

The single order quantity model is very well suited to demand that is noncontinuous, changeable, and short-lived. It is specifically applicable to the following two categories of demand: (1) demand which exists for an item at infrequent intervals and (2) uncertain demand which exists for a short-lived item at frequent intervals. The first category is typified by promotional and fad items ordered by retail stores and by spare parts for maintenance repair. The second category is associated with highly perishable items (fresh fish, flowers) and short-lived, obsolescent items (newspapers, periodicals). Due to its common association with the second category, the single order quantity problem is frequently referred to in the literature as the Christmas tree problem or the newsboy problem.

Single order quantity items have a demand pattern with a limited sales (or usage) period. An item is ordered (procured or produced) at the beginning of the period, and there is no opportunity for a second order during the period, since a second order would not arrive before the end of the period. With no repeat orders during the period considered, there is insufficient time to replenish the stock to fill unsatisfied demand. If the demand during the period considered is greater than the order size, an opportunity-profit loss results. If the demand is less than the order size, the overstock is usually disposed of at a loss after the sales period ends. The excess stock might be (1) discarded because of spoilage (dairy products) or obsolescence (newspapers), (2) sold at a reduced price (chocolate Easter rabbits), or (3) stored until the next season (snow tires), with each of these alternatives incurring an associated cost.

The single order quantity problem can be classified according to source, demand, and lead time, as shown in Figure 1. The source of the single order quantity may be self-supply or outside supply. Self-supply exists when the organization produces the item itself, whereas outside supply exists when another organization is the supply source. With self-supply, the lead time is mainly composed of production scheduling, manufacturing, and assembly time. With outside supply, the lead time also includes the transit and receipt times. An organization has greater control over the lead time if an item is self-supplied.

The determination or estimation of the demand is critical in dealing with a single order. If the demand is known, the problem is simplified. If the demand follows some specified or empirical distribution, the problem can

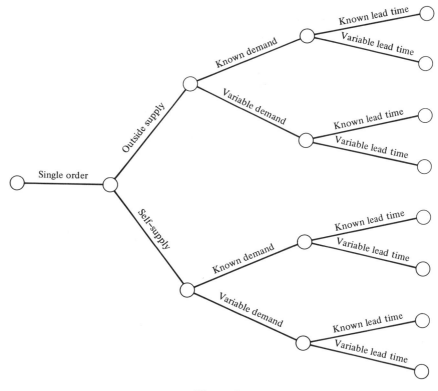

Figure 1

be solved by the techniques of decision making under risk. With no information concerning the demand, it becomes necessary to do market analysis or market research.

The lead time has a different significance with the single order than with the repeat order. With a repeat order and ongoing demand, the lead time is a complication, since demand occurs during the lead time. With a single order, there is no demand, or at any rate there is no stock available to satisfy demand, during the lead time. The lead time is thus the waiting time until goods are available to meet demand. Until the goods arrive, there is no stock available. If the lead time is longer than expected, some sales may be lost. If the lead time is shorter than expected, the stock is available prior to demand.

KNOWN DEMAND, KNOWN LEAD TIME

When the demand is known and the lead time is known, there is no single order inventory problem. The quantity of goods ordered matches the demand, and they arrive on the day of demand origination. A condition of certainty exists which rarely occurs in practice. For this condition to exist, all demand must result in backorders from patient customers, or all planning must be perfect with no unusual occurrences or delays.

KNOWN DEMAND, VARIABLE LEAD TIME

Since the demand is known, the size of the single order is known. With a variable lead time, the decision maker wants to ensure that the order is received prior to demand, so there is no idle production time or lost sales. If no lost sales are to be tolerated, orders are placed prior to the maximum possible lead time. If a lead time distribution can be ascertained, a lead time can be selected which has a high probability of arrival prior to demand. Alternatively, if the demand is fixed regardless of when the goods are delivered, a late delivery only delays an activity. This situation could exist in the construction of a building, where a delivery delay would only result in a construction delay.

EXAMPLE 1

The Norfolk Boys Club plans to sell Christmas trees for the building fund. Local merchants have placed orders for the trees to be delivered on specified dates, starting with the earliest lot on 1 December. When should the order be placed if an 85% chance of the trees arriving on time is desired? The lead time distribution in Table 1 is known.

Table 1

Lead Time (Days)	Number of Occurrences
10	10
11	10
12	15
13	20
14	30
15	10
16	5
	100

To satisfy all demand, the largest lead time would be selected, which is 16 days. The trees would be ordered 16 days prior to 1 December.

From Table 2, it is seen that if an 85% chance of the trees arriving on time is desired, the lead time must be 14 days. Trees would be ordered 14 days prior to 1 December.

When self-supply exists, the variable lead time is a result of uncertainties in scheduling and in the production processes. A service level policy on the

Table 2

Lead Time L	Probability $P(L)$	Probability of Lead Time $\leq L$
10	.10	.10
11	.10	.20
12	.15	.35
13	.20	.55
14	.30	.85 ←
15	.10	.95
16	.05	1.00

lead time can be obtained from a PERT analysis. A description of PERT analysis is beyond the scope of this section, but it can be found in any production/operations textbook.

VARIABLE DEMAND, KNOWN LEAD TIME

When the demand is variable and the lead time is known, the single order inventory problem is in ascertaining the order size. If the demand is not known but a probability distribution of demand is available, the problem can be solved as decision making under risk. The order size that results in the largest expected profit or lowest expected cost is selected.

The procedure for decision making under risk is to determine the demand strategy with the optimum expected value. The probability that the demand will be less than or equal to the single order quantity for a discrete distribution is as follows:

$$P(M \leq Q) = \sum_{M=0}^{Q} P(M) = 1 - \sum_{M=Q+1}^{M_{max}} P(M),$$

where

$$Q = \text{single order quantity in units,}$$

$$M = \text{demand in units (a random variable),}$$

$$P(M) = \text{probability of a demand of } M \text{ units,}$$

$$M_{max} = \text{maximum demand in units.}$$

The probability that the demand will exceed the single order quantity is as follows:

$$P(M > Q) = \sum_{M=Q+1}^{M_{max}} P(M) = 1 - \sum_{M=0}^{Q} P(M).$$

The procedure for calculating the expected value of each discrete demand strategy Q_i is as follows:

$$E(Q_i) = P(M_0)F(Q_iM_0) + P(M_1)F(Q_iM_1) + \cdots + P(M_n)F(Q_iM_n)$$

$$= \sum_{j=0}^{n} P(M_j)F(Q_iM_j) = \text{expected value of strategy } Q_i,$$

where $F(Q_iM_j)$ is the outcome of following the demand strategy Q_i when the actual demand is the state of nature M_j. The determination of outcomes can take on two forms, depending on whether the amount ordered (Q_i) is less than or greater than the demand level (M_j). When the outcomes are expressed in profit or benefit terms, the following relationships apply:

$$F(Q_iM_j) = Q_iJ \qquad \text{for} \quad Q_i \leq M_j \quad \text{(understock condition)},$$

$$F(Q_iM_j) = M_jJ - (Q_i - M_j)l \quad \text{for} \quad Q_i > M_j \quad \text{(overstock condition)},$$

where

$$J = \text{unit profit or benefit},$$
$$l = \text{loss from disposition of unutilized unit},$$
$$Q_i = \text{single order quantity of } i \text{ units},$$
$$M_j = \text{demand level of } j \text{ units},$$
$$Q_i - M_j = \text{number of units overstocked}.$$

When outcomes are expressed in cost or sacrifice terms, the following relationships apply:

$$F(Q_iM_j) = Q_iP \qquad \text{for} \quad Q_i \geq M_j \quad \text{(overproduction condition)},$$

$$F(Q_iM_j) = Q_iP + (M_j - Q_i)A \quad \text{for} \quad Q_i < M_j \quad \text{(underproduction condition)},$$

where

$$P = \text{unit cost},$$
$$A = \text{stockout cost per unit},$$
$$M_j - Q_i = \text{size of stockout in units}.$$

The matrix in Table 3 depicts the previously established discrete mathematical relationships.

Table 3

Strategy	Probability: State of Nature:	$P(M_0)$ M_0	$P(M_1)$ M_1	$\cdots$ $\cdots$	$P(M_n)$ M_n	Expected Value $E(Q_i)$
Q_0		$F(Q_0 M_0)$	$F(Q_0 M_1)$	$\cdots$	$F(Q_0 M_n)$	$E(Q_0)$
Q_1		$F(Q_1 M_0)$	$F(Q_1 M_1)$	$\cdots$	$F(Q_1 M_n)$	$E(Q_1)$
$\vdots$		$\vdots$	$\vdots$		$\vdots$	$\vdots$
Q_m		$F(Q_m M_0)$	$F(Q_m M_1)$	$\cdots$	$F(Q_m M_n)$	$E(Q_m)$

EXAMPLE 2

A merchant wishes to stock Christmas trees for sale during the Christmas season. He must determine how many trees to order, since only one order can be filled during the short time. He pays $2.00 for each tree delivered, and he sells the trees for $6.00. His ordering costs are negligible, and he can sell any unsold tree for $1.00 as firewood. The merchant's probability distribution for Christmas tree demand during the season is given in Table 4. (The merchant must order trees in multiples of ten.) How many trees should the merchant order?

Table 4

Demand M	Probability $P(M)$
10	.10
20	.10
30	.20
40	.35
50	.15
60	.10
	1.00

A payoff matrix is developed (Table 5) with the profit from each strategy and state of nature. The expected value of each strategy is obtained by multiplying its

Table 5

Strategy	Probability: State of Nature:	0.10 10	0.10 20	0.20 30	0.35 40	0.15 50	0.10 60	Expected Value
10		40	40	40	40	40	40	$40.00
20		30	80	80	80	80	80	75.00
30		20	70	120	120	120	120	105.00
40		10	60	110	160	160	160	125.00
50		0	50	100	150	200	200	127.50 ←
60		−10	40	90	140	190	240	122.50

probability of occurrence by the value of its outcome and summing the products. The final selection is based on the strategy with the highest expected value. The best strategy is to order 50 trees with the expected value of $127.50.

Benefit (Marginal) Analysis

The preceding section outlined an exhaustive tabulation of each prospective order quantity to determine the lot size with the optimum expected value. Although the method is applicable to single order quantity analysis involving discrete (integer) units of demand, it can be a tedious process when the number of alternatives is large. In this section, a simpler optimizing relationship will be derived to indicate the most profitable order quantity. The objective is to determine the order size (Q) that should be purchased at the beginning of the period (assuming no initial inventory) to maximize the expected profit at the end of the period:

$$\text{expected profit (EP)} = \text{expected revenue (ER)} - \text{expected cost (EC)};$$

$$\text{expected revenue (ER)} = \text{expected sales revenue}$$

$$+ \text{expected salvage revenue},$$

$$\text{ER} = P_1 \left[Q - \int_0^Q (Q - M) f(M)\, dM \right]$$

$$+ V \int_0^Q (Q - M) f(M)\, dM$$

$$= P_1 Q + (V - P_1) \int_0^Q (Q - M) f(M)\, dM;$$

$$\text{expected cost (EC)} = \text{purchase cost} + \text{order cost}$$

$$+ \text{expected stockout cost},$$

$$\text{EC} = PQ + C + A \int_Q^\infty (M - Q) f(M)\, dM,$$

$$\text{EP} = P_1 Q + (V - P_1) \int_0^Q (Q - M) f(M)\, dM - PQ$$

$$- C - A \int_Q^\infty (M - Q) f(M)\, dM$$

$$= P_1 Q + (V - P_1)(Q - \overline{M}) - (P_1 - V + A)$$

$$\times \int_Q^\infty (M - Q) f(M)\, dM - PQ - C,$$

where

$$A = \text{stockout cost per unit}$$
$$\text{(a goodwill cost in addition to any lost profit)},$$
$$C = \text{ordering cost per order},$$
$$M = \text{demand in units (a random variable)},$$
$$f(M) = \text{probability density function of demand},$$
$$M - Q = \text{size of stockout in units},$$
$$Q = \text{single order quantity in units},$$
$$Q - M = \text{amount of excess inventory in units},$$
$$P = \text{unit purchase cost},$$
$$P_1 = \text{unit selling price},$$
$$P(M > Q) = \text{probability of a stockout}$$
$$\text{(probability of a demand greater than } Q),$$
$$V = \text{salvage value per unit},$$
$$\int_0^Q (Q - M) f(M) \, dM = \text{expected number of excess (salvage) units},$$
$$\int_Q^\infty (M - Q) f(M) \, dM = \text{expected stockout quantity in units}.$$

To determine the maximum expected profit for a continuous distribution requires taking the derivative of the expected profit with respect to the order quantity and setting it equal to zero:

$$\frac{d\,\text{EP}}{dQ} = P_1 + V - P_1 + (P_1 + A - V)P(M > Q) - P = 0,$$

$$P(M > Q) = P(s) = \frac{P - V}{P_1 + A - V} = \frac{\text{ML}}{\text{MP} + \text{ML} + A}$$

$$= \text{optimum stockout probability},$$

where

$$\text{ML} = P - V = \text{marginal loss},$$
$$\text{MP} = P_1 - P = \text{marginal profit}.$$

For discrete demand distributions where the optimum probability of a stockout is not exactly attainable, select the stock level with the next lower probability of a stockout. Then the above optimum expression can be used for both discrete and continuous demand distributions. Frequently, in single order problems, there will be no stockout cost associated with excess demand. In this situation, the stockout cost per unit (A) is assumed to be zero.

EXAMPLE 3

Using the marginal approach, how many Christmas trees should be ordered from the information given in Example 2?

$$P(s) = \frac{ML}{MP + ML + A} = \frac{1}{4 + 1 + 0} = 0.20.$$

From Table 6, the optimum stockout probability is between 0.25 and 0.10, so the smaller value is selected and 50 trees should be ordered.

Table 6

Demand M	Probability	Probability of Demand $> M$
10	0.10	0.90
20	0.10	0.80
30	0.20	0.60
40	0.35	0.25
50	0.15	0.10 ←
60	0.10	0.00
	1.00	

EXAMPLE 4

The Evergreen Company owns acreage of shrub trees to be harvested and sold each spring. The company estimates the costs of cutting and trimming the trees to be $2.50 per tree. The average cost of shipping the trees to the retailer is about $.50 per tree. The company receives about $5.00 per tree ordered by the retailer. However, if the trees are cut and not sold to the retailer, they are a total loss. Shipping costs are not incurred if trees are not sold. The historical demand distribution is shown in Table 7. How many trees should be cut in order to maximize profit if the demand occurs in lots of 10,000?

$$P(s) = \frac{ML}{MP + ML + A} = \frac{2.50}{2.00 + 2.50 + 0} = 0.55.$$

Table 7

Level of Demand, M (Thousands)	Probability, $P(M)$
10	.10
20	.20
30	.25
40	.30
50	.15

Table 8

Level of Demand, M	Probability	Probability of Demand $> M$
10	0.10	0.90
20	0.20	0.70
30	0.25	0.45 ←
40	0.30	0.15
50	0.15	0.00

From Table 8, the optimum stockout probability is between 0.70 and 0.45, so the smaller value is selected and 30,000 trees should be cut to maximize profits.

Cost Analysis

When items are intended for internal use with no generation of revenue, the selection of the single order size is based on the lowest expected cost. The cost components are the order cost, purchase cost, stockout cost, and salvage value. The following formula is for the expected cost of a single order for a continuous distribution:

expected cost = (order cost) + (purchase cost) + (expected stockout cost)

$\qquad$ − (expected salvage),

$$EC = C + PQ + A \int_{Q}^{\infty} (M - Q)f(M)\, dM$$

$$- V \int_{0}^{Q} (Q - M)f(M)\, dM,$$

$$= C + PQ + (A - V) \int_{Q}^{\infty} (M - Q)f(M)\, dM + V(\overline{M} - Q),$$

where

$\qquad C$ = order cost per order or setup cost,

$\qquad P$ = unit purchase cost,

$\qquad Q$ = single order quantity in units,

$\qquad A$ = stockout cost per unit,

$\qquad M$ = demand in units (a random variable),

$M - Q$ = size of stockout in units,

$\qquad f(M)$ = probability density function of demand,

$\qquad V$ = salvage value per unit.

To determine the minimum expected cost for a continuous distribution requires taking the derivative of the expected cost with respect to the order size and setting it equal to zero:

$$\frac{d\,EC}{dQ} = P - (A - V)P(M > Q) - V = 0,$$

$$P(M > Q) = P(s) = \frac{P - V}{A - V} = \text{optimum stockout probability.}$$

Observe that if the purchase cost is equal to or greater than the stockout cost, the desired stockout probability is 1. Under these conditions, no orders would be instituted until a known demand existed. Also, if an item has no salvage value, the optimum probability of a stockout is $P(s) = P/A$.

The expression $1 - P(s)$ is the service level, and $P(s)$ is the stockout probability. Thus, if the demand for the item is normally distributed with a

Table 9. Standard normal distribution

Standard Normal Deviate Z	Probability of a Stockout	Standard Normal Deviate Z	Probability of a Stockout
− 3.00	.999	1.20	.115
0.00	.500	1.25	.106
0.05	.480	1.30	.097
0.10	.460	1.35	.088
0.15	.440	1.40	.081
0.20	.421	1.45	.073
0.25	.401	1.50	.067
0.30	.382	1.55	.060
0.35	.363	1.60	.055
0.40	.344	1.65	.049
0.45	.326	1.70	.045
0.50	.308	1.75	.040
0.55	.291	1.80	.036
0.60	.274	1.85	.032
0.65	.258	1.90	.029
0.70	.242	2.00	.023
0.75	.227	2.25	.012
0.80	.212	2.50	.006
0.85	.198	2.75	.003
0.90	.184	3.00	.001
0.95	.171		
1.00	.159		
1.05	.147		
1.10	.136		
1.15	.125		

known mean $\overline{M}$ and standard deviation σ, the following expression determines the lowest expected cost single order quantity:

$$Q_0 = \overline{M} + Z\sigma = \text{optimum single order size},$$

where Z is the standard normal deviate obtained from the normal table for a stockout probability of $P(s)$. Table 9 exhibits the standard normal distribution which permits conversion from stockout probabilities to standard normal deviates.

EXAMPLE 5

A large department store has just purchased a new central air conditioning unit. The lifetime of the air conditioner is estimated at 12 years. The manager must decide how many spare compressors to purchase for the unit. If he purchases the compressors now, they will cost $100 each. If he purchases them when they fail, the cost will be $1000 each. Table 10 gives the probability distribution of the number of failures of the part during the life of the air conditioner, as supplied by the manufacturer.

Table 10

No. of Failures M	Probability	Probability of No. of Failures $> M$
0	.30	.70
1	.40	.30
2	.25	.05 ←
3	.05	.00

The installation cost of the compressor, as well as its salvage value, is assumed to be negligible. How many compressors should be purchased if the holding cost is neglected? How many compressors should be purchased now if the holding cost, which is mainly the opportunity cost of the money invested, is 10% (assume failures occur at equal intervals—the single failure occurs at the end of the 6th year, the two

Table 11

Strategy	Probability: State of Nature:	0.30 0	0.40 1	0.25 2	0.05 3	Expected Cost
0		0	1000	2000	3000	$1050
1		100	100	1100	2100	450
2		200	200	200	1200	250 ←
3		300	300	300	300	300

Table 12

Failure at End of Year	Factor
3	0.751
4	0.683
6	0.564
8	0.467
9	0.424

failures occur at the end of the 4th and 8th years, and the three failures occur at the end of the 3rd, 6th, and 9th years)?

With holding costs neglected, the cost matrix can be developed, as shown in Table 11.

Since strategy 2 has the lowest expected cost, the manager should order two spare compressors at the present time. An easier method to obtain the same solution as with the expected value approach is as follows:

$$P(s) = \frac{P - V}{A - V} = \frac{100 - 0}{1000 - 0} = 0.1.$$

Referring to Table 10, there are two failures associated with a 0.05 stockout probability and one failure with a 0.30 probability, so two compressors should be purchased.

In the case of a holding cost of 10%, the manager must correct his matrix costs according to the time value of money. Consulting a present value table for future single payments results in the factors shown in Table 12. A payment that must be made in the future must be multiplied by the respective time correction factor. The cost matrix of Table 13 results. For strategy 0, the cost for state of nature 1 is $0.564(1000) = 564$; the cost for state of nature 2 is $0.683(1000) + 0.467(1000) = 1150$; and the cost for state of nature 3 is $0.751(1000) + 0.564(1000) + 0.424(1000) = 1739$. The costs for each strategy are obtained in a similar manner. Since strategy 2 results in the lowest expected cost, the manager should order two spare compressors at the present time.

Table 13

Strategy	Probability: State of Nature:	0.30 0	0.40 1	0.25 2	0.05 3	Expected Cost
0		0	564	1150	1739	\$600.25
1		100	100	567	1088	266.15
2		200	200	200	624	221.20 ←
3		300	300	300	300	300.00

EXAMPLE 6

If the demand for an item is normally distributed with a mean of 100 and a standard deviation of 20, what should be the size of the single order if the unit cost is \$100 and the stockout cost is \$1000?

$$P(s) = \frac{P - V}{A - V} = \frac{100 - 0}{1000 - 0} = 0.1,$$

$$Q_0 = \overline{M} + Z\sigma$$

$$= 100 + 1.29(20) = 126 \text{ units.}$$

VARIABLE DEMAND, VARIABLE LEAD TIME

When both demand and lead time are variable, the problem is more complex. Since no product is being used during the lead time, a delay in delivery could result in lost demand. It is possible to treat demand and lead time as independent variables. The demand can be determined independently of the lead time, as in the variable demand, constant lead time case. The lead time can be set at its maximum level or at some acceptable service level, as in Example 1. The peculiarities of the single order problem would dictate what policy to follow in reference to lead time determination. Contractual stipulations can simplify the lead time problem when outside supply is utilized.

CONCLUSION

The major emphasis in inventory analysis tends to be on items for which there are repeat orders. Single order items are frequently a greater source of difficulty, since errors in ordering cannot be corrected by an ongoing demand. Seasonal, religious, and cultural events have imposed the need for single order inventory analysis.

Single order models are referred to as static inventory models; repeat order models, as dynamic inventory models. The static or one time period model applies when only a single inventory decision is made in anticipation of demand. Static models have a simpler structure than their dynamic counterparts and are easier to apply. They are, however, far more sensitive to forecasting errors, since there is no opportunity to reorder or alter the operation.

For several types of activities, single order inventory analysis is the major mode of the inventory system. In job shops, construction, and special projects (shipbuilding, space vehicles, and research) single order analysis is much more important than repeat order analysis. Single order inventory analysis is likely to receive much more attention in practice than it has in the past as its economic significance becomes better understood and appreciated.

QUESTIONS

1. Describe the inventory situations for which the single order quantity model is suited.

2. Give some examples of items which may be controlled according to a single order quantity model, and give a reason why that is so for each.

3. What may result in one time period when items are ordered according to a single order quantity, and what are the cost consequences of each result?

4. What constitutes the lead time for a single order under self-supply? under outside supply?

5. What is the significance of lead time with the single order?

6. What is the single order quantity problem under conditions of variable demand and known lead time?

7. What is the premise of marginal analysis in establishing single order quantities?

8. In cost analysis, what are the relevant parameters in the selection of the single order quantity?

9. Why are models for single order quantities referred to as static inventory models? In what way are static inventory models more restrictive than dynamic inventory models?

10. What are some examples of types of activities for which single order inventory analysis is the major mode of the inventory system?

PROBLEMS

1. A wholesale bakery provides lemon cookies in gross containers to a discount food chain. The bakery is attempting to determine the number of gross of lemon cookies to bake each day. Any containers of cookies not sold at the end

of the day are worthless. Each container costs $10.00 and is sold for $12.00 by the bakery. Over the last 100 days, the bakery has kept daily sales records, and they reveal the following distribution:

Containers Sold	Number of Days
26	10
27	20
28	40
29	20
30	10

What is the optimum number of containers of lemon cookies to bake each day? Solve this problem by the expected value method.

2. Solve Problem 1 by marginal analysis.

3. The owner of the bakery in Problem 1 is able to sell any unsold containers of lemon cookies to a local orphanage for $8.00 a container. What is the optimum number of containers of lemon cookies to bake each day? What is the optimum expected profit?

4. The Parker Flower Shop promises its customers delivery within 4 hours on all flower orders. All flowers are purchased on the prior day and delivered to Parker by 8:00 the next morning. Parker's daily demand for roses is as follows:

Dozens of Roses	Probability
7	.1
8	.2
9	.4
10	.3

Parker purchases roses for $5.00 per dozen and sells them for $15.00. All unsold roses are donated to a local hospital. How many dozens of roses should Parker order each evening to maximize its profits? What is the optimum expected profit?

5. The Parker Flower Shop must stock some orchids for the upcoming high school prom. Most of the boys will purchase gardenias, but a few orchids will be requested. An orchid costs Parker $10.00 and sells for $25.00. Only one orchid order can be placed, and any unsold orchids will have no salvage value. Past proms' sales records reveal the data in the table. How many orchids should be ordered for the prom?

Orchid Demand	Number of Occurrences
12	5
13	5
14	10
15	15
16	30
17	20
18	15
	100

6. As president of the senior class you are responsible for planning activities for the ten-year class reunion. The planning committee has decided on a hamburger cookout. It is your task to determine the number of one pound hamburgers to purchase for the event. Demand for the dinner is normally distributed with a mean of 200 people and a standard deviation of 40. An out-of-town supplier will sell you meat at $1.50 per pound for large orders placed two weeks in advance. If you do not have enough meat you will have to purchase additional meat from a local supplier at $2.00 per pound. What should be the size of the meat order to the out-of-town supplier?

7. A food broker is trying to decide how many bushels of apples to purchase from the orchards to maximize his profits. His potential sales are estimated to be normally distributed with a mean of 1000 bushels and a standard deviation of 100 bushels. The apples can be purchased for $5.00 per bushel and sold for $7.00. Any unsold apples can be sold for $4.00 per bushel for cider. Determine by marginal analysis the quantity of apples to purchase.

8. You are having a new furnace installed. The dealer offers to sell you spare fuel pumps at $20 each if you buy them during installation. The pumps sell for $50 retail. Manufacturer's records indicate the following probability of fuel pump failures during the furnace's lifetime:

Failures	Probability
0	.1
1	.3
2	.4
3	.1
4	.1

Ignoring installation and holding costs, how many spare fuel pumps should be purchased during installation?

9. A supermarket must decide how much bread to purchase for the weekend (Friday and Saturday). Past history has shown that weekend demand can be considered normally distributed with a mean of 300 and a standard deviation of 40 loaves. A loaf of bread sells for $.50 and costs the store $.42. Any bread not sold over the weekend can be sold on Sunday for $.30 a loaf. How many loaves should be purchased to maximize expected daily profit?

10. Solve Problem 9 above if there is a goodwill loss of $.60 for every loaf of bread demanded when the store is out of stock.

11. A fashionable department store must order chocolate rabbits for the Easter season. They must be ordered three months in advance, and there is no possibility of a reorder. Each rabbit costs $5.00 and sells for $14.50. The manager feels he can sell at least 100 rabbits but not more than 500. Any number between 100 and 500 rabbits is felt to be equally likely (distribution of demand is uniform from 100 to 500 rabbits). How many chocolate rabbits should be ordered if unsold rabbits are donated to a children's hospital?

12. If all unsold rabbits in Problem 11 are sold on Easter Monday for $3.00, what is the single order quantity?

13. Spare parts for an experimental aircraft are made at the time of production. Once production is terminated, the cost of spare parts increases substantially. The experimental aircraft will have an operational lifetime of 8 years, and the demand for a specific part is Poisson distributed with a mean rate of 0.75 per year. The spare part costs $2000 per unit if ordered during production. If the spare part is purchased after production has ceased, its cost is $13,072 per unit. There will be no scrap value for any unused spare parts at the end of the aircraft's operational life. How many spares should be purchased while the aircraft is in production?

14. A buyer for a large southern department store must decide what quantity of expensive women's leather handbags to procure in Italy for the Easter season. The handbags cost the store $48 each and will retail for $75. Any unsold handbags can be sold at a sale price of $40 after the holiday. The buyer feels she is losing $2.50 additional on any unsold bags, since the money could have been invested to yield a profit. The buyer estimates demand to be normally distributed with a mean of 150 bags and a standard deviation of 30. How many leather bags should be purchased in Italy?

15. The buyer in Problem 14 believes she can sell more than 50 bags but not more than 250. If she considers the sale of any number between the limits as equally likely, how many bags should be purchased for the Easter holiday?

16. Instant Cement and Concrete Company mixes concrete for use at a nuclear power-plant construction site. One cubic yard of concrete costs $26, and it sells for $43. Under the contract established with the site contractor, daily orders are placed for concrete to be used on the following day. Any concrete not used by the end of the day is poured into a waste pit. Records of previous jobs result in the data in the table. How any cubic yards of concrete should be planned for mixing each day?

Concrete Demand (Cubic Yards)	Number of Occurrences
250	5
260	8
270	11
280	20
290	22
300	19
310	15
	$\overline{100}$

17. Solve Problem 16 with the additional stipulation that concrete remaining at the end of the day can be sold to a paving contractor for $20 per yard.

18. An amusement park must decide how many hot dogs to purchase for the upcoming three-day holiday weekend. Each hot dog costs the park $.12 and sells for $.35. Any hot dogs remaining at the end of the weekend are sold to employees for a nickel each. Past years have resulted in the following:

Demand M	4500	4600	4700	4800	4900	5000	5100
Probability $P(M)$	.07	.10	.18	.25	.16	.13	.11

How many hot dogs should be purchased to maximize the expected profit if there is a loss of goodwill of $.20 for each hot dog demanded when the concessions are out of stock?

19. The demand for an item is normally distributed with a mean of 1560 and a standard deviation of 80. What should be the size of the single order if the unit cost is $250 and the stockout cost is $1200?

20. If the salvage value is $50 in Problem 19, what should be the size of the single order?

CASE 1: HARBORFEST

Harborfest is the summer gala event in San Mateo in which the local residents and businesses participate in a sea-oriented extravaganza. Each year tens of thousands of people congregate at the downtown harbor to view a water spectacle. Locals and tourists come to converse, view art works and displays, watch sailing craft of all types, and witness the largest fireworks show on the coast. The event has become so famous that crews of foreign ships join American seamen in the festivities.

The highlight of the celebration is the Harborfest Seafood Feast. Large crowds come to sample crabs, scallops, shrimp, oysters, and clams. The seafood is prepared at the waterfront and distributed from booths scattered throughout the main harbor area. Only one seafood item is available at each booth, but there are usually several booths serving each item. The food is eaten in covered or open picnic areas or as one walks the boardwalk. One admission price is charged, and the customer can eat all he wants.

Until this year all the clams were shipped from a northern seaport. The festival officials have not been pleased with the size or flavor of the clams and have decided to buy the clams from a local bay fisherman. The problem of selecting the vendor and ordering the bay clams rests with Anne Cooney, the Regional Seafood Commission's home economics expert.

Anne is familiar with Captain Ben Edwards, an old-timer in the clam business. He knows the bay waters better than most and manages to locate the most succulent clams. Anne is positive that Captain Ben's catches are not overrated and a pound of his clams would contain fewer but larger and tastier clams than pounds purchased elsewhere. Anne, however, is unsure of the correct number of pounds to order.

Anne is to receive $1.50 from each ticket sold. Captain Ben has quoted her a price of $2.50 per pound. Based on past consumption, Anne estimates that $\frac{1}{3}$ pound of clams will be consumed for each ticket sold. However, her estimate is based on a correlation of past tickets sold and the number of pounds purchased. She is unable to locate statistics on the number of pounds overage or on the frequency or level of dissatisfaction due to insufficient clams. Anne does have accurate data on the number of tickets sold. She has rounded the numbers and plotted the following distribution of ticket sales for the past 25 festivals:

Tickets Sold	Probability
17,500	.10
20,000	.10
22,500	.40
25,000	.20
27,500	.15
30,000	.05

Because of his large contract with a leading soup company, Captain Ben has only a two-day opening left in his fishing schedule. The opening, however, is just prior to the festival and would enable him to provide fresh clams for the feast. Captain Ben promises Anne that he can provide up to 12,000 pounds if he allocates his fleet of resources to the project. Captain Ben needs a firm commitment from Anne within the week.

Anne's extreme apprehension over the correct number of pounds to order is not unfounded. The Harborfest Seafood Festival and the Regional Seafood Commission have both come under severe criticism. The community and the media have not been laudatory, and the credibility of both groups is at stake. Inclement weather has caused extensive overages and waste on some occasions; on others, there have been complaints of insufficient quantities. One newspaper article called the feast a hoax, because those who did not attend early went home hungry.

Because of the difficulties experienced in past Harborfests, the Festival Commission is declaring strict accountability. Each seafood item will be handled as a separate profit unit. If some items show a considerable loss this year, they may be dropped in upcoming feasts. Anne is determined to protect her reputation as well as the Commission's. She is desperate to find a quantitative method to calculate the number of pounds of clams so that she can show a profit and protect the clams from cancellation as a festival seafood item.

1. Taking into account statistical changes, do Anne's 25 years of data give a good indication of ticket sales?

2. How reliable are Anne's portion estimates?
3. What impact will adversities such as foul weather, more competition from other profit units, or strict accountability have on ordering practices?
4. What method should be used to order the clams and what quantity should be ordered?

CASE 2: LACTIC ACID

Hannifin's Dairy is under contract to four fast food chains to supply the Memphis franchises with containerized milk and milk products. While the milk products business appears undifferentiated, Hannifin's in reality does not serve a homogeneous market. Hannifin's must blend milk products to the specifications of McDonald's, Burger King, Wendy's, and Dairy Queen; each chain requires a different formula for milk shake and ice milk products.

The fast food chains make periodic checks on Hannifin's to ensure they are receiving the proper formulas. Samples are analyzed and rated for quality and consistency. Because of the sizable investments these companies have in product identification, they are unwavering in their requirements. For example, Wendy's builds a large portion of its reputation on the thickness of its "Frostie"; any consistency less than promised could obliterate the Wendy's image.

Containerized milk and coffee creamers are the only products Hannifin's distributes that are homogeneous in composition. Although the milk and creamers are packaged in the same assortment of container sizes, each company's logo is stamped on the carton, making sale to another chain impossible. In addition, some companies prefer to use some container sizes more than others. Therefore, the orders for containerized milk come in various proportions.

The milk products have shelf lives of eight days. The products are blended and packaged in a continuous process in one day for next day delivery. The standard contract that Hannifin's has with the chains does not stipulate the amount of products to be delivered within a given period; but it does specify that Hannifin's will deliver to the franchises twice a day. When the deliverymen run their routes, they fill the orders they have received from the franchise managers.

Because their customers practice product differentiation, Hannifin's product line cannot be completely standardized. Although the chains' marketing strategies distinctly segment and lower individual product sales, the total sales potential is substantial enough for Hannifin's to require methods to supply this market efficiently. The need for efficient and economical supply of nonstandard, perishable products burdens the production and inventory planners with many problems.

In the past Hannifin's has packaged more products than it has sold; it has repeatedly had to dispose of milk products that were beyond the expiration dates. Various methods to eradicate the problem were tried unsuccessfully. Hannifin's manager, Frederick Holsteiner, appealed to his production supervisor, Charles Guernsey, to invent a solution.

Guernsey has tried rescheduling the production, but the method is proving futile. There is too much delay in receiving the feedback from the deliverymen. Aside from the delays, Guernsey is not receiving accurate information from the deliverymen on their stock levels on the trucks. Since the deliverymen are paid on commission, they keep their levels inordinately high.

Even when correct inventory level data are received, their translation into a revised schedule is proving to be a rushed and disorderly means of dealing with the problem. What usually results is a jumbled schedule that cannot be followed precisely or on time. The irregularity of this method has led to gross negligence and disarray.

At this point, Holsteiner is in an extremely excitable state. The issue has become divisive; Guernsey wants to continue with his method in hopes of working out the kinks, while Holsteiner is ready to reject the rescheduling method immediately. Holsteiner wants to test other schemes before the summer season is upon them. Hannifin's has suffered some of its greatest losses during times when enormous profits were possible. The peak summer season and the numerous fast food promotional events have caught Hannifin's wholly unprepared. Holsteiner knows that if operations do not improve this season, the fast food chains may take their trade elsewhere.

1. Where does the overage problem lie? Could seasonality and forecasting be contributing factors?
2. Is the production rescheduling method a muddled plan? How could it be leading to gross negligence?
3. What type of production and inventory system does Hannifin's need?
4. What other changes could mitigate Hannifin's problem?

CASE 3: AN EDUCATED GUESS

Henning's Bookstore, located adjacent to the main campus of the University of Oklahoma, is the oldest bookstore in Norman. Its name has become synonymous with bookstore: the faculty and students use the terms interchangeably. This unqualified acceptance is due in part to the completeness of the store's stock of textbooks and course materials. Traditionally Henning's has carried all textbooks on the university textbook adoption list. For over 40 years the store and the university have had a mutually beneficial relationship.

Supplemental to textbooks and course materials, Henning's has ancillary lines of school and office supplies. Additionally, it offers an assortment of O.U. commemoratives, memorabilia, and knickknacks bearing the university insignia. One of the more popular lines of university bric-a-brac is a selection of O.U. T-shirts, sweatshirts, and other athletic wear.

Presently, Henning's is making plans for the upcoming school year and is restocking the depleted line of T-shirts and sweatshirts. In past years, the task of ordering these garments has not been viewed as an onerous job by the store owner, Harold DeWitt. Mr. DeWitt, following in the parsimonious footsteps of his predecessors, has always used the same fundamental ordering system. He has never anticipated his competitors in purchasing clothing or bric-a-brac items; he waits and sees what they buy and then tries to duplicate the selections in his fall order. His order quantity is based on an inventory expenditure allowance. Mr. DeWitt releases orders for shirts until the amount of his expenditures plus the value of the stock on hand equals a predetermined upper limit. The limit typically has been set low enough so that the bulk of the inventory has been sold by summer vacation. At that time the store closes for four weeks and then reopens to prepare for the coming year.

Upon his return this year, Mr. DeWitt has recruited the services of a stock clerk, Debbie Dodd, a management major at the university. Debbie spent many tutorial sessions with Mr. DeWitt during the last semester. She advised him on the relative benefits of adopting optimizing techniques for all areas of his operation. Debbie was able to convince Mr. DeWitt that he could minimize costs if he would order for the shirt department according to a periodic inventory system that she designed as a course project. The system is structured to work effectively in situations where there are to be reorders on basic items. Obviously, the scope of Debbie's lectures included the merits of ordering basic styles in advance of demand. Debbie coaxed Mr. DeWitt into ordering some basic shirts as well as periodically ordering newer styles as special inventory items. The system incorporated a category of eight special inventory items, and each item in this group would have a set economic order interval and maximum inventory level. However, at the order interval the inventory items were subject to style change, so that a newer style could be purchased in lieu of the existing item.

Mr. DeWitt's willingness to implement Debbie's system was a result of his priorities and Debbie's concessions. Mr. DeWitt has emphasized the textbook end of his business and always will, leaving areas of lesser importance to subordinates. Also, Debbie capitulated on two issues. First, she dropped her semester long argument against Mr. DeWitt's system for ordering textbooks, strictly according to the adoption list and in quantities that are a rigid percentage of the class sizes set by the university. Second, she admitted that her system cannot accommodate all items. In particular, a specialty item that Mr. DeWitt added to the T-shirt line two years ago defies Debbie's ordering policies.

Acting on the recommendation of a marketing major who worked for Henning's, Mr. DeWitt decided to take an innovative step. The marketing major had had a brainstorm for capitalizing on the largest annual O.U. football event. Her idea was to sell T-shirts commemorating the O.U.–Texas game, a game that incites one of the wildest weekends of the fall season. The T-shirts colorfully displayed the O.U. logo with lettering proclaiming the big event. Last year's shirts had a different design from the year before but advertised the same message—"O.U.–Texas Weekend." The shirts were sold at $9.00 each and were sacrifice priced at $3.00 each after the football weekend.

Mr. DeWitt has requested that Debbie apply her educated methods and devise a unique solution to the specialty item ordering problem. However, he has told Debbie that if she cannot concoct an educated guess by the time the order needs to go to the shirt printers, he will. Either Mr. DeWitt will order according to his set limit of expenditures method as previously used with the entire T-shirt line, or he will use a system similar to the one he uses in ordering textbooks. In the latter case, the quantity of shirts ordered will be a fixed fraction of the total student enrollment figure.

The important factor for Debbie to consider is an appropriate method for the determination of the order quantity and the quantity of shirts in each size. The newness of the item makes the determination very difficult, particularly since Mr. DeWitt has not used very scientific methods on past orders. The only information Debbie has is the order quantities for each of the two previous years and scanty information from Mr. DeWitt's wife as to her estimate of the number of sacrifice sales. Alternatively, Debbie is considering a change in the item itself, to something with less style dependence.

1. Evaluate Mr. DeWitt's ordering methods in practice at Henning's and their appropriateness to his needs.
2. Considering Mr. DeWitt's lack of emphasis on the sportswear line, does Debbie's system sound reasonable? Are there other factors that affect her system, such as the store's vacation schedule and the historical inventory investment policy?
3. What method should Debbie prescribe for the O.U.–Texas shirt? What assumptions must she make?
4. What qualitative factors need consideration?

MATHEMATICAL ABBREVIATIONS AND SYMBOLS USED IN CHAPTER 7

A	Stockout cost per unit
C	Ordering cost per order
EC	Expected cost
EP	Expected profit
ER	Expected revenue
$E(Q_i)$	Expected value of demand strategy Q_i
$f(M)$	Probability density function of demand
$F(Q_iM_j)$	Outcome of strategy Q_i when demand M_j occurs
J	Unit profit or benefit
L	Lead time in days
l	Loss from disposition of unutilized unit
M	Demand in units (a random variable)
$\overline{M}$	Average demand in units
M_{max}	Maximum demand in units
ML	Marginal loss
MP	Marginal profit
P	Unit purchase cost
P_1	Unit selling price
$P(M)$	Probability of a demand of M units
$P(M > Q)$	Probability of a stockout
$P(s)$	Optimum probability of a stockout
Q	Single order quantity
Q_0	Optimum single order quantity
V	Salvage value per unit
Z	Standard normal deviate
σ	Standard deviation of demand

SUMMARY OF FORMULAS IN CHAPTER 7

Model	Formula
Marginal analysis	$P(s) = P(M > Q) = \dfrac{ML}{MP + ML + A}$
Cost analysis	$P(s) = P(M > Q) = \dfrac{P - V}{A - V}$
	$Q_0 = \overline{M} + Z\sigma$

8 Dependent Demand Systems: Material Requirements Planning (MRP)

CLOSED-LOOP MRP

MRP INPUTS

MRP OUTPUTS

PRODUCT STRUCTURES
  Low Level Coding

MRP COMPUTATIONS

AN EOQ-MRP COMPARISON

MRP TYPES

MRP OVERVIEW

CAPACITY PLANNING AND CONTROL

CONCLUSION
QUESTIONS
PROBLEMS
CASES
APPENDIX A: BILLS OF MATERIALS (BOM)

Demand for an item may be classified as either independent or dependent. Demand is considered independent when no relationship exists between the demand for an item and any other item. Independent demand customarily exhibits a continuous and definable pattern but fluctuates because of random influences from the marketplace. The demand for independent items is subject to customer preferences and needs, as in the case of finished products (end items) and spare parts.

In contrast, demand is classified as dependent when a direct, mathematical relationship exists between the demand for an item and another "higher level" or "parent" item. Demand for dependent items is the result of the requirements generated for their use in the manufacture of another item, as in the case of raw materials, parts, and subassemblies used in the manufacture of a finished product. For example, a two to one relationship exists between wheels and bicycles; two wheels are needed for every bicycle to be produced. Thus, the demand for the final product (bicycle) may be continuous and independent, while the demand for the lower-level, subordinate items (wheels) composing the product tends to be discrete, derived, and dependent.

Dependent demand is not random but occurs in a lumpy, on-again, off-again pattern. The lumpiness stems from the practice of scheduling manufacturing in lots. Although independent items are demanded on an almost continuous basis, they are more economically produced in lots. Specific quantities of items needed to produce a lot usually are withdrawn from inventory all at once; quantities are not withdrawn again until another lot is produced. Lumpy demand can be described as discontinuous (having periods of zero demand) and irregular (having varying sizes of lumps). This means that large quantities may be used at some times, and little or none at other times.

The lumpy demand pattern of components is very unlike the constant demand rate assumption of the basic EOQ as it applies to end items. In principle, the EOQ replenishes inventory when levels run low, so that inventory is available at all times. Except for the observance of lot sizing economies, dependent demand items should be available only when needed (not before and not after); they do not need to be replenished when no manufacturing requirements exist (when demand is zero). In EOQ systems, independent demand for inventory items is forecasted and used to determine stock level replenishments. On the other hand, the requirements of dependent demand items can be derived from the "higher level" items. Because the uncertainty about the extent of dependent demand can be removed, these items need not be forecasted for replenishments. Thus, the demand for independent items should be forecasted, while the demand for dependent items should be calculated from the production requirements for independent demand items.

The distinctions between independent and dependent demands are important both in classifying inventory items and in developing systems to manage items within each classification. Because the demand for work-in-process and raw materials is dependent on the production of independent demand items, a different basis should be used for planning their usage. Material requirements planning (MRP) systems were developed to help manufacturing and fabrication organizations cope better with their dependent demand items than they could with previous systems built upon inappropriate demand assumptions. MRP is a computer-based system. It is designed to release production and purchase orders to regulate the flow of raw materials and in-process inventories necessary to meet the production schedules for finished products. It enables manufacturing organizations to maintain minimum levels of dependent demand items, yet assures that production schedules for the independent items can be met. It does so through the proper timing of order placement, and thus also is known as "time-phased requirements planning."

CLOSED-LOOP MRP

Material requirements planning (MRP), as an information processing system, has made possible planning and controlling both the materials and the capacity required to manufacture end items. A "closed-loop" MRP system is flow diagrammed in Figure 1. This general overview is one of a broad, integrated information system which goes beyond the simpler order launch inventory control systems which first applied materials planning logic. Supported by numerous files, it enables organizations to develop realistic plans and to coordinate resources to:

1. ensure the availability of materials, components, and products for planned production and for customer delivery,
2. maintain the lowest possible level of inventory, and
3. plan manufacturing activities, delivery schedules, and purchasing activities.

Figure 1 shows that a master production schedule is determined from customer orders, forecasts, and an aggregate production plan. The master production schedule (MPS) stipulates the products that are to be produced in specific time periods. MRP's role is to schedule all the dependent components that are required to meet the master production schedule through a materials "explosion" process. Referring to the product structure records and the inventory status records, MRP determines what components will be required and when they will be required. It systematically works backward from the scheduled completion dates of end items to derive the planned purchase and production orders and order dates for dependent demand items.

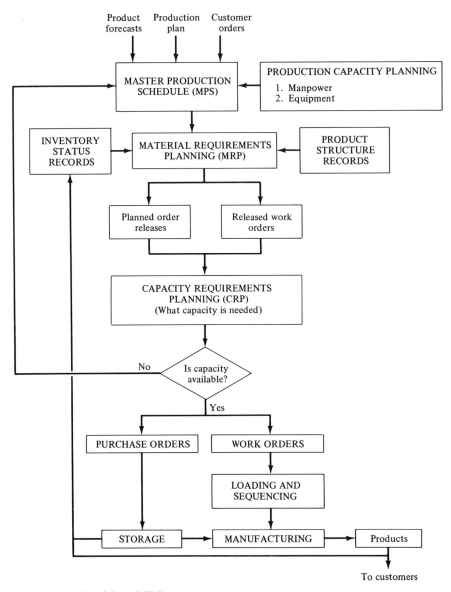

Figure 1. A closed-loop MRP system.

The MRP schedule must be subsequently checked for capacity feasibility before any orders are released. If sufficient capacity will not be available to meet the planned work orders as well as the shop orders already released, it may be necessary to revise the MPS or increase capacity. Adjustments are made as shown through the feedback loop until the plan complies with valid capacity projections.

Once the work orders are placed under the shop-floor control system, their status and progress become the responsibility of that system. It is up to shop-floor controllers to see that orders are completed on time. MRP also is updated as orders are sent to vendors. Once vendors acknowledge orders with specific delivery dates, the MRP system will update the inventory status records to ensure that delivery dates coincide with need dates. If they do not, expediting and other vendor followup actions may be used to maintain schedule integrity.

When closed-loop MRP systems are used effectively, they can be a good basis for manufacturing control. Information is processed through the system to support management decisions in many areas—purchasing, shop-floor control, capacity planning, financial planning, etc. If the information provided by the system is timely and accurate, the system can be an excellent tool for controlling inventories, costs, and service levels. As information is fed into the system and updated on a continuing basis, it dynamically plans and coordinates organizational resources.

In general, the key features of the closed-loop MRP system are the generation of lower-level requirements, the time phasing of requirements, the planning of order releases, and the rescheduling of orders to meet realistic schedules. It manages to order the right part in the right quantity at the right time. Since closed-loop systems are extended to include feedback from and control of vendor orders and manufacturing, it is an information system which addresses inventory investment levels, facility capacity needs, and work force requirements.

MRP INPUTS

The three major inputs of an MRP system are the master production schedule (MPS), the inventory status records, and the product structure records. These are diagrammed in Figure 2, and each is explained further in this section. Without these basic inputs, the MRP system cannot function.

The *master production schedule* (MPS) outlines the production plan for all end items; it expresses how much of each item is planned and when it is wanted.[1] This end item output is developed from end item forecasts and

---

[1] The term end item w̶i̶l̶l̶ be used in reference to the master schedule. The end item may be the final product, a product module, or a major assembly. When a product consists of numerous options, it is frequently desirable to master schedule below the product level at a lower level that disentangles the options.

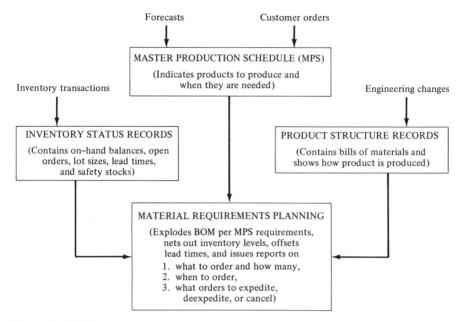

Figure 2. MRP inputs.

customer orders. Master scheduling is a basic input to and driving force behind the MRP system. MRP takes the master schedule and translates it into individual time-phased component requirements.

The MRP parts explosion process assumes that the MPS is capacity feasible. In closed-loop MRP systems, the orders generated from the parts explosion process are put into a capacity requirements planning routine to evaluate their feasibility. If sufficient capacity is unavailable, the MPS must be revised or capacity must be added until the MPS can be accomplished. The MPS must project a realistic plan of production that is leveled to accommodate available capacity.

The MPS generally is stated in terms of time-phased requirements. The time increments found to be most practical are weeks, so the planning horizon can comprise several one-week planning periods or "time buckets." The time period in which an entry (requirement) appears usually indicates that this quantity is scheduled to be available at the beginning of (or during) that respective period. How far a schedule extends into the future (the number of time buckets included) depends on the requirements of the organization. The minimum planning horizon should be long enough to cover the cumulative procurement and production lead times ("stacked lead times") for all components and assemblies composing end items. For example, if the cumulative lead times for the products of a three-product firm are 7, 10, and 12 weeks, the MPS must be at least 12 weeks long. The maximum length of the planning horizon will depend on forecasting practices, aggregate production planning, etc., but it might well extend to one year or more.

As mentioned, the MPS is developed from end item forecasts, but it is clearly not the same as the forecast; they may differ because (1) the forecast may exceed plant capacity, (2) it may be desirable to increase or decrease inventory levels, or (3) the firm may decide to operate uniformly, using inventory as a buffer against demand fluctuations. Firm demands, usually in the form of customer orders, reasonably occur in the closest time buckets of the planning horizon, and actual orders may replace forecasted sales as the schedule is updated. Frequently, the MPS is "frozen" (solidified and left intact) within the production lead time or (especially) the final assembly lead time portion of the schedule. This is done to prevent costly expediting, scrapping, etc. An organization has more latitude in planning and modifying the time periods beyond the production lead time. These plans are left more general, and the time periods themselves may be extended to months instead of weeks.

The *product structure records*, also known as the *bill of materials* (BOM) records, contain information on all materials, components, or subassemblies required to produce each end item (or master scheduled item). While the master production schedule plans how much of each end item must be available on particular dates to satisfy independent demand, the product structure records are used to derive the quantities of dependent components required to build the end items. Moreover, the bill of materials is not just a simple listing of dependent demand items, but a structured list which describes the sequence of steps in manufacturing the product. The product structure record contains the materials for the end item in levels representing the way they are actually placed in the manufacturing process. Each level in the structure represents a distinct stage of the overall manufacturing process: from the conversion of raw materials into subassemblies at the lowest level, to the subsequent steps involved in building assemblies, and lastly to the final assembly of the end item at the highest level in the structure.

Information on each end item must be meticulously kept, or the wrong materials will be ordered and required materials overlooked. The BOM file must be updated as products are redesigned, new products are added, and product sequencing or assembly is changed. The BOM should be used as a materials planning and scheduling tool and not as an engineering or accounting reference document in this context. Additionally, information on every component at every level of the product structure must include a unique part number for the item, an item description, the quantity used per assembly, the next higher assembly in the structure, and the quantity used per end item.

The *inventory status records* contain the on-hand and on-order status of each inventory item. Whereas the MPS informs the MRP system what end items are to be produced and the BOM is accessed by the system to find what components will be required to produce the end items, the inventory status records are checked to determine what inventory will be available to meet the production schedule and if more will be needed to cover requirements in a particular period. The gross component requirements in any time period are compared to the available inventory (on-hand plus on-order) to determine a need to produce it or acquire it. Quantities of items in inventory at the start of an MRP planning horizon are available for use and are referred to as "on-hand." "On-order" quantities are those that are expected to become available during a planning horizon from open work orders or open purchase orders. If available inventory is projected to be less than requirements, MRP will recommend the item be ordered.

The inventory status part of each record contains a thorough materials plan for each item, indicating in a time-phase format the planned inventory status over the planning horizon. For this reason, these records must be kept up to date, with each receipt, disbursement, and withdrawal documented to maintain record integrity. The data stored in the inventory status section should be periodically verified by a physical count. Cycle counting, where a small number of items are counted each day, commonly is used to eliminate errors, ensure that the on-hand figures are correct, and exclude defective items. Acknowledgements from vendors concerning scheduled delivery dates and quantities of released purchase orders also should be kept current, so that the scheduled receipts will be correct when the MRP program is run.

Besides information on quantities on hand and on order, the records in the inventory status file contain data on lead times for lead time offsetting (adjusting of orders to take account of the lead time period). Other subsidiary information, such as lot size, item description, list of vendors, usage to date, demand history, vendor delivery performance, notes on orders outstanding, and scrap rates may appear on these records. File maintenance should be done to safeguard the accuracy of this information.

MRP OUTPUTS

As stated previously, MRP takes the master production schedule for end items and determines the gross quantities of components according to the requirements given in the product structure records. Gross requirements are obtained by "exploding" the end item product structure record into its lower level requirements. The exploding process is simply a multiplication of the number of end items by the quantity of each component required to produce a single end item. The explosion identifies *what* components are required, as well as *how many*, to produce a given quantity of end items (the term explosion is used because each level in the product structure tends to create more requirements than the previous one). By referring to the inventory status records, the gross quantities will be netted by subtracting the available inventory items. The actual order quantity for an item may be adjusted to a suitable lot size, or it may simply be the net requirement.

Just as important as "what" and "how many" is *when*. The timing of orders is based on scheduling order releases for the purchase or the manufacture of component parts in a sequence which assures their availability in proper conjunction with the total manufacturing process. The orders are planned far enough ahead to allow adequate time for scheduled completion of the final product without having materials waiting unnecessarily for entry into a particular stage of the production process. Considering when components are scheduled to be purchased or produced and the lead times for their supply, MRP time-phases orders by lead time offsetting or setbacks. For purchased components, the lead time is the time interval between the placement of the purchase order and its availability in inventory. For manufactured items, it is the interval between the release of the work order and its completion. To make sure the component is available when needed, the planned order is offset (moved back) so that it is placed at the beginning of the lead time. Normally, all components to an assembly are planned to be available before the start date and therefore are set back at least to the beginning of their lead time period.

Thus, the material requirements for each component are phased over time in a pattern determined by lead times and parent requirements. MRP plans orders (planned order releases) for purchasing and shop scheduling for the quantity of items that must be available in each time period to produce the end items. The planned order release provides the quantity and time period when work orders are to be released to the shop or purchase orders placed with suppliers. A schematic of planned order releases as MRP outputs is contained in Figure 3. When the order (work or purchase) is released or placed, it changes from being "planned" to being "scheduled," "open," or "on order." The two basic purposes of planned orders are:

1. to generate material requirements at the next lower level,
2. to project capacity requirements.

Although MRP is an excellent tool for initial planning and scheduling, its greatest benefit may be its ability to replan and reschedule in view of unforeseen contingencies. The MRP system can predict shortages and overages soon enough so that something can be done to prevent them. It can keep order priorities up to date by planning and replanning order due dates. MRP provides exception reporting whenever a mismatch of timing between demand and supply exists. It is a priority system: typical messages are to delay, expedite, or cancel an existing order, launch a new order, etc. It attempts to make the due date and need date coincide, so operations

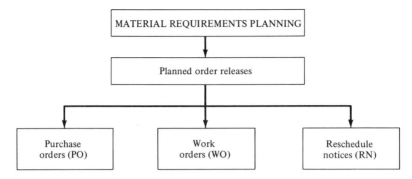

Figure 3. MRP outputs.

proceed as planned while inventory investment is minimized. If a component to an assembly will not be available when planned, MRP can reschedule all other components to the same assembly to a later date while rescheduling shop priorities. MRP will not actually reschedule orders, but it will print messages specifying exactly where changes are appropriate. The decision to make changes remains with management personnel.

PRODUCT STRUCTURES

MRP is well suited for fabrication and/or assembly type operations. A fabricated part has had manufacturing operations performed on it such as bending, cutting, grinding, milling, drilling, blanking, polishing, or coating. An assembly is a collection of parts and/or subassemblies that are put together. A subassembly is an assembly that is used at a higher level to make up another assembly. The term "component" in MRP refers to all inventory items below the product level, including subassemblies, parts, and raw materials, whether they are produced internally or obtained from suppliers. In MRP, only assembly and component relationships are considered; other terms such as subassembly, fabricated part, purchased part, or raw material are subsumed under "components."

A bill of materials (BOM) is a list of the items, ingredients, or materials needed to produce an end item or product. It lists all of the subassemblies, parts, and raw materials that go into a parent assembly, showing the quantity of each required to make an assembly. It shows how much of what materials is needed and in what order to manufacture a product. An accurate formal bill of materials is needed for every master scheduled item. The BOM will contain information on each input to the product, such as part numbers, descriptions, quantity needed for each part number, and the unit of measure. All items in the BOM must be uniquely numbered and identified.

When a product is designed, an engineering drawing (blueprint) is made, and the bill of materials is created at the same time. This initial design information is used by a process planner to develop route and operation sheets on how to make the product and by a purchasing agent to procure an adequate supply of parts for production. Originally, the function of a bill of materials was to define a product from a design point of view only. However, a product may not be assembled the way it is designed. For MRP to be effective it is necessary to generate a BOM that represents the way the product is manufactured. Frequently, an existing BOM must be modified or restructured so it is a manufacturing as well as an engineering document.

The traditional bill of materials for a product defines its structure by listing all the components that go into making it. A structured bill of materials specifies not only the composition of a product, but also the process stages in its manufacture. It defines the product structure in terms of levels of manufacture, each of which represents a completion state in the buildup of the product. It shows the "as built" as opposed to the "as designed" condition. In a schematic form, a structured bill of materials is known as a product structure, product tree, or Christmas tree. A more thorough discussion of the types of BOM is contained in Appendix A at the end of this chapter.

EXAMPLE 1

Suppose 100 units of product A (see Figure 4) must be available in period 8. If no stock is on hand or on order, determine when to release orders for each component shown and the size of each order. Product A is made from components B and C; C is made from components D and E. By simple computation the quantity requirements of each component are:

component B: (1) (number of A's) = 1(100) = 100,
component C: (2) (number of A's) = 2(100) = 200,
component D: (1) (number of C's) = 1(200) = 200,
component E: (2) (number of C's) = 2(200) = 400.

Now the time element for all the items must be considered. Table 1 creates a material requirements plan based on the demand for A, the knowledge of how A is made, and the time needed to obtain each component. It shows which items are needed, how many are needed, and when they are needed to complete 100 units of A in period 8.

The material requirements plan developed for product A is based on the product structure of A and the lead time needed to obtain each component. Planned order releases of the parent item are used to determine gross requirements for its component items. Planned order releases generate requirements in the same time period for its lower level components. In order to have 100 units of product A

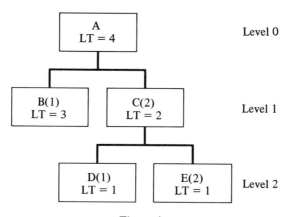

Figure 4.

Table 1. MRP plan for 100 units of product _A_ in period 8

Lead Time			1	2	3	4	5	6	7	8
4	_A_	Gross requirements								100
		Planned order releases				100				
3	_B_	Gross requirements				100				
		Planned order releases	100							
2	_C_	Gross requirements				200				
		Planned order releases		200						
1	_D_	Gross requirements		200						
		Planned order releases	200							
1	_E_	Gross requirements		400						
		Planned order releases	400							

available in period 8, it is necessary to release orders for 100 units of _B_ in period 1, 200 units of _C_ in period 2, 200 units of _D_ in period 1, and 400 units of _E_ in period 1. Planned order release dates are simply obtained by offsetting the lead times (moving the requirement one lead time earlier in the schedule). A component's gross requirements time period is the planned order release period of its parent. Planned order releases indicated for the first period are those that are in "action buckets" where immediate action is mandatory. Planned order releases for two or more periods into the future do not require immediate action.

Low Level Coding

Before MRP can net requirements (subtract projected available inventory from planned gross requirements), the system must accumulate *all* of the (gross) requirements for an item in a particular time bucket. To accumulate requirements, MRP systematically works through all of the product structures level by level. If a component is used on multiple products or appears at various levels in a single BOM, it is necessary to use low level coding to determine when an item is eligible for netting. When a component appears at more than one level, it is customary to assign it to its lowest level—i.e. the level farthest down the product structure (lower levels are designated by higher numbers). Its low level code will indicate when to generate requirements and when to finally net requirements. This ensures that the item is netted only after all higher level requirements have been calculated and only once during processing. MRP keeps accumulating requirements for an item until it arrives at the lowest level at which the item appears. At this level, MRP calculates its net requirements, because no more requirements will be generated. Once an item is netted, it too can generate lower level requirements for itself.

MRP connects parent items to lower level items as it proceeds down the product structure during the parts explosion process. It is necessary to explode the numbers of level 0 items needed in order to find out how many level 1 components are required, because level 1 items are the ones which go directly into level 0 items. In a similar fashion, it is necessary to explode the numbers of level 1 items to find out how many level 2 components are required and so forth. This process of generating lower level requirements is continued until all the product levels have been treated. If an item appears on both level 2 and level 4 of a BOM and is netted along with level 2 components, its requirements would include only those generated by its parent on level 1. It would have to be recalculated at level 4 in order to include requirements generated from its level 3 parent. Its final order schedule should be completed only after processing arrives at level 4. The total gross requirement for the item is the sum of the requirements from all its parents or sources.

MRP COMPUTATIONS

The computations and steps required in the MRP process are not complicated. They involve only simple arithmetic. The MRP process is outlined in Figure 5. The format for a typical MRP matrix is shown in Table 2 along with a description of the meaning of each term. An example of MRP component computations is shown in Table 3 along with an explanation of how the quantities were determined. A thorough understanding of the MRP matrix and component computations is necessary before MRP can be mastered.

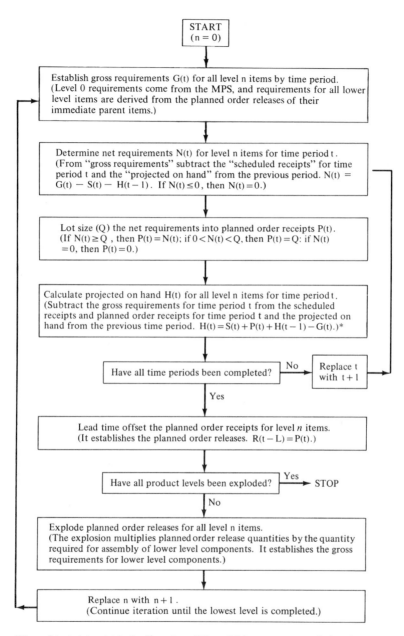

START
(n = 0)

Establish gross requirements G(t) for all level n items by time period.
(Level 0 requirements come from the MPS, and requirements for all lower level items are derived from the planned order releases of their immediate parent items.)

Determine net requirements N(t) for level n items for time period t.
(From "gross requirements" subtract the "scheduled receipts" for time period t and the "projected on hand" from the previous period. $N(t) = G(t) - S(t) - H(t-1)$. If $N(t) \leq 0$, then $N(t) = 0$.)

Lot size (Q) the net requirements into planned order receipts P(t).
(If $N(t) \geq Q$, then $P(t) = N(t)$; if $0 < N(t) < Q$, then $P(t) = Q$: if $N(t) = 0$, then $P(t) = 0$.)

Calculate projected on hand H(t) for all level n items for time period t.
(Subtract the gross requirements for time period t from the scheduled receipts and planned order receipts for time period t and the projected on hand from the previous time period. $H(t) = S(t) + P(t) + H(t-1) - G(t)$.)*

Have all time periods been completed? — No → Replace t with t + 1

Yes

Lead time offset the planned order receipts for level *n* items.
(It establishes the planned order releases. $R(t-L) = P(t)$.)

Have all product levels been exploded? — Yes → STOP

No

Explode planned order releases for all level n items.
(The explosion multiplies planned order release quantities by the quantity required for assembly of lower level components. It establishes the gross requirements for lower level components.)

Replace n with n + 1.
(Continue iteration until the lowest level is completed.)

*When safety stock is maintained and/or units are "allocated," these amounts must also be subtracted to obtain the "projected on hand."

Figure 5. The MRP process.

Table 2. Typical MRP matrix

Lot size	Lead time	On hand	Safety stock	Allocated	Low level code	Item		Period								
								PD	1	2	3	4	5	6	7	8
							Gross requirements									
							Scheduled receipts									
							Projected on hand									
							Net requirements									
							Planned order receipts									
							Planned order releases									

The column entries are self-explanatory. The row entries have the following meanings:

Gross requirements: the total anticipated production, use, or withdrawals during each time period. For end items (independent demand items), this quantity is obtained from the MPS; for components (dependent demand items), it is derived from the "planned order releases" of their immediate parents.

Scheduled receipts (also known as on-order, open orders, or scheduled orders): material that is already ordered (orders already released) and expected to arrive.

Projected on hand: the expected quantity in inventory at the end of the period to be available for demand in subsequent periods. This is calculated by adding the "projected on hand" from the previous period to the receipts for the period ("scheduled receipts" and "planned order receipts") and subtracting the "gross requirements" for the same period.

Net requirements: the difference between the "gross requirements" for the period and the total of the "scheduled receipts" in the period and the "projected on hand" from the previous period. This indicates the net number of items that must be provided to satisfy the parent or master schedule requirements. (The net requirement is zero if the projected available inventory exceeds "gross requirements.")

Planned order receipts: the size of the planned order (the order has not been placed yet) in the period in which it is needed. This appears in the same time period as the "net requirements," but its size is modified by the appropriate lot sizing policy. With lot sizing, the planned order quantity will generally exceed the "net requirements." Any excess beyond the "net requirements" goes into "projected on hand" inventory. With lot-for-lot ordering, the "planned order receipts" is always the same as the "net requirements."

Planned order releases: when the order should be placed (released) so the items are available when needed by the parent. This is the same as the "planned order receipts" offset for lead time. "Planned order releases" at one level generate material requirements at lower levels. When the order is placed, it is removed from the "planned order receipts" and "planned order releases" rows and entered in the "scheduled receipts" row. "Planned order releases" show the *what*, *how many*, and *when* of MRP.

Table 3. Example of MRP component computations

Lot size	Lead time	On hand	Safety stock	Allocated	Low level code	Item		Period									
								PD	1	2	3	4	5	6	7	8
							Gross requirements		10	15	25	25	30	45	20	30
							Scheduled receipts		10	25						
25	2	10	0	0	1	Z	Projected on hand	10	10	20	20	20	15	0	5	0
							Net requirements				5	5	10	30	20	25
							Planned order receipts				25	25	25	30	25	25
							Planned order releases		25	25	25	30	25	25		

Item Z with a low level code of 1 has an on hand quantity of 10, a lead time of 2 weeks, and a lot size of 25 units. The numbers in each time period are interpreted as follows:

In the past due (PD) period, the "projected on hand" is the present on hand quantity of 10.

In period 1, the "gross requirements" are 10, which are satisfied from the 10 "projected on hand" from the previous period. The "scheduled receipts" of 10 will then become the "projected on hand."

In period 2, the "gross requirements" for 15 are satisfied by the 10 "projected on hand" from the previous period and 5 of the 25 from "scheduled receipts." The rest of the "scheduled receipts" of 20 become the "projected on hand."

In period 3, the "gross requirements" for 25 are satisfied partially by the 20 "projected on hand" from the previous period. The "net requirements" for 5 generate the need for "planned order receipts" of 25, the lot size. Offsetting for two weeks of lead time, the "planned order release" is for period 1.

In period 4, the situation is exactly the same as in period 3 except the "planned order release" is for period 2.

In period 5, the "gross requirements" for 30 are satisfied by the 20 "projected on hand" from the previous period. The "net requirements" for 10 generate the need for "planned order receipts" of 25, the lot size. Thus, the "planned order release" for 25 is planned for period 3. The rest of the "planned order receipts" of 15 become the "projected on hand."

In period 6, the "gross requirements" for 45 are satisfied by the 15 "projected on hand" from the previous period. The "net requirements" for 30 generate the need for "planned order receipts" of 30. Since the "net requirements" exceed the lot size, the "planned order receipts" are for the larger or the "net requirements." The "planned order release" is for period 4. Since the "planned order receipts" equal the "net requirements," the "projected on hand" becomes zero.

In period 7, the "gross requirements" of 20 become the "net requirements," since there are no units "projected on hand" from the previous period. The "net requirements" for 20 generate the need for "planned order receipts" of 25, the lot size. Thus, the "planned order release" is for period 5. The rest of the "planned order receipts" of 5 become the "projected on hand."

In period 8, the "gross requirements" of 30 are satisfied by the 5 "projected on hand" from the previous period. The "net requirements" for 25 generate the need for "planned order receipts" of 25, which is the lot size. The "planned order release" is for period 6. Since the "planned order receipts" equal the "net requirements," the "projected on hand" becomes zero.

EXAMPLE 2

In the MRP table below, indicate the projected on hand, the planned order receipts, and the planned order releases. The lead time is two periods, and the lot size is the same as the net requirements (lot size = 1).

	PD				Period				
		1	2	3	4	5	6	7	8
Gross requirements		5	10	18	0	10	6	0	14
Scheduled receipts			20						
Projected on hand	20								
Net requirements									
Planned order receipts									
Planned order releases									

Solution:

	PD				Period				
		1	2	3	4	5	6	7	8
Gross requirements		5	10	18	0	10	6	0	14
Scheduled receipts			20						
Projected on hand	20	15	25	7	7	0	0	0	0
Net requirements						3	6		14
Planned order receipts						3	6		14
Planned order releases				3	6		14		

The preceding example illustrates how to net the gross requirements and establish planned order releases with lot-for-lot ordering (the order quantity is the same as the net requirements). The following example will require the same process except with a fixed lot size.

EXAMPLE 3

Redo Example 2 in the MRP table below with the lot size equal to 15 units.

		Period							
	PD	1	2	3	4	5	6	7	8
Gross requirements		5	10	18	0	10	6	0	14
Scheduled receipts			20						
Projected on hand	20								
Net requirements									
Planned order receipts									
Planned order releases									

Solution:

Gross requirements		5	10	18	0	10	6	0	14
Scheduled receipts			20						
Projected on hand	20	15	25	7	7	12	6	6	7
Net requirements						3			8
Planned order receipts						15			15
Planned order releases				15			15		

The next example shows the explosion process where the gross requirements for a dependent item are derived from a parent item. The planned order release of the parent is exploded into the gross requirements of its component items. The release date of the parent item dictates when the lower level or component items must be available. Hence, the gross requirements for component items are due in the same time period as the planned order release of the parent (they "line up" or appear in the same time bucket).

EXAMPLE 4

Product K has the product structure shown below. Complete the MRP tables if the lot sizes are equal to one.

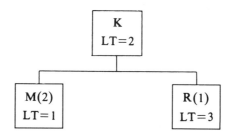

	PD	\multicolumn{8}{c}{Period}
	PD	1	2	3	4	5	6	7	8

K

	PD	1	2	3	4	5	6	7	8
Gross requirements		25	15	120	0	60	0	15	0
Scheduled receipts									
Projected on hand	50								
Net requirements									
Planned order receipts									
Planned order releases									

M

	PD	1	2	3	4	5	6	7	8
Gross requirements									
Scheduled receipts		30							
Projected on hand	225								
Net requirements									
Planned order receipts									
Planned order releases									

		Period							
PD	1	2	3	4	5	6	7	8

Solution:

K

	PD	1	2	3	4	5	6	7	8
Gross requirements		25	15	120	0	60	0	15	0
Scheduled receipts									
Projected on hand	50	25	10	0	0	0	0	0	0
Net requirements				110		60		15	
Planned order receipts				110		60		15	
Planned order releases		110		60		15			

M

	PD	1	2	3	4	5	6	7	8
Gross requirements		220		120		30			
Scheduled receipts		30							
Projected on hand	225	35	35	0	0	0	0	0	0
Net requirements				85		30			
Planned order receipts				85		30			
Planned order releases			85		30				

The preceding example illustrates the explosion process for a single product. The next example shows that a particular dependent item may have "needs" or gross requirements placed on it from more than one source. MRP will combine (accumulate) the gross requirements placed on items, regardless of their source or number of parents.

EXAMPLE 5

Two products, J and K, have the product structures shown below. Complete the MRP tables below with the lot sizes of $J = 1$, $K = 1$, and $M = 30$.

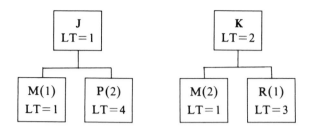

		Period							
	PD	1	2	3	4	5	6	7	8

J

Gross requirements		0	50	80	10	0	60	10	25
Scheduled receipts									
Projected on hand	15								
Net requirements									
Planned order receipts									
Planned order releases									

K

Gross requirements		25	15	120	0	60	0	15	0
Scheduled receipts									
Projected on hand	50								
Net requirements									
Planned order receipts									
Planned order releases									

M

Gross requirements									
Scheduled receipts		30							
Projected on hand	225								
Net requirements									
Planned order receipts									
Planned order releases									

Solution:

	Period							
PD	1	2	3	4	5	6	7	8

J

	PD	1	2	3	4	5	6	7	8
Gross requirements		0	50	80	10	0	60	10	25
Scheduled receipts									
Projected on hand	15	15	0	0	0	0	0	0	0
Net requirements			35	80	10		60	10	25
Planned order receipts			35	80	10		60	10	25
Planned order releases		35	80	10		60	10	25	

K

	PD	1	2	3	4	5	6	7	8
Gross requirements		25	15	120	0	60	0	15	0
Scheduled receipts									
Projected on hand	50	25	10	0	0	0	0	0	0
Net requirements				110		60		15	
Planned order receipts				110		60		15	
Planned order releases		110		60		15			

M

	PD	1	2	3	4	5	6	7	8
Gross requirements		255	80	130	0	90	10	25	0
Scheduled receipts		30							
Projected on hand	225	0	0	0	0	0	20	25	25
Net requirements			80	130		90	10	5	
Planned order receipts			80	130		90	30	30	
Planned order releases		80	130		90	30	30		

EXAMPLE 6

Develop an MRP plan for products A and Q with the product structures given in Figure 6. There are orders for 103 units of product A in period 8 and 200 units of product Q in period 7. The on hand inventory levels for each item are $A = 18$,

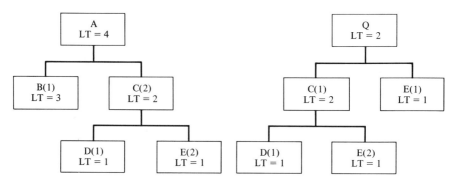

Figure 6.

Table 4

Item	Low Level Code
A	0
Q	0
B	1
C	1
D	2
E	2

$Q = 6$, $B = 10$, $C = 20$, $D = 0$, and $E = 30$. A safety stock of 5 units is maintained on product A and 6 units on product Q; there is no safety stock on other components. Additionally, 10 of the 18 units on hand of product A are already allocated. There are no open orders (scheduled receipts) on any item. The lot size for items A, Q, B, and C is the same as the net requirements (lot-for-lot ordering), while the lot size for D is 200 units and E is 500 units. What should be the size of the orders for each item, and when should the orders be released?

The low level code (LLC) for each item is as shown in Table 4. Since item E appears at level 1 and level 2 in product Q, and also at level 2 in product A, it is assigned the lowest level code of 2.

The MRP plan for 103 of product A and 200 of product Q is shown in Table 5. It shows *what* is needed, *how many* are needed, and *when* they are needed. The table was developed in the following manner:

1. The first step is to establish the gross requirements for items A and Q, which are given as 103 and 200 units. Items A and Q are netted, since they have low level codes of 0. By lead time offsetting, planned order releases for A and Q of 100 and 200 units in periods 4 and 5 are obtained.
2. The planned order releases for A and Q in periods 4 and 5 are exploded (multiplied by use quantities of items B, C, and E) and accumulated as gross

requirements for items B, C, and E. Only items B and C have a low level code of 1. Items B and C are netted. A planned order release of 90 units is scheduled for B for period 1. Similarly, planned order releases for 180 and 200 units are scheduled for C for periods 2 and 3.

3. The planned order releases for B and C in periods 1, 2, and 3 are exploded (multiplied by use quantities of items D and E) and accumulated as gross requirements for items D and E. Item E already has a gross requirement of 200 units in period 5 from item Q's explosion. Items D and E, with low level codes of 2, are netted. Planned order releases for 200 units are scheduled for D for periods 1 and 2. Planned order releases for 500 units are scheduled for E for periods 1 and 2.

The planned order release is exploded into gross requirements of its component items. It "lines up" (appears in same time period) with the gross requirements generated by it. Thus, the planned order release is responsible for the dependent item requirements. In Table 5, note how the planned order release for 100 units of product A in period 4 was exploded into gross requirements of 100 units for component B and 200 units for component C in the same period 4. Similarly, in Example 6, the planned order release for 200 units of product Q in period 5 was exploded into gross requirements of 200 units each of components C and E in the same period. The process of planned order releases creating requirements at the next lower level continues to the end of the product structure, when all the component requirements have been satisfied.

Planned order release quantities in MRP may be lot size quantities or identical to the net requirements for a given period. Ordering the same quantity as the net requirements, as in Example 1, is called lot-for-lot ordering. Safety stocks can be used with MRP, but it does not consider them available for regular use. Safety stock is recommended at the end item level but not the component level in MRP. The need for safety stock of components is reduced by MRP, since it calculates the exact quantities and when they are needed. As an alternative to safety stock, some organizations use safety lead time. With safety stock, replenishments are planned for periods when stock levels (net requirements) dip below the safety stock level. Alternatively, safety lead time plans replenishments a number of time periods before they normally would have been placed.

Reasons of economy or convenience may dictate the ordering of inventory items in excess of net requirements. Although MRP emphasizes the timing of orders more than the size of orders, lot sizing techniques based on balancing the costs of ordering and holding inventory commonly are used with MRP systems. There are several different types of lot sizing tech-

Table 5. MRP plan for 103 product A and 200 product Q

Lot size	Lead time	On hand	Safety stock	Allocated	Low level code	Item
1	4	18	5	10	0	A

		Period								
A		PD	1	2	3	4	5	6	7	8
	Gross requirements									103
	Scheduled receipts									
	Projected on hand	3	3	3	3	3	3	3	3	0
	Net requirements									100
	Planned order receipts									100
	Planned order releases					100				

Lot size	Lead time	On hand	Safety stock	Allocated	Low level code	Item
1	2	6	6	0	0	Q

		Period								
Q		PD	1	2	3	4	5	6	7	8
	Gross requirements								200	
	Scheduled receipts									
	Projected on hand	0	0	0	0	0	0	0	0	
	Net requirements								200	
	Planned order receipts								200	
	Planned order releases					200				

Lot size	Lead time	On hand	Safety stock	Allocated	Low level code	Item
1	3	10	0	0	1	B

		Period								
B		PD	1	2	3	4	5	6	7	8
	Gross requirements					100				
	Scheduled receipts									
	Projected on hand	10	10	10	10	0				
	Net requirements					90				
	Planned order receipts					90				
	Planned order releases		90							

Item C — Lot size: 1, Lead time: 2, On hand: 20, Safety stock: 0, Allocated: 0, Low-level code: 1

C	1	2	3	4	5	6	7	8
Gross requirements							200	200
Scheduled receipts								
Projected on hand	20	20	20	20	20	20	0	0
Net requirements							180	200
Planned order receipts							180	200
Planned order releases					180	200		

Item D — Lot size: 200, Lead time: 1, On hand: 0, Safety stock: 0, Low-level code: 2

D	1	2	3	4	5	6	7	8
Gross requirements					180	200		
Scheduled receipts								
Projected on hand	0	0	0	0	20	20		
Net requirements					180	180		
Planned order receipts					200	200		
Planned order releases				200	200			

Item E — Lot size: 500, Lead time: 1, On hand: 30, Safety stock: 0, Low-level code: 2

E	1	2	3	4	5	6	7	8
Gross requirements			360	400	200			
Scheduled receipts								
Projected on hand	30	30	170	270	70			
Net requirements			330	230				
Planned order receipts			500	500				
Planned order releases		500	500					

niques, such as the economic order quantity (EOQ), the Wagner-Whitin algorithm, the Silver-Meal heuristic algorithm, and the part-period algorithm. Numerous discrete lot sizing techniques were outlined in Chapter 4.

Lot sizing which relies on forecasted demand may result in unstable lot sizes in dynamic situations. As the forecast signals change in response to irregular demand, the lot sizes are adjusted upward and downward. The ordering system becomes "nervous"; it reacts frequently to change and may initiate recomputation of MRP outputs in many of these instances. Lot sizing at upper levels of the product structure can cause aggravated "nervousness" in order sizes for lower level components, particularly for complex products with several levels. A "nervous" system typically has a high volume of exception messages as manifestations of distorted or exaggerated lot sizing priorities.

Many exception messages will be generated if many orders are past due or scheduled too early or too late. With MRP logic, it is possible to have low level items scheduled "past due." However, it is not logical, operationally speaking, to schedule a component in a time period that has already passed. Therefore, the exception message will come to the attention of an analyst, who may revise the master schedule for the end item to a later period, or else compress the lead time by expediting the item if possible. Some managerial replanning is necessary when action is required in the past due time period.

When it is desired to supersede MRP logic, a *firm planned order* (FPO) is used. It freezes an order in a particular time bucket. It does not allow the normal MRP gross to net and lead time offset logic to take place. A firm planned order is a manual intervention mode to override typical MRP logic so a planner can expedite a past due order, compress lead time, change the lot size, or perform other changes.

MRP performs its procedures from the top of the product structure downward, exploding requirements level by level. There are times when it is desirable to identify the parent item that generated the component (dependent) requirement. This is possible through what is called "pegged" requirements. The pegging of requirements permits a retracing upward in the product structure to identify each parent that created the component demand. Single-level pegging locates the immediate parents; full pegging determines the end items that generated the component requirement. If a component will be delayed, it is then possible to indicate the impact on the delivery of the end item to the customer. Pegged requirements are very important in determining the significance of rescheduling alternatives.

AN EOQ-MRP COMPARISON

The MRP system has numerous advantages over the fixed order size system for control of production items. A comparison of the fixed order size and

Table 6. Comparison of fixed order size and MRP systems

Fixed Order Size System (EOQ/EPQ)	MRP system
Part oriented (every item)	Product/component oriented
Replenish supply	Actual requirements
Independent demand	Dependent (derived) demand
Continuous item demand	Discrete/lumpy item demand
Random demand pattern	Known lumpy demand pattern
Continuous lead time demand	No lead time demand
Reorder point ordering signal	Time-phased ordering signal
Historical demand base	Future production base
Forecast all items	Forecast master schedule items
Quantity-based system	Quantity- and time-based system
Safety stock for all items	Safety stock for end items
End items/spare parts	Raw materials/work-in-process
Just-in-case	Just-in-time

the MRP systems is contained in Table 6. Some disadvantages of the fixed order size system are as follows:

1. It requires a very large inventory investment.
2. It is unreliable with a highly varying demand rate.
3. It requires a large investment in safety stock.
4. It requires forecasts for all items.
5. It is based on past demand data.
6. Material obsolescence is more likely.

The use of EOQ or EPQ when demand is dependent can create serious operational problems and an excessive inventory investment. For dependent demand items, demand should be calculated from a bill of materials explosion. Demand should not be forecasted when it can be calculated. Independent demand items must be forecasted, but dependent demand items should be calculated. It is much more efficient to order components from product requirements and to drive the component inventory to zero between requirements. MRP will substantially reduce inventory investment in dependent demand items while improving operational efficiency by removing the automatic (built-in) risk of shortages associated with the EOQ or EPQ. Independent demand inventory models when used for dependent demand items generate excessive inventory when it is not needed and insufficient inventory when it is needed. A few examples will illustrate the benefits of the MRP system.

EXAMPLE 7

A toy manufacturer assembles a small wagon composed of the following components (quantities): frame(1), wheels (4), axles (2), body (1), and handle (1). All of the

Table 7

Component	Service level
Frame	.90
Wheels	.90
Axles	.90
Body	.90
Handle	.90

components are maintained on an EOQ system with the service levels[2] shown in Table 7. What is the probability that all the components will be in stock when production is scheduled to commence? What must be the component service level to maintain a 90% service level for the complete wagon?

Since the EOQ system assumes independent component demand, the probability of all the components being available is obtained as follows:

$$(0.90)(0.90)(0.90)(0.90)(0.90) = (0.90)^5 = 0.5904 = 59.04\%.$$

While service appears to be high at the component level, it is not high at the assembly (product) level. Very few production managers would agree that a service level of 59% is acceptable. To maintain a 90% service level on the wagon, each component must have a service level as follows:

$$\sqrt[5]{0.90} = 0.98 = 98\%.$$

Now the production manager may be pleased with being able to produce a complete wagon 90% of the time, but the financial manager would argue relentlessly against a 98% service level on components because of the large quantity of safety stock required to maintain such a high service level. An extremely high level of investment would be required in safety stock. Thus, the example illustrates the operational difficulties in using an independent demand EOQ as well as the large inventory investment required to make the system work. When the final product is composed of many components (many more than five used in the example), the EOQ is practically impossible to use.

=====

EXAMPLE 8

An end item is fabricated from a single component supplied by a local distributor. The end item is produced on a cycle every fourth week, or 13 times per year, during weeks 3, 7, 11, 15, 19, 23, 27, 31, 35, 39, 43, 47, and 51. Annual demand for the end item is 52,000 units. Each component costs $3.50, and the order cost is $125 per lot. The annual inventory holding cost is 20% of the unit cost, and the lead time is a constant one week. What is the total annual cost with EOQ? What is the total annual cost of MRP with lot-for-lot ordering? Compare the EOQ and MRP costs.

---

[2] The service level may be viewed as that fraction (percentage) of the time components are available in the storage area (90% of the time the frame is available, and 10% of the time it is out of stock).

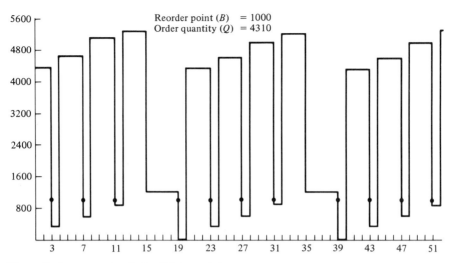

Figure 7. Inventory levels for EOQ model.

With the EOQ model, the inventory policy would be as follows:

$$\text{EOQ} = Q_0 = \sqrt{\frac{2CR}{PF}} = \sqrt{\frac{2(125)(52,000)}{0.20(3.50)}} = 4310 \text{ units,}$$

$$\text{reorder point} = B = \frac{RL}{52} = \frac{52,000(1)}{52} = 1000 \text{ units.}$$

The performance of the EOQ model on inventory levels is shown graphically in Figure 7 based on production runs of 4000 units. Note how inventory levels go through a cyclical pattern every 20 weeks, with a stockout occurring at least twice and sometimes three times in a year. Instead of inventory peaks there are plateaus (for three weeks after each order is received, inventory lies dormant in the storage area awaiting production).

Table 8 develops the average inventory level for the EOQ model:

$$\text{average inventory} = \frac{172,610}{52} = 3319 \text{ units.}$$

Neglecting stockout cost, the total annual cost using the EOQ model is as follows:

$$\begin{aligned}
\text{total annual cost} &= \text{purchase cost} + \text{order cost} + \text{holding cost} \\
&= (52,000)(3.50) + (125)(11) + (3319)(0.20)(3.50) \\
&= 182,000.00 + 1375.00 + 2323.30 \\
&= \$185,698.30.
\end{aligned}$$

Now consider an MRP system with the same variables except that orders are scheduled to arrive the day before they are needed for production. The performance of the MRP system on the inventory levels is shown graphically in Figure 8. Table 9

Table 8

Week	Inventory level	Week	Inventory level
1	4,310	27	620^a
2	4,310	28	4,930
3	310^a	29	4,930
4	4,620	30	4,930
5	4,620	31	930^a
6	4,620	32	5,240
7	620^a	33	5,240
8	4,930	34	5,240
9	4,930	35	1,240
10	4,930	36	1,240
11	930^a	37	1,240
12	5,240	38	1,240
13	5,240	39	0^a
14	5,240	40	4,310
15	1,240	41	4,310
16	1,240	42	4,310
17	1,240	43	310^a
18	1,240	44	4,620
19	0^a	45	4,620
20	4,310	46	4,620
21	4,310	47	620^a
22	4,310	48	4,930
23	320^a	49	4,930
24	4,620	50	4,930
25	4,620	51	930^a
26	4,620	52	5,240
		Total	172,610

^{a} Order placed.

develops the average inventory level for the MRP system:

$$\text{average inventory} = \frac{52,000}{365} = 143 \text{ units.}$$

To avoid complicating the computations, no attempt will be made to determine if savings could be realized by combining some orders and reducing the number of orders required from 13 to some lesser amount. However, discrete lot sizing techniques could be applied. Note that with MRP no stockouts occurred. The total annual cost with MRP is as follows:

total annual cost = purchase cost + order cost + holding cost

$= (52,000)(3.50) + (125)(13) + (143)(0.20)(3.50)$

$= 182,000.00 + 1625.00 + 100.10$

$= \$183,725.10,$

MRP cost savings = EOQ annual cost − MRP annual cost

$= 185,698.30 - 183,725.10$

$= \$1973.20.$

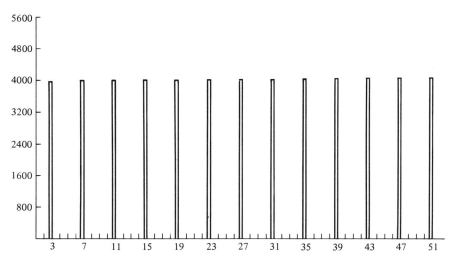

Figure 8. Inventory levels for MRP model.

Table 9

Week	Inventory level[a]	Week	Inventory level
1	0(7)	27	4,000(1); 0(6)
2	0(7)	28	0(7)
3	4,000(1); 0(6)	29	0(7)
4	0(7)	30	0(7)
5	0(7)	31	4,000(1); 0(6)
6	0(7)	32	0(7)
7	4,000(1); 0(6)	33	0(7)
8	0(7)	34	0(7)
9	0(7)	35	4,000(1); 0(6)
10	0(7)	36	0(7)
11	4,000(1); 0(6)	37	0(7)
12	0(7)	38	0(7)
13	0(7)	39	4,000(1); 0(6)
14	0(7)	40	0(7)
15	4,000(1); 0(6)	41	0(7)
16	0(7)	42	0(7)
17	0(7)	43	4,000(1); 0(6)
18	0(7)	44	0(7)
19	4,000(1); 0(6)	45	0(7)
20	0(7)	46	0(7)
21	0(7)	47	4,000(1); 0(6)
22	0(7)	48	0(7)
23	4,000(1); 0(6)	49	0(7)
24	0(7)	50	0(7)
25	0(7)	51	4,000(1); 0(6)
26	0(7)	52	0(7)
		Total	52,000

[a] The number of days in the week at the given level follows in parentheses.

In this example, a cost saving of $1973.20 was realized through the use of MRP when compared with EOQ. In addition, no stockouts occurred with MRP. The example dealt with only one end item with only one component; evidently, far greater savings can be obtained with numerous products with several components. The advantages of MRP for dependent demand items should now be apparent.

EXAMPLE 9

An organization produces an end item from a single purchased component. The existing inventory system is based on EOQs for both the end item and the purchased component. The data in Table 10 pertain to the existing inventory system. What difference would an MRP system with lot-for-lot ordering make in the average inventory level of the purchased component? What would be the cost saving of an MRP system for the purchased component? Assume all end item stockouts are lost sales.

Figure 9 illustrates a few cycles of the end item and component inventory levels with the EOQ system. The average inventory levels for the EOQ and MRP systems are calculated in Table 11. It is assumed the end item demand is stable at 10 units per week. It is further assumed that the MRP system delivers purchased components to the storeroom one week before required. Unsatisfied end item demand results in a lost sale, while unsatisfied component demand results in a backorder. The end item is not produced unless the required lot size of components is available. The average weekly component inventory with the EOQ system is 55 units, whereas with the MRP system it is only 10 units. With the EOQ system, there are 18 weeks (over 11% of the time) when there are shortages in end items that result in lost sales. The end item shortages result from the EOQ system not providing sufficient quantities of purchased components for production needs. There are no end item shortages with the MRP system, and component inventory levels are much smaller.

The total annual cost of the component with the EOQ system is as follows:

$$TC = \text{purchase cost} + \text{order cost} + \text{holding cost} + \text{stockout cost}$$

$$= \$28.80(520) + \frac{16(\$50)52}{155} + \$28.80(0.25)55 + \frac{180(\$5.00)52}{155}$$

$$= \$14,976.00 + \$268.39 + \$396.00 + \$301.94$$

$$= \$15,942.33.$$

The total annual cost of the component with the MRP system is as follows:

$$TC = \text{purchase cost} + \text{order cost} + \text{holding cost} + \text{stockout cost}$$

$$= \$28.80(520) + \frac{\$50(19)52}{155} + \$28.80(0.25)10 + 5(0)$$

$$= \$14,976.00 + \$318.71 + \$72.00 + 0$$

$$= \$15,366.71.$$

Table 10

	End Item	Component
Cost/unit	$65.00	$28.80
Annual demand (units)	520	520
Order/setup cost	$100.00	$50.00
Holding cost fraction	0.25	0.25
Stockout cost/unit	$5.00	—
Lead time (weeks)	3	4
Safety stock (units)	5	5
EOQ (Q_0)	80	85
Reorder point B	35	45

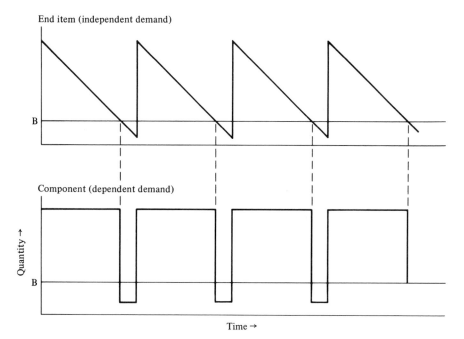

Figure 9. Inventory levels with EOQ.

Thus,

$$\text{MRP annual cost saving} = (\text{EOQ annual cost}) - (\text{MRP annual cost})$$
$$= \$15,942.33 - \$15,366.71$$
$$= \$575.62.$$

Thus, the MRP system not only provided better service (no stockouts) to production, but it reduced the inventory investment.

Table 11. EOQ and MRP inventory levels

		EOQ			MRP	
Week	End Item Demand	End Item Inventory Level	Component Demand	Component Inventory Level	End Item Inventory Level	Component Inventory Level
0	—	80	—	85	80	0
1	10	70	0	85	70	0
2	10	60	0	85	60	0
3	10	50	0	85	50	0
4	10	40	0	85	40	0
5	10	30^a	80	5^a	30	80
6	10	20	0	5	20	0
7	10	10	0	5	10	0
8	10	80^b	0	5	80^b	0
9	10	70	0	90^b	70	0
10	10	60	0	90	60	0
11	10	50	0	90	50	0
12	10	40	0	90	40	0
13	10	30^a	80	10^a	30	80
14	10	20	0	10	20	0
15	10	10	0	10	10	0
16	10	80^b	0	10	80^b	0
17	10	70	0	95^b	70	0
18	10	60	0	95	60	0
19	10	50	0	95	50	0
20	10	40	0	95	40	0
21	10	30^a	80	15^a	30	80
22	10	20	0	15	20	0
23	10	10	0	15	10	0
24	10	80^b	0	15	80^b	0
25	10	70	0	100^b	70	0
26	10	60	0	100	60	0
27	10	50	0	100	50	0
28	10	40	0	100	40	0
29	10	30^a	80	20^a	30	80
30	10	20	0	20	20	0
31	10	10	0	20	10	0
32	10	80^b	0	20	80^b	0
33	10	70	0	105^b	70	0
34	10	60	0	105	60	0
35	10	50	0	105	50	0
36	10	40	0	105	40	0
37	10	30^a	80	25^a	30	80
38	10	20	0	25	20	0
39	10	10	0	25	10	0
40	10	80^b	0	25	80^b	0
41	10	70	0	110^b	70	0
42	10	60	0	110	60	0
43	10	50	0	110	50	0
44	10	40	0	110	40	0
45	10	30^a	80	30^a	30	80

(*continued*)

Table 11. EOQ and MRP inventory levels *(continued)*

Week	End Demand Demand	EOQ End Item Inventory Level	EOQ Component Demand	EOQ Component Inventory Level	MRP End Item Inventory Level	MRP Component Inventory Level
46	10	20	0	30	20	0
47	10	10	0	30	10	0
48	10	80^b	0	30	80^b	0
49	10	70	0	115^b	70	0
50	10	60	0	115	60	0
51	10	50	0	115	50	0
52	10	40	0	115	40	0
53	10	30^a	80	35^a	30	80
54	10	20	0	35	20	0
55	10	10	0	35	10	0
56	10	80^b	0	35	80^b	0
57	10	70	0	120^b	70	0
58	10	60	0	120	60	0
59	10	50	0	120	50	0
60	10	40	0	120	40	0
61	10	30^a	80	40^a	30	80
62	10	20	0	40	20	0
63	10	10	0	40	10	0
64	10	80^b	0	40	80^b	0
65	10	70	0	125^b	70	0
66	10	60	0	125	60	0
67	10	50	0	125	50	0
68	10	40	0	125	40	0
69	10	30^a	80	45^a	30	80
70	10	20	0	45	20	0
71	10	10	0	45	10	0
72	10	80^b	0	45	80^b	0
73	10	70	0	130^b	70	0
74	10	60	0	130	60	0
75	10	50	0	130	50	0
76	10	40	0	130	40	0
77	10	30^a	80	50	30	80
78	10	20	0	50	20	0
79	10	10	0	50	10	0
80	10	80^b	0	50	80^b	0
81	10	70	0	50	70	0
82	10	60	0	50	60	0
83	10	50	0	50	50	0
84	10	40	0	50	40	0
85	10	30^a	80	$(-30)^a$	30	80
86	10	20	0	(-30)	20	0
87	10	10	0	(-30)	10	0
88	10	0	0	(-30)	80^b	0
89	10	0	0	55^b	70	0
90	10	0	0	55	60	0

(continued)

Table 11. EOQ and MRP inventory levels *(continued)*

		EOQ			MRP	
Week	End Demand Demand	End Item Inventory Level	Component Demand	Component Inventory Level	End Item Inventory Level	Component Inventory Level
91	10	0	0	55	50	0
92	10	70[b]	0	55	40	0
93	10	60	0	55	30	80
94	10	50	0	55	20	0
95	10	40	0	55	10	0
96	10	30[a]	80	(-25)[a]	80[b]	0
97	10	20	0	(-25)	70	0
98	10	10	0	(-25)	60	0
99	10	0	0	(-25)	50	0
100	10	0	0	60[b]	40	0
101	10	0	0	60	30	80
102	10	0	0	60	20	0
103	10	70[b]	0	60	10	0
104	10	60	0	60	80[b]	0
105	10	50	0	60	70	0
106	10	40	0	60	60	0
107	10	30[a]	80	(-20)[a]	50	0
108	10	20	0	(-20)	40	0
109	10	10	0	(-20)	30	80
110	10	0	0	(-20)	20	0
111	10	0	0	65[b]	10	0
112	10	0	0	65	80[b]	0
113	10	0	0	65	70	0
114	10	70[b]	0	65	60	0
115	10	60	0	65	50	0
116	10	50	0	65	40	0
117	10	40	0	65	30	80
118	10	30[a]	80	(-15)[a]	20	0
119	10	20	0	(-15)	10	0
120	10	10	0	(-15)	80[b]	0
121	10	0	0	(-15)	70	0
122	10	0	0	70[b]	60	0
123	10	0	0	70	50	0
124	10	0	0	70	40	0
125	10	70[b]	0	70	30	80
126	10	60	0	70	20	0
127	10	50	0	70	10	0
128	10	40	0	70	80[b]	0
129	10	30[a]	80	(-10)[a]	70	0
130	10	20	0	(-10)	60	0
131	10	10	0	(-10)	50	0
132	10	0	0	(-10)	40	0
133	10	0	0	75[b]	30	80
134	10	0	0	75	20	0
135	10	0	0	75	10	0

(continued)

Table 11. EOQ and MRP inventory levels *(continued)*

		EOQ			MRP	
Week	End Demand Demand	End Item Inventory Level	Component Demand	Component Inventory Level	End Item Inventory Level	Component Inventory Level
136	10	70^b	0	75	80^b	0
137	10	60	0	75	70	0
138	10	50	0	75	60	0
139	10	40	0	75	50	0
140	10	30^a	80	$(-5)^a$	40	0
141	10	20	0	(-5)	30	80
142	10	10	0	(-5)	20	0
143	10	0	0	(-5)	10	0
144	10	0	0	80^b	80^b	0
145	10	0	0	80	70	0
146	10	0	0	80	60	0
147	10	70^b	0	80	50	0
148	10	60	0	80	40	0
149	10	50	0	80	30	80
150	10	40	0	80	20	0
151	10	30^a	80	0^a	10	0
152	10	20	0	0	80^b	0
153	10	10	0	0	70	0
154	10	80^b	0	0	60	0
155	10	70	0	85^b	50	0
				8520		1520
	Weekly average			55		10

^{a} Reorder point.
^{b} Stock replenishment.

As was previously illustrated in Table 6, an MRP system has several advantages over an EOQ system. However, the systems are not really competing, for each has a different area of application. For continuous, uniform, and independent demand the EOQ system is desirable. For discontinuous, nonuniform, and dependent demand the MRP system is desirable. For production, manufacturing, fabrication, or assembly industries the majority of inventory items dictate an MRP approach.

A dependent demand item can experience a fairly uniform demand rate. This can occur when an item is used at several different production stages, or when it is used to make several different products. In both cases, the summing of many separate lumpy demands can result in a demand pattern that is fairly uniform. When this happens, it may be more appropriate to treat the demand as independent. Basic raw materials and components with a large number of uses can exemplify this situation. Contrariwise, a dependent demand item can also be subjected to independent demands. This occurs when an item not only is used to produce a product but also is sold separately as a repair or replacement part. The result is an item with both a dependent and independent side to its demand.

Historically, many organizations have used statistical inventory control via EOQ models when they should have been using MRP. Since the statistical approach does not ensure the availability of components for production, they instituted expediters and support departments to ensure material availability. Expediters were required tò make an inadequate system meet scheduling and delivery needs. In accounting for the system's shortcomings, everybody had his own idea who was the culprit, and recriminations were common. The real culprit was an inappropriate system that did not serve the needs of the organization. Not only will the wrong system hamper operations and increase costs, but it can result in serious conflicts between the various parts of the organization.

It should be apparent by now that a manual MRP system is untenable except for very simple products. Computerized MRP systems are necessary because of the massive number of lower level items and the tedium of manual computations. Numerous organizations have highly sophisticated MRP systems, which have been implemented in the last decade. Software packages are readily available to ease the pain of conversion from other systems. However, MRP systems must be tailored to meet the specific needs of an organization.

MRP TYPES

There are two basic types of MRP systems, the regenerative and the net change systems, geared to different frequencies of replanning. With *regenerative systems*, the entire MRP (full explosions) is recalculated periodically (usually once a week), based on the latest master schedule requirements. The regenerative approach is designed for low-frequency replanning and employs batch-processing techniques. Regeneration starts over with a "new slate" and reexplodes the entire master schedule. After each planning period the planning horizon is extended one more period into the future. One advantage of the regenerative system is that it permits efficient use of data processing equipment. Another benefit is that fewer data errors are compounded over time, since it is checked and corrected on a regular basis.

With *net change systems*, the entire requirements for every component are not recalculated periodically; only additions and subtractions from the master schedule are entered. The requirements change is then calculated for only those components affected (partial explosions). The net change system can be applied instantly or at the end of each day. This system is designed for high-frequency replanning. In a stable environment (master production schedule) the regenerative MRP functions satisfactorily; in a volatile environment with frequent change the net change MRP is more desirable.

MRP OVERVIEW

MRP originally was seen as a superior method of ordering inventory. As it evolved, its major emphasis shifted to scheduling (establishing and maintaining valid due dates on orders). Today, it has been expanded further into manufacturing resource planning (MRP II) to include the effective planning of all the resources of a manufacturing organization. As illustrated in Figure 10, manufacturing resource planning is a much more sophisticated system which incorporates information from manufacturing, marketing, engineering, and finance into a total operations plan for the organization. The evolution of MRP to closed-loop MRP to MRP II results in a single game plan to meet the overall goals of an organization. This is possible because it ties together strategic, financial, and capacity planning areas.

Thus, the term MRP has meant different things to different people at different times. Some think of it as an inventory system, others as a scheduling system, and still others as a complete closed-loop production system. It can be all of these things, depending on the organization and the stage of its development with MRP. Most would agree that MRP fosters systems thinking and tends to become the cornerstone of the production system. Within the limits of its methodology, it will reveal (1) what is needed, (2) how many are needed, (3) when they will be needed, and (4) when they should be ordered.

The time horizon in MRP is composed of equal time periods called "time buckets." The "time buckets" are usually weeks or some other convenient time increment. The time horizon is usually longer than the longest sequence of component lead times of any product. It should be long enough to obtain all materials and produce all components before a planned order release for end items. It is also possible to have "bucketless MRP," where equal time periods are not used but specific dates are developed for every order.

The effective operation and efficiency of an MRP system depend on the integrity of the files and records of relevant data. The quality is directly influenced by data accessibility, up-to-dateness, and accuracy. Lack of record integrity is a major reason for the failure of MRP systems to live up to expectations. Computer-based MRP, even more than manual, will not perform satisfactorily with poor files and records. File integrity is not a one-time affair, but must have constant maintenance. The outputs from a computer-based MRP system cannot be better than its inputs.

When inventory decisions cannot be separated from production decisions, they must be considered part of aggregate planning for the total

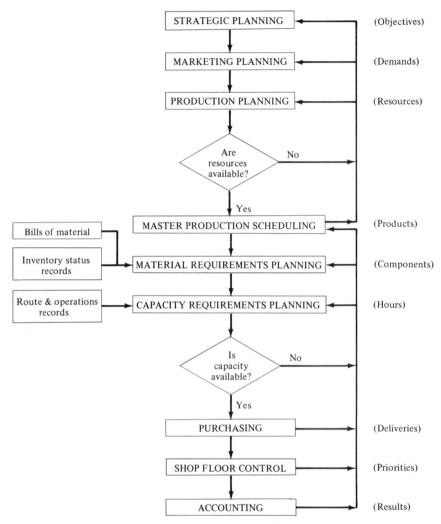

Figure 10. Manufacturing resource planning.

production system. Dependent demand inventory items are in this category, since they are production dependent. The function of an MRP system is to translate the overall plan of production (master production schedule) into detailed component requirements and orders. It determines what is to be manufactured and when, as well as what is to be procured and when. For end items, it is useful to hold extra inventory to provide for customer service. To hold extra inventory of components with a dependent demand normally serves no function.[3] While the demand for end items may be uncertain, the demand for components is certain (deterministic) and dictated by the production schedule.

When the following conditions hold, MRP is usually superior to other inventory systems:

1. The final product is complex and contains several other items.
2. The specific demand for the product in any time period is known.
3. The final product is expensive.
4. The demand for an item is tied in a predictable fashion to the demand for other items.
5. The forces creating the demand in one time period are distinguishable from those in other time periods.

CAPACITY PLANNING AND CONTROL

Capacity planning determines how many persons, machines, and physical resources are required to accomplish the tasks of production. It defines, measures, and adjusts the levels of capacity so they are consistent with the needs of production. Capacity must be planned in terms of some unit of measure that is common to the mix of products encountered (units, tons, meters, standard hours, etc.). The unit of measure selected must translate all products into a common equivalent unit related to time.

There are many factors that affect capacity. Some factors are completely under management control, while others are not. The management controlled factors include:

1. land,
2. labor,
3. facilities,
4. machines,
5. tooling,
6. shifts worked per day,
7. days worked per week,
8. overtime,
9. subcontracting,
10. preventive maintenance.

Other, less controllable factors include:

1. absenteeism,
2. personnel turnover,

[3] Safety stocks for components may be desirable to cushion uncertain lead times, scrap losses, and shrinkage.

3. labor performance,
4. equipment breakdown,
5. scrap and rework.

Capacity can be affected by a change in any of the above factors.

Capacity refers to the production capability of a work center, department, or facility. It is important because (1) sufficient capacity is needed to provide the output for current and future customer demand, (2) it directly influences the efficiency (cost) of operations, and (3) it represents a sizable investment by the organization.

Operations managers must address the conflicting objectives of efficient plant operation, minimum inventory investment, and maximum customer service. They must answer the questions:

1. What should I be working on?
2. Do I have the capacity to work on it?

The first question deals with *priorities* and the second with *capacities*. It is necessary to plan and control both priority and capacity. Priority is the ranking by due date of an order relative to other orders. It determines what material is required and when it is required. MRP is a form of priority planning. Capacity is the quantity of work that can be performed at a work center and is frequently expressed in hours.

Capacity planning relates to labor and equipment requirements. It determines what labor and equipment capacity is required and when it is required. It is usually planned on the basis of labor or machine hours available within the plant. Capacity has a direct influence on customer service. Excess capacity results in low resource productivity, while inadequate capacity may mean poor customer service.

Within the framework of MRP II, capacity management validates the feasibility of manufacturing plans with respect to capacity in each stage of the planning process (production plan, master production schedule, and MRP) so major problems can be anticipated and avoided. As illustrated in Figure 11 and Table 12, the three levels of capacity planning are resource requirements planning (RRP), rough-cut capacity planning (RCCP), and capacity requirements planning (CRP). All three are time-phased predictions of resources required, but each differs in the amount of detail that is produced.

Capacity decisions really start with the production plan, which establishes the output for each time period in aggregate terms. The production plan should be leveled so it is realizable within capacity constraints. The time horizon of the production plan is usually long enough that capacity can be changed (expanded or contracted) to meet expected demand. While the production plan deals in aggregate terms, the master schedule, which is

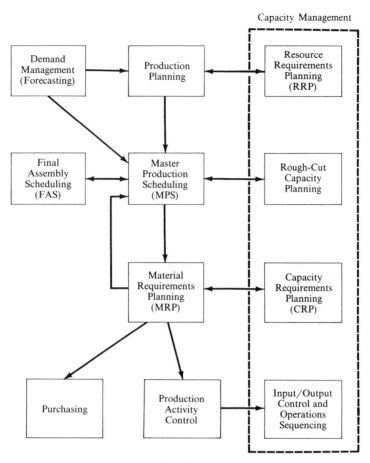

Capacity Management

Figure 11. Capacity planning and control.

Table 12. Capacity planning

Capacity Tool	Time Horizon	Plan	Change Options
Resource requirements planning (RRP)	Long range	Production plan (PP)	Land, facilities, equipment, work force
Rough-cut capacity planning (RCCP)	Medium/long range	Master production schedule (MPS)	Work force, routings, make/buy, tooling, subcontract
Capacity requirements planning (CRP)	Short/medium range	Material requirements planning (MRP)	Work force, routings, overtime, subcontract

derived from it, contains more specific detail on products and product modules.

The objective of *resource requirements planning* is to identify the aggregate level of major resources required to meet the production plan. Resource profiles are developed to indicate the usage of key resources at the product family level. Resource profiles (also known as capacity bills, time-phased bills of capacity, load profiles, capacity planning factors, and bills of labor or resources) contain three data: (1) identification of the resource, (2) estimated capacity impact of each product family, and (3) time estimates to predict when resources will be required. By extending the production plan quantities over the resource profiles, management has an estimate of the requirements for critical resources throughout the planning horizon.

The objective of *rough-cut capacity planning* is to identify the resources required to meet the master production schedule. It converts the MPS to a prediction of the load on the factory.[4] Resource profiles are constructed for· each master scheduled item, similar to those in RRP but in more detail. By extending the master scheduled quantities over the resource profiles, management has an estimate of the requirements for critical resources over the master production schedule horizon. Thus, RCCP is used to verify that the MPS is realistic in terms of gross capacity. If it is not, management is provided with enough lead time to adjust the MPS or change the capacity without impeding current operations. The emphasis is on bottleneck resources or work centers that might cause trouble.

The master schedule must also be a realizable schedule. MRP plans priorities, and it assumes that sufficient capacity is available to execute the master schedule. If the master schedule is overstated (overloaded), MRP priorities will be invalid and impossible to attain. For this reason, it is necessary to verify that sufficient capacity is available after the material requirements plan is obtained.

Through each of the capacity planning stages, the amount of detail has been increasing, while the time increments of planning and the planning horizon have been decreasing. Although major capacity problems have been resolved during the higher level planning process, the day-to-day capacity problems will still exist. *Capacity requirements planning* (CRP) is the tool used to identify those problems and to validate the material plan generated by material requirements planning (MRP). CRP determines the amount of specific labor and equipment resources required to meet the material plan over the short- to medium-range horizon. The required capacity is then compared with the available capacity to identify potential overloads or underloads.

---

[4] Capacity is the rate at which work is withdrawn from a system, while load is the volume of work in a system.

MRP is not a capacity plan, it does not solve capacity problems, and it does not level work loads in the shop. It tends to utilize capacity in a lumpy manner. Leveling the MPS can attenuate capacity fluctuations, but then the netting of demands against existing stocks, previous order actions, and lot sizing policies tends to generate fluctuations in capacity requirements at the lower shop level.

The output from MRP will be planned order releases and released (open) orders, which are the inputs into capacity requirements planning (CRP). As shown in Figure 12, the combination of planned orders and released orders will be converted into their capacity requirements by time period. From route sheets, the operations required and their standard time can be ascertained. The capacity requirements plan will calculate the standard hours of production by work center and time period required to satisfy the master schedule. The objective is to indicate if existing capacity is adequate to support the master schedule. If sufficient capacity is not available, the master schedule must be revised or capacity expanded. If sufficient capacity is available, the material requirements plan can be executed.

The ability to see capacity requirements ahead of time is especially important in manpower planning. CRP enables an organization to anticipate overloads, underloads, or bottlenecks in work centers in time to take corrective action. It takes material requirements from MRP and converts them into standard hours of load on the labor and equipment in the various work centers for future time periods.

Figure 12. Capacity requirements plan.

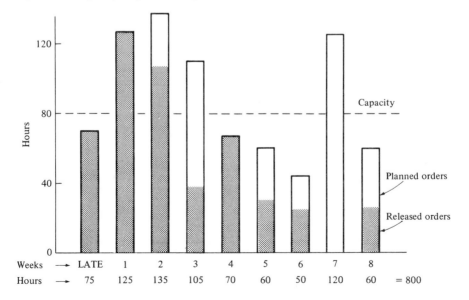

Thus, capacity planning is performed at various stages with different degrees of exactness. Before MRP, capacity planning is rough cut (performed in broad aggregate terms). After MRP, capacity planning, in the form of CRP, measures the work load at each work center, based on both planned and released orders. Capacity planning is really an iterative process of comparing available capacity with future capacity requirements. When there is an imbalance the following steps can be taken:

1. If available capacity is less than required capacity, either increase available capacity (utilize overtime, extra shifts, subcontracting, etc.) or reduce required capacity (reduce master schedule requirements, select alternate routings, etc.).
2. If available capacity is greater than required capacity, either reduce available capacity (shift or lay off manpower, reduce shift hours, etc.) or increase required capacity (increase master schedule requirements, release orders early, reduce subcontracting, etc.).

Frequently organizations have critical work centers that limit production. Critical work centers are bottleneck work centers where capacity is limited and flow restricted. In job shops, critical work centers may change from time period to time period. Frequently, work center loading is based only on released orders. With MRP, capacity requirements on work centers are based on planned orders as well as released orders. Thus, critical work centers can be planned more effectively.

The role of capacity management is to verify that plans (family, product, and component plans) are realistic. To ensure plans are executed, capacity control is needed via input/output control. It monitors the flow of work through the designated work centers and provides performance information. If capacity is overstated or understated, plans may be implemented that either cannot be met or result in poor utilization of resources.

MRP is a material-dominated scheduling technique which backward schedules material through time from end item due dates. After the time and quantity of material requirements have been determined, a capacity analysis (CRP) is performed to evaluate capacity feasibility. Problems are identified and solutions initiated by rescheduling materials or changing capacity. If either material or capacity is inadequate, the master production schedule is revised until an acceptable schedule is developed.

MRP is an input to capacity requirements planning, which must assess the workload at work centers and determine if capacity is sufficient. MRP systems assume that the master production schedule is feasible and adequate capacity exists to meet its requirements. If capacity is insufficient, changes must be made. Usually, capacities in key work centers are continuously monitored, for they indicate capacity limitations. Adjustments to labor and machine utilization may be necessary in critical work centers. The

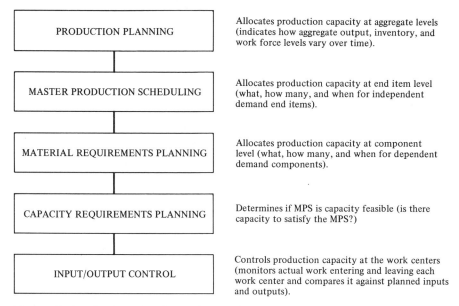

Figure 13. Production planning and control systems.

major modules in a production planning and control system are outlined in Figure 13.

CONCLUSION

Production planning and master scheduling establish the manufacturing plan of products or end items to be produced during a given time frame. MRP takes the master schedule for end items and calculates the plan for all dependent demand items composing the end items. Manufacturing and purchasing are responsible for executing the overall material plans as portrayed in Figure 14.

MRP combines product explosions, netting, lot sizing, time phasing, and other operations into one coordinated procedure. It can be compared to a person who makes a menu each day and buys groceries according to the menu. Items are purchased only as the menu requires them. Non-menu items are not purchased or prepared, so inventory is held very low.

Although MRP primarily calculates material requirements, it can be used to calculate machine time and labor needs. Once the MRP plan is established, route and operation sheets can be utilized to determine labor and machine times. This additional extension is called capacity requirements planning. Thus, MRP is a valuable tool for (1) inventory control (time

Figure 14. Material planning.

phasing orders to needs), (2) scheduling (setting priorities), and (3) capacity requirements planning (determining MPS capacity feasibility).

MRP is normally implemented as a computer-based system because of the quantity of transactions and simple calculations required. It is practically impossible to plan and replan hundreds of subassemblies with many-leveled product structures on a manual basis. Without a computer it is impossible to keep up-to-date records on the status of thousands of inventory items.

QUESTIONS

1. Differentiate between independent and dependent demand items by pointing out the defining characteristics of each. To which category of items is MRP better suited?

2. What are the key features of an MRP system?

3. List and describe briefly the three major inputs to an MRP system.

4. Explain the phrase " 'exploding' the end item product structure record."

5. How does MRP time-phase net requirements?

6. To what items does the term "component" refer in MRP systems?

7. What is the purpose of low level coding? Does the product (end item) have the highest or lowest level code? Why?

8. Give the rules for lot sizing the net requirements into planned order receipts.

9. Distinguish between planned order receipts and planned order releases.

10. How are gross requirements obtained for end items? for components?

11. How does a net change system differ from a regenerative system?

12. What is the appropriate time horizon for an MRP system?

13. Give a concise discussion of the relationship of MRP to capacity planning.

14. What short-term steps can be taken to correct a capacity imbalance where available capacity is less than required capacity?

15. What are the uses for a bill of materials (BOM)?[5]

16. Why would a BOM generate both an explosion and an implosion format for the same product structure data? Give an example of both format types and the uses of each example.[5]

17. In what situation would a modular BOM be appropriate? Why?[5]

PROBLEMS

1. Compute the net requirements for the three items listed below:

	Item A	Item B	Item C
Gross requirements	175	30	140
On hand	35	5	70
On order	40	0	50
Safety stock	18	3	0

2. From the information given below for product A, draw the product structure:

Parent:	A	B	C
Components:	$B(1)$	$E(2)$	$D(1)$
	$C(1)$	$F(1)$	$G(3)$
	$E(1)$	$G(1)$	
	$F(4)$		

3. Make an indented bill of materials with low level coding for the product in Problem 2.

4. An indented parts list for product Z is given next. How many component F's are required for product Z? How many component 50's are required?

[5] Requires information contained in Appendix A.

Part Number			Quantity/Assembly
Z			—
·	A		1
·	·	80	6
·	·	110	6
·	·	F	3
·	G		2
·	·	50	4
·	·	70	4
·	·	90	1
·	K		2
·	M		2
·	Q		1
·	R		1
·	·	50	4
·	·	70	4
·	·	D	1
·	50		1

5. Subic Marine, Inc. manufactures power packages for the U.S. Navy. An order for 200 power packages has been received. Each power package contains two engines, each of which contains one gearbox; each gearbox contains five gears, and each gear is forged from one forge of high tensile strength steel. The available inventory is as follows:

Engines	13
Gearboxes	22
Gears	215
Steel forges	67

Determine the net requirements for each item.

6. After reviewing reliability data, the production manager in Problem 5 decides that a safety stock of five engines is necessary. What are the new net requirements for each item?

7. A manufacturer of one-half ton trucks offers its customers a number of options. The options available are as follows:

5 engines	15 colors
3 transmissions	4 bodies
2 rear ends	3 frames

How many unique truck configurations are possible? At what level of the product structure would the organization perform its master scheduling?

8. The lead time to purchase a steel spring from a supplier is four weeks. There are currently 42 springs available with an additional scheduled receipt of 20 springs in four weeks. The gross requirements for the steel spring over the next

eight weeks are as follows:

Week	1	2	3	4	5	6	7	8
No. of units	12	17	0	14	2	28	9	18

If the order quantity is 20 units, when should orders be released for the spring?

9. An order has been received for 200 units of product A with the product structure shown next. If no stock is available or on order, determine the size of each order and when to release each order.

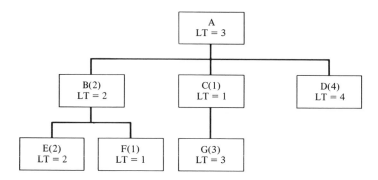

10. An order has been received for 150 units of product A with the product structure shown below. If no stock is available or on order, determine the size of each order and when to release each order.

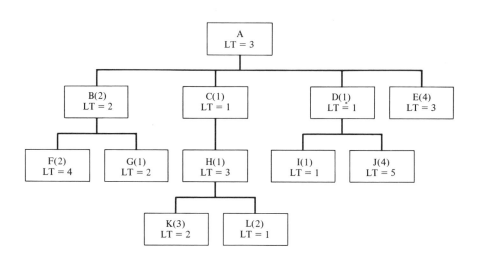

11. Orders have been received for 20 units of product A and 50 units of product R with the product structures shown below for period 8. The on hand stock levels are $A = 1$, $R = 4$, $B = 74$, $C = 19$, $D = 190$, and $E = 160$. What is the low level code for each item? If components are ordered as required (no fixed lot sizes), what should be the size of each order? When should orders be released for each item?

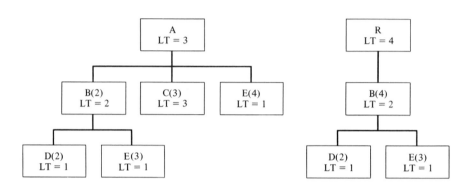

12. The A and B Manufacturing Company produces two products with the product structures shown below. It has orders for 150 units of product A in period 8 and 135 units of product B in period 7. The on-hand inventory levels for each item are $A = 5$, $B = 2$, $C = 135$, $D = 300$, and $E = 356$. When should orders be released for each item, and what should be the size of the order?

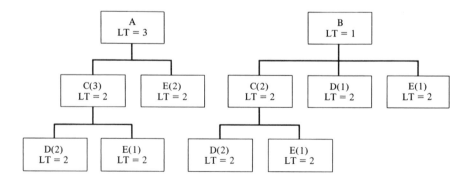

13. The XYZ Corporation assembles three products as shown in the product structures below. It has orders for 50 units of product X for period 8, 20 units of product Y for period 6, and 10 units of product Z for period 7. The on-hand stocks of each item are $X = 7$, $Y = 3$, $Z = 2$, $A = 3$, $B = 12$, $C = 30$, $D = 3$, and $E = 40$. When should each order be placed, and what should be the size of each order?

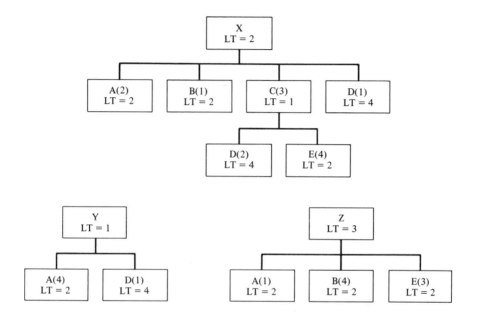

14. Joe Breakdown, the maintenance manager for XYZ Corporation, has just informed you that he will need ten item E in period 4. How would this change affect the orders planned in Problem 13?

15. The supplier of item E in Problem 13 indicates that its lead time will be one period longer (3 periods) due to a strike. What impact will this change have on the delivery of the product orders?

CASE 1: SUBVERSION OR TERRITORIAL RIGHTS

Polymerics Corporation was still attempting to work the "bugs" out of its recently installed computerized MRP system. It had been six months since the system was put into operation. Ed Explode, the production control manager, disagreed with Sue Structure, the computer programmer. It seemed that the two could not agree on the format and design of the reports the computer was to generate. Ed insisted, on behalf of his two production supervisors, that the report be printed with an additional space between lines. Each line represented a separate part number. Sue Structure argued that providing additional space would only increase the cost of the report. Sue exclaimed it would take a very good reason to convince her to modify the reports.

In an attempt to gather additional information for his argument Ed discussed the situation with his supervisors. After meeting several hours with them, he uncovered the real reason behind their request for more space in the report. It seemed the supervisors wanted the extra space so they could write in their own numbers regarding planned production and parts requirements. The supervisors apparently had little faith in the new computerized system. They both had been involved in an earlier system that was a complete failure. As he left his office to meet with Sue, Ed was not sure what position he should take.

1. What strategy would you recommend to Ed Explode?
2. Who should make the decision on the format of the reports?
3. Is the resistance of the supervisors warranted?

CASE 2: TROUBLE DOWN BELOW

Riff Manufacturing was founded twenty-four years ago and until recently had a steady record of growth in sales, assets, and profits. The company manufactures four products, and each product has over twenty options. Until three years ago, profit margins were satisfactory and the company's main objective was growth into other geographical areas. Now profit margins have fallen dramatically because of higher production costs and increased competition from foreign firms.

George Riff, the founder and president, faces the additional problem of raising capital for plant expansion into the growing southeastern section of the country. Unfortunately, the company's stock is selling below book value, and interest rates are approaching an all-time high. It was in such an atmosphere that the year-end meeting was called to review the past and draw up plans for the future. After brief presentations by several managers, Mr. Riff asked for a brief statement from the production vice president on their problems in holding down costs. The following is a summary of the points presented:

a. The forecasting techniques developed should produce excellent results. Over-capacity in the new computer installation has permitted extensive experimentation with exponentially weighted moving averages.
b. A production plan is now prepared for eighteen months and will be updated quarterly.
c. A master schedule is now prepared for twelve months and will be updated monthly.
d. Inventory remains excessive. Holding costs are high, and the availability of components remains a problem.
e. Manufacturing disruptions and stoppages are common.
f. Purchasing costs are high because of constant rush orders, while deliveries are erratic.

As the production vice president was sitting down, Mr. Riff wondered if their strategies were sufficient to solve the problem.

1. Are the actions by the production vice president sufficient for effective cost control? Why or why not?
2. What action should be taken on geographical expansion into the southeast?
3. What recommendations would you make to Mr. Riff?

CASE 3: WILDCAT OPERATIONS

Gulf Coast, Inc. is a Texas manufacturer that engages in the production and distribution of equipment for the oil-producing industry. Gulf Coast is regarded as a component manufacturer by the petroleum industry and especially so by the front-line production employees, who boast a high rate of success with G.C. products. The confidence shown in Gulf Coast is attributed to the generally faultless field installation of the company's pumping units and the outstanding performance and maintenance records of both the pumping units and the well heads. The major product lines are two critical pieces of equipment: well heads (casing and tubing types and Christmas-tree assemblies) and pumping units (hydraulic-powered sucker-rod pumps, subsurface hydraulic pumps, and plunger lifts). Gulf Coast is adding another artificial lift to the pump line this year, an electrical submersible centrifugal pump. Production design changes are occurring very rapidly due to technological advances, and additions to the major lines are being made frequently as a result of the dynamic nature of the industry.

The petroleum industry and all its subsections are presently undertaking projects that could drastically alter current operating methods. The industry is in perpetual motion and is investing ever more capital in research and development in order to promote further technological advance. Gulf Coast is an active participant in the change process. The company is dedicated to improving oil-producing equipment both to retain its competitive edge and to keep abreast of methods that extract the precious resource by the most efficient means.

Other changes occurring in oil-producing equipment and practices are an outcome of external regulations. The EPA, for instance, is becoming a very strong voice against the numerous and disastrous accidents that are plaguing drilling operations. Legislation governing the allowance for depletion is being scrutinized with a view to a reduction in the percentage rate of depletion. Laws are also being enacted to regulate exploration, transport, refinement, and sale of oil products; these newer and stricter measures could have adverse effects. Further, Congress has passed legislation to levy taxes on the income of the producers, i.e., windfall profits. Those particularly vulnerable to such taxation laws appear to be the integrated companies and the independent producers, who are Gulf Coast's largest customers.

Some legislation is on the horizon that could benefit the industry. One such act that could mitigate the onslaught of deleterious regulations is a proposed measure to support secondary recovery methods. Legislation of this type could foster the acquisition of new equipment and supplies. A second such change is the American Petroleum Institute's increasing leniency regarding the specifications that have been set as to size, grade, weight per foot, type, etc. of the many casings used throughout the industry.

All factors considered, the industry is experiencing phenomenal growth. The growth of the independent producers is unprecedented. Gulf Coast is in the remarkable position of having sold all the pieces of equipment that it could possibly produce under present conditions for the next two years. With capacity and supplier constraints both being critical, the firm is unable to promise any more equipment within this period. However, the firm's management is in hope of increasing the supply by the implementation of an MRP system to replace the fixed order size system now in use.

Gulf Coast executives feel that an MRP system could be a more efficient way to order and control inventory. The present method of ordering every item—even valves, gauges, casings, tubings, etc.—independently is unsatisfactory. Computerized reports are seen as better control devices. In addition, the MRP system is considered to be a superior method for production scheduling. Given the frequent design changes, the increasing costs in the oil-producing industry, and the volatility of the energy related fields, MRP seems to be the safeguard that Gulf Coast management desires. Therefore, a shift to an MRP system appears to be a solution to Gulf Coast's problems of having parts on hand at necessary times and of being able to schedule and deliver by customer due dates.

However, in conjunction with the MRP system, Gulf Coast is also considering a companion system for the spare parts division. Because of the need for a large stock of spare parts, i.e., tubings and casings, for field installations and repairs, Gulf Coast knows it would be an impossibility to supply these needs from a dependent demand system. Thus, it is expected that a scaled-down version of the present EOQ system would be operational for spare parts after implementation of an MRP system to handle orders for finished products.

1. Does Gulf Coast management seem to be considering many of its circumstances as exceptional?
2 What effects does the demand side of the industry have on Gulf Coast's situation?
3 Is an MRP system a practical solution to the capacity and supply problems?
4 What purposes could an MRP system serve at Gulf Coast?

CASE 4: PROMISES, PROMISES

Sinthetics Corporation has two separate product lines. In one there are four "major" products, each composed of over six subassemblies of varying value. Most of the subassemblies have multiple configurations; in other words, the customer may select different product options (subassemblies) and hence define his own final product configuration. Because of the seemingly infinite number of possible end items (final product configurations), Sinthetic does no demand forecasting for this product line. Instead, it fabricates options and assembles end items after receipt of customer orders. The options are fabricated from parts which are planned using reorder point techniques. Consequently, the customer is given a delivery date based on the cumulative lead time of subassembly and final assembly processes (lead times are derived from actual average throughput times for unexpedited components and orders).

For the line of products with optional features, Sinthetic has excellent engineering drawings and reasonably accurate parts lists. Every drawing has a part number, and every part and assembly has a drawing. Whenever two or more parts are joined together, an assembly drawing is made and a unique part number assigned. Many of the "assemblies" have different part numbers but consist of the same components. A vast majority of subassemblies never flow in and out of the stockroom. The skilled assembly technicians, for example, will cut tubing, drill holes, mount fittings, etc. as they "build up" the end item (carry out the sequence of manufacturing steps). Wiring harnesses and other electrical assemblies similarly are prepared during the final assembly process. Because Sinthetics already possesses detailed engineering drawings of its uniquely identified parts and components, the production manager, Jim Wickersham, has decided that their incorporation into a computerized MRP system would facilitate inventory control and improve customer service. After these bills of materials are properly input into the system, it is thought that lead time offsetting and lot-for-lot ordering will lead to simplified scheduling and more economical parts ordering.

The second line of products is not composed of customer selected options, but still is not forecasted, due to low and irregular levels of demand. This line has five products, each with a set of uniquely numbered parts and components. Figure 15 represents the engineering product structure for one of the items belonging to this line, a power supply assembly. This item's lead time is based on "stacked" lead times, but in this case the delivery lead time is the accumulation of purchase, fabrication, and assembly lead times. Judging from its product structure, delivery cannot be promised any sooner than 15 weeks from order receipt. Even with excessively long lead times quoted to customers, scheduled delivery dates commonly are protracted. Not only do the long lead times invariably result in unreliable delivery promises, but they indirectly are blamed for insufficient components. The shortages frequently are traced to the chaotic cannibalization of parts from one order to another in an effort to speed up the long delivery process for preferred customers.

The assembly supervisor, John Brody, does not agree with the practice of stacking lead times. He sees the long process as creating increased inventory levels, proliferating work orders, and adding unnecessary indirect costs. He would rather shorten the cumulative lead times by eliminating the separate fabrication of some of the assemblies shown on the engineering BOM. He asserts that the entire product practically could be put together at final assembly. The wiring harnesses, presently used in the fabrication of the fan housing assemblies, could be scheduled for completion prior to the actual start of the final assembly process. The harness subassemblies could be delivered directly to final assembly. The power supply component also would be delivered to final assembly by virtue of an automatic issuance policy whereby power supplies are given priority at the receiving dock and sent immediately to the power assembly area. The wiring harness and the power supply would become level 1 items along with a newly created power supply subassembly. The power supply subassembly is to be composed of items promoted to low level code 2—namely, the fan housing, fans, chassis, connectors, and mother board. The items to be designated as level 2 would retain their original part numbers, but the power supply subassembly would be assigned a unique number.

All purchased parts would still have purchase lead times, but a possibility exists where individual lead times could be shortened due to new methods for receiving,

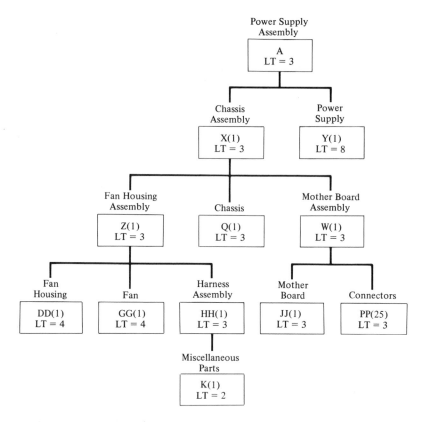

Figure 15. Engineering product structure for power supply assembly.

releasing, staging, and issuing parts for assembly orders. Three assembly lead times would be eliminated by the removal of the three assemblies from the present product structure (the fan housing, mother board, and chassis assemblies). In place of these separate processes will be a power supply subassembly with a lead time of two weeks. The final assembly lead time is estimated to be shortened by one week due to superior policies regarding the issuance of components directly to the final assembly area. Indeed, the power supply, given priority because of its high value, is expected to be ready for assembly in six weeks from order release rather than eight weeks, due to improved and speedier receipt and acceptance policies.

Thus, three assemblies will be eliminated and replaced by one. Fewer separate assembly processes will have to be scheduled, and the new assembly will not have to be moved in and out of storage as with the present subassembly processes. Production is expected to flow more in a continuous fashion, reducing waiting and lead times. For instance, the fan housing components now pass from storage to fan housing assembly to chassis assembly to final assembly, with storage sequences in between. Under the proposed sequence, the fan housing component would be delivered almost immediately to the power supply subassembly and then to final assembly; this could change its minimum total time in the facility from nine weeks to only four weeks.

John Brody calculates a considerable time saving in order deliveries and a reduction in inventory levels and their associated carrying costs. Furthermore, he foresees an unprecedented flexibility for Sinthetics in both of its product lines. Transferring the concept to the line with optional features, John anticipates that Sinthetics finally will be able to react to changes in final product demand for individual configurations which use certain multiple use components.

1. Will the reliance upon the engineering BOM as inputs to an MRP system lead to the outcomes Jim Wickersham expects?
2. What else should be done in conjunction with the implementation of MRP to bring about system improvements? Be sure to consider the forecasting and parts numbering aspects of the situation.
3. Comment on the workability of John Brody's proposal for reducing lead times. Include what assumptions must be made and what tasks must be carried out to execute his plan (do not ignore forecasting, supplier, and MRP input considerations).
4. If John's technique is applied to the power supply assembly, how should the modified BOM be structured?

APPENDIX A. BILLS OF MATERIALS (BOM)

A bill of materials (BOM) is a list of the items, ingredients, or materials needed to produce a parent item, end item, or product. It can take several different forms and be used in many ways. It may be (1) a simple parts list, (2) structured to indicate how a product is produced, or (3) structured to simplify forecasting and master scheduling. The BOM is called a product structure when it indicates how a product will be produced. The specific format for the BOM depends upon its intended use. Some of its important uses are to:

1. define the product and distinguish it from other products,
2. facilitate the forecasting of optional product features,
3. permit the master schedule to be stated in terms of the fewest possible end items,
4. allow easy order entry from customers,
5. provide the basis for product costing,
6. facilitate material procurement,
7. aid manufacturing planning and final assembly scheduling,
8. permit efficient file storage and maintenance.

Bills of materials can be structured to provide information by either tracing down (exploding) or tracing up (imploding) a product structure. Explosion begins with the parent and breaks it into its lower level components; implosion begins with the component and builds into the parent or higher level items. The explosion of end item requirements or master scheduled items into component requirements is vital in MRP to establish all lower level component scheduling. When scheduling problems exist at the component level, implosion permits the identification of the parent item generating the requirement.

Traditional Bills of Materials

When product structure data are stored in a computer system, they can be retrieved and displayed in a variety of formats for the benefit of the various users. The objective is to load one bill that can generate numerous formats to satisfy different users in the organization. Six popular formats are:

1. single-level explosion,
2. indented explosion,
3. summary explosion,
4. single-level implosion,
5. indented implosion,
6. summary implosion.

Each of the six formats is described briefly in this section. Following each general description is an illustration of the format style. All of the example illustrations use the information from the multilevel product structure for product A shown in Figure 16.

1. The *single-level explosion* format displays the components used at a specific level of assembly. Several single-level bills are designed to represent completely the product structure of a multilevel product. The four level product structure given in Figure 16 results in four single-level bills:

Single-level explosion BOM for assemblies A, B, C, and D

Assembly	Component Part Number	Quantity per Assembly	Description
A	B	1	
	C	1	
	10	3	
B	D	2	
	20	1	
C	30	2	
	40	1	
	50	1	
D	10	1	
	30	1	

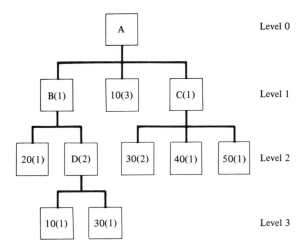

Figure 16. Multilevel product structure.
The letters represent assemblies and subassemblies, and the numerals represent parts. The numbers in parentheses are the quantities required for assembly.

2. The *indented explosion* format lists components on all lower levels by indentation under their respective parents. Indentation signifies levels. All components of a given level are shown with their part numbers beginning in the same column. The indented format represents the product in the manner in which it is manufactured. Figure 16's product structure appears as follows when arranged in an indented explosion format:

Indented explosion BOM for product *A*

Part Number				Quantity	Unit of
Level 1	2	3	Description	per Assembly	Measure
B				1	
.	20			1	
.	D			2	
.	.	10		1	
.	.	30		1	
C				1	
.	30			2	
.	40			1	
.	50			1	
10				3	

3. The *summary explosion* format lists all items which go into an end item along with their total quantities. As can be seen from the next example, it includes all the components of an end item, irrespective of level, with

the quantities reflecting use per end item rather than per immediate parent. When a component is used in more than one assembly, the summary explosion bill aids purchasing in the procurement of the proper quantity of items. This format does not indicate the way the product is produced, but it does assist in product costing, procurement, and other related activities:

Summary explosion BOM for product *A*

Assembly	Component[a]	Description	Quantity Required	Unit of Measure
A	10		5	
	20		1	
	30		4	
	40		1	
	50		1	
	(*B*)		(1)	
	(*C*)		(1)	
	(*D*)		(2)	

[a]Subassemblies are indicated by parentheses. This listing of subassemblies is optional.

4. The *single-level implosion* format displays the assemblies that directly use a component at the next higher level. It is a where-used list that indicates all the immediate parents of an item. The items and their immediate parents for the multilevel structure of product *A* can easily be incorporated into the next example format:

Single-level implosion BOM for components 10, 20, 30, 40, and 50

Component Part Number	Assembly Used on	Quantity per Assembly	Description
10	*A*	3	
	D	1	
20	*B*	1	
30	*C*	2	
	D	1	
40	*C*	1	
50	*C*	1	

5. The *indented implosion* format indicates the usage of a component to all higher levels. It traces both the direct and indirect usage of a given component to all higher levels until the end product is reached. It is valuable in determining the parent that generated the component requirement as well as in evaluating the effects of engineering design changes. Component 30 from the product structure in Figure 16 is used

to illustrate this format:

Indented implosion BOM for component 30

Component Part Number	Assembly Used on	Quantity	Description
30	D	1	
	·B	2	
	··A	1	
	C	2	
	·A	1	

6. The *summary implosion* format shows all higher level items which contain the component along with the total quantity used in each. It is an expanded where-used list in which all higher levels that contain the component are listed. The "quantities per" are total quantities of the component used in each of the higher level assemblies. The identification of higher level requirements by summary implosion is depicted for components D, 10, and 30 of product A:

Summary implosion BOM for components D, 10, and 30

Component Part Number	Assembly Used on	Quantity Required	Description
D	A	2	
	B	2	
10	A	5	
	B	2	
	D	1	
30	A	4	
	B	2	
	C	2	
	D	1	

Matrix BOM

A matrix BOM is a consolidation of product summary data for families of items with a large number of common components. This format is used to identify and group the common parts found on the models in a family. The components are listed down the left hand side, and the models or end items across the top. The numbers in the body of the matrix indicate the total number of components used to produce a single end item (it is the same information listed as "quantity required" in the summary explosion BOM for product A). An X is used to indicate a component is not used on a given item.

This bill is useful for products having many common components among products. However, the matrix format does not specify the manner in which the products are built. It cannot be used as manufacturing instructions for multilevel products, since it does not indicate the levels of assembly. An example for three products is as follows:

Matrix BOM for products A, W, and Z

Component Part Number	Description	Unit of Measure	Product		
			A	W	Z
10			5	5	2
20			1	2	X
30			4	7	2
40			1	1	X
50			1	1	X
60			X	X	3
(B)			(1)	(2)	(1)
(C)			(1)	(1)	(X)
(D)			(2)	(1)	(2)

Add / Delete BOM

This bill, sometimes called a "comparative" or "same as, except" bill, defines a special product in terms of a standard product and specifies which components are to be added and which components are to be removed. New or unique products are stated as a standard product with some items added and others subtracted. Figure 17 shows that special product B15 is produced by putting together standard product B12 with components F and G and removing component A. It is an effective way to explain how one product differs from another. This bill cannot be utilized in making forecasts and is not well suited for MRP.

Modular BOM

Modular bills of materials are used for complex products that have many possible configurations and are made from a number of common parts. For example, in vehicle manufacturing, where choices of engines, transmissions,

Figure 17. Add/delete BOM.

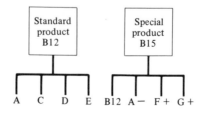

bodies, interiors, trim, and many other features are available, the several variations can be combined into a tremendous number of final configurations. Modularization provides a wide choice of products to the customer while keeping component inventories down. It has been used extensively in the automotive and farm equipment industries.

When a product line has many variations (optional features), their combinations can be astronomical and forecasting them for the master schedule becomes impossible. If a separate BOM were used for each unique end product for MRP purposes, the file records would be excessive (too costly to store and maintain). The solution to this problem is the modular bill of materials. A modular BOM is stated in building blocks or modules from which the final product is assembled. The process of modularizing breaks down the bills of products into lower level modules. The demand for these modules can be forecasted separately with much more accuracy than the final configurations. Modules can achieve two different purposes:

1. to disentangle combinations of optional product features,
2. to segregate common parts from unique parts.

The first purpose facilitates forecasting, while the second minimizes inventory investment in components common to optional units.

An example will illustrate the concept of modularity. Suppose a manufacturer offers his customers 10 engines, 30 colors, 4 bodies, and 2 frames. By assembling the optional features in various combinations, it is possible to build $(10)(30)(4)(2) = 2400$ models or unique configurations:

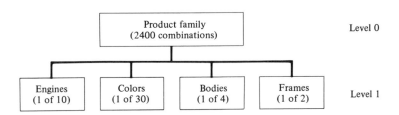

It would be irrational to set up separate bills for each end product (level 0); 2400 would be needed. Furthermore, the development of a master schedule showing the quantity of each model needed in specific time periods would be arduous. The solution is to disregard specific end item forecasts and proceed with a single forecast for the product family. From it, forecasts for each option can be derived from *popularity percentages*, defined as the probability of option selection based on past customer orders or expectations. These will make it possible to decompose the family forecast into the forecasts for each option. For example, past sales may indicate that 75% of orders call for frame *A* and 25% for frame *B*. If the forecast is for 100 products per period, orders for 75 *A* frames and 25 *B* frames would be scheduled. In using the modular method, each of the options or modules would have a BOM, but there would be a total of $10 + 30 + 4 + 2 = 46$ bills instead of 2400.

If commonality of components within the product family exists, further analysis can reduce inventory investment by segregating common parts from unique parts. To illustrate this procedure, the previous example is scaled down so the restructuring process can be seen more clearly. Assume the product has only two optional features, the body and the frame, each with only two choices. The customer can select between body 1 and body 2, and between frame 1 and frame 2. Figure 18 represents the four bills of materials (B1 & F1, B1 & F2, B2 & F1, and B2 & F2). Only level 0 and level 1 are shown; lower levels are excluded for clarity. To restructure these bills into modules, they first are broken down into components. The components then are analyzed and compared with respect to usage on level 1 items (bodies and frames); they subsequently are grouped according to use. The analysis reveals that components C20 and P46 are common to all products, so they are assigned to the common group. Components F25 and Q64 are used only on B1F1 and B1F2, so they are unique to body option B1; components F29 and T53 are used only on B2F1 and B2F2, so they are unique to body option B2; components G12, J87, and V54 are used only on

Figure 18. Product structures for four end items.

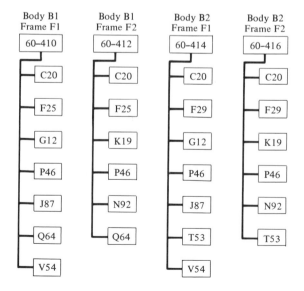

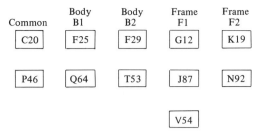

Figure 19. Modular bills of materials.

B1F1 and B2F1, so they are unique to frame option F1; and components K19 and N92 are used only on B1F2 and B2F2, so they are unique to frame option F2. Reorganization of the components according to their product options and common usages results in the modular bills shown in Figure 19.

Modularity does away with BOM at the product level (level 0) for purposes of MRP. Instead, assembly components (level 1 or lower) are promoted to end item status. This procedure establishes a new modular planning bill suitable for forecasting, master production scheduling, and MRP.

The BOM that cites the options necessary to build a specific end item is called a *manufacturing bill* or M-bill. It is simply a conglomeration of all the individual modular BOM that are selected by a customer or included in a specific warehouse order. This bill is not a direct part of the MRP system. It integrates with the MRP system by defining the items to be assembled against the final assembly schedule (FAS), given that these items use the components planned and provided by the MRP system.

Pseudo BOM

Pseudo BOM are imaginary components which are never actually produced. They sometimes are called "phantom bills," "super bills," or "S-bills." As was illustrated in Figure 19, many assemblies and subassemblies become end items in modularizing the bills. This increases the number of items that will have to be forecasted and identified in the master schedule. The set of components in any related group is assigned an artificial part number. In Figure 20, the five groups of items in the modular bills of Figure 19 are assigned to imaginary part numbers S-70, S-72, S-74, S-76, and S-78. These artificial assembly numbers are not actually assembled, but are used in forecasting and master scheduling operations. The "quantity per" relationship of the pseudo bill is the popularity percentage of each module.

Another type of pseudo bill is the "K-bill." In building a product, a large number of small loose parts such as nuts, bolts, and fastners frequently are

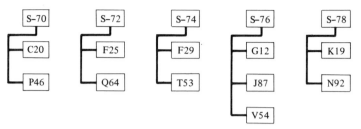

Figure 20. Super bills of materials.

used. Rather than identify each of the items individually, they are grouped together under an artificial part number called a kit. Thus, with one number an entire group of components that goes with a particular feature can be properly scheduled.

Conclusion

The BOM specifies the material content of an item, and multiple levels reflect the manufacturing processes for the item. Different BOM formats are used within an organization to explode requirements for MRP, prepare material purchase requisitions, assist product costing, make engineering changes, and so forth.

MRP information is usually stored in the single level format. It requires that the product be defined in such a manner as to express a valid master schedule in terms of BOM part numbers. It works with products and the relationship of their component items, using the BOM as the planning guide. Each component must be uniquely identified by part number. The BOM should signify the composition as well as the process stages in the product's manufacture in terms of levels. Without an accurate, up-to-date, complete, and properly structured file, MRP cannot work properly.

Restructuring of the traditional bill of material format can substantially simplify master scheduling for many organizations. If a firm order backlog does not cover the cumulative lead times, it is necessary to forecast master schedule requirements. Most organizations either make to stock, so that all planning is based on forecasts, or use customer orders in the short range and forecasts to fill out the remainder of the planning horizon. Thus, the product must be defined in forecastable terms in the master schedule. It is simple to see that in a make-to-order environment, end items are not the best thing to forecast. Some specific BOM is needed to link the master schedule to its dependent components that have to be obtained prior to receiving the customer orders. Planning bills perform this function and substantially reduce the number of items to be forecasted and master scheduled.

9 Just-in-Time and In-Process Inventory

IN-PROCESS INVENTORY
  Lead Time
  Setup Time
  Time Cycle Charts
  Bottleneck Work Centers
  Input / Output Control
  Critical Ratio Technique

JUST-IN-TIME
  Elimination of Waste
  Inventory as Waste
  Pursuit of Perfection
  Repetitive Manufacturing and JIT

CONCLUSION
QUESTIONS
PROBLEMS
CASES

This chapter is divided into two major sections—in-process inventory and just-in-time (JIT). The first section gives a generalized discussion of the various dimensions of in-process inventory along with examples of a few standard in-process inventory control techniques. The second section integrates the topic of in-process inventory into the broader framework of JIT. In this context, JIT has definite implications for in-process inventory which extend beyond any narrowly defined inventory function to include logistical, financial, and other organizational functions. The examination of JIT takes a critical look at the conventional view of the inventory function as it relates to specific categories of inventory. Since JIT encompasses the successful execution of all activities necessary to provide a product, it treats inventory as a part of a synchronized system of production. Its focus is not on the control of individual types of inventory but on the control of all the stages of production and the materials at each point in the total production process—from the acquisition of raw materials through the various stages until the final delivery of the product. Together the two sections provide a glimpse of the inventory control problems associated with manufacturing or materials processing.

IN-PROCESS INVENTORY

Except for the previous chapter on material requirements planning (MRP), the primary focus of this text has been on three main categories of inventory—finished goods, raw materials, and supplies. Attention is now turned to an important fourth category known as in-process goods. It consists of all the items in a partial state of completion. Work has been started, but further processing steps are required before the product becomes available as a finished or end item. In-process goods are thus an inventory category peculiar to organizations that engage in the manufacture or production of physical products.

In manufacturing organizations, in-process inventory may account for a substantial part of the total inventory investment. In fact, it may represent as much as 50% of the entire investment in inventory for organizations which manufacture their products to order. The investment assessed as in-process inventory is the accumulation of direct material, direct labor, and applied manufacturing overhead costs of the products in the manufacturing process. The accumulation of these costs begins with the transfer of the raw materials to production and ends with the movement of completed products into storage or shipping.

This means that in-process inventory and its associated costs bear a direct relationship to most facets of the production process. The efficiency of the production process can affect in-process inventory and vice versa. From a cost control standpoint, the management of in-process inventory can provide production economies in terms of capacity utilization. Since idle workers and facilities represent a loss of productivity, the regulation of in-process inventory can protect against underutilization of manpower and facilities. With such regulation, two opposing costs are involved: too little work in process results in underutilization costs, while too much results in excessive inventory costs.

The characteristics of the production process dictate to a large extent the kind of in-process inventory regulation possible. *Continuous production processes* use sequences of operations that are inseparably tied together. The output rates of the operations are the same, so little in-process inventory usually is present. This fixed flow of operations is typical of assembly lines with balanced operations. The major disadvantage of assembly lines is their inflexibility. If one operation runs out of material or breaks down, the whole line must sit idle until material is supplied or equipment is repaired. *Intermittent production processes* perform a variety of operations in an independent manner. Not all orders require the same number or type of operations. These production processes decouple their operations and have a queue of orders that permits them to function efficiently and independently. However, the cost of independence is a queue of in-process inventory. Given the nature of their operations, continuous production processes regard in-process inventory control as a relatively minor problem. On the other hand, the regulation of in-process inventory is a major challenge in intermittent production processes.

A classical example of an intermittent production process is a job shop: an organization where a wide variety of products with significant differentiation is produced in batches at intermittent intervals. Because the products require varying processing tasks, there is an irregular flow of work between successive operations. In-process inventory compensates for the different output rates and sequences of operations, and protects against work stoppages. In order to do this, adequate in-process inventory is required to keep work at each work station. As a result, the process time (the time when productive operations are performed) is small in relation to the total time needed to complete an order. An order spends most of its time waiting to be processed.

The economies of in-process inventory are primarily derived when the rate of flow of orders between work stations cannot be controlled. When these rates can be controlled at "gateway" work stations or "bottleneck" work stations, the amount of in-process inventory is determined by the control of inputs to these stations. If perfect control is possible, the proper amount is very small. At "intermediary" work stations where the degree of control is not as certain, the need for in-process inventory is much greater.

Controlling work in process is largely a matter of moving orders through production as fast as possible. If orders are not moved through the facility at an efficient pace, excess in-process inventory results. Although it would seem that direct labor and equipment utilization are maximized when there

Table 1. Manufacturing cycle time

Setup time	Process time	Move time	Wait time	Queue time

is plenty of work in process, other penalties are incurred, such as:

1. a long manufacturing cycle time,
2. a complex and costly production control system,
3. high materials movement cost,
4. high floor space requirement for work in process and movement.

In short, excess in-process inventory increases the manufacturing cycle time and represents a costly investment.

Lead Time

Lead time can take on different meanings depending on the range of items and/or activities included in the interpretation. It may apply to particular items or operations, individually or collectively. The total time to procure all the raw materials and purchased components, process them, test them, and package the finished product is the *production cycle time*. The total manufacturing time needed to perform all necessary operations exclusively in the plant (from the start of the earliest to the completion of the last) is the *manufacturing cycle time*.[1] Each of these is the sum of many individual lead times.

For further clarification, the manufacturing cycle time is the time elapsed between the release of an order and its completion; this is the time a job or order spends in the manufacturing process. As shown in Table 1, the manufacturing cycle time comprises the following five elements:

1. *Setup time*. The material, machine, or work center is prepared for an operation.
2. *Process time*. The productive operations are performed.
3. *Move time*. Transportation occurs from storage, to storage, or between work centers.
4. *Wait time*. Material is waiting to be moved to its next location.
5. *Queue time*. Material waits because another order is being processed at a work center.

The process time represents a small fraction of the manufacturing cycle time for most orders. The greatest portion of lead time (sometimes up to

---

[1] The cycle time is also referred to as the "flow time" or "manufacturing lead time" by some authors.

90%) usually comes from queue time, the time a job spends waiting because another order is being processed ahead of it. Setup time, wait time, and queue time all are periods of inactivity within the manufacturing cycle time, due to some type of delay. Typical reasons for such delay are:

1. waiting for machine or work center availability,
2. waiting to be moved,
3. waiting to be inspected,
4. hot jobs receiving priority,
5. shortages of tools, materials, or information,
6. machine breakdown,
7. absenteeism.

On the assumption that material cost and labor cost are adequately controlled, it is necessary to reduce the manufacturing cycle time in order to reduce in-process inventory levels. If the cycle time is reduced, the in-process inventory investment will be decreased in direct proportion. Since the queue time is usually larger than the combination of all the other time elements, the major opportunity for reducing the cycle time is to reduce the queue time.

For a specific order or job, the queue time is a function of its priority. A high priority order will spend less time in queues and have a shorter manufacturing cycle time. Thus, priorities can dramatically affect an order's manufacturing cycle time in either direction. High priority orders leapfrog all or part of existing queues, which compresses their cycle time but tends to expand the cycle time of lower priority orders.

As with most delays, queue time is related to planning and scheduling. To reduce delay, it is necessary to plan and schedule operations more efficiently. Queue time can best be reduced by eliminating physical backlogs in production. Backlogs can be reduced by better scheduling of operations and planning of the release of work to production. Reduction of the backlog or queue at each work center results in parts waiting less time for their "turn" to be worked.

The lead time stretches as the backlog grows. To control the lead time, it is necessary to control the backlog. To control the backlog, release no more work into a facility than it has shown it can turn out. When the output consistently falls short of the input, either an expansion of capacity or a reduction of input is necessary.

The flow of work through a shop is limited by its capacity. An order should not be released into the shop unless the capacity *and* the material for the job are available. Increasing the input without increasing the capacity will only increase the manufacturing cycle time. If an organization has a capacity problem, there is a temptation to increase the lead time. This action would only result in larger in-process inventory and likely prove counterproductive. The answer is to solve the capacity problem, not lengthen the lead time.

Manufacturing lead time should be considered a variable for management to control instead of a constant. Shortening it can improve customer service, reduce inventory costs, and shave product costs. Shorter lead times improve responsiveness to schedule changes, thereby softening the effects of forecasting errors and economic cycles. The size of in-process inventory is related to lead times. A reduction of lead times reduces this inventory and may improve schedule performance. Whether it does help schedule performance depends on how much in-process inventory the organization is carrying. If it is excessive, the priorities of orders probably change frequently. This results in excessive setups and teardowns that reduce throughput and raise product costs.

In short, lead time should be managed by proper short-term planning and scheduling and by appropriate capacity planning. Lead time can best be reduced by shortening those periods of time where orders are inactive. Queue time is one of those periods and also happens to be the major constituent of the manufacturing cycle time. Shortening queue time can provide an enormous competitive edge through lower costs and faster responses. The final effect of reducing the queue time is improved turnover of the cash investment in inventory.

Setup Time

Setup time is another element of the manufacturing cycle time when no output is being produced. Therefore, an excellent opportunity for reducing the lead time is by reducing the setup time. This action directly reduces in-process inventory. Moreover, reduced setup time has a multiplicative effect that favorably influences the other elements of the manufacturing cycle time (process time, move time, wait time, and queue time). The most obvious effect of reduced setup time is reduced cost per setup. Reduced setup costs favor small lot sizes, so process time is thereby shortened. Although move and wait times may not be changed by setup time reduction, they can be under certain circumstances. If lot sizes are reduced substantially, fewer trips for movement from one work center to another may be required. Under these conditions, move and wait times can be abbreviated. Queue time for an item is the sum of the setup and process times for those lot sizes ahead of it at a work center. Reduced setup time decreases the average unproductive time that items wait in queues. Furthermore, no output is being produced when a work center is being set up. Translating less setup time into process time, more output can be produced, which effectively expands the capacity of a work center. In conclusion, reducing setup time can substantially increase productivity and contribute to lower levels of in-process inventory. The aggregate benefits are increased operational flexibility, reduced storage space requirements, early detection of quality problems, and lower investment in inventory.

Time Cycle Charts

A time cycle chart shows how much time it would take to produce a product starting from scratch (assuming no expediting of orders or processes, no inventory available or on order, and no special orders or any other measures to hasten the process). It indicates the full extent of the lead time requirements, and therefore also illustrates the minimum planning horizon which should be used for the master production schedule. If customer delivery is to be made in less than the maximum time on the time cycle chart (the time to produce the product from scratch), inventories must be maintained.

Each material, component, and assembly requires some lead time. Starting with the final product, the time cycle chart works backwards through each manufacturing step, assembly operation, and purchase to map the time relationships. A typical time cycle chart is shown in Figure 1. Product 1 is assembled from subassemblies 2 and 6 and purchased part 21. Subassembly 2 consists of manufactured components 3, 4, and 5, which in turn are made from purchased parts 22, 23, and 24 respectively. Similarly, subassembly 6 consists of manufactured components 7 and 8 and purchased part 27. Manufactured components 7 and 8 are made from purchased parts 25 and 26 respectively. The bottleneck item is purchased part 25, which sets the no inventory lead time at approximately 22 weeks.

Obviously, an organization must have inventories if it is going to offer customer delivery in less than 22 weeks for the product shown in Figure 1. If the organization is going to offer instantaneous customer service, inventory of the finished product must be maintained. If customer service time is not instantaneous, inventory of the finished product should not be maintained, since it frequently includes large production costs which should not be incurred until a firm demand exists.

Suppose a six week lead time is available to all customers who purchase the finished product in Figure 1. Inventories could be maintained at every stage of manufacture and assembly, as well as for each purchased part, but there is an easier way that involves less control and smaller inventories. Stocks are maintained for only a few critical items; others are purchased or manufactured only when there is a definite demand for them. To determine the critical inventory items, a horizontal line is drawn across the time cycle chart at six weeks. The critical items are those items that are crossed by the horizontal line. In Figure 1, the critical items are 3, 4, 5, 7, 8, 21, and 27. The first five critical items are manufactured parts, and the last two are purchased parts. (If there were a ten week sales lead time, there would be a different group of critical items.)

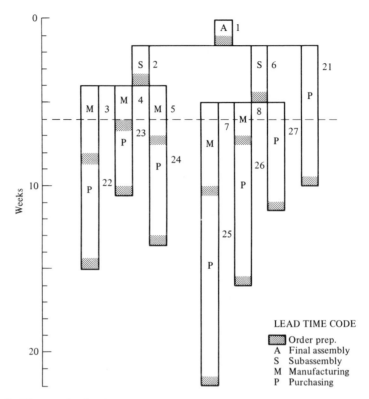

Figure 1. Time cycle chart

The product structure or bill of materials for a product as revealed by the time cycle chart affects the manufacturing cycle time. The greater the number of levels in the product structure, the longer it takes to produce the end item. A restructuring of a bill of materials to fewer levels can reduce a product's cycle time.

Additional approaches to reducing cycle time for an individual order include (1) *overlapping*—sending items to subsequent work centers before the entire order is completed at a given work center—and (2) *operations splitting*—dividing the order and sending it to two (or more) different machines for the same operation (although this method necessitates additional setups).

Bottleneck Work Centers

Many factories have natural bottleneck (critical) work stations whose throughput capacity determines the output for the factory. At these points, the output to downstream work centers is controlled, so that all subsequent processing is dependent upon their rate of output. For this reason, bottleneck work centers should never sit idle because they have run out of work; the queues in front of them should never be allowed to disappear. This does not imply that the queues should build excessively. It is also at bottlenecks that lead times are lengthened when the queues in front of them are allowed to build. The queues are only the symptoms of the problem; the actual problem is the bottlenecks themselves. Since the bottlenecks cause the queues, they should be alleviated or eliminated if possible.

To summarize: The presence of bottleneck work centers places obvious physical limitations on the throughput capacity of an organization. Where bottlenecks are permitted to exist, they should be operating to their capacity. But more importantly, efforts to expand the capacity of these restrictive work centers can increase the capacity of the total operation. Along with increasing the output to downstream work centers, it shortens the manufacturing cycle time.

Bottleneck work centers establish the output rate for a facility and influence the utilization of nonbottleneck centers. If the output rate of nonbottleneck centers exceeds those of bottleneck centers, the inevitable outcome is increased queues and in-process inventory. The output rate in nonbottleneck centers should be governed by the output rate of the slower bottleneck centers. This means the utilization rate of nonbottleneck centers should be lower; these centers should be servants to bottleneck centers.

Increasing output in noncritical centers is a waste of resources that generates additional inventory. High utilization is critical in bottleneck centers but not so in nonbottleneck centers; idle time in noncritical centers is even desirable. The idea is not to use each center to its capacity but to balance the flow rate. Without a balanced flow, high capacity utilization in all work centers will generate excessive in-process inventory.

Input / Output Control

Input/output control regulates (1) the flow of work into a work center by comparing actual input with planned input, and (2) the flow of work from a work center by comparing actual output with planned output. The objective is to highlight deviations before they become acute. Minor divergences are to be expected as work progresses. Delays and disruptions are corrected so the *average input* of new jobs does not differ substantially from the *average output* of completed jobs. If work is released that exceeds the output of completed jobs, backlogs will develop and lead times will increase. If work is released that is less than the output of completed jobs, the backlog will drop and the lead time will be reduced.

It should be noted that the input rate cannot really be "controlled" at any work center except an entry (gateway) work center. Here, work is fed in, and it is possible to increase or decrease the input rate. At subsequent

Table 2. Input / output report. All quantities are in standard hours. There was a released backlog of 240 hours at work center 5 at the beginning of week 12.

Work Center 5

Week	12	13	14	15	16	17	18	19	20	21
Planned input	540	540	540	540	540	540	540	540	540	540
Actual input	540	530	500							
Cumulative deviation	0	−10	−50							
Planned output	600	600	600	600	540	540	540	540	540	540
Actual output	610	520	600							
Cumulative deviation	+10	−70	−70							
Planned backlog	180	120	60	0	0	0	0	0	0	0
Actual backlog	170	180	80							

work centers, the input rate is controlled by regulating the output rates at the feeding work centers.

Table 2 shows an input/output report for a typical job shop work center. The *planned input* of jobs to a work center includes both released ("open") orders that have not arrived yet and unreleased ("planned") orders. The *planned output* is the objective or available capacity for the period, and it equals the planned input plus or minus any desired change in the backlog. The *actual input* is simply the number of standard hours of work that have arrived. The *actual output* is simply the number of standard hours of work completed. The *planned backlog* is the previous period's planned backlog plus the planned input minus the planned output. The *actual backlog* is the previous period's actual backlog plus the actual input minus the actual output.

The report in Table 2 is in abbreviated form: in practice it typically would extend for 12 or more weeks. The planned output rate is 600 hours per week for the first four weeks and thereafter 540 hours per week. The planned input rate is 540 hours per week as far as the plan goes. The planned output of 600 for the first four weeks is higher than the planned input of 540. This is intended to reduce the existing backlog by 240 standard hours. The latest week for which data are available is week 14. The report clearly indicates whether or not the backlog is building. It measures capacity in total hours rather than late orders in the work center.

Table 3 shows an input/output report for another work station. Work center 11 is not an entry point (a starting or gateway work center) for orders, but receives its inputs from the outputs of other work centers. It is a secondary or downstream work center. Against a planned average output rate of 220 standard hours, actual output has fallen short by a cumulative

Table 3. Input / output report. All quantities are in standard hours. There was a released backlog of 60 hours at work center 11 at the beginning of week 21.

Work Center 11

Week	21	22	23	24	25	26	27	28	29	30
Planned input	220	220	220	220	220	220	220	220	220	220
Actual input	110	150	140	130						
Cumulative deviation	−110	−180	−260	−350						
Planned output	220	220	220	220	220	220	220	220	220	220
Actual output	150	140	160	140						
Cumulative deviation	−70	−150	−210	−290						
Planned backlog	60	60	60	60	60	60	60	60	60	60
Actual backlog	20	30	10	0						

total of 290 standard hours. From reviewing output figures only, a logical conclusion would be that work center 11 needs more capacity. However, input figures reveal the real problem lies in the work centers feeding work center 11. The actual input has fallen short by a cumulative total of 350 hours behind the plan. The work is not arriving at work center 11. To expand capacity would only compound the problem.

Table 4 shows an input/output report for a different work station. Work center 13 is not an entry point for orders, but receives its inputs from numerous other work centers. Actual inputs have been fairly close to planned inputs, but actual output has consistently fallen short of planned

Table 4. Input / output report. All quantities are in standard hours. The released backlog at work center 13 at the beginning of week 5 was 200 hours.

Work Center 13

Week	5	6	7	8	9	10	11	12	13	14
Planned input	100	100	100	100	100	100	100	100	100	100
Actual input	110	105	95	95						
Cumulative deviation	+10	+15	+10	+5						
Planned output	100	100	100	100	100	100	100	100	100	100
Actual output	75	85	75	70						
Cumulative deviation	−25	−40	−65	−95						
Planned backlog	200	200	200	200	200	200	200	200	200	200
Actual backlog	235	255	275	300						

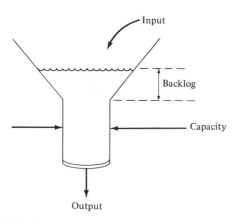

Figure 2. Capacity limitations.
Input must equal or be less than output, or the backlog will increase.

output. The work center suffers from a capacity constraint. Something should be done to improve the capacity problem. The key to using input/output techniques is to establish a planned backlog and a tolerance level, such as $\pm 15\%$, for each work center. When the backlog tolerance level is exceeded, the work center's capacity should be altered.

Problems in input force the examination of upstream work centers, or in the case of gateway or primary work centers, the examination of the order release system. The gateway work centers are easier to control in terms of input. The input to secondary or intermediate work centers is more difficult to control because input is coming from multiple sources. Problems in output are usually associated with capacity unless they are the direct result of input problems.

As shown in Figure 2, input/output control deals with the throughput (the flow in and the flow out) rather than focusing only on backlogs. Input/output control checks lead time by developing a planned queue length at each work center and then regulating the relationship between input and output to each work center to achieve planned queues. Its prime function is capacity control, which results in backlog and lead time control.

The actions that can reduce the in-process inventory levels for an organization are as follows:

1. Schedule delivery of purchased materials as near as possible to the required first operation start date. Refuse to accept delivery of items that arrive outside defined reasonable limits.

2. Withdraw materials from storerooms as late as possible before their required date. This action keeps materials cost from being applied to work in process and keeps materials under control until it is needed by production.
3. Balance the input rate of orders with the output rate of completed orders. If the input rate exceeds the output rate, backlogs will increase, as well as the cycle time.
4. Do not release work to production unless personnel, materials, tooling, and support services are available in the needed quantities.
5. Schedule work to the shortest possible cycle time that does not result in excessive underutilization of facilities. Do not prerelease orders (the backlog) unless serious underutilization of resources will otherwise occur.
6. Use time increments that are compatible with actual requirements. The use of weeks is not appropriate for routings that actually require a day or two. Too large a time increment can inflate the cycle. It is not uncommon for the time scheduled to be the time taken.

The reaction to large visible backlogs is frequently an attempt to increase capacity in some way. If the backlog consists of early release of orders or jobs for which there is no immediate demand, it is artificial and can only be aggravated by increasing capacity. If schedules are not being met, the bottleneck work centers can be expanded by additional manpower, more shifts, overtime, subcontracting, or more equipment. A consistently high backlog can indicate the need for capacity expansion if it is due to an increase in demand.

Critical Ratio Technique

A major function of MRP systems is the establishing and updating of due dates for shop orders. The shop must then determine the sequence in which these orders are to be processed. When several orders simultaneously compete for the services of a given machine, some type of priority rule must be used based on due date information. Numerous priority dispatching rules have been proposed for use in job shops. There are many simulation studies which compare the relative performance of such rules. There is no one best priority rule for all situations. One priority rule that has received considerable attention is the critical ratio technique.

The critical ratio rule is a dynamic priority rule that facilitates the constant updating of priorities. It is used in conjunction with MRP systems and has broad industrial application. The critical ratio is a measure of the urgency of any order in comparison with the other orders for the same facility. It is based on when the completed order is required and how much time is required to complete it. It is a dimensionless index and is calculated as follows:

$$\text{critical ratio} = \frac{\text{demand time}}{\text{supply time}} = \frac{\text{time remaining until needed}}{\text{time needed to complete work}}$$

$$= \frac{(\text{date required}) - (\text{today's date})}{\text{days needed to complete the job}}.$$

From the critical ratios, it is possible to determine the orders that are behind schedule, the orders that are ahead of schedule, the orders that are on schedule, the orders that should be processed next, and whether processing rates should be increased. Orders with the lowest critical ratio are processed before orders with higher ratios. If the critical ratio is greater than one, the order is ahead of schedule; if it is equal to one, the order is on schedule; and if it is less than one, the order is behind schedule. The lower the critical ratio, the more critical the order is.

EXAMPLE 1

Sequence the jobs listed in Table 5 by the critical ratio technique. Today is day 43 on the production calendar.

Table 5

Job	Date Required	Process Time Remaining (days)
A	50	3
B	45	2
C	44	2
D	53	5
E	46	4

Table 6

Job	Critical Ratio
C	$(44 - 43)/2 = 0.50$
E	$(46 - 43)/4 = 0.75$
B	$(45 - 43)/2 = 1.00$
D	$(53 - 43)/5 = 2.00$
A	$(50 - 43)/3 = 2.33$

Table 6 lists the jobs in the order in which they should be performed according to their critical ratios. Jobs C and E are behind schedule and must be speeded up if they are to be completed by the date required; job B is on schedule; and jobs D and A are ahead of schedule.

When the critical ratio is used to schedule warehouse operations or determine what items should be shipped on the next delivery truck, the appropriate formulae are as follows:

$$\text{critical ratio} = \frac{\text{days of supply}}{\text{lead time remaining}},$$

$$\text{days of supply} = \frac{(\text{stock on hand}) - (\text{safety stock})}{\text{average daily demand}}.$$

In practice, all the items being shipped should have their critical ratio calculated and ranked. All items with a critical ratio less than one should be shipped on the next truck. To obtain a full truckload, the next items in order of criticality should be shipped.

JUST-IN-TIME

Just-in-time is an organizational philosophy which strives for excellence (indeed, perfection). The term JIT is frequently used interchangeably with "zero inventory" and "stockless production," but it represents a production strategy and not just an inventory control technique. It identifies a philosophical pursuit or set of goals that apply to any type of production organization. In the broadest sense, its aim is the elimination of all waste and consistent improvement of productivity. Other JIT goals are listed in Table 7.

JIT encompasses the successful execution of all production activities required to produce a product from design engineering to delivery. It encourages solving the entire spectrum of production problems, not cover-

Table 7. Just-in-time goals

Zero defects
Zero setup time
Zero lot excesses
Zero handling
Zero surging
Zero breakdowns
Zero lead time

Table 8. Conventional vs. JIT attitudes

Conventional	Just-in-Time
Some defects are acceptable	Zero defects are necessary and attainable
Large lots are efficient (more is better)	Ideal lot size is one (less is better)
Fast production is efficient	Balanced production is efficient (faster production is a waste)
Inventory provides safety	Safety stock is a waste
Inventory smooths production	Inventory is undesirable
Inventory is an asset	Inventory is a liability
Queues are necessary	Queues should be eliminated
Suppliers are adversaries	Suppliers are partners
Multiple supply sources lead to safety	Fewer sources of supply lead to control
Breakdown maintenance is enough	Preventive maintenance is essential
Long lead time is better	Short lead time is better
Setup time is given	Setup time should be zero
Management is by edict	Management is by consensus
Work force is specialized	Work force is multifunctional

ing them up with excess inventory, safety stock, or padded lead times. Among the targets for elimination are large lot sizes, quality rejects, machine breakdowns, and excessive lead times. JIT production means making and buying just enough, no more or less, of the right items just in time, no sooner or later.

It may be easier to explain just-in-time by what it is not. Its opposite, the more conventional just-in-case approach, manages operations expecting something (not sure of what) to go wrong. It provides contingencies to cover all eventualities, and the contingency is usually excess inventory. Buffering the impact of uncertainty instead of eliminating it is misguided. It is more desirable to smooth the flow of product than to maintain inventory buffers. The goal of JIT, if achieved to perfection, is a balanced, continuous flow of the product through the organization. There would be no idle inventory, only that to which value is being actively added. A contrast of conventional and JIT attitudes is given in Table 8.

Elimination of Waste

JIT attempts the virtual elimination of all costs (waste) that do not add value to a product. Waste is defined as anything other than the absolute minimum resources of materials, machines, and personnel required to add value to the product. Machining, assembling, finishing, and packaging add value to a product. Activities such as moving, storing, counting, sorting, and scheduling add cost to a product but no value. Inspections, backup sources, expediters, safety stocks, and safety time add cost but not value. Cost without value is waste.

The general idea is to eradicate all encumbrances to the smooth flow of product through the facility. Inventory is considered an undesirable cost, and by lowering its level, hidden quality and productivity impediments are revealed. By working to eliminate costs that do not add value, opportunities to synchronize and link operations become apparent. It must be emphasized that JIT is a long term approach that cannot be installed quickly; it can take years for effective implementation. Inventory and lot sizes are reduced incrementally (month after month). The result is sustained productivity and quality improvements with greater operational flexibility and delivery responsiveness.

The essence of JIT is simplification and elimination through problem solving. Continuous improvement and attention to any barrier to product flow (smooth production) is the key. JIT does not use automation and robotics *until* all that can be done to rearrange, synchronize, and balance operations is completed. Initial savings are in overhead reduction of indirect labor (stockroom personnel, material handlers, planners, controllers, inspectors, etc.). These functions do not add value to the product. Direct labor reductions occur subsequently when automation takes place. JIT makes automation easier and more effective, but automation is not the main thrust.

Inventory as Waste

Inventory hides or conceals many types of problems, such as:

1. machine breakdowns,
2. poor quality or high scrap,
3. bad raw materials,
4. worn tools,
5. worker absences or tardiness,
6. late delivery of parts,
7. unavailable materials handling equipment,
8. unavailable inspectors or setup persons.

Such problems are *impediments to flow*. The logic is to observe the symptoms, then find the causes, and finally correct the problems (not the symptoms).

JIT assumes the following goals are desirable:

1. Lot sizes should be as small as possible.
2. Quality must be consistently high.

3. People must perform reliably.
4. Inventory is inherently wasteful and should be minimized.
5. Machines must run reliably.
6. Production plans should be level and stable.
7. Space is a scarce resource, too valuable to be used for storage.

In order to achieve the above goals, pressure is applied to:

1. shorten setup times,
2. develop multifunctional employees (no restrictive work rules),
3. commit employees to total quality control (zero defects),
4. control quality at the source,
5. assure machine reliability via preventive maintenance,
6. group machines sequentially and dedicate them to part families,
7. use reliable sole source suppliers,
8. have suppliers deliver frequently in small lots.

Tradeoffs between inventory holding costs and setup costs are the usual reason for lot sizes larger than one. JIT seeks to drive setup time to zero (usually less than 10 minutes), so setup costs are low and small lot sizes are economical. Methods analysis and quick-change tooling, such as quick disconnects, hinged bolts, clamps, roller platforms, and tool carousels, can be used to generate setup reductions. Initial emphasis is on changes that involve minimal costs. Time and motion studies, such as simply videotaping a setup and reviewing it with several employees, usually discloses many possible time saving alternatives.

Safety stocks are never planned to be used, and thus amount to planned waste. They usually exist because of uncertainty of demand and supply (delivery performance). Uncertainty of demand can be reduced if not eliminated through lead time reduction. By reducing setup times, queue lengths, and lot sizes, lead time is shortened. By working with suppliers on delivery reliability, supply uncertainty can be diminished. Another need for safety stock comes from an inconsistent quality of the supply (defective parts). By improving material quality standards, this uncertainty can be abated.

Pursuit of Perfection

JIT attacks anything that slows or disrupts its planned activity, but refuses to plan more activity than is necessary. Quality must be near perfect; materials must move, not sit; people and equipment must only be used to produce what is needed. Performance evaluations based on capacity utilization become less appropriate. The issue is whether there is an immediate need for the part being produced, not whether the workers meet or exceed standards, nor whether the machines are fully utilized. Employees should make *only* what is needed when it is needed. Early production and excess production imply that more materials and people are being used than are needed. Likewise, late production and underproduction result in late deliveries, excessive shipping costs, etc.

Along the same lines, equipment should be dedicated to the production of groups of parts or products and arranged in compact configurations to promote short, constant movement. Group technology cells can reduce or eliminate transit (move) time and queue time as well as setup time, which substantially decrease throughput time and work-in-process. Since large lot sizes are inconsistent with smooth material flows, every effort is made to reduce setups to make changeovers possible at will. Similarly, materials do not move when equipment is down for repair, so high machine uptime is obtained through preventive machine maintenance. Several JIT suggestions are contained in Table 9.

An objective of JIT is to flow materials through a facility with a minimum of intervening queues. In-process and supplier quality must be at very high levels because of reduced protective stocks. Inspection of incoming materials and outgoing products is an "after the fact" discovery of defects: the defect already has occurred and cannot be prevented. You cannot inspect quality into a product; it must be built in. JIT quality directions are shown in Figure 3. High quality is obtained through never-ending programs to eliminate defects in the pursuit of perfection (zero defects, or only a few per million). Small lots enhance the early detection of quality problems. Substantial cost savings accrue directly from reduction of in-process scrap and rework. Emphasis is placed on preventing defects from

Table 9. JIT suggestions

1. Avoid interrupted work flow:
   Decrease setup time
   Control quality at source
   Eliminate machine breakdowns

2. Eliminate material handling and stocking:
   Arrange equipment to product flow
   Reduce space between operations
   Eliminate stocking points

3. Synchronize production:
   Cross train operators
   Uniform plant loading
   Schedule only what is needed
   Eliminate queues and banks
   Frequent vendor delivery

4. Pull scheduling:
   Only make what is used

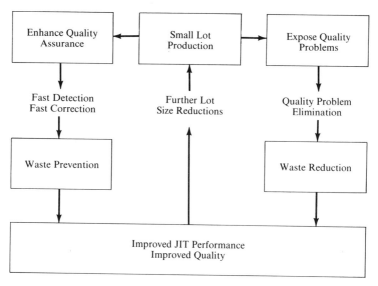

Figure 3. JIT quality directions.

occurring. Failing to prevent defects with complete certainty, the next option is to discover defects when they occur (or as quickly thereafter as possible) and make corrections immediately. Defect levels should never go up; they should go down, or at the worst, stay level.

Unless there is a capacity problem, establishing multiple sources violates the principle of absolute minimum resources. Suppliers must be few and deliver virtually 100% good parts. The principles are:

1. fewer but better suppliers,
2. long term partnerships with a few suppliers,
3. quality at the source by preventing defects and doing it right the first time,
4. eliminating incoming inspections,
5. using local suppliers to reduce lead times,
6. frequent delivery of parts directly to the point of use.

JIT attitudes are better suited for a "pull" execution system of shop floor control than a "push" execution system. A "push" system is where orders are launched and pushed through the system to meet some established due date. The order is moved to the next work center upon completion, with the expectation that the next work center needs it. If the rate of flow of materials from level to level of the product structure is controlled or determined by the *lower levels*, it is a push system. Push execution authorizes production or procurement independent of, or in anticipation of, higher level materials needs. A "pull" system is where orders are placed at the end item level and work is pulled through the facility to satisfy the demand of the end item. The order is not moved to the subsequent work center until it is needed or demanded by it. If the rate of flow of materials from level to level of the product structure is controlled or determined by the *higher levels*, it is a pull system. Top down on the product structure is equivalent to "pull," and bottom up to "push." Toyota's kanban system is an example of a "pull" system, since consuming work centers request more material from the feeding work centers, and nothing is processed by the feeding work centers without authorization.

Continuous processes (flow shops) are most efficient in terms of equipment utilization, throughput time, and work-in-process inventory. Intermittent processes (job shops) are more flexible but much less cost efficient than continuous processes, because they can produce a wider variety of outputs. The JIT logic attempts to operate a job shop more like a flow shop with its attendant cost efficiencies.

Repetitive Manufacturing and JIT

Although JIT concepts can apply to any type of production process, they are well suited to repetitive manufacturing. In repetitive manufacturing, discrete units are manufactured by a continuous process. In this environment, JIT takes a number of seemingly unconnected concepts and techniques and binds them together in such a way that they not only begin to pull together toward a common goal, but they multiply, with each one building on and amplifying the results of the others. They include uniform plant loading, group technology, quality control at the source, minimized setup times, and a kanban type production control system.

Uniform plant loading is accomplished by establishing a firm production plan in which output is fixed (usually for a month). The same mix of products are produced every day, even though the total quantities are small. For example, with a monthly requirement for 100 units, five might be built each day (presuming a 20 day month). Those five units would be intermixed with other products and not necessarily produced in exact sequence. Every day's schedule must be very nearly the same, or JIT will not work efficiently. The rated speed of equipment is ignored, and only daily requirements are produced.

Uniform plant loading attempts to produce products at the rate they are demanded. There are costs and side effects from producing more than is demanded. If products are produced faster than the demand rate, then containers are needed to hold them, trucks are needed to move them, warehouse space is needed to store them, money is needed to finance the inventory, cycle counters are needed to count it, accountants are needed to keep track of it, and schedulers are needed to indicate when to produce more. All this because products were produced faster than the demand rate.

Group technology clusters dissimilar machines into work centers for a given part or family of parts. One operator may run several machines, which eliminates the move and queue time between operations in a given cluster or cell. Group technology is used to physically link and overlap as many operations as possible. Pieces of equipment are placed very close to each other, as in an assembly line. Balance, synchronization, and smooth flow are achieved, while lead times are reduced from days to minutes, which all but eliminates work-in-process inventory.

Quality control at the source means each worker is the quality inspector of his or her tasks. Every individual is responsible personally for the quality of the work that he or she produces. If a quality problem develops, the work is stopped and everybody in the area concentrates on resolving the problem. Work is not started again until the problem is corrected. Workers are responsible for feeding only good quality parts to the downstream operations they supply. Poor quality is not tolerated; the emphasis is on quality instead of quantity. Quality circles frequently are used to improve quality and productivity. Quality at the source is predicated on three principles: (1) defect-free output is more important than mere output, (2) defects, errors, and breakdowns can be prevented, and (3) prevention costs less than doing things a second time.

Minimized setup times aim for single digit (less than ten minutes) setup times on every machine. Small lots cannot be run if setups take hours. Reduced setup times increase equipment utilization, which is equivalent to a capacity expansion. Time saving devices like hinged bolts, roller platforms, and folding brackets are used to reduce setup times. Time and motion studies are helpful in meeting this goal. A large number of setups must be made with JIT, so unless setup times are at an absolute minimum, its benefits falter.

Kanban type production control systems are simple, self-regulatory, and paperless systems for scheduling and shop floor control. (Kanban is a Japanese word meaning card.) Kanban is a "pull" type of reorder system where authority to produce or supply comes from the final assembly schedule (usually the master production schedule). It is a material flow control system that functions in the following manner:

1. Production control gives a final production schedule to final assembly.
2. Final assembly withdraws parts in small quantities at the time required from the work centers which feed final assembly.
3. The work centers feeding final assembly then manufacture parts to replace those withdrawn by final assembly.
4. In order to do this, these work centers withdraw small quantities of parts as required from the upstream work centers which feed them.

5. Continuing in this manner, each work center withdraws parts at the time needed and in the quantities required from the work centers feeding them. Thus, the entire network is engaged in production synchronized to final assembly.

Kanban provides JIT production without the use of work orders for parts. In the Toyota kanban system, two types of cards are attached to the standard containers used to move parts. The conveyance kanban (cards) are used to move parts from feeding work centers to the using work centers (they are a form of move ticket); production kanban are used to authorize the production of parts to replace those which are withdrawn. These cards are prepared by hand and always circulated between the work centers and stock points for which they are designated.

Not every part can be controlled by kanban. Large components and irregular optional parts require special attention, but repetitively used parts are regulated by kanban.

The flow of kanban between two work centers is simple. When an assembly center starts to use part X, a worker takes the conveyance kanban and travels to the machine center storage area, where he finds a full container of part X. He removes the production kanban and replaces it with the conveyance kanban which authorizes him to move the container. The liberated production kanban is then placed in a rack by the machine center as a work authorization for another lot of material. Parts are manufactured in the machine center in the order in which cards are placed on the rack (the sequence of cards in the rack indicates the priority list for the machine center). No more parts are built than called for by the kanban cards in circulation. When the container of parts is completed, the production kanban is inserted into the container, which is moved into a storage area. The result is essentially a "pull" system. Each action by the assembly center results in a ripple effort back through the feeding work centers.

If a work center does not have any production kanban cards, no parts are produced. No parts are built in anticipation, so in-process inventory is kept low.

Kanban is a manual pull system. Ordering is triggered by actual usage rather than planned usage, so planning errors are avoided. In contrast, MRP is a computerized push system in which the schedule pushes material forward based on average planned usage rather than actual usage.

With JIT, it is desirable to have reliable local (nearby) suppliers. The policy of quality control at the source is extended to suppliers. They are expected to deliver good materials in small and frequent batches as close to their use in production as is possible. This avoids costly inventory buildups and permits rapid responses to changes in market demand. The result is usually closer supplier relations, fewer suppliers, sole sources, and large contracts. Since contracts are larger and for longer time duration, supplier economies should be achieved that result in lower unit cost. The clustering of suppliers nearby shortens the logistical chain, with attendant economies.

CONCLUSION

This chapter addresses the problem of controlling in-process inventory in a job shop. Inventory results when inputs are greater than outputs. In job shops, control of in-process inventory is difficult, since it involves input and output control of each work center. Since the work center workload is not balanced, queues or backlogs of work are required for efficient utilization of resources. The control of backlogs is the key to efficient operations which directly influence the manufacturing cycle time. Capacity control is achieved by input/output control at each work center, which results in backlog and lead time control.

JIT has two basic tenets—(1) eliminate waste (anything that does not add value to the product) and (2) produce only what is sold (if you do not need it now, do not make it now). It includes continual efforts to reduce defects, inventory, space requirements, and labor content in the final product. It involves designing, producing, and distributing products with little wasted time, material, and effort and doing all this at a minimal cost. Obviously the goals of zero waste, making only what is sold, and zero inventory are unachievable in the near term, if indeed ever, but continual movement toward these goals can produce significant benefits. It is unlikely that a large percentage of U.S. manufacturers can completely convert to JIT; it is likely that every manufacturer can find some part of its operations where JIT concepts are applicable.

QUESTIONS

1. What costs are associated with in-process inventory?

2. State an apparent benefit to an organization from the proper management of in-process inventory.

3. List some of the negative consequences of holding excess in-process inventory.

4. Name the five time elements that make up the manufacturing cycle time. Which of these usually represents the largest fraction of the total manufacturing cycle time?

5. How does the priority of an order influence its process time? its queue time?

6. Why is the reduction of setup times desirable?

7. Of what value are time cycle charts?

8. How is lead time regulated through input/output control?

9. If an individual work center is not obtaining its output goals, what may be the reasons?

10. In broad terms, describe the application of the critical ratio technique.

11. List a few of the specific goals of just-in-time (JIT).

12. In order to achieve the stated goals of JIT, what actions are recommended?

13. If a job shop wants to reduce its in-process inventory levels, where should it concentrate its initial reduction efforts?

14. Distinguish between the "pull" and the "push" execution systems of shop floor control.

15. What impact does a short manufacturing cycle time have on finished goods inventory?

PROBLEMS

1. Determine critical ratios for the following jobs and sequence them accordingly. This is the 12th day on the production calendar:

Job	Date Required	Process Time Remaining (Days)
A	13	5
B	20	9
C	15	4
D	18	6
E	14	1
F	25	4
G	22	12
H	30	19

2. Use the critical ratio technique to schedule the following warehouse operations:

Job	Days of Supply on Hand	Lead Time Remaining
A	4	5
B	7	5
C	3	5
D	10	5
E	1	5
F	8	5

3. Use the critical ratio technique to determine in which sequence the following items should be shipped for delivery:

Item	Stock on Hand	Safety Stock	Avg. Daily Demand	Lead Time Remaining
A	20	10	5	3
B	18	4	3	4
C	350	50	275	1
D	100	10	20	5
E	72	6	10	7
F	23	18	1	3

4. Complete the input/output report in Table 3 using the following data, and analyze the results:

Week	21	22	23	24	25	26	27	28	29	30
Actual Input	110	150	140	130	180	170	200	200	190	210
Actual Output	150	140	160	140	150	170	180	210	210	220

5. Complete the input/output control report in Table 2 using the following data, and analyze the results:

Week	12	13	14	15	16	17	18	19	20	21
Actual Input	540	530	500	520	540	540	560	550	540	530
Actual Output	610	520	600	580	530	520	540	540	530	530

CASE 1: THE SOLUTION

Acacia Company produces a line of solid wood furniture. The production process is such that only about 20% of the process remains after the component parts are produced and ready for assembly. In other words, 80% of the process is making component parts, and 20% is final assembly and finishing. Some of the parts, which require excessive setups and long lead times, are produced in double order quantities. A typical production run for these parts would entail 33% of annual demand or four months' production supply. For this reason in-process inventory is high. The manufacturing of components incurs large storage space requirements, a costly inventory control system, and long cycle times.

The problem that is perplexing to the company is that all of the component parts of a unit are frequently not ready for final assembly at the scheduled time. Typically, some of the more elaborate components requiring the longest manufacturing lead times arrive late, but this has not been the rule for the basic parts. Mr. Bart was recently employed to apply modern techniques in the solution of this problem. Mr. Bart's original contention was that the firm needed to create an even more complete in-process inventory of component parts ready for final assembly. He also planned an alternative action in the event the increased inventory proposal was rejected: he felt the problem could be resolved equally well by increasing production rates. However, while continuing to research his proposals, he made the following observations:

1. Establishment of an increased parts inventory would be difficult because of lack of available production time. All of the production facilities are fully utilized at present. Often, parts in process are held up to let rush orders continue through.
2. Production of some component parts is not in accord with economic production quantities, either because of insufficient raw materials or because of competition for production capacity.
3. Expansion of the component inventory seems inadvisable because of the likelihood of deterioration. Large expansion also appears risky, since the type of modern furniture produced by Acacia is subject to a higher rate of obsolescence than is typical in the furniture industry.

After considering these points, Mr. Bart wondered if the real problem might be production capacity and not insufficient inventories of components. Consequently, he decided that his second proposal was the better. In order to solve the capacity problem the production rate for components must be increased.

1. Would the proposed increase in component production be a workable solution?
2. Does the structuring of a capacity requirements plan seem integral to Mr. Bart's proposal? Might raw material requirements also be crucial to the firm's capacity?
3. Are there other aspects of Acacia's operation that need analysis, e.g., schedules?

CASE 2: MULTIFACETED

Octagon was founded in 1968 by John Tuxley, who was an established builder and general contractor. He developed the idea of a prefabricated home which could be built cheaply and assembled easily. The home was extremely heavy and awkward to move, so John came up with the idea of a tower crane. He built a prototype which performed excellently and soon found that people were far more interested in his crane than his prefab house. As a result, he started Octagon Manufacturing Company and began to produce tower cranes for industry.

When Octagon first went into production, operations ran smoothly. In more recent years the plant has experienced a rash of bottlenecks, late deliveries, customer cancellations, increased costs, reduced quality, and increased manufacturing cycle times (the usual four weeks increased to seven or eight weeks). The updated load reports continually revealed increased backlogs. What worsened the work load status was the rise in the volume of customer orders and government contracts. Orders had risen by approximately 25% in each of the preceding two years, but firm orders for the first production period of the current year were down for the first time in over ten years.

When operations were progressing methodically, most jobs were dealt with on a first-come, first-served basis. Nowadays orders often accumulate over several weeks. The accumulated orders plus any incoming orders are classified by type and size and then assigned to the work centers. The loading or assignment of tasks to a particular work center is done so as to minimize the number of times the machinery has to be set up. For each machine center (i.e., cutting, welding, casting, etc.), a list is prepared of all orders to be processed in the next two week period. The sequencing of orders at each work center is arranged to reduce setups and to shorten queue time with the saving of setup costs as the number one priority.

Setups have an average cost of $250, so any rush jobs which require additional setups are deemed too costly. The setup priority schedule is rarely altered once it is completed, and tampering with it is protectively disallowed. However, some members of Octagon management think that the tight schedules are the primary cause of delays and bottlenecks. Manufacturing lead times have become excessively long, and they assert this is due to the large accumulations of in-process inventory. It is also their assertion that proper scheduling could reduce in-process inventory by at least 30%. Although limiting setups may have kept production economical from one standpoint, it is causing inefficient compromises of competing goals, e.g., reduction of inventory costs.

This group of adversaries is pushing for a new scheduling system based on a restructuring of goals and priorities. Their position rests with the following assumptions: first, Octagon's situation is faltering due to poor scheduling, and second, Octagon is failing due to the adoption of misdirected goals. It is their belief that the basic criteria on which job shops compete, specifically cost, delivery, and quality, are not receiving sufficient focus. These adversaries have issued a challenge: "All of the competitive criteria will be improved within a trial phase of a scheduling technique that incorporates unprecedented setups."

As preliminary steps to devising the new schedule, studies are being performed on various aspects of plant activity, and process times are being computed at the work centers. A mean time for each job shop center is to be formulated by averaging a sample of the activities. These estimates will determine capacity. Plant personnel are being questioned as to which operations have proven to cause bottlenecks, and these particular operations will receive isolated study with subsequent closer estimation of time ranges. Job completion dates will be based on forward scheduling, but the actual way to sequence the orders is still under consideration. Lastly, the new scheduling method will reflect the following policies: changing priorities, use of overtime, tracking of progress, and necessary revisions:

1. How is competition affected by the old policies? Could the "challenge" be more effective?
2. Are the dispatching rules acceptable under the old plan? What are some suggestions for the new plan?
3. Since it is practically impossible to develop "the" optimal schedule in a job shop, would the new plan at least be satisfactory?
4. How will in-process inventory be affected by any changes?

CASE 3: THE UNCONTROLLABLE SHOP JUNGLE

Dave Conservative was reviewing the year-end financial statements of Wilson Manufacturing Company, a job shop operation which recently moved into a spacious new facility. Dave noted with alarm the changes that occurred in current assets during the first accounting period following the move. Specifically, he was alarmed by the decline in the cash balance and the growth in inventory.

Dave realized that as the company financial manager, he viewed things differently from John Lathe, who was vice president for production. He recalled John insisting on large stabilization stocks in order to keep production levels high. John scheduled long production runs in centers where frequent production changes had proven expensive. He also realized the disruption of production because of inventory shortages could be more costly than the extra holding costs. Furthermore, the large stocks allowed John to continue the use of flexible scheduling. He felt it important to maintain different input/output rates at work centers so as to maximize the efficiency and productivity of each center. So as a consequence of stabilization stocks, the centers enjoyed independent planning, and the firm as a whole could have flexibility in scheduling different products through the facility.

On Friday morning at the weekly department head meeting, Dave broached the subject of cash and inventory control with John. John proceeded to highlight areas where he saw problems. He said certain costs had definitely increased since the move, but most of these would be remedied in due course. Large cash outlays had gone to compensate the maintenance crew for overtime. The new machinery had many operational problems that were not covered under the purchase warranties. Another enlarged expense was the rise in materials handling costs. The materials handlers were slow in acquainting themselves with the new facility and its more spacious layout. The materials personnel were still confused on the locations of partially processed goods; more in-process goods were going to temporary storage so the accumulation on the shop floor would be reduced. The storage and retrieval of in-process goods were unfamiliar to the materials handlers.

John also thought that his direct labor costs were up, but he was sure this would also be self-correcting. The employees were having a hard time adjusting their pace to their workload. The employees had always been in the habit of judging the amount of work to be processed through their center by the inventory coming in and going out. With the new layout they were having difficulty estimating workloads, and their actual workload was greater than they perceived. For instance, as the firm reduced the input to some centers by leaving more inventory in storage, the workers were slackening their pace in response to the reduced inventory at their centers. Also contributing to the slower pace was the smaller amount of waste and damaged goods, which gave the appearance of little in-process inventory.

In defense of other inventory control areas, John was quick to point out that a new purchasing and raw materials inventory control system installed this year had reduced raw material inventory levels. The finished goods inventories were also down. "Look, Dave, marketing is doing a superb job of forecasting demand. To reduce the finished goods any more will only result in excess stockouts, and with the competition we have, we just can't afford that."

Dave, after reviewing the figures on the raw materials and finished goods inventory, had to agree that they were both down. "You're right. The problem is with the in-process inventory. John, I guess you are doing all you can. In-process inventory is just part of the manufacturing process and beyond our control. We can only deal with these labor and maintenance costs that will improve with some training and adjustment. Have a nice weekend, John, I'll see you Monday."

1. Discuss how such diverse things as maintenance, scheduling, and materials handling affect in-process inventory.

2. How do behavioral considerations affect Wilson's cash or inventory problems?
3. Should Dave overlook the inventory problem and concentrate on the cash outlays, or is there some overlap?
4. What recommendations would you make to Dave?

CASE 4: BREAKAWAY

The Breakaway plant in Tulsa, Oklahoma manufactures medium voltage circuit breakers to customer specifications. The company understates its product line when it advertises it offers two basic models. Because of the many options available to customers, numerous product configurations can be built and sold to a broad customer base. Thus, Breakaway is recognized for its wide selection despite its simplistic appeal. It also is known for its unique, innovative designs and for the high quality of its products.

The Tulsa plant is departmentalized into the following areas: fabrication, machine shop, plating and painting, subassembly, final assembly, and testing and packing. Parts fabrication, subassembly, and final assembly all do their own weekly scheduling of production, and each operates duplicate lines for processing. Furthermore, all three areas are trying to increase lot sizes in order to gain economies of scale. The production planners charged with determining the lot sizes are very enthusiastic about improving productivity. Department heads have set forth productivity goals for their respective areas.

One reason the department heads are keen on long production runs is the prevailing attitude at Breakaway toward production changeovers. Setups at Breakaway are viewed as production interferences. For example, a typical setup in sheet metal fabrication is estimated to take one hour away from production time. Changeovers in metal fabrication are done by individuals who must adjust different dies without assistance. Because of the many differences in the heights of the dies, the changeovers vary in procedure and duration. Changeovers are complicated not only by the compensations for die heights but also by the awkwardness and rigidity of some of the clamping devices which must be adjusted.

One of Breakaway's corporation consultants thinks the Tulsa plant would be a good starting place for studying productivity improvements which eventually could be copied at other plants. The consultant wants to focus on inventory reduction as a key to improving productivity throughout the entire organization. Because of recent familiarity with the potential benefits of just-in-time (JIT), the consultant wants the Tulsa plant to commit itself to a JIT program. The JIT principle to receive the greatest emphasis is the elimination of inventory waste.

1. What problems will be encountered in implementing a JIT program at the Tulsa plant? Are any of these common to most organizations embarking on a JIT program?
2. What factors may be critical to the success of a JIT program (at Breakaway in particular and at any other organization)? If such a program were successful, what results could be expected?
3. Do you recommend a JIT program for Breakaway's Tulsa plant? If so, on what scale? What introductory steps should be taken during a JIT implementation?

10 Distribution Inventory Systems

PUSH VS. PULL DISTRIBUTION SYSTEMS

TIME-PHASED ORDER POINT

DISTRIBUTION REQUIREMENTS PLANNING

FAIR SHARES ALLOCATIONS

LOT SIZING AND SAFETY STOCK

CONCLUSION

QUESTIONS

PROBLEMS

CASES

Because customers for products commonly are geographically dispersed (sometimes hundreds or thousands of miles from where the product is produced), it may be necessary to store inventory in several locations. An organization that produces or provides products for a local market may have a single factory warehouse at the production site or a single outlet to serve its customers. As the target market increases in geographic expanse, more locations are added along with more levels (echelons). When a single organization is in control of more than one level of distribution, it has a multiechelon distribution system or network. This chapter explores inventory systems for organizations which control more than one level of distribution and must provide prompt and efficient service to diverse geographical areas.

The terms echelon, layer, and level all indicate the stratification and hierarchical structure of a distribution network and are used interchangeably. The top echelon is the master (central) distribution center that is supplied by a manufacturing facility and/or vendors outside the distribution network. The central distribution center is the primary source of supply for the distribution system and is the focal point in the network. Regional distribution centers are replenished by the central distribution center and serve as sources of supply to subordinate distribution centers. At the lowest echelon are the local distribution centers. These centers are closest to the customers; it is from these points that the products leave the distribution network to directly satisfy customer demands.

The example of a multiechelon (trilevel) distribution network shown in Figure 1 illustrates numerous local distribution centers fed from regional distribution centers fed in turn from a master or central distribution center. The graphical representation of a distribution network is analogous to a product structure (bill of materials) in an MRP system. Source or parent distribution centers deliver products to subordinate distribution centers in the same network. The master center represented in the diagram may well be a factory warehouse, while the local distribution centers found at the ends of the structure are very likely retail outlets.

When production is separated from consumption by several echelons, demand oscillations are amplified through the network. These undulations are caused by the ordering and lot sizing policies used at each location, which themselves are influenced by individual lead times. This phenomenon of variations in demand becoming amplified in a multistage system is covered in Chapter 1 in the section on business cycle influence. Because time lags are a major factor in creating this circumstance, the amplification is attenuated when lead times are very short. Hence, the lot sizing and ordering policies associated with single item, single location inventory control methods are known to have serious shortcomings when applied to multiechelon networks.

427

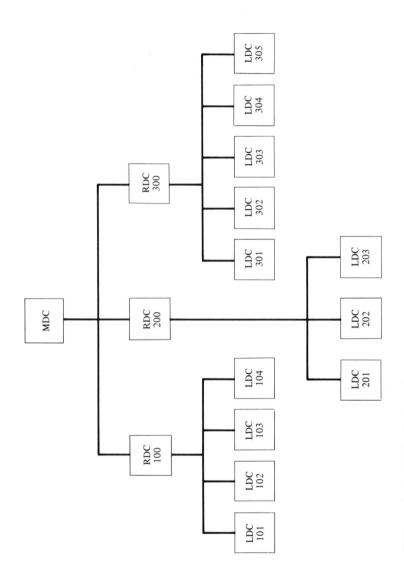

MDC = master (central) distribution center
RDC = regional distribution center
LDC = local distribution center

Figure 1. Trilevel distribution network.

Multiechelon distribution networks exist to support customer service and to provide transportation economies. Transportation costs are often the largest cost element of a distribution system and thus deserve careful consideration. Techniques, such as using less expensive bulk shipments to central supply centers and then breaking bulk for local deliveries, are sought in order to reduce this major cost item. Beyond the obvious need to reduce transportation costs are other cost reduction and customer service goals. Keeping in mind all of these objectives, the critical issues confronting distribution inventory systems are (1) where to locate the distribution centers, (2) what products to stock at each location, and (3) how to replenish stocks at each distribution center. It will be assumed in this treatment of the subject that the first two issues have been decided on some rational basis. Thus, only the issue of stock replenishment will be addressed.

PUSH VS. PULL DISTRIBUTION SYSTEMS

Distribution inventory systems can be classified as "pull" or as "push" systems. In a pull system, each distribution center decides what is needed and orders its own requirements from its source (pulling inventory to itself). In a push system, the master (central) distribution center determines the needs of each location and sends these requirements or orders through the network (pushing inventory to the local center).

Distribution centers draw stock from their parent supply sources if they are operating in a pull system. Each location acts independently of others in the network and replenishes stock without regard to the inventory at any other location. Despite its level in the network, each location performs its own planning and usually maintains an individual safety stock. Acting to isolate themselves even further, similar centers generally engage only in limited stock transfers if they transfer inventory at all. Traditional pull systems include the fixed order size system, two-bin system, and fixed order interval system. All of these operate on an independent replenishment principle, treat demand as continuous, require some form of forecasting, do not use time phasing, and lack visibility beyond the immediate replenishment order.

A traditional pull system reacts to demand without anticipating it. The parent center does not know of replenishment orders until they are received. In the typical operation, the parent centers receive erratic demands from the distribution centers they supply. When unpredicted and simultaneous orders are received from several local centers, a deficiency of inventory results. For example, local centers might operate for several weeks without placing a replenishment order for an item and then impose a large demand on the parent center. Sometimes several centers order the same item at about the same time and deplete the stock at the source. The possibility of drastic stock depletion results in a requirement for large safety stocks at the source of supply. The local centers are unconcerned with the replenishment habits of their sources and assume these supply sources have plenty of inventory available. Obviously, communications in this type of system characteristically flow one way, from the bottom to the top (up to the parent level).

In the actual operation of a distribution network, demands at local distribution centers may be independent, continuous, and quite unlike the demands for item replenishment at parent supply centers. Because stock actually leaves the distribution network from the local distribution centers, it is only at these outlets that demand is truly independent and subject solely to market influences. Regardless of their own continuous demand patterns, the local centers use ordering policies which place erratic demands on their sources. At source levels in the network (at the central and regional distribution centers), the demand pattern is dependent and discontinuous. Since demand at these levels is inherently lumpy (occurs intermittently and unevenly), it is desirable to be able to predict future orders from subordinate centers to avoid a potential overload of replenishment orders. Due to its dependent nature, demand at the parent centers (those which feed other centers) can be calculated more effectively than it can be forecasted.

With erratic demands coming from local centers, pull systems based on average demands do not operate satisfactorily in multiechelon systems. Because of the time-varying demands associated with the source levels in multiechelon systems, the timing of requirements rather than an appropriately held inventory level is the paramount consideration. Since the timing and magnitude of peaks can be anticipated, it is more economical to keep minimal inventory in stock and schedule the amount and timing of requirements to coincide with peak conditions rather than to replenish inventory blindly. Unable to use their replenishment (reorder) policies effectively, traditional pull systems do not adequately establish requirement order policies suited to the levels in a multiechelon system.

In direct opposition to pull systems, push systems have replenishment allocations that are centrally planned at the master distribution center (not at local centers). The stock status of the total network is used to determine individual location stock replenishments. Forecast requirements for all local distribution centers are summed by period, and the available inventory is allocated. Lot sizes are determined centrally and are fair share allocations made on the basis of current balances at each location. Rather than flowing in only one direction, communications flow in both directions as the master distribution center decides what to send through the network.

Under the push system, the central distribution center may be eliminated and replenishments be sent directly to the local distribution centers from the factory. In this situation, disproportionate local stock quantities may be leveled by transfers between centers. For slow-moving items, a national safety stock may be maintained at the local center which has the largest requirements or variability.

Push systems are most appropriate where materials and/or capacity are limited or inflexible, while pull systems are appropriate when material and capacity are readily available.

Many important savings are possible if the distribution network is viewed and controlled in its entirety (through centralization). Although the push approach offers several advantages over the pull approach, a pure push system can be difficult to implement where local managers have customer service and marketing responsibilities. Its institution can result in a disintegrated "soft push" with the following characteristics:

1. forecasts are developed at local centers,
2. the master center plans orders that are reviewed by local center managers,
3. local center managers can accept, alter, or cancel orders (silence is acceptance).

TIME-PHASED ORDER POINT

Time phasing is the scheduling of inventory requirements and replenishments by need date over a specified time horizon. It focuses on the management of stock flows as opposed to the more traditional management of stock levels. It transforms the replenishment decision from a quantity to a time dimension. With time phasing, bottlenecks and shortages become apparent before rather than after the fact, so it is possible to avoid the "feast or famine" cycle.

The conventional fixed order size system always reorders items whenever the inventory position reaches a reorder point regardless of whether more is needed. It blindly keeps a certain amount of inventory on hand at all times (even though it may not be required). It never looks beyond the next order and is equipped only to indicate when to place the next order. It reacts to rather than anticipates demand, and hence has limited capabilities for coping with time-varying demand.

In contrast, the time-phased order point (TPOP) gives visibility to replenishment orders beyond the lead time period. It indicates when to place orders and has an additional feature that signals when to reschedule an order to an earlier or later time period. Its ability to predict allows planners to anticipate what may change in the future rather than merely react to something that has actually happened. It can identify problems while there is still time to do something about them. Lacking the rigid demand assumptions of traditional reorder point systems, the TPOP permits forecasts to vary period by period and thus is designed to be responsive to time-varying demand. Moreover, it can accommodate less ordinary demand conditions (promotions, export orders, or any kind of lumpy demand can be put into a time-phased format).

The TPOP applies the logic of MRP to independent demand items in a distribution setting. TPOP is not only an outgrowth of MRP, but it may be used along with MRP. By using the same technique in both distribution and manufacturing, only one system is needed with one set of data.

The TPOP logic is simple. It uses the forecast for an item directly as gross requirements. When the net requirements quantity is projected to fall below the safety stock, a planned order receipt is scheduled [net requirements = (gross requirements + safety stock) − (scheduled receipts + previous period's projected on hand)]. The lead time is subtracted from the planned order receipt date, and the planned order release date is determined. Thus, planners know the planned releases and receipts out as far as the planning horizon extends.

With TPOP an entire schedule of planned replenishment orders is developed rather than one order at a time. The name is actually a misnomer, since no order point as such is used. Instead, MRP logic takes over and provides for ordering at the right time. TPOP constantly reexamines the need dates on orders to determine if they should be rescheduled to another date based on changing requirements. Schedule changes can be implemented up until an order is actually shipped. This rescheduling capability of TPOP deals favorably with forecast errors and demand undulations so that inventory levels can be kept low.

EXAMPLE 1

Develop the time-phased order point for an end item with a forecasted weekly demand of 30 units, a lot size of 100 units, a safety stock of 10 units, a lead time of 2 weeks, and a stock level of 80 units.

Solution:

	PD	\multicolumn{8}{c}{Period}
	PD	1	2	3	4	5	6	7	8
Gross requirements		30	30	30	30	30	30	30	30
Scheduled receipts									
Projected on hand	80	50	20	90	60	30	100	70	40
Net requirements				20			10		
Planned order receipts				100			100		
Planned order releases		100			100				

The forecast of 30 units per week is projected over the entire planning horizon of 8 weeks and represents gross requirements. The current quantity on hand of 80 will drop below the safety stock of 10 in period 3, and a replenishment order of 100 is planned to arrive at that time. Offsetting for lead time, a planned order release is scheduled for period 1. In period 6, there is a net requirement for 10 units to replenish the safety stock, so another planned order is scheduled for replenishment by ordering in period 4. Notice the results are the same as would result with a reorder point of 70 units, but with TPOP an entire schedule of planned replenishment orders is developed instead of one order at a time. It indicates when orders for an item are likely to be placed during the entire planning horizon.

DISTRIBUTION REQUIREMENTS PLANNING

Distribution requirements planning (DRP) is the application of MRP logic to distribution inventories. A derivative of MRP, it plans requirements for finished goods through distribution networks. The bill of materials used in MRP is replaced with a bill of distribution (the network). DRP uses time-phased order point (TPOP) logic to determine network replenishment requirements, while MRP applies time-phased logic to subassemblies and components to products in a manufacturing bill of materials network. DRP is an "implosion" process from the lowest levels of the network to the central distribution center. MRP is an "explosion" process from the master production schedule to the detailed scheduling of component replenishments. DRP, like MRP, distinguishes between independent and dependent demand.

DRP relies on forecasts at the lowest level in the network to derive inventory demand at all higher levels. Although gross requirements must be forecasted at the local distribution level, it can be calculated at all the other levels. Gross requirements for items are developed from forecasts in a time-phased manner at all local distribution centers in a TPOP format. The planned order releases for a given item in each time period at the local centers are accumulated and become gross requirements at the parent center. Thus, parent centers no longer have to forecast lumpy requirements but can accumulate them from their demand sources. In a similar time-phased manner, at each level in the distribution network, planned order releases from all subordinate distribution centers are summed to become gross requirements for the parent center.

DRP is a method of handling stock replenishment in a multiechelon distribution environment. It takes the point of independent demand—the point where forecasting must be done—and structures the requirements for supply sources. The only place for independent demand is at the customer level. No matter how many levels exist in the distribution network, they are all dependent except the level that serves the customer.

DRP places emphasis on scheduling rather than on ordering. Inventory items are not replenished unless there are future requirements to be met. DRP anticipates future requirements by forward planning at all levels of a distribution network. Periods of potential shortage can be identified early enough to develop alternative plans. It can predict problems before they actually occur and provide visibility to the distribution network.

The basic logic of DRP is as follows:

1. From forecasts at local distribution centers, it calculates the time-phased net requirements. The net requirements indicate when the stock level (scheduled receipts + projected-on-hand from the previous period) will be consumed by gross requirements (drop below its safety stock level). For a given period, net requirements = (gross requirements + safety stock) − (scheduled receipts + projected-on-hand for the previous period). Only positive values of net requirements are recorded.
2. It creates a planned order receipt for the net requirements quantity (or a specified lot size) in the period of net requirements.
3. It calculates the planned order release date (shipping date) by offsetting the planned order receipt date by the lead time. In other words, stock must be ordered one lead time prior to its need.
4. It revises the projected-on-hand quantity at the end of each period. For a given period, projected-on-hand = (projected-on-hand of the prior period + scheduled receipts + planned order receipts) − (gross requirements).
5. The planned order release quantity becomes a gross requirement in the same time period for the parent supply center at the next higher level of the distribution network.

EXAMPLE 2

A distribution system consists of a central distribution center that supplies three local distribution centers (A, B, and C). The forecasted demand for a product over an eight-week time horizon at each of the local distribution centers is shown in Table 1 along with the product's lot size, safety stock, lead time, and stock on hand. When are replenishment orders for the product planned at each of the centers?

The completed DRP tables for the unnamed product are shown in Table 2. Center A has orders planned for periods 1 and 5; center B has orders planned for periods 2 and 6; center C has orders planned for periods 2 and 6; and the central center has a replenishment order planned for period 2. Note how the planned order releases at the local centers become gross requirements for the central center. The time-phased format provides eight weeks of future visibility to distribution planners.

Table 1

Center A; Safety stock 30
Lot size 120; Lead time 1

	PD	Period 1	2	3	4	5	6	7	8
Gross requirements		30	30	30	30	30	30	30	30
Scheduled receipts									
Projected on hand	70								
Net requirements									
Planned order receipts									
Planned order releases									

Center B; Safety stock 10
Lot size 100; Lead time 1

Gross requirements		20	20	20	40	20	20	20	50
Scheduled receipts									
Projected on hand	50								
Net requirements									
Planned order receipts									
Planned order releases									

Center C; Safety stock 5
Lot size 70; Lead time 2

Gross requirements		40	15	20	30	10	5	30	10
Scheduled receipts		70							
Projected on hand	15								
Net requirements									
Planned order receipts									
Planned order releases									

Center Central; Safety stock 0
Lot size 400; Lead time 3

Gross requirements									
Scheduled receipts									
Projected on hand	300								
Net requirements									
Planned order receipts									
Planned order releases									

Table 2

Center A; Safety stock 30 Lot size 120 ; Lead time 1	Period								
	PD	1	2	3	4	5	6	7	8
Gross requirements		30	30	30	30	30	30	30	30
Scheduled receipts									
Projected on hand	70	40	130	100	70	40	130	100	70
Net requirements			20				20		
Planned order receipts			120				120		
Planned order releases		120				120			

Center B; Safety stock 10
Lot size 100 ; Lead time 1

	PD	1	2	3	4	5	6	7	8
Gross requirements		20	20	20	40	20	20	20	50
Scheduled receipts									
Projected on hand	50	30	10	90	50	30	10	90	40
Net requirements				20				20	
Planned order receipts				100				100	
Planned order releases			100				100		

Center C ; Safety stock 5
Lot size 70 ; Lead time 2

	PD	1	2	3	4	5	6	7	8
Gross requirements		40	15	20	30	10	5	30	10
Scheduled receipts		70							
Projected on hand	15	45	30	10	50	40	35	5	65
Net requirements					25				10
Planned order receipts					70				70
Planned order releases			70				70		

Center Central; Safety stock 0
Lot size 400; Lead time 3

	PD	1	2	3	4	5	6	7	8
Gross requirements		120	170	0	0	120	170	0	0
Scheduled receipts									
Projected on hand	300	180	10	10	10	290	120	120	120
Net requirements						110			
Planned order receipts						400			
Planned order releases			400						

DRP works well both in an integrated manufacturing distribution environment and in a pure distribution environment. For organizations that produce and distribute products, manufacturing and distribution are united through the master production schedule into one comprehensive plan. For organizations that only distribute products, distribution operates in a unified system. By time-phasing inventory requirements at each level in the distribution network, DRP has the predictive power to identify potential problems before they are encountered.

For manufacturing organizations that produce to stock and sell through their own distribution network, performance can be improved by an integrated system that combines DRP and MRP. As shown in Figure 2, DRP and MRP are linked through the master production schedule. The accumulation of planned order releases for items from the master distribution center are a major input to the master production schedule. This linking meshes the customer service goals of distribution with the production priorities at the master scheduling level. In a sense, DRP "drives" the master production schedule, which in turn "drives" MRP. The forecasting of demand occurs only once, at the lowest level of the distribution network. DRP manages finished goods inventory in distribution, while MRP manages materials and in-process goods for production. Together they provide concise control over material flow from raw materials suppliers all the way to customers.

Many wholesalers and large retailers operate chains of distribution centers to distribute products obtained from suppliers to retail outlets. DRP can efficiently replenish what has been consumed in succeeding levels of the distribution network, based on its ability to predict requirements. The tangible benefits are improved service, reduced inventory levels, and lower handling costs.

The planning horizon of DRP should extend out to at least the longest cumulative lead time. Typically it is six months to a year in length. The replanning of the network is performed periodically—usually at least once a week.

In addition to scheduling replenishment requirements, time-phased systems can assist planners in developing efficient transportation plans. With advanced knowledge of what is expected to be shipped, transportation modes can be filled to as close to capacity as possible. If a particular shipment is scheduled at less than capacity, the load can be completed with future schedule requirements. Potential overload shipments can be moved forward or backward in time to optimize capacity utilization.

Just as MRP (material requirements planning) has been expanded into MRP II (manufacturing resource planning), so has DRP (distribution requirements planning) been expanded into DRP II (distribution resource planning). Distribution resource planning deals with the entire distribution function. In addition to controlling inventory, it projects inventory and

437

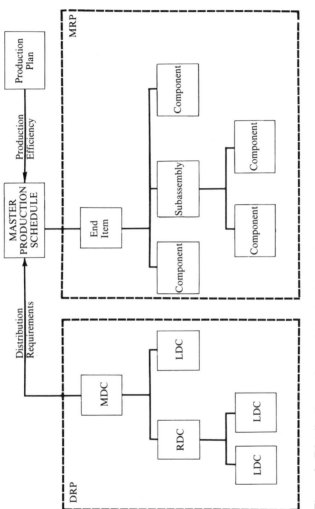

Figure 2. Distribution and manufacturing integration.

resource requirements which are useful for operational and financial planning. It can

1. manage the entire distribution function including inventory, transportation, warehousing, and personnel,
2. improve the integration between an organization's manufacturing function and distribution function,
3. provide forward (future) visibility for scheduling operations, so priorities are kept valid.

DRP is a system and not a technique. It must be tailored to the specific distribution network it is to simulate. It functions as a decision support system. Although DRP is computer-based, its overall performance is determined by the human interface.

FAIR SHARES ALLOCATIONS

Pull systems can be appropriate where materials and capacity are readily available with few limitations on flexibility and supply. Push systems are appropriate where materials and/or capacity are in short supply so that allocation must be made centrally to optimize aggregate performance. DRP is an advanced type of pull system that time-phases replenishment requirements established at local distribution centers. An advanced pull system anticipates future demand, while a traditional pull system only reacts to it. By modifying DRP, it is possible to make it a push system based on fair shares allocation. Although DRP is a pull system and fair shares allocation is a push system, both are time-phased systems that can anticipate demand (quantity based systems must inherently react).

If items are in short supply (and something always is), the conventional pull system will prevent the organization from getting the best overall use of its limited inventory. In such cases, it is desirable for the central location to replenish local center inventory on an allocation basis rather than give local centers the liberty of establishing their own replenishments (letting them order whatever they want whenever they want).

The fair shares allocation uses the same requirements philosophy as DRP, except that lot sizing is done by a central location and not each individual local center. DRP pulls inventory through the system from one level to the next; fair shares allocation pushes material from the factory or central supply facility. Since both DRP (advanced pull) and fair shares allocation (push) are time-phased, they both give each source knowledge of future requirements. A comparison of DRP and fair shares allocation is given in Table 3.

Fair shares allocation, conforming to a crucial requirement of any push system, must have accurate and timely information on the stock status at all locations (as well as in transit). Opportunely, it waits until the last moment

Table 3. Comparison of distribution requirements planning and fair shares allocation

Factor	DRP	Fair Shares
Forecasts	Local	Local
Replenishments	Time-phased	Time-phased
System	Advanced pull	Push
Lot sizing	Localized (destination)	Centralized (source)
Shipping quantity	Planned order releases	Fair shares allocation
Visibility	Planned order releases	Net requirements

before determining shipment sizes. Rather than parceling out inventory according to planned orders in local distribution centers (as in DRP), it allocates on-hand inventory according to aggregate net requirements for the network. The inventory status at the parent center and the current net requirements at each local center are considered. Replenishment lot sizes are determined at the time of shipment at the source (central planning and control). The quantity shipped is a fair share of what is available to the total system. If more than sufficient stock is available to meet total system requirements, the additional stock is allocated so each location has the same time supply (though it may be advisable to limit the maximum order size for space reasons). If insufficient stock is available for total system requirements, each location is allocated the same time supply of available stock. The logic is that if every location has the same time supply stock, the total system will give better service than with any other way of allocating stock.

EXAMPLE 3

A two echelon distribution network (one central distribution center and three local distribution centers) has 126 units of product X at the central center, and no additional receipts are expected for at least a week. The on-hand inventory and the requirements (forecasts) for the three local centers are listed below. How many units of product X should be shipped to each local center based on a fair shares allocation?

Local Center	On Hand	Unit Requirements/Week of Product X					Daily Usage
		1	2	3	4	5	
A	10	20	20	20	20	20	4
B	30	50	50	50	50	50	10
C	14	30	30	30	30	30	6
Total	54	100	100	100	100	100	20

The system has a total of 180 units (126 at the central center and 54 units at the three local centers). Since 20 units are needed each day, there are 9 days' supply in the system. The objective is to ship each local center the quantity required to bring its stock to a 9 day supply. The fair shares shipping quantity for each local center is calculated as follows:

$$Q_i = (\text{requirements during runout period}) - (\text{stock on hand}).$$

Local Center	Fair Shares Allocation Q_i
A	$4(9) - 10 = 26$
B	$10(9) - 30 = 60$
C	$6(9) - 14 = 40$
	$\overline{126}$

Thus, the 126 units have been allocated to provide coverage for an equal time period in all local centers.

LOT SIZING AND SAFETY STOCK

Lot sizing in distribution is influenced by a variety of factors—(1) frequency of shipment, (2) economic order quantities, (3) shipping container sizes, and (4) total weight and cube. When there are infrequent shipments (such as monthly), the lot size should be a time supply that is an integer multiple of the replenishment lead time (a one-month supply, a two-month supply, etc.). With frequent shipments, frequency of shipments is not as important in determining lot sizes, so economic order quantities can be calculated for them. Moreover, lot sizes can vary from exact economic order quantities without significantly deviating from their minimum total cost (due to their cost insensitivity).

The usual methods of determining lot sizes do not apply to stock transfers within a distribution network. Since the total amount of inventory within a system is not affected by changes in location, total system holding costs are not necessarily affected. Lot sizes cannot be based on the usual minimization of ordering and holding costs, unless holding costs are redefined on a marginal or incremental basis. Since the cost of transportation is usually the largest cost element in a distribution system, lot sizes are frequently based on transportation efficiency.

Sometimes there are shipping quantities that are economical from a materials handling and storage standpoint. It may be a quantity that conveniently fits on a pallet, tray, or other storage container. It is desirable to have shipping quantities that are multiples of their container quantities. Freight rates and transportation charges are usually based on total weight and cube (volume). It is advantageous to meet freight requirements in an economically efficient manner.

Pipeline inventory can be large in a multilocation inventory system. A tradeoff exists between inventory investment and speed of order processing and of transportation. Safety stock requirements in multiechelon systems are not the same as in single locations. In general, safety stock should not be duplicated at each echelon and should be decentralized. The safety stock held at upper echelons should be a backup to the stock held at lower (retail) echelons. Theoretically, less total safety stock is needed if it is held at a central location, but this can result in a loss of sales and stockouts at the lower levels. It is acceptable for high cost, low demand items to have a high service level centrally with little if any safety stock at the lower level. Expensive items with low demand are candidates for centralization. In contrast, low cost, high demand items typically have a high service level at the lower level with little safety stock at the central location.

The only locations where requirements must be forecasted are at the local level, so major safety stocks should be kept primarily at the local distribution centers. Since requirements above the local level are derived, only lead time variance is relevant at these locations. Safety stocks only have to be large enough to cover demand variations during the lead time. When only demand is uncertain, safety stock should be held at the location closest to the demand; when only supply is uncertain, safety stock should be held at locations closest to the supply.

In time-phased systems, the emphasis shifts from safety stocks to the proper scheduling of orders. It is most important to have shipping schedules to distribution centers and to adhere to them faithfully. The shipping schedule is the control over lead time. By placing bounds on replenishment lead times, the shipping schedule affects safety stock requirements for lead time demand variations. If replenishments to distribution centers are on a fixed periodic pattern (perhaps once a week), the lead time is deterministic. Erratic replenishment patterns seriously jeopardize customer service at local distribution centers and necessitate greater safety stock requirements.

CONCLUSION

The most commonly encountered problems with distribution inventory systems are (1) too much inventory, (2) inventory at the wrong location, (3) poor customer service, and (4) lost sales due to lack of product availability. Traditional inventory systems treat each location as an independent entity. These systems are inadequate for multiechelon distribution networks, because they ignore lumpy demand patterns and do not provide visibility of future demand requirements. Time-phased order points predicated on MRP logic and applied to a distribution structure (network) provide the mechanism for overcoming these shortcomings. DRP and fair shares allocation have evolved as distinct approaches to stock replenishment. DRP establishes lot sizes at the local level and pulls inventory from supplying sources; fair shares allocation determines lot sizes centrally based on an equal runout time supply to each location.

QUESTIONS

1. Differentiate between push and pull distribution systems.

2. Name several examples of pull distribution systems.

3. Describe demand patterns at different levels of a distribution network.

4. What advantages does the time-phased order point (TPOP) system provide to a distribution network?

5. What happens in TPOP when net requirements are projected to fall below the safety stock level?

6. How are net requirements calculated in TPOP?

7. Does DRP operate more effectively in an integrated manufacturing and distribution environment or in a pure distribution environment?

8. In an integrated manufacturing and distribution system, how are DRP and MRP linked?

9. What determines the minimum planning horizon in DRP?

10. Contrast the lot sizing logic of DRP and of fair shares allocation when the available supply exceeds the demand for an item.

PROBLEMS

1. A product is distributed through the network below with the listed replenishment lead times. What is the minimum planning horizon for a time-phased system for the product?

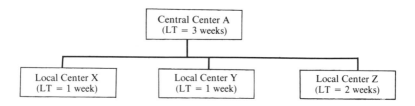

Table 4

Center X; Safety stock 5 Lot size 40; Lead time 1	PD				Period				
		1	2	3	4	5	6	7	8
Gross requirements		20	20	20	20	20	20	20	20
Scheduled receipts									
Projected on hand	40								
Net requirements									
Planned order receipts									
Planned order releases									

Center Y; Safety stock 10
Lot size 180; Lead time 1

Gross requirements		60	60	60	60	60	60	60	60
Scheduled receipts									
Projected on hand	190								
Net requirements									
Planned order receipts									
Planned order releases									

Center Z; Safety stock 10
Lot size 200; Lead time 2

Gross requirements		50	50	50	50	60	60	70	70
Scheduled receipts									
Projected on hand	160								
Net requirements									
Planned order receipts									
Planned order releases									

Center A; Safety stock 40
Lot size 400; Lead time 3

Gross requirements									
Scheduled receipts									
Projected on hand	600								
Net requirements									
Planned order receipts									
Planned order releases									

2. Develop a DRP material plan for the product in Problem 1 for the next 8 weeks from the data given in Table 4.

3. Develop a fair shares allocation plan for the product in Problem 1 from the data given in Table 4.

CASE 1: ADVANCE WARNING

Marlex Corporation has several distribution centers across the United States, a central supply facility in Oklahoma City, and one manufacturing plant near the central supply facility. The plant inventory in Oklahoma City is controlled by reorder points. The inventory system in use is based on the average demand forecasts for the distribution centers in Denver, Omaha, and Phoenix. Currently, there are no orders outstanding within the distribution system. Other pertinent and up-to-date data on the central supply facility and the three distribution centers are given in the table below:

Center	Inventory on Hand[a]	Reorder Point	Order Quantity	Lead Time (weeks)	Forecast (units/wk)
Denver	450	450	1200	2	150
Omaha	300	200	670	2	65
Phoenix	550	500	1300	2	170
OK City	2000	1500	3000	3	—

[a] The amount on hand at the beginning of the current period (week). Note that the amount on hand is currently equal to or greater than the reorder point for each center.

1. (a) Analyze the situation at Marlex for the next few weeks. Assume Marlex continues operating under its reorder point system and the demands for the coming weeks are equal to the forecasts. (In other words, simulate orders and inventory levels at each center for several weeks, using deterministic reorder points.)
   (b) What problems surface, and at what time are they detected?
   (c) Why do these problems arise?
2. (a) Now develop an 8-week DRP plan for each center using the data given. Assume the gross requirements for the three distribution centers are the same as the forecasts. Develop the gross requirements for the central supply facility and the planned order releases for all four facilities using DRP logic.
   (b) What problems are evident?
   (c) What does the DRP plan do that the reorder point system did not?

CASE 2: THE LINK

Selbyco, a manufacturer and distributor of health food products, links its DRP system to its MRP system in order to provide the best service to its nationwide network of customers. Its distribution requirements end at the master production schedule (MPS). That is, the total distribution system demands are fed into the master production scheduling process. All of the supporting manufacturing schedules are based on the MPS.

Assume the following table displays the MPS for 10 oz. bottles of Tonic X:

MASTER PRODUCTION SCHEDULE
10 oz. Tonic X

	PD	1	2	3	4	5	6	7	8
Mast. sched. receipts					1800				
Mast. sched. releases			1800						

Now suppose the next display is the MRP plan for ingredient Z. Selbyco holds the patent on ingredient Z and is the only manufacturer of this item. Selbyco uses ingredient Z in the final mixing stages of Tonic X. Notice that the requirements for ingredient Z come not only from the production of Tonic X but also from the production of other Selbyco products.

MRP PLAN
Units of Ingredient Z

Lead Time 2 weeks

Lot Size 4000	PD	1	2	3	4	5	6	7	8
Gross requirements		0	5000	3000	0	3500	6000	4000	0
Scheduled receipts				4000					
Projected on hand	3000	3000	−2000	3000	3000	3500	1500	1500	1500
Net requirements			2000	1000		500	2500	2500	
Planned order rec.				4000		4000	4000	4000	
Planned order rel.		4000		4000	4000	4000			

MRP is used to plan the component parts and ingredients in a manner similar to that used in DRP to plan and coordinate the products in the distribution system. The scheduled receipts indicate released orders due to arrive at the beginning of the period in which they appear. In the case of the scheduled receipt in period 3, it is a released manufacturing order for ingredient Z.

1. What problem is evident? State a number of possible causes.
2. Give some suitable solutions to this problem, assuming different reasons for its occurrence. Which of these solutions would be most appropriate if the problem tends to recur?

11 Inventory Valuation and Measurement

FLOW OF COSTS
  FIFO
  LIFO
  Average Cost
  Specific Cost

INVENTORY RECORDS
  Periodic Count Method
  Cycle Count Method

INVENTORY SECURITY

QUESTIONS

PROBLEMS

CASES

Inventory has physical and financial characteristics. The physical characteristics (flow of goods) are factual and objective, whereas financial characteristics (flow of costs) are more subjective. The physical and financial attributes usually are separate, distinct, and independent problem areas for an organization. In this section, emphasis will be placed on the financial characteristics associated with the flow of costs.

The financial significance of inventory is attributable to the need for measuring operating performance or income over a particular time period (month, quarter, or year) as well as to the need to measure and analyze an organization's relative financial position. Inventory, in an accounting sense, represents value assigned to goods either acquired or produced for subsequent sale or consumption. Inventory accounts at a particular point in time are a snapshot view of the total value of inventory items either on hand or in process. The valuation of these accounts is used in assessments of present financial conditions and to anticipate future financial conditions. As a corollary, the amounts deducted from inventory accounts during any particular period of time are the basic data for determining the cost of goods sold during the period. Obviously, consistent policies and methods of inventory valuation are imperative for the meaningful measurement of performance between time periods and for the undistorted interpretation of a firm's financial position at any given time.

Inventory costs and expenses will depend on the accounting procedures adopted. Accounting procedures determine when and how a change in assets owned should be recognized, and when and how assets are transformed into costs and expenses. Facts are not altered, but accounting procedures govern the recognition of events which affect periodic income determination and financial ratio analysis.

The primary basis for inventory accounting is cost. The cost for inventory purposes may be determined under any one of several assumptions as to the flow of costs. Material is ordered, not just once, but on a continuing basis. Therefore, organizations have to plan on the same basis. There is no one prescribed procedure to be used in the determination of inventory costs for accounting purposes. There are a number of standard procedures, together with combinations and variations of each. The major objective in selecting a method is to clearly reflect periodic performance. To determine the dollar amount of inventory at any given point in time, the quantity of inventory items on hand must be known and a value must be assigned to those quantities. The quantity of items on hand is obtained by counting or measuring. The value assigned to individual items is based on one of several accounting methods. The accounting method used is very important, since it can significantly affect the total dollar amount of inventory and the related cost of goods sold. Inventory influences performance additionally in that suboptimal inventory policies will reduce income by incurring unnecessary expenses.

The inventory methods for accountability can be subdivided into the method of valuation and the inventory flow method. In most cases, the method of valuation is based on the original cost of the item. There would be no problem if unit costs were constant, but during a period of time, items are frequently purchased or manufactured at different unit costs. This poses a problem, since the items sold must be costed for the income statement (cost of goods sold), and unsold items must be valued for the balance sheet (inventory).

FLOW OF COSTS

The inventory flow method refers to the way items are added to and taken from inventory. The assumed flow for accounting purposes may not be the same as the actual physical flow of goods. The selection of the assumed inventory flow method by management will determine the flow of costs. There are various inventory flow assumptions in practice today, four of which account for more than 90% of current usage. Listed in order of frequency of use (for internal accounting purposes) beginning with the most frequent, they are:

1. FIFO (first in, first out),
2. LIFO (last in, first out),
3. average cost,
4. specific cost.

The above inventory flow methods are primarily concerned with the flow of costs rather than the flow of physical goods. The selection of a flow method will depend upon several factors, including the type of organization, the projected economy, industry practices, the tax rules, and other regulations. Once a flow method is adopted, it is not easy to change to another method because of income tax requirements and accountants' concerns for consistency in reporting to outsiders.

All of the inventory flow methods are simply schemes to carry costs from the balance sheet to the income statement as expenses. The costs allocated do not have to match the actual physical flow of goods. Goods can be sold by physically removing the oldest items first, yet assigning costs according to the last unit produced. The flow of goods does not have to be related in any way to the flow of costs.

FIFO

The most widely used inventory flow method is called FIFO, which stands for "first in, first out." It is assumed that materials are issued from the oldest supply in stock, and units issued are costed at the oldest cost listed on the stock ledger sheets, with materials on hand at all times being the most recent purchases. Under FIFO, the inventory cost is computed on the assumption that goods sold or consumed are those which have been on hand longest and that those remaining in stock represent the latest purchase or production.

FIFO tends to coincide with the actual physical movement of goods through many organizations. It is scrupulously followed for goods that are subject to deterioration and obsolescence. The ending inventory from FIFO closely approximates the actual current value, as the costs assigned to the goods on hand are the most recent. While this technique tends to produce inventory assets at current costs during inflationary periods, it understates the value of cost of goods sold on the income statement. When the price of materials and other costs are subject to change, FIFO is not likely to result in matching costs against revenues on a current basis. Thus, cost changes can create income statement distortions from what would be obtained if current costs were applied.

FIFO is fairly simple and compatible with the operations of many organizations. Inventory records are usually kept on a perpetual or a periodic basis. With perpetual systems, all changes to stock (additions, subtractions, or deletions) are recorded for each incoming or outgoing transaction. With periodic systems, a physical count of stock is made at specific time intervals to determine stock status, and records are kept of the costs associated with each inflow of goods. Costs are then assigned to each outgoing item, with the oldest costs being assigned to units first. FIFO is adaptable to either perpetual or periodic inventory systems. The use of FIFO simplifies record keeping requirements, as the actual flow usually coincides with record keeping activities. A few simple examples can best illustrate the FIFO method.

EXAMPLE 1

The periodic inventory record shown in Table 1 is available on an item. A physical count of the items on 1 April reveals an ending inventory of 300 units. What is the value of the ending inventory? What is the cost of goods sold for the period?

Table 1. Periodic inventory record (FIFO)

Date	Type of Transaction	Units	Unit Price	Total Cost
1 Jan.	Beginning inventory	200	$1.00	$ 200
31 Jan.	Purchase	300	1.10	330
28 Feb.	Purchase	400	1.16	464
31 Mar.	Purchase	100	1.26	126
	Total	1000		$1120

A periodic count reveals that the ending inventory is 300 units.

Units Sold	Unit Price	Total Cost
200	$1.00	$200
300	1.10	330
200	1.16	232
700		$762

Ending Inventory	Units	Unit Price	Total Cost
Feb. Purchases	200	$1.16	$232
Mar. Purchases	100	1.26	126
Total	300		$358

The cost of goods sold with FIFO is $762, and the value of ending inventory is $1120 − $762 = $358 for 300 units.

EXAMPLE 2

From the perpetual inventory record in Table 2, what are the values of the ending inventory and the cost of goods sold?

Table 2. Perpetual inventory record (FIFO)

Date	Received			Issued			Balance		
	Units	Unit Cost	Total Cost	Units	Unit Cost	Total Cost	Units	Unit Cost	Total Cost
1 Jan.							200	$1.00	$200
31 Jan.	300	$1.10	$330				200	1.00	200
							300	1.10	330
3 Feb.				200	$1.00	$200	100	1.10	110
				200	1.10	220			
28 Feb.	400	1.16	464				100	1.10	110
							400	1.16	464
1 Mar.				100	1.10	110	200	1.16	232
				200	1.16	232			
31 Mar.	100	1.26	126				200	1.16	232
							100	1.26	126

The cost of goods sold for the quarter under the perpetual system is $762 ($200 + $220 + $110 + $232), and the value of ending inventory is $358 ($232 + $126) for 300 units.

When preparing a perpetual inventory record, it is essential to carry information concerning each individual transaction separately in the balance column. Note how the perpetual inventory record is more complex and time-consuming than the periodic inventory record. However, FIFO is readily adaptable to either method.

LIFO

LIFO, which stands for "last in, first out," assumes that the most current cost of goods should be charged to the cost of goods sold. Under LIFO, the cost of units remaining in inventory represents the oldest costs available, while the units issued are costed at the latest costs available. The underlying purpose of LIFO is to match current revenues against current costs, so the method charges current revenues with amounts approximating replacement costs.

Like FIFO, LIFO can be used with either perpetual or periodic inventory systems. The following examples are illustrations of the LIFO method.

EXAMPLE 3

The periodic inventory record shown in Table 3 is available on an item. A physical count of the item on 1 April reveals an ending inventory of 300 units. What is the value of the ending inventory? What is the cost of goods sold for the period?

Table 3. Periodic inventory record (LIFO)

Date	Type of Transaction	Units	Unit Price	Total Cost
1 Jan.	Beginning inventory	200	$1.00	$ 200
31 Jan.	Purchase	300	1.10	330
28 Feb.	Purchase	400	1.16	464
31 Mar.	Purchase	100	1.26	126
	Total	1000		$1120

Units Sold	Unit Price	Total Cost
100	$1.26	$126
400	1.16	464
200	1.10	220
700		$810

Ending Inventory	Units	Unit Price	Total Cost
1 Jan. Inventory	200	$1.00	$200
Jan. Purchases	100	1.10	110
Total	300		$310

452   11. Inventory Valuation and Measurement

The cost of goods sold with LIFO is $810, and the value of ending inventory is $310 for 300 units. Note that this same item under FIFO in Example 1 had a cost of goods sold of $762 and an ending inventory of $358.

EXAMPLE 4

From the perpetual inventory record in Table 4, what are the values of the ending inventory and the cost of goods sold?

Table 4. Perpetual inventory record (LIFO)

Date	Received			Issued			Balance		
	Units	Unit Cost	Total Cost	Units	Unit Cost	Total Cost	Units	Unit Cost	Total Cost
1 Jan.							200	$1.00	$200
31 Jan.	300	$1.10	$330				200	1.00	200
							300	1.10	330
3 Feb.				300	$1.10	$330	100	1.00	100
				100	1.00	100			
28 Feb.	400	1.16	464				100	1.00	100
							400	1.16	464
1 Mar.				300	1.16	348	100	1.00	100
							100	1.16	116
31 Mar.	100	1.26	126				100	1.00	100
							100	1.16	116
							100	1.26	126

The cost of goods sold for the quarter under the perpetual system is $778 ($330 + $100 + $348), and the value of ending inventory is $342 ($100 + $116 + $126) for 300 units. Note that this same item under FIFO in Example 2 had a cost of goods sold of $762 and an ending inventory value of $358. It should also be noted that generally differences in the cost of goods sold and ending inventory will arise between a periodic inventory system and a perpetual inventory system when using the LIFO method, in contrast with using the FIFO method.

The importance of matching costs with revenue for the income statement is generally acknowledged. In periods of rapid price change (inflation), a part of the increase in earnings during the upward cycle is attributable to the rise in prices. During an inflationary period, the goods on hand at the beginning of the period will generally be sold at a higher price than contemplated at the time they were purchased. This increase in revenues will be reflected in the income for the period; however, if inventory is maintained at the same quantity levels, the additional revenues received will have been expended to a substantial extent in purchasing the replacement inventory units. Thus, the increase in income, frequently termed "inventory profits," is illusory. LIFO protects against "inventory profits," because its use (as compared to the use of other valuation methods) decreases income during periods of rising prices by assigning a higher cost to goods sold. LIFO provides less benefit to organizations with a high inventory turnover, since their costs already are closely matched to revenues.

LIFO often is preferred during periods of rising prices due to its favorable effect on income taxes and cash on hand. It does not ignore the need of an organization to replenish inventory at higher prices and does not create the "ballooning" effect on apparent income caused by goods costed much lower than actual replacement costs. Despite its desirability with respect to the income statement, some criticize LIFO for its unrealistic valuation of inventory for balance sheet purposes. It is felt that the valuation of inventory units at the oldest cost available distorts the current ratio and the other current asset relationships in assessing the near-term financial position.

Average Cost

In an attempt to provide the elusive perfect combination of a realistic ending inventory and cost of goods sold, the average cost method was developed. This method does not attempt to indicate what unit went out first or last, but rather to determine the average cost for each item during a time period. There are three types of averages that can be used:

1. simple average,
2. weighted average,
3. moving average.

All three averages can be used with a periodic inventory system, but only the moving average is well suited to the perpetual inventory system.

The simple average is determined by dividing the sum of production or purchase unit costs by the number of production runs or orders. The simple average neglects the size of the lot (number of units) and gives the unit production or purchase cost of each lot equal weight. The weighted average corrects the distortion of the simple average by considering quantity as well as unit cost. The weighted average divides the cost of goods available for sale or use by the total number of units available during the period. The moving average computes an average unit cost after each purchase or addition to stock, making it better suited for computerized inventory operations. Since the simple average and the weighted average cannot be calculated until the period is over, they are not well suited to perpetual inventory systems. All of the averages are suitable for periodic inventory systems, since in them costs are not allocated until the end of the period.

With the average cost method, the costs of all like items available during the period are averaged to obtain the ending inventory value. During periods of increasing or decreasing costs, the average cost method tends to damp out the extremes: it responds more gradually than the other inventory flow methods. While the average cost method is simple to apply, it reflects all the limitations of any average figure. The unit cost cannot be equated to any tangible figure, and it does not reveal price changes as clearly as may be desired. The average cost method is shown in the two examples which follow.

EXAMPLE 5

The periodic inventory record shown in Table 5 is available on an item. A physical count of the item on 1 April reveals an ending inventory of 300 units. What are the values of the ending inventory and the cost of goods sold using the (a) simple average, (b) weighted average, and (c) moving average?

a:

$$\text{simple average} = \frac{1.00 + 1.10 + 1.16 + 1.26}{4} = \$1.13 \text{ unit cost,}$$

$$\text{ending inventory value} = (\text{ending inventory})(\text{unit cost}) = 300(1.13) = \$339,$$

$$\text{cost of goods sold} = (\text{units issued})(\text{unit cost}) = 700(1.13) = \$791.$$

b:

$$\text{weighted average} = \frac{\sum\limits_{i=1}^{4} P_i Q_i}{N}$$

$$= \frac{1.00(200) + 1.10(300) + 1.16(400) + 1.26(100)}{1000}$$

$$= \$1.12 \text{ unit cost,}$$

$$\text{ending inventory value} = (\text{ending inventory})(\text{unit cost}) = 300(1.12) = \$336,$$

$$\text{cost of goods sold} = (\text{units issued})(\text{unit cost}) = 700(1.12) = \$784.$$

Table 5. Periodic inventory record

Date	Type of Transaction	Units	Unit Price	Total Cost
1 Jan.	Beginning inventory	200	$1.00	$ 200
31 Jan.	Purchase	300	1.10	330
28 Feb.	Purchase	400	1.16	464
31 Mar.	Purchase	100	1.26	126
	Total	1000		$1120

Table 6

Date	Units	Unit Price	Total Cost	Moving Average
1 Jan.	200	$1.00	$200	$1.00
31 Jan.	300	1.10	330	1.06
28 Feb.	400	1.16	464	1.10
31 Mar.	100	1.26	126	1.12

c: See Table 6. The moving average for each addition to stock is obtained by summing the total cost column and dividing by the number of units. The moving average for the period is the last moving average, which is $1.12. Thus

$$\text{ending inventory value} = (\text{ending inventory})(\text{unit cost})$$
$$= 300(1.12)$$
$$= \$336,$$
$$\text{cost of goods sold} = (\text{units issued})(\text{unit cost})$$
$$= \$700(1.12)$$
$$= \$784.$$

Note how the weighted average and the moving average are true averages that result in the same costs. On the other hand, the simple average results in a slight distortion of costs.

EXAMPLE 6

From the perpetual inventory record in Table 7, what are the ending inventory value and the cost of goods sold for the item?

Table 7. Perpetual inventory record (moving average)

Date	Received			Issued			Balance		
	Units	Unit Cost	Total Cost	Units	Unit Cost	Total Cost	Units	Unit Cost[a]	Total Cost
1 Jan.							200	$1.00	$200
31 Jan.	300	$1.10	$330				500	1.06	530
3 Feb.				400	$1.06	$424	100	1.06	106
28 Feb.	400	1.16	464				500	1.14	570
1 Mar.				300	1.14	342	200	1.14	228
31 Mar.	100	1.26	126				300	1.18	354

[a] The balance unit cost is the moving average which is obtained by dividing the number of units on balance into the balance total cost.

The cost of goods sold is the sum of the total costs for issues, or $766 ($424 + $342). The value of ending inventory is obtained from the final amount in the balance total cost column: $354 for 300 units.

The average cost methods match the average costs of the period against revenue and assign average costs to ending inventory. Characteristically, the values (COGS and ending inventory) derived under the average cost methods will fall between the extreme values found under FIFO and LIFO. These less exaggerated valuations of the average cost methods make them extremely appealing.

Specific Cost

Of all the inventory flow assumptions, the specific cost method provides the most realistic valuation of ending inventory and cost of goods sold. The procedure consists of tagging or numbering each item as it is placed into inventory so its exact cost is readily discernable. Since an item is both valued and expensed at its specific cost, the cost flow and the physical flow are identical with this method. The cost of maintaining records under this method can mount very quickly, so it is most appropriate for goods of significant value which are few in number.

The specific cost method has the added flexibility of being suitable for either perpetual or periodic inventory systems. It is employed frequently in job shops for the valuation of inventory items used in custom-made products. If the number of custom orders being processed is large, its implementation can be extremely expensive and difficult. Thus, its use is more commonly confined to small operations.

Evidently, there are many methods of inventory costing or valuation that may be used by organizations. The method chosen should be practical, reliable, and as easy to apply as possible. As long as unit costs remain the same, all the methods are essentially equivalent. When unit costs change dramatically, major differences among the methods occur. If the inventory turnover is very high, the differences among the methods are diminished. There is no standard recommended practice for inventory costing. The best method depends upon the nature and objectives of the organization.

EXAMPLE 7

An organization that produces a single product has the production and sales record given in Table 8. The following data also are relevant:

Operating expenses	$5000/year
Opening inventory	400 units at $2.00/unit
Tax rate	50%
Inventory method	Periodic
Ending inventory	210 units, all made in November

Determine the net income for the organization under the FIFO, LIFO, average cost (simple and weighted), and specific cost methods.

The results are shown in Table 9.

Table 8

Month	Production Quantity	Production Unit Cost	Production Total Cost	Sales Quantity	Sales Unit Price	Sales Total Revenue
Jan.	600	$2.04	$1,224.00	500	$3.00	$1,500
Feb.	570	2.05	1,168.50	610	3.00	1,830
Mar.	550	2.10	1,155.00	650	3.00	1,950
Apr.	610	2.08	1,268.80	590	3.00	1,770
May	580	2.15	1,247.00	600	3.20	1,920
June	490	2.17	1,063.30	400	3.20	1,280
July	450	2.25	1,012.50	470	3.20	1,504
Aug.	480	2.30	1,104.00	540	3.20	1,728
Sept.	540	2.50	1,350.00	570	3.50	1,995
Oct.	610	2.57	1,567.70	650	3.50	2,275
Nov.	600	2.59	1,554.00	670	3.50	2,345
Dec.	580	2.60	1,508.00	600	3.50	2,100
Total	6660	$27.40	$15,222.80	6850		$22,197

Table 9

Method:	FIFO	LIFO	Average Cost Simple	Average Cost Weighted	Specific Cost
Sales	$22,197	$22,197	$22,197	$22,197	$22,197
Beginning inventory	800	800	800	800	800
Production	15,223	15,223	15,223	15,223	15,223
Goods available for sale	16,023	16,023	16,023	16,023	16,023
Less: ending inventory	546[a]	420[b]	479[c]	480[d]	544[e]
Cost of goods sold	15,477	15,603	15,544	15,543	15,479
Gross income	6,720	6,594	6,653	6,654	6,718
Less: operating expenses	5,000	5,000	5,000	5,000	5,000
Income before taxes	1,720	1,594	1,653	1,654	1,718
Less: income taxes	860	797	827	827	859
Net income	$ 860	$ 797	$ 826	$ 827	$ 859

[a](Number of units)(last-in cost) = (210)($2.60) = $546.

[b](Number of units)(first-in cost) = (210)($2.00) = $420.

[c](Number of units)(cost) = (210)($27.40/12) = $479.

[d](Number of units)(cost) = (210)($15,223)/6660 = $480.

[e](Number of units)(Nov. cost) = (210)($2.59) = $544.

As can be seen, costs were rising. As was previously stated, during a period of rising costs, the LIFO method will result in a higher cost of goods sold and therefore lower profit and taxes than the FIFO method. It is important to note, however, that just the opposite holds true in a period of falling prices. The amounts used in this example did not result in a significant difference between the simple and weighted average computations, but it is important to note the difference in the method of calculation.

No two methods result in exactly the same ending inventory dollar value. If the example were multipled by 1000, the dollar difference that could result from the use of the various methods might be appreciable. Fluctuations in the example are generally upward; should any other significant fluctuations take place during the period, the differences could be changed significantly. Thus, the manager needs to know what inventory flow method is in use and what its impact on performance will be.

INVENTORY RECORDS

No inventory system will work efficiently unless records are accurate. All decisions on when or how much to order are based on the inventory balance of individual items. If the inventory balance is overstated, there is a risk of stockouts. If the inventory balance is understated, there will most likely be excess inventory accumulated. Inaccurate inventory records trigger a chain reaction of problems: lost sales, shortages, missed schedules, low productivity, late delivery, excessive expediting, premium freight costs, and so on. To overcome some of these problems, organizations frequently order more than needed, creating excess inventory and high obsolescence.

Appropriate control of inventory items and record-keeping accuracy require a periodic verification of items and records. Inventory items should be classified and properly identified so they can be located for verification. This means that proper control over inventory must also include the methods of storage and handling. Control is necessary to ensure against errors in item status, such as inaccurate counts and items lost to embezzlement, damage, spoilage, and obsolescence. Control usually is accomplished through a series of inventory records and reports that provide information on usage, balances, and receipts. It is desirable for record verifications and physical counts to be conducted by an independent agency with no interest of its own in the operations.

Some of the basic data required to keep meaningful and useful inventory records are as follows:

1. item identification and/or classification,
2. item location(s),
3. unit costs and net prices,
4. interchangeable and/or substitute items,
5. shelf life,
6. end item (what it is used on or with),
7. dates item entered inventory,
8. dates of withdrawal,
9. supply sources,
10. unit balance.

Accurate inventory records are an important aspect of financial accounting as well as a cornerstone of inventory control. The foundation of any inventory control system is the information contained in records upon which decisions are made. Without record accuracy, the best-designed system is destined for major problems if not failure.

Albeit every inventory system must be concerned with inventory record accuracy, it is not uncommon for more attention to be given to the more interesting technical aspects of a system while overlooking the tedious aspects of inventory record accuracy. Whether the system is manual or computerized, record accuracy is critical to operations. Three certain requirements for accurate inventory records are:

1. a good system for recording all receipts and disbursements,
2. a good system for auditing record accuracy that discovers and corrects the causes of errors,
3. trustworthy, responsible personnel.

The condition of inventory records is influenced by the personnel involved, the physical control, and the system. The *personnel involved* are the people who physically receive, issue, and store material as well as the first line of supervision of these people. The stockroom supervisors must accept responsibility for and take pride in maintaining record accuracy. Without their full support, their subordinates cannot be expected to strive fully for record integrity. Operatives must be instructed and trained in stockroom operating procedures so they recognize the importance of accuracy. It is desirable to set accuracy goals, measure accuracy, and post records of performance in comparison with goals.

An important aspect of *physical control* is to limit and control access to the storeroom. Each time a part is added to the stockroom or withdrawn from it, the transaction should be logged in the appropriate record. Unauthorized and undocumented transactions must be stopped or control is virtually impossible. An enclosed and locked storeroom with access only to authorized personnel can do much to control undocumented transactions. It is desirable for all parts to be identified by part number and geographical location in the storeroom. A clean and well-ordered storage area will reduce lost and misplaced items.

An efficient way to utilize space in the stockroom is to use a locator system. The stockroom is divided into sections and subsections with an appropriate numbering scheme. Parts are stored in the same location or in an available section, with the location noted on the receipt card along with the part number. As part issues are required, the warehouseman proceeds to the designated location of the part. A well-devised locator system can contribute much to data integrity.

Fixed locations, random location, and zoned locations can be used to store inventory items. With *fixed locations*, each item is permanently assigned a specific, single location (space). This minimizes problems in finding items but can lead to inefficient space utilization. With *random location*, items do not have a specific location but are assigned to the easiest open space, and the same item may be stored in more than one location. While space is utilized more efficiently, the location of an item must be updated with each transaction (receipt or withdrawal). Naturally, this method of location involves exact records and careful reporting of stock location. *Zoned locations* are a hybrid of fixed and random locations. A grouping of similar items is assigned to a designated zone. An item is located anywhere in the space available within the given zone. Space is used more efficiently, and each item has a general but not a specific location.

A physical count of items is necessary to verify the integrity and accuracy of inventory records. Differences between book (record) and physical inventories must be ascertained. Any differences (variances) must be adjusted and the amount of overage or underage properly accounted for. A periodic physical count of inventory can be made for all items, or a cycle count program can be instituted. A physical count of all items usually involves closing the facility for a time while the quantities of all items are substantiated and the records are updated. The cycle count method involves the continuous counting of inventory throughout the year.

Thus, inventory accuracy is a fundamental requirement of any inventory system. True record integrity requires a management policy intolerant of errors. Management must establish a climate of accuracy and the necessary tools for its achievement.

Periodic Count Method

The periodic count method refers to the periodic auditing of the inventory balances on hand to verify and maintain accurate inventory records. The inventory record may be manually posted, machine posted, or maintained by a computer. The periodic count method requires a complete count of all categories of inventory over a short time period. For most organizations, an annual or semiannual verification is adequate. If only one physical inventory is taken in a year, it must be at the end of the fiscal year and is usually timed to coincide with the yearly low point in production and inventory levels.

Taking an annual physical inventory is like selecting a marriage partner: the time spent in preparation can pay off handsomely in the final results. A written standard procedure should be prepared that can also serve as a training document. Preparation for the physical inventory should involve the following:

1. *Housekeeping.* The arrangement of material in its proper location so it can be easily inventoried.

2. *Identification.* The proper identification of all items with part number and nomenclature.
3. *Instruction.* Review of inventory-taking forms and procedures with personnel prior to taking inventory.
4. *Training.* Instruction of appropriate personnel in the use of scales, counters, and measurement procedures.
5. *Teams.* The establishment of inventory teams of two or more members and the assignment of responsibility for counting, checking, and recording the inventory levels.

On the day of the count, operations in the storage areas should be terminated. A holding area should be designated to retain all material received during the actual counting period so it is excluded from the count. All items sold, but not yet shipped, should be segregated and not counted on the loading dock. All internal movements and shipments should be suspended for the duration except for emergencies. If the physical count will require several days, customers should be advised of the shutdown dates.

The tag method of recording inventory levels is universally used. The inventory teams will take the count, one fills out the tags and places them on the materials, and the other re-counts and checks the accuracy of the tags (amount as well as part number). The tags are used for both manual and computer systems. When an area has been completed by an inventory team, it should be checked to ensure that all items are tagged (spot checked for accuracy), and then the tags are collected. Items in the shipping dock not yet sold, as well as those in the export holding area, returned goods area, marketing displays, and so forth, should also be included in the count.

The inventory records and the physical inventory should be reconciled with the inventory tags. The inventory data from the tags are transferred to inventory summary sheets. An auditing team should check any significant variations and reconcile discrepancies before materials start to move again. Appropriate adjustments should be made to inventory records and to general ledgers so that the record balance agrees with the quantity actually on hand.

The frequency of physical inventory is often determined by the value of the item and the ease of disposing of the item in the open market. Expensive or precious items may be inventoried much more frequently than general inventory items.

Cycle Count Method

Cycle counting is a physical inventory-taking technique performed continuously rather than periodically. It is a basic step toward controlling the accuracy of inventory records and maintaining it at a high level. Major profit improvements can be achieved by effective cycle counting through a reduction in production disruptions, improved customer service, reduced obsolescence, elimination of the annual physical inventory, and less inventory shrinkage. Frequently, the cycle count method is less expensive than the disruptive periodic count method.

The goals of cycle counting are to (1) identify the causes of errors, (2) correct the conditions causing the errors, (3) maintain a high level of inventory record accuracy, and (4) provide a correct statement of assets. Historically, organizations conducted an annual physical inventory (periodic count) to attest to the dollar accuracy of the inventory as an asset on the balance sheet. This was usually required by the accounting profession in its audit of the annual financial statements for external reporting purposes. The primary objective of cycle counting is accurate inventory records for internal purposes of operating the organization. The primary emphasis is not dollar accuracy but piece count accuracy.

This method involves a continuous counting of stock throughout the year. A limited number of items are checked every day, or at some other time interval. Personnel can be assigned to cycle count on a full-time or part-time basis. The stock items to be checked may be selected at random or according to a predetermined plan. The cycle count method does not require a disruptive termination of operations as is required with the periodic count method.

The cycle count method is becoming more widely used by organizations. It permits the use of specialists or regularly assigned stores personnel to conduct the physical count. When regularly assigned personnel are used, they can perform the cycle count during lulls in their assigned duties; when specialists are used, they are full-time personnel who continually count inventory items. In large organizations specialists are desirable, since they become familiar with items, the locator system, the storage system, and "peculiar" things that can occur.

The cycle count tests the condition of inventory records and provides a measure of record accuracy. Record accuracy can be measured by the percentage of items in error and the relative magnitude of the errors. The significance of the error relates to the relative value of the item. An error of one unit for an expensive item is significant, while an error of plus or minus 2% might be acceptable for low cost items.

Cycle counting can prioritize concentration on the integrity of inventory items with high annual dollar usage (*ABC* principle). The "*A*" items (highest annual usage items) should be counted most frequently, "*C*" items least frequently. "*A*" items might be counted every one or two months, "*B*" items every three or four months, and "*C*" items every year. Since "*C*" items may represent the bulk of the inventory, but a small percentage of investment, less effort is expended on them. Each organization must establish a cycle count based on its own peculiarities.

Several procedures have been developed to vary the cycle count frequency. Some of the more prevalent systems are as follows:

1. *ABC system.* The stratification of items based on the *ABC* principle with the highest frequency on "*A*" items and the lowest on "*C*" items.
2. *Reorder system.* The counting of items at the time of reorder.
3. *Receiver system.* The counting of items when a replenishment order is received.
4. *Zero balance system.* The counting of items when the balance on hand is zero or negative (backorder).
5. *Transaction system.* The counting of items after a specific number of transactions have transpired.

Of course, various combinations of the above systems can also be used.

The reorder system, receiver system, and zero balance system have "trigger rules," such as count when an order is placed, count when a replenishment order is received, or count when the item balance is zero. If the item balance is low, the accuracy of the count should be high. If the count is taken when an item stocks out, the accuracy should be greatest; however, with a high safety stock (service level), the count may not be taken often enough. Including the count in either the requisitioning or receiving process means the average number of counts will equal the average inventory turnover.

With cycle counting only a small portion of the total stock is being investigated at a given time. This reduces the magnitude of the problem substantially. Each day's count can be reconciled without delay. Cycle counts can be established so that all inventory items are counted at least once during a year, or on a statistical sampling basis. With statistical procedures, a random sample of items in a given category is counted, and the results are generalized to the population of items.

The procedure for determining the average number of items to count per day with an *ABC* analysis is relatively simple. A cycle is the time required to count all items in inventory at least once, and it is often a year. The count frequency is the number of times an item is counted in each cycle. For example, *A* items might be counted monthly, *B* items quarterly, and *C* items annually.

$$\text{Items counted/day} = \frac{\Sigma(\text{number of items in a class})(\text{count frequency})}{\text{number of days per cycle}}$$

EXAMPLE 8

A supplier has 5000 items in stock of which 500 are class *A*, 1000 are class *B*, and 3500 are class *C*. There are 300 operating days per year, and the respective count frequencies for the classes are 5, 2, and 1 times per year. How many items should be cycle counted each day?

Solution:

The following table determines the total number of annual counts:

Class	Number of Items	Count Frequency	Total Annual Counts
A	500	5	2500
B	1000	2	2000
C	3500	1	3500
			8000

$$\text{Items counted/day} = \frac{\text{total annual counts}}{\text{number of days/year}}$$

$$= \frac{8000}{300} = 26.67 \text{ or } 27.$$

Approximately 27 items should be counted each day.

The cycle count method is an excellent method for maintaining the accuracy of records. Some of the more apparent advantages are as follows:

1. Operations do not have to be terminated during the cycle count, and the annual physical inventory is eliminated.
2. Errors are discovered quickly, inventory records adjusted throughout the year, and the cause of errors eliminated.
3. Record accuracy improves, and a more correct statement of assets results. Inventory counts are not performed under pressure, resulting in more accurate measurements. Year-end inventory write-offs can be eliminated, and a correct statement of assets be obtained throughout the year.
4. Specialists become efficient in obtaining good counts, reconciling differences, and finding solutions to systematic errors.
5. Efforts are concentrated in problem areas.

INVENTORY SECURITY

Security requirements vary widely among organizations and are dependent upon the nature of the material, its value, size, weight, application, utility, and resaleability. Generally, the more valuable an item, the greater the need for security. However, some expensive items require relatively little protection because of their size, weight, and limited utility (large castings, special molds).

Materials can be safeguarded by establishing and enforcing storeroom regulations. A periodic auditing of storeroom operations can reveal existing or potential security problems. The following measures should apply to storeroom operations:

1. Limit access to storage areas to authorized personnel.
2. Count, weigh, or measure all materials on receipt.
3. Require authorized orders and requisitions for all transactions.
4. Store valuable items in locked cabinets or in safes if necessary.
5. Keep storerooms locked and enclosed except during working hours.
6. Periodically spot-check stock on hand against inventory records.
7. Investigate unusual consumption for improper use.
8. Periodically check the authenticity of signatures and authorizations.
9. Provide security bonds for storeroom personnel to protect against losses through negligence or theft.

The effort, time, and money spent on the security of inventory should be allocated among the items in proportion to their relative importance. At no time should the cost of security exceed the benefits that accrue from it.

QUESTIONS

1. What is the financial significance of inventory valuation?
2. Upon what factors does the selection of an inventory flow method depend?
3. Which valuation method is most suitable for goods that are subject to deterioration and obsolescence? Why?
4. Give the primary disadvantage of the FIFO inventory flow method.
5. How does the LIFO inventory flow method protect against "inventory profits"?
6. According to some critics, what is recognized as a weakness of the LIFO method?
7. Name three types of averages that can be used in the average cost inventory flow method. To which types of inventory systems does each apply?
8. State the limitations of the average cost inventory flow method.
9. Describe the most appropriate situation for the application of the specific cost inventory flow method.
10. Under what conditions are the four inventory flow methods essentially equivalent?
11. List three requirements for maintaining accurate inventory records.
12. Differentiate between the periodic count and cycle count methods of taking a physical inventory count.
13. Describe some of the procedures which have been developed to vary the cycle count frequency.

PROBLEMS

1. At the end of football season, Big Red Sports Supply conducted a physical count of footballs. An ending inventory of 15 footballs was indicated. During the season the inventory reports revealed the following data:

	Quantity	Unit Cost	Total Cost
Beginning Inventory	50	$30.00	$1,500.00
1st receipt	10	31.00	310.00
2nd receipt	25	31.50	787.50
3rd receipt	30	32.00	960.00
4th receipt	20	33.00	660.00
Total	135		$4,217.50

   If FIFO is used, what is the value of cost of goods sold for Big Red Sports Supply? What is the value of the ending inventory?

2. What would be the value of cost of goods sold and ending inventory in Problem 1 if the simple average method were used?

3. What would be the value of cost of goods sold and ending inventory in Problem 1 if the weighted average method were used?

4. What would be the value of cost of goods sold and ending inventory in Problem 1 if the LIFO method were used?

5. Using the answers obtained in Problems 1–4, which method would you use during a period of rising costs if you were concerned with taxes? If you were concerned with maximizing profits?

6. Sheep farmer Smith uses a perpetual inventory system to keep track of his sheep as he buys and sells them at the stockyards. Below is a table of the sales and purchases of sheep for the month of May. (Assume no loss of herd to wolves.) What would be the value of cost of goods sold and ending inventory, utilizing the FIFO method?

Date	Sheep Purchased	Unit Price	Sheep Sold	Unit Balance
1				100[a]
4	200	$110.00		300
10			175	125
12	250	120.00		375
19			275	100
21	100	125.00		200
22			50	150
27			100	50
31	150	130.00		200

[a]At $100.00.

7. From the issues and receipts data in Problem 6, develop a perpetual inventory record on the LIFO basis for the month of May. What would be the value of cost of goods sold and ending inventory for the month of May?

8. The Irwin Manufacturing Corporation maintains a periodic inventory system. A physical count of one of its products indicated an ending inventory of 650 units. During the time interval, the inventory card revealed the following data:

	Quantity	Unit Cost	Total Cost
Beginning inventory	1200	$14.00	$16,800
1st receipt	800	15.50	12,400
2nd receipt	950	15.60	14,820
3rd receipt	900	15.80	14,220
4th receipt	1100	17.00	18,700
Total	4950		$76,940

If the FIFO method is used, what is the value of the ending inventory? What is the cost of goods sold for the product?

9. What would be the ending inventory value in Problem 8 if the LIFO method were used? What would be the cost of goods sold for the product?

10. The issues and receipts on an item for the month of October are shown in the table. Develop a perpetual inventory record on the FIFO basis for the month of October. What is the value of the ending inventory? What is the cost of goods sold?

Date	Unit Receipts	Unit Cost	Unit Issues	Unit Balance
1				50[a]
2	400	$2.60		450
8			375	75
9	50	2.80		125
11	175	2.85		300
20			255	45
25	75	2.95		120
31			50	70

[a]At $2.50.

11. From the issues and receipts data in Problem 10, develop a perpetual inventory record on the LIFO basis for the month of October. What is the value of the ending inventory? What is the cost of goods sold?

12. L and S Imports sells custom made sports cars to the elite of Nichols Hills. Because of the high unit cost, a small number are kept in inventory. Which inventory method should be used?

Receipt Date	Item	Unit Cost
5	Car #12345	$35,000
10	Car #12350	40,000
15	Car #12355	63,000
20	Car #12360	22,000
25	Car #12365	51,000
30	Car #12370	49,000
		$260,000

On the 16th, car #12355 was sold, and on the 29th, car #12365 was sold. Given your answer above, determine the value of the cost of goods sold and the ending inventory for the company.

CASE 1: LOOSE SECURITY AND EMPLOYEE THEFT

The Westside Automotive Company repairs automobiles and sells related parts and equipment. The owner, Bill Westside, recently read an article in a newspaper about employee theft. He decided to conduct a study to see if Westside had a theft problem. Bill was shocked when he discovered a substantial amount of money was being lost due to theft. He immediately began a program to tighten control.

Part of the new control procedure was to spot check employees' vehicles as they left work for the day. When the contents of one mechanic's pickup truck were examined, ten boxes of spark plugs, ten sets of points, three distributor caps, and two sets of new spark plug wires were discovered. Further investigation revealed that Bob Gavin, the mechanic, was operating a small repair shop in his garage with parts and equipment stolen from Westside.

Because Gavin had been with the company 15 years and was one of the best mechanics in the area, the company decided to handle the matter internally, instead of reporting it to local authorities. Gavin was asked to appear before a group of three people: Bill Westside; John Stephens, a union representative; and Alan Jones, the personnel manager. Gavin's only defense was that everybody took parts and supplies from the company quite frequently. A thorough investigation found this to be correct. The company accountant estimated that about $6000 in supplies and equipment had been stolen within the last 12 months.

After considering all the factors and implications of the situation, the personnel manager recommended that Gavin be fired. This, he claimed, would set an example for the other employees. John Stephens argued against firing Gavin. He contended that, through lax control procedures, Westside actually encouraged theft. He also argued that since theft was so widespread, it would be unfair to single out Bob Gavin. Bill Westside was very concerned about losing his best mechanic.

1. What action would you recommend against Gavin? Why?
2. Could the situation have been prevented? How?
3. Is this type of theft common in organizations?
4. What security precautions would you implement for the company?

CASE 2: A NEW NEIGHBOR

Harold Hosiner is the director of material for Conforma Foams Inc., a producer of styrofoam forms used in floral and holiday decorations. Harold's neighbor is Gerry Burns, a junior executive with a local accounting and auditing organization. Gerry recently moved to the area, so, to get acquainted, Harold invited him to his next backyard cookout.

At the cookout Harold and Gerry began to talk shop. Gerry was enthusiastic about his last two assignments, auditing a small plumbing distributor and a producer of eyeglass frames. Gerry's most interesting comments concerned inventory valuations:

"From what I have seen in the past few weeks, I see no reason why all businesses don't switch to LIFO. The profits realized by our clients more than pay for our services. With the economy the way it is today, we are recommending LIFO across the board."

Since Conforma was not using LIFO, Harold had some questions, but the hamburgers had to be turned and Gerry began to mingle with other guests.

The next morning Harold sat in his office pondering the conversation of last evening. He knew Gerry's firm had a good reputation, and he thought Gerry was an intelligent young man. Could a switch in inventory valuation policy improve Conforma's profit picture? Was Gerry's experience applicable to Conforma? Harold began to analyze these questions when he received a call from the director of finance. This would be an excellent opportunity to begin discussions on the feasibility of moving to LIFO.

1. Do you agree with Gerry Burns's comments on LIFO?
2. What advice would you offer to Harold Hosiner?

CASE 3: EVAPORATION OR SHRINKAGE

E. G. Truck Rental is a large national truck leasing and rental company. Although located primarily in the northeastern United States, it has districts in every state except Alaska and Hawaii. For the last ten years E. G. has maintained an edge over its competition by providing better service to its customers. One key aspect of this better service is always being able to supply its long-term lease customers with fuel. E. G. guarantees lease customers that none of their vehicles will sit idle during any fuel shortage.

Prior to a major fuel crisis E. G. purchased all its diesel and gasoline fuel from one major supplier. Fuel was delivered in drops of either 6500 or 8500 gallons. Deliveries were made on a regular basis (usually three times per week), and underground fuel tanks were checked daily. Dipstick readings were recorded and compared weekly against inventory records kept by the office personnel. Pricing of the fuel inventory was also done by office personnel and was a fairly routine task when the price of diesel and gasoline fuel was stable.

When the fuel shortage hit its peak, E. G.'s major fuel supplier refused to fulfill its commitment and supply all the fuel needed. In an attempt to keep its promise to its long-term lease customers, E. G. purchased fuel from several national and local suppliers. Deliveries were made at all hours of the day and night, including weekends. Although dipstick readings of E. G.'s underground fuel tanks were still taken daily, it became very difficult to match the inventory records maintained by the office personnel to the actual gallons of fuel received. Also, some small local suppliers actually pumped fewer gallons of fuel into the underground tank than they billed for.

Due to the fuel shortage the price of diesel and gasoline fuel began to fluctuate by as much as twenty cents per gallon. Many suppliers sent duplicate billings to E. G.'s home office in New Jersey requesting payment, even though they had already billed the location to which the fuel was delivered. In a six month period, approximately 15,000 gallons of fuel were unaccounted for or stolen.

1. How could the fuel shrinkage have been prevented?
2. During times of rising prices what inventory flow method is desirable?
3. Will the shrinkage influence the dollar value of inventory?

CASE 4: HOLDING GAINS

Sara O'Keefe is becoming furious about the understatement of inventory prices on her company's balance sheet. The balance sheet presentation of Vladimar China Company is becoming meaningless under the company adopted LIFO inventory-costing method. Initially, Sara agreed that her accountant's arguments to adopt LIFO had appeal—the influencing of net income and the aftereffect on income tax expense. However, hindsight is causing some disagreement with the decision. The fundamental reason for acceptance of the method is being discounted as Sara begins to stress LIFO's inability to reflect current prices on the balance sheet.

Vladimar is a growth firm that produces and sells fine quality china and glassware in the United States and also exports 25% of its production to northern European countries. The inventory accounts are growing yearly due to steady expansion and to company policies of maintaining considerable safety stock levels of raw materials. Coincidental with the total dollar value increase in inventory is an enlarging undervaluation of the current asset. Sara is blaming unexpectedly fast inflation. At various stages of growth Vladimar has encountered cost problems.

Secondary to the strictly inflationary effects on the inventory accounts is the effect of the stock of obsolete items in the finished goods inventory. Vladimar is carrying large stocks of goods from discontinued lines. These goods are withdrawn to fill replacement orders, but their existence and relative market value make the inventory portion of the balance sheet even more suspect.

A further complication is the distrust between management and stockholders. The major shareholders are unanimously of the opinion that management is manipulating net income so as to decrease distributable earnings. Part of this conspiracy, they feel, is finagling the cost of goods sold. They also are suspicious of the net decrease in income from foreign sales and openly dispute with management that it is attributable to devaluation of the dollar.

Since these problems have arisen, Sara is contemplating a change of technique for valuing inventory. For financial purposes, Sara recognizes that the Internal Revenue Code accepts the LIFO method almost without qualification. Sara's conversations with IRS agents have shown that the agency would not allow an inventory method based on replacement costs for reporting purposes but would allow this method for internal use. Sara knows her company would have to undergo federal red tape to make an inventory valuation change, and in practice it could only be done once.

Even with this information, Sara is asking her accountant to check the ramifications of reversing the LIFO decision. Sara wants to adopt a generally accepted accounting practice that is more conservative. She feels if the company would switch to FIFO, the balance sheet would reflect current prices, but there would be a poorer job of matching current costs with revenues on the income statement. Because she wants both a realistic current asset account and a theoretically close match between costs and revenues, she suggests the firm might look either to an average cost method or a specific cost method. In her investigation, Sara does not want to neglect implementation problems.

1. Do the stockholders have cause for complaint concerning dividend payouts?
2. Given Vladimar's present economic environment, would the inventory costing methods give dramatically different financial pictures? How would a large increase in sales change the financial picture?
3. What are the pros and cons of switching to alternative valuation methods?
4. What qualitative factors could impinge upon the choice?

CASE 5: PICKARD MOTOR COMPANY

The Louisville Assembly Plant of the Pickard Motor Company is the site of the "Launch Program" for the newly engineered S-cars. The Louisville plant has been chosen to build these energy efficient compacts because of superior quality control records and a location central to suppliers and support facilities. Louisville is producing the S-car line three months prior to scheduled production in two other plants and is responsible for finalizing engineering and production aspects of the most massive engineering change the motor company has experienced in ten years.

In executing the Launch Program, one of the most complicated tasks is stocking the new parts inventory. Ordering and delivery of parts for the S-line are naturally more complex than in ordinary model year changes. Inventory building has engaged the staff for almost two months and is now at its height. So far the most annoying problem has been expediting of parts orders, and the most costly has been payment of premium freight costs for company and privately chartered aircraft to deliver critical and substitution parts. Because of the fury in the Parts Control and Traffic Departments, morale is low, and tension is building.

Similar to the agitation in the inventory offices is the frenzy at the receiving docks. New parts are being delivered by truck, railcar, and aircraft. Extra personnel have been hired and borrowed from other assembly sites to ease the hurried receipt and check-in of parts. Even with the additional personnel, the work pace seems to be the quickest in five years. The beleaguered receivers are starting to show signs of inability to cope with the burgeoning workload. They are complaining about the demanding task of deciphering bills of lading and packing slips. Because there is no universal standard for packing slips, the receivers are often confused about part numbers, indicated quantities, and other printed information. In this turmoil, they are disregarding mandatory routines for receipt of goods, and in keeping with the nonstandardization of incoming documents, are themselves using dissimilar markings and exception symbols.

From the receiving station the packing slips are input by punched cards to the computerized MRP system. The keypunchers assume the roles of major transcribers of the inventory data. Due to the current confusion over the receiving documents, they are openly dubious about record accuracy. Given this situation, they have come to rely on the Engineering Specifications and Inventory Audit Department to detect and correct inventory errors.

Spec and Audit has the critical job of ultimate verification of inventory data. Each day they receive and audit computerized inventory error lists that are output from a programmed system designed to detect inventory input discrepancies, e.g., duplicate inputs, quantities varying from invoiced quantities, etc. They have every record at their disposal, but in this situation, they must rely on the packing slips that are forwarded from the keypunchers. At the time of error recognition and subsequent verification, an authorized audit person may input the necessary information and/or back out erroneous input that was previously entered. Any audit person can enter information into the system. Thus far, the entire department has held the confidence of upper management because of its past performance in overseeing enormous amounts of inventory data.

In an attempt to gain more control over an inordinately large influx of materials, the audit staff has temporarily changed the cycle count procedure. Because they suspect a high error rate, the number of full-time cycle counters has been increased. The incoming parts are counted more frequently, albeit not more thoroughly. The new cycle counters are working under the direction of the more qualified counters, which has resulted in greater supervision but less physical counting by expert personnel. In addition, there is some rechecking of questionable counts, not to affix blame, but to identify gross errors and to evaluate personnel.

The most spectacular part of the Launch is the presence and participation of the engineers from the home office. The large, imported staff of 200 is remaking, redesigning, and substituting parts almost daily. The inventory personnel are working nearly full time keeping track of the part substitutions and the paperwork associated with both the permanent and temporary changes. The greatest havoc is keeping track of part numbering and inputting the revised information into the computer so that the system can function properly.

Amid all the commotion, production has just begun and already is plagued with shortages, poor productivity, and rescheduling. The production supervisor wants to issue a general statement to vindicate himself. He wants it known from the beginning that he is not responsible for a "cripple" rate of 1 out of 3 cars produced. He intends to shift the blame to two culprits—the inadequate inventory system and the new hires in the Launch.

1. What inventory problems are resulting from the Launch?
2. What could be causing the production problems?
3. What improvements could be made?

12 Simulation

SIMULATION CATEGORIES

MONTE CARLO SIMULATION

PERPETUAL INVENTORY SIMULATION PROBLEM

PERIODIC INVENTORY SIMULATION PROBLEM

SIMULATION OF JOINT PROBABILITY DISTRIBUTIONS

LENGTH OF SIMULATION RUN

CONCLUSION
QUESTIONS
PROBLEMS
CASES
MATHEMATICAL ABBREVIATIONS AND SYMBOLS

Management decision approaches embody many effective means of evaluating alternatives. Possessing various degrees of reliability, acceptable approaches may range from pure intuition and judgment to experimentation with real systems and include experience and analogy with similar situations, analysis with the aid of analytical models, and experimentation with a model of a real system. The simulation of different phases of an operation is associated with the last approach. Typically, a simulation study manipulates a model of a real system for the purpose of evaluating alternative design characteristics or decision rules. Through a systematic trial-and-error method, simulation solves complex problems by changing the key variables in its formulation of a real system. It imitates the behavior of a real system as it responds to an assumed situation over time, until it reaches a satisfactory solution to the problem under study.

Simulation makes available an experimental laboratory for the manager by permitting him to test various alternatives without risking or committing organizational resources. The effects of numerous alternative policies can be ascertained without tampering with the actual system. This form of system experimentation can reduce the risk of upsetting the existing structure with changes that would not be beneficial. Simulation gives the manager an opportunity to test and evaluate proposals without running the risk of actually installing new approaches and absorbing the costs associated with the changes. With simulation, "trial-and-error" need not become "trial-and-catastrophe."

A simulation model does not produce an optimum solution. The manager selects the alternatives to evaluate by simulation, but is not sure that the best alternative has been included. The simulation indicates possible solutions based only on the input of alternatives selected by the manager; it does not indicate which alternatives to evaluate. Simulation models usually develop heuristic rather than analytical solutions to a problem, but they can deal with very complex situations that defy solution by analytical methods.

No analytical solution can be extricated from its premises and assumptions. Simulation can investigate the effect of a relaxation of assumptions. When problems involve risk or uncertainty, an analytical solution may be difficult or impossible to obtain. Simulation is also useful in situations where analytical solutions are not appropriate because the models are either too complex or too costly. A mathematical model using the analytical approach can become incredibly complex because of numerous interacting variables. Simulation offers an alternative. Its ability to handle dependent variable interactions renders it a very powerful tool of systems analysis.

Simulation is used to reproduce a typical series of events (usually in mathematical form) which could have occurred in practice. If enough events are simulated and mean values determined, it can be assumed that they represent what would probably have happened in practice if the real situation existed.

Initial transient phenomena such as oscillations, rapid growth, and sudden decay are not unusual in simulation (or in reality). If system stability is desired, a sufficient startup period should be allowed for stability to develop. In real life such transient phenomena are commonplace occurrences. Whereas analytical methods are usually based on steady state conditions, simulation need not be limited by these assumptions.

The use of simulation techniques would not be very feasible if it were not for the availability of computing equipment. While the design of many simulation models is not very complicated and does not involve a large amount of advanced mathematics, a large number of variables and equations is not uncommon. Thousands of simple manipulations and computations are usually required for each simulation, and the arithmetic operations are usually too numerous for hand computation. With the aid of the computer, simulation has become an important tool to the manager because it allows the manipulation of many variables and constants associated with a problem in an artificial environment.

SIMULATION CATEGORIES

Simulation models can be classified into two basic types—deterministic and probabilistic. Deterministic models have properties that can be stated explicitly and use the expected values of variables as model inputs. The classical approach to dynamic systems is deterministic: it does not include probability distributions, its variables must be continuous, and the relationships among the variables must be stable over time. Equations are the modeling framework for the classical approach. Probabilistic models have key variables defined by probability distributions and not expected values. In these models, variables need not be continuous, and relationships can vary with time. While it is not uncommon for management simulation games to be deterministic, business situations in the real world usually are probabilistic.

EXAMPLE 1

A supply attendant at a tool crib distributes hand tools to mechanics. It takes him exactly 3 minutes to serve each mechanic. Simulate 15 minutes (10:00 to 10:15) of toolroom operation if the mechanics arrive at 10:00, 10:01, 10:04, 10:10, and 10:15. At any given time, indicate the idle time of the attendant, the waiting time of the mechanic, and the number of mechanics in the queue.

Table 1 develops the relevant information. The attendant is idle $\frac{3}{15}$ or 20% of the time.

Table 1

Arrival Time of Mechanics	Service Begins at	Service Ends at	Idle Time of Attendant	Waiting Time of Mechanics	No. of Mechanics in Queue
10:00	10:00	10:03	0	0	0
10:01	10:03	10:06	0	2	1
10:04	10:06	10:09	1	2	1
10:10	10:10	10:13	2	0	0
10:15	10:15	10:18	0	0	0
			$\overline{3}$	$\overline{4}$	

MONTE CARLO SIMULATION

Monte Carlo simulation is a probabilistic type of simulation that approximates the solution to a problem by sampling from a random process. It involves determining the probability distributions of the variables under study and then randomly sampling from the distributions to obtain data. A series of random numbers is used to describe the movement of each random variable over time and allows an artificial but realistic sequence of events to occur. Monte Carlo simulation permits the manager to determine how varied policies or organizational conditions will be modified by the behavior of random or transient influences. A general approach to solving problems by Monte Carlo simulation is given in Figure 1.

Monte Carlo simulation establishes a stochastic model of a real situation and then performs sampling experiments on the model. This technique generates a vast number of data that might otherwise take a very long time period to obtain. Following the generation of data, analytical computations can be made and then a problem solution derived.

The major steps in Monte Carlo simulation are as follows:

1. Define the known probability distributions of certain key variables. They may be standard distributions such as the Poisson, normal, or exponential, or they may be empirical distributions obtained from historical records.
2. Convert the frequency distributions to cumulative probability distributions. This assures that only one variable value will be associated with a given random number.
3. Sample at random from the cumulative probability distributions to determine specific variable values to use in the simulation. A way to sample is to use numbers from a table of random numbers. The random numbers are inserted in the cumulative probability distributions to obtain specific variable values for each observation. The sequence of assigned random numbers will imitate the pattern of variation expected to be encountered.

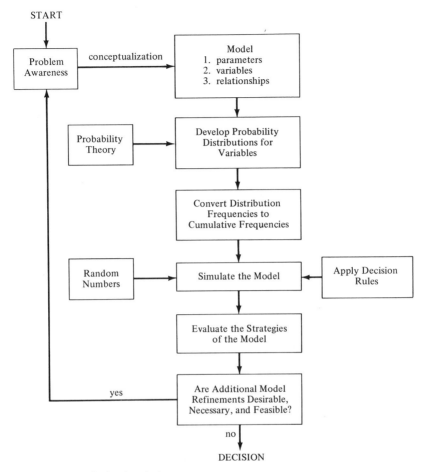

Figure 1. Monte Carlo simulation.

4. Simulate the operation under analysis for a large number of observations. The appropriate number of replications is determined in the same manner as the appropriate size of a sample in an actual experiment in the real world. The ordinary statistical tests of significance can be used. With computerized simulation the size of the sample can be very large, and it is often economical to run large samples with very small sampling errors.

Everything depends on the choice of frequency distributions. Unless there is some assurance they are well chosen, the entire simulation can be worthless. Distributions can be obtained from historical records or experimentation, or established *a priori* on a quasisubjective basis.

Table 2

Time (minutes)	Frequency
5	20
6	30
7	20
8	10
9	10
10	10
	100

Random numbers are numbers of equal long-run frequency. They have a complete lack of sequential predictability, and each number has an equal opportunity to be selected. The randomness of tabulated numbers can be validated by a chi-square test. The stream of random numbers can be obtained from a published table or created by the computer. In the latter case, the computed numbers are termed "pseudorandom numbers." Table 16 at the end of this chapter is a typical random number table.

Monte Carlo simulation has many practical uses, such as waiting line problems where standard distributions for arrival rates and service rates are inadequate, layout problems of multiphase assembly lines, inventory problems determining reorder points and order quantities, equipment replacement problems, and so forth.

EXAMPLE 2

The probability distribution of pogo stick assembly times is given in Table 2. Determine the average assembly time by simulating the performance time for ten replications with the following random numbers: 04, 95, 45, 21, 44, 57, 03, 98, 98, and 10.

Convert the frequency distribution to a cumulative frequency distribution, as in Table 3. The simulated assembly time can be obtained by referring each random

Table 3

Time	Frequency	Cumulative Frequency	Random Numbers
5	20	20	01–20
6	30	50	21–50
7	20	70	51–70
8	10	80	71–80
9	10	90	81–90
10	10	100	91–00
	100		

Table 4

Replication	Simulated Assembly Time (minutes)
1	5
2	10
3	6
4	6
5	6
6	7
7	5
8	10
9	10
10	5
	$\overline{70}$

number to the cumulative frequency distribution. Random numbers in the range 01–20 give a performance time of 5, 21–50 give 6, 51–70 give 7, 71–80 give 8, 81–90 give 9, and 91–00 give 10 minutes. The simulated times are given in Table 4. The average assembly time is $70/10 = 7$ minutes.

PERPETUAL INVENTORY SIMULATION PROBLEM

The assignment at hand is to establish a minimum cost inventory policy for an item which historically has been subject to both variable demand (in units per week) and variable lead time (in weeks from order to delivery). Having access to the historical demand and lead time data contained in Table 5, the following information on the costs associated with inventory

Table 5

Quantity Demanded (Units/Week)	Frequency (No. of Weeks)	Lead Time[a] (Weeks)	Relative Frequency
0	2	1	60
1	4	2	30
2	14	3	9
3	20	4	1
4	8		$\overline{100}$
5	1		
6	1		
	$\overline{50}$		

[a] From order to delivery.

Table 6

Reorder Point	Order Quantity:	1	2	3	4	5	6	7	8
0		C_{01}	C_{02}	C_{03}	C_{04}	C_{05}	C_{06}	C_{07}	C_{08}
1		C_{11}	C_{12}	C_{13}	C_{14}	C_{15}	C_{16}	C_{17}	C_{18}
2		C_{21}	C_{22}	C_{23}	C_{24}	C_{25}	C_{26}	C_{27}	C_{28}
3		C_{31}	C_{32}	C_{33}	C_{34}	C_{35}	C_{36}	C_{37}	C_{38}
4		C_{41}	C_{42}	C_{43}	C_{44}	C_{45}	C_{46}	C_{47}	C_{48}
5		C_{51}	C_{52}	C_{53}	C_{54}	C_{55}	C_{56}	C_{57}	C_{58}
6		C_{61}	C_{62}	C_{63}	C_{64}	C_{65}	C_{66}	C_{67}	C_{68}

activity is also available to aid the task:

$10.00 = order placement cost,

$ 5.00 = holding cost per unit per week,

$20.00 = stockout cost per week of occurrence

(assuming that a stockout cost is encountered only once in a given week). A minimum cost inventory policy requires the determination of a specific order quantity and reorder point combination. (The establishment of a specific combination implies that when the balance at the end of a week falls at or below the reorder point, units are reordered in the predetermined quantity.)

This problem can be handled by simulation with little difficulty. Using reorder points of 0 through 6 and order quantities from 1 through 8, fifty-six possible simulations (combinations) can be run. Each cell in the matrix of Table 6 would contain the results of a simulation. The cell with the smallest cost would indicate the best reorder point and order quantity combination of those examined. For simplicity, only the computations for a single cell, C_{38}, are shown. These computations are based on 25 replications or the simulation of 25 weeks of data.

Converting the frequency distributions to cumulative frequency distributions, Table 7 is obtained.

In Table 8, twenty-five replications of order quantity 8 and reorder point 3 are run. From these data,

$$\text{average cost} = \frac{(\text{holding cost}) + (\text{order cost}) + (\text{stockout cost})}{N}$$

$$= \frac{545 + 70 + 60}{25} = \frac{675}{25} = \$27.00,$$

average cost = $27.00/week.

The simulation gives the cost which would be placed in cell C_{38} in the matrix if 25 replications were considered suitable. To determine the most

Table 7

Quantity Demanded	Relative Frequency	Cumulative Frequency	Random Numbers
0	4	4	01–04
1	8	12	05–12
2	28	40	13–40
3	40	80	41–80
4	16	96	81–96
5	2	98	97–98
6	2	100	99–00

Lead Time	Relative Frequency	Cumulative Frequency	Random Numbers
1	60	60	01–60
2	30	90	61–90
3	9	99	91–99
4	1	100	00

desirable cell in the matrix, all cells must be simulated in a like manner. The simulation example has built into it the following assumptions:

1. Holding costs are determined from the number of units in stock at the end of each week.
2. If the demand for the item exceeds the balance on hand, the consumer will accept the items available even though he desires a larger quantity.
3. If the demand for an item is not satisfied in the given week, it is lost and not recoverable in the following weeks.
4. The stockout cost is a maximum of $20 per week regardless of the number of units of demand which are unfulfilled. (It may be feasible in some cases to include the stockout cost on a per unit basis.)
5. All orders for additional units are received at the beginning of the work week.
7. If the unit balance plus the number of units on order (but not received) exceeds the reorder point, no new order will be initiated for additional units. If the unit balance plus the number of units on order (but not received) is less than the reorder point, a new order will be initiated for additional units.

The simulation example begins with an initial unit balance of 8 units. A demand value for the first period is obtained from the random number by referring to the demand cumulative frequency distribution. The synthetic demand value is subtracted from the unit balance of 8 units from the previous period, which results in an end-of-period unit balance. At the end

Table 8

Simulated Week	Random Numbers		Simulated Activity				Simulated Cost		
	Demand	Delivery	Demand	Order Time	Units Received	Unit Balance	Hold Cost	Order Cost	Stockout Cost
0						8			
1	19	20	2			6	30		
2	3	19	0			6	30		
3	80	14	3	1		3	15	10	
4	15	34	2		8	9	45		
5	61	10	3			6	30		
6	74	2	3	1		3	15	10	
7	19	39	2		8	9	45		
8	5	49	1			8	40		
9	32	98	2			6	30		
10	24	21	2			4	20		
11	62	55	3	1		1	5	10	
12	19	78	2		8	7	35		
13	93	40	4	1		3	15	10	
14	44	99	3		8	8	40		
15	26	55	2			6	30		
16	21	82	2			4	20		
17	78	66	3	2		1	5	10	
18	40	37	2			0	0		20
19	84	7	4		8	4	20		
20	55	97	3	3		1	5	10	
21	98	80	5			0			20
22	91	9	4			0			20
23	87	53	4	1	8	4	20	10	
24	38	36	2			2	10		
25	39	63	2		8	8	40		
Total							545	70	60

of each period (replication), the stock position (stock on hand plus stock on order) is compared with the reorder point. If the reorder point has been reached or exceeded, a lead time value is obtained from the random number by referring to the lead time cumulative frequency distribution, and an order is placed. If the reorder point has not been reached or exceeded, no order is placed. Since one period (replication) has expired, 1 is added to the number of periods and 1 is subtracted from all outstanding lead time values. With the start of a new period, any orders scheduled for delivery are added to the unit balance from the previous period, and the process continues for the specified number of replications, which is 25. Appropriate inventory costs are entered at the end of each simulated time period. The average cost for the simulated cell is obtained by adding all the inventory costs and dividing by the number of replications or simulated time periods.

The preceding simulation of a single cell in the matrix indicated the vast number of simple computations associated with a simulation. While the computations are simple, their quantity dictates the use of a computer. It is an easy matter for a computer to run thousands of replications on each cell in a matrix and indicate a most desirable alternative.

EXAMPLE 3

If stockout costs are $20 per unit per week in the inventory evaluation of cell C_{38}, what is the average cost per week for the 25 replications? (All other aspects of the problem are unchanged.)

The order and holding costs are unchanged, and the only difference will be in the stockout costs for weeks 18, 21, and 22 when stockouts occurred (Table 9). Thus

$$\text{average cost} = \frac{(\text{holding cost}) + (\text{order cost}) + (\text{stockout cost})}{N}$$

$$= \frac{545 + 70 + 180}{25} = \$31.80/\text{week}.$$

Table 9

Simulated Week	Units Short	Stockout Cost
18	1	20
21	4	80
22	4	80
		$\overline{180}$

PERIODIC INVENTORY SIMULATION PROBLEM

The task of establishing a minimum cost inventory policy for the item identified in the previous section (perpetual inventory simulation problem) now must be restructured for a periodic inventory system. This requires the determination of a specific reorder cycle and maximum inventory level combination. Due to space limitations on the system, the maximum number of units that can be stored at any given time is set at 50. Restricting the maximum inventory level to the range 20–50 units in steps of 5, and the reorder cycle to the range 1–5 weeks in steps of 1, the matrix of possible combinations is shown in Table 10.

To determine the best policy, each cell would be simulated. The cell with the lowest cost would be selected as the best strategy. As an example, using the distributions and cost data from the previous section, the computations for a single cell will be displayed: a reorder cycle of 5 weeks and a maximum inventory of 30 units which correspond to cell C_{530}. The simulation will start at time 0 with 25 units on hand. At each review period, an order will be placed for 30 units less the number of units in stock and on order. Table 11 contains 25 replications of cell C_{530}. From these data,

$$\text{average cost} = \frac{(\text{holding cost}) + (\text{order cost}) + (\text{stockout cost})}{N}$$

$$= \frac{2250 + 50 + 0}{25} = \$92/\text{week}.$$

To actually determine the best periodic inventory policy, it is necessary to evaluate each cell in the matrix. The 25 replications given would not be sufficient. Several hundred replications of each cell in the matrix would ensure a reliable estimate. With the use of a computer, it is a simple matter to determine a desirable periodic inventory policy by such a simulation.

Throughout the use of Monte Carlo simulation, the solution procedures for establishing a perpetual and periodic inventory system have been outlined for a single product. The technique was illustrated for a very simple problem. Although not illustrated, many other factors could have

Table 10

Reorder Cycle (weeks)	Maximum Inventory (units):	50	45	40	35	30	25	20
1		C_{150}	C_{145}	C_{140}	C_{135}	C_{130}	C_{125}	C_{120}
2		C_{250}	C_{245}	C_{240}	C_{235}	C_{230}	C_{225}	C_{220}
3		C_{350}	C_{345}	C_{340}	C_{335}	C_{330}	C_{325}	C_{320}
4		C_{450}	C_{445}	C_{440}	C_{435}	C_{430}	C_{425}	C_{420}
5		C_{550}	C_{545}	C_{540}	C_{535}	C_{530}	C_{525}	C_{520}

Table 11

Simulated Week	Random Nos.		Simulated Activity					Simulated Cost		
	Demand	Delivery	Demand	Order Size	Order Time	Units Recd.	Unit Bal.	Holding Cost	Order Cost	Stockout Cost
0							25			
1	19	20	2				23	115		
2	3	19	0				23	115		
3	80	14	3				20	100		
4	15	34	2				18	90		
5	61	10	3	12	1		15	75	10	
6	74	2	3			12	24	120		
7	19	39	2				22	110		
8	5	49	1				21	105		
9	32	98	2				19	95		
10	24	21	2	11	1		17	85	10	
11	62	55	3			11	25	125		
12	19	78	2				23	115		
13	93	40	4				19	95		
14	44	99	3				16	80		
15	26	55	2	14	1		14	70	10	
16	21	82	2			14	26	130		
17	78	66	3				23	115		
18	40	37	2				21	105		
19	84	7	4				17	85		
20	55	97	3	13	3		14	70	10	
21	98	80	5				9	45		
22	91	9	4				5	25		
23	87	53	4			13	14	70		
24	38	36	2				12	60		
25	39	63	2	18	2		10	50	10	
Total								2250	50	0

been introduced and varied, such as quantity discounts, price changes, expediting costs, strikes, material shortages, pilferage, and partial back-ordering. Additional factors are comparatively easy to include in a simulation, although they are forbiddingly complex in analytical form.[1]

SIMULATION OF JOINT PROBABILITY DISTRIBUTIONS

The interdependence of demand and lead time can be approximated for independent distributions by using Monte Carlo simulation. When demand and lead time are variables in an inventory problem, it is necessary to develop their combined probability so order quantities and reorder points can be set. The resultant joint probability distribution will define the demand during the lead time period.

Although demand and lead time variables can be combined numerically, it involves the algebra of multinomial equations for summing all the possible combinations of variables. With Monte Carlo, the joint behavior of the distribution is simulated by random numbers. The numerical method is exact, but the Monte Carlo method is quicker and sufficiently accurate for practical purposes.

The Monte Carlo method consists of selecting values of lead time and demand on a random basis. Although the procedure requires a large number of replications to establish the joint distribution, it can be extremely useful when standard distributions do not apply. A simple example can best illustrate the procedure.

EXAMPLE 4

Using Monte Carlo simulation, establish the joint probability of lead time demand for 20 replications using random numbers from Table 16 at the end of the chapter (start with the last two digits from column 1 in Table 16). The independent demand and lead time distributions are shown in Table 12.

The Monte Carlo process consists of selecting a random number for each lead time period. Additional random numbers will be used to generate demand during the lead time. The lead time demand will consist of the summation of the individual demands during the lead time. The independent distributions are modified to accept random numbers in the manner shown in Table 13.

---

[1] See Arnold Reisman, *Industrial Inventory Control*, New York: Gordon and Breach Science Publishers, 1972, Chapter 6, for multi-item simulation analysis of inventory.

Table 12

Daily Demand D (units)	Probability $P(D)$	Lead Time L (days)	Probability $P(L)$
0	0.40	1	0.25
1	0.30	2	0.50
2	0.20	3	0.25
3	0.10		$\overline{1.00}$
	$\overline{1.00}$		

Table 13

Daily Demand D	Probability	Cumulative Probability	Random Numbers
0	0.40	0.40	01–40
1	0.30	0.70	41–70
2	0.20	0.90	71–90
3	0.10	1.00	91–00

Lead Time L	Probability	Cumulative Probability	Random Numbers
1	0.25	0.25	01–25
2	0.50	0.75	26–75
3	0.25	1.00	76–00

Table 15 contains the 20-replication simulation. From it, the joint probability distribution in Table 14 is obtained.

Table 14

Lead Time Demand M	Frequency	Probability $P(M)$
0	2	0.10
1	4	0.20
2	6	0.30
3	5	0.25
4	2	0.10
5	1	0.05
6	0	0.00
7	0	0.00
8	0	0.00
9	0	0.00
	$\overline{20}$	$\overline{1.00}$

Table 15

Simulated Lead Time	Random Numbers		Simulated Activity		
	Lead Time	Demand	Lead Time	Daily Demand	Lead Time Demand
1	63	58	2	1	
		66		1	2
2	35	09	2	0	
		72		2	2
3	92	70	3	1	
		14		0	
		27		0	1
4	77	44	3	1	
		80		2	
		21		0	3
5	23	58	1	1	1
6	6	56	1	1	1
7	28	13	2	0	
		91		3	3
8	30	94	2	3	
		7		0	3
9	37	44	2	1	
		20		0	1
10	42	42	2	1	
		99		3	4
11	5	16	1	0	0
12	8	93	1	3	3
13	51	30	2	0	
		34		0	0
14	28	56	2	1	
		85		2	3
15	96	14	3	0	
		92		3	
		57		1	4
16	9	81	1	2	2
17	45	85	2	2	
		1		0	2
18	68	78	2	2	
		32		0	2
19	74	75	2	2	
		91		3	5
20	99	27	3	0	
		3		0	2
		83		2	

The above example was for only 20 replications. In practice, to establish a joint probability distribution of lead time demand would require several hundred replications to assure a reliable estimate. See Appendix E to Chapter 5 for the numerical method of establishing the joint distribution for the preceding problem.

LENGTH OF SIMULATION RUN

A simulation run is the same as a statistical sample of a process under study or a process being simulated. The information gained from a simulation is dependent on the length of the simulation run, just as that from statistical sampling depends on the size of the sample taken. The usual method for estimating the needed length of a simulation run (number of replications) is to perform a few short trial runs using different random numbers to obtain the mean and standard deviation of the variable being measured. By assuming that the measured variable is normally distributed, the length of the simulation run can be determined for a given accuracy and a statistical confidence level. The following formula can be used to determine the desired length of the simulation run:

$$N = \frac{Z^2 s^2}{K^2} = \text{desired length of simulation run},$$

$$s^2 = \frac{\Sigma(X - \overline{X})^2}{n - 1} = \frac{\Sigma X^2 - (\Sigma X)^2/n}{n - 1},$$

where

$K = p\overline{X} =$ desired accuracy of simulated variable,

$p =$ accuracy fraction,

$s =$ standard deviation of n sample runs of simulated variable X,

$X =$ simulated variable,

$\overline{X} =$ arithmetic mean of sample runs of simulated variable X,

$Z =$ standard normal deviation for a specified confidence level

($Z = 1.0$ for 68.3% confidence level; $Z = 2.0$ for 95.5% confidence level; $Z = 3.0$ for 99.7% confidence level).

The desired length (sample size) of a simulation run is a function of three things: (1) the variability of the simulated variable, (2) the desired accuracy, and (3) the specified confidence level. A 95% confidence level and a $\pm 5\%$ accuracy fraction indicate the analyst wants the simulated variable average to be within (plus or minus) 5% of the population average 95 out of 100 times.

EXAMPLE 5

A series of simulation runs of ten years' duration to determine the average inventory for a perpetual inventory system gives a mean value of 120 units with a standard deviation of 40 units. What would be the minimum length of simulation runs (replications) to specify an average inventory level of 120 units with an accuracy of ± 5 units and a confidence level of 95%?

$$Z = 1.96 \qquad \text{for the 95\% confidence level,}$$

$$N = \frac{Z^2 s^2}{K^2} = \frac{(1.96)^2 (40)^2}{(5)^2} = 246 \text{ years.}$$

At least 246 replications would be required.

CONCLUSION

Simulation serves the dual purposes of system analysis and the improvement of system design. Simulation serves system analysis by generating information on how a system operates and the significance of particular variables and their interrelationships in a system. For system design, it provides insights into potential improvement areas. Simulation can indicate which variables are more important in generating a desirable output.

Simulation can be used to help solve simple, narrowly defined problems or complex multivariable problems. In almost all cases a computer is desirable. The essence of simulation does not lie in its structure, for it lacks structure. The structure for a simulation problem must be defined by its user. For this reason, the development of a simulation model requires a basic understanding of the system under study and a degree of conceptual creativity.

QUESTIONS

1. What is simulation? What are its advantages?

2. Describe two types of simulation models. What are the characteristics of the variables in them?

3. What is involved in Monte Carlo simulation?

4. What are the major steps in Monte Carlo simulation?

5. How are frequency distributions selected for use in Monte Carlo simulation?

6. What are some practical uses for Monte Carlo simulation?

7. How can variable demand and variable lead time be approximated for independent distributions by using Monte Carlo simulation?

8. On what does the accuracy of information gained from a simulation depend?

9. What two purposes are served by simulation?

10. What capabilities are required for the development of a simulation model?

PROBLEMS

1. A small construction company owns two backhoes that cost $50.00 a day whether they are used or not. Each additional backhoe required can be rented for $50.00 per day. Actual use figures are listed below:

No. of Backhoes Used	No. of Days
0	13
1	22
2	38
3	16
4	11
	100

Using the random numbers below, simulate 15 days of construction to determine the daily backhoe cost.

56, 10, 40, 65, 45, 01, 69, 16, 13, 12, 78, 88, 62, 43, 67.

2. A manager of a new warehouse operation must determine the number of workers to hire. The daily workload varies from 40 to 70 labor-hours as indicated in the table. Pertinent data are as follows:

Hours	Probability	Cumulative Probability
40	0.05	0.05
45	0.13	0.18
50	0.21	0.39
55	0.27	0.66
60	0.17	0.83
65	0.11	0.94
70	0.06	1.00
	1.00	

Regular pay	$4.00/hour
Overtime pay	$6.00/hour
Max. allowed overtime	4 hours per person
Temporary help	$40.00/day per person

If the backlog is over 20 hours, two temporary workers are hired by the day until the backlog goes back below 20 hours. Assuming that all of the regular employees volunteer for all overtime, test work forces of 4, 5, and 6 over a period of 15 days to determine the minimum cost level. Use the random numbers given below in your computations.

4 workers: 77, 44, 80, 21, 23, 58, 06, 56, 28, 13, 91, 30, 94, 07, 37.
5 workers: 30, 66, 63, 53, 56, 80, 10, 47, 23, 53, 96, 00, 29, 87, 22.
6 workers: 31, 67, 84, 96, 72, 85, 03, 34, 74, 44, 85, 13, 35, 42, 26.

3. In determining the total inventory cost for a periodic inventory system, a sample of ten simulation replications was performed which yielded an average cost of $85 with a standard deviation of $10. What is the minimum number of replications to yield an average cost of $85, accurate to $\pm$$2, with a confidence level of 99%?

4. A particular product with a perpetual inventory system has an order quantity of 8 units and a reorder point of 3 units. Past records indicate the demand and lead time data given in the table. Pertinent inventory costs are given below.

Quantity Demand (units/week)	Frequency (weeks)	Lead Time[a] (weeks)	Frequency (weeks)
0	3	1	46
1	6	2	41
2	8	3	11
3	22	4	2
4	7		$\overline{100}$
5	4		
	$\overline{50}$		

[a] From order to delivery.

Order placing cost	$10.00
Holding cost	$10.00/week per unit
Stockout cost	$20.00/week.

You have been assigned the task of determining the average inventory cost if the order quantity and the reorder point were changed to 6 and 4 respectively. With an initial balance of 6 units at time 0, simulate 10 replications with the following random numbers:

Demand: 10, 24, 38, 25, 07, 86, 66, 07, 65, 89.
Delivery: 22, 44, 06, 99, 11, 35, 35, 50, 79, 46.

5. The company in Problem 4 is considering shifting to a periodic inventory system. The possible reorder cycles range from 1 to 5 weeks, and the possible maximum inventory levels range from 15 to 50 units. You have been given the assignment of evaluating a reorder cycle of 2 weeks and a maximum inventory level of 15 units. Simulate 10 replications using the same random numbers used in Problem 4. (Assume there are 15 units on hand at time 0.)

6. An organization's demand for one of its products is as follows:

Demand per Month (units)	Probability of Demand
2200	.09
2300	.38
2400	.31
2500	.22

The lead time for the item is very short, and orders are placed at the end of the month for the next month's demand. All stockouts are lost sales, with no backorders. Management is considering the use of a fixed order size each month equal to the expected demand per month. To test this alternative, the following random numbers are to be used: 16, 3, 82, 97, 13, 45, 56, 73, 90, 61, 33, and 20. Simulate the proposed ordering rule from the random numbers and determine the following: (a) number of orders per year; (b) number of months per year in which a stockout will occur, and percentage of months; (c) average shortage in units per month; (d) percentage of total demand satisfied, and percentage unsatisfied.

7. A firm owns three copiers which cost $25 per day whether they are used or not. Each additional copier required can be rented for $30 per day. Actual use figures are as follows:

No. of copiers used	0	1	2	3	4	5
No. of days	7	12	25	30	18	8

Using the random numbers below, simulate eighteen days of copying to determine the daily copier cost.

13, 97, 63, 90, 36, 02, 57, 72, 97, 35, 15, 68, 29, 53, 77, 07, 64, 18.

8. In determining the total inventory cost for a periodic inventory system, a series of simulation runs of 13 years was performed which yielded an average cost of $60 with a standard deviation of $8. What is the minimum number of replications needed to yield an average cost of $60, accurate to $\pm$ $3 with a confidence level of 95%?

9. What is the minimum number of replications needed in Problem 8 for a confidence level of 99%?

10. If it is possible to run 1000 years of replications in Problem 8, how accurately can the average be estimated with 95% confidence?

11. The retail manager of a large department store decided to analyze costs associated with his major product. Researching sales files from the last four

years, he compiled the following data:

Quantity Demanded	No. of Weeks	Quantity Demanded	No. of Weeks
4	2	12	18
5	8	13	22
6	10	14	18
7	12	15	14
8	18	16	8
9	24	17	2
10	24	18	4
11	20	19	4

The carrying costs of inventory are estimated to be $10 per unit, while the cost of placing an order is $5. The manager estimates that 50% of the customers will purchase elsewhere if the store is out of stock. Each unit contributes $80 to profit. An order is placed the first day of every week, and it takes four weeks for delivery. If the beginning inventory is 4, simulate the cost of order quantities of 10 and 11 units with the following random numbers: 234, 753, 709, 792, 582, 231, 768, 091, 365, 248, 472, 176.

CASE 1: DEMAND DEPENDENCE

Konacolor Corporation and Laminado Company located in the same industrial park several years ago because of the conveniences of the park and the inducements offered by the park developer. The move was fortunate for the two companies, since it began a cooperative undertaking that resulted in a joint venture. What started as a bulk shipping arrangement between the firms led to a full-fledged production agreement. Konacolor, a producer of electrical equipment and television components, was ripe for a television production line of its own; Laminado, a company skilled in special order cabinetry, had some capital to invest. The enterprise that ensued allowed Konacolor to open a TV production line with Laminado capital and afforded Laminado the opportunity to supply the cabinets for the two sizes of portable sets that composed Konacolor's line.

The startup costs of the venture were less than Laminado anticipated. The unused capital was expended on a sophisticated computer system for Laminado. The capacity of the system was in excess of needs, so Laminado worked a deal with Konacolor to share computer time. Interestingly enough, Konacolor came to depend on the system more than Laminado. Since it got on the system, Konacolor has implemented an MRP system for all four present styles of TV sets.

The problem that bothered both companies, Laminado as the supplier and Konacolor as the production unit, was the erratic demand for the TV sets. On balance, sales for the six year period had been good to excellent, but the undulations in the demand for the primary items translated into various problems for the dependent items. Because there are several levels of dependence at Konacolor, the market factor dependence of the primary item rippled from final assembly, to subassembly, and to manufacturing of components. Demand for some production periods had been grossly overestimated. As soon as this situation revealed itself, Konacolor made changes. The master schedule was promptly revised, and the MRP system regenerated. This change, combined with what appeared to be inflated requirements schedules, gave the company a large buffer of production parts so that during certain intervals the inventory of dependent items was uncharacteristically high.

A computer analyst for Laminado examined the problem and pinpointed the culprit as the forecasting technique abetted by the lot sizing policy. She stated that the inputs were faulty: a master production schedule which based independent demand on an exponentially weighted moving average with a smoothing constant of 0.4 was inadequate for the seasonally popular portables. She also recommended a computer simulation of the multistage environment to determine lot sizing policies for end items. The analyst asserted that once the misapplication of the forecasting technique was corrected, and the company switched from the present EOQ system to an experimentally determined lot sizing policy, all would be well.

The simulation was approved, and in came the results. However, they did not imply a clear-cut solution to the problem. The test pitted EOQ against EOI and the part-period method, given the final assembly schedule set in relation to end item demand. The outcome of the run showed the EOQ as a slight favorite over the part-period but with no clear dominance in total number of stockouts for final products, total number of setups, or the average dollar value of inventory. While it was a photo finish for EOQ and the part-period, both clearly surpassed EOI.

The analyst was unhappy that the simulation did not resolve the lot sizing policy question and was sure this was due to her assumptions. She ran the simulation under the following conditions: requirements covered normal usage during supply lead time with no buffer stock, no lot splitting was allowed, and Konacolor was loaded under capacity. In reality, Konacolor had operated with projected overloads and with frequent lot splitting.

1. Given the decision rules, is the simulation of any value?
2. Are the usually high levels of dependent items understandable?
3. Should Konacolor accept the fate of being at the mercy of erratic demand, or can it counteract the situation?
4. What lot size policy could be expected to perform best under periods of variable demand? How do the alternative methods fail to recognize much of the information given in the requirements schedule?

CASE 2: WHEELER DEALER

During his ten years as manager of a seaside resort hotel, Sid Smee had seen the small town become one of the boom towns that lie between New York City and Cape Cod. The village previously had catered to the older "urbanites" from the eastern metropolitan districts, but a younger, more energetic crowd had begun to monopolize the resort community, seeking satisfaction, escape, and thrills during short breaks from the city.

Sid had known for some time that the tempo and composition of the stodgy town were changing, and the urbane guests would soon be a thing of the past. Being a very progressive person, Sid felt he should invest in a business that would serve the new breed of visitors. He realized that the pleasures the newcomers were seeking included the town's scenic views. Therefore, he decided to open a moped shop and rent motorbikes that could be driven along the narrow shoreline paths and over the back roads which lead to the elevated coastline.

This was a business about which Sid knew very little. He had read some brochure sketches on similar types of shops located in southern regions, but he needed to gain information on their operating details. For this purpose, Sid decided to take a short holiday combined with a fact-finding mission to a southern rental shop featured in one of the travel brochures. This shop, he thought, would be the perfect business to duplicate.

Sid visited the South Carolina firm and learned that it had become successful under the management of a retired motor pool sergeant. The veteran was an ardent believer in military fashioned organizations and operations research. He was well schooled in vehicular matters, and his knowledge in the fields of maintenance and security was abundant. However, Sid did not find much immediate application of these types of information. Instead, he was searching for ways to ascertain the level of investment required as well as an approximation of the number of mopeds needed to operate his 5–6 month a year rental service. On this matter, the sergeant was of little use. Specifically, the sergeant's firm operated practically year round, his acquisition of goods appeared unorthodox, and his operating costs seemed to be lower than normal.

The sergeant's son and operations expert, however, had done some quantitative investigation of equipment usage. He had provided statistical data that had been used to plan personnel, workloads, and equipment acquisition and replacement. The son had done two simulation studies that were interesting to Sid from a numerical standpoint, but did not indicate any detailed transferability to Sid's organizational design.

The first of the studies, conducted two years ago, was a simulation of two eight-hour day rental operations. The study was used to indicate the idle time of the shop attendant who checked out the mopeds, the waiting time of the customers, and the number of customers in the queue. He used a service time of 5 minutes, which was fairly close to the actual time it would take to prepare rental forms and collect deposits. At the conclusion of the simulated days, he calculated attendant idle times at 8% and 37%. The study, executed twice, once for a typically busy day and once for a slower day, was used to determine manpower needs for the two seasons.

The second and more recent study was more complex and of greater value to the firm. Although it was a simplification of their real conditions, it was being used to structure their business decisions. Initially, the son prepared probability distributions using historical rental records, which are given below:

1 Hour Rentals		2 Hour Rentals	
Number of People	Probability	Number of People	Probability
1	.04	1	.03
2	.13	2	.16
3	.16	3	.09
4	.10	4	.14
5	.06	5	.04
6	.03	6	.02

The probability distributions were used in conjunction with the following frequency table obtained by taking observations over a 4-day summertime period:

Minutes between Arrivals	Frequency
0–2	6
3–5	13
6–8	17
9–11	24
12–14	21
15–17	14
18–20	5

Using this information, he ran a 30-day simulation. He chose random numbers for arrivals and for the type of customer rental. The simulation revealed the percentage of usage of the mopeds, the number of stockouts, the percentage of demand satisfied, and the total amount of rental time.

Sid saw no relevance to his situation. In addition, he felt there were obvious shortcomings in the information provided; e.g., there were:

a. no calculations to determine moped requirements,
b. no provisions for costs in the model, and
c. no resource constraints (whereas Sid could obtain licenses for a maximum of 50 mopeds under a city ordinance).

Furthermore, he had not received information on lease versus purchase acquisitions, nor any ways to compensate for the off season.

1. Was the fact-finding mission of any use to Sid? Could any of the firm's experience be transferred to his operation?
2. What simulations would you recommend he try? How could they be structured to his rental service?
3. Would simulation alone be the key to his inventory planning, particularly for investment decisions?

CASE 3: COMBINING PROBABILITIES

Adolph Nolting has been assigned the task of developing an ordering system for inventory item R2D3, which has a variable demand and lead time. He has been given historical demand and lead time data, contained in two independent probability distributions as follows:

Demand		Lead Time	
Units/Day	Probability	Days	Probability
0	.05	2	.27
1	.18	3	.45
2	.23	4	.18
3	.27	5	.10
4	.16		
5	.09		
6	.02		

Table 16. Random numbers

.6663	.0696	.6964	.6935	.3077	.6821	.8774	.1951	.9228	.9856
.8558	.8714	.9132	.3207	.6221	.8776	.9366	.5563	.6306	.2010
.8666	.5692	.0397	.7806	.3527	.5242	.3519	.8278	.9806	.9540
.4535	.3457	.0319	.6396	.0550	.8496	.8441	.2896	.5307	.2865
.7709	.0209	.1590	.1558	.7418	.6382	.7624	.8286	.4225	.7145
.7472	.0681	.9746	.4704	.5439	.7495	.4156	.4548	.4468	.7801
.5792	.0245	.8544	.2190	.6749	.6243	.9089	.5974	.4484	.8669
.5370	.4385	.9413	.4132	.8888	.9775	.8511	.6520	.1789	.0816
.4914	.1801	.9257	.3701	.3520	.0823	.5915	.5341	.2583	.0113
.6227	.8568	.1319	.0681	.8898	.9335	.3506	.4813	.5271	.5912
.7077	.0878	.1730	.0093	.9731	.6123	.6100	.0389	.0522	.7478
.8044	.7232	.7466	.0349	.3467	.0174	.1140	.5425	.2912	.7088
.4280	.3474	.3963	.5364	.7381	.8144	.7645	.5116	.0300	.6762
.8821	.4375	.9853	.9138	.0596	.6294	.3415	.4358	.2713	.8343
.8523	.5591	.3956	.3516	.8472	.2884	.8550	.3524	.3919	.3967
.6558	.3999	.0480	.3046	.8285	.1693	.2330	.7610	.2674	.3679
.1806	.3227	.9710	.8548	.5003	.6345	.6815	.9612	.3378	.5091
.9256	.0103	.1347	.8074	.4534	.0373	.9885	.1182	.0795	.7094
.6128	.2383	.9223	.4459	.8974	.4525	.0441	.7379	.0677	.6135
.4913	.6686	.4453	.0223	.7344	.6333	.8080	.1075	.5077	.2590
.3491	.9060	.0496	.5251	.2385	.3425	.7426	.0827	.7816	.3100
.1530	.7750	.1800	.5491	.4713	.3572	.8914	.3287	.3518	.4199
.5894	.9256	.1529	.4922	.7235	.9046	.5771	.3954	.6794	.1984
.7107	.7293	.5387	.9880	.4642	.6092	.4389	.3820	.4119	.5821
.5337	.8973	.0322	.7474	.5526	.7386	.3476	.0762	.9613	.8789
.9644	.9317	.7214	.9388	.5131	.7891	.6504	.8672	.4880	.1557
.3820	.4209	.4876	.6906	.9257	.4447	.8541	.5250	.8272	.9513
.7142	.7821	.9281	.0016	.4180	.2971	.7259	.3844	.3801	.5372
.3342	.0695	.3189	.7217	.0428	.6227	.8967	.1417	.4771	.0137
.7599	.6804	.3587	.7765	.9790	.5331	.8654	.5337	.8883	.1268
.5905	.5242	.3262	.2409	.1039	.8727	.2752	.3265	.1110	.6722
.9016	.0268	.2134	.8633	.9959	.8970	.2688	.9149	.8124	.3244
.3508	.3038	.3095	.6480	.3089	.7948	.7897	.4792	.9238	.5206
.9393	.2211	.6921	.8622	.2688	.7890	.1363	.1282	.9525	.5299
.8151	.0355	.0688	.3432	.8580	.9888	.2402	.0000	.1307	.1611
.6730	.6635	.9948	.3730	.5977	.6089	.6678	.7734	.1086	.1435
.1834	.3191	.4042	.7264	.9511	.0549	.4267	.2888	.9166	.1935
.9028	.7539	.3215	.9958	.7826	.7569	.0633	.4506	.0807	.5650
.6556	.7547	.1155	.1975	.7882	.5929	.1493	.7455	.4865	.2179
.4285	.8922	.8721	.3307	.6236	.6329	.5228	.7599	.6689	.1966

He has been informed further of the following costs associated with inventory activity: ordering cost = \$15.00/order; holding cost per day = \$1.00/unit; and stockout cost per day of occurrence = \$5.00/unit.

Adolph has considered two techniques to determine his ordering strategy. The first alternative is to form joint probability distributions using the enumeration approach. This method of combining probabilities would define the demand during lead time, and consequently could be used to meet his objective of setting the reorder point at its lowest expected cost.

On the other hand, Adolph is considering the use of simulation techniques, and as yet is undecided between his two options, the perpetual or the periodic inventory simulation. To date, the firm has used a perpetual system for R2D3, but Adolph is ready to experiment with both types. What is confusing to Adolph is the structuring of the simulations. He is fully aware that Monte Carlo simulation involves determining the probability distribution of the variables under study and then sampling from the distribution by using random numbers to obtain data. He is uncertain, however, how to perform the simulation and generate the requisite data. More specifically, Adolph does not have definitive decision rules or a predetermined number of replications.

For methodology determination Adolph has chosen the following selection criteria: optimality, suitability, facility, and accommodation to introduction of other factors, e.g., real life occurrences.

1. Which technique should he use (simulation or joint probabilities)?
2. In using the different techniques, will he arrive at similar policies?
3. What benefit would lie in running both perpetual and periodic inventory system simulations?

MATHEMATICAL ABBREVIATIONS AND SYMBOLS USED IN CHAPTER 12

D	Daily demand in units
K	Desired accuracy of simulated variable
L	Lead time in days
M	Lead time demand in units
N	Number of replications or length of simulation run
$P(D)$	Probability of a demand of D units
$P(L)$	Probability of a lead time of L days
$P(M)$	Probability of a lead time demand of M units
s	Standard deviation of sample runs
Z	Standard normal deviate

13 Aggregate Inventory Control

TYPES OF CONTROL SYSTEMS
  Perpetual Inventory System
  Two-Bin Inventory System
  Periodic Inventory System
  Optional Replenishment Inventory System
  Distribution Requirements Planning Inventory System
  Single Order Quantity Inventory System
  Material Requirements Planning Inventory System
  Just-in-Time Inventory System

SELECTIVE INVENTORY CONTROL

INVENTORY SYSTEM DEVELOPMENT

INVENTORY SYSTEM IMPROVEMENT

AGGREGATE INVENTORY MEASUREMENT

AGGREGATE INVENTORY REDUCTION
  Raw Materials, Supplies, and Finished Goods
  In-Process Inventory

CONCLUSION
QUESTIONS
CASES

Inventory is ubiquitous in today's organizations but varies widely in the number and nature of materials held. Inventory in a manufacturing firm may take the form of raw materials waiting to enter the production process, work in process in some intermediate form of transformation, finished goods already completely transformed by the production system, or supplies used to support the process. It also may be found as retail and wholesale finished goods located at distinct parts of a distribution system, or as service industry materials or supplies. Thus inventory performs many functions throughout any organization.

The management of inventory is a management of diversity. A typical organization may have over 10,000 items in inventory. The items may differ in cost, weight, shape, volume, and color. They may be packaged separately or together and stored in boxes, crates, pallets, barrels, bottles, bags, or bins. The storage facilities may require strict environmental control (over dust, temperature, humidity, etc.), only covered protection from the elements, or no particular shelter. Transportation into, within, and from the organization may be via various types of conveyances (e.g., train, boat, truck, aircraft, pipeline, conveyor, etc.) and involve quantities of thousands, dozens, or single units.

The large number of physical units of inventory requires that they be classified into a smaller number of relatively homogeneous categories for control purposes. The complexity and diversity of inventory are made more manageable by applying similar procedures to each category. Inevitably, the type of inventory control systems selected will have an impact on almost all other organizational activities.

The starting point in developing a control system is an analysis of the objectives of the intended system. This procedure discloses the critical activities in the operation where control can be most effective. It is imperative that the control mechanism satisfy the service and operating objectives of the institution at the lowest possible cost. For this reason it is the responsibility of top management to select the control system (or systems) and to establish aggregate inventory levels. However, an inventory control system, with guidelines on inventory policies, often is converted to rules for specific items by the operations personnel who implement and monitor the system.

By definition the operating system should indicate how routine and nonroutine situations are to be treated via predetermined rules and procedures. A good control system provides for self-control and only requires attention to exceptions. Adjustments are made as the system operates to

1. ensure that sufficient goods and materials are available,
2. identify excess and fast- and slow-moving items,
3. provide accurate, concise, and timely reports to management,
4. expend the least amount of resources in accomplishing the above.

The establishment of inventory operating policies usually is based on cost analysis which is rational, logical, and unemotional. It involves factors which can be analyzed and set forth in precise mathematical formulations. In spite of their apparent exactness, however, the use of sophisticated mathematical techniques does not necessarily result in an effective system. Precise techniques are of little value unless the information to feed into the models is available at a realistic cost. On these grounds, an inventory control system may vary in complexity and accuracy from absence of any noticeable control to a highly sophisticated data processing system. Systems that select approximate, reasonable levels with low data processing costs often are preferable.

Without minimizing the importance of quantitative techniques, it should be understood that a comprehensive inventory system involves much more than refined inventory models. All aspects of the system must be considered, and not just the specific model(s). Six areas are vital in the development and maintenance of the system, and a breakdown in any one can undermine the efficiency of the entire system:

1. the development of demand forecasts and the treatment of forecast errors,
2. the selection of inventory models (EOQ, EOI, EPQ, DRP, and MRP),
3. the measurement of inventory costs (order, holding, stockout),
4. the methods used to record and account for items,
5. the methods for receipt, handling, storage, and issue of items,
6. the information procedures used to report exceptions.

TYPES OF CONTROL SYSTEMS

There are various types of inventory control systems, and there are special hybrids of the common ones. It is difficult to classify them in an orderly fashion and still demarcate their defining characteristics. Nevertheless, a depiction of the systems used most frequently is given in Figure 1. It segregates the major systems by demand situation and operating doctrine. Included in the diagram are the perpetual, two-bin, periodic, optional replenishment, and distribution requirements planning systems, which usually apply to end items, in addition to the material requirements planning and just-in-time systems, which apply to materials and components used to produce end items. The single order quantity system also is categorized but remains unique in that it lacks a reorder dimension.

The perpetual and two-bin systems are referred to as fixed order size systems (quantity-based). The periodic and optional replenishment systems are referred to as fixed order interval systems (time-based). The distribution requirements planning system is a time-phased system for replenishments of items in a distribution network (distribution-based). The material re-

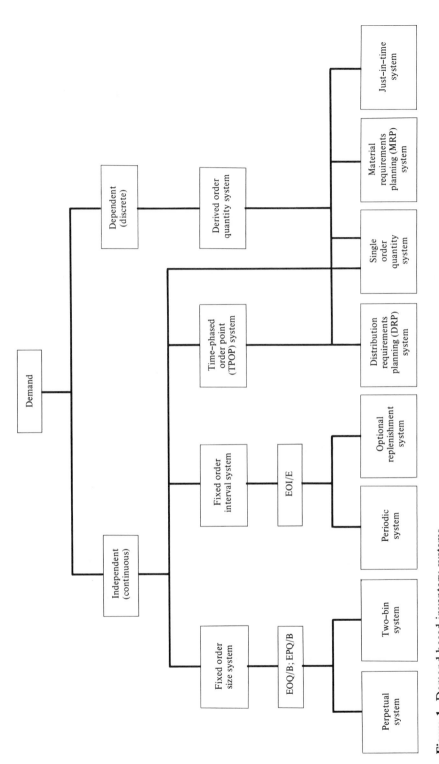

Figure 1. Demand-based inventory systems.

quirements planning and just-in-time systems are derived order quantity systems for production environments (production-based). Quantity-based systems are checked continually (with each demand) to determine if an order should be placed. With time-based systems, a count of stock is only made on designated review dates, and orders are placed at that time. A distribution-based system predicts distribution requirements and schedules orders to meet them. Production-based systems order stock only to meet manufacturing requirements.

Perpetual Inventory System

A perpetual system keeps a running record of the amount in stock. Each time a unit (or units) is issued from stock, the withdrawal is logged and the stock position is compared with the reorder point. If the stock position is equal to or less than the reorder point, an order is prepared for a fixed number of units. If the stock position is more than the reorder point, no action is taken.

This system is based on the economic order quantity (EOQ) and the reorder point. The perpetual system is completely defined by knowing the order size (Q) and the minimal stock level that signals the placing of an order (B). Under this system the reorder point and order quantity are fixed, the review period and demand rate are variable, and the lead time can be fixed or variable. Figure 2 describes the behavior of the perpetual inventory system for a single item.

The major disadvantage of the perpetual system is that it requires perpetual auditing of the inventory in stock to know as quickly as possible when the reorder point is reached. The review may consist of analyzing perpetual records (manual or computerized) as they are posted. Since an order can occur at any time, this prevents the economies that result from the amalgamation of several items from one supplier into one order. These potential savings can be considerable.

Further weaknesses of the perpetual system may become evident if:

1. Managers do not take the time to study inventory levels of individual items and allow order quantities to be established by clerical personnel alone.
2. Reorder points, order quantities, and safety stocks are not restudied or changed for years.
3. Delays in posting transactions render the system useless for control.
4. Clerical errors or mistakes in posting transactions make the system impotent.
5. Numerous independent orders result in high transportation and freight costs.
6. Supplier discounts based on the dollar volume of individual orders are forfeited.

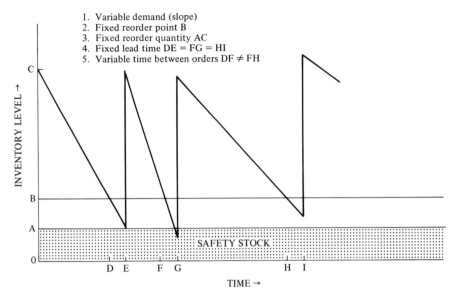

1. Variable demand (slope)
2. Fixed reorder point B
3. Fixed reorder quantity AC
4. Fixed lead time DE = FG = HI
5. Variable time between orders DF ≠ FH

Figure 2. Perpetual inventory system.

On the positive side, the fixed order size system with perpetual records is excellent for high cost items needing close control. It is extremely useful in these situations as well as others, because:

1. An efficient, meaningful order size is used.
2. Safety stock is needed only for the lead time period.
3. The system is relatively insensitive to forecast and parameter changes.
4. Inventory checks are related to usage; slow moving items receive less attention.

Two-Bin Inventory System

As indicated before, the two-bin system is a version of the fixed order size system which operates without perpetual record keeping. Inventory usually is stored in two bins; upon order receipt, an amount equal to the reorder point is put into one bin, and the remainder of the order is placed in another bin. Stock is taken first from the bin which contains the difference between the order quantity and the reorder point. When stock in this bin is depleted, an order is released. Demands then are filled from the second bin, containing the expected lead time quantity plus any safety stock (reorder point quantity). Due to this procedure, records need not be maintained of each withdrawal, and the signal for a replenishment order comes about by visual observation. Hence, it represents an obvious reduction in clerical work.

The system actually can be used with only one bin. An order can be triggered when the inventory level reaches some attention-getting device. The device may be a physical mark, such as a line painted at the reorder volume level on a tank of gasoline or other liquid, or it may be a partition placed in front of or on top of the reorder point quantity when stock is stored in a bin or container. Any similar markings or apparatus can be used to signal when stock is drawn down to the reorder point quantity.

Since the two-bin system does not provide open order information, it can only be used when no more than one replenishment order is outstanding. Therefore, the order quantity must always be greater than the reorder point. The two-bin system is suited best for items of low value of fairly consistent use and short lead times, such as office supplies, nuts, bolts, and so forth.

Periodic Inventory System

In a periodic inventory system the number of items in storage is reviewed at a fixed time interval T. A count must be taken of the goods on hand at the designated inventory review date.[1] The size of the replenishment order depends upon the number of units in stock at that time. Therefore, the order quantity varies from period to period, and the decision maker changes the quantity ordered to reflect changes in the demand rate.

Figure 3 describes the behavior of the periodic inventory system for a single item. A maximum inventory level E is established for each item. The order quantity is the maximum inventory level minus the inventory position on the review date (review dates are at points F, H, and J in the illustration). Under this system, the review period is fixed; the order quantity, demand rate, and reorder point are variable; and the lead time can be fixed or variable.

The presumption in the periodic system is that some sort of physical count is made at the time of review. In many instances records of transactions (sales slips) are available, but the accuracy of the information system may require an actual count for verification (lost or stolen items are not apparent from transaction records). Automatic data processing equipment can provide perpetual inventory records with order decisions still being made on a prescribed basis without the need for an actual physical count of items. Some accommodation must be made in these systems for the return of sale items, errors in transaction accounting, lost items, and stock shrinkage.

In the perpetual (continuous review) system, a replenishment order is initiated as soon as the inventory level drops to the reorder point; an actual

---

[1] The count may be from an information system relying on a perpetual inventory record, or through an inspection that includes an actual physical count. New point of sale registers and business machines maintain inventory records as well as register sales. The new machines serve many functions and are part of a management information system.

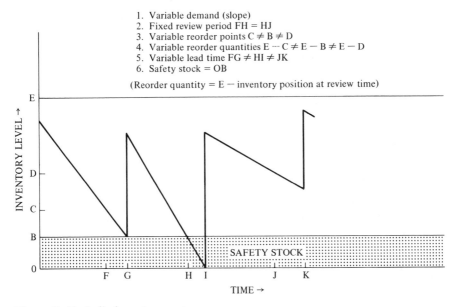

1. Variable demand (slope)
2. Fixed review period FH = HJ
3. Variable reorder points C ≠ B ≠ D
4. Variable reorder quantities E -- C ≠ E - B ≠ E - D
5. Variable lead time FG ≠ HI ≠ JK
6. Safety stock = OB

(Reorder quantity = E - inventory position at review time)

Figure 3. Periodic inventory system.

count is not required, since the inventory records contain receipts, issues, and balances on hand. In the periodic (discrete review) system, the inventory position is checked only at specified time intervals. Thus, the perpetual system treats inventory item reviews continuously and independently, while the periodic system treats item reviews discretely and dependently.

Frequently, it is worthwhile to consolidate orders for items. Coordination of replenishments can be desirable when items are produced on the same equipment, purchased from the same supplier, shipped in the same transportation mode, or supplied from a centralized source. Consequently, the periodic system can provide the following benefits of joint orders:

1. A reduction in ordering cost may be possible because items are processed under a single order.
2. Suppliers may offer discounts for purchases exceeding a given dollar volume. The lumping of several items into a single order can make the discount more attainable.
3. Shipping costs may be significantly decreased if an order is of a convenient size such as a boxcar. This can often be accomplished by the simultaneous ordering of several items.

The manner (or timing) in which the perpetual and periodic systems customarily initiate replenishment orders not only affects their ability to engage in consolidated ordering but also holds implications for their safety stock requirements. In the perpetual system, safety stock represents protection against demand fluctuations during the lead time period.[2] With a fixed order period, the periodic system requires safety stock for protection against demand fluctuations during both the review period and the lead time. This means that the periodic system will require a larger safety stock for a given item than the perpetual system. However, some or all of the additional safety stock expense may be justified by the economies achieved from joint orders.

Optional Replenishment Inventory System

The optional replenishment inventory system is a hybrid of the perpetual and periodic systems. Stock levels are reviewed at regular intervals, but orders are not placed until the inventory position has fallen to a predetermined reorder point. When placing an order is expensive, it may be advantageous not to order at every review time. Figure 4 typifies the optional replenishment system for a single item with its three defining parameters:

1. the length of the review period T,
2. the maximum inventory level E,
3. the reorder point B.

A maximum inventory level is established for the item. If the inventory position is above the reorder point on the review date (e.g., at points F, I, L, and M in the illustration), no order is placed. If the inventory position is at or below the reorder point on the review date (e.g., at points G, J, and N), an order is placed. The order quantity is the maximum inventory level minus the inventory position at the review date.

Remember that both the perpetual and the periodic systems are defined by only two parameters, in contrast to three for the optional replenishment system. The instatement of the reorder point as a third defining parameter permits orders to be placed in efficient quantities; it reduces the costs which may result from frequent placements of small orders in the two-parameter periodic system. However, the optional replenishment system is indistinguishable from the periodic inventory system when the review period is so long that an order is triggered at almost every review.

The computational effort to obtain the best values of the three control parameters is prohibitive. Thus, control values are usually set in a rather arbitrary fashion in practical applications.

---

[2] It can be shown that the average inventory will be lower if orders are placed when needed rather than only at set times. However, the cost of operating the continuous record system may far exceed the advantages to be gained from it.

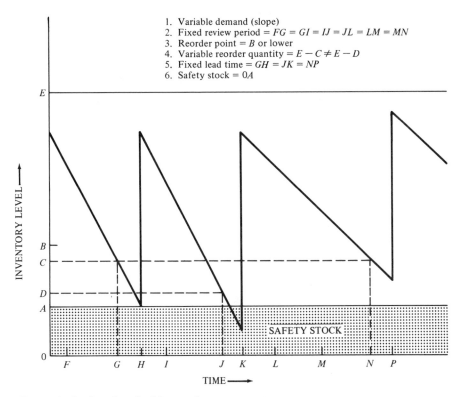

1. Variable demand (slope)
2. Fixed review period = $FG = GI = IJ = JL = LM = MN$
3. Reorder point = B or lower
4. Variable reorder quantity = $E - C \neq E - D$
5. Fixed lead time = $GH = JK = NP$
6. Safety stock = $0A$

Figure 4. Optional replenishment inventory system.

Distribution Requirements Planning Inventory System

Distribution requirements planning (DRP) is a method of handling stock replenishment in a multiechelon distribution environment. It applies time-phased logic to products in a distribution network in a way similar to the way MRP applies it to the subassemblies and components of products in a manufacturing bill of materials network. While MRP is an "explosion" process from the master production schedule to the detailed scheduling of component requirements, DRP is an "implosion" process from the lowest levels of a network to the central distribution center.

DRP, like MRP, distinguishes between independent and dependent demand. All demands in a distribution network are dependent except at the level where products leave the network. DRP relies on forecasts at the lowest level in the network to derive inventory demand at all higher levels. Although gross requirements must be forecasted at the local distribution level, they can be calculated at all the other levels.

Gross requirements for items are developed from forecasts at all local distribution centers in a time-phased order point (TPOP) format. The planned order releases for a given item in each time period at the local centers are accumulated and become gross requirements at the parent center. Thus, parent centers no longer have to forecast lumpy requirements, but can accumulate them from their demand sources. Based on the future visibility of requirements, DRP replenishes what has been consumed in succeeding levels of a distribution network.

Single Order Quantity Inventory System

The single order quantity system is not really an inventory system but a general category for handling the variety of items that are ordered infrequently or only once. They tend to be unique and require special attention. Items fall in this category when (1) demand is nonrepetitive and occurs at infrequent intervals or (2) an uncertain demand exists for a short-lived item. The first situation is typified by promotional, fad, or seasonal items ordered by retail outlets; occasionally needed spare parts for maintenance; and materials required in the construction of special projects. The second situation is typified by highly perishable items (fresh fish, flowers) or short-lived, obsolescent items (Christmas trees, newspapers, periodicals). Lot sizes for single order items are determined by marginal analysis, cost analysis, calculation from specific project requirements, or management judgment.

Material Requirements Planning Inventory System

Most classical inventory systems assume that inventory items should be available at all times. They replenish inventory with a lot size that is triggered by a reorder point or a time interval. These systems are appropriate for items that exhibit a continuous and independent demand. Items sold by retailers, wholesalers, and distributors usually meet these requirements, as do products sold by manufacturers.

For items that exhibit a discrete and dependent demand, classical systems are less desirable. These items are more appropriately controlled under a material requirements planning (MRP) system. This system does not try to make inventory items available at all times. It plans inventory lot sizes so they are time phased to when they are needed. Inventory levels can be lower, and holding costs reduced substantially, if inventory is not held during time periods of zero demand. In order to achieve these economies, MRP must develop an elaborate scheduling system that indicates when each dependent demand item is needed. Items suitable for MRP are components of products that are listed on a product's bill of materials; they usually constitute the majority of items held in inventory by a manufacturing organization.

Time phasing is the essential ingredient of an MRP system. Time phasing requires *known future requirements* and *sufficient time to react* (lead time). MRP is impossible without these conditions, but even these conditions are not sufficient to ensure its success.

Known future requirements are ascertained from forecasts and customer orders that are translated into a capacity-feasible master production schedule (MPS). The master schedule indicates those products that should be produced in future periods. It applies predominately to the end items that the organization produces for its customers. It does not include all the components that are necessary to make the end item. Once the MPS is established, the exact quantities of these dependent or derived demand components needed to make the end items can be calculated from the bills of materials for end items. Thus, all of these components will have known future requirements.

The number of end items will be small in comparison with the number of components in a manufacturer's inventory. This is desirable, since forecasts need not be developed for dependent demand components but only for independent demand items. All dependent demand is derived and can be calculated from its parents' requirements. All components that make up an end item have dependent demand.

The demand for a component is dependent in the sense that the end item demand generates a known, exact requirement for each of its components. Thus, once the master production schedule is developed for end items (products), the specific number of its components can be deterministically calculated from bill of materials explosions.

Sufficient time to react is another vital ingredient for an MRP inventory system. Lead times must be established for every material order, fabrication, subassembly, and assembly. If a sufficient time horizon exists, it is possible to start without any inventory for end items and purchase exactly what is needed, fabricate just those components needed, and assemble the precise requirements with no surpluses or shortages. The lead times of all items and their interrelationships are vital to the success of time phasing.

MRP is a backward scheduling system that starts with the finished product. It then works back to the raw materials, through all levels of subassembly and fabrication. Its goal is to plan inventory so it is available when needed (not before and not after).

Just-in-Time Inventory System

The just-in-time (JIT) inventory system, developed by the Japanese, is used in repetitive manufacturing. It controls raw materials and in-process inventory levels for dependent demand items. It logistically links work centers so there is an even flow of materials similar to that found in an assembly line.

It attempts to drive all queues toward zero and achieve an ideal lot size of one unit.

For JIT to be feasible, the preconditions are uniform plant loading (usually for one month), group technology, quality control at the source (zero defects), minimized setup times (less than ten minutes), a kanban type production control system, and local (nearby) suppliers. JIT is a philosophy of production where inventory is considered undesirable.

SELECTIVE INVENTORY CONTROL

Materials management involves thousands or even millions of individual transactions each year. To do their job effectively, materials managers must avoid the distraction of unimportant details and concentrate on significant matters. Inventory control procedures should isolate those items requiring precise control from other items that can be controlled with less precision. Selective inventory control can indicate where the manager should concentrate his efforts.

It is usually uneconomical to apply detailed inventory control analysis to all items carried in an inventory. Frequently, a small percentage of inventory items accounts for most of the total inventory value. It is usually economical to purchase a large supply of low cost items and maintain little control over them. Conversely, small quantities of expensive items are purchased, and tight control is exercised over them. It is frequently advantageous to divide inventories into three classes according to dollar volume (the product of annual quantity and the unit purchase cost or production cost). This approach is called *ABC* analysis. The *A* class is high value items whose dollar volume typically accounts for 75–80% of the value of the total inventory, while representing only 15–20% of the inventory items. The *B* class is lesser value items whose dollar volume accounts for 10–15% of the value of the inventory, while representing 20–25% of the inventory items. The *C* class is low value items whose volume accounts for 5–10% of the inventory value but 60–65% of the inventory items. Figure 5 shows a typical *ABC* inventory classification. The breakdown into *A*, *B*, and *C* items is arbitrary, and further divisions may be established.

The inventory value for each item is obtained by multiplying the annual demand by the unit cost. Annual demand is used to avoid distortions from seasonal changes. The entire inventory is listed in descending order of value. The items are then classified as described above.

The same degree of control is not justified for all items. The class *A* items require the greatest attention, and the class *C* items the least attention. Class *C* items need no special calculations, since they represent a low inventory investment. The order quantity might be a one year supply with a

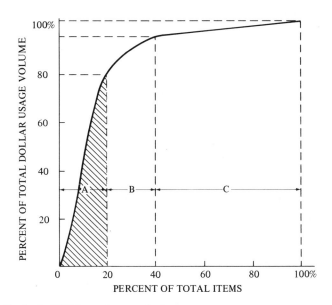

Figure 5. Typical *A BC* inventory analysis.
Key: *A* = High value items; *B* = Medium value items; *C* = Low value items.

periodic review once a year. Class *B* items could have EOQs developed with a semiannual review of the variables. Class *A* items could have EOQs developed with a review of the variables each time an order is placed. The major concern of an *ABC* classification is to direct attention to those inventory items that represent the largest annual expenditures. If inventory levels can be reduced for class *A* items, it will result in a significant reduction in inventory investment.

The purpose of classifying items into groups is thus to establish appropriate levels of control over each item. The *ABC* analysis is useful for any type of independent demand system (perpetual, periodic, optional replenishment, and so forth). With the periodic system, the *ABC* analysis can be subdivided so high-volume items receive a short review and low-volume items receive a much longer review. On a periodic basis, class *A* items might be ordered weekly, *B* items might be ordered biweekly, and *C* items might be ordered quarterly or semiannually. Note that the unit cost of an item is not related to the classification. An *A* item may have a high dollar volume through a combination of either low cost and high quantity or high cost and low quantity. Likewise, *C* items may have a low dollar volume because of low demand or low cost.

If items are on a fixed order size system with an EOQ, the EOQ automatically adjusts the lot sizes to an *ABC* configuration. A low annual

Table 1. Comparison of A, B, and C classes

Class	Degree of Control	Type of Records	Lot Sizes	Frequency of Review	Size of Safety Stocks
A	Tight	Accurate and complete	Low	Continuous	Small
B	Moderate	Good	Medium	Occasional	Moderate
C	Loose	Simple	Large	Infrequent	Large

demand results in a smaller lot size, while a low unit cost results in a larger lot size. When an item is a C because of low unit cost, that automatically results in a larger lot size. When an item is a C because of a high unit cost and a low unit demand, it may be advisable to order it on a one-for-one basis or order only when a known demand occurs. Perhaps only one unit may be kept in stock, and the item is reordered when the existing unit is removed from stock.

The A, B, and C classes are artificial strata. Each organization should tailor its inventory system to its own peculiarities. Organizations may choose to group their inventory into more than three classifications, but the principle is the same: high value items receive the most attention and low value items the least. A comparison of the A, B, and C classes is contained in Table 1.

EXAMPLE 1

A small firm inventories only ten items, but decides to set up an ABC inventory system with 20% A items, 30% B items, and 50% C items. The company records provide the information shown in Table 2.

Table 2

Item	Annual Usage	Cost	Annual Dollar Usage	Rank
G-1	40,000	$.07	$ 2,800	5
G-2	195,000	.11	21,450	1
G-3	4,000	.10	400	9
M-1	100,000	.05	5,000	3
M-2	2,000	.14	280	10
M-3	240,000	.07	16,800	2
M-4	16,000	.08	1,280	6
P-1	80,000	.06	4,800	4
P-2	10,000	.07	700	7
P-3	5,000	.09	450	8
			$53,960	

Table 3

Item	Annual Dollar Usage	Cumulative Dollar Usage	Cumulative Percentage	Class
G-2	$21,450	$21,450	39.8	A
M-3	16,800	38,250	70.9	A
M-1	5,000	43,250	80.2	B
P-1	4,800	48,050	89.0	B
G-1	2,800	50,850	94.2	B
M-4	1,280	52,130	96.6	C
P-2	700	52,830	97.9	C
P-3	450	53,280	98.7	C
G-3	400	53,680	99.5	C
M-2	280	53,960	100.0	C

Table 4

Class	Dollars per Group	Percentage of Items	Percentage of Dollar Usage
A = G-2, M-3	$38,250	20	70.9
B = M-1, P-1, G-1	12,600	30	23.4
C = all others	3,110	50	5.7

Tables 3 and 4 stratify the items into the *ABC* classification.

Before items can be classified, factors other than financial ones must be evaluated. Additional considerations can drastically change an item's classification as well as its control procedure. Some important factors might be:

1. a difficult procurement problem (long and erratic lead time),
2. the likelihood of theft,
3. a difficult forecasting problem (large changes in demand),
4. a short shelf life (due to deterioration and obsolescence),
5. a large storage space requirement (very bulky),
6. the item's operational criticality.

The *ABC* system does not apply directly to demand items controlled under MRP or JIT systems. Its primary application is to end items with demand independent of other end items. Dependent demand items tend to be of equal operational importance for continuity of the production function. Lack of even the lowest cost item can totally disrupt dependent organizational activities. Therefore, operational criticality overrides the item's financial influence.

INVENTORY SYSTEM DEVELOPMENT

The development and implementation of an inventory control system to meet the needs of a specific organization is a customizing operation. Since inventory management is not an island unto itself, the system must serve the goals of the organization as well as the service objectives of other departments. It is usually easier to develop an inventory system for a new company. If a revised system is planned for an existing company, the period of change can be traumatic. When a new system is introduced, operational procedures must be revised, new forms and reporting techniques are changed, employee work patterns are disrupted, and operating efficiency is usually diminished.

The decision to implement and, subsequently, to redesign an inventory system rests with top management. However, the ultimate fate of an inventory control system usually lies in the hands of lower level operations personnel. To avoid resistance to change and implementation difficulties, the affected departments should be included in the design of the inventory system. Their inclusion usually results in a better system with fewer behavioral problems when it is installed. Departments that help create the inventory system tend to nurture it during the implementation phase and correct unanticipated design flaws. Without employee support, any inventory system is subject to demise or at least a turbulent future.

Should the system be manual or computerized? Just as with any prospective investment, a cost-benefit analysis should be conducted. The decision will be influenced by many factors, the most important probably being the volume of work to be handled. Microcomputers and similar business machines are making electronic control a viable alternative for more and more organizations. Since electronic systems are providing additional benefits (accounting, control, and administration) beyond stock control, it is no surprise that they are popular.

A popular retail and wholesale device is called a point-of-sale terminal. There are two types: code readers and keyboards. The code reader automatically inserts information in a terminal by reading magnetic strips on specially designed tapes when the product is passed over a sensing device. The keyboard is similar to a cash register, but it maintains records of inventory status with each sale or withdrawal.

The use of the computer in materials management is growing rapidly. Manual methods (in many cases) have reached their limit. The computer can perform and develop forecasts, reorder points, order quantities, order intervals, product explosions, record maintenance, customer billing, inventory status, and supplier payments. However, manual systems with clerical control are still appropriate for small organizations with fewer material needs.

When initiating an inventory system, the following hints can be helpful:

1. Inventory will invariably increase. Items whose order quantity is increased will be ordered at once, and the stock will increase. Items whose order quantity is decreased will take time for their level to be worked off.
2. Forecasting should be based on daily or weekly data, since lead times are frequently shorter than a month. Monthly forecasting data can conceal patterns of demand occurring during the month and complicate estimates of lead time of shorter duration.
3. The system should be tried on a limited number of items initially to solve any unforeseen problems before it is implemented totally.
4. Run the initial pilot study manually (with a calculator) on a small number of items so personnel can understand it thoroughly. If the final system will be computer-based, the pilot can be studied manually as well as on an automated basis.
5. Before the total system is to be implemented, verify that all personnel involved understand it and are committed to its success.

There are many approaches to designing an inventory system; this section will cover a single approach that can provide a general framework. The general procedure is outlined in Figure 6.

A necessary precondition for developing the inventory system is forecasts of all end items produced or used by the organization. Item forecasts are developed from forecasting models such as were covered in a previous chapter. After item forecasts are obtained, an *ABC* analysis of the inventory will indicate what system or systems would be preferable. If a perpetual or two-bin inventory system is indicated, the EOQ and EPQ models can be employed. If conglomerate orders are necessary, the EOI model can be utilized for the periodic or optional replenishment inventory system. If items fall into the single order category, the SOQ model can be incorporated. If items are needed to support scheduled production operations, the MRP model can be applied.

From the various models and an understanding of the peculiarities of the organization, inventory decision rules can be established for all items. When inventory decision rules indicate items should be ordered, purchase requisitions are transmitted for the appropriate supplier. For external suppliers, purchase requisitions are transmitted to the purchasing department, which then contracts for the items. With internal suppliers, production requisitions are transmitted to the production control department, which then schedules the production of items.

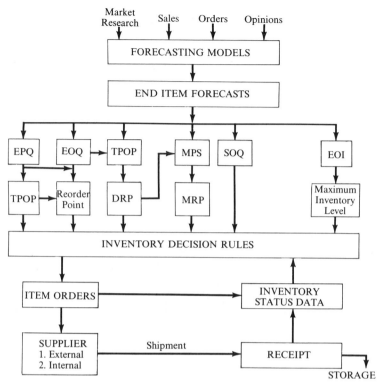

Figure 6. An inventory control system.

Key: EOQ = economic order quantity, EPQ = economic production quantity, EOI = economic order interval, SOQ = single order quantity, TPOP = time-phased order point, DRP = distribution requirements planning, MRP = material requirements planning, MPS = master production schedule.

When ordered items are received from the suppliers, they are quality accepted and put into inventory. Needless to say, all of the transactions involve the generation of paper for accountability and control. Inventory systems are best maintained from a central control location that can indicate the status of any item. These records become the data base for forecasting models. Because of the quantity of items and the proliferation of paperwork, inventory systems are natural candidates for computer control.

The ultimate success of an inventory system depends on turning inventory theory into workable detailed procedures. Any inventory system requires the collection and processing of vast quantities of data. The design of forms and procedures can be as important as precise quantitative accuracy.

The foundations of any inventory control system are input data and control records, which must be current and accurate. Inventory control is based on the accuracy of records of inflows and outflows. Poor records and data can destroy a perfectly designed control system. Inadequate records result in operating personnel finding informal methods (usually to the subversion of the formal procedures) for satisfying inventory needs (hoarding, stockpiling, overordering, early ordering, and so forth). Accurate and up-to-date records permit an inventory system to function efficiently and effectively.

Modern analytical techniques have taken much, but not all, of the guesswork out of inventory management. No longer need stock levels be determined solely by habit, hunch, or accident. Formulas are available to establish order quantities and order intervals, while statistical probability theory can be applied to safety stock determination. Intelligent and informed management judgment has not been replaced, but has been supplemented. Both qualitative and quantitative evaluations, involving considerable study and collaboration, are usually required before intelligent decisions can be made and effective systems implemented.

The design of inventory systems must include sufficient flexibility to permit growth, expansion, and internal change without upsetting the operational system. The system must be able to cope with the exceptional item or event. The inventory system should be capable of being integrated into the other organizational systems with little difficulty.

INVENTORY SYSTEM IMPROVEMENT

Each purchase or production situation must be preceded by a decision making process. The number of items involved can range from scores to millions, and the number of transactions is far in excess of the number of items. The decision making process may be simple or complex, programmed or nonprogrammed, intuitive or mathematical, hasty or deliberate. There are many ways an inventory manager can reduce costs. Some of the more apparent methods are as follows:

1. *Reduce lead times.* By selecting local suppliers or suppliers close to the organization's geographical location, substantial reductions in cost can be achieved. Local supply can reduce lead times, which lowers the reorder point and safety stock.
2. *Inform suppliers of expected annual demand.* If suppliers are aware of annual needs, they can plan their production to have sufficient inventory available to meet the expected demand. This action can reduce lead time and permit the supplier to better plan and schedule production operations.

3. *Contract with suppliers for minimum annual purchases.* Contract to purchase a fixed annual quantity from suppliers with payment to coincide with the receipt of materials. Quantity discounts can be obtained in this manner while materials are ordered and received in economic quantities. This approach can also be a hedge against future price increases.

4. *Offer customers a discount on preordered items.* If customers order items before they need them, inventory reductions can be achieved by specially ordering components. If customers receive a discount on items ordered before they are needed, the price reduction can frequently offset the increase in holding costs associated with higher inventory levels.

5. *Use fewer suppliers.* Multiple suppliers can increase costs by reducing bulk purchases. With fewer suppliers, there can be greater provision for quality, price, and inventory control. Frequently, reliability and quality of supply are more important than short-term, minor price differences. Smaller order quantities with more frequent deliveries are more likely with "favored suppliers."

6. *Buy on consignment.* Arrange with suppliers to pay for their items as they are sold or used. This action will transfer a large portion of the holding costs to the supplier.

7. *Consider transportation costs.* Failing to consider transportation costs and the most economical mode of transportation can increase unit cost considerably.

8. *Order economical quantities.* Overbuying in relation to needs results in excessive holding costs.

9. *Control access to storage areas.* Protect against losses from theft, spoilage, unauthorized withdrawals by employees, and the ravages of the elements.

10. *Obtain better forecasts.* More reliable and precise forecasts can substantially reduce safety stocks.

11. *Standardize stock items.* Inventories can be reduced by a reduction in the quantities of each item or by a reduction in the number of different items used in stock. Inventory investment can be lowered by carrying one standard item instead of five different items that are used for essentially the same purpose.

12. *Dispose of inactive stock.* On a regular basis all stock should be reviewed to identify obsolete, poor quality, surplus, and slow-moving items. Disposal alternatives include return to vendor, scrap, rework, salvage, and reduced-price sale.

13. *Adopt cycle counting.* Inaccurate inventory records result in numerous problems (too much of the wrong stuff, not enough of the right stuff, low turnover rate, excessive expediting and staging, and ineffective scheduling). Cycle counting can improve record accuracy and

reduce the need for disruptive shutdowns of operations for physical inventory counts.

14. *Improve capacity planning.* Overloading a facility results in backlogs and poor customer service. The master production schedule should not be loaded beyond the capacity of the facility (bottleneck work centers).

15. *Minimize setup times.* The unencumbered flow of work through a production facility is limited by setup times. When a work center is being set up, no output is being produced and other arriving jobs must wait in a queue. With shorter setup times, smaller lot sizes are possible.

Frequently the quickest, most effective way to reduce inventory is better priority planning and control of operations. A poorly devised operating system may appear efficient with the aid of excessive inventory. Improved planning and scheduling of operations can reduce the investment in inventory.

Organizationally, the inventory control function is usually assigned to the purchasing or the production control department. Purchasing feeds the inventory reservoir, while production control draws from it. Because department managers tend to neglect the significance of costs outside their own departments, the materials management concept has developed. The materials manager consolidates purchasing, inventory control and production control into a single operating unit. The materials management concept grew out of the frustration of many companies at not being able to control inventory effectively. It is not uncommon for departments to continually find fault with each other, when the true culprit is an inadequate organizational structure. Decisions to add new products, purchase foreign components, and add distribution points can have a dramatic effect on inventory investment. Likewise, uncontrolled product proliferation, errors in transaction documentation, and outdated bills of materials create serious problems.

The number of items in inventory has been growing because of the increasingly technical nature of the items, a demand for greater variety by customers, and requirements for better service. The number of dollars invested in inventory is growing at a faster rate than the number of items. Computerization may hold the key to the solution of these problems. The computer aspect of materials management has been intentionally downplayed so as not to divert the reader from the really important subject matter. The computer's contribution lies in its power to execute a multitude of straightforward procedures in a very short time. The computer, while an essential tool of materials management, is not essential to understanding the subject. Computer routines and analytical techniques do not eliminate the need for good management.

AGGREGATE INVENTORY MEASUREMENT

Aggregate inventory measurement relates to the overall level of inventory and the techniques for its measurement. In essence it "looks at the forest and not each tree." Four common ways to measure aggregate inventory are as follows:

1. aggregate inventory value,
2. ratio of aggregate inventory value to annual sales,
3. days of supply,
4. inventory turnover.

An organization may use one or more of the above for aggregate inventory measurement.

Aggregate inventory value is simply the total value of inventory at cost. Many organizations set dollar limits or budgets on the amount which can be invested in each general class of materials. They are usually applied to broad classes and not to individual items. The dollar limits indicate the upper investment limit which aggregate inventory value should not exceed. Aggregate inventory value is very simple and easy to use, but it neglects the dynamic nature of inventory and its other financial interactions.

The *inventory to sales ratio* is the aggregate inventory at cost divided by annual sales. This ratio recognizes the dynamic relation between inventory and sales, but it can vary substantially due to cost and/or selling price changes. If profit margins change, the ratio can become distorted and useless for comparison purposes.

The number of *days of supply* (time supply of inventory) is the total value of inventory at cost divided by the sales per day at cost. This measure is dynamic in nature, but it can become confounded if the cost of sales is not maintained and controlled.

Inventory turnover refers to the cycle of using and replacing materials. It is the ratio of the annual cost of goods sold (annual sales at cost) to the average inventory. It indicates the number of "turnovers" of the investment in inventory for a given time period (usually a year). If an organization has sales such that its cost of goods sold is $600,000 a year and has an average inventory valued at $300,000, it has two turnovers per year. If the organization could generate the same sales with an average inventory worth $150,000, it would have four turnovers per year. High turnover reduces the inventory investment and also saves holding costs. But it can be harmful if the low inventories cause frequent stockouts. A high inventory turnover at the cost of customer service and manufacturing expense is of dubious value. Inventory turnover recognizes the dynamic nature of inventory, but like most ratios it can easily become distorted.

Aggregate inventory measurement techniques usually reduce inventory items to the common financial measure of dollars. The techniques measure results in absolute terms or ratios. The desirable range of performance is established historically by industry data, or by management judgment. While measurement in financial terms is desirable, inventory should also be viewed through other dimensions (composition, flexibility, contribution to organizational objectives).

AGGREGATE INVENTORY REDUCTION

In uncertain economic environments it may not be possible to achieve desired growth rates in profitability and return on assets simply by increasing sales volumes. Consequently, management may be forced to look for ways to improve performance within the organization. Usually the attention of top management focuses on cash flow and return on assets. Inventory represents a substantial asset in most firms, and many times the goal will be to reduce inventory in order to improve performance.

A starting point for inventory reduction is an analysis of the current composition of the inventory. As shown in Figure 7, an aggregate inventory

Figure 7. Aggregate inventory profile.
It is the total inventory level that appears on the balance sheet in aggregate dollars.

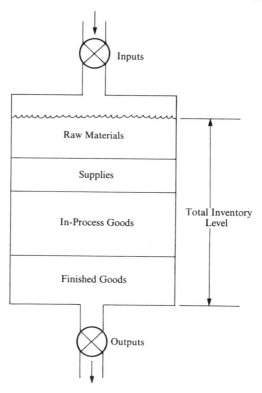

profile will reveal the financial composition by type of inventory. Reduction strategies should begin with the inventory type that represents the largest investment or fraction of inventory investment and then focus on the other types in descending order.

Pressures for inventory reductions frequently emanate from top management following periods of unsatisfactory performance. Since there is no perfect inventory control system appropriate to all situations, temporal distortions are to be expected occasionally. Often this condition results in an edict to materials managers to achieve a lower aggregate level by a given point in time or a higher turnover rate for a given period of time.

Raw Materials, Supplies, and Finished Goods

Profiles of raw materials and supplies and of finished goods are illustrated in Figures 8 and 9. For these profiles, it is important to understand the distinction between productive and nonproductive (sometimes referred to as active and inactive) inventory. Productive inventory is that which is serving a purpose or for which there is an anticipated demand within the foreseeable future. Nonproductive inventory consists of items currently on the books for which there is no reasonable expectation of a use or customer requirement within the foreseeable future. A reduction of a dollar's worth of productive inventory is worth one dollar in positive cash flow with little impact on profits and taxes. On the other hand, a reduction in nonproductive inventory only affects cash flow through the tax savings, but it has a major impact on profit and taxes. Thus, if a nonproductive inventory item is scrapped, the inventory writedown reduces profits by the full value of the item. With a 50% tax rate, every dollar of nonproductive writedown produces a cash tax saving of about $.50. The conclusion to be reached is that inventory reduction in both productive and nonproductive inventory produces a significant improvement in cash flow.

The initial way to reduce inventory and generate cash is to identify and dispose of all nonproductive inventory (surplus and excess stock). Any loss taken from selling at a price below book value is still tax deductible, and any cash received simply increases the yield above the tax rate. For example, if a $1.00 item is sold for $.40, a $.60 loss per item is taken, which will save approximately $.30 in taxes (assuming a 50% tax rate). The net result is a 70% yield ($.40 in cash and $.30 in reduced taxes).

Surplus items for which there are no known future requirements should be sold or salvaged. For other items, it is necessary to determine if excessive levels exist. Even when there is a future demand for an item, its level may exceed what should be available. The accrued holding costs of these excessive quantities for extended periods of time can be a financial burden. It may be economically advantageous to sell or salvage a fraction of such

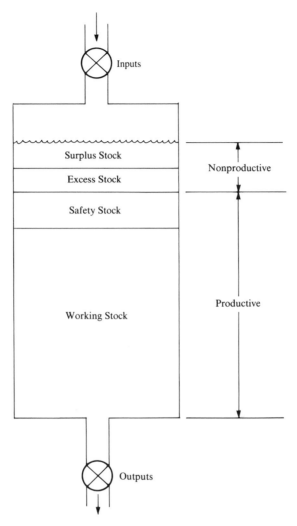

Figure 8. Raw materials and supplies inventory profile.

stock levels. Periodic review can identify items that need not be carried in stock or items whose quantity should be reduced.

Safety stock, lot sizes, and lead times are the parameters that must change if significant reductions are to be made in productive inventory. Safety stock levels can be lowered by decreasing service levels, improving quality control, and shortening lead times. If seasonal (anticipation) stock is built during some time periods, it can also serve as safety stock until it is depleted by seasonal demand. Lot size (working stock) levels can be

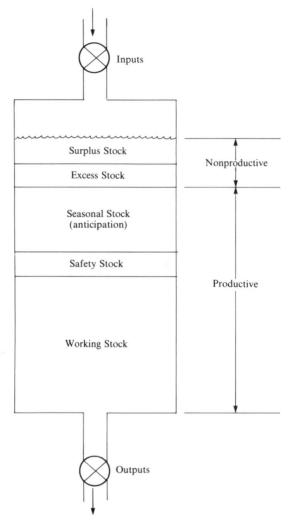

Figure 9. Finished goods inventory profile.

lowered by increasing the holding cost fraction and reducing setup (ordering) costs.

The holding cost fraction F can be used as a management policy variable to control stock levels. A high fraction makes inventory more expensive, so there will be less of it. A low fraction makes inventory less expensive, so there will be more of it. For this fraction to have an impact, it must be changed in large increments. A change of 1 or 2% will not usually be noticed. Also, there is a limit to how low you can drive inventory by increasing the holding cost fraction. Since service levels may take account of the number of replenishments, a high F can result in more orders being placed, which increases the exposure to stockouts. Thus, a high F will decrease the working stock inventory.

It takes some time before the inventory investment will respond to a change in F. Its effect is fast for active items that are replenished frequently. For slower moving items it will have no effect until the items are ordered. Thus, the reaction to a change in F can be varied and sluggish.

In-Process Inventory

The level of work-in-process (WIP) inventory is determined by the amount of work released to the shop and the output rate from it. The in-process inventory profile is illustrated in Figure 10. To reduce WIP, reduce the number of orders released to the shop, decrease the throughput time (lead time), or increase the capacity of critical (overloaded or bottleneck) work centers. Typically, input considerations include

1. keeping backlogs off the shop floor (do not overload the shop beyond bottleneck capacity limitations);
2. releasing an order at the latest possible moment (the shorter the scheduling period, the lower the WIP, because of the decrease in handling, congestion, and conflict).

The majority of WIP is represented by work waiting in queues; the time spent in such queues usually amounts to 80–90% of the manufacturing cycle time. If queues can be shortened, WIP and lead times can be correspondingly reduced.

Growing WIP and excessive lead times are symptoms of poor capacity planning. Since the output of a facility is dictated by its bottleneck work centers, they should be loaded to capacity with little if any planned idle time (except maintenance). There should always be a queue in front of bottleneck centers to ensure their complete utilization. Nonbottleneck work centers should not be loaded to capacity, but their utilization rate should be dictated by the bottleneck centers. Capacity utilization at bottleneck work centers is of paramount benefit, while capacity utilization at nonbottleneck work centers builds unneeded inventory and is of no benefit. Overloaded conditions at critical centers can be resolved through alternate routings, schedule revisions, and overtime. Additionally, reduced setup times will result in a reduction of lot sizes and lead times. These ideas are embodied in the just-in-time (JIT) philosophy.

The basic concept of JIT is to eliminate waste—of time, energy, and material—so as to produce only what is needed when it is needed. Follow-

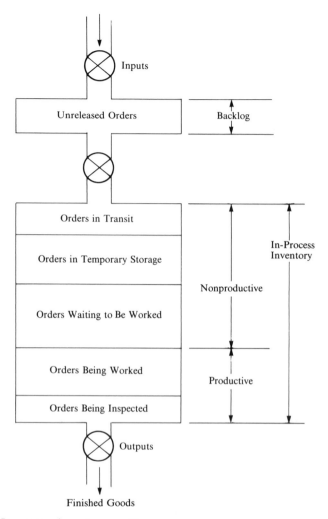

Figure 10. In-process inventory profile.

ing this concept to its ideal, the ultimate lot size is *one* and there is *no* excess inventory. It is a goal to strive for, even though it is not achievable. The idea is to operate with as little inventory as possible.

CONCLUSION

An effective inventory system should be relative, dynamic, and truthful. *Relative* refers to meeting the needs of other organizational functions or departments. *Dynamic* refers to the time variation of inventory needs. Any

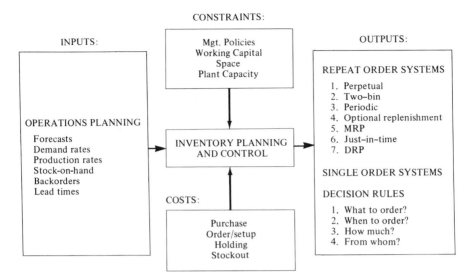

Figure 11. The inventory function.

system must react to expected and unexpected changes. *Truthful* refers to the ability to report accurately the stock or position of inventory when required.

Management's responsibility is to manage the organization's assets, both human and nonhuman, in the light of preconceived goals and objectives. Inventory bears upon all the functional areas. Thus it should not be surprising that inventories are troublesome and controversial.

The inventory function is outlined in Figure 11.

Control can be a two-edged sword. Intense overcontrol is just as undesirable and costly as undercontrol. A *carte blanche* attitude towards new sophisticated control systems can be costly. New systems that save hundreds and cost thousands of dollars are unhealthy investments. A control system (or systems) should be installed on the basis of its cost-benefit relationship and not to achieve control as an end in itself.

The design of aggregate materials management systems can be approached from different angles. It is common for emphasis to be put on specific control models rather than the relevant systems. A broad based aggregate program should include at least the following elements:

1. determination or delineation of organizational goals,
2. assessment of the significance of materials management to organizational goals,
3. determination of aggregate materials needs,

4. design of appropriate material control models,
5. design of forecasting models,
6. measurement and collection of model parameter inputs,
7. model testing and implementation,
8. variable reporting and model redesign,
9. operationalization of the materials management system.

Most systems fail because the fundamentals or basics are forgotten. The basics must be operating in order for the sophisticated tools to be successful. Just like football, the game is won or lost on the line. With so much emphasis on computers, we often are tempted to believe they are the solution to all of the problems. Computerized techniques can very quickly and efficiently turn a little bit of nonsense into a whole lot of nonsense.

The problems of inventory and materials management are ubiquitous and complex. No simple formula takes into account all of the variables encountered in real situations. The value of good approximations in permitting a practical and understandable solution to a problem is often far greater than any loss caused by a lack of accuracy or precision. Aggregate inventory analysis is not a precise science.

QUESTIONS

1. What should an effective inventory control system accomplish? What vital areas should be considered in developing a comprehensive control system?

2. Identify the most frequently used inventory systems, and indicate the basis on which each operates.

3. What is the major disadvantage of the perpetual inventory system? What other problems may occur with the use of this system?

4. How does the two-bin inventory system differ from the perpetual system?

5. Compare the potential ordering practices and safety stock requirements of the periodic inventory system with those associated with the perpetual system.

6. What is the benefit derived from using a reorder point parameter in conjunction with the two other parameters of the optional replenishment system?

7. Discuss independent and dependent demand as they occur in a distribution requirements planning (DRP) system.

8. How does DRP determine requirements at the central distribution level?

9. Name some of the vital ingredients for an MRP inventory system.

10. To what manufacturing environment does just-in-time (JIT) apply?

11. What considerations can drastically affect an item's classification as well as its control procedure in an *ABC* inventory analysis?

12. With what organizational group does the ultimate success of an inventory system lie? Why?

13. Give two or three hints which might be useful in initiating an inventory control system.

14. How can reducing lead times, offering customers a discount on preordered items, and using fewer suppliers reduce inventory costs?

15. Where is a good starting point for inventory reduction?

16. How can overloaded conditions at critical work centers be resolved?

17. Discuss the types of inventory control systems used in your home for food, clothing, medicines, and other household items.

CASE 1: MATERIAL SHORTAGES AND DELAYED PRODUCTION

Zoom Equipment, Inc., produces a full line of earth moving equipment including tractors, dirtmovers, and shovels. It manufactures all component parts for the machines with a few exceptions. Sam Irwin, the new production manager, realized quickly that a major problem existed in the production department. A shortage of parts on the assembly lines was costing Zoom thousands of dollars.

Sam's first step in attempting to alleviate the problem was to investigate the company's make or buy decision procedures. He started his investigation in the accounting department. After some searching he realized he'd have to get actual out-of-pocket costs from the manufacturing department itself. There he was told the actual costs of parts varied considerably from one run to another for several reasons, the main one being that when it came time to assemble a piece of equipment there was seldom a sufficient quantity of all parts needed. The result was usually a schedule-upsetting rush order through the machine shop to make needed parts.

Sam decided to track down the reasons for the parts shortages on the assembly lines. He spent the next several days talking to the workers and supervisors. Sam learned that the marketing department forecasted sales of all equipment and parts about nine months in advance. The production control supervisor then prepared a list of all parts required and added a manufacturing spoilage allowance to the quantities needed. This allowance was as follows:

a. large items, 1%;
b. costly or intricate parts, 2%;
c. other parts, 3%.

The quantities of parts in inventory were compared with this list. If requirements exceeded inventory, a purchase order or manufacturing order was placed to bring inventory up to the required level.

Sam got the impression that the shortage problem had gone unnoticed for some time, because the cost accounting department actually budgeted for excess labor costs resulting from shortages on the assembly lines. After completing his investigation Sam made a list of reasons for the shortages:

a. inadequate spoilage allowances,
b. errors in annual physical inventory count,
c. incorrect count of parts put into production,
d. poor machine loading,
e. insufficient raw materials purchased,
f. foremen performing clerical tasks.

1. Are any of Sam's reasons for shortages on the assembly line valid?
2. How would you correct for the shortages?
3. What type of inventory control system should be adopted by Zoom?

CASE 2: CONTROL AND OPERATING METHODS

Automobile dealerships have a large and continuing need for supplies and materials in their function of selling and servicing automobiles. Facilities usually include buildings spread over several acres of land. Below are listed the departments that have special needs for supplies:

a. *Office*: office supplies and special forms.
b. *New car predelivery service*: cleanup materials and lubricants.
c. *Used car reconditioning*: cleanup materials and lubricants.
d. *Body shop*: paint and materials, including thinner, sandpaper, files, tape, etc.
e. *Mechanical shop*: supplies and materials.

At Tidewater Motors, salesmen from various suppliers make regular calls, check inventory levels, and recommend purchases. Normally the dealership parts manager acts as purchasing agent. However, salesmen go directly to the foremen of the different departments, since in most cases the supplies are stored at the department location. In this case, the foreman is the real purchasing authority who instructs the parts manager to issue the necessary purchase orders.

The advantages of the existing system are that the salesmen can solve any problems with their products, salesmen can check inventory levels, and little of the parts manager's time is required. Disadvantages of the system are that the salesmen try to sell the foreman and workers on their products as being best (this often creates problems when brands are changed), the salesmen tend to oversell actual needs, and price increases frequently go unnoticed.

Recently, Dick Terry took over as owner of the Tidewater Motors dealership. Upon reviewing his investment in inventory, he concluded that his inventory turnover was too low. He decided to investigate new control and operating procedures that might reduce his inventory investment.

1. Should all materials and supplies be kept in one central location instead of being stored in close proximity to where they are used?
2. Should the parts manager make all decisions concerning the purchase of supplies?
3. Should salesmen be able to deal directly with foremen and workers, or should they deal only with the parts manager?

CASE 3: POOR RECEPTION

Warwick Electronic Services (WES) is a service company that services all types of home entertainment equipment. Seventy percent of the revenue is derived from television set repairs.

WES is an authorized Zenith service center, which must stock a complete line of spare parts for Zenith TV sets. The spare parts are purchased from Zenith in a kit and then exchanged for new and rebuilt parts as they are used. If the exchange of parts is the result of warranty service, they are replaced at no charge. The Zenith repairs account for 30% of total revenue. Another 40% of revenue is derived from servicing television sets manufactured by other companies, but there are no service agreements with them. The remaining revenue comes from stereo and miscellaneous equipment repairs.

The commonly used parts are stocked by a local distributor (parts house), which is three miles from the repair shop. The slower moving items have to be ordered through the distributor with a lead time of two weeks. The service records show that $60,000 was spent on parts last year. The annual inventory holding cost is 20%, and the inventory level averages $40,000. The consumption of parts is directly related to the gross revenue, and the revenue is forecasted to increase at a rate of 10% during the next three years.

The present inventory system is unorganized and inefficient. As parts are needed, a few extra ones are ordered and stored until they are needed. This practice has led to a large accumulation of obsolete parts. The manager wants to formalize the inventory system and is ready to implement a new system.

1. What inventory system options are available to WES?
2. What inventory system or systems would you recommend? Why?
3. Does the dollar size of the inventory investment influence the type of system?

CASE 4: DEFENSIVE PURCHASING

The Propulsion Division of Tinker Air Force Base is a government operated facility for reworking military aircraft engines. The division supports five families of engines plus component parts. The disassembled engines flow through a series of continuous and intermittent process shops by means of an automated conveyor system with selected inventory control and feed points. The actual route and replacement work for an individual part entering the overhaul process is dependent on its condition as determined by nondestructive inspections.

The purchasing function to support the rework facility is encumbered with several obstacles. The quantities of required parts vary greatly. Not only do work loads tend to be sporadic (partly a budgetary effect), but the types of rework necessary to repair or rebuild the incoming engines are also subject to extreme variation. Furthermore, purchasing, as a legislated procurement procedure, is done by contract with the recipients promising least cost delivery of federally specified parts. Many suppliers are becoming reluctant to submit bids because of the competitive pressure. Other peculiarities are also increasing supplier reluctance, e.g., fear of short-term agreements after expensive setups, tight governmental guidelines, costs that restrict profit potential, and worse yet, a recent wave of favoritism. Therefore, as either a cause or an effect, an extension of the already successful in-house production of replacement parts is expected.

Tinker has an excellent staff of six civil service purchasing agents, skilled in public purchasing and experienced in make-or-buy decisions. The total budget for the purchasing department is $425,000 annually, with 50% allocated to staff salaries. The agents typically process 12,500 purchase orders per year, amounting to a total annual expenditure of $60 million. A work measurement study conducted in the purchasing department disclosed that preparation and followup on orders is required at the 90% performance level for rework operations.

There are other costs of particular importance to the purchasing department. Materials and expediting expenses are $12 per order for phone calls, forms, etc. Obsolescence costs are approximated at 3% of total inventory value, and costs for insurance, deterioration, and warehouse space are roughly 6%. Presently, the annual expense to operate the stores for inventory storage is budgeted at $125,000, the interest rate the military is assumed to pay on borrowed capital is 10%, and the required return on investment used for performance evaluation is set at 15%. These costs are used as in private enterprise to determine operating and inventory policies. The purchasing department calculates EOQs for purchased replacement parts and orders.

These costs are expected to change as the nation confronts an economic crisis. The administration and congressional bodies are formulating a comprehensive revitalization program. A significant part of the program is massive Federal restraint. Tinker is not certain how this will affect operations directly, but cutbacks in personnel and operating budgets seem imminent. With drastic cutbacks, the purchasing department feels it will have to cope in the short run by cutting some variable costs.

However, there is another administrative program that appears to be receiving popular support—increased defense spending. Provided this program receives approval, activity at Tinker could increase measurably. The not so invisible hand of the government could change rework orders substantially.

With operations so tightly predicated on government policies, the purchasing department cannot predict future circumstances. If cutbacks are severe, are changes in ordering strategies necessary or are changes in inventory systems preferred, e.g., from EOQ to two-bin? If defense spending is a priority item, are EOQs changed proportionately and are fixed costs likely to increase? If either or both situations occur, how is inventory management affected? These and more unanswered questions abound.

1. What ordering costs and holding costs are relevant prior to a revitalization program?
2. How might purchasing and inventory management change with stringent budgetary controls? With military proliferation?
3. What operating practices might come into play with the new program? Could another inventory control system be better in the deployment of the revitalization plan?
4. What effect could the federal programs have on suppliers and on in-house production?

CASE 5: SECOND-HAND GOODS

The Pickard Motor Company is imperiled by the contemporary problems that have nearly destroyed much of the American automobile industry. With the depressed domestic economic situation, sales are falling dramatically, and ability to compete with foreign auto makers is seriously hampered. Proof of their financial jeopardy comes with the announcement of the latest quarterly earnings; Pickard is declaring the largest losses in corporate history. Witnessing the rapid decline of corporate solvency, Pickard is undertaking a recovery program whereby drastic changes are being instituted in product offerings. Pickard is converting a large portion of passenger car production to energy efficient cars. To do so, Pickard is paying enormous retooling and inventory replacement costs with capital borrowed at record high interest rates.

The Louisville Assembly Plant of Pickard Motors (Case 5, Chapter 11) is nearing the production "launch" of the newly engineered S-cars, Pickard's first energy efficient compacts. Since the Louisville plant is the site for finalizing engineering and production changes, the model year changeover to introduce the new line to production precedes operations at the other assembly plants by three months. Current model year production ends company-wide in four months, and all aspects of capital and procedural modification at Louisville must occur within that time.

Currently, Louisville has over $2.6 million worth of parts that are technologically acceptable for the present production year. Calculations show that these parts will carry over well beyond the final four weeks of scheduled production. Unfortunately, most of these parts are obsolete for the S-line, which is the only line to remain in production at the Louisville site. The number of obsolete parts is inordinately high even after subtraction of the few "carryover" parts. The only possibilities of parts that could carry over to next year's line are certain sizes of tires and spark plugs, a few incidental nuts and bolts, some standard paint colors, and other parts with negligible dollar values.

Pickard headquarters is greatly disturbed about the dollar value of excess materials and is demanding prompt disposition of all surplus parts. The Louisville staff also recognizes the need for immediate disposition in order for the plant to attain operational status for the S-car "Launch Program." Louisville is more interested in getting the parts "off the books" than in the losses that will be suffered through quick disposition. The corporate headquarters, on the other hand, is taking an opposing view, stressing reasonable cash recovery from the disposition of the goods.

Customarily, Pickard's initial disposition step would be return of the excess parts to the supplier and assumption of a small loss on the transaction. The present difficulty with this disposition route is time consumption and the predatory attitude the suppliers have taken in the current hard times for automobile producers. Pickard feels there has been systematic and conspired erosion of supplier repurchase prices, and therefore would rather choose an alternative route.

In the past, Pickard has also sold excess materials to employees. Recently, the company has considered forbidding this practice, because it has been used discriminately and has become a perquisite of top management. Furthermore, many of those who have participated in employee surplus sales have used the materials to start side-line businesses rather than for personal repairs or avocations.

Jim Jones, Louisville's scrap materials manager, seems to have been left with the bulk of the disposition task and has been instructed to get rid of as much dollar value of inventory as possible. As his first sources of solutions, he has been phoning friends in scrap materials businesses in automobile related fields. However, most of his hopes lie internally with great expectations of his counterpart at the San Jose Assembly Plant; he is sure he can ride to laurels on the proven disposition paths of the San Jose expert.

Ironically, San Jose, Louisville's sister plant, is found to seldom face excesses but chronically experience shortages. So, with little assistance from surplus materials personnel with understandably good track records and given headquarters's apprehensions concerning customary routes, Jim may have to push to pursue the old disposition means or quickly find new ones.

1. What disposition options are available?
2. Given their orientation, what would Louisville and the corporate headquarters most likely want done?
3. Should Louisville sacrifice sell and take the tax writeoff?
4. Could an *ABC* approach be applicable to Jim Jones's task?

Bibliography

Alfandary-Alexander, Mark. *An Inquiry into Some Models of Inventory Systems*, Pittsburgh, PA: University of Pittsburgh Press, 1962.

Aljian, George W., and P. V. Farrell, ed. *Aljian's Purchasing Handbook*, New York: McGraw-Hill, 1982.

American Management Association. *Company Approaches to Production Problems*: *Inventory, Warehousing, Traffic*, New York: American Management Association, 1955.

_____. *Key Consideration to Inventory Management*, New York: American Management Association, 1953.

American Production and Inventory Control Society. *Management of Lot-Size Inventories*, Washington, DC: APICS, 1963.

_____. *Material Requirements Planning by Computer*, Washington, DC: APICS, 1971.

Ammer, D. S. *Materials Management and Purchasing*, Homewood, IL: Richard D. Irwin, 1980.

Arrow, K. J., et al. *Studies in the Mathematical Theory of Inventory and Production*, Stanford, CA: Stanford University Press, 1958.

Baily, P. J. *Design of Stock Control Systems and Records*, London: Gower Press, 1970.

Baily, Peter, and David Farmer. *Managing Materials in Industry*, London: Gower Press, 1972.

Ballot, Robert P. *Materials Management*, New York: American Management Association, 1971.

Ballou, Ronald H. *Business Logistics Management*, Englewood Cliffs, NJ: Prentice-Hall, 1978.

Barrett, D. A. *Automatic Inventory Control Techniques*, London: Business Books Limited, 1972.

Bierman, Harold, et al. *Quantitative Analysis for Business Decisions*, Homewood, IL: Richard D. Irwin, 1969.

Blanchard, B. S. *Logistics Engineering and Management*, Englewood Cliffs, NJ: Prentice-Hall, 1986.

Bourke, R. *Bill of Materials*, Pasadena, CA: Bourke & Associates, 1975.

Bowersox, Donald J. *Logistical Management*, New York: Macmillan Publishing Company, 1974.

Bowman, Edward H., and Robert B. Fetter. *Analysis for Production and Operations Management*, Homewood, IL: Richard D. Irwin, 1967.

Box, G. E. P., and G. M. Jenkins. *Time Series Analysis: Forecasting and Control*, San Francisco: Holden-Day, 1970.

Briggs, Andrew J. *Warehouse Operations Planning and Management*, New York: John Wiley and Sons, 1960.

Brown, R. G. *Advanced Service Parts Inventory Control*, Norwich, VT: Materials Management Systems, 1982.

_____. *Materials Management Systems*, New York: John Wiley and Sons, 1977.

_____. *Decision Rules for Inventory Management*, New York: Holt, Rinehart and Winston, 1967.

_____. *Smoothing, Forecasting, and Prediction of Discrete Time Series*, Englewood Cliffs, NJ: Prentice-Hall, 1963.

_____. *Statistical Forecasting for Inventory Control*, New York: McGraw-Hill, 1959.

Buchan, Joseph, and Ernest Koenigsberg. *Scientific Inventory Management*, Englewood Cliffs, NJ: Prentice-Hall, 1963.

Buffa, E. S., and J. G. Miller. *Production-Inventory Systems: Planning and Control*, Homewood, IL: Richard D. Irwin, 1979.

Carroll, Phil. *Practical Production and Inventory Control*, New York: McGraw-Hill, 1966.

Cavinato, J. L. *Purchasing and Materials Management*, St. Paul, MN: West Publishing, 1984.

D'Anna, John P. *Inventory and Profit: The Balance of Power in Buying and Selling*, New York: American Management Association, 1966.

Davis, Grant M., and Stephen W. Brown. *Logistics Management*, Lexington, MA: Lexington Books, 1974.

Deis, P. *Production and Inventory Management in the Technological Age*, Englewood Cliffs, NJ: Prentice-Hall, 1983.

Dobler, D. W., et al. *Purchasing and Materials Management*, New York: McGraw-Hill, 1984.

Dudick, T. S., and R. Cornell. *Inventory Control for the Financial Executive*, New York: John Wiley and Sons, 1979.

England, Wilbur B. *The Purchasing System*, Homewood, IL: Richard D. Irwin, 1967.

England, Wilbur B., and Michiel R. Leenders. *Purchasing and Materials Management*, Homewood, IL: Richard D. Irwin, 6th edition, 1975.

Enrick, Norbert Lloyd, *Inventory Management*, San Francisco, CA: Chandler Publishing Company, 1968.

Fabrycky, W. J., and Jerry Banks. *Procurement and Inventory Systems: Theory and Analysis*, New York: Reinhold Publishing Corp., 1967.

Fetter, Robert B., and Winston C. Dalleck. *Decision Models for Inventory Management*, Homewood, IL: Richard D. Irwin, 1961.

Fogarty, D. W., and T. R. Hoffman. *Production and Inventory Management*, Cincinnati, OH: South-Western, 1988.

Forrester, Jay W. *Industrial Dynamics*, Boston: M.I.T. Press, 1961.

Fourre, James P. *Applying Inventory Control Techniques*, New York: American Management Association, 1969.

Fuchs, J. H. *Computerized Inventory Control Systems*, Englewood Cliffs, NJ: Prentice-Hall, 1978.

Greene, James H. *Production and Inventory Control Handbook*, New York: McGraw-Hill, 1987.

———. *Production and Inventory Control*, Homewood, IL: Richard D. Irwin, 2nd edition, 1974.

Gross, Harry. *Make or Buy*, Englewood Cliffs, NJ: Prentice-Hall, 1966.

Hadley, G., and T. M. Whitin. *Analysis of Inventory Systems*, Englewood Cliffs, NJ: Prentice-Hall, 1963.

Hall, R. W. *Zero Inventories*, Homewood, IL: Dow-Jones Irwin, 1983.

Hanssmann, Fred. *Operations Research in Production and Inventory Control*, New York: John Wiley and Sons, 1962.

Hasting, N. A. J., and J. B. Peacock. *Statistical Distributions*, London: Butterworths, 1975.

Hax, A. C. and D. Candea. *Production and Inventory Management*, Englewood Cliffs, NJ: Prentice-Hall, 1984.

Hedrich, Floyd D. *Purchasing Management in the Smaller Company*, New York: American Management Association, 1971.

Heinritz, Stuart F., and Paul V. Farrell. *Purchasing: Principles and Applications*, Englewood Cliffs, NJ: Prentice-Hall, 6th edition, 1981.

Heskett, James L., et al. *Business Logistics*, New York: The Ronald Press, 2nd edition, 1973.

Hobbs, John A. *Control over Inventory and Production*, New York: McGraw-Hill, 1973.

Hoffman, Raymond A., and Henry Gunders. *Inventories: Control, Costing and Effect upon Income and Taxes*, New York: Ronald Press, 2nd edition, 1970.

Holt, Charles C., et al. *Planning Production, Inventories, and Work Force*, Englewood Cliffs, NJ: Prentice-Hall, 1960.

——— et al. *Operations Research in Production and Inventory Control*, New York: John Wiley and Sons, 1962.

Jannis, C. P., et al. *Managing and Accounting for Inventories*, New York: John Wiley and Sons, 1980.

Janson, R. L. *Handbook of Inventory Management*, Englewood Cliffs, NJ: Prentice-Hall, 1986.

Jenkins, Creed H. *Modern Warehouse Management*, New York: McGraw-Hill, 1968.

Johnson, Lynwood A., and Douglas C. Montgomery. *Operations Research in Production Planning, Scheduling, and Inventory Control*, New York: John Wiley and Sons, 1974.

Killeen, Louis M. *Techniques of Inventory Management*, New York: American Management Association, 1969.

Leenders, M. R., et al. *Purchasing and Materials Management*, Homewood, IL: Richard D. Irwin, 1985.

Lewis, C. D. *Scientific Inventory Control*, New York: American Elsevier, 1970.

Lipman, Burton E. *How to Control and Reduce Inventory*, Englewood Cliffs, NJ: Prentice-Hall, 1973.

Love, S. F. *Inventory Control*, New York: McGraw-Hill, 1979.

Magee, John F. *Physical Distribution Systems*, New York: McGraw-Hill, 1967.

Magee, John F., and David M. Boodman. *Production Planning and Inventory Control*, New York: McGraw-Hill, 1967.

Magee, John F., et al. *Modern Logistics Management*, New York: John Wiley and Sons, 1985.

Martin, A. J. *DRP Distribution Resource Planning*, Englewood Cliffs, NJ: Prentice-Hall, 1983.

Mather, H. *Bills of Materials, Receipts, and Formulations*, Atlanta, GA: Wright Publishing Co., 1982.

Mathews, Lawrence M. *Control of Materials*, London: Industrial and Commercial Techniques, Ltd., 1971.

McGarrah, Robert E. *Production and Logistics Management*, New York: John Wiley and Sons, 1963.

McLeavey, D. W., and S. L. Narasimhan. *Production Planning and Inventory Control*, Boston, MA: Allyn and Bacon, 1985.

McMillan, Claude, and Richard F. Gonzalez. *Systems Analysis: A Computer Approach to Decision Models*, Homewood, IL: Richard D. Irwin, 2nd edition, 1968.

Mills, Edward S. *Price, Output, and Inventory Policy*, New York: John Wiley and Sons, 1962.

Mize, Joe H., et al. *Operations Planning and Control*, Englewood Cliffs, NJ: Prentice-Hall, 1971.

Montgomery, D. J., and L. A. Johnson. *Forecasting and Time Series Analysis*, New York: McGraw-Hill, 1976.

Morse, Philip M. *Queues, Inventories, and Maintenance*, New York: John Wiley and Sons, 1958.

Mossman, Frank H., and Newton Morton. *Logistics of Distribution Systems*, Boston: Allyn and Bacon, Inc., 1965.

Mudge, Arthur E. *Value Engineering: A Systematic Approach*, New York: McGraw-Hill, 1971.

Naddor, Eliezer. *Inventory Systems*, New York: John Wiley and Sons, 1966.

National Association of Accountants. *Techniques in Inventory Management*, Research Report No. 40, New York: NAA, 1964.

Nelson, C. R. *Applied Time Series for Managerial Forecasting*, San Francisco: Holden-Day, 1973.

New, Colin. *Requirements Planning*, New York: John Wiley and Sons, 1973.

Niland, Powell. *Production Planning, Scheduling, and Inventory Control*, London: Macmillan, 1970.

Orlicky, Joseph. *Material Requirements Planning*, New York: McGraw-Hill, 1975.

_____. *The Successful Computer System*, New York: McGraw-Hill, 1969.

Oxenfeldt, Alfred R. *Make or Buy*: *Factors Affecting Decisions*, New York: McGraw-Hill, 1965.

Peckham, Herbert H. *Effective Materials Management*, Englewood Cliffs, NJ: Prentice-Hall, 1972.

Plossl, G. W. *Manufacturing Control*, Reston, VA: Reston Publishing, 1973.

Plossl, G. W., and W. E. Welch. *The Role of Top Management in the Control of Inventory*, Reston, VA: Reston Publishing, 1979.

Plossl, G. W., and O. W. Wight. *Production and Inventory Control*, Englewood Cliffs, NJ: Prentice-Hall, 1985.

Prabhu, N. *Queues and Inventories*, New York: John Wiley and Sons, 1965.

Prichard, James W., and Robert H. Eagle. *Modern Inventory Management*, New York: John Wiley and Sons, 1965.

Putnam, Arnold Q., et al. *Unified Operations Management*, New York: McGraw-Hill, 1963.

Raymond, Fairfield E. *Quantity and Economy in Manufacturing*, New York: McGraw-Hill, 1931.

Reisman, Arnold, et al. *Industrial Inventory Control*, New York: Gordon and Breach Science Publishers, 1972.

Sampson, Roy J., and Martin T. Farris. *Domestic Transportation*: *Practice, Theory, and Policy*, Boston: Houghton Mifflin Co., 1971.

Scarf, Herbert E., et al. *Multistage Inventory Models and Techniques*, Stanford, CA: Stanford University Press, 1963.

Schary, P. B. *Logistics Decisions*, Chicago, IL: Dryden Press, 1984.

Schonberger, R. J. *Japanese Manufacturing Techniques*, New York: The Free Press, 1982.

Silver, E. A., and R. Peterson. *Decision Systems for Inventory Management and Production Planning*, New York: John Wiley and Sons, 1985.

Sims, E. Ralph. *Planning and Managing Materials Flow*, Boston: Industrial Education Institute, 1968.

Smykay, Edward W. *Physical Distribution Management*, New York: Macmillan Publishing Co., Inc., 3rd edition, 1973.

Starr, Martin K., and David W. Miller. *Inventory Control*: *Theory and Practice*, Englewood Cliffs, NJ: Prentice-Hall, 1962.

Stelzer, W. R. *Materials Management*, Englewood Cliffs, NJ: Prentice-Hall, 1970.

Stock, J. R., and D. M. Lambert. *Strategic Logistics Management*, Homewood, IL: Richard D. Irwin, 1987.

Stockton, R. Stansbury. *Basic Inventory Systems*: *Concepts and Analysis*, Boston: Allyn and Bacon, 1965.

Sussams, J. E. *Industrial Logistics*, Boston: Cahners Books, 1972.

Taff, Charles A. *Management of Physical Distribution and Transportation*, Homewood, IL: Richard D. Irwin, 6th edition, 1984.

Tersine, R. J. *Production/Operations Management: Concepts, Structure, and Analysis*, New York: North-Holland, 1985.

Tersine, R. J., et al. *Problems and Models in Operations Management*, Columbus, OH: Grid Publishing, 1980.

_____. *Modern Materials Management*, New York: North-Holland, 1977.

Thomas, Adin B. *Inventory Control in Production and Manufacturing*, Boston: Cahners Publishing Company, 1970.

Tyler, Elias S. *Material Handling*, New York: McGraw-Hill, 1970.

Van DeMark, R. L. *Inventory Control Techniques*, Dallas, TX: Van DeMark, Inc., 1981.

_____. *Managing Material Control*, Dallas, TX: Van DeMark, Inc., 1970.

_____. *Production Control Techniques*, Dallas, TX: Van DeMark, Inc., 1970.

_____. *New Ideas in Materials Management*, Dallas, TX: Van DeMark, Inc., 1963.

Van Hees, R. N., and W. Monhemius. *Production and Inventory Control: Theory and Practice*, New York: Harper and Row Publishers, Inc., 1972.

Vollman, T. E., et al. *Manufacturing Planning and Control Systems*, Homewood, IL: Richard D. Irwin, 1984.

Wagner, Harvey M. *Statistical Management of Inventory Systems*, New York: John Wiley and Sons, 1962.

_____. *Principles of Operations Research*, Englewood Cliffs, NJ: Prentice-Hall, 1975.

Ward, R. E. *Fundamentals of Inventory Management and Control*, New York: American Management Association, 1983.

Warman, J. *Warehouse Management*, London: William Heinemann, Ltd., 1971.

Welch, W. E. *Tested Scientific Inventory Control*, Greenwich, CT: Management Publishing Company, 1956.

Westing, J. E., et al. *Purchasing Management: Materials in Motion*, New York: John Wiley and Sons, 3rd edition, 1969.

Whitin, T. M. *Theory of Inventory Management*, Princeton, NJ: Princeton University Press, 1957.

Wight, O. W. *MRP II: Unlocking America's Productivity Potential*, Williston, VT: Oliver Wight Publications, Inc., 1981.

_____. *Production and Inventory Management in the Computer Age*, Boston: Cahners Publishing Company, 1974.

Willets, Walter E. *Fundamentals of Purchasing*, New York: Appleton-Century-Crofts, 1969.

Zenz, G. J. *Purchasing and the Management of Materials*, New York: John Wiley and Sons, 1981.

Zimmerman, Hans-Jurgen, and Michael G. Sovereign. *Quantitative Models in Production Management*, Englewood Cliffs, NJ: Prentice-Hall, 1974.

Index

A

ABC inventory classification (analysis). *See also* Selective inventory control
  used in control, 512–516
  used in physical count, 463–464
Accelerator effect, 25–26
Accounting methods used in inventory, valuation, 447–458
Accumulated holding costs, 170, 173
Accuracy
  desired level of, 34, 462–463, 487, 502
  of records, 458–460
Aggregate inventory control, 500–530
  measurement techniques of, 522–523
Aggregate inventory value, 522
Aggregate planning, for total production systems, 328–330, 365–372
Aggregate runout time (AROT) method, 133–134
Algebraic sum of errors, 44, 67
Algorithms. *See* Lot sizing (discrete)
All-units quantity discount, 99–103
American Production and Inventory Control Society (APICS), 280
Analysis techniques
  benefit (marginal), 307–310
  cost, 263–264, 310–314
  expected value, 304–307
  ratio, 20–25, 522–523
  sensitivity, 114–121
Anticipation stock, 7, 525–526
Arithmetic average forecasting technique, 46
Arithmetic mean. *See* Mean
Autocorrelation, 51
Automation, and inventory planning, 27
Autoregressive coefficient, 69
Autoregressive integrated moving average method (ARIMA), 69
Average cost inventory flow method, 453–456
Average inventory, 91, 93, 96–97, 123, 128, 137, 188, 266–268, 274, 278

B

Backlog(ging)
  effect on lead time, 399
  planned, 404–406
Backorder(ing)
  dependence of parameters in model, 249–250
  economic order quantity derivation with, 95–99
  economic production quantity derivation with, 125–126
  stockout cost per outage model of, 198–203
  stockout cost per unit model of, 195–198
Balance sheet, 22, 448, 453
  distortion, 452–453, 456–458
Banks, Jerry, 125
Base series, 61
Batch-type production systems, 121–132
  aggregate runout time method, 133–134
  economic production quantity (multiple items), 128–131
  economic production quantity (single item), 121–126
  runout time method, 131–133
Bias, 45
Bierman, Harold, 250
Bill of distribution, 432
Bill of materials (BOM), 332, 385–394. *See also* Product structure record
  add/delete, 390
  coding, 338
  explosion, 332 (*see also* Explosion)
  matrix, 389–390
  modular, 390–391
  pseudo, 393
  restructuring, 394
  traditional, 386–394
Binomial expansion, 241–242
Bonini, Charles, 250
Bottleneck centers, 372, 397, 402–403, 527
Box-Jenkins method, 69–70

Brown, Robert G., 56, 157, 209
Buffer stock. *See* Safety stock
Business cycle, influence on inventory, 25–26

C

Capacity, expansion of, 129, 371–372
Capacity control, 399–400, 402–407, 527
Capacity planning, 330–332, 334, 438
    factors, 367–368
    rough-cut, 368–370
Capacity requirements planning (CRP),
    367–373
Cash flow, 523
Central tendency, measure of, 189, 192
Chi-square test, 192, 245–248
Classification of materials. *See* ABC
    inventory classification
Component, 511
    definition of, 335
Computerization
    need for, 453, 516, 521
    used in material requirements planning, 364
    used in simulation, 475
Confidence limit, 44, 489–490
Constrained functions, optimizing, 296–299
Constraints, 113. *See also* Inventory system
    constraints
    active, 280
    capacity, 13, 126–127, 368
    equality function, 297–298
    inequality function, 275, 277, 298–299
    on inventory investment, 266–268
    of inventory system, 266–280
    storage space, 274–279
    working capital, 126–127, 272–274,
        277–279
Control. *See* Inventory control
Control limits, 51, 67
Control system. *See* Inventory control system
Conversion, inventory system, 263–264
Convexity of function, 299
Convolution, 195
    of probability distribution, 208–210, 215,
        241–242
Correlation coefficient
    multiple, 74
    partial, 74
    simple, 49–50, 71
Cost accumulation profile, 15–16
Cost analysis, 263, 502
Cost-benefit analysis, 263, 516, 529
Cost curve
    continuous, 91–93
    discontinuous, 100–101
Cost of goods sold, 447–448, 451, 456
    realistic valuation of inventory for, 449
Costs
    annual, 92

backordering, 96–98
    current, 449
    expected, 189, 304, 310
    flow of, 447–458
    holding, 14, 91, 93, 163, 165, 170, 173, 194
        (*see also* Holding cost fraction)
    incremental, 126, 173, 263
    marginal, 161, 308
    minimum total annual, 94, 124, 129
    obsolescence, 301
    opportunity, 301
    ordering, 14, 91, 93, 163, 165, 170
    production, 123
    purchasing, 13, 91, 93, 99–101, 103–106,
        311
    replacement, 451
    safety stock, 194, 198, 204–205
    setup, 14, 121, 123
    stockout, 14, 95, 189, 193–194, 203–206,
        223, 308
    total annual, 91, 97, 101, 107, 111, 123,
        128, 136
    total relevant, 168–169
    total variable, 114, 117, 165–167
Critical ratio technique, 407–409. *See also*
    Scheduling
Cumulative frequency distribution, 243, 476,
    478
Cycle count
    advantages, 464
    method(s), 461–464
    procedures for varying, 463
Cycle time. *See also* Time cycle charts
    manufacturing, 398
    production, 121–125, 131–134, 398
    reduction of, 399–401, 402–403
Cyclical variations, 41–42

D

Days of supply, 409, 522
Decision-making under risk, 304–307
Decoupling stock, 8
Delphi technique, 70
Demand
    average, 185, 188, 213
    captive, 95
    certain, 90, 302
    constant, 91, 161, 184, 194, 206
    continuous, 90, 161, 192, 363, 429
    cumulative frequency of, 197
    dependent, 90–95, 161, 327, 353, 363, 429,
        432, 511
    derived, 327–328
    deterministic, 161, 184
    discrete, 161–163, 175–177, 185, 327
    distributions, 184 (*see also* Distribution[s])
    error, 43–45, 114–121
    forecasting, 34–80

independent, 161, 241, 327, 363, 429, 432
knowledge of future, 10, 90
lead time (*see* Lead time, demand)
low levels of, 193
mean lead time (*see* Mean lead time
  demand)
noncontinuous, 301
pattern, 12
probabilistic, 184, 189–193
rate, 12, 504
without reordering, 300
size, 12
time-varying, 161–162, 176–177, 431
variable, 71, 184, 194, 208, 304, 431, 479
variance, 44, 50, 190–192, 199
Demand items
  continuous, 90
  dependent, 327–328, 353
  discrete, 176
  independent, 327–328, 431
  infrequent or short-lived, 300–301
Demand variations, 68, 161, 194
  cyclical, 41–42
  levels, 41, 53–56
  random, 43
  seasonal, 41, 60–65
  trends, 43, 57–60, 63–65
DeMatteis, J. J., 162
Dependency, of order quantity and reorder
  point, 248–253
Dependent demand. *See also* Demand,
  dependent
  definition of, 10, 327
Dependent variable, 48–51, 71–74
Deseasonalization, of demand, 61–65
Design, of inventory system. *See* Inventory
  system design
Deterioration, 14, 449
Deterministic, 90, 161, 475
Diminishing returns, 186, 212
Direct labor, 123, 396
Direct materials, 123, 396
Discount(s)
  all-units quantity, 99–103
  incremental quantity, 103–106
  temporary, 106–110
Discount (quantity), approximation, 156–157
Discrete distribution. *See* Distribution,
  discrete
Dispersion, measure of, 189–190
Disposal routes, 282
Disposition, 524–525
Distribution(s)
  Chi-square, 245
  continuous, 189, 191, 308
  convolution of, 195, 241–242
  cumulative, 476
  discrete, 189, 191, 197, 241, 308
  exponential, 476

frequency, 194
joint probability, 208–211, 253–260,
  486–488
negative exponential, 193, 216–217
normal, 191–193, 200–201, 214, 219, 242,
  247, 476
Poisson, 193, 202, 215–216, 246, 476
probability, 189–193, 304, 476
standard normal, 245, 311
Distribution inventory system(s), 425–442
  centers (distribution points) in, 426
  fair shares allocation, 438–440
  push vs. pull, 428–430
  time phased order points used in, 430–432
Distribution requirements planning (DRP),
  11, 432–438, 509–510
  application of MRP logic to, 432–433
  comparison with fair shares allocation,
    438–439
  in an integrated manufacturing
    environment, 436–437
  lot sizing in, 438–441
  in a pure distribution environment, 426,
    436
Distribution requirements planning II
  (DRP II), 436
Donaldson, W. A., 162
Durbin-Watson statistic, 51
Dynamic programming, 164

E

Echelon, 426
Econometric model, 74–75
Economic indicator, 71–74
Economic order interval (EOI). *See also*
  Fixed order interval
  assumptions of, 135–136, 141
  concept applied to periodic inventory
    system, 135–136, 506
  deterministic model, 135–141
  and discrete lot sizing, 163–164
  multiple items model of, 139
  probabilistic model, 224–226
Economic order quantity (EOQ). *See also*
  Fixed order size system
  assumptions of, 94, 184, 301
  basic model of, 90–95
  comparison to material requirements
    planning, 352–364
  concept applied to perpetual inventory
    system, 504
  with dependence, 248–253
  derivation with backordering, 95–99,
    249–250
  deterministic model(s), 90–114
  independence, 189
  known price increase model of, 110–113
  probabilistic model, 184–224

Economic order quantity (EOQ) [*cont.*]
  quantity discount model(s), 99–106
  sensitivity, 114–121
  service level, 212–224
  single item model of, 91–95
  special sale price model of, 106–110
Economic production quantity (EPQ),
    121–141
  with backordering, 125–126
  multiple items model of, 128–131
  single items model of, 121–128
Economic time supply, 282–286
  lead time influence on, 288–289
Effectiveness 25. *See also* Inventory ratio(s);
    Inventory ratio analysis
Efficiency, 25–27
End item, 511
  definition of, 76, 327, 330
Ending inventory, 449, 456
Environmental factors, 35
Error(s)
  in estimation of parameters, 114–120
  forecast, 43–45, 65–68, 71–72
  in records, 365, 458–459
Error factor, 114–120
Excess materials, 280–289, 524–528
  expected, 308
  obsolete, 281
  scrap, 281
  surplus, 281, 524
Exchange curves, 268–272
Expected cost, 189, 307, 310
Expected cost approach, 310–314
Expected profit approach, 310–314
Expected value, as decision criterion, 304–307
Explosion, 333–334, 343–344, 385–388. *See*
    also Bill of materials (BOM)
Exponential decay, 55
Exponential smoothing constant, 53, 59, 62,
    65–68
Exponentially weighted moving average
    technique (EWMA), 53–69
  advantages of, 53, 68
  models, 66
  overview, 65–69
  with seasonal correction, 60–62
  with trend and seasonal corrections, 63–65
  with trend correction, 57–60

F

Fabrycky, W. J., 125
Fair shares allocation, 438–440
Families (of items), 75, 128, 131, 389–394
File integrity, 365–366, 459, 519. *See also*
    Inventory record
Finished goods, definition of, 4
First in, first out (FIFO), 448–452

Fixed order interval (T-system). *See also* EOI
  assumptions of, 135–136
  deterministic model, 135–142
  probabilistic model, 224–226
Fixed order size (Q-system), 90–134, 227. *See*
    also EOQ
  assumptions of, 90, 184
  compared with MRP, 352–364
  deterministic, 90–134, 210
  disadvantages of, 353
  probabilistic, 184–224
Flow methods. *See* Inventory flow methods
Forecast error, 39, 43–45, 49–51, 65–68,
    71–72, 186
  bias, 45
  mean absolute deviation (MAD), 43–45,
    65–67
  mean squared error, 43–44
  model sensitive to, 314
  tracking signal, 44, 67
Forecast methods, 37–41
  arithmetic average, 46
  Box-Jenkins, 69–70
  econometric model, 74–75
  economic indicator, 71–74
  exponential smoothing, 53–69
  last period demand, 45
  moving average (simple), 46–47
  qualitative, 70
  quantitative, 41–70
  regression analysis, 48–52, 71–74
  soliciting opinions, 70
  time series, 41–69
Forecast precision, 34, 43–45, 67
Forecasting, 34–80
  aggregate, 36, 75–76
  base, 35–36
  bottom-up, 36
  components, 41
  definition of, 34
  in distribution systems, 432, 441
  established product demand, 40–41
  EWMA models for, 66
  external factors, 35, 78
  function, 37–41
  group, 75–77
  independent demand, 330, 332, 511
  levels, 53–54, 66
  model selection, 38–41, 77–79
  multiperiod, 49, 52, 56, 59, 62, 63, 66
  for new products, 40, 70
  as a precondition to system development,
    517
  reliability, 43–45, 50, 67–68
  short-range, 36, 68
  top-down, 36
  trends, 49, 57, 63
  uses of, 34

Forecasts used as requirements in TPOP, 431
F-test, 73–74
Functional classifications (of inventory), 7–8
Functional factors (of inventory), 6–7

G

Gaussian distribution (normal), 192
Generic items, 75–76
Gonzales, Richard F., 210
Goodness-of-fit test, 192
Goodwill loss, 187
Greene, James H., 280
Groff, G. K., 162
Groff's marginal cost algorithm, 161–162
Gross requirements. *See* Requirements, gross
Group forecasting, 75–76
Group technology, 413, 416

H

Hadley, G., 104, 241, 296
Hausman, Warren, 250
Heuristic approaches, for lot sizing. *See* Lot sizing
Holding cost fraction, 266
  determination of new, 266–274
  as a management policy variable, 268, 526–527

I

Implosion
  of BOM, 385–391
  in distribution requirements planning, 432, 509
Imputed service level, 223–224. *See also* Service level; Stockout cost
Income determination, 447
Income statement, 22, 448, 449
Income taxes
  effects of inventory flow methods on, 449, 452–453
  surplus inventory losses impact on, 281, 523–525
Incremental cost analysis, 173, 263. *See also* Costs, incremental
Incremental part-period algorithm, 173–174
Incremental quantity discounts, 103–106
Independent demand, 327. *See also* Demand, independent
Independent variable, 48–51, 71–74
Inefficiency
  in inventory systems, 409–415
  signals of, 262
Inflation
  effect on inventory valuation, 452–453
  price increase model as a result of, 110

In-process inventory, 395–409. *See also* Input/output control
  control of, 20, 397
  costs, 15–16, 22, 396
  definition of, 4, 396
  economies of, 6–8, 397
  purposes of, 396–398
  reduction of, 399–401, 406–407, 527–528
  relationship to cycle time, 24, 398, 402
Input. *See also* Material requirements planning input
  forecast, 38
  planned, 403–407
Input/output control, 403–407
  effect on lead time, 403, 406–407
  function of, 403
Input/output forecasting models, 75
Input/output report, 404–405
Intercorrelation, of variables, 74
Interdependence
  of demand and lead time, 208–211, 486
  of order quantity and reorder point, 226, 248
Interperiod dependency, 75
Intraperiod dependency, 75
Inventory. *See also* Management (inventory)
  build-up, 123
  characteristics of, 501
  control, 3 (*see also* Inventory control)
  costs, 13–15
  definitions of, 3, 447
  financial characteristics of, 447–448
  financial considerations of, 20–25, 522–523
  flow of costs, 447–458
  functions of, 6–8, 521, 529
  goals, 15–19
  investment, 15, 20–25, 189, 266–274, 353, 516
  maintenance, 3, 5–6
  management, 2–28, 501 (*see also* Management [inventory])
  organizational categories of, 4–6
  position, 94, 135–136
  productive and nonproductive types of, 523
  properties, 11–13
  significance of, 2–3
  turnover, 23–24, 522 (*see also* Inventory ratio analysis)
  types of, 4
  viewed as a waste, 411
Inventory control
  aggregate, 262, 268–272, 279, 500–530
  aggregate measurement of, 20–25, 447–448, 522–523
  elements of aggregate program for, 501–502
  in organizational structure, 3, 16–19, 521
  physical, 447
  record integrity and, 458–460

Inventory control [*cont.*]
  record keeping for, 458–464
  relationship to planning and scheduling, 121–128, 131, 133, 365–367, 399–400, 402–403, 407, 415 (*see also* Scheduling)
  selective, 512–516
  significance of, 2–4, 521
Inventory control system, 501–519. *See also* Systems
  decision rules, 517
  definition of, 501
  development, 516–519
  features, 501
  improvement, 519–521
  kanban, 416–418
  overview, 528–530
  selection of, 501–502
  types of, 11, 502–519
  vital areas of, 502
Inventory costs, 16. *See also* Costs
  definition of, 13–15
  valuation of, 447
Inventory flow cycle, 19–20
Inventory flow method, 448–458
  average cost, 453–456
  first in, first out (FIFO), 448–452
  last in, first out (LIFO), 451–453
  specific cost, 456–458
Inventory investment, 15, 20–25, 189, 266–274, 353. *See also* Inventory ratio analysis
  relationship to aggregate performance, 22–25, 447, 522–523
Inventory management. *See* Management (inventory)
Inventory position, 508
Inventory problems, classification of, 4–6, 8–11
Inventory profits, 453
Inventory ratio
  aggregate inventory value, 522
  critical, 407
  current, 23
  days of supply, 522
  inventory to sales, 522
  inventory turnover, 23, 262, 522
  quick, 23
  throughput time, 24
Inventory ratio analysis, 20–25, 522–523
Inventory records, 458–464
  accuracy of, 458–459
  establishment of methods for maintaining, 460–464
  resultant problems from errors in, 458
Inventory reduction, 396–418, 431, 523–527
Inventory security, 464–465
Inventory status records, 328, 333. *See also* Material requirements planning inputs

Inventory system(s). *See also* Systems
  behavior of, 501–512
  distribution based, 425–442
  ideal, 90–114, 184–185
  just-in-time (JIT), 26–27, 409–418
  production planning and control based, 121–134, 327–374
  quantity based (*see* Fixed order size [Q-systems])
  time based (*see* Fixed order interval [T-systems])
  types of, 11
Inventory system constraint(s), 13, 266–280. *See also* Constraints
Inventory system design, general framework for, 262–289
Inventory system evaluation, 262
Inventory system redesign, 263–266, 516–521
Inventory turnover, 522. *See also* Inventory ratio, turnover
Inventory valuation, 20–25, 446–458
  methods of, 448

J

Job shop. *See* Production processes, intermittent
Johnson, L. A., 196, 204, 250
Joint order, 139, 507
Joint probability distributions, 208–211, 253–260
  simulations, 486
Just-in-time (JIT), 26–27, 409–418, 511–512, 527–528
  elimination of waste in, 410–418, 527
  goals, 409, 527
  repetitive manufacturing and, 415–418
  suggestions, 413
  tenets, 412, 418
  versus conventional attitudes, 410

K

Kanban, 415–418
Kicks, P., 162
Known price increase. *See* Price increase
Kuhn–Tucker conditions, 277, 296

L

Lagrange multipliers, 272, 277, 279, 296–299
Last in, first out (LIFO), 451–453
  effect on income taxes, 452–453
Last period demand forecasting technique, 45
Lead time, 511. *See also* Cycle time
  characteristic to type of control system, 94
  components, 12–13, 398
  constant, 90, 182, 194, 302
  definition of, 10, 331
  demand, 98, 138, 140, 184–185, 192, 203, 302

demand variance, 184, 190
expected, 185
expression, 94
influence on economic time supply, 288
knowledge of, 10
offsetting, 333–334, 338
probabilistic, 185, 206
production, 123–124, 398
reduction, 399–402, 409–418
replenishment, 12
stacked, 331
stockout occurrence, 185, 188, 195
variable, 206, 208, 303, 479
zero, 113
Lead time (manufacturing). *See also*
    Input/output control
delays, 398–400
reduction of, 519, 527
Lead time (demand) distribution, 189–193,
    195, 199, 207, 209, 214–215. *See also*
    Mean lead time demand; Standard
    deviation
Least squares method, 49, 71
Least total cost approach (LTC), 172. *See
    also* Part-period algorithm
Length of production run, 122–124, 129–130
Level (inventory), 359
maximum, 97, 123, 135–138, 140, 225, 484,
    506
restrictions on, 266–280
Levels (demand), 41, 53–54
Linear association, 48, 71
Liquidity
    restrictions, 266, 272, 277, 280
Locations (stockroom), 460
Locator system, 459–460
Longest delay time, 98
Look-ahead and look-backward refinements,
    172–173
Lost sale
    stockout cost per outage model, 205–206
    stockout cost per unit model, 203–205,
    250–251
Lot-for-lot ordering, 163, 343, 349
Lot size, 27
    reduction, 266, 409–418
Lot size inventory management interpolation
    technique (LIMIT), 280
Lot sizing (discrete), 160–177
    in DRP, 429–430, 438–441
    fair shares allocation, 438–439
    implications, 174–177
    incremental part-period algorithm,
    173–174
    lot-for-lot ordering, 163
    in MRP, 343–346, 349–352
    part-period algorithm, 170–173
    periodic order quantity, 163–164
    reduction, 400, 526

Silver-Meal algorithm, 168–170
Wagner–Whitin algorithm, 164–168
Low level coding, 338

M

McMillan, Claude, Jr., 210, 299
Maintenance, of inventory, 5–6
Make or buy decision, 126–128
Management (inventory), 16–19
    compared with other functional areas, 2
    future challenges for, 27–28
    historical overview, 3
    structure of, 19
Manufacturing/assembly system, 5, 21, 175,
    436
Manufacturing bill (M-bill), 393, 509
Marginal analysis, 307–310
Master production schedule (MPS), 328–332,
    368–371. *See also* Material
    requirements planning input
    leveling, 370, 415
    as a link between MRP and DRP, 436–438
Matching principle, 453
Material requirements planning (MRP),
    326–374, 510–511
    advantages of, 328, 330, 334, 363
    areas of application, 328–330
    basic types of, 364–365
    and capacity requirements planning,
    367–372
    computations, 336, 339, 341–352
    as a control system, 11, 365–367
    cost savings of, 358–359
    and demand, 327–328, 363
    key features of, 328, 330
    logic applied to DRP, 432–438
    logic applied to TPOP, 431
    net change vs. regenerative systems, 364
    objectives of, 328
    overview, 365–367
    priority dispatching rules used with, 407
    use of lot sizing in, 161, 176, 343–346,
    349–352
    use of safety stock in, 349
Material requirements planning II (MRP II),
    365, 368
Material requirements planning comparison
    with economic order, quantity,
    352–364
Material requirements planning explosion
    process, 328, 333–334, 343–344
Material requirements planning input(s),
    330–333
    inventory status records, 333, 335–338
    master production schedule, 330–332 (*see
    also* Master production schedule)
    product structure records, 332 (*see also*
    Bill of Materials)

Material requirements planning output,
333–335
net requirements, 334 (*see also*
Requirements, net)
planned order releases, 334, 340 (*see also*
Planned order releases)
Materials management, 2–28
elements of aggregate program of, 529–530
financial considerations of, 20–25
objectives, 15–19
organizational structure, 3, 16, 521
significance of, 2–3, 20–22, 27–28
Maximum inventory level, 95–96, 98,
122–123, 135–136, 138, 140, 159, 225,
506, 508
simulated, 484–486
Meal, H. C., 161, 168
Mean, 312, 489
arithmetic, 189–190, 244
Mean absolute deviation (MAD), 43–45,
65–67, 192–193. *See also* Forecast
error
Mean demand during order interval and lead
time, 225
Mean lead time demand, 184–185, 189–193,
195–196, 202–206, 209–210, 213, 216
Mean squared error (MSE), 43–44
Mendoza, A. G., 162
Miller, D. W., 199, 250
Minimum service level. *See* Service level
Model
dynamic, 314
integrated, 69
static, 314
stochastic, 476
Modeling, 474
Modularization, 390–394
Monte Carlo simulation, 476–477
major steps in, 476–479
uses of, 478
vs. joint probability distributions, 210, 260
Montgomery, D. C., 196, 250
Moving average, 69
used in inventory valuation, 453–456
used in time series analysis, 46–47
Multicollinearity, 74
Multiechelon distribution network, 426–428,
509

N

Negative exponential distribution, 193
Negative exponential distribution table, 217
Net benefit of excess sales, 282–285
Net change MRP system, 364
Netting. *See* MRP, computations;
Requirements, net
Normal probability distribution, 191–193,
243–245, 247. *See also* Distribution(s)

O

Objective
function, 99
organizational, 263, 501
Obsolescence, 14, 281, 301, 449. *See also*
Excess material
shelf life, 301
technical, 281
Opportunity-profit loss, 187, 301
Optional replenishment inventory system,
508–509
Order
cost (as a management variable), 268
cycle, 90, 93, 106, 135, 267–269, 484
frequency, 10
joint (*see* Joint order)
open, 334, 340, 404
outstanding, 94
releases, 333–334, 340, 349, 371, 439
Order interval, 134, 225. *See also* Economic
order interval (EOI)
simulated, 484
Order quantity (lot size), 90, 307, 504. *See
also* Economic order quantity (EOQ)
constrained, 273, 275
with dependence, 248
dynamic, 161, 164
simulated, 480
Ordinate, 199
Organizational categories and inventory
problems, 4–6
Organizational functions, 2
Outage, 198, 205
Outcomes, 305
Output, planned, 403–407

P

Parameter(s)
errors, 114–120
of distributions, 192–193
of inventory systems, 90
of lead time demand, 192
Parent centers, 428, 432
Parent items, 327
Partial expectation, 219, 243
Part-period
accumulated, 171
economic, 171, 173
incremental, 173
Part-period algorithm
incremental, 173–174
refinements to simple, 172–173
simple, 170–172
Payoff matrix, 306
Pegged requirements (pegging), 352
Performance. *See also* Inventory ratio
analysis
measures, 22–25, 447, 522–523
Periodic count method, 460–462

Periodic inventory simulation, 484–486
Periodic inventory system, 506–509
  advantages of, 507
  defining parameters of, 135–136, 506
  description of, 11, 135–141, 506–509
  suitability to flow methods, 449–450,
    451–458
Periodic order quantity, 163–164
Perpetual inventory simulation, 479–483
Perpetual inventory system, 504–505
  advantages and disadvantages, 504
  compared to periodic system, 265
  defining parameters of, 504
  description, 11, 504–505
  suitability to flow methods, 450–451, 458
Peterson, R., 63
Physical control, 459
Physical count, 460–464
Physical flow, 448
Pipeline stock, 8, 441
Planned order release, 333–334, 340, 349,
    371, 439
  firm, 352
Planned order schedule, 334, 431
Planned receipts, 340, 349, 431
Planning horizon, 331, 365, 401, 436
Poisson probability distribution, 193,
    215–216, 246. See also Distribution,
    Poisson
Poisson probability distribution table(s), 202
  cumulative, 216
Popularity percentages, 76, 391–392
Present value, 312–313
Price
  determination, 122–123
  discounts, 106–110
  escalation, 110
  escalation and inventory valuation, 448,
    452–453
Price break (quantity), 101, 104
Price increase (known), 110–113
Priority dispatching rules, 407
Priority planning, 368, 399
Probability density function, 243
Probability distribution. See Distributions
Probability simulation model, 475
Process. See Production process
Production, aggregate planning of, 328–332,
    334, 365–372
Production order quantity, 121–140. See also
    Economic production quantity
Production plan, 328–332, 334, 365–372
Production process(es), 4–6, 121, 128, 131,
    327–328, 335, 396–397, 409, 415
Production rate, 123–124, 128
Production run, 130
  optimum length and number of, 124, 129
  scheduling, 415–418
Production scheduling, 131–134
  related to inventory planning, 365

Production systems (batch-type), 121–141
Product structure, 335–338
  coding, 338
  levels, 175
Product structure record, 328. See also Bill
    of materials (BOM)
Profit (expected), 304, 307
Program evaluation and review technique
    (PERT), 304
Projected on hand, 340
Pull system, 414–417
  in a distribution network, 428–430, 438
Purchase order quantity, 91. See also Order
    quantity; EOQ
Purchasing, 126
  function, 5, 10, 16–19
  growing importance of, 2, 27–28
Push system, 414–415
  in a distribution network, 428–430, 438

Q

Qualitative forecasting techniques, 70. See
    also Forecast methods
Quality control, 413–414, 525
Quantitative forecasting techniques, 41–70
Quantity discount
  all-units, 99–103
  incremental, 103–106
Queue
  inventory, 398
  time, 399, 527

R

Random number (used in simulation), 476,
    478
Random number table, 498
Random sampling, 476
Random variations, 43, 194
Ratio. See also Inventory ratio
  critical, 407–409
Ratio analysis. See Inventory ratio analysis
Raw materials, definition of, 4
Receiver system, 463
Record keeping, 365, 458–464. See also
    Inventory record
  simplification of, 449
Reduction. See Inventory reduction
Regenerative MRP system, 364
Regression analysis, in forecasting, 48–52,
    71–74
Reisman, Arnold, 486
Reorder point, 190
  characteristic to type of control system, 90,
    124, 504, 508
  with dependence assumption, 248–253
  determination of, 94, 185, 192, 197, 199,
    205, 208, 214, 219
  with known stockout costs, 194–211
  negative, 98

Reorder point [*cont.*]
production, 124, 130
service level approach to, 211–224
simulated, 480
Replenishment, 12, 505. *See also* Lead time
continuous, 121
continuous review, 135, 504
cycle, 106 (*see also* Order, cycle)
discrete, 90, 511
discrete review, 135, 508
independent, 428
lead time, 12, 90, 185
pattern, 12
policies, 268
size, 12, 506
Replenishment rate, 122
Requirements
aggregate net, 439
gross, 333, 340, 431–432, 509
low level, 333, 338, 432
net, 338, 340, 431
Resource
need for efficient management of, 27–28
scarcity problems, 2
Resource requirements planning (RRP),
368–370
Retail system, 5
Review period, characteristic to type of
control system, 135, 504, 508
Risk and uncertainty, 302
accounted for in probabilistic model, 184
safety stock provision for (*see* Safety stock)
simulation in an environment of, 474
Rolling the schedule, 161, 175–176
Rough-cut capacity planning (RCCP),
368–370
Runout time (ROT) method, 131–133

S

Safety stock, 184–189
costs of, 185, 194, 196
definition of, 7, 184
determination by service level method,
211–224
determination with known stockout costs,
193–211
in JIT, 412
at levels in a distribution system, 429–430,
441
minimum level for, 195, 199
need for, 185–188
reduction, 525
relative requirements for inventory systems,
505, 507–508
and service levels, 188–189
setting levels for, 192, 203
used in material requirements planning, 349
Safety stock quantity, 195, 199, 203, 213
Sales forecast. *See* Forecasting, demand

Salvage value, 307–308, 524
minimum economic, 286–288
Sampling
random, 476
statistical, 489
Scatter diagram, 50
Scheduled receipts, 340, 371
Scheduling. *See also* Production scheduling
critical ratio technique for, 407–409
for input/output control, 403–407
for material requirements planning,
333–335, 511
master, 328–332, 368–371, 436
order releases, 161, 175–176, 433, 441
responsiveness, 400
Seasonal
correction, 60–65
index, 61
variation, 41
Seasonalization, 60
Security (inventory), 464–465
Selective inventory control, 463–464, 512–516
Sensitivity analysis, economic order quantity,
114–121
Serial correlation, 51
Service level, 188, 211, 225, 311
comparison, 354
decreasing, 525
definition of, 211–212
fraction of operating days method for,
222–223
fraction of units demanded method for,
219, 226
safety stock relationship to, 188
service per order cycle method for, 212–218
service per order interval method for, 226
service per year method for, 218, 226
Setup
cost, 14, 121
minimization of, 400–401, 412–418, 526
Shadow price, 297. *See also* Imputed values
Shop floor control, 414–415
Shortage, 187. *See also* Stockout
Silver, E. A., 63, 161, 168
Silver-Meal heuristic algorithm, 168–170, 352
Simple average cost method, 453
Simulation
joint probability distribution, 486–488
Monte Carlo, 476–478, 484
periodic inventory problem, 484–486
perpetual inventory problem, 479–483
system design and, 263
uses of, 474, 490
Simulation run (length), 477, 489–490
Single order quantity (SOQ), 300–315, 510
determined by benefit (marginal) analysis,
307–310
determined by cost analysis, 310–314
determined by expected value approach,
304–307

Smoothing. *See* Exponential smoothing
Smoothing constant. *See* Exponential
    smoothing constant
Soliciting opinions, 70
Special (one time) order cost size
    of known price increase, 112
    of temporary discount, 106–110
Special project. *See* Production process
Special sale prices, 106–110
Specific cost inventory flow method, 456–458
Standard deviation, 189–190, 489
    of forecast errors, 44, 72
    used in determining safety stock, 219, 243
    used in determining single quantity orders,
        312–314
Standard normal deviate, 199, 311–312
Standard normal table(s), 200–201, 214, 311
Starr, Martin K., 199, 250
Stock
    safety (*see* Safety stock)
    working, 184
Stockless production. *See* JIT
Stock level review, 139
Stock position, 94, 140, 483, 504
Stockout, 187, 217
    probability of, 190–191, 203, 204, 219–221,
        243, 308
    size, 95–96 (*see also* Stockout quantity)
Stockout cost, 14
    expected, 307
    finite, 95, 125
    imputed, 223–224, 225
    infinite, 125
    known, 189, 193, 225
    per outage, 198–203, 205–206
    per unit, 195–198, 203–205
    unknown, 189
Stockout quantity (expected), 190–191, 203,
    204, 219–221, 243, 308
Storage space restriction, 274–279
Storeroom operations, 459, 464
Structural relationship, 74
Suboptimization, 17, 266
Sum of the squares of the deviations, 49
Supplies, 4
Supply sources, 10, 301, 414, 417–418
Surplus. *See* Excess material
Survey approach, 40, 70
System(s)
    actual, 185–187
    closed-loop, 328–329
    discrete demand, 160–177
    distribution based, 425–442, 502, 509–510
    failure, 262
    ideal, 184–185
    in general, 11
    just-in-time (JIT), 26–27, 511–512
    manufacturing based, 121–134, 175,
        326–374, 502, 510–511
    pull vs. push, 428–430

quantity based, 90–114, 184–224, 502–506
time based, 135–142, 224–226, 502,
    506–509

T

Tag method, 461
Tax savings, 523
Technological change, impact on inventory
    planning and control, 2–3, 397
Tersine, R. J., 101, 279, 281
Tests for convexity, 299
Throughput time, 24, 527
Time bucket, 331, 365
Time cycle chart, 401–402
Time-phased order point (TPOP), 430–438,
    509
Time-phasing, 331, 334, 430, 509, 511
Time series analysis, 41–69
    components of, 41–43
Toelle, R. A., 101, 281
Tolerance range, 406
Tracking signal, 44, 67
Transaction system (of counting), 463
Transportation efficiency and lot sizing,
    440–441
Trend, 41
    correction, 57–60, 63–65
    effect, 49–51
t-test, 72–74
Turnover. *See* Inventory, turnover
Two-bin inventory system, 505–506

U

Uniform plant loading, 415

V

Valuation. *See* Inventory valuation
Van DeMark, R. L., 13
Variable
    dependent, 48
    in simulation, 474
    independent, 48
Variance, lead time demand, 190, 244
von Neumann ratio, 51

W

Wagner, H. M., 161
Wagner–Whitin algorithm, 164–168, 352
Waste, 410–412
Whitin, T. M., 104, 161, 241, 296
Wholesale distribution system, 5, 426,
    436–438
Working capital, 266
    restrictions on, 272–274
Working stock, 7, 184

Z

Zero balance system, 463
Zero inventory. *See* JIT